Psyche

Volume II

James M. Buchanan
11 vi 67

ERWIN ROHDE

Psyche

THE CULT OF SOULS AND BELIEF IN IMMORTALITY AMONG THE GREEKS

Volume II

Introduction to the Torchbook edition
by W. K. C. GUTHRIE

Translated from the Eighth edition by W. B. Hillis

HARPER TORCHBOOKS The Cloister Library
Harper & Row, Publishers, New York

PSYCHE: Volume II

Printed in the United States of America.

This book was originally published in one volume in 1925 by Kegan Paul, Trench, Trubner & Co., Ltd., London and Harcourt, Brace & Company, Inc., New York. It is here reprinted by arrangement.

First HARPER TORCHBOOK edition published 1966 by
Harper & Row, Publishers, Incorporated
49 East 33rd Street
New York, N.Y. 10016.

The Library of Religion and Culture
General Editor: BENJAMIN NELSON

CONTENTS

VOLUME II

PAGE.

PART II

APPENDIX

PART II

CHAPTER VIII

ORIGINS OF THE BELIEF IN IMMORTALITY

THE THRACIAN WORSHIP OF DIONYSOS

The popular conception of the continued existence of the souls of the dead, resting upon the cult of the dead, grew up and coalesced with a view of the soul derived from Homeric teaching on the subject, which was in essential, though unrecognized, contradiction with the cult of souls. The popular conception, unchanged in all essentials, remained in force throughout the coming centuries of Greek life. It did not contain within itself the seeds of further development; it did not make any demand for better and deeper ideas of the character and condition of the soul in its independent life after its separation from the body. Still more, it had nothing in it that could have led beyond the belief in the independent future life of those souls to the conception of an everlasting, indestructible, immortal life. The continued life of the soul, such as was implied in and guaranteed by the cult of souls, was entirely bound up with the remembrance of the survivors upon earth, and upon the care, the cult, which they might offer to the soul of their departed ancestor. If that memory dies out, if the venerating thoughtfulness of the living ceases, the soul of the departed is at once deprived of the sole element in which it still maintained its shadow of an existence.

It was impossible, then, that the cult of the souls should produce out of itself the idea of a true immortality of the soul or of the independent life of the soul indestructible by its very nature. Greek religion as it existed among the people of Homer could not shape such a belief of its own accord, and even if it were offered from outside could not have accepted it. It would have meant giving up its own essential character.

If the soul is immortal, it must be in its essential nature like God; it must itself be a creature of the realm of Gods. When a Greek says "immortal" he says "God": they are interchangeable ideas. But the real first principle of the religion of the Greek people is this—that in the divine ordering of the world, humanity and divinity are absolutely divided in place and nature, and so they must ever remain. A deep gulf is fixed between the worlds of mortality and divinity. The relations between man and God promoted by religion depend entirely upon this distinction. The ethical ideas of the Greek popular conscience were rooted in the frank admission of the limitations proper to human capacity which was conditioned by an existence and a fate so different from that enjoyed by the gods; in the renunciation of all human claims to happiness and independence. Poetic fancies about the "Translation" of individual mortals to an unending life enjoyed by the soul still united to the body might make their appeal to popular belief; but such things remained *miracles* in which divine omnipotence had broken down the barriers of the natural order on a special occasion. It was but a miracle, too, if the souls of certain mortals were raised to the rank of Heroes, and so promoted to everlasting life. The gulf between the human and the divine was not made any narrower on that account; it remained unbridged, abysmal. The bare idea that the gulf did not in reality exist, that actually in the order of nature the inner man, the "Soul" of man belonged to the realm of gods; that as a divine being it had everlasting life—such an idea would involve further consequences about which no one can be in much doubt: it would have contradicted every single idea of Greek popular religion. It never could have become widely held and believed in by the Greek populace.

Nevertheless, at a certain period in Greek history, and nowhere earlier or more unmistakably than in Greece, appeared the idea of the divinity, and the immortality implicit in the divinity, of the human soul. That idea belonged entirely to *mysticism*—a second order of religion which, though little remarked by the religion of the people and by orthodox believers, gained a footing in isolated sects and influenced certain philosophical schools. Thence it has affected all subsequent ages and has transmitted to East and West the elementary principles of all true mysticism: the essential unity of the divine and the human spirit; their unification as the aim of religion; the divine nature of the human soul and its immortality.

The theory and doctrine of mysticism grew up in the soil of an older cult-practice. Greece received from abroad a deeply emotional religious cult, accompanied by practices that stimulated mysterious and extraordinary imaginings. The sparks of momentary illumination struck out by this faith were fed and fanned by mysticism till they became a vivid and enduring flame. For the first time, clearly discernible through its mystical wrappings, we meet with the belief in the indestructibility and eternal life of the soul: we meet it in the doctrines of a mystical sect which united in the worship of Dionysos. The worship of Dionysos must have sown the first seed of the belief in an immortal life of the soul. To explain how this may have happened; to make clear to the mind of the reader how the essence and inner reality of that worship was bound to stir up the belief in an immortal life—such is our next task.

§ 2

In the spiritual life of men and nations, it is not by any means the extravagant or, in one sense or another, the abnormal that is most difficult for our sympathetic understanding to grasp. By clinging to a traditional and too narrow formula for the Greek spirit we make difficulties for ourselves; but it is not really a matter of serious perplexity, if we reflect upon it, to understand how Greek religion at the height of its development regarded "madness" (μανία) as a religious phenomenon of wide-reaching importance. Madness, in this sense, is a temporary destruction of physical balance, a condition in which the self-conscious spirit is overwhelmed, "possessed" by a foreign power, as our authorities explain it to us. This madness "which comes not from mortal weakness or disease, but from a divine banishment of the commonplace"[1] found effective application in the *mantic* and *telestic* arts. Its effects were so common and well recognized that the truth and importance of such religious madness (entirely distinguishable from bodily disease) was treated as a fact of experience not merely by philosophers, but by the doctors themselves.[2] For us it only remains obscure how such "divine mania" was fitted into the regular working order of the religious life; the sensations and experiences themselves belonging to this condition are made intelligible enough by a whole host of analogies. In fact if the truth were told we should rather have to admit that it is easier for us to sympathize with such overflowing of sensation and all that goes with it than with the opposite pole of Greek religious life, the calm and measured composure with which man lifted up heart and eye to the gods, as the patterns of all life and the patrons of a serenity as brilliant and unmoved as that of the clear heavens themselves.

But how came it that in the character of a single people such extravagance of emotion was combined with a fast-bound and regulated equilibrium of temper and behaviour? The answer is that these opposing features sprang from two different sources. They were not originally combined in Greece. The Homeric poems hardly give any hint of that overflowing of religious emotion which later Greek peoples knew and honoured as a heaven-sent madness. It spread among the Greeks themselves in the train of a religious agitation, we might almost say revolution, of which Homer records, at most, only the first faint essays. It had its origin in the religion of Dionysos, and in company with this religion enters as something new and strange into Greek life.

The Homeric poems do not recognize Dionysos as belonging to the gods of Olympos, but they are aware of his existence. It is true they nowhere plainly [3] refer to him as the wine-god honoured in joyful festivals, but we read (in the narrative of Glaukos' meeting with Diomedes) of the "frenzied" Dionysos and his "Nurses" who were attacked by the Thracian Lykourgos.[4] The *Mainas*, the frenzied woman of the Dionysos-cult, was such a well-known phenomenon, so familiar in men's minds, that the word could be used in a simile to explain the meaning of something else.[5] In this form the worship of the god first came to the notice of the Greeks: this was the origin of all the other festivals of Dionysos that later Greece developed in so many different directions.[6] They learnt to know Dionysos Bakcheios, "who makes men frenzied,"[7] as he was worshipped in his own country.

That the original home of Dionysos-worship was in Thrace, that his cult, popular among many of the Thracian peoples,[8] was particularly honoured among the southernmost of the Thracian stocks who were best known to the Greeks and lived on the coast between the mouths of the rivers Hebros and Axios and in the mountainous country behind—to all this the Greeks themselves bore frequent and manifold witness.[9] The god whose name the Greeks knew in its Greek form "Dionysos" had, it appears, among the numerous and divided Thracian peoples various appellations of which those most familiar to the Greeks were Sabos and Sabazios.[10] The Greeks must have known and remarked on the nature and worship of the god at an early period of their history. They may have met with him in Thrace itself. At all periods they had an extensive and varied intercourse with this country and must in the early days of their wanderings have passed through it on their way to their future home. They may have had further opportunities of knowing it from the Thracian races or tribes who, according to a few isolated legends, had dwelt in primitive times in certain localities of Central Greece. The ethnographical material of these legends was regarded as founded on fact by the great historians of the fifth and fourth centuries.[11]

The cult of this Thracian divinity differed in every particular from anything that we know of from Homer as Greek worship of the gods. On the other hand, it was closely related to the cult paid by the Phrygians, a people almost identical with the Thracians, to their mountain-mother Kybele. It was thoroughly orgiastic in character. The festival was held on the mountain tops in the darkness of night amid the flickering and uncertain light of torches. The loud and troubled sound of music was heard; the clash of bronze cymbals; the dull thunderous roar of kettledrums; and through them all penetrated the "maddening unison" of the deep-toned flute,[12] whose soul Phrygian *aulêtai* had first waked to life. Excited by this wild music, the chorus of worshippers dance with shrill crying and jubilation.[13] We hear nothing about singing:[14] the violence of the dance left no breath for regular songs. These dances were something very different from the measured movement of the dance-step in which Homer's Greeks advanced and turned about in the *Paian*. It was in frantic, whirling, headlong eddies and dance-circles[15] that these inspired companies danced over the mountain slopes. They were mostly women who whirled round in these circular dances till the point of exhaustion was reached;[16] they were strangely dressed; they wore *bassarai*, long flowing garments, as it seems, stitched together out of fox-skins;[17] over these were doeskins,[18] and they even had horns fixed to their heads.[19] Their hair was allowed to float in the wind;[20] they carried snakes sacred to Sabazios[21] in their hands and brandished daggers or else thyrsos-wands, the spear-points of which were concealed in ivy-leaves.[22] In this fashion they raged wildly until every sense was wrought to the highest pitch of excitement, and in the "sacred frenzy" they fell upon the beast selected as their victim[23] and tore their captured prey limb from limb. Then with their teeth they seized the bleeding flesh and devoured it raw.

It is easy enough, by following poets' descriptions and plastic representations of such scenes, to elaborate still further the picture of this nocturnal festival of fanatic enthusiasm. But, we must ask, what was the *meaning* of it all? We shall get nearest to the truth if we will exclude as far as possible all theories imported from unrelated provinces of thought and fix our attention solely on what, for the participants, was the result of it all—the result anticipated and consciously proposed by them, and therefore the recognized object, or, at least, one of the recognized objects of these strange proceedings. The participators in these dance-festivals induced intentionally in themselves a sort of mania, an extraordinary exaltation of their being. A strange rapture came over them in which they seemed to themselves and others " frenzied ", " possessed ".[24] This excessive stimulation of the senses, going even as far as hallucination,[25] was brought about, in those who were susceptible to their influence, by the delirious whirl of the dance, the music and the darkness, and all the other circumstances of this tumultuous worship.[26] This extreme pitch of excitement was the result intended. The violently induced exaltation of the senses had a religious purpose, in that such enlargement and extension of his being was man's only way, as it seemed, of entering into union and relationship with the god and his spiritual attendants. The god is invisibly present among his inspired worshippers. At any rate, he is close at hand, and the tumult of the festival is to bring him completely into their midst.[27] There are various legends about the disappearance of the god into another world and his return thence to mankind.[28] Every second year his return is celebrated, and it is just this Appearance, this " Epiphany " of the god, that gives the reason and the motive of the festival. The Bull-God, in the most ancient and primitive form of the belief, appeared in person among the dancers,[29] or else the imitated roaring of a bull produced by hidden " Mimes of Terror " served to suggest the invisible Presence.[30] The worshippers, too, in furious exaltation and divine inspiration, strive after the god; they seek communion with him. They burst the physical barriers of their soul. A magic power takes hold of them; they feel themselves raised high above the level of their everyday existence; they seem to *become* those spiritual beings who wildly dance in the train of the god.[31] Nay, more, they have a share in the life of the god himself; nothing less can be the meaning of the fact that the enraptured servants of the god call themselves by the name of the god. The worshipper who in his exaltation has become one with the god, is himself now called Sabos, Sabazios.[32] The superhuman and the infra-human are mingled in his person; like the frenzied god [33] he throws himself upon the sacrificial animal to devour it raw. To make this transformation of their nature outwardly manifest, the participants in the dance-festival wear strange dress: they resemble in their appearance the members of the wild *thiasos* of the god; [34] the horns they set on their heads recall the horned, bull-shaped god himself, etc.[35] The whole might be called a religious drama, since everything is carefully arranged so as to suggest to the imagination the actual presence of the mysterious figures from the spirit world. At the same time, it is something more than mere drama, for it can hardly be doubted that the players themselves were possessed by the illusion of living the life of a strange person. The awe-inspiring darkness of night, the music, especially that of the Phrygian flute, to which the Greeks attributed the power of making its hearers " full of the god ",[36] the vertiginous whirl of the dance—all these may very well, in suitably disposed natures,[37] have really led to a state of visionary exaltation in which the inspired person saw all external objects in accordance with his fancy and imagination. Intoxicating drinks, to which the Thracians were addicted, may have increased the excitement ; [38] perhaps they even used the fumes derived from certain seeds, with which the Scythians and Massagetai knew how to intoxicate themselves.[39] We all know how even to day in the East the smoke of hashish may make men visionaries and excite religious raptures [40] in which the whole of nature is transformed for the enthralled dreamer. " Only when thus possessed did the Bakchai drink milk and honey out of the rivers ; their power ceased when they came to themselves again," says Plato.[41] For them the earth flowed with milk and honey, and the air was filled with the sweet odours of Syria.[42] Hallucination was accompanied by a state of feeling in which pain itself was only an added stimulus to sensation or in which the visionary became completely insensible to pain, as is not unusual in such states of exaltation.[43]

Every detail confirms the picture of a condition of wild excitement in which the limitations of ordinary life seemed to be abolished. These extraordinary phenomena transcending all normal experience were explained by saying that the soul of a person thus " possessed " [44] was no longer " at home " [45] but " abroad ", having left its body behind. This was the literal and primitive meaning understood by the Greek when he spoke of the " ekstasis " of the soul in such orgiastic conditions of excitement.[46] This ekstasis is " a brief madness ", just as madness is a prolonged ekstasis.[47] But the ekstasis, the temporary *alienatio mentis* of the Dionysiac cult was not thought of as a vain purposeless wandering in a region of pure delusion, but as a *hieromania*,[48] a sacred madness in which the soul, leaving the body, winged its way to union with the god.[49] It is now with and in the god, in the condition of *enthousiasmos* ; those who are possessed by this are ἔνθεοι ; they live and have their being in the god.[50] While still retaining the finite Ego, they feel and enjoy to the full the infinite powers of all life.

In *ekstasis* the soul is liberated from the cramping prison of the body; it communes with the god and develops powers of which, in the ordinary life of everyday, thwarted by the body, it knew nothing. Being now a spirit holding communion with spirits it is able to free itself from Time and see what only the spiritual eye beholds—things separated from it in time and space. The enthusiastic worship of the Thracian servants of Dionysos gave birth to the *inspiration mantikê*,[51] a form of prophecy which did not (like prophecy as it invariably appears in Homer) have to wait for accidental, ambiguous and external signs of the god's will, but on the contrary entered immediately into communion with the world of gods and spirits and in this heightened spiritual condition beheld and proclaimed the future. This power belonged to men only in *ekstasis*, in religious madness, when " the God enters into men ". The *Mainads* are the official exponents of this *mantikê* of inspiration.[52] It is simple and intelligible enough that the Thracian cult of Dionysos, which was throughout a means of stimulating men to a condition of extreme exaltation that they might enter into direct communion with the spirit-world, also encouraged the prophesying of inspired seers, who in their rapt exaltation and frenzy became clairvoyant. Among the Thracian Satrai there was a tribe called the Bessoi who produced *prophêtai*, and these were in charge of an oracle of Dionysos situated on the top of a high mountain. The prophetess of this temple was a woman who gave prophecies like the Pythia at Delphi, that is to say, in a state of rapt ecstasy. This, at least, is what Herodotos says,[53] and we have many other accounts of Thracian *mantikê* and its close connexion with the orgiastic cult of Dionysos.[54]

§ 3

The Greek type of religion, perhaps from its very origin, certainly at the earliest period of its development in which it becomes accessible to our observation—the period to which the Homeric poems belong—had no leaning to anything resembling an excited emotional worship like that practised by the Thracians in their orgiastic cult of Dionysos. The whole movement wherever it came to their notice must have struck the Greeks of Homer as something strange and barbaric, attractive only through the interest ever attached to the unknown. And yet—the fact is certain—the thrilling tones of this "enthusiastic" worship awoke an answering chord deep in the hearts of many Greeks; in spite of all that was strange they must have recognized a familiar accent in it—something that, however outlandishly expressed, could appeal to the common nature of mankind.

This enthusiastic Thracian cult was in fact only a special expression, conforming to their peculiar national characteristics, of a religious impulse that is to be found all over the earth, and which breaks out in every stage of civilization. It must, indeed, answer to an instinctive need of human nature, and be rooted in the physical and psychical constitution of man. In moments of supreme exaltation man felt the presence above him and around him of mighty powers that seemed to express themselves even in his own personal life. These he was no longer to confront in pious and fearful awe, passively confined within the limits of his own separate personality; he was to break down every barrier and clasp them to his heart, making them his own in unconditional surrender. Mankind needed not to wait for that strange product of poetry and thought, Pantheism, before it could experience this instinctive need to lose its own private existence, for a moment, in the divine. There are whole races of men, not otherwise among the most distinguished members of the human family, who have a special tendency and gift for such expansion of the human consciousness into the supra-personal. They have an urgent impulse to such rapt and visionary states, and they regard the enticing or horrifying visions that visit them in those states as actual experiences of another world into which their "souls" have for a brief while been transported. In every part of the world there are peoples who regard such ecstatic exaltation as the only true religious act, the only way of intercourse with the spirit-world available to man, and base their religious performances principally upon such ceremonial as experience has shown to be most capable of inducing the ecstasies and visions. The means most commonly adopted by such peoples to produce the desired intensity and stimulation of feeling is a violently excited dance prolonged to the point of exhaustion, in the darkness of night, to the accompaniment of tumultuous music. Sometimes whole companies of the people induce in themselves a state of religious excitement by wild and furious dancing.[55] More often selected individuals, specially susceptible to such impressions, suffer their "souls" to be drawn out by music and dancing and every other sort of stimulating influence, and made to visit the world of spirits and gods.[56] Such "magicians" and priests who can place themselves in immediate contact of soul with the spirit world, are to be found all over the globe. The shamans of Asia, the "medicine men" of North America, the Angekoks of Greenland, the Butios of the Antilles, the Piajes of the Caribbees are merely special cases of a universal type, essentially the same in all its different manifestations. Africa, Australia, and the island world of the Pacific are equally familiar with them. Both their performances and the range of ideas that lie behind them belong to a type of religious experience that occurs with the regularity of a natural phenomenon, and must therefore not be regarded as abnormal. Even among Christian peoples of long standing, the smouldering fires of this primitive and emotional type of religion are ever ready to burst out again in renewed flames, and those who feel their warmth are kindled to a more than human sense of life and vigour.[57] Conventionality and traditionalism, even the substitution of a cold and spurious mimicry for real feeling, are of course quite compatible with a form of religion which consists so much in the display of emotion. But even so, the most cautious observers [58] have declared that by such violent stimulation of every sense the "magicians" are thrown into a state of quite unfeigned exaltation. In accordance with the character and content of their normal modes of thought, the hallucinations to which the magicians are subject differ in different cases; but as a general rule their frenzy opens to them a way of immediate intercourse, frequently of complete communion of being, with the gods. This is the only explanation which will account for the fact that, like the inspired Bakchantes of Thrace, the magicians and priests of so many peoples are called by the name of the divinity to whom their "enthusiastic" worship elevates them.[59] The impulse to union with God, the extinction of the individual in the divine—these are what form the fundamental points of contact between the mysticism of the most highly cultivated and talented peoples and the emotional religion of primitive "savages". Even the external machinery of excitement and stimulation are not always dispensed with by the mystics: [60] they are always the same as those with which we are already familiar in the orgiastic religion of primitive peoples—music, the giddy whirl of the dance, narcotic stimulants. Thus (to take the most striking example out of many that might be given) the dervishes of the Orient whirl round in their violent dances to the rattle of drums, and the sound of flutes till the last stages of excitement and exhaustion are reached. The purpose of it all is vividly expressed by the most fearless of all the mystics, Jelaleddin Rumi, in the words: " He that knows the power of the dance dwells in God; for he has learnt that Love can slay.[61] Allah hu! . . . ."

§ 4

Wherever a cultus of this kind, making its aim and object the evocation of ecstatic raptures, has taken root—whether in whole races of men or in religious communities—there we find in close alliance with it, whether as cause or effect or both, a peculiarly vital belief in the life and power of the soul of man after its separation from the body. Our comparative glance over the analogous phenomena of other lands has shown us that the exalted worship offered to " Dionysos " among the Thracians was only a single variety of a method, familiar to more than half the human race, of getting into touch with the divine by a religious " enthousiasmos ". We therefore expect to find among the Thracians a specially strong and well-developed belief in the life of the " soul ". And in fact we find Herodotos telling us of a Thracian tribe, the Getai, whose belief " made men immortal ".[62] They had only one god, Zalmoxis by name.[63] To this god, who dwelt in a cavernous mountain, all the dead of their race, they believed, would one day be gathered and have immortal life.[64] The same belief was held by other Thracian tribes, too.[65] This creed seems to have had in view the " transplantation "[66] of the dead to a blessed life in the hereafter. But, it would seem, this transplantation was not perhaps for ever. We hear of the belief that the dead would " return "[67] from the other world; and that this idea existed among the Getai is implied (though the narrator does not clearly understand this) by the absurd pragmatizing fable which Herodotos got from the Greek settlers on the Hellespont and the Pontos.[68] In this story (as often in later accounts too) Zalmoxis is actually a slave and pupil of Pythagoras of Samos. Whoever invented this fairy-tale was led to it by observing the close relationship between the Pythagorean doctrine of the soul and the Thracian belief. In the same way later observers of the same fact reversed the positions and made Pythagoras the pupil of the Thracian.[69] In any case the fact cannot to be doubted that in Thrace people thought they had found again the special doctrine of Pythagoras as to the *transmigration of souls*. The belief in the " return " of the soul must be interpreted as meaning that the souls of the dead return to life in new bodies and resume their life on earth, to this extent being "immortal". Only so interpreted could it have been held for a moment without coming into conflict with obvious appearances. An allusion in Euripides seems to regard as Thracian such a belief in a recurrent incarnation of the soul.[70]

We should be justified in expecting to find an inner connexion between this Thracian belief in immortality, which seems to have made such an impression on our Greek informants, and the religion and "enthousiastic" worship of the same people. Nor are traces lacking of a close association of the Thracian worship of Dionysos and Thracian cult of the Souls.[71] But if we ask why the religion of the Thracian Dionysos was attended by a belief in the independent, indestructible life of the soul, a life not confined to the period of its sojourn in the body which at present envelopes it, the answer must be sought not in the nature of the god to whom the cult was offered (that nature being, in fact, insufficiently known to us) but in the nature of the cult itself. The object of that cult—we might almost say its special task—was to exalt its worshippers to a state of "ekstasis" in which their "souls" should be forcibly delivered from the normal circle of their human and circumscribed being, and raised as pure spirits to communion with the god and his company of spirits. The true "Bakchai"[72]—those who were really cast into a state of religious madness—found in the rapture of these orgies a new province of experience open before them: they experience things of which they could give no account in the fully conscious light of ordinary day. There can be no doubt that the experiences and visions that their "ekstasis" gave them were regarded by them as the plainest and most literally real of facts.[73] The belief in the existence and life of a second self distinct from the body and separable from it was already encouraged by the "experiences" of the separate existence and independent behaviour of that self in dreams and fainting fits.[74] How much more strongly and vividly must this belief have been confirmed for those who in the intoxication of those delirious dances had "experienced" for themselves how the soul, freed from the body, could participate in the joys and terrors of the divine existence; not indeed the whole man, body and soul together, but the soul by itself and in separation from the body—the spiritual being invisibly living within the man. The sense of its own divinity, its eternity, which had been blindingly revealed to it in "ekstasis", might be developed by the soul into a lasting persuasion that it was indeed of a divine nature, and called to a divine life which it would enjoy for ever as soon as it was freed from the body, just as it had then enjoyed it for a moment. No mere intellectual arguments could give such powerful support to a spiritualism of this kind as the personal experience itself which, even in this life supplied a foretaste of what the individual was one day to enjoy as his own for ever.

In some such way as this, the persuasion of an independent, continued existence of the soul after the death of its body was developed into a belief in the divinity and immortality of the soul. In all such cases it was almost inevitable that the naïve distinction between " body " and " soul ", natural to simple-minded peoples and individuals, should harden into an *opposition* between the two. The descent from the heights where the ecstatic and emancipated soul enjoyed its thrilling delights was too sudden: the body could not but seem a burden and a hindrance, almost an enemy of the heaven-born soul. Disparagement of the ordinary existence of every day, a turning aside from this life—these are the natural results of such an advanced spiritualism, even though it may have no speculative basis, when it influences so profoundly the religious temperament of a people as yet untroubled by the subtleties of a scientific culture. A trace of such a depreciation of the earthly life of mankind in comparison with the joys of a free spirit-existence is to be found in what Herodotos and other narrators tell of certain Thracian tribes [75] who receive the new-born among their kinsfolk with mourning, and bury their dead with joyful acclamation, for the latter are now beyond the reach of all pain, and are living " in perfect happiness ".[76] The cheerfulness with which the Thracians faced death in battle [77] was explained by the persuasion which they held that death was only an entrance into a higher life for the soul. They were even credited with a real desire for death, for to them " dying seemed so fair ".[78]

§ 5

Further than this the Thracians—who never quite outgrew a sort of semi-animated torpor of the intellect—could not go on the way marked out for them. The seed of a mystical form of religion that existed in the ecstatic dance-orgies of Dionysos-worship never came to fruition. We never feel with them that we are being taken beyond the region of vague unconscious emotion; it is but a passing illumination that for a moment of wild excitement reveals the near presence of overwhelming spirit-forces.

Not until the flames of such ecstatic worship were fed and nourished by a people of more independent and developed spiritual life, could fitful suggestions be welded into deep and enduring thought. Reflexion upon the nature of the world and of God, the changing and deceptive flow of appearance with the indestructible One Reality behind it; the conception of a divinity that is One, a single light that, divided into a thousand rays and reflected from everything that is, achieves its unity again in the soul of man: such thoughts as these, allied to the dim half-conscious impulse of an enthusiastic dance-worship, might allow the pure waters of the stream of mysticism to run clear at last, freed from the turbid and unsatisfying enthusiasm of popular religious practices.

Thus, for example, among the stern and rigid-minded peoples of Islam, with their stiff, uncompromising Monotheism, there arose, no one knows whence, the inspired dance-orgies of the Dervishes, which then spread far and wide carrying with them the mystical doctrine of the Sûfis, that child of the profound mind of India. Man is God; God is All: such was the pronouncement of the inspired poetry—the special contribution in particular of Persia to this religion of mystic ecstacy—now in the most transparent simplicity, now in the most gorgeous magnificence of imagery. In the ecstatic dance, which in this case remained in organic connexion with the mystical doctrine (as the soil of the maternal earth with the flowers which she puts forth) new strength was ever being added to the spiritual superstructure. Mystical theory was invigorated by the practical experience, in heightened consciousness, of an internal and unquenchable source of undying power and might. The veil of the world was torn aside for the inspired worshipper; the All-One became sensible and intelligible for him; it poured into his own being; the "deification" of the Mystai was realized in him. "Who knows the power of the Dance dwells in God"...

Many years before all this, a process of development was completed on Greek soil which has no closer parallel than the special phase of Oriental religion just referred to. Greek religion never indeed (so long at least as the independence of Greek life lasted) went to the extravagant lengths of Oriental mysticism. Even the sense of the infinite had to be expressed by the Greek imagination in plastic form. But for all that, on Greek soil, in the ecstatic Cult of Dionysos, under the influence of Greek reflexion upon God, the world and mankind, the seeds which previously lay undeveloped in the womb of that cult were unfolded in a mystical doctrine, whose guiding principle was the divinity of the human soul and the infiniteness of its life in God. It was from this source that Greek philosophy found the courage to advance a doctrine of the immortality of the soul.

NOTES TO CHAPTER VIII

[1] Pl., *Phdr.* 265 A.

[2] e.g. Cael. Aurel. (i.e. Soranos), *Morb. Chr.* i, § 144 ff.; Aret. *Chron. Pass.* i, 6, p. 84 Kühn [vol. 24].

[3] Even the late interpolated passages *Ξ* 325, *ω* 74, are not quite conclusive. Apart from these the statement of Sch. *ι* 198 applies strictly throughout both poems: *τὸ μὴ παραδιδόναι Ὅμηρον Διόνυσον οἴνου εὑρετήν*, Lehrs, *Arist.*[3], p. 181.

[4] *Z* 132 ff. The scene is evidently meant to be a Bacchic festival. This is shown by the *θύσθλα*, which the *Διωνύσοιο τιθῆναι* let fall out of their hands. All the rest is obscure. Even in antiquity no one knew who the *τιθῆναι* of Dionysos really were, and hence alternative suggestions were all the more numerous: cf. Nauck, *Fr. Trag.*[2], p. 17. Voigt, in Roscher's *Mythol. Lex.* i, 1049. It can hardly be necessary (with Sch. A on *Z* 129) to deduce from the reference to *τιθῆναι* that Dionysos himself was regarded as *νήπιος ἔτι καὶ παῖς*. His former *τιθῆναι* follow him in the Bacchic festival even after he has grown up, exactly as in *h. Hom.* xxvi, 3, 7–10. *αἱ Διονύσου τροφοί* as the frenzied mob worshipping the god, *τῷ θεῷ ὀργιάζουσαι* (in Thessaly), come in D.S. 5, 50, 4, in a parallel narrative to the story of Lykourgos and the Mainads. With the conception of the god as *λικνίτης* neither his leap into the sea (*Z* 135 ff.), nor esp. the adj. *μαινομένοιο* (132) are in harmony. This last word does certainly give us pause. The accounts provided by later ages of the madness of Dionysos are obviously made up from the lines of Homer and are therefore of no use to us (already ap. Eumelos in the *Εὐρωπία*, Schol. AD. *Z* 131; then Pherekydes, Achaios *ἐν Ἴριδι*: Phld., *Piet.*, p. 36 [Nauck, *Fr. Trag.*[2], p. 751]; E., *Cyc.* 3. [Apollod.] iii, 5, 1, is prob. derived from Pherec. as are also Philistos *fr.* 57, *FHG.* i; Pl., *Lg.* 672 B; Nic. *Ὀφιακ. fr.* 30 Schn., etc.). Scholastic interpreters even thought of a hypallage: *μαινομένοιο = μανιοποιοῦ, βακχείας παρασκευαστικοῦ*, Schol. A, *Z* 132; cf. Sch. B, p. 182a, 43 f. Bk. And, indeed, there is certainly in this case a sort of mythological or sacramental hypallage: the state of mind brought about by the god in those who surround him is reflected back on to the god himself (*μαινόμενοι Σάτυροι*, E., *Ba.* 130; cf. the mad nurses of Dionysos, Nonn., *D.* ix, 38 ff.). It would not be hard to parallel this (e.g. Dionys. who makes men drunk is represented as himself drunk, Ath. 428 E, etc.).

[5] *X* 460, *μεγάροιο διέσσυτο μαινάδι ἴση, παλλομένη κραδίην.* The evidence of this passage for the familiarity of Homer's audience with the nature of the Mainads cannot be set aside as Lob., *Agl.* 285, tries to do. The word could only be used as an *εἰκών* if the thing were often before men's eyes. *μαινάς*, indeed, is even something different from, and more specialized than *μαινομένη* (*Z* 389).

[6] The view that *μαίνεσθαι* was primitive in the cult of D., the wine, etc., being added later, was definitely put forward in 1825 by O. Müller (*Kl. Schr.* ii, 26 ff.) arguing against J. H. Voss. But it is only in quite recent times that in tracing the origin of the religion of Dionysos occasional inquirers have taken this view as their starting point: cf. esp. Voigt in his noteworthy treatment of Dionysos in Roscher's *Myth. Lex.* i, 1029 ff.

[7] *ὃς μαίνεσθαι ἐνάγει ἀνθρώπους*, Hdt. iv, 79.

[8] E.g. the Odrysai, who, however, lived further north in the Hebros valley; Mela, ii, 17, mentions distinctly the mountain chains of Haimos, Rhodope, and Orbelos as sacris Liberi patris et coetu Maenadum celebratos.

[9] Lob., *Agl.* 289 ff.

[10] Sabazios: *Σαβάζιον τὸν Διόνυσον οἱ Θρᾷκες καλοῦσιν* Sch. Ar., *Ves.* 9; cf. Sch. Ar., *Lys.* 388; D.S. 4, 4, 1; Harp. *Σαβοί*; Alex. Polyh. ap. Macr. i, 18, 11 (*Sebadius*: cf. Apul., *M.* viii, 25, p. 150, 11 Ey. The original form of this name seems to have been *Savos*, *Savadios*, Kretschmer, *Einleitung in. d. griech. Spr.* 195 f.; Usener, *Götternamen* 44). Sabos, Phot. p. 495, 11–12 Pors. Hesych. s.v.; Orph., *H.* 49, 2, etc. The fact that others could call Sabazios a Phrygian god (Amphitheos *π. Ἡρακλείας β'* ap. Sch. Ar., *Av.* 874; Str. 470; Hsch. s.v.), only serves to bring out more clearly the opinion, unanimously held even in antiquity, that the Thracians and the Phrygians were closely related. Sabazios (besides being identified with Helios: Alex. Polyh. l.c.; cf. Soph. *fr.* 523 N.), as the supreme and almighty god of the Thracians, was even called *Ζεὺς Σαβάζιος* (Val. Max. i, 3, 2), esp. on inss. (a few are given in Rapp, *Dionysoscult* [Progr.] p. 21); cf. also ins. from Peiraeus *Ἐφ. Ἀρχ.* 1883, p. 245; *Ins. Per am.* i, 248, 33, 49; from Pisidia, *Papers of the Amer. School at Athens*, ii, p. 54, 56. *Jovi Sabazio*, Orelli, *Ins.* 1259). We even find *Ζεὺς Βάκχος, Ζεὺς Ἥλιος* (*BCH.* vi, 189).—The name *Σαβάζιος* was derived from *σαβάζειν = εὐάζειν, διὰ τὸν γενόμενον περὶ αὐτὸν εὐασμόν* (*θειασμόν*): Sch. Ar., *Av.* 874; *Lys.* 388. So, too, *Βάκχος* was on this view only another way of expressing the same meaning; since this name also was derived by the ancients from *βάζειν = εὐάζειν* (it is really from the root *Ϝαχ* (*ἀχέω*) *Βάκχος*, with "affrication"; a reduplicated form of it is *ϜιϜαχος, Ἴακχος, ἰαχέω, ἰακχέω*; cf. Curtius, *Griech. Etym.*[5], p. 460, 576). Other names of the Thracian Dionysos are the following: *Βασσαρεύς* (*Βάσσαρος*, Orph., *H.* 45, 2), derived from *βασσάρα* the long dress (made of skin ?) worn by the *Βασσαρίδες = Θρᾴκιαι βάκχαι, AB.* 222, 26 f.; Hsch. s.v. *Βασσάραι* and *EM.* s.v. (the last compiled from Orion and Sch. Lyc. 771). Other accounts (not contradicting in this point the statement of Hsch.) made it the dress worn by the god himself: Sch. Pers. i, 101. (The *Βασσαρεύς* was generally described as bearded and even *senili specie*, like the representation of Dionysos himself in the oldest Greek art: Macr. i, 18, 9.) If *Βασσαρεύς* means "the wearer of the long fox-skin" we should be strongly reminded of the—also Thracian—god *Ζάλμολξις* (*Ζάλμοξις*), whose name was derived from *ζαλμός = δορὰ ἄρκτου* (Porph., *VP.* 14, though this comes only from Antonius Diogenes 6), and probably means "he who is cloaked in the bearskin" (see Fick, *Spracheinh. d. Indog. Europ.*, p. 418; Hehn, *Culturpflanz.* 428 E.T.).—*Γίγων* a name of Dionysos, *EM.* 231, 28: perhaps a name given to the god in the city Gigonos mentioned in the same passage, and the *ἄκρα Γίγωνις* at the western end of the Thracian Chalkidike.—*EM.* 186, 32, is too short to be intelligible: *βαλιά. διαποίκιλος. καὶ τὸν Διόνυσον Θρᾷκες.—Δύαλος Διόνυσος παρὰ Παίοσιν*, Hesych.

[11] At any rate the people whom Thuc., Ephoros, and others call Thracians and regarded as having been once settled in Phokis, Boeotia, etc., are undoubtedly to be considered Thracians—and not the impossibly honest and exemplary people, a creation of the fancy, the "Thracians of the Muses", alleged to be quite distinct from the real Thracian peoples, of whom we have heard so much since K. O.

Müller (*Orchom.* 379 ff.) introduced the idea. Antiquity only knew of one kind of Thracian. In the Homeric poems they are not so different from the Greeks in civilization as they were in later times, when we know them from the accounts of Herod. and Xen. For all that they are the same people. They seem in the course of time to have degenerated, or rather they have not shared in the progress made by others and so have remained backward (even behind their Phrygian relatives who wandered to Asia Minor and achieved a higher culture under Semitic influence). In fact, like the Keltoi, they were never able to get beyond a condition of semi-civilization.

[12] μανίας ἐπαγωγὸν ὁμοκλάν. Aesch. in the Ἠδωνοί ap. Str. 470–1 (*fr.* 57), is the locus classicus for the music in the *Thracian* festival of Dionysos. Apart from this it is impossible to distinguish in the accounts given by our ancient authorities, between the strictly Thracian festival and the *ideal* generalized festival of Dionysos (not the mitigated ceremonial actually used in the festival in Greece). They merge completely into each other.

[13] σαβάζειν = εὐάζειν, Schol. Ar., *Av.* 874 ; *Lys.* 388.

[14] αἱ Βάκχαι σιγῶσιν. Diogen., *Prov.* iii, 43.

[15] Complete revolution round one's own axis, as in the dance of a dervish, is known at least only in the more fanatic dance-festivals of antiquity : στροφὴν ὁλοσώματον ὥσπερ οἱ κάτοχοι δινεύοντες, Heliod. 4, 17, p. 116, 1 Bk. δίνησις τῶν θεοφορήτων in Phrygia : Horus ap. *EM.* 276, 32. Crusius, *Philol.* 55, 565, compares besides Verg., *A.* vii, 377 ff. ; Alex. Aphr., *Prob.*, p. 6 Us. In the Spartan dance διαμαλέας (?) Seilenoi and Satyrs appeared ὀρχούμενοι ὑπότροχα [περίτροχα acc. to Meineke : perhaps better]. Poll. 4, 104.

[16] E., *Ba.* 116 ff., 664 ff. Thracian : assiduis Edonis fessa choreis qualis in herboso concidit Apidano, Prop. 1, 3, 5 f.

[17] Bassaris : Thracian acc. to Sch. Pers. i, 101 ; worn by βάκχαι Hsch. βασσάραι. Lydian, too : ὅστις χιτῶνας βασσάρας τε Λυδίας ἔχει ποδήρεις, A. ἐν Ἠδωνοῖς, *fr.* 59 ; cf. Poll. 7, 59. " Perhaps a Phrygian word that has penetrated into Lydia," Kretschmer, *Einleitung*, 390. The worship of Dionysos which had also presumably come from Phrygia, was esp. popular in Lydia.

[18] Familiar in the Bacchic ceremonial of Greece ; but occurring already in Thrace : Aesch. in Ἠδωνοί (dealing entirely with Thracian customs) mentions the νεβρίδες, and in the same place has αἰγίδας as well (*fr.* 64).

[19] The Βάκχαι of Macedonia and the Μιμαλλόνες, in all respects resembling the Thracian Bacchants, κερατοφοροῦσι κατὰ μίμησιν Διονύσου : Sch. Lyc. 1237 (Λαφυστίας κερασφόρους γυναῖκας).

[20] Mentis inops rapitur, quales audire solemus Threicias passis Maenadas ire comis, Ov., *F.* iv, 457 f.

[21] Thphr. *Ch.* 16 (28, p. 141 Jebb) ; Artemid. 2, 13, p. 106, 9 H.

[22] Snakes and daggers are found in the hands of the μιμαλλόνες καὶ βασσάραι καὶ λυδαί in the train of Ptol. Philad. : Kallixenos ap. Ath. 198 E. Snakes and θύρσοι belong to the paraphernalia of the ἔνοχοι τοῖς Ὀρφικοῖς καὶ τοῖς περὶ τὸν Διόνυσον ὀργιασμοῖς γυναῖκες in Macedonia, and of the Κλώδωνες καὶ Μιμαλλόνες who πολλὰ ταῖς Ἠδωνίσι καὶ ταῖς περὶ τὸν Αἷμον Θρῄσσαις ὅμοια δρῶσιν, Plu., *Alex.* 2 (in connexion with the snake of Olympias. She was especially given to the Thrako-Dionysian mysteries : cf. the letter of Olympias to Alexander, Ath. 659 F).—θύρσοι of the Macedonian Μιμαλλόνες : Polyaen. 4, 1 ; Sch. Pers. 1, 99.—" Even now " the thyrsos wands are decked with ivy in the *Thraciae populis sollemnibus sacris*, Plin.,

NH. xvi, 144.—The νάρθηξ of the thyrsos is really a shepherd's staff: Clem. Al., *Protr.* ii, p. 14 P.

[23] Eur., *Ba.* 735 ff. and frequently.

[24] κατοχαὶ καὶ ἐνθουσιασμοί in the Thrako-Macedonian worship of Dionysos: Plu., *Alex.* 2. (The Mimallones *imitantur furorem Liberi*, Sch., Pers. i, 99.) οἱ τῷ Σαβαζίῳ κάτοχοι: Porph. ap. Iamb. *de Myst.* 3, 9, p. 117, 16. βάκχος· ὁ μανιώδης, Eust. δ 249; β 16. Κλώδωνες is the name given to the μαινάδες καὶ βάκχαι ἀπὸ τοῦ κατόχους γινομένας κλώζειν, *EM.* 521, 50. οἱ κάτοχοι τοῖς περὶ τὸν Διόνυσον ὀργιασμοῖς, Plu., *Is. et Os.* 35, p. 364 F.

[25] οἱ βακχευόμενοι καὶ κορυβαντιῶντες ἐνθουσιάζουσι μέχρις ἂν τὸ ποθούμενον ἴδωσιν, Philo, *Vit. Cont.* 2, ii, p. 473 M.

[26] So too the wild shaking and whirling-round of the head, which acc. to innumerable literary and pictorial descriptions was a regular feature of the Bacchic dance and cult, must have contributed—and was so intended—to bring about the condition of ecstasy and frenzy (ῥιψαύχενι σὺν κλόνῳ, Pi., *fr.* 208; κρᾶτα σεῖσαι, E., *Ba.* 185, etc.).—How such fanatic shaking of the head, if kept up for along time, is by itself sufficient, in persons naturally predisposed to it, to bring on complete religious ἔκστασις, may be learnt from a remarkable account in Moreau *du hachisch*, p. 290 ff., derived from personal observation in the East.

[27] The object of the trieteric festival of Dionysos (repeated every second year) held in so many places in Greece (cf. Weniger, *Dionysos-dienst in Elis*, Progr. 1883, p. 8) was to celebrate the *presence* of the god. This is clearly shown by D.S. 4, 3, 2, who also attributes the trieteric festival to the Thracians: τοὺς Βοιωτοὺς καὶ τοὺς ἄλλους Ἕλληνας καὶ Θρᾷκας . . . καταδεῖξαι τὰς τριετηρίδας θυσίας Διονύσῳ καὶ τὸν θεὸν νομίζειν κατὰ τὸν χρόνον τοῦτον ποιεῖσθαι τὰς παρὰ τοῖς ἀνθρώποις ἐπιφανείας. At this time women and maidens celebrated τὴν παρουσίαν τοῦ Διονύσου. (In the archaic song of the Elean women the Bull-god is thus called upon: Plu., *QG.* 36, 299 A; *Is. et. Os.* 35, p. 364 F; whereupon the Eleans believed that τὸν θεόν σφισιν ἐπιφοιτᾶν ἐς τῶν Θυίων τὴν ἑορτήν: Paus. 6, 26, 1.)—For Bakchos amongst the dancers see E., *Ba.* 185 ff., 306 f., and often. At the trieteric festival at Delphi Διόνυσος . . . Παρνασὸν κάτα πηδᾷ χορεύει παρθένοις σὺν Δελφίσιν, E., *Hypsip. fr.* 752. And so often in poetry: see Nauck on S., *OT.* 213; *Ant.* 1126 ff.—Thracian trieteric festival: tuo motae proles Semeleia thyrso Ismariae celebrant repetita triennia bacchae, Ov., *M.* ix, 641 f.; tempus erat, quo sacra solent trieterica Baccho Sithoniae celebrare nurus; nox conscia sacris, etc., vi, 587.

[28] ἀφανισμός followed by ἐπιφάνεια of Dionysos represent, as we frequently learn, the varying relationship of the god with mankind. These are alternating and periodically repeated, and they are reflected in the trieteric period of the festivals. It is customary to explain this disappearance and return of the god as an allegorical typification of the destruction and restoration of vegetation. There is no reason at all to believe this, except for those who regard the doctrines of the Greek " Religion of Nature " as infallible axioms. The god is simply, and in the literal sense of the words, regarded as removed for a time from the world of men, during which period he is in the world of spirits. In the same way Apollo, according to the Delphic legend, is carried away from the human world for certain periods: he lives during that time among the Hyperboreans, whose land is inaccessible to mortal foot or ship. We ought not to be afraid to make use of the light thrown on these matters by parallel legends of the temporary disappearance

of gods among uncivilized peoples (the god may be sometimes asleep or under constraint; cf. Plu., *Is. et Os.*, 69 fin. 378 F); cf. what we are told in Dobrizhoffer's *Gesch. d. Abip.* ii, p. 63 (E.T.), about the beliefs held by the Abipones of Paraguay; or, again, what is said of the negro races of West Africa, according to whom the god normally lives in the depths of the earth, but at regularly recurring intervals comes up to visit men; whereupon the members of a mystical society build him a house, receive his oracles, etc.; Réville, *Rel. des peuples non-civil.* i, 110–11. Thus Dionysos, too, is for a time in the underworld, in the world of spirits and the *souls.* This is clearly presupposed by the festival at Lerna, in which Dionysos is called up out of the bottomless spring Alkyonia by which there was an entrance to Hades (just as the inhabitants of Kos every year ἀνακαλοῦνται Hylas out of his spring, i.e. from the underworld: H. Türk, *De Hyla*, p. 3 f.; Welcker, *Kl. Schr.* i, 12; and see Maass, *Litt. Ztg.* 1896, 7–8). Hence also in Lerna a lamb was offered as a victim τῷ πυλαόχῳ, i.e. to Hades himself, and was thrown into the spring (Plu., *Is. et Os.* 35, p. 368 F, quoting Sokrates περὶ τῶν Ὁσίων; *Smp.* 4, 6, 2, p. 671 E; Paus. 2, 36, 7; 37, 5–6). Because he is in the realm of the dead a pragmatical myth represented him as slain by Perseus and thrown into the spring of Lerna: Lob., *Agl.* 574. In Delphi, too, something was known of the death and reawakening of Dionysos, but we have in Orph., *H.* 53, a quite unambiguous expression of the real conception, acc. to which D. " rested in the house of Persephone ", and appears again in the upper world at the time of the trieteric festival when he ἐγείρει his κῶμον, εὐάζων κινῶν τε χορούς. We may be all the more certain that the same idea is to be attributed to the trieteric festival in Thrace, since the same belief exactly occurs again in the legend of the Thracian (Getic) god Zalmoxis (see below)—he was believed to have disappeared into his infernal kingdom among the spirits and souls and to have made periodical returns to the world of the living. The reason why Dionysos, as worshipped both in Thracian and Greek trieteric festivals, stops for a time in the underworld of the souls, is clear enough: that too was his realm. We can now understand why it is that Dionysos is also ruler over the souls and can be called Ζαγρεὺς, Νυκτέλιος, Ἰσοδαίτης: i.e. he is simply given names of Hades himself (Plu., *E ap. D.* ix, p. 389 A). His real character of master of the souls and spirits (ἄναξ, ἥρως), as it had been originally in the Thracian cult, was thus perserved, in spite of much alteration in its Greek form, partly in Greek local cults, partly in the Orphic cult of Dionysos.—There is a legend which is based on a reminiscence of this periodic disappearance of Dionysos to the underworld, viz. the thoroughly Greek story of his descent on a single occasion into Hades in order to bring back Semele. Elsewhere his disappearance into the realm of the spirits gave rise to the legend of his escape and flight to the Muses; this was spoken of in the *Agrionia* at Chaironeia (Plu., *Smp.* 8 Praef.).

[29] Cf. Eur., *Ba.* 920 ff., 1020 f.

[30] ταυρόφθογγοι δ' ὑπομυκῶνταί ποθεν ἐξ ἀφανοῦς φοβεροὶ μῖμοι: A. Ἠδωνοί describing the Thracian worship of D. (*fr.* 57). This was " certainly intended to increase for the participants in the festival the feeling of the god's presence and thus to add to the wildness of their orgies ", as Rapp, *Dionysosc.*, 19, very rightly observes. The invisible bellowing bull is the god himself. (Dionysos appears as a bull to the insane Pentheus: E., *Ba.* 920 ff.).—" The Batloka, a tribe in the Northern Transvaal, hold a yearly festival of the dead in which

hidden magicians make weird sounds with flutes which the people take for the voice of spirits: they say 'Modimo is there'." Schneider, *Relig. d. Afrikan. Naturv.* 143.

[31] The women taking part in the trieteric festival of the god play the part of the μαινάδες in his train: D.S. 4, 3, 3. Imitation of the *Νύμφαι τε καὶ Πᾶνες καὶ Σειληνοὶ καὶ Σάτυροι* in the *βακχεία*: Pl., *Lg.* 815 C. What was afterwards merely a piece of traditional ritual was originally without doubt a real hallucination of the *κάτοχοι*.—The idea that a throng, *θίασος*, of wood-spirits Satyrs and Seilenoi danced about the God must also have been common in the Thracian cult (*συγχορευταὶ Διονύσου*, Ael., *VH.* iii, 40; *ὁ τῷ Διονύσῳ παρεπόμενος ὄχλος*, Ath. 362 E). *σαυάδαι* (obviously related to *Σαβάζιος*; cf. Usener, *Götternamen*, 44 f.) was the name given to *οἱ σειληνοί* by the Macedonians, who in the practice of Dionysos-worship were entirely dependent upon the Thracians. Hsch. s.v., cf. Hdt. viii, 138 fin.

[32] The *βακχεύοντες τῷ θεῷ* (i.e. Sabazios, Sabos) are called *σάβοι καὶ σάβαι καὶ σαβάζιοι*: Phot. *σαβούς*; cf. Eust., *β* 16, p. 1431, 46. Harp. (Phot.) s. *σάβοι*; Phot. *παρασαβάζειν* (p. 383, 16 Pors.); Sch. Ar., *Av.* 874. This identification of the god with his ecstatic worshippers belongs to the Phrygian cult of Kybele as well. Just as the goddess is called *Κυβήβη* so *ὁ κατεχόμενος τῇ μητρὶ τῶν θεῶν* is called *Κύβηβος*: Phot. *Κύβηβος, κύβηβον*, Eust. *β* 16. Thus the Greeks in calling the ecstatic worshippers of Bakchos by the name of the god were only adopting the conceptions and vocabulary of the Thracian religion of inspiration into their Dionysos-worship which was modelled on the Thracian cult. *Βάκχος* is their name for the *ὀργιαστὴς τοῦ θεοῦ* (etymologically connected is *βαβάκτης* [*κραύγασος, ὅθεν καὶ Βάκχος* Hsch.] a Phrygian word for the frenzied priest of Kybele: and therefore = *Κύβηβος*; cf. Ribbeck, *Alazon*, p. 86). It appears that the *βάκχοι* of Dionysos were often called by the old Thracian name *σάβοι*: *σάβους καὶ νῦν ἔτι πολλοὶ τοὺς βάκχους καλοῦσιν*, Plu., *Smp.* 4, 6, 2, p. 671 F (*Λαφύστιοι* is also a name given, after *Διόνυσος Λαφύστιος*, to the *Βάκχοι* who worship him: Lyc. 1237 with Sch.).

[33] *Διόνυσος ὠμάδιος* (Porph., *Abs.* ii, 55), *ὠμηστής* (Plu., *Them.* 13), *λαφύστιος, ταυροφάγος* (Soph. *fr.* 607 N.).—At other times we catch a glimpse of the idea that the god himself is the torn and devoured bull (just as in many ancient worships the proper victim of the god is the animal most homogeneous with him): this is evidently the most primitive form of *ἐν—θουσιασμός*, the primeval symbolism of a mystic worship that, like all mysticism, desires to take personal possession of the God.

[34] Dionysos himself also carries the thyrsos (as often in sculpture): E., *Hyps. fr.* 752, etc.

[35] See above, n. 19 (*ὁ βούκερως Ἴακχος*, Soph., *fr.* 874, *ταυρόκερως θεός*, E., *Ba.* 100). The Greek Dionysos is often described as bull-shaped and horned: this, too, in imitation of Thracian belief. It is *Sabazios* whom they *κεραστίαν παρεισάγουσι*, D.S. 4, 4, 2; cf. 3, 64, 2. *Ὕῃ ταυροκέρωτι*, Euphor. *fr.* 14.—An allusion in D.S. 4, 4, 2, seems to suggest that the god, the *μυριόμορφος*, was also (like Attis) regarded as a herdsman. Something of the sort may be referred to in the unintelligible lines quoted by Cl. Al., *Prot.* ii, p. 14 P., apparently in connexion with the Sabazios mysteries. So Dionysos, too, is sometimes thought of as a *βουκόλος*: *ποιμένι δ' ἀγραύλων ταύρων, Διὸς αἰγιόχοιο υἱέι κισσοχίτωνι* are words used of him in [Orph.] *Lith.* 260. Again, in imitation of the god himself his *μύσται* are *βουκόλοι* on the inscriptions from Asia Minor (*Ins. Perg.* ii, 485–8) and Thrace, of

which R. Schöll speaks, *de commun. et. coll. Graecis* (Satura philol. Saupp.), p. 178 ff. *βουκολικός* occurs among the cult officials in the *Iobakcheia* at Athens: *Ath. Mitth.*, 1894, p. 260, l. 122; *archibucolos dei Liberi* on inscriptions of the city of Rome. *βουκόλος* and *βουκολεῖν* occur in connexion with Bacchic worship as early as Kratinos, Aristoph., and Eurip.: *νυκτιπόλου Ζαγρέως βούτας*, E., *Cret. fr.* 472, 11 (acc. to Diels). See Crusius, *Rh. M.* 45, 266 f.; Dieterich *de hymnis Orph.* (Marb. 1891), p. 3 ff.

[36] The special flute-melodies going under the name of Olympos were called *θεῖα* ([Pl.] *Min.* 318 B); *κατέχεσθαι ποιεῖ* (Pl., *Smp.* 215 C); *ὁμολογουμένως ποιεῖ τὰς ψυχὰς ἐνθουσιαστικάς* (Arist., *Pol.* 1340a 10). Cic., *Div.* i, 114: ergo et ei quorum animi, spretis corporibus, evolant atque excurrunt foras, ardore aliquo incitati atque inflammati, cernunt illa profecto quae vaticinantes praenuntiant: multisque rebus inflammantur tales animi qui corporibus non inhaerent: ut ei qui sono quodam vocum et Phrygiis cantibus incitantur. An unmistakable description of what was meant by *ἔκστασις* and Korybantic frenzy (see below).

[37] i.e. those who are *ἐνθουσιασμοῦ κατακώχιμοι*, as Aristotle knew them; certain *μανικαὶ διαθέσεις* are known to Plato. Somewhat similar is the *φύσις θειάζουσα* which according to Demokritos [D. Chr. 36, 1] *fr.* 21 Diels, belongs to the inspired poet.

[38] The drunkenness of the Thracians and their ancient cultivation of the vine are well known. They even brewed beer from barley: Ath. 547 BC (cf. Hehn, *Culturpflanzen*, p. 121 E.T.). The prophetai (prophesying in "enthusiasm") of a Thracian oracle prophesied *plurimo mero sumpto*, Aristot. ap. Macr. 1, 18, 1.—Even the women drank unmixed wine in Thrace: Pl., *Lg.* 637 E.

[39] Mela, 2, 21 (and from him Solin. 10, 5, p. 75, 16 Mom.) says of the Thracians epulantibus ubi super ignes quos circumsident quaedam semina ingesta sunt, similis ebrietati hilaritas ex nidore contingit (cf. [Plu.] *de Flu.* 3, 3). There can be no doubt that it was hempseed (*κάνναβις*) which had this effect. Hdt. iv, 74, says expressly that the Thracians knew hemp. It was thus with a sort of hashish that they intoxicated themselves (hashish is an extract of *cannabis indica*). The Scythians did something similar: Hdt. tells of their vapour-baths in tightly closed huts (iv, 75): they produced a smoke by laying hempseeds on red-hot stones and—though Hdt. does not say so—must necessarily have got into a state of wild intoxication. This may have been a religious performance. Drunkenness is generally regarded by savage tribes as a religiously inspired condition. Further, the Scythian practice has the most striking parallel in the use of "vapour-huts" among the North American Indians, in which case the religious intention is certain (see the account in Klemm, *Culturg.* ii, 175–8; J. G. Müller, *Amerik. Urrelig.* 92). Hdt. i, 202, also mentions intoxication from the fumes of certain "fruits" among the Massagetai; these last, after they had completely bemused themselves, stood up to dance and sing. The Thracians, too, may very well have used intoxication through hashish-fumes as a means of exciting themselves to their ecstatic religious dances.—The ancients were quite familiar with the practice of inhaling aromatic smoke to produce religious hallucinations: [Galen] *ὅρ. ἰατρ.* 187 (xix, p. 462 K.) *ἐνθουσιασμός ἐστι καθάπερ ἐξίστανταί τινες ἐπὶ* (*ὑπὸ*?) *τῶν ὑποθυμιωμένων ἐν τοῖς ἱεροῖς*, < *φάσματα* (om. edd.) > *ὁρῶντες ἢ τυμπάνων ἢ αὐλῶν ἢ συμβόλων* (scr. *κυμβάλων*) *ἀκούοντες*; cf. odorum delenimento potest animus humanus externari, Apul., *Ap.* 43.—For the use of smoke in the

Korybantic ceremonies see below.—The γαγάτης λίθος ὑποθυμιαθείς is useful as an ἐπιληπτικῶν ἔλεγχος (Dioscor. v, 145); it brings on the convulsions of the victim of ἱερὰ νόσος (epilepsy) [Orph.] *L.* 478 ff. (cf. further Damigeron, *de Lap.* 20, p. 179 Ab.; Plin., *NH.* 36, 141; and also Gal. xii, p. 203 K.).

[40] Polak, *Persien*, ii, 245 ff.—We have only to read the accounts derived from personal experience of the sensations and hallucinatory states accompanying hashish-smoking—such as those given, for instance, by Moreau (de Tours) *Du hachisch et de l'aliénation mentale* (Paris, 1845), esp. pp. 23 ff., 51 ff., 59 ff., 90, 147 ff., 151 ff., 369 ff.—to have a complete parallel to the condition which underlay Bacchic excitement. There, too, is the complete ἔκστασις of the spirit, a waking dream-state, an ὀλιγοχρόνιος μανία. It only requires the special tone and character given to the hallucinations and illusions by deep-rooted religious or fanciful conceptions—and the external machinery for cultivating such illusions—to make them an exact equivalent of the delirious condition of the real βάκχοι at the nightly festival of Dionysos. (The helpless state of impressionability to outward—e.g. musical—and inward influences is a marked feature of the intoxication and *fantasia* of hashish.) Other narcotics also have similar effects (Moreau, p. 184 ff.).

[41] Pl., *Ion*, 534 A (perhaps an allusion to the words of Aischines Socr. in the Ἀλκιβιάδης [Aristid. *Rh.* ii, 23 f. Dind.]).

[42] E., *Ba.* 142 f., 706 ff. (144 Συρίας δ' ὡς λιβάνου καπνός).

[43] Anaesthesia of the Bakchai: ἐπὶ δὲ βοστρύχοις πῦρ ἔφερον οὐδ' ἔκαιεν, *Ba.* 757 f.—suum Bacche non sentit saucia volnus, dum stupet Edonis exululata iugis, Ov., *Tr.* 4, 1, 41 f. qualis deo percussa maenas . . . atque expers sui volnus dedit nec sensit, Sen., *Troad.* 682 ff. Similar insensibility to pain (certainly not always feigned) was shown in their ekstasis by the self-wounding *galli* of Kybele, the priests and priestesses of Mâ (Tibull. 1, 6, 45 ff.)—something of the sort is reported of the prophets of Baal (1 *Kings* xviii, 28). See in general on the subject of anaesthesia and the ὀρθῶς κατεχόμενοι ὑπὸ τῶν θεῶν, Iamb., *Myst.* 3, 4, p. 110 Par. In the case of the shamans, the Indian Yogis, the dervishes, and the natives of North America the existence of such states of insensibility in religious excitement has been actually observed.

[44] κατεχόμενος ἐκ τοῦ θεοῦ (Pl., *Men.* 99 D; X., *Sym.* i, 10. κατεχόμενοι ὥσπερ αἱ βάκχαι, Pl., *Ion*, 534 A; *Sym.* 215 C. μανέντι τε καὶ κατασχομένῳ *Phdr.* 244 E). ἡ δ' ἀφρὸν ἐξιεῖσα καὶ διαστρόφους κόρας ἑλίσσουσ', οὐ φρονοῦσ' ἃ χρῆν φρονεῖν, ἐκ Βακχίου κατείχετο, E., *Ba.* 1122 ff. κάτοχοι above, n. 24.

[45] ἔνθεός τε γίγνεται καὶ ἔκφρων καὶ ὁ νοῦς οὐκέτι ἐν αὐτῷ ἔνεστιν, Pl., *Ion*, 534 B (where it is applied to the inspired poet but properly belongs to the Bakchai).

[46] ἔκστασις, ἐξίστασθαι is often used of the inspired state. μαίνεσθαι, ἐνθουσιᾶν, ἔνθεον γίνεσθαι, ἐκστῆναι are all used in the same sense and apply to the "inspired" prophets (Βάκιδες, Σίβυλλαι) and the poets: Arist., *Prob.* 30, 1, p. 954a, 34–9. ἐξίσταται καὶ μαίνεται, Arist. *HA.* 6, 22, p. 577a, 12. The religious ὀργιασμοί, ἐκστάσιας ψυχᾶς ἐπάγοντι: Phintys ap. Stob., *Fl.* iv, 23, 61a, p. 593 H. ἔκστασις is a state in which the soul seems estranged from itself; when the οἰκεῖαι κινήσεις οὐκ ἐνοχλοῦνται ἀλλ' ἀπορραπίζονται (Arist., *Pa. Nat.* 464a, 25). The word became weak and commonplace enough in later usage, but it was evidently meant, originally, to express the "exit" of the "soul" from its body. In the same way the phrase used of one who

goes off into a faint : τὸν δ' ἔλιπεν ψυχή originally meant the same thing and was so understood, see above (chap. i, n. 8). The same idea occurs again in *P. Mag. Par.*, l. 725, p. 63 Wessely : ὑπέκλυτος δ' ἔσει τῇ ψυχῇ καὶ οὐκ ἐν σεαυτῷ ἔσει ὅταν σοι ἀποκρίνηται [the god conjured up].

[47] ἔκστασίς ἐστιν ὀλιγοχρόνιος μανία [Galen] ὅρ. ἰατρ. 485 (xix, p. 462). μανίη ἔκστασίς ἐστι χρόνιος Aretaeus, *Chr. Pass.* 1, 6, p. 78 K.

[48] Διόνυσον μαινόλην ὀργιάζουσι βάκχοι, ὠμοφαγίᾳ τὴν ἱερομανίαν ἄγοντες, καὶ τελίσκουσι τὰς κρεωνομίας τῶν φόνων ἀνεστεμμένοι τοῖς ὄφεσιν ἐπολολύζοντες εὐάν, Clem. Al., *Protr.* ii, p. 11 P.

[49] The ἐνθουσιῶντες ἐκ θεοῦ τινος become like the god, λαμβάνουσι τὰ ἔθη καὶ τὰ ἐπιτηδεύματα (τοῦ θεοῦ), καθόσον δυνατὸν θεοῦ ἀνθρώπῳ μετασχεῖν, Pl., *Phdr.* 253 A. More boldly ἑαυτῶν ἐκστάντας ὅλους ἐνιδρῦσθαι τοῖς θεοῖς καὶ ἐνθεάζειν, Procl. *in Rp.* ii, 108, 23 Kr.—οὐκ ἔκστασις ἁπλῶς οὕτως ἐστίν, ἀλλὰ (in its positive sense) ἐπὶ τὸ κρεῖττον ἀναγωγὴ καὶ μετάστασις, Iamb. *Myst.* 3, 7, p. 114, 9 Parth.

[50] ἔνθεοι γυναῖκες of the Bakchai, S. *Ant.* 963. αἱ Βάκχαι ὅταν ἔνθεοι γένωνται—Aesch. Socr. ap. Aristid., *Rh.* (ii, 23 Dind.). ἔνθεος ἥδε ἡ μανίη (the religious sort) Aret., p. 84 K. The essential meaning of ἔνθεον εἶναι (*plenum esse deo*) is clearly defined in Sch., E., *Hip.* 141 : ἔνθεοι λέγονται οἱ ὑπὸ φάσματός τινος ἀφαιρεθέντες τὸν νοῦν, καὶ ὑπ' ἐκείνου τοῦ θεοῦ τοῦ φασματοποιοῦ κατεχόμενοι καὶ τὰ δοκοῦντα κείνῳ ποιοῦντες. The ἔνθεος is completely in the power of the god ; the god speaks and acts through him. The ἔνθεος has lost his consciousness of himself : like the θεῖοι ἄνδρες (which phrase in Plato has the same meaning as ἔνθεοι ἄνδρες) esp. the θεομάντεις, λέγουσι μὲν ἀληθῆ καὶ πολλά, ἴσασι δ' οὐδὲν ὧν λέγουσι, Pl., *Men.* 99 C. (Philo, *Spec. Leg.* ii, p. 343 M., says of the inspired prophet : ἐνθουσιᾷ γεγονὼς ἐν ἀγνοίᾳ, μετανισταμένου μὲν τοῦ λογισμοῦ. . . , ἐπιπεφοιτηκότος δὲ καὶ ἐνῳκηκότος τοῦ θείου πνεύματος καὶ πᾶσαν τῆς φώνης ὀργανοποιΐαν κρούοντος κτλ. ; cf. Iamb., *Myst.* 3, 4, p. 109.)

[51] ἔνθεοι μάντεις (Bakides, Sibyllai) Arist., *Prb.* 30, 2, 954a, 37. θεομάντεις Pl., *Men.* ad fin. μαντικὴ κατὰ τὸ ἔνθεον, ὅπερ ἐστὶν ἐνθεαστικόν [Plu.] *Plac. Phil.* 5, 1, 1 [*Dox.*, p. 415].

[52] μάντις δ' ὁ δαίμων ὅδε (Dionysos)· τὸ γὰρ βακχεύσιμον καὶ τὸ μανιῶδες μαντικὴν πολλὴν ἔχει· ὅταν γὰρ ὁ θεὸς εἰς τὸ σῶμ' ἔλθῃ πολύς, λέγειν τὸ μέλλον τοὺς μεμηνότας ποιεῖ, E., *Ba.* 298 ff. Here the inner relationship of the inspiration *mantikê* and the " possession " which took place in ecstatic frenzy is expressed with all possible clearness (drunkenness is surely not referred to !). This is how Plu., *Smp.* 7, 10, p. 716 B, also understood Eur. Prophesying Mainads : μαινάδας θυοσκόους E., *Ba.* 224—οὐδεὶς ἔννους ἐφάπτεται μαντικῆς ἐνθέου καὶ ἀληθοῦς, ἀλλ' ἢ καθ' ὕπνον τὴν τῆς φρονήσεως πεδηθεὶς δύναμιν ἢ διὰ νόσον ἢ διά τινα ἐνθουσιασμὸν παραλλάξας, Pl., *Ti.* 71 E. νοσήματα μαντικὰ ἢ ἐνθουσιαστικά make inspired μάντεις what they are : Arist. *Prob.* 954a, 35. Such *mantikê* takes place in the state of furor, cum a corpore animus abstractus divino instinctu concitatur, Cic., *Div.* i, 66. A famous case is that of Kassandra from whom the deus inclusus corpore humano, non iam Cassandra loquitur, § 67 ; cf. the Sibyl who prophesies μαινομένῳ στόματι (Heraclit. *fr.* 12 By. = 92 D.) and the Pythia at Delphi prophesying in a state of μανία. For the prophecy of Korybantic Phrygians possessed and " frenzied ", see Arrian ap. Eust., on D.P. 809.

[53] Hdt. vii, 111 (for Hdt. the Βησσοί seem to be a division, perhaps a clan, of the Satrai. Polyb., Strabo, Pliny, Dio C., and others know them as an independent Thracian tribe) : πρόμαντις γυνὴ χρέουσα κατάπερ ἐν Δελφοῖσι—which means that she prophesied in ecstasy, for that is what the Pythia at Delphi did. (See Sch. Ar., *Plut.* 39 ;

Plu., *Def. Or.* 51, p. 438 B. Lucan vi, 166 ff., clearly describes the phenomena supposed to attend their religious *ekstasis*: artus Phoebados irrupit Paean, mentemque priorem expulit, atque hominem toto sibi cedere iussit pectore. bacchatur demens aliena, etc.)

[54] ὁ Θρῃξὶ μάντις Διόνυσος, E., *Hec.* 1267. Rhesos dwelling in Mt. Pangaios is Βάκχου προφήτης, *Rh.* 972. ἀφικέσθαι τοῖς Λειβηθρίοις παρὰ τοῦ Διονύσου μάντευμα ἐκ Θρᾴκης, Paus. 9, 30, 9. Aristoteles qui Theologumena scripsit, apud Ligyreos (?) ait in Thracia esse adytum Libero consecratum, ex quo redduntur oracula. Macr. 1, 18, 1. The wife of Spartacus, herself a Thracian, was μαντική τε καὶ κάτοχος τοῖς περὶ τὸν Διόνυσον ὀργιασμοῖς, Plu., *Crass.* 8. Octavian in Thrace consulted in Liberi patris luco barbara caerimonia, i.e. an oracle: Suet., *Oct.* 94. Even in 11 B.C. the Bessoi still had a ἱερεὺς τοῦ Διονύσου, Vologeses, who by means of prophesyings (πολλὰ θειάσας) and τῇ παρὰ τοῦ θεοῦ δόξῃ stirred up his people to rebel against the Odrysai: D.C. 54, 34, 5. In 29 B.C. M. Crassus had handed over to the Odrysai the piece of land occupied by the Bessoi ἐν ᾗ καὶ τὸν θεὸν ἀγάλλουσι, D.C. 51, 25, 5.—The spirit of the old Thracian ecstatic cult reappeared in the character of the Bacchic worship introduced from Greece into Italy whose excesses (in 186 B.C.) are narrated by Livy: 39, 8 ff.; among these being viros velut mente capta cum iactatione fanatica corporis vaticinari: 39, 13, 12.

[55] Compare, for example, what we are told of the religious dances of the Ostiaks (Erman, *Travels in Siberia*, ii, 45 f., E. T., Cooley), the Haokah dance of the Dakota, the " medicine-dance " of the Winnebago in North America (Schoolcraft, *Indian Tribes*, iii, 487 ff., 286 ff.), the dance of voodoo negroes in Haiti (*Nouv. annales des voyages*, 1858, iii, p. 90 ff.). For the violent religious dances of the people in ancient Peru see Müller, *Amerik. Urrelig.* 385; in Australia, R. Brough-Smith, *Aborigines of Victoria*, i, 166 ff. (1878). Among the Veddas of Ceylon there was a dance of the " devil's priests " (called Kattadias) dressed up as demons: see Tennent, *Ceylon*, i, 540 f.; ii, 442.—In antiquity the following have the closest relationship to the ecstatic cult of the Thracians: the dance festivals in honour of the " Syrian Goddess ", of the Kappadocian Mâ, of the Phrygian Mountain Mother, and of Attis (the last having much the same origin as the Thracian festival, but being more strongly affected by Semitic influences, and perhaps by the religious practices of the prehistoric inhabitants of Asia Minor). Besides these we may remember the account given by Poseidonios ap. Strabo, 198, D.P. 570 ff., of the excited nocturnal festival celebrated in honour of " Dionysos " in an island at the mouth of the Loire by the women of the Namnites (Samnites, Amnites) Διονύσῳ κατεχόμεναι in the wildest delirium (λύττα).

[56] This is regularly the meaning of such excesses practised by " magicians ". The shaman (with his " soul ") voyages out into the spirit-world: see the remarkably vivid account of Radloff, *Siberien*, ii, 1–67; and also Erman, *Zschr. f. Ethnologie*, ii, 324 ff.; A. Krause, *Tlinkitindianer*, p. 294 ff., 1885. So does the Lapp magician (Knud Leem, *Lappen in Finmarken* [E.T. in Pinkerton's *Voyages*]). The Angekok enters into communion with his Torngak (Cranz, *Hist. of Greenland*, i, p. 194, E.T., 1820); the Butio with the Zemen (Müller, *Amerik. Urrelig.*, 191 f.); the Piajes with the spirits (Müller, 217). Thus, too, communication with the divine " grandfather " of the people is established by means of dances, etc., among the Abipones (Dobrizhoffer, *Abipones*, ii, 64, E.T.). The expulsion of the soul to visit the spirit-world is also practised (in their convulsions) by the

magicians of the North American Indians, the people of the Pacific Islands (Tylor, ii, 133), etc. Such practices start out from a commonly held conception of the nature of body and soul and of their relations with the unseen. The magicians believe "that in their ecstatic condition they can break through the barrier between this world and the next", Müller 397. To facilitate this process they employ the various means alluded to of stimulating their senses.

[57] The most remarkable case of this is provided by the history of a religious sect of our own day widely spread in Russia, who call themselves "the Christs", i.e. sons of God. The sect was founded by a holy man named Philippov in whose body God one day took up his abode; after which the man spoke as the living God himself and gave commandments. The sect particularly stood for the idea that the divine dwells in mankind, Christ in men and Mary in women, and that the sense of their presence can be awakened in men by the action of the Holy Ghost, through the force of strong belief, by saintliness and by religious ecstasy. To produce the ecstasy dances are held in common. About midnight, after long prayers, hymns, and religious addresses, the participators in the secret festival, both men and women, dressed in strange costumes begin to dance. Soon the ranks and circles of the dancers and singers break up; individuals begin to turn round and round, revolving on their own axis with incredible speed, balancing meanwhile on their heels. The excitement of the dancing and leaping crowd grows continually greater. Finally one of them calls out "He comes: He is near—the Holy Ghost". The wildest ecstasy takes hold of every one. Details may be found in N. Tsakni's *La Russie sectaire*, p. 63 ff. (cf. what is said in the same work, p. 80 ff., of the religious dances of the Skopzes, and p. 119 f. of the sect of the "Leapers").—All this is true *Bacchanalia christiana* and therefore mentioned here.

[58] e.g. Mariner, *Tonga Islanders*, i, 108 (1817); Wrangel, *Reise in Siberien*, i, 286 (i, 267 f., French trans.); Radloff, *Siberien*, ii, 58. Even the respectable Cranz, whose own point of view made it impossible for him to appreciate properly the Angekok practices so clearly observed by him, admits that many of them really saw visions that suggested "something supernatural" to them: *Hist. of Greenland*, p. 197 E.T. Something similar is said about ecstatically dancing dervishes by Lane, *Modern Egyptians*, ii, 197.

[59] Magicians called by the name of the god (*Keebet*) among the Abipones: Dobrizhoffer, ii, 248. Similar cases elsewhere: Müller, 77. In Tahiti the person inspired by the god so long as the "inspiration" lasted (several days sometimes) was himself called "god" or given the name of some particular god: Waitz, *Anthropol.* vi, 383. In the case of an African tribe dwelling on the banks of Lake Nyanza the chief spirit sometimes takes temporary possession of one of the magicians (man or woman) who then bears the name of the spirit: Schneider, *Relig. d. Afrik. Naturv.* 151. Sometimes the identity of the magician with the god is expressed by the wearing of the god's distinguishing dress and imitation of his outward appearance (in the manner of the Thracian *Βάκχοι*); cf. the devil-dancers in Ceylon, etc.

[60] When it acquires a more philosophical temper mysticism seeks its unification with the highest (the *ἔλλαμψις τῆς φύσεως τῆς πρώτης*) more by means of the completest passivity of mind and body. It employs the *εἰς αὑτὴν ξυλλέγεσθαι καὶ ἀθροίζεσθαι* of the soul (Plato), or its withdrawal from all that is finite and particular (the *recojimiento* of the Spanish mystics). The profoundest quietude of spirit brings

about the unification with the One behind all multiplicity; cf. the Neoplatonic mystics, the Buddhists, etc. Sometimes both are found together; absorption and passivity of the spirit side by side with wild excitement. Both methods were practised by the Persian Sufis. Chardin, *Voyage en Perse*, iv, 458 (ed. Langlés) says of them, cependant ils se servent plus communément du chant de la danse et de la musique, disant qu'ils produisent plus sûrement leur extase. It may be that the cult of religious exaltation is always the real origin of these ecstatic states. Though the cult sometimes falls into decay itself, its offspring the ἔκστασις survives.

[61] In the language of these mystics the words mean: he knows that the passionate longing for reunion with God, the Soul of the universe, breaks down the individual personality and its limitations—"for where Love awakes to life the Self dies, that gloomy tyrant."

[62] *Γέται οἱ ἀθανατίζοντες*, Hdt. iv, 93–4 (*ἀπαθανατίζοντες*, Plato and others, see Wesseling on D.S. i, p. 105, 32).

[63] . . . *οὐδένα ἄλλον θεὸν νομίζοντες εἰ μὴ τὸν σφέτερον* (the Zalmoxis just mentioned) Hdt. iv, 94 fin. There we are told that the Getai *πρὸς βροντήν τε καὶ ἀστραπὴν τοξεύοντες ἄνω ἀπειλεῦσι τῷ θεῷ, οὐδένα κτλ.* If it were true (as most people seem to think) that the god (*ὁ θεός*) threatened by the Getai during thunder was their own god Zalmoxis, then it certainly is difficult, or, indeed, impossible, to understand the point of explaining the threatening of this god by the statement that they hold him for the only true god. The truth is that the *τῷ θεῷ* refers simply to the "sky" during a thunderstorm. The usage is common in Greek and is only transferred to the Getai by a rather awkward extension. This thundering *θεός* is not Zalmoxis at all (hence Z. is not as some have thought a "sky-god"). The Getai regarded Zalmoxis as the only god: the Thunderer is no real god to them (at the most a bad demon or a magician or something of the kind). To show that they are not afraid of him they shoot arrows against him, probably in the hope of breaking the thundercloud. (Parallels in other countries: Grimm, p. 1088; Dobrizhoffer, ii, 78. In India, Oldenberg, 491–4. Excitement during an eclipse of the moon: Weissenborn on Livy, 26, 5, 9. Reminiscence of such customs in the myth of Herakles: [Apollod.] 2, 5, 10, 5. From Hdt. by indirect channels comes Isig., *Mir.* 42 [p. 162 West.]; cf. also the account of D.C. 59, 28, 6 about Caligula.—Pallad., *RR.* i, 35 [*contra grandinem*].)

[64] *ἀθανατίζουσι δὲ τόνδε τὸν τρόπον . . . οὔτε ἀποθνήσκειν ἑωυτοὺς νομίζουσι, ἰέναι τε τὸν ἀπολλύμενον παρὰ Ζάλμοξιν δαίμονα (οἱ δὲ αὐτῶν τὸν αὐτὸν τοῦτον ὀνομάζουσι Γεβελέϊζιν)*, Hdt. iv, 94. Here, as regularly in Greek use of the words, we must not understand by *ἀθάνατον εἶναι* a mere shadowy (if timeless) survival of the soul after death as in the Homeric Hades. Such a belief if it had been held by the Getai would not have struck Hdt. or his readers as remarkable in the slightest degree. It must therefore imply an unending and fully conscious existence, in this last respect resembling the life on earth.

[65] *ἀθανατίζουσι δὲ καὶ Τέριζοι (τερετιζοι* Phot.) *καὶ Κρόβυζοι καὶ τοὺς ἀποθανόντας ὡς Ζάλμοξίν φασιν οἴχεσθαι*, Phot. Suid., *EM. Ζάμολξις*. The Krobyzoi are a well-known Thracian stock. The Terizoi are not elsewhere mentioned; perhaps they may be placed in the neighbourhood of *Τίριστις, Τίριζις ἄκρα* = C. Kaliakra (cf. C. Müller on Arrian, *P. Eux.* 35); there we also hear of a *Τίριστις πόλις*, Ptolem. With this Tomaschek also agrees (*D. alten Thraker, Ber. Wien. Ak.* 128, iv, p. 97). In this case they would be neighbours of the Krobyzoi.

[66] οὐκ ἀποθνήσκειν ἀλλὰ μετοικίζεσθαι νομίζοντες is what we hear of the Getai in Julian, *Caes.* 327 D. animas (putant) non extingui sed ad beatiora transire, Mela, ii, 18.

[67] . . . τοὺς ἀποθανόντας ὡς Ζάλμοξίν φασιν οἴχεσθαι, ἥξειν δὲ αὖθις. καὶ ταῦτα ἀεὶ νομίζουσιν ἀληθεύειν. θύουσι δὲ καὶ εὐωχοῦνται ὡς αὖθις ἥξοντος τοῦ ἀποθανόντος, Phot. Suid., *EM.* Ζάμολξις. Mela, ii, 18 : alii (among the Thracians) redituras putant animas obeuntium.

[68] Hdt. iv, 95, Zalmoxis, a slave of Pythagoras in Samos, is set free and comes back a rich man to his poverty-striken country. He collects together the leading men of the race in a room, where he entertains them and seeks to persuade them of the belief that neither he nor they nor their descendants will die but that they will all come after death to a place where they will enjoy all good things in abundance. Thereupon he withdraws into a secret underground chamber and lives there for three years. In the fourth year he comes to light again and " the Thracians are persuaded of the truth of what Zalmoxis had told them." This implies—though Hdt. omits to say so, and so does [Hellan.] π. νομ. βαρβ. (following Hdt.) ap. Phot., etc., s. Ζάμολξις—that he had also promised that he and his adherents should *return* to earth alive after the expiry of a definite period (three years). That such a belief in the " return " of the dead was actually held by the Thracians is clear enough from the quotations given in the last note. The story of Zalmoxis' trick (which was perhaps intended humorously by its inventors) seemed suspicious even to Hdt., but it is not pure invention (any more than the analogous stories about Pythagoras, Trophonios, and later Empedotimos) : it is rather a euhemerist version of a miraculous legend. The disappearance of Zalmoxis into a subterranean chamber is a distortion of the belief in his permanent abode in a hollow mountain-side, an ἀντρῶδές τι χώριον in Mt. Kogaionon of which Str. 298 speaks plainly enough. In that mountain the god dwells ; just as Rhesos κρυπτὸς ἐν ἄντροις τῆς ὑπαργύρου χθονός of Mt. Pangaios, dwells there as an ἀνθρωποδαίμων [E.], *Rh.* 970 ; cf. chap. iv, n. 36. He lives there undying like the Βάκχου προφήτης, who has become a god, to whom the tragedy obscurely alludes in ll. 972 f. as living on Mt. Pangaios (this may perhaps refer to Lykourgos—see G. Hermann, *Op.* v, 23 f.—surely not to Orpheus as Maass, *Orpheus*, p. 68 [1895], suggests). The obvious parallel is Amphiaraos and Trophonios in their caves, and Orig., *Cels.* iii, 34 (see above, chap. iii, n. 13), puts them and Zalmoxis together. We may safely complete Hdt.'s account of how the ἀπολλύμενοι of the Getai go away and have everlasting life παρὰ Ζάλμοξιν δαίμονα (iv, 94), by saying that they reach this same hollow mountain, a subterranean place of delight where they dwell with the god. Mnaseas compares Zalmoxis with Kronos (*FHG.* ; Phot. Suid. *EM.*, as before) and the similarity doubtless resides in the fact that both rule over the spirits of the blest in another world. But besides this the Thracian belief must also have included the idea of a periodical appearance of the god in the upper world. Hdt.'s story of the trick practised by Zalmoxis shows this (the return of the souls to which the story also points, is a sort of counterpart of this). Are we to suppose that the ἐπιφάνεια of the god was expected after the expiry of three years (just as it was after two years in the Dionysos festival ; see above, n. 27) ? We do not know whether these Thracian tribes celebrated the ἐπιφάνεια of the god with " enthusiastic " worship. Such an element in the cult of Zalmoxis seems to be suggested by the fact that we hear of " physicians of Zalmoxis " (Pl., *Charm.* 156 D) and of *mantikê*—which is generally closely bound up with ἰατρική—

in the cult of this god. This must be the meaning of calling Zalm. himself μάντις: Str. 762, 297; cf. also the otherwise valueless account of Ant. Diog. ap. Porph. *VP.* 14–15. Finally, the enthusiastic character of the cult seems to be implied in the identifying of the priest with the god by the Getai (as in the similar cases mentioned above, notes 32 and 59). Thus, the high priest is himself called "god": Str. 298 (he has authority over both king and state: cf. the ἱερεὺς τοῦ Διονύσου among the Bessoi, above, n. 53; cf. Jordanes, *Get.* 71). This made it easy for the "god" Zalmoxis, whom even Hdt. quite rightly regarded as δαίμων τις Γέτῃσι ἐπιχώριος (iv, 96) to be metamorphosed into a man of the historical past (he is this in D.S. 1, 94, 2; Str. vii, 297; cf. Jordanes, *Get.* 39). If the contemporary priest was called "god" it might naturally be concluded that the "god" Zalmoxis was once only a priest too.

[69] Hermip. ap. Jos., *Ap.* i, 22.

[70] In E., *Hec.* (1265 ff.) the Thracian Polymestor prophecies to Hekabe that she shall become a dog after her death, πύρσ' ἔχουσα δέργματα. Hekabe asks πῶς δ' οἶσθα μορφῆς τῆς ἐμῆς μετάστασιν; Pol.: ὁ Θρῃξὶ μάντις εἶπε Διόνυσος τόδε. It looks as if Eur. in this allusion to a belief in metempsychosis was intending to give a realistic touch of Thracian national character. He was well informed in such matters.

[71] The connexion between Thracian Dionysos-worship and the belief in immortality and cult of the dead is vouched for, acc. to Rapp, *Dionysosc,* 15 ff., by the insc. found by Heuzey in Thracian districts. An epitaph found at Doxato (near Philippi) says of one who has died young (ll. 12 ff.): reparatus vivis in Elysiis. Sic placitum est divis aeterna vivere forma qui bene de supero lumine sit meritus.—nunc seu te Bromio signatae (see Anrich, *Antike Mysterienwesen,* 123 f.) mystides ad se florigero in prato congregem uti Satyrum, sive canistriferae poscunt sibi Naïdes aeque, qui ducibus taedis agmina festa trahas . . . (*CIL.* iii, 686). It is true that this remarkable fantasy contains nothing directly alluding to specifically Thracian worship. On the other hand this is certainly suggested and both the Thracian god and his connexion with a cult of the dead is implied in the use of the local cult-title of Dionysos in an offering made by Bythos and Rufus to the thiasi Liberi patris Tasibasteni of 300 denarii ex quorum reditu annuo rosalibus (and so at the yearly festival of the dead) ad monimentum eorum vescentur. *CIL.* iii, 703; cf. 704. Even the conjunction by E., *Hec.* 1265 ff., of the belief in palingenesia with the oracle of the Thracian Dionysos seems to imply a connexion between that belief and the cult of Dionysos.

[72] πολλοὶ μὲν ναρθηκοφόροι, παῦροι δέ τε Βάκχοι, ap. Pl., *Phd.* 69 C. The strict meaning of this Orphic verse (Lob., *Agl.* 813 ff.) is that out of the multitudes who take part in the Bacchic festival only a few have any real right to call themselves by the name of the god—as having become one with him through their ecstasy and exaltation. A special morbid state was necessary for that: the same state which in other circumstances made the real shamans, Piajes, etc.

[73] Even when their ἔκστασις had ceased the ecstatic worshippers still regarded as real the visions which they had enjoyed in that condition: οἷον συνέβη 'Αντιφέροντι τῷ 'Ωρείτῃ καὶ ἄλλοις ἐξισταμένοις. τὰ γὰρ φαντάσματα ἔλεγον ὡς γενόμενα καὶ ὡς μνημονεύοντες, Arist. π. μνήμης, 1, p. 451a, 8. "Magicians who had subsequently been converted to Christianity were still convinced of the reality of their earlier visions: they thought they had seen something perfectly real."

Müller, *Amerik. Urrelig.* 80. Add: Tylor, ii, 131; Cranz, *Greenland*, p. 197.

[74] See above, chap. i, p. 7 ff.

[75] Hdt. v, 4 (speaking of the *Τραυσοί*. Hsch. has the same, s.v. *Τραυσός*). The story was then added to the regular list of *νόμιμα βαρβαρικά* used for illustrating the variability of *νόμος*. It was soon after told of the *Κρόβυζοι*: Isig., *Mir.* 27 (they were also regarded as strong adherents of a belief in immortality; see above, n. 65); then of the *Καυσιανοί*: Nic. Dam., *Mir.* 18 West. Zenob., *Prov.* v, 25, p. 128, 5 L.-Schn. (*Καύσιοι, Καυσιανοί*). It occurs again in a fragment of some collection of *νόμιμα βαρβαρικά* written before the third century (there is no reason to ascribe it to Aristotle) given by Mahaffy, *On the Flinders Petrie Papyri, Transcript.*, p. 29: *Καυσιανοῖς δὲ νόμιμον τοὺς μὲν γιγνομένους θρηνεῖν τοὺς δὲ τελευτῶντας εὐδαιμονίζειν ὡς πολλῶν κακῶν ἀναπεπαυμένους* (*κακῶν* as above or *πόνων* must be supplied to fill the gap; cf. the well-known fragment of Eur. *Cresph.*: *ἐχρῆν γὰρ ἡμᾶς* . . . *fr.* 449, which perhaps alludes to Hdt.'s account). It is told of Thracians in general, or of some tribe not particularly named, by S. E., *P.* iii, 232; Val. Max. 2, 6, 12 (both clearly drawing on collections of *νόμιμα βαρβαρικά*); Mela, ii, 18; *AP.* ix, 111 (Archias). There were thus three sources of the story: Besides Hdt.'s, two in which either the Krobyzoi or the Kausianoi were named as the Thracian tribe instead of Hdt.'s Trausoi.

[76] *ὅσων κακῶν ἐξαπαλλαχθεὶς ἔστι ἐν πάσῃ εὐδαιμονίᾳ*, Hdt. v, 4.

[77] See Jul., *Caes.* 327 D, Mela, ii, 18. Likewise of the *Καυσιανοί* in Anon. ap. Mahaffy (see n. 75), p. 29, 10–12. Iamb., *VP.* 173: as a result of the (Pythagorean) doctrine of immortality taught by Zalmoxis *ἔτι καὶ νῦν οἱ Γαλάται* (because they had been instructed by Zalm.; from a similar fabulous source comes Hippol., *RH.* i, 2, p. 14, 93 D.-S.) *καὶ οἱ Τράλεις καὶ πολλοὶ τῶν βαρβάρων τοὺς αὐτῶν υἱοὺς πείθουσιν ὡς οὐκ ἔστι φθαρῆναι τὴν ψυχήν* . . . *καὶ ὅτι τὸν θάνατον οὐ φοβητέον, ἀλλὰ πρὸς τοὺς κινδύνους εὐρώστως ἐκτέον.*—*Τράλλεις* Scaliger for the MS. *τραλις*, rightly as far as sense goes. But we find the name ΤΡΑΛΕΙΣ given to the Pergamene mercenaries called after the Thracian tribes: *Ins. Perg.* i, n. 13, 23, 59. These had already served as infantry in 331 in the army of Alexander the Great: D.S. 17, 65, 1; cf. Hsch. *Τραλλεῖς*. They were a South Thracian tribe: Plu., *Ages.* 16; *Ap. Lac.* 42; Str. 649 (where read *Τραλλέων*); Tralli Thraeces, Liv. 38, 21, 2, who elsewhere calls them Illyriorum genus, 27, 32, 4; 31, 35, 1. It appears that a branch of the Thracian tribe of the Tralles reached Illyria in their wanderings; there Theopompos, too, knew them: Steph. Byz. *Τραλλία*; cf. also s.vv. *Βῆγις, Βόλουρος* (cf. Tomaschek, *Sitzb. Wien. Ak.*, 128, iv, p. 56 f.).

[78] Appetitus maximus mortis, Mart. Cap. 6, 656. The Thracians esp. are meant by Galen when he speaks of *βαρβάρων ἐνίοις* who entertained the belief *ὅτι τὸ ἀποθνήσκειν ἐστὶ καλόν* (xix, p. 704 K.)

CHAPTER IX

DIONYSIAC RELIGION IN GREECE

Its Amalgamation with Apolline Religion. Ecstatic Prophecy. Ritual Purification and Exorcism. Asceticism

The Greeks received from the Thracians and assimilated to their own purposes the worship of Dionysos, just as, in all probability, they received the personality and worship of Ares and the Muses. Of this assimilation we cannot give any further particulars; it took place in a period lying before the beginnings of historical tradition. In this period a multiplicity of separate tendencies and conceptions, freely mingled with features borrowed from foreign creeds, were welded together to form the religion of Greece.

Homer is already acquainted with the fanatical worship of Dionysos; the god is called by the name under which Greek worshippers made themselves familiar with the stranger.[1] But in Homer, Dionysos appears only once or twice for a moment in the background. He is not the bountiful giver of wine; he does not belong to the Round Table of the great gods assembled on Olympos. Nowhere in the story told in either of the Homeric poems does he influence the life and destiny of human beings. There is no need to seek far for the reason of Dionysos' subordinate position in the Iliad and the Odyssey. Homer's silence makes it quite plain that at that time the Thracian god had not yet emerged from a position of insignificance or merely local importance in the life and faith of Greece. Nor is this hard to understand: the cult of Dionysos only gradually won recognition in Greece. Many legends tell of the battles that had to be fought by the new worship and of the opposition that met the invader. We hear how the Dionysiac frenzy and the *ekstasis* of the Dionysiac dance-festival took possession of the whole female population of many districts of Central Greece and the Peloponnese.[2] Sometimes a few women would venture to join the wandering choruses of wild Bacchants who danced upon the mountain tops; here and there the king of the land would oppose the progress of this tumultuous worship. Such stories are told of the daughters of Minyas in Orchomenos, of Proitos in Tiryns, of King Pentheus at Thebes, and Perseus at Argos;[3] their opposition to the Dionysiac form of worship, occurring in reality at no precise date, assumed a deceptive distinctness in the artificial systems of the mythologists and developed the character of historical events. In reality what we are told of these individuals—how the opponents of Dionysos themselves fell into even wilder frenzy and in Bacchic delirium slew and tore in pieces their own children instead of the victim-animal, or (as in the case of Pentheus) became themselves the victim slain and torn in pieces by the raging women—all this belongs to the class of *ætiological* myth. They are legends in which special features of worship (for example, the existing or dimly remembered sacrifice of human beings at the feasts of Dionysos) are provided with a mythical prototype in the supposed historical past of mythology, and thus receive their justification.[4] Still, there remains a substratum of historical fact underlying such stories. They all presuppose that the cult of Dionysos arrived from abroad and entered into Greece as something foreign. This presupposition notoriously corresponds to the actual facts of the case, and we are bound to assume that the account which they immediately proceed to give of the violent opposition which this cult, and only this cult, met with in many parts of Greece, is not pure fiction.[5] We are obliged to recognize that such stories preserved a trace of real historical memory expressed in the one form which was invariably assumed by the earliest Greek tradition, namely mythology, in which all the accidents and varieties of earthly experience were condensed into types of universal applicability.

It was then not without opposition, it appears, that the worship of Dionysos, descending from the north into Boeotia, spread from thence to the Peloponnese and at an early period invaded even some of the islands as well. In truth, even if we had no evidence at all on the point, we should have expected the Greeks to feel a profound repugnance to this disorderly and tumultuous Thracian worship; a deep-seated instinct must in their case have resisted such extravagance of emotional excitement and refused to lose itself in the limitless abyss of mere feeling. This unchecked roaming over the mountain sides in nocturnal revelry might be suitable enough for Thracian women-folk, but respectable Greek citizens could not give themselves up to such things without a struggle—without, indeed, a break with all inherited propriety and decorum.[6] It seems to have been the women who were the first to give in to the invading worship,[7] carried away in a real frenzy of inspired enthusiasm, and the new cult may really have owed its first success chiefly to them. What we are told of the irresistible progress and widespread success [8] of the

Bacchic dance-worship and its exaltation reminds us of the phenomena which have attended similar religious epidemics such as have in more recent times occasionally burst out and overflowed whole countries. We may in particular recall to mind the accounts which we have of the violent and widespread dance-madness which, soon after the severe mental and physical shock suffered by Europe in the Black Death of the fourteenth century, broke out on the Rhine and for centuries could not be entirely stamped out. Those who were attacked by the fever were driven by an irresistible impulse to dance The bystanders, in convulsions of sympathetic and imitative fury joined in the whirling dance themselves. Thus the malady was spread by contagion, and soon whole companies of men, women, and girls, wandered dancing through the country. In spite of the insufficiency of the surviving records, the religious character of this dance-enthusiasm is unmistakably apparent. The Church regarded it as a " heresy ". The dancers called upon the name of St. John or of " certain demons " ; hallucinations and visions of a religious nature accompanied their ecstasies.[9] Can it have been another such popular religious malady which attacked Greece—perhaps in the train of the disturbance of spiritual equilibrium caused by the destructive migrations which take their name from the Dorians ? The circumstances of the time must have predisposed men's minds in that direction and made them ready to accept the Thracian Dionysos and his enthusiastic dance-worship. In any case this invasion did not, like its mediæval counterpart, break down by coming into conflict with a well-established religion and an exclusive ecclesiastical organization of a very different temper from its own. In the deceptive twilight of myth we can only dimly discern the arrival and progress of the Dionysiac religion in Greece. But so much at least is evident : the Bacchic cult, though it had to overcome many obstacles, at last established itself in Greece and triumphantly overran both mainland and islands, until in the course of time it obtained a profound and far-reaching importance in Greek life of which Homer could scarcely give a hint.

§ 2

It was no longer simply the old Thracian Dionysos who now took his place beside the other great gods of the Greek Olympos as one of themselves. He had become Hellenized and humanized in the meantime. Cities and states celebrated him in yearly festivals as the giver of the vine's inspiring fruit, as the daimonic patron of vegetation, and the whole of Nature's rich and flourishing growth. He was worshipped as the incarnation of all natural life and vigour in the fullest and widest sense; as the typical exponent of the most eager enjoyment of life. Even Art, the highest expression of the courage and pride of life, drew much of its inspiration and its aspiration towards the infinite from the worship of Dionysos; and the drama, that supreme achievement of Greek poetry, arose out of the choruses of the Dionysiac festival.

Now the art of the actor consists in entering into a strange personality, and in speaking and acting out of a character not his own. At bottom it retains a profound and ultimate connexion with its most primitive source—that strange power of transfusing the self into another being which the really inspired participator in the Dionysiac revels achieved in his *ekstasis*. The essential features of the god as he first arrived in Greece from foreign lands, in spite of much alteration and transformation of the primitive type, were thus not entirely lost. There remained also, in addition to the cheerful festivity of the daylight worship of Dionysos, as it was celebrated more particularly in Athens, certain vestiges of the old ecstatic worship which drove men and women over the mountains in nocturnal revelry. In many places there were still celebrated the *trieteric* festivals [10] in which at recurrent intervals the "Epiphany" of Dionysos, his appearance in the world of men and ascent from the underworld, was solemized by night. The primitive character of Dionysos the Lord of Spirits and of the Souls of the dead—a very different figure indeed from the tender and delicate Wine-God of later times—was still obscurely present in many features of the Dionysiac festivals, in those of Delphi especially, but even to some extent at Athens too.[11] The ecstasy and the violence, even the dark savagery of the ancient cult did not quite die out in the midst of all the refinements of Greek civilization; recognizable traces of such things were preserved in the *Nuktelia* and *Agrionia* and in the various trieteric festivals that were offered to the god in many different localities.[12] In Greece the awful god received the blood of human victims.[13] Nor did the outward signs of delirious frenzy, such as the eating of raw flesh, the killing and tearing in pieces of snakes, entirely disappear.[14] So little, indeed, did the Bacchic frenzy that could exalt and lift the worshipper to communion with the god and his train, disappear before the gentler attractions of the gracious wine-god and his festival, that the raving and "possession" which characterized the cult of Dionysos were now actually regarded by foreign peoples as the essentially *Hellenic* form of the worship of the god.[15]

Thus, a sympathetic understanding of the orgiastic cult and its tremendous capabilities lived on. The " Bacchants " of Euripides still preserves for us a breath of its magic, a trace of the enthusiasm and exaltation that overwhelmed the senses and enthralled the will and consciousness of those who gave themselves up to the powerful Dionysiac influence. Like an irresistible current that overwhelms a swimmer or like the mysterious helplessness that frustrates the dreamer, the magic power emanating from the neighbourhood of the god took complete possession of the worshipper and drove him whither it willed. Everything in the world was transformed for him ; he himself was altered. Every character in the play falls under the spell as soon as he enters into the magic circle. Even the modern reader who turns over the pages of Euripides' poem feels something of that strange power to subdue the soul wielded by the Dionysiac mysteries and experiences in his own person a faint reflexion of these extraordinary states of mind.

Probably as a result of this profound Dionysiac fever which had once raged through Greece like an epidemic and was liable to periodic returns in the nocturnal festivals of the god, there remained in the constitution of the Greek people a certain morbid weakness, a susceptibility to suddenly appearing and as suddenly disappearing crises in which the normal powers of perceiving and feeling were temporarily overthrown. A few stray accounts have come down to us in which we read how such brief attacks of passing insanity ran through whole cities like an infectious disease.[16] The Korybantic form of the malady, which was religious in character[17] and took its name from the daimonic companions of the Phrygian Mountain Mother, was a phenomenon quite well-known to doctors and psychologists. Those affected by such fevers saw strange figures that corresponded to no objective reality, and heard the sound of invisible flutes, until at last they were excited to the highest pitch of frenzy and were seized with a violent desire to dance.[18] The initiation festivals of the Phrygian deities were specially directed to the discharge and so eventually to the cure and " purgation " of such emotional states; the means employed being principally dance and music—more especially the music composed for the flute by the old Phrygian masters ; music that could fill the soul with inspiration in suitably disposed natures.[19] By such methods the ecstatic element was not simply suppressed or expelled, it was taken up as a special disciplinary process by the physician-priesthood who recognized in it a vital movement and added it to the regular worship of the god.

In a similar fashion Greece in its most enlightened period accepted and practised the " enthusiastic " cult of Dionysos. Even the tumultuous night-festivals of the Thracian god—festivals closely related to those of Phrygia from which they had borrowed and to which they had given so many features—were made to serve the " purgation " of the ecstatically exalted soul. The worshipper in such festivals " initiated his soul into the company of the god in holy purifications, while he raged over the mountains in Bacchic frenzy ".[20] The purification consisted in this case, too, of violent excitement in which the soul was stimulated to the highest pitch of religious ecstasy. Dionysos as " Bakcheus " awoke the holy madness which he himself again, after it had reached its highest point of intensity, stilled and tranquillized as Lysios and Meilichios.[21] The old Thracian cult of ecstasy has here been modified in a fashion that belonged only to Greek soil and to Greek modes of thought. Legend, allegorizing the facts, threw back this final development of the Dionysiac worship into the remotest antiquity. Even Hesiodic poems [22] related how the daughters of King Proitos of Tiryns wandered in the holy frenzy of Dionysos [23] over the mountain of Peloponnesos, until at last they and all the multitide of women who had joined them were healed and " purified " by Melampous the Seer of Pylos famed in legend.[24] The cure was effected through the intensification of the Dionysiac frenzy " with loud crying and inspired dancing," [25] and, further, by the use of certain special purificatory devices.[26] Melampous did not put an end to the Dionysiac cult and its " enthusiasm "; he rather regulated and developed it. For this reason Herodotos can even call him the " Founder " of the Dionysiac cult in Greece.[27] Legend, however, always recognized in this " founder " of the Dionysiac festival an adherent of the specifically *Apolline* form of religion. " Apollo had favoured him especially," and bestowed upon him the Seership which became ancestral in his family.[28] Legend used him as a type in which the reconciliation between the Apolline and the Dionysiac was figuratively expressed. The reconciliation is an historical fact, but it did not happen in the primitive past of legend.

It is a fact, however, that Apollo did at last, doubtless after prolonged resistance, enter into the closest alliance with this remarkable divine brother of his, the Hellenized Dionysos.

The covenant must have been made at Delphi. There at least on the heights of Parnasos, in the Korykian Cave, the trieteric festival of Dionysos was held every second year in the close neighbourhood of Apollo the Lord of Delphi. Nay, more, in Apollo's own temple the " grave " of Dionysos was shown,[29] and at this grave, while the Thyiades of the god rushed over the mountain heights, the priests of Apollo celebrated a secret festival of their own.[30] The festal year of Delphi was divided, though unequally it is true, between Apollo and Dionysos.[31] To such an extent had Dionysos taken root at Delphi,[32] so closely were the two gods related, that while the front pediment of the temple showed the form of Apollo, the back pediment represented Dionysos—and the Dionysos of the nocturnal ecstatic revels. Apollo, too, shared in the trieteric festival of Dionysos,[33] while Dionysos in later times at the penteteric festival of the Pythia, received, as well as Apollo, his share of sacrifice and the contests of cyclic choruses.[34] The two divinities have many of their titles and attributes in common ; in the end the distinction between them seems to disappear entirely.[35]

Antiquity never forgot that at Delphi, the radiating centre of his cult, Apollo was an intruder. Among the older deities whom he supplanted there, the name of Dionysos also occurred ;[36] but the Delphic priesthood thought it wise to tolerate the Thracian god and his ecstatic cult that at first seemed so opposed to that of their own deity. Dionysos may have been too vigorous a spirit to allow his worship to be suppressed like that of the Earth divinity who sent the prophetic dreams. Apollo is the " Lord of Delphi " ; but the priesthood of the Delphic Apollo, following in this the tendency to religious syncretism which is so recognizable in them, took the worship of Dionysos under their protection. The Delphic Oracle in fact introduced Dionysos into localities where he had hitherto been a stranger, and nowhere so successfully or with such momentous consequences as at Athens.[37] It was this promoting of the Dionysiac form of religion by the great corporation which had the leadership in Greece in all matters of religion, that did more than anything else to secure for the god and his worship that profound, wide-reaching influence on Greek religion that Homer, who knows little even of the Delphic Oracle, completely ignores.

But it was a gentler and more civilized Dionysos whom Delphi popularized and even helped to re-shape ; the extravagance of his ecstatic abandonment was pruned and moderated to suit the more sober temper of ordinary city-life, and the brighter, daylight festivals of urban and countryside worship. Hardly a trace of the old Thracian worship of ecstasy and exaltation is discoverable in the Dionysiac worship of Athens. In other places, and especially in the districts ruled over by the Delphic Apollo himself, Dionysiac worship preserved more of its primitive nocturnal wildness. Even Athens, in obedience to an oracular command, sent a religious embassy of elected women to the Delphic Trieteria. It is plain enough however, that in all this there was nothing but a dim counterpart of the former tumultuous mountain-worship of the god, and its profound soul-stirring ceremonies; the worship of Athens and Delphi had reduced all that to a vague ritual traditionalism.[38]

§ 3

But in spite of all attempts to moderate and civilize it outwardly, the cult of Dionysos retained as its most enduring feature a tendency to the ecstatic and the extravagant that was continually breaking out in threatening or alluring guise. So strong indeed was the ecstatic element in Dionysiac worship, that when the Apolline and Dionysiac forms of religion became united, as at Delphi, it was the Apolline worship—once so hostile to anything in the nature of ecstasy—that had to accept this entirely novel feature.

The "prophecy of inspiration", deriving its knowledge of the unseen from an elevation of the human soul to the divine, was not always a part of Greek religion. Homer, of course, knows of the prophetic *art* in which specially instructed seers explained such signs of the gods' will as occurred accidentally or were purposely sought out by men, and by this means claimed to discover the will of heaven both at the moment and for the future. This is, in fact, the sort of prophecy that Apollo bestowed upon his seers.[39] But the prophecy of which there was no "art" and which "no man could be taught"[40] (for it came in a moment by "inspiration")—of this Homer shows no trace.[41] In addition to professional and independently working prophets the Odyssey, and even the Iliad, too, are aware of the enclosed oracular institutions belonging to the temple of Zeus at Dodona and that of Apollo at Pytho.[42] Both these used the names of the gods with whose service they were concerned to increase the effect and the credit of their utterances. In the Odyssey (but not the Iliad) there is a reference to the influence wielded by the oracle of Apollo in the more important circumstances of a people's life. But whether at that time it was an inspired prophetess who gave replies at Delphi we cannot be sure from the poet's words. There must have been oracles of sortilege [43] at that place from an early period under the protection of the god and it is these we should naturally expect a poet to mean who nowhere [44] shows any knowledge of the striking phenomena of ecstatic *mantikê*.[45]

In any case this new *mantikê* of inspired prophets, which subsequently enjoyed such enormous development and gave the Delphic oracle such peculiar power, was a late-coming innovation in the Apolline cult. Over the chasm in the rock at Pytho, out of which arose a strange and potent vapour from the depths of the earth, there had once existed an oracle of Gaia at which perhaps inquirers had received their instruction through the means of premonitory dreams by night.[46] The earth-goddess was displaced by Apollo here as at many other oracular sites.[47] The accuracy of this tradition is confirmed by the Delphic temple legend which speaks of the overthrow of the oracular earth-spirit Python by Apollo.[48] The change may have been gradually brought about; in any case, where once the earth-divinity had spoken directly in dreams to the souls of men, there Apollo now prophesied—no longer indirectly through the intervening medium of signs and omens, but directly answering those who, in open-eyed wakefulness, inquired of him, and speaking to them out of the mouth of his ecstatically inspired prophetess.

This Delphic prophecy of inspiration is as far removed from the old Apolline art of interpreting omens as it is closely allied to the *mantikê* which we found attached from the earliest times to the Thracian cult of Dionysos.[49] It appears that in Greece Dionysos but rarely obtained an official priesthood that could have organized or maintained a permanent oracular institute attached to a particular place or temple. In the one Dionysiac oracle in Greece, however, of which we have certain knowledge a priest gave prophecies in a state of "enthusiasm" and "possession" by the god.[50] Enthusiasm and ecstasy are invariably the means of the Dionysiac prophecy just as they were the means of all Dionysiac religious experience. When we find Apollo in Delphi itself—the place where he most closely allied himself with Dionysos—deserting his old omen-interpretation and turning to the prophecy of *ekstasis*, we cannot have much doubt as to whence Apollo got this new thing.[51]

With the mantic *ekstasis*, Apollo received a Dionysiac element into his own religion. Henceforward, he, the cold, aloof, sober deity of former times, can be addressed by titles that imply Bacchic excitement and self-abandonment. He is now the "enthusiastic", the Bacchic god: Aeschylus strikingly calls him "ivy-crowned Apollo, the Bacchic-frenzied prophet" (*fr.* 341). It is now Apollo, who more than any other god, calls forth in men's souls the madness [52] that makes them clairvoyant and enables them to know hidden things. At not a few places there are founded oracular sites at which priests or priestesses in frenzied ecstasy utter what Apollo puts into their mouths. But the Pythian oracle remained the pattern of them all. There, prophecy was uttered by the Pythia, the youthful priestess who sat upon the tripod over the earth-chasm and was inspired by the intoxicating vapour that arose from it, until she was filled with the god, and with his spirit.[53] The god, so ran the belief, entered into the earthly body; or else the soul of the priestess, "released" from her body, received the heavenly revelation with spiritual sense.[54] What she then "with frenzied mouth" proclaimed, that the god spoke out of her; when she said "I", Apollo was speaking of himself and of what concerned him.[55] It is the god who lives, thinks, and speaks in her so long as the madness lasts.

§ 4

A profound and compelling tendency of the human mind must have been the source of the great religious movement that could succeed in establishing, with the ecstatic prophecy of the Delphic priestess, a seed of mysticism in the very heart of Greek religion. The introduction of *ekstasis* into the ordered stability of the Delphic mode of religion was only a symptom of that religious movement and not its cause. But now, confirmed by the god himself, and by the experience which the mantic practice seemed to make so evident, the new belief, so long familiar to Dionysiac religion and worship, must have at last invaded the older and original type of Greek religion, and taken hold of it in spite of that religion's natural antipathy to anything of the kind. And this belief was that a highly exalted state of feeling could raise man above the normal level of his limited, everyday consciousness, and could elevate him to heights of vision and knowledge unlimited; that, further, to the human soul it was not denied, in very truth and not in vain fancy, to live for a moment the life of divinity. This belief is the fountain-head of all mysticism, and tradition still records a few traces of the way in which it grew and spread at that time.

It is true that the formal and official worship of the gods in Greece (where their cults were not obviously affected by foreign influence) remained as fast-bound as ever within the confines of order and lucidity. We hear very little of the entrance of ecstatic exaltation into the constitution of the older cults.[56] The irresistible religious impulse to such things found an outlet through other channels. Men and women began to appear who on their own initiative began to act as intermediaries between the gods and the needs of individual men. They were natures, we must suppose, of unusual susceptibility to "enthusiastic" exaltation; having a strange capacity for projecting themselves into the infinite. Nothing in the organization of Greek religion prevented such men and women, if they could not obtain authority from any religious community of the state itself, from acquiring a real influence in religious matters simply from their own experience of divine favour,[57] their own inward communion with divine powers.

In the darkness and ferment of this period of growth, from the eighth to the sixth centuries, we can vaguely discern many such shadowy figures; they look uncommonly like those strange products of the earliest infancy of Christianity when prophets, ascetics, and exorcists wandered from land to land, called to their work by nothing but the immediate grace of god (χάρισμα), and not attached to any permanent religious community. It is true that what we hear of Sibyls and Bakides—men and women who wandered from land to land prophesying the future, independently of and uncommissioned by any particular oracular institute—is mostly legend; but these are the sort of legends that preserve real historical tradition condensed into single types and pictures. The nomenclature itself tells us much: Sibyls and Bakides are not individual names, but *titles* belonging to various types[58] of ecstatic prophet, and we are entitled to suppose that the types so named once existed. The appearance in many places of Greek Asia Minor and the old mainland of Greece of such divinely inspired prophets is among the distinguishing marks of a clearly defined period in Greek history: the age of promise that came immediately before the philosophic period of Greece. The later age, entirely given up as it was to the pursuit of philosophic enlightenment, made so little claim to the inheritance in their own time of the divine favour that had once enabled the Sibyls and Bakides to see their visions and utter their wisdom, that there actually began to appear in large numbers prophets at second-hand, who were satisfied with preserving the traditional wisdom of the inspired prophets of the past, and with the judicious interpretation of their treasures.[59] The age of *enthusiastic* prophets was evidently a thing of the past. The very literature of Sibylline and Bakid oracles, which began to appear just at that time and showed itself capable of an almost indefinite extension, was itself largely responsible for the veil of myth and legend which completely enveloped the original bearers of the prophetic title. Earlier and earlier became the historic events of the past which they had foretold; further and further into the mythical past, *before* the time of the events prophesied, receded the imaginary period of the great prophets.[60] In spite of which the scientific chronologists of antiquity, who were far from being imposed upon by the delusive anticipations of prophetic poems, found reason for fixing the date of particular Sibyls—which means for our purpose the whole prophetic age of Greece—in the fully historical period of the eighth and seventh centuries.[61]

We may recognize, in what we hear of these prophets, the shadowy representatives of a once real and living past; they are reminiscences of a striking and therefore never quite forgotten phase of Greek religious life. The Bakids and Sibyls were independent agents—though not entirely without connexion with the regular worship of the gods, they were not attached to any particular temple—who wandered from land to land according to the needs of those who sought their counsel. In this respect, at least, they resembled the Homeric omen-interpreters,[62] and continued their work; but they differed from them profoundly in the mode of their prophesying. They were "seized by the god" and in ecstatic clairvoyance saw and proclaimed unseen things. It was no academic skill that they possessed, enabling them to interpret the meaning of signs and omens that anyone could see—they saw what was visible only to God and to the soul of man filled with God.[63] In hoarse tones and wild words [64] the Sibyl gave utterance to what the divine impelling power within her and not her own arbitrary fancy suggested; possessed by the god, she spoke in a divine distraction. An echo of such daimonic possession, and of the horrible reality and terror that it had for the possessed, can still be heard in the cries and convulsions which Aeschylus in the *Agamemnon* gives to his Kassandra—a true picture of the primitive Sibyl, and a type that the poets of that prophetic generation had reflected backwards into the earlier past of legend.[65]

§ 5

The activity of the seer was not confined to foreseeing and foretelling the future. We hear of a "Bakis" who "purified" and delivered the women of Sparta from an attack of madness that had spread like an epidemic among them.[66] The prophetic age of Greece must have seen the origin of what later became part of the regular duties of the "seer": the cure of diseases, especially those of the mind; [67] the averting of evil of every kind by various strange means, and particularly the supply of help and counsel by "purifications" of a religious nature.[68] The gift or art of prophecy, the purification of "the unclean", the healing of disease, all seem to be derived from one source. Nor can we be long in doubt as to what the single source of this threefold capacity must have been. The world of invisible spirits surrounding man, which ordinary folk know only by its effects, is familiar and accessible to the ecstatic prophet, the *Mantis*, the spirit-seer. As exorcist he undertakes to heal disease; [69] the *Kathartic* process is also essentially and originally an exorcism of the baleful influences of the spirit-world.

The wide popularity and elaboration given to the notion—hardly hinted [70] at as yet in Homer—of the universally present menace of "pollution", which is only to be averted or got rid of by means of a religious process of purification—this is one of the chief distinguishing features of the over-anxious piety that marked the post-Homeric age when men could no longer be content with the means of salvation handed down to them by their fathers. If we confined our attention to the fact that now we find purification required for such actions as murder and the spilling of blood which seem to imply a moral stain to the doer of them,[71] we might be tempted to see in the development of Kathartic practices a fresh step in the history of Greek ethics, and to suppose that the new practices arose out of a refinement and deepening of the "conscience" which now desired to be free from the taint of "sin" by the help of religion. But such an interpretation of Katharsis (favourite as it is) is disposed of by a consideration of the real essence and meaning of the thing. In later times the methods of Katharsis were nearly always in competition and conflict (rarely in friendly alliance) with "conscience", with the independently developed ethical thought that based itself upon the unchanging requirements of a moral law transcending all personal will and feeling, and even the will of daimonic powers. In its origin and essence Katharsis had nothing whatever to do with morality or with what we should call the voice of conscience. On the contrary, it usurped the place which in a more advanced and morally developed people would have belonged to a true morality based on an inner feeling for what is right. Nor did it fail to hinder the free and unfettered development of such a morality. Kathartic practices required and implied no feeling of offence, of personal guilt, of personal responsibility. All that we know of these practices serves to bring this out and set the matter in a clearer light.

Ceremonies of " purification " accompany every step of a man's life from the cradle to the grave. The woman with child is " unclean " and so is anyone who touches her ; the new-born child is unclean ; [72] marriage is fenced about with a series of purificatory rites ; the dead, and everything that approaches them, are unclean. Now, in these instances of the common and almost daily occurrence of purification ceremonies, there can be no moral stain involved that requires to be washed off, not even a symbolical one. Equally little can there be any when ritual purifications are employed after a bad dream,[73] the occurrence of a prodigy,[74] recovery from illness, or when a person has touched an offering made to deities of the lower world or the graves of the dead ; or when it is found necessary to purify house and hearth,[75] and even fire and water [76] for sacred or profane purposes. The purification of those who have shed blood stands on exactly the same footing. It was necessary even for those who had killed a man with just cause, or had committed homicide unknowingly or unwillingly ; the moral aspect of such cases, the guilt or innocence of the doer, is ignored or unperceived. Even in the case of premeditated murder, the remorse of the criminal or his "will to amend " [77] is quite superfluous to the efficacy of purification.

It could not be otherwise. The " stain " which is wiped out by these mysterious and religious means is not " within the heart of man ". It clings to a man as something hostile, and from without, and that can be spread from him to others like an infectious disease.[78] Hence, the purification is effected by religious processes directed to the *external* removal of the evil thing ; it may be washed off (as by water from a running spring or from the sea), it may be violently effaced and obliterated (as by fire or even smoke alone), it may be absorbed (by wool, fleece of animals, eggs),[79] etc.

It must be something hostile and dangerous to men that is thus removed ; since this something can only be attacked by religious means, it must belong to the daimonic world to which alone Religion and its means of salvation have reference. There exists a population of spirits whose neighbourhood or contact with men renders then " unclean ", for it gives them over to the power of the unholy.[80] Anyone who touches their places of abode, or the offerings made to them, falls under their spell; they may send him sickness, insanity, evils of every kind. The priest with his purifications is an " exorcist " who sets free those who have fallen victims to the surrounding powers of darkness. He certainly fulfils this function when he disperses diseases, i.e. the spirits who send the diseases, by his ministrations ; [81] when he employs in his purificatory ritual hymns and incantatory formulæ which regularly imply an invisibly listening being to whom they are addressed ; [82] when he uses the clang of bronze instruments whose well-known property it is to drive away ghosts.[83] Where human blood has been shed and requires " purification " the Kathartic priest accomplishes this " by driving out murder with murder ", [84] i.e. he lets the blood of a sacrificed animal fall over the hands of the polluted person. Here, the purification is plainly in the nature of a substitution-sacrifice (the animal being offered instead of the murderer).[85] In this way the anger of the dead is washed away—for this anger is itself the pollution that is to be removed.[86] The famous scapegoats were nothing but sacrifices offered to appease the anger of the Unseen, and thereby release a whole city from " pollution ". At the *Thargelia* or on extraordinary occasions of need in Ionic cities, and even in Athens, unfortunate men were in ancient times slain or stoned to death or burnt " for the purification of the city ".[87] Even the materials of purification that in private life served to free the individual and his house from the claims of invisible powers, were thought of as offerings to these powers : this is proved clearly enough by the custom of removing such materials, when they had served their purpose as " purifications ", to the cross-roads, and of making them over to the unearthly spirits who have their being there. The materials of purification so treated are in fact identical with offerings to the dead or even with " Hekate's banquets ".[88] In this case we can see most clearly what the forces are which Kathartic processes essentially aim at averting. In them no attempt was made to satisfy a heartfelt consciousness of sin or a moral sense that has become delicate ; they were much rather the result of a superstitious fear of uncanny forces surrounding men and stretching out after them with a thousand threatening hands in the darkness.

It was the monstrous phantasies of their own imagination that made men call upon the priests of purification and expiation for much-needed aid and protection.

§ 6

It is simply the invasion of human life by the sinister creatures of the daimonic world that the clairvoyant *mantis* is supposed to avert with his "purifications". Among these sinister influences Hekate and her crew are particularly noticeable. This is without doubt an ancient product of religious phantasy—though it is not mentioned by Homer—which did not till a late period emerge from the obscurity of local observance and obtain general popularity: even then it only here and there ceased to be a private and domestic cult and reached the dignity of public city-worship.[89] The cult of Hekate fled the light of day, as did the wild farrago of weird and sinister phantoms that surrounded her. She is *chthonic*, a goddess of the lower world,[90] where she is at home; but, more easily than other lower-world creatures, she finds her way to the living world of men. Wherever a soul is entering into partnership with a body—at birth or in child bed—she is at hand; [91] where a soul is separating from a body, in burials of the dead, she is there. Amidst the dwelling-places of the departed, the monuments of the dead and the gloomy ritual of their worship, she is in her element.[92] She is the queen of the souls who are still fast bound to the upper world. It shows her deep-seated connexion with the primeval worship of the dead at the household hearth,[93] when we hear of Hekate as dwelling "in the depth of the hearth",[94] and being honoured together with the underworld Hermes, her masculine counterpart, among the domestic gods who "were left to us by our forefathers".[95]

This domestic cult may be a legacy from times when in familiar intercourse with the lower world men did not yet fear "pollution" therefrom.[95a] To later ages Hekate was the principal source and originator of all that was ghostly and uncanny. Men came upon her suddenly and to their hurt by night, or in the dreamy solitudes of midday's blinding heat; they see her in monstrous shapes that, like the figures in a dream, are continually changing.[96] The names of many female deities of the underworld of whom the common people had much to say—Gorgyra (Gorgo), Mormo, Lamia, Gello or Empousa, the ghost of midday—denote in reality so many different personifications and variations of Hekate.[97]

She appeared most frequently by night, under the half-light of the moon, at the cross-roads. She is not alone but is accompanied by her " crew ", the hand-maidens who follow in her train. These are the souls of those who have not had their share of burial and the holy rites that accompany it; who have been violently done to death, or who have died " before their time ".[98] Such souls find no rest after death; they travel on the wind now, in the company of Hekate and her daimonic pack of hounds.[99] It is not without reason that we are reminded of the legends of " wild hunters " and the "furious host", so familiar in modern times in many countries.[100] Similar beliefs produced similar results in each case; perhaps there is even some historical connexion between them.[101] These night-wandering spirits and souls of the dead bring pollution and disaster upon all who meet them or fall into their hands; they send evil dreams, nightmares, nocturnal apparitions, madness and epilepsy.[102] It is for them, the unquiet souls of the dead and Hekate their queen, that men set out the " banquets of Hekate " at the cross-roads.[103] To them men consign with averted faces the remains of the purificatory sacrifices[104] that they may not come too close to human dwelling places. Puppies, too, were sacrificed to Hekate for " purifications ", i.e. " apotropaic " sacrifices.

Gruesome inventions of all kinds were easily attached to this province of supernaturalism; it is one of the sources which, with help from other Greek conceptions and many foreign creations of fancy, let loose a stream of anxious and gloomy superstitiousness that spread through the whole of later antiquity and even reached through the Middle Ages to our own day.

Protection and riddance from such things were sought at the hands of seers and " Kathartic priests " who, in addition to ceremonies of purification and exorcism had other ways of giving help—prescriptions and recipes of many strange sorts which were originally clear and natural enough to the fantastic logic of superstition and were still credited and handed down as magic and inexplicable formulæ after their real meaning had been entirely forgotten. Others, again, were driven by a fearful curiosity to attempt to bring the world of surrounding spirits—of whose doings such strange stories were told in legend[105]—even closer to themselves. By magic arts and incantations, they compelled the wandering ghosts and even Hekate herself to appear before them:[106] the magic power forces them to do the will of the spirit-raiser or to harm his enemies.[107] It was these creatures of the spirit-world that magicians and exorcists claimed to banish or compel. Popular belief was on their side in this, but it is hardly possible that they never resorted to deceit and imposture in making good their claims.

§ 7

The mantic and Kathartic practices, together with what arose out of them, are known to us almost exclusively as they were in the time of their decay. Even in the brief sketch just attempted of this notable by-way of Greek religion, many details have had to be taken from the accounts left to us by later ages that had quite outgrown the whole idea of mantic and Kathartic procedure. Compared on the one hand with science, seriously engaged in studying the real and inward sources of being and becoming throughout the world, together with the limitations of man's estate, and on the other hand with the practical and cautious medical study of the physical conditions of human life in health and sickness, the mantic and Kathartic practices and all the myriad superstitions arising from them seemed like a legacy from a forgotten and discredited past. But such things persisted in many circles of old-fashioned and primitive-minded people, though by the emancipated and cultured they were despised as the silly and dangerous quackery of mendicant priests and wizards.

But this product of the religious instinct cannot always have appeared in such a light ; it certainly was not so regarded when it first came into prominence. A movement that was zealously taken up by the Delphic oracle, which influenced many Greek states in the organization of their religious cults, must have had a period when its right to exist was incontestable. It must have answered to the needs of a time when the dawning sense of the profound unity and interconnexion of all being and becoming in the world still contented itself with a religious explanation of what seemed mysterious, and when a few chosen natures were seriously credited with the power to communicate with the all-embracing spirit-world. Every age has its own ideal of Wisdom ; and there came a time when the ideal of the Wise Man, who by his own innate powers has achieved a commanding spiritual position and insight, became embodied in the persons of certain great men who seemed to fulfil the highest conceptions of wisdom and power that were attributed to the ecstatic seer and priest of purification. The half-mythical stories in which later ages preserved the memory of the times lying just before the age of the philosophic exploration of nature tell us of certain great masters of a mysterious and occult Wisdom. It is true that they are credited with powers over nature of a magical kind rather than with a purely intellectual insight into the laws of nature; but even in the scanty accounts of them which have come down to us there are clear indications that their work already included the first attempts at a mode of study based on theory. We cannot call them philosophers—not even the forerunners of Greek philosophy. More often their point of view was one which the real philosophic impulse towards self-determination and the freedom of the soul consciously and decisively rejected, and continued to reject, though not indeed without occasional wavering and back-sliding. These men must be counted among the magicians and exorcists who so often appear in the earliest dawn of the spiritual history of civilized nations, and, as primitive and marvellous types of the spirit of inquiry, precede the philosophers. They all belong to the class of ecstatic seers and Kathartic priests.

Legend related how, out of the country of the Hyperboreans, that distant Wonderland where Apollo hid himself in winter, there came to Greece one Abaris, sent by the god himself. He was a saint and needed no earthly food. Carrying in his hand the golden arrow, the proof of his Apolline origin and mission, he passed through many lands dispelling sickness and pestilence by sacrifices of a magic kind, giving warning of earthquakes and other disasters. Even in later times prophecies and " purifications ", going under his name, were still to be read.[108]—This man, and also another like him, called Aristeas, were already mentioned by Pindar (*fr.* 271). Aristeas, a man of high rank in his native city of Prokonnesos, had the magic gift of prolonged *ekstasis*. When his soul left his body behind, being " seized by Phoibos ", it (as his second self made visible) was seen in distant places.[109] As Apollo's attendant he also appeared together with the god in Metapontum. A bronze statue in the market-place of that city remained to testify to his presence there, and to the astonishment awakened by his inspired utterances.[110] But among all these examples of the type,[111] Hermotimos of Klazomenai is the most striking. His soul could desert his body " for many years ", and on its return from its ecstatic voyages, brought with it much mantic lore and knowledge of the future. At last, enemies set fire to the tenantless body of Hermotimos when his soul was away, and the latter returned no more.[112]

The greatest master of all these magically gifted men was,

according to tradition, Epimenides. His home was in Crete, an ancient centre of Kathartic wisdom,[113] where Epimenides was instructed in this lore as an adherent of the cult of the underworld Zeus.[114] Through a mist of legend and fable we hear of his prolonged stay in the mysterious cave of Zeus on Mt. Ida, his intercourse with the spirits of the darkness, his severe fasting,[115] the long ecstasy of his soul,[116] and his final return from solitude to the light of day, much experienced and far-travelled in "enthusiastic wisdom".[117] Next he journeyed through many lands bringing his health-giving arts with him, prophesying the future as an ecstatic seer,[118] interpreting the hidden meaning of past occurrences, and as Kathartic priest expelling the daimonic evils that arose from specially foul misdeeds of the past. The Kathartic activity of Epimenides in Delos and other Greek cities was famous.[119] It was in particular never forgotten how in Athens at the end of the seventh century he brought to a satisfactory close the expiation of the godless murder of the followers of Kylon.[120] With potent ceremonies of which his wisdom alone knew the secret, with sacrifice of animals and men, he appeased [121] the anger of the offended spirits of the depth who in their rage were "polluting" and harming the city . . .

It was not without reason that later tradition, undeterred by questions of chronological possibility, brought all the names just mentioned into connexion with Pythagoras or his adherents,[122] and was even accustomed to refer to Pherekydes of Syros, the latest of the band, as the teacher of Pythagoras. The practice, if not the philosophy, of the Pythagorean sect grew up among the ideas and what may be called the teaching of these men, and belongs to the epoch which honoured them as Wise Men. We still possess a few scraps of evidence to show that the conceptions guiding their life and work tended to reach some sort of unification in the minds of these visionaries who were yet something more than the mere practicians of a magical species of religion. We cannot, indeed, tell how far the fanciful pictures of the origin of the world of men which Epimenides [123] and Pherekydes drew were connected with the business and professional activity of these men; [124] but when it is related of Hermotimos that he, like his countryman Anaxagoras, attempted a distinction between pure "mind" and matter,[125] we can see very clearly how this theory might arise out of his special "experiences". The ecstasies of the soul of which Hermotimos himself and this whole generation had such ample experience seemed to point to the separability of the soul from the body [126]—and, indeed, to the superiority of the soul's essence in its separate state over that of the body—as to a fact of the most firmly established authenticity. In contrast with the soul the body could hardly help appearing as an encumbrance, an obstacle to be got rid of. The conception of an ever-threatening pollution and " uncleanness " which was nourished by the teaching and activities of those innumerable purification-priests of whom Epimenides is known to us as the supreme master, had gradually so penetrated the whole of the official religion itself with purification-ceremonies that it might very well have seemed as though, in the midst of this renovation and development of a type of religious thought that had been more than half forgotten in the Homeric period, Greek religion was fast approaching the condition of Brahmanism or Zoroastrianism and becoming essentially a religion of purification. Those who had become familiar with the contrast between body and soul, especially if they lived in the atmosphere of Kathartic ideas and their practical exercise, were almost bound to proceed to the idea that even the " soul " required to be purified from the polluting embarrassment of the body. That such ideas were almost a commonplace is shown by many stories and turns of phrase which represent the destruction of the body by fire as a " purification " of the man himself.[127] Wherever these ideas—the precise opposite and contrary of the Homeric conception of the relation between body and soul-image—had penetrated more deeply they must have led to the idea that even in the lifetime of the body the purification of the soul should be prepared by the denial and inhibition of the body and its impulses. The first step was thus taken towards a purely negative system of morality, not attempting the inner reformation of the will, but aiming simply at averting from the soul of man a polluting evil threatening it from without—in fact to a morality of religious *asceticism* such as later became such an important and decisive spiritual movement in Greece. In spite of all the inadequacy of our information about these Wise Men of the early pre-philosophic period, we can still dimly make out the fact that their natural bent lay in this ascetic direction (the abstention from food practised by Abaris and Epimenides are distinct cases of it).[128] How far, exactly, they went in this direction is indeed more than we can say.

Thus, the ascetic ideal was not absent even from Greece. It remained, however—in spite of the influence it had in some quarters—always a foreign thing in Greece, having its obscure home among sects of spiritualistic enthusiasts, and regarded in contrast with the normal and ruling view of life, as a paradox, almost a heresy. The official religion itself is not entirely without the seeds of an ascetic system of morality; but the ascetic ideal, fully developed and distinguished from the simple and normal religious attitude, was in Greece found only among minorities who cut themselves off in closed and exclusive conventicles of a theological or philosophical temper. The "Wise Men", as idealized in the legends of Abaris, Epimenides, etc., were as individuals not far removed from the ideal of asceticism. Nor was it long before the attempt was made to use these ideals as the basis on which to found a society.

NOTES TO CHAPTER IX

[1] We may safely take it for granted that *Διόνυσος* is the *Greek* name of the god, though a completely convincing etymology for the word has yet to be found. Recent attempts to derive it from the Thracian language are not very convincing. (Tomaschek, *Sitzber. Wien. Ak.* 130, 41; Kretschmer, *Aus der Anomia*, 22 f.; *Einl.* 241.) Acc. to Kretschmer a Thracian origin for the name is proved by the appearance of the form *Δεόνυσο—* on inss. found in a few Greek towns surrounded by Thracian influences, e.g. Abdera, Maroneia. Acc. to him the transition from ι to ε before a vowel is regular in Thrako-Phrygian, while on the other hand "it is completely incompatible with all the laws of Greek phonetics". Others have disagreed with this view, e.g. G. Curtius, certainly an *auctor probabilis*, to whom the occasional appearance of the transition from ι to ε before a vowel (side by side with the much commoner reverse process) seemed quite compatible with the laws of Greek phonetics. He even counted *Διόνυσος—Δεύνυσος* (Anakreon) among the examples of this vowel change within the limits of the Greek language (*Gr. Etym.*[5], p. 608 f.). At any rate *Ἐάσων* = *Ἰάσων*, and *πατρουέαν* = *πατρωίαν* are certain cases of it (see Meister, *Gr. Dial.* i, 294; G. Meyer, *Gr. Gramm.*[2], p. 162). Kretschmer himself, *Einl.* 225, supplies *Ἀσκληπεόδωρος*, *Δεί* = *Διί*. To account for these forms he postulates the influence of Thracian surroundings on Greek pronunciation; but in the case of such a purely Greek word as *Ἀσκληπιόδωρος* the Thracian influence must have been a *secondary* phenomenon operating to cause the alteration of the old $\overline{ιο}$ into $\overline{εο}$. Why should we not use the same explanation in accounting for the change from *Διόνυσος* to *Δεόνυσος* and (*if* Thracian influence is to be presumed—by no means probable in view of the statement of *EM.* 259, 30, *Δεόνυσος, οὕτω γὰρ Σάμιοι προφέρουσιν*) say that this Thracian influence was a secondary one acting upon the original *Greek* form of the name *Διόνυσος*?—It is evident that the ancients had no idea that *Διόνυσος* (*Διώνυσος, Διόννυσος*) was the indigenous name of the Thracian god, for they would in that case have said so without hesitation. They derived the conception, figure, and cult of the god from Thrace but not this particular name, which they regularly regard as the Greek name of the daimon whom the Thracians spoke of as *Σαβάζιος* or otherwise. (So too Hdt. regards *Διόνυσος* as the Greek name of the god whose essential nature is Egyptian.) This is by no means without importance; on the contrary, it provides cogent reason for doubting the (otherwise insecurely founded) derivation of the name from the Thracian.

[2] The women in Boeotia *ἐνθεώτατα ἐμάνησαν* (cf. Eur., *Ba.*). *ταῖς Λακεδαιμονίων γυναιξὶν ἐνέπεσέ τις οἶστρος βακχικὸς καὶ ταῖς τῶν Χίων*, Ael., *VH.* iii, 42. Hdt. ix, 34, speaks inclusively of the madness of the women in Argos (*τῶν ἐν Ἄργεϊ γυναικῶν μανεισέων*), where others speak only of the frenzy attacking the daughters of Proitos. Neither is incompatible with the other: they simply represent two different stages of the story. The *μαίνεσθαι* which attacks the entire female population is not (as later accounts generally make out) the punishment sent by Dionysos: it is simply another way of expressing the general acceptance of his worship which essentially consisted in

μαίνεσθαι (= βακχεύειν in Ant. Lib. 10). The μαίνεσθαι of individual women who try to resist the contagious enthusiasm of the Dionysiac revelry going on around them (e.g. the daughters of Eleuther: Suid. μελαναιγ. Διόν.) is, however, a punishment sent by the angry god when it leads them to murder their own children.—The regular and widespread "mania" of the newly introduced cult of Dionysos is referred to also by D.S. 4, 68, 4; [Apollod.] 2, 2, 2, 5; Paus. 2, 18, 4; cf. also Nonn., *D*. 47, 481 ff.

[3] Resistance of Perseus to Dionysos who in this account arrives with the Mainads from the islands of the Aegean Sea (so Paus.); victory of Perseus, followed, however, by a reconciliation with the god whose worship is established and a temple built for Dionysos Kresios: Paus. 2, 20, 4; 22, 1; 23, 7–8. So, too, Nonn., *D*. 47, 475-741; [Apollod.] 3, 5, 2, 3; Sch. V., Ξ 319; cf. Meineke, *An. Alex*. 51. (Dionysos is slain in the war with Perseus: Dinarchos "the poet" ap. Eus., *Chr*. ii, pp. 44–5 Sch. = an. 718 Abr.; Lob., *Agl*. 537 f.).—Lykourgos does not properly belong to this series: his legend, as told by [Apollod.] 3, 5, 1 (apparently following the direction given to it by Aesch.), is a late transformation of the story preserved by Homer, in which stories of Pentheus or the Minyads or the Proitides are imitated.

[4] This is esp. clear in the legend dealing with Orchomenos; cf. the account in Plu., *Q.Gr*. 38, p. 293 D. It is very probable that the other stories, too, were founded upon sacrificial ritual; cf. Welcker, *Gr. Götterl*. i, 444 ff.

[5] Cf. also Sch. Ar., *Ach*. 243.

[6] Cf. Eur., *Ba*. 217 ff., 487, 32 ff. The daughters of Minyas ἐπόθουν τοὺς γαμέτας (see Perizon. ad loc.) καὶ διὰ τοῦτο οὐκ ἐγένοντο τῷ θεῷ μαινάδες, Ael., *VH*. iii, 42. Throughout all these legends the contrast between Dionysos and Hera, who is the patroness of marriage, is very marked.

[7] ὀρσιγύναικα Διόνυσον—unknown poet ap. Plu., *Exil*. 17, p. 607 C; *Smp*. 4, 6, 1, p. 671 C; *E ap. D*. 9, 389 B. ἴλαθι, εἰραφιῶτα, γυναιμανές, *h. Hom*. 34, 17.

[8] Like an infection or a conflagration. ἤδη τόδ' ἐγγὺς ὥστε πῦρ ἐφάπτεται ὕβρισμα Βακχοῦ, ψόγος ἐς Ἕλληνας μέγας, Pentheus in E., *Ba*. 778.

[9] See the accounts reported ap. Hecker, *Epidemics of the M.A.*, pp. 88, 153 Babington, esp. those of Petrus de Herental (ap. Steph. Baluz., *Vit. Pap. Avinion*. i, 483): quaedam nomina daemoniorum appellabant. The dancer cernit Mariae filium et caelum apertum.—"The masters of the Holy Scripture who exorcized the dancers regarded them as being possessed by the devil." (Limburg Chronicle; see *Mon. Germ., Chron*. iv, 1, ed. Tilemann: p. 64, ed. Wyss.)

[10] Details given by Weniger, *Dionysosdienst in Elis*, p. 8 (1883).

[11] At Delphi there was a festival called ἡρωΐς in which the Dionysiac *Thyiades* took part; a Σεμέλης ἀναγωγή was the chief feature of the δρώμενα φανερῶς (Plu., *Q.Gr*. 12). The name ἡρωΐς points to a general festival of the dead (cf. Voigt in Roscher's *Lex*. i, 1048); for another general festival of "Heroes" at Delphi see chap. iv, n. 82. At Athens the great festival of the dead, the Choes and Chytrai (chap. v, p. 168) formed part of the Anthesteria. It is precisely in these ἀρχαιότερα Διονύσια (Thuc. ii, 15, 4) that Dionysos appears as he was in primitive belief, the "master of the souls". Thus, too, in Argos one of the most ancient seats of the worship of Dionysos, the Dionysiac festival of the Agriania was at the same time a festival

of the dead, νεκύσια: Hsch., ἀγριάνια (it was specially ἐπὶ μιᾷ τῶν Προίτου θυγατέρων [Iphinoë: Apollod. 2, 22, 8], Hsch. s.v.: even so it was a festival of the dead).—In Plu., *E ap. D.* 9, 389 A, in view of the hopeless confusion shown by Plutarch in that chapter between Delphic cult-procedure and the opinions of certain unspecified θεολόγοι, it is unfortunately impossible to say with certainty whether it is the Delphians who Διόνυσον καὶ Ζαγρέα καὶ Νυκτέλιον καὶ Ἰσοδαίτην ὀνομάζουσιν or whether this only applies to the θεολόγοι (in which case they are probably Orphics).

[12] The *Agrionia* to the "savage" god (ὠμηστὴς καὶ ἀγριώνιος as contrasted with the χαριδότης καὶ μειλίχιος, Plu., *Ant.* 24) were celebrated in Thebes and Argos. ἀγριώνια καὶ νυκτέλια ὧν τὰ πολλὰ διὰ σκότους δρᾶται are opposed to the ὀλύμπια ἱερά, by Plu., *QR.* 112, p. 291 A. Bacchic din, ψόφος, at the νυκτέλια, Plu., *Smp.* 4, 6, p. 672 A. —Temple of D. Νυκτέλιος at Megara: Paus. 1, 40, 6. Nocturnal festivities (νύκτωρ τὰ πολλά, Eur., *Ba.* 486) at the Dionysia at Lerna = Paus. 2, 37, 6, at the festival of Διόνυσος Λαμπτήρ in Pellone: Paus. 7, 27, 3. ὄργια of D. at Melangeia in Arcadia 8, 6, 5; at Heraia 8, 26, 1. The orgiastic cult of D. seems to have been preserved particularly in Sparta. We hear of the οἶστρος βακχικός that once attacked the women of Sparta from Aelian, *VH.* iii, 42; some lines of Alkman (*fr.* 34) allude to the fanatical Bacchic revels on the mountain tops (quite misunderstood by Welcker, *Kl. Schr.* iv, 49). It became proverbial: virginibus bacchata Lacaenis Taygeta, Vg., *G.* ii, 487. A special word is applied to the Bacchic fury of these Spartan Mainads: δύσμαιναι (Philarg. on Vg., *G.* ii, 487; Hsch. s.v.; Meineke, *An. Alex.* 360). In view of these ecstatic mountain-revels we need not be surprised at the prohibition of drunken roaming about the city and countryside, of which Pl., *Lg.* 637 AB speaks.

[13] Welcker, *Gr. Götterl.* i, 444.—But human sacrifice in the Thracian worship of D. is nevertheless suggested by the remarkable story of Porph. (*Abs.* ii, 8) about the Βάσσαροι (whom he seems to take for a Thracian tribe).

[14] Clem. Al., Arn., Firm. all speak of the ὠμοφαγία of the Bakchai as a still-prevailing cult-practice. Bernays, *Heraklit. Briefe*, 73. Galen, too, speaks in the same way of the tearing in pieces of snakes at the Bacchic festivals (quoted Lob., *Agl.* 271 a); to snare vipers κάλλιστός ἐστι καιρός, ὃν καὶ αὐτὸς ὁ Ἀνδρόμαχος (79 ff. of his poem) ἐδήλωσεν, ἡνίκα καὶ οἱ τῷ Διονύσῳ βακχεύοντες εἰώθασι διασπᾶν τὰς ἐχίδνας, παυομένου μὲν τοῦ ἦρος οὔπω δ' ἠργμένου τοῦ θέρους (*Antid.* i, 8 = xiv, p. 45 K.). ἡνίκα—ἐχίδνας are Gal.'s words not Andromachos'. Cf. also Prud., *Sym.* i, 130 ff.

[15] We need only recall the remarkable story of Hdt. (iv, 79) about the Scythian king who in Borysthenes was initiated into the mysteries of Dionysos Bakcheios ὃς μαίνεσθαι ἐνάγει ἀνθρώπους. His Scythian subjects took exception to this. For them the religion was specifically Greek. A Borysthenite says to the Scythians: ἡμῶν γὰρ καταγελᾶτε, ὦ Σκύθαι, ὅτι βακχεύομεν καὶ ἡμᾶς ὁ θεὸς λαμβάνει. νῦν οὗτος ὁ δαίμων καὶ τὸν ὑμέτερον βασιλέα λελάβηκε καὶ βακχεύει καὶ ὑπὸ τοῦ θεοῦ μαίνεται.

[16] Cf. the remarkable account given by Plu., *Mul. Virt.* 11, p. 249 B; *fr. de An.* ap. Gell. 15, 10; Polyaen. 8, 63; and Lucian in *H. Conscr.* (25), 1.

[17] Of a different description are the attacks of temporary insanity accompanied by similar features but not religious in complexion described by Aretaeus, p. 82 K., and Gal. vii, pp. 60–1 K. (the case of Theophilos).

[18] Phenomena of κορυβαντιασμός: hearing the sound of flutes Pl., *Crit.* 54 D, Max. T., *Diss.* 38, 2, p. 220 R.; cf. Cic., *Div.* i, 114; seeing φαντασίαι, D.H., *Dem.* 22. It is this waking dream-condition, a condition related to hypnosis, which Pliny probably means: patentibus oculis dormiunt multi homines, quos corybantiare Graeci dicunt, *NH.* xi, 147. Excitement, beating heart, weeping: Pl., *Smp.* 215 E. Maddened dance: οἱ κορυβαντιῶντες οὐκ ἔμφρονες ὄντες ὀρχοῦνται, *Ion*, 534 A. "Sober drunkenness" μέθη νηφάλιος of the κορυβ., Philo, *Mund. Op.* 23, i, p. 16 M.—The name shows that those attacked by the disease were regarded as "possessed" by the Korybantes. κορυβαντιᾶν· τὸ Κορύβασι κατέχεσθαι, Sch. Ar., *V.* 9. The Korybantes μανίας καὶ ἐνθειασμοῦ εἰσιν ἐμποιητικοί, ib. 8. ἔνθεος ἐκ σεμνῶν Κορυβάντων, E., *Hip.* 142; Sch. ad loc.: Κορύβαντες μανίας αἴτιοι. ἔνθεν καὶ κορυβαντιᾶν.—Arrian gives an unusually good account of the Korybantic frenzy of the Phrygians in a little noticed passage ap. Eust. on D.P. 809: μαίνονται τῇ Ῥέᾳ καὶ πρὸς Κορυβάντων κατέχονται, ἤγουν κορυβαντιῶσι δαιμονῶντες (i.e. possessed by the δαίμων, see Usener, *Götternamen*, 293). ὅταν δὲ κατάσχῃ αὐτοὺς τὸ θεῖον, ἐλαυνόμενοι καὶ μέγα βοῶντες καὶ ὀρχούμενοι προθεσπίζουσι τὰ μέλλοντα, θεοφορούμενοι καὶ μαινόμενοι. The complete similarity between this condition and that of the Bacchic worship is sufficiently obvious.

[19] Use of dance and music to cure those who are attacked by Korybantic excitement: Pl., *Lg.* 790 DE, 791 A. More especially the melodies for the flute composed by Olympos, being θεῖα, were able to discover and cure those liable to Korybantic *ekstasis* (by means of the *inspiring* effect which they had on such persons). This is shown particularly by a passage in Plato (*Smp.* 215 C–E); where it is evident that the κορυβαντιῶντες of 215 E are not to be distinguished from the θεῶν καὶ τελετῶν δεόμενοι of 215 C (C states the general rule of which E is a particular application). This homoeopathic cure of the κορυβαντιῶντες by the intensification and subsequent discharge of the disorder is implied in all that we hear of the character of the Phrygian mode as ἐνθουσιαστική and of the μέλη Ὀλύμπου as exciting the souls of men to "*enthousiasmos*"; Arist., *Pol.* 1340b, 4, 5, 1342b, 1 ff., 1340a, 8; [Pl.], *Min.* 318 B; Cic., *Div.* i, 114. The κορυβαντιῶντες are also meant in Arist., *Pol.* 8, 7, 1342a, 7 ff. . . καὶ γὰρ ὑπὸ ταύτης τῆς κινήσεως (i.e. τοῦ ἐνθουσιασμοῦ) κατακώχιμοί τινές εἰσιν· ἐκ δὲ τῶν ἱερῶν μελῶν ὁρῶμεν τούτους, ὅταν χρήσωνται τοῖς ὀργιάζουσι τὴν ψυχὴν μέλεσι, καθισταμένους ὥσπερ ἰατρείας τυχόντας καὶ καθάρσεως. Plato's analysis (*Lg.* 790 D ff.) is exactly parallel: the cure for the μανικαὶ διαθέσεις of the Korybantic patients is οὐχ ἡσυχία ἀλλὰ τοὐναντίον κίνησις, whereby they are assisted to regain their ἕξεις ἔμφρονες. (It is from this religio-musical procedure and not from strictly medical experience or practice that Aristotle, taking a hint from Plato, *Rp.* 606, derived his idea of the κάθαρσις τῶν παθημάτων by violent discharge of the emotions and transferred it to tragedy—not, as in the explanation to which some have recently returned, by a tranquilization of the emotions in "a final reconciliation".) This κάθαρσις and ἰατρεία of the κορυβαντιῶντες is the object of the initiation ceremony of the Korybantes (whose true βάκχοι are the κορυβαντιῶντες, i.e. the worshippers who are in need of and capable of cure); of the Κορυβάντων μυστήρια which are held ἐπὶ καθαρμῷ τῆς μανίας (Sch. Ar., *V.* 119–20, ἐκορυβάντιζε); cf. the τελετὴ τῶν Κορυβάντων (Pl., *Euthd.* 277 D, including θρόνωσις: D. Chr. 12, p. 388 R., § 33 Arn.; Lob., *Agl.* 116, 369. There is a parody of θρόνωσις in the initiation scene of Ar., *Nub.* 254, where Streps. sits ἐπὶ τὸν ἱερὸν σκίμποδα. τεθρονισμένος τοῖς θεοῖς = initiated

in *P. Mag. Lond.* 747 f. = Kenyon, *Greek Papyri in B.M.* i, p. 108); and cf. the μητρῷα καὶ κορυβαντικὰ τέλη: D.H., *Dem.* 22. At the initiation ceremony (κορυβαντισμός· κάθαρσις μανίας Hsch.) held in the Κορυβαντεῖον (Hdn. Gr. 1, 375, 15 Lentz; *App. Prov.* ii, 23) the famous music of "inspiration" was played; there was also χορεία (Pl., *Euthd.*), ἦχοι e.g. the sound of τύμπανα (Ar., *Ves.* 120 f.; Luc. *DD.* 12, 1), and also it appears incense-burning: ὀσμαί, D.H., *Dem.* 22; cf. above, chap. viii, n. 39. All these stimulants intensified the pathological tendency of the κορυβαντιῶντες and gave them relief by the violent discharge of their emotions.—There is no need to doubt the actual occurrence of such pathological states and their medical treatment by music, etc. It was clearly the same type of psychopathical malady that invaded Italy in the Middle Ages under the name of Tarantism, repeating its attacks for several centuries: in this case, too, music (and even the sound of a particular melody) served both to excite and eventually to cure the violent dance-mania; cf. Hecker 172, 176 ff. —There seems to be a fabulous element in other stories current in antiquity about the cure of madness, love-passions, and even sciatica by the music of the flute (Pythagoras, Empedokles, Damon, Thphr. *fr.* 87). Such belief in the curative powers of music, esp. of the flute, seems to have been derived originally from actual experience of the καθάρσεις practised in Korybantic festivals, and then to have been exaggerated into a fable. Even doctors had no doubt that μανία was curable by the *cantiones tibiarum*; see Cael. Aur., *Morb. Chr.* i, 5, 175, 178 (Asklepiades); Cael. Aur. (i.e. Soranos), ib. 176, however, denies it. It depended entirely upon the theory, originally derived from κορυβαντισμός, of cure by intensification and discharge of the emotional state.

[20] ὦ μάκαρ ὅστις . . . θιασεύεται ψυχάν, ἐν ὄρεσσι βακχεύων, ὁσίοις καθαρμοῖσιν, E., *Ba.* 72 ff.—dicunt sacra Liberi ad purgationem animae pertinere Serv. on Vg., *G.* ii, 389; cf. also on *A.* vi, 741.

[21] Διόνυσος λύσιος (like Δ. μειλίχιος ἐλευθερεύς and σαώτης) is rightly taken as the "freer from orgiastic frenzy" (and not in the ordinary political sense) by Klausen, *Orpheus*, p. 26 [Ersch-Gruber] and Voigt in Roscher's *Lex.* i, 1062. That this is the proper meaning of λύσιος is shown by its being contrasted with βακχεῖος, which by common consent means the god ὃς μαίνεσθαι ἐνάγει ἀνθρώπους (Hdt.); e.g. in Korinth, Paus. 2, 2, 6; Sikyon, Paus. 2, 7, 5–6. And Δ. βακχεύς and μειλίχιος in Naxos, *Ath.* iii, 78 C.

[22] In the κατάλογος γυναικῶν as it seems; *fr.* 54 Rz. But perhaps also in the *Melampodia* (*fr.* 184 Kink.).

[23] ἐμάνησαν, ὡς Ἡσίοδός φησιν, ὅτι τὰς Διονύσου τελετὰς οὐ κατεδέχοντο. [Apollod.] 2, 2, 2, 2, and cf. 1, 9, 12, 8. The same story (only with the name Anaxagoras substituted for that of his grandfather Proitos—doubtless on chronological grounds) with the words τὰς Ἀργείας γυναῖκας μανείσας διὰ τὴν Διονύσου μῆνιν: D.S. 4, 68, 4. (μανία—in the reign of Anaxagoras—Paus. 2, 18, 4; Eust., on *B* 568, p. 288, 28).—Otherwise, it is generally Hera who sends the μανία Akousil. ap. [Apollod.] 2, 2, 2, 2 [*fr.* 14 Diels]. Pherekyd. ap. Sch. on ο 225. Probus and Serv. on *Ecl.* vi, 48. This is a later version of the legend depending upon a different interpretation of the "insanity".

[24] [Apollod.] 2, 2, 2. Acc. to Hdt. ix, 34, the treatment of Melamp. was applied generally to all the Ἀργεῖαι γυναῖκες (who acc. to [Apollod.] § 5, were also attacked by the madness); cf. D.S. 4, 68, 4. (. . . τὰς Ἀργείας ἢ ὥς τινες μᾶλλόν φασι, τὰς Προιτίδας Eustath. κατὰ τὴν ἱστορίαν). θεραπεύειν is D.S.' word; ἐκάθηρεν, Sch. Pi., *N.* ix, 30; *purgavit* Serv.

[25] Μελάμπους παραλαβὼν τοὺς δυνατωτάτους τῶν νεανιῶν μετ' ἀλαλαγμοῦ καί τινος ἐνθέου χορείας ἐκ τῶν ὀρῶν αὐτὰς ἐς Σικυῶνα συνεδίωξε (i.e. the frenzied women who had eventually become very numerous: § 5, 6) [Apollod.] 2, 2, 2, 7. The account in Pl., *Phdr.* 244 D, E, corresponds closely with the proceedings of Melampous and perhaps refers to them: ἀλλὰ μὴν νόσων γε καὶ πόνων τῶν μεγίστων, ἃ δὴ παλαιῶν ἐκ μηνιμάτων ποθὲν ἔν τισι τῶν γενῶν ἡ μανία ἐγγενομένη καὶ προφητεύσασα οἷς ἔδει ἀπαλλαγὴν εὕρετο, καταφυγοῦσα πρὸς θεῶν εὐχάς τε καὶ λατρείας, ὅθεν δὴ καθαρμῶν τε καὶ τελετῶν τυχοῦσα ἐξάντη ἐποίησε τὸν ἑαυτῆς ἔχοντα πρός τε τὸν παρόντα καὶ τὸν ἔπειτα χρόνον, λύσιν τῷ ὀρθῶς μανέντι καὶ κατασχομένῳ τῶν παρόντων κακῶν εὑρομένη. This is a description of the remedial methods used in the Bacchic and Korybantic *enthousiasmos* but applied to special circumstances of the mythical past which are regarded as the standard of all later kathartic methods.

[26] καθαρμοί [Apollod.] § 8. The regular kathartic materials are σκίλλα, ἄσφαλτος, water, etc.; Diphilus, *fr.* 126 K., employs them all for his own purpose, ap. Clem. Al., *Str.* vii, p. 844 P. The black hellebore (ἐλλέβορος μέλας) was popularly known as μελαμπόδιον because Melampous had first gathered and employed it for the purpose (Thphr., *HP.* 9, 10, 4), esp. when he cured and purified the Προίτου θυγατέρας μανείσας (Gal., *Atrabile* 7 = v, p. 132 K.; it can only be by mistake that he calls it the white hellebore; cf. also Diosc. 4, 149, where the old καθαρτής becomes Μελάμπους τις αἰπόλος [hence Plin., *NH.* 25, 47]; the reason may be elicited from Thphr., *HP.* 9, 10, 2). The place where the καθαρμοί took place and where the καθάρσια were thrown away differed acc. to the natural features of the locality and the convenience they offered: thus in Arcadia it was at Lousoi, in Elis at the river Anigros, etc.; Ov., *M.* xv, 322 ff.; Vitr. 8, 3, 21; Paus. 5, 5, 10; 8, 18, 7–8; cf. Call., *H. Art.* 233 f.; Str. 346, etc.

[27] Melampous Ἕλλησιν ὁ ἐξηγησάμενος τοῦ Διονύσου τό τε οὔνομα καὶ τὴν θυσίην καὶ τὴν πομπὴν τοῦ φαλλοῦ, Hdt. ii, 49. Hdt.'s elaborate theory in this passage of a connexion between Mel. and Egypt, etc., is of course historically quite worthless, but the fact that he pitched upon Melamp. especially as the introducer of the Dionysiac religion can only have been due to the existence of ancient tradition (i.e. legendary tradition of course). There can be no doubt that he, like Hesiod, regarded as *Dionysiac* the frenzy in which the Argive women were said μανῆναι and to have been healed by Melamp. (ix, 34).

[28] Μελάμπους φίλτατος ὢν Ἀπόλλωνι, Hes., *Eoiai*, (168 Rz.) ap. Sch. A.R. i, 118. φίλος Ἀπόλλωνι, D.S. 6, 7, 7 Dind. The poet of the family tree of the Melampodidai given in ο 244 ff. undoubtedly regarded Melamp. as an Apolline μάντις (like all μάντεις in Homer). This poet at least knows nothing of the Dionysiac side of Melampous' activities. How Mel. met Apollo on the banks of the Alphaios and from him received his consecration as true μάντις, we learn from [Apollod.] 1, 9, 11, 3. The same is said of Polypheides, a descendant of Mel. ο 252: αὐτὰρ ὑπέρθυμον Πολυφείδεα μάντιν Ἀπόλλων θῆκε βροτῶν ὄχ' ἄριστον, ἐπεὶ θάνεν Ἀμφιάραος. Another descendant of Melamp., Polyeidos, comes to Megara to purify Alkathoös from the murder of his son, and founds there a temple of *Dionysos*: Paus. 1, 43, 4.

[29] See above, chap. iii, n. 32.

[30] Plu., *Is. et O.* 35, p. 365 A. Sacrifice made by Agamemnon to Dionysos ἐν μυχοῖς Δελφινίου παρ' ἄντρα κερδῴου θεοῦ, Lyc. 207 ff.

[31] Plu., *E ap. D.* ix, p. 388 F. Three winter months were sacred to Dionysos (cf. the three chief Dionysiac festivals at Athens which

occurred in the months Gamelion, Anthesterion, Elaphebolion). Only during these three months is the god on earth. So, too, Kore shared her rule over the underworld with Aïdoneus for three months (or six); the rest of the year she is on earth παρὰ μητρὶ καὶ ἄλλοις ἀθανάτοισι.

[32] Διονύσῳ τῶν Δελφῶν οὐδὲν ἧττον ἢ τῷ Ἀπόλλωνι μέτεστιν, Plu., *E ap. D.* ix, 384 D.

[33] τὰ δὲ νεφῶν τέ ἐστιν ἀνωτέρω τὰ ἄκρα (τοῦ Παρνασοῦ), καὶ αἱ Θυιάδες ἐπὶ τούτοις τῷ Διονύσῳ καὶ τῷ Ἀπόλλωνι μαίνονται, Paus. 10, 32, 7. Parnasus gemino petit aethera colle, mons Phoebo Bromioque sacer, cui numine mixto Delphica Thebanae referunt trieterica Bacchae, Luc., v, 72 ff. We hear of a Delphos the son of Apollo and Thyia the first priestess and Mainad of Dionysos at Delphi: Paus. 10, 6, 4.

[34] Apollo himself in an oracular command Πυθιάσιν πεντετήροισιν . . . ἔταξε Βάκχου θυσίαν χορῶν τε πολλῶν κυκλίαν ἅμιλλαν; so says Philodamos of Skarpheia in the Paian (second half fourth century B.C.), *BCH.* 1895, p. 408. We must suppose, too, that this command (i.e. decree of the Delphic priesthood) was actually carried out.

[35] Δελφοὶ δὲ διπλῇ προσηγορίᾳ τιμῶσιν (σέ, i.e. Apollo), Ἀπόλλωνα καὶ Διόνυσον λέγοντες, Men. Rhet., p. 446, 5 Sp.

[36] *Arg.*, Sch. Pi., *P.*, p. 297, Böckh [p. 2, 5 ff. Drch.]: . . . τοῦ προφητικοῦ τρίποδος (in Delphi) ἐν ᾧ πρῶτος Διόνυσος ἐθεμίστευσε. And again . . δάκτυλον (a part of the νόμος Πυθικός) ἀπὸ Διονύσου, ὅτι πρῶτος οὗτος δοκεῖ ἀπὸ τοῦ τρίποδος θεμιστεῦσαι. As it has been previously said that at the Delphic μαντεῖον πρώτη Νὺξ ἐχρησμῴδησεν, Dionysos seems to be here regarded as πρόμαντις of Nyx. Thus, at Megara there was a temple of Διόνυσος Νυκτέλιος in the immediate neighbourhood of, and in all probability closely associated with a Νυκτὸς μαντεῖον: Paus. 1, 40, 6.

[37] Paus. 1, 2, 5; Ribbeck, *Anf. d. Dionysoscult in Att.*, p. 8 (1869); cf. Dem. 21, 52. Regulation of a festival of Dionysos in Kolone by the Oracle: Paus. 3, 13, 7; in Alea, Paus. 8, 23, 1 (at which women were scourged, a substitution for primitive human sacrifice, as at the διαμαστίγωσις in Sparta, of which Paus. is reminded). Introduction of the worship of Διόνυσος Φαλλήν at Methymna by the oracle: Paus. 10, 19, 3.—At Magnesia on the Maeander a plane-tree split by a storm revealed a statue of Dionysos (a true Διόνυσος ἔνδενδρος). The Delphic oracle commanded the ambassadors sent by the city to build a temple to Dionysos (who had hitherto been without one in Magnesia) and put a priest in charge of it; then, for the institution of the cult they were to introduce from Thebes Mainads of the family of Ino: Μαινάδας αἳ γενεῆς Εἰνοῦς ἄπο Καδμηείης. (The cult of Dionysos was evidently traditional at Thebes in this family which traced its descent from Ino, the foster-mother of Dionysos.) The three Mainads obtained from Thebes (called Kosko, Baubo, and Thettale) instituted the cult of the god and founded three θίασοι arranged according to locality (there were three θίασοι in Thebes, too, E., *Ba.* 680 ff.). They themselves remained in Magnesia till their death and were buried with great ceremony by the city, Kosko on the "Hill of Kosko", Baubo ἐν Ταβάρνει, Thettale πρὸς τῷ θεάτρῳ. See the ἀρχαῖος χρησμός with explanatory notes in prose, restored by Ἀπολλώνειος Μοκόλλης, ἀρχαῖος μύστης (of Dionysos): *Ath. Mitth.* 15 (1890), p. 331 f.

[38] See Rapp, *Rhein. Mus.* 27. In spite of his quite correct emphasis in general upon the ritual and purely formal character of this sacred embassy and the dance-festival that followed, Rapp makes the mistake of underestimating the ecstatic side of the Dionysiac festivals—a side

which was once predominant and was always liable to recur. (If this element had not been real there would have been no need for a symbolical ritualistic imitation of such ἔκστασις). How even in later times a true ekstasis and self-forgetfulness seized upon the Thyiades in their sacred night-festivals and in consequence of the numerous stimulating influences of the occasion, we can learn very clearly from Plutarch's description of the Thyiads who wandered in their frenzy to Amphissa (*Mul. Virt.* 13, 249 E). Rapp., p. 22, tries in vain to upset the historical value of this account. Other points have already been mentioned incidentally.

[39] ἣν διὰ μαντοσύνην τήν οἱ πόρε Φοῖβος Ἀπόλλων, *A* 72.

[40] τὸ ἄτεχνον καὶ ἀδίδακτον (τῆς μαντικῆς) τουτέστιν ἐνύπνια καὶ ἐνθουσιασμούς [Plu.] *Vit. Poes. Hom.* ii, 212. The only form known to Homer is ἡ τῶν ἐμφρόνων ζήτησις τοῦ μέλλοντος διά τε ὀρνίθων ποιουμένη καὶ τῶν ἄλλων σημείων (Pl., *Phdr.* 244 C).

[41] The Ps.-Plutarch of the last note does, however, find in Theoklymenos' position among the suitors, *υ* 345–57 (in any case a passage added by a later hand), a proof that he is an ἔνθεος μάντις, ἔκ τινος ἐπιπνοίας σημαίνων τὰ μέλλοντα. But in that story the abnormal state belongs rather to the suitors than the seer. See Lob., *Agl.* 264. Still less can we (with Welcker, *Götterl.* ii, 11) deduce Homer's knowledge of ecstatic prophecy from *A* 91 ff. or *H* 34–53. The derivation of the word μάντις from μαίνεσθαι, frequently repeated since the time of Plato, would make the ecstatic element predominant in the idea of the prophet. But this derivation is quite uncertain and a connexion with μανύω is much more probable.

[42] Pytho: *θ* 80, *I* 405. Dodona: *Π* 234, *ξ* 327 f., *τ* 296 f. An oracle is questioned perhaps in *π* 402 f. See Nägelsbach, *Hom. Theol.*, p. 181 f.

[43] See Lob., *Agl.* 814 f. (even the regular use of the expressions ἀνεῖλεν ὁ θεός, ἡ πυθία suffice to prove it). Cf. also Bgk., *Gr. Lit.* i, 334. *h. Hom. Merc.* in its own fashion (552–66) tells how the god deserted the "lot" oracle at Delphi as too unreliable and unworthy of the god.

[44] Even the case of Helenos is no real example of this: *H* 44 ([Plu.] *Vit. Hom.* ii, 212, seems to regard it as one). Cic., *Div.* i, 89, expressly distinguishes the prophesying of Helenos from the "enthusiastic" frenzy of Kassandra.

[45] Even the *h. Hom. Merc.* to the Pythian Apollo, though it describes the institution of the cult and oracle of Apollo at Delphi, nowhere mentions the Pythia (as Lob., *Agl.* 264, very pertinently remarks). (Acc. to 306 f. we must suppose that at that time the prophesying was done exclusively by male μάντεις or προφῆται.)

[46] See Eur., *IT.* 1234 ff. Oracles of earth-divinities were always given by *Incubation*. Even Cicero (*Div.* i, 38, following Chrysippos it seems) refers to vis illa terrae, quae mentem Pythiae divino afflatu concitebat (as something that has disappeared). It is often referred to by later authors. The placing of the tripod over the chasm from which the vapour of inspiration came, is certainly, with Welcker, *Götterl.* ii, 11, to be regarded as a reminiscence of the ancient method of the earth-oracle which was thus continued in the direct inspiration of Apollo. (The ἐνθουσιασμός does not exclude other stimulants. The Pythia drinks from the inspired spring—like the μάντεις at Klaros: *Ath. Mitth.* xi, 430—and thereupon becomes ἔνθεος: Luc., *Herm.* 60. The prophetess of Apollo Deiradiotes at Argos by drinking the sacrificial blood κάτοχος ἐκ τοῦ θεοῦ γίγνεται: Paus. 2, 24, 1. The Pythia chews the sacred laurel-leaves to become inspired: Luc., *Bis Acc.* 1; also

the δάφνη, ἧς ποτε γευσάμενος πετάλων ἀνέφηνεν ἀοιδὰς αὐτὸς ἄναξ σκηπτοῦχος: *H. Mag.* ap. Abel, *Orphica*, p. 288. The holy plant contains the *vis divina* which one absorbs into oneself by chewing. This is the crude, primitive idea underlying such actions, as plainly appears in a similar case mentioned by Porph., *Abs.* ii, 48.)

[47] e.g. in Sparta: ἔστιν ἐπονομαζόμενον Γάσηπτον ἱερὸν Γῆς. Ἀπόλλων δ' ὑπὲρ αὐτοῦ ἵδρυται Μαλεάτης, Paus. 3, 12, 8.—The legend of Apollo and Daphne symbolizes the overthrow of the earth-oracle by Apollo and his own kind of prophecy.

[48] See above, chap. iii, p. 97. Welcker, *Götterl.* i, 520 ff.

[49] See above, p. 260 ff.

[50] At Amphikleia in Phokis there was an oracle of Dionysos: πρόμαντις δὲ ὁ ἱερεύς ἐστι, χρᾷ δὲ ἐκ τοῦ θεοῦ κάτοχος, Paus. 10, 33, 11. The words of Cornutus probably refer to Greece (chap. xxx, p. 59, 20 Lang): καὶ μαντεῖα ἔσθ' ὅπου τοῦ Διονύσου ἔχοντος . . . cf. Plu., *Smp.* 7, 10, 17, p. 716 B: οἱ παλαιοὶ τὸν θεὸν (Dionysos) μαντικῆς πολλὴν ἔχειν ἡγοῦντο μοῖραν.

[51] Dionysos the first giver of oracles at Delphi: Arg., Pi. *Pyth.*, p. 2, 7 Drch. (see above, n. 36). Voigt ap. Roscher, i, 1033–4, regards Apollo at Delphi as the heir of the Dionysiac *mantikê*; but he considers Dionysos to have been in the same condition as the Python who was overthrown and killed by Apollo—a view that can hardly be justified. My own view is that Apollo, after destroying the chthonic (dream) Oracle adopted from the *mantikê* of Dionysos the prophecy by *furor divinus* which had been hitherto unknown to him.—No one can seriously claim to have a clear certain insight into the intricate and kaleidoscopic changes of power and authority that finally led to the supremacy of the composite Apolline cult in the violently disputed centre of Greek religion.

[52] . . . ὅσους ἐξ Ἀπόλλωνος μανῆναι λέγουσι (i.e. the ancient χρησμολόγους), Paus. 1, 34, 4. μανία τοῦ χρησμολόγου, Diogen., *Pr.* 6, 47. So, too, ἐπίπνοια: Sittl, *Gebärden der Gr. u. R.* 345. ὁ ἐνθουσιασμὸς ἐπίπνευσίν τινα θείαν ἔχειν δοκεῖ, Str. 467.—οἱ νυμφόληπτοι καὶ θεόληπτοι τῶν ἀνθρώπων, ἐπιπνοίᾳ δαιμονίου τινὸς ὥσπερ ἐνθουσιάζοντες, *Eth. Eud.* i, 1, 4, 1214a, 23.

[53] Ecstatic condition of the Pythia: D.S. xvi, 26; misconstrued in a Christian sense, Sch. Ar., *Plu.* 39 (see Hemsterh. ad loc.). ὅλη γίγνεται τοῦ θεοῦ, Iamb., *Myst.* 3, 11, p. 126, 15 Parthey. Description of a case in which the prophesying Pythia became completely ἔκφρων: Plu., *Def. Or.*, 51, p. 438 B.

[54] In the inspired *mantikê* the soul becomes " free " from the body: animus ita solutus est et vacuus ut eo plane nihil sit cum corpore, Cic., *Div.* i, 113; cf. 70. (καθ' ἑαυτὴν γίγνεται ἡ ψυχή in dreaming and μαντεῖαι: Arist. ap. S.E., *M.* 9, 21 [*fr.* 10 R.]. ἔοικε ἡ ἀρχὴ (of νοῦς) ἀπολυομένου τοῦ λόγου ἰσχύει μᾶλλον in *enthousiasmos*, *EE.* 1248a, 40; cf. 1225a, 28.) This is ἔκστασις of the understanding itself: see above, p. 260 ff. At other times it is said that the god enters into men and fills their souls; whereupon the man is ἔνθεος: see above, chap. viii, n. 50; cf. *pleni et mixti deo vates*, Minuc. 7, 6. The priestess at the oracle of Branchidai δέχεται τὸν θεόν, Iamb., *M.* 3, 11, p. 127, 7 Par. —ἐξοικίζεται ὁ ἐν ἡμῖν νοῦς κατὰ τὴν τοῦ θείου πνεύματος ἄφιξιν, κατὰ δὲ τὴν μετανάστασιν αὐτοῦ πάλιν ἐσοικίζεται κτλ: Philo, *Q. rer. div.* 53, i, p. 511 M., speaking of the ἔνθεος κατοχωτική τε μανία, ᾗ τὸ προφητικὸν γένος χρῆται (p. 509 M.); cf. also *Spec. Leg.* i, p. 343 M. This also was the idea prevailing at Delphi. Plu., *Def. Or.* 9, p. 414 E, rejects as εὔηθες, τὸ οἴεσθαι τὸν θεὸν αὐτόν, ὥσπερ τοὺς ἐγγαστριμύθους,

ἐνδυόμενον εἰς τὰ σώματα τῶν προφητῶν ὑποφθέγγεσθαι, τοῖς ἐκείνων στόμασι καὶ φωναῖς χρώμενον ὀργάνοις. But this was evidently the ordinary and deep-rooted opinion (τὸν θεὸν εἰς σῶμα καθειργνύναι θνητόν, Plu., *Pyth. Or.* 8, p. 398 A). The primitive idea is naively expressed by a late magic papyrus (Kenyon, *Gk. Pap. in BM.* i, p. 116 [1893], No. 122 [fourth century B.C.] l. 2 ff. : ἐλθέ μοι, κύριε Ἑρμῆ ὡς τὰ βρέφη εἰς τὰς κοιλίας τῶν γυναικῶν κτλ.—Neither in *mantikê* nor in ἔκστασις is any great distinction made between the out-going of the soul and the in-coming of the god : the two ideas merge together. The condition is regarded as one in which two persons are united and become one ; the human being οἷον ἄλλος γενόμενος καὶ οὐκ αὐτός, θεὸς γενόμενος μᾶλλον δὲ ὤν, no longer experiencing a sense of division between himself and divinity μεταξὺ γὰρ οὐδέν, οὐδ' ἔτι δύο ἀλλ' ἓν ἄμφω (as the subtle mysticism of Plotinos describes ἔκστασις, 6, 9, 9–10 ; 6, 7, 34–5). In the above-mentioned magic invocation of Hermes the γόης who has conjured the god into himself says to the god (l. 36 ff., p. 117) σὺ (σοι MSS.) γὰρ ἐγώ, καὶ ἐγὼ σύ (σοι MSS.) · τὸ σὸν ὄνομα ἐμὸν καὶ τὸ ἐμὸν σόν · ἐγὼ γάρ εἰμι τὸ εἴδωλόν σου κτλ. [Cf. Swinburne, *Songs before Sunrise* ii, 74 f.]

[55] So Bergk, *Gr. Lit.* i, 335, n. 58. The verses of the oracle are regarded as the god's own : Plu., *Pyth. Or.* v, 396 C ff. Since the god himself speaks out of her the Pythia can properly speaking only give true oracles οὐκ ἀποδάμου Ἀπόλλωνος τυχόντος, Pi., *P.* iv, 5 ; i.e. when Apollo is present at Delphi and not (as he is in winter) far away among the Hyperboreans. This was why oracles were originally only given in the spring month *Bysios* (Plu., *Q. Gr.* 9) in which apparently the θεοφάνια occurred (Hdt. i, 51). Just as in the case of the old oracular earth-spirits (see above, chap. iii, n. 12) who were confined to special localities, so in the case of the gods who work through the ἐνθουσιασμός of an inspired prophetess, their personal presence in the temple at the time of the prophesying is requisite. This presence is thought of as actual and corporeal in the primitive form of the belief (though it was got over and reinterpreted in later times), and therefore in the case of the gods can only be temporary. When, in summer, Apollo is in Delos (Vg., *A.* iv, 143 ff.), no χρηστήριον takes place in the temple of Apollo at Patara in Lykia (Hdt. i, 182). And so in general φυγόντων ἢ μεταστάντων (τῶν περὶ τὰ μαντεῖα καὶ χρηστήρια τεταγμένων δαιμονίων) ἀποβάλλει τὴν δύναμιν (τὰ μαντεῖα), Plu., *DO.* 15, p. 418 D.

[56] The cult of Zeus in Crete was held μετ' ὀργιασμοῦ : Str. 468 The same applies to the cult offered in many places to the various and very different female deities who were generally combined together under the name of Artemis : Lob., *Agl.* 1085 ff. ; Meineke, *An. Al.* 361. In their case Asiatic influence was at work sometimes, but by no means always : Welcker, *Götterl.* i, 391 ; Müller, *Dorians*, i, 404 ff. The worship of Pan was also orgiastic. Otherwise we find it principally in foreign worships that had made their way at an early period into private cults : e.g. the Phrygian worship of Kybele, etc. These easily combined with the Bacchic worship and became almost indistinguishable from it ; sometimes they even allied themselves with true Greek cults, with that of Pan, for example, which was closely assimilated both to the worship of Kybele and that of Dionysos. It remains obscure how far the Cretan cult of Zeus was affected by Phrygian elements.

[57] A remarkable example is given by Herod. (ix, 94), who tells us of the blind Euenios in Apollonia who suddenly became possessed of

ἔμφυτος μαντική (not acquired by learning). He is a true *θεόμαντις* (Pl., *Ap.* 22 C).

[58] The ancients knew quite well that *Βάκις* and *Σίβυλλα* were really *common nouns* denoting inspired *χρησμῳδοί*: thus *Σίβυλλα* is the *παρωνυμία* of Herophile, Plu., *P. Or.* 14, p. 401 A, and *Βάκις* an *ἐπίθετον* of Peisistratos, Sch. Ar., *Pax* 1071. The words are clearly used to denote whole classes of individuals by Arist., *Prob.* 954a, 36 : *νοσήματα μανικὰ καὶ ἐνθουσιαστικά* are liable to attack *Σίβυλλαι καὶ Βάκιδες καὶ οἱ ἔνθεοι πάντες.* And in general when the ancients speak in the singular of " the Sibyl " or " Bakis ", the word is generally meant as a class-name ; just as for the most part when *ἡ Πυθία, ἡ Πυθίας* occurs it is not a particular individual Pythia who is meant but the class-concept of " the Pythia " (or some particular member of the class actually functioning at the moment). Hence it is by no means certain that Herakleitos, etc., when they speak simply of *ἡ Σίβυλλα,* and Herod. when he says *Βάκις* were of the opinion that there was only one Sibyl and one Bakis.—It must be admitted that we do not know the real meaning of these adjectival words themselves, their etymology being quite uncertain. Was the ecstatic character of these prophets already expressed in their titles ? *σιβυλλαίνειν,* of course = *ἐνθεάζειν* (D.S. 4, 66, 7), but the verb is naturally enough derived from the name *Σίβυλλα,* just as *βακίζειν* is from *Βάκις, ἐρινύειν* from *Ἐρινύς* and not vice versa. Nor can we tell how far the personal names attached to certain Sibyls and Bakides have real historical significance. Sibyl names are Herophile, Demophile (abbreviated to Demo), *Φυτώ* or perhaps rather *Φοιτώ* ; cf. *φοιτὰς ἀγύρτρια,* A., *Ag.* 1273 (so Lachmann on Tib. 2, 5, 68) : the Arcadian Bakis was called Kydas or Aletes (cf. *Φοιτώ*) acc. to Philetas Eph. ap. Sch. Ar., *Pa.* 1071. It is impossible to extract from the by no means scanty materials any real element of historical fact with respect to these stories of individual Sibyls. Most untrustworthy of all in this as in all he says on this subject is Herakleides Pont. and his story of the Phrygian (or Trojan) Sibyl : we might be more inclined to believe what Eratosthenes reported acc. to the *antiquis annalibus Samiorum* of a Samian Sibyl (Varro ap. Lactant., *Inst.* 1, 6, 9)—if it had not included so entirely worthless a story as that preserved in Val. M. 1, 5, 9.—Clem. Al., *Str.* i, 21, p. 398 P., gives after Bakis a whole list of *χρησμῳδοί* with names : they evidently do not all belong to legend, but hardly one of them is otherwise known to us. The following are possibly real persons belonging to the prophetic period : Melesagoras of Eleusis who prophesied in Athens like another Bakis *ἐκ νυμφῶν κάτοχος*: Max. Tyr. 38, 3 (there is not a shadow of a reason for identifying him with Amelesagoras, the author of an alleged ancient Atthis : Müller, *FHG.* ii, 21) ; Euklos of Cyprus whose *χρησμοί* written in the old Cypriote language inspire a certain confidence (M. Schmidt, *Kuhns Ztschr.* 1860, p. 361 ff.) ; unfortunately he wrote before Homer : Paus. 10, 24, 3 ; Tat., *Gr.* 41, which makes his personality dubious again.

[59] Of this description were the *χρησμολόγοι* of the fifth and fourth —even of the expiring sixth—centuries (Onomakritos belongs entirely to this class). Lob., *Agl.* 978 ff., 932. It is very rarely that we hear in these times of real prophets on their own account, prophesying in the *furor divinus,* like that Amphilytos of Acarnania who met Peisistratos as he returned from Eretria before the battle *ἐπὶ Παλληνίδι* and prophesied to him *ἐνθεάζων* (Hdt. i, 62 f. ; he is an Athenian in [Pl.] *Thg.* 124 D—where he is mentioned side by side with *Βάκις τε*

καὶ Σίβυλλα—and in Clem. Al., *Str.* i, 21, p. 398 P.). In the same way occasional " Sibyls " occur even in late times (Phaennis, Athenais: see Alexandre, *Or. Sib.*[1] ii, p. 21, 48).

[60] Herakl. Pont. ap. Cl. Al., *Str.* i, 21, p. 384 P., seems to have been the first to speak definitely of *two* Sibyls, Herophile of Erythrai and the Phrygian Sibyl (whom he identifies with the Marpessian Sibyl or the S. of Gergis: Lact. 1, 6, 12, see Alexandre, ii, p. 25, 32. Philetas ap. Sch. Ar., *Av.* 962, follows him except that he adds a third, the Sardian). The Phrygian-Trojan Sibyl is dated by Herakleides in the times of " Solon and Cyrus " (Lact.); we cannot tell what date he assigned to the Erythraean. Perhaps it was only after his times that the χρησμοί of Herophile first appeared in which she prophesied the Τρωϊκά. From these verses it was now deduced that she lived before the Trojan war: so Paus. 10, 12, 2, and even Apollodoros of Erythrai (Lact. 1, 6, 9). Thenceforward the name of Herophile was associated with the idea of extreme antiquity. (The Libyan Sibyl of Paus. who is said to be the oldest of all is merely an invention of Euripides and never really obtained currency: Λίβυσσα = Σίβυλλα anagrammatically. See Alexandre, p. 74 f.) Herophile was identified also with the πρώτη Σίβυλλα who came to Delphi and prophesied there: Plu., *P.Or.* 9, 398 C; expressly so by Paus. 10, 12, 1, and Bocchus ap. Solin. 2, p. 38, 21–4 Mom. Acc. to Herakleides (ap. Clem. Al.) it was rather the Φρυγία who calling herself Artemis prophesied in Delphi (so, too, Philetas following Herakl. and see also Suid. Σιβ. Δελφίς). This is due to the local patriotism of the inhabitants of the Troad. Their Sibyl is the Marpessian (= the Φρυγία of Herakl.). The artificial sort of interpretation and forgery that enabled a local historian of the Troad (it cannot have been Demetrios of Skepsis) to identify the Marpessian Sibyl, who also called herself Artemis, with Herophile and turn her into the true ἐρυθραία, may be guessed from Paus. 10, 12, 2 ff. (The same source as that of Paus. is used by St. Byz. s. Μερμησσός, as Alexandre, p. 22, rightly remarks.) The Erythraean claim to Herophile was also disputed from other directions. The Erythraean is distinguished from Herophile as being later by Bocchus ap. Solin. 2, p. 38, 24; and in a different fashion the same is done by Mart. Cap. ii, 159. Acc. to Eus., *Chr.* 1305 Abr. (not Eratosthenes in this case) even the Samian Sibyl was identified with Herophile—to say nothing of the Ephesian Herophile in the fragg. of the enlarged Xanthos, *FHG.* iii, 406–8. From the fable of the Marpessian Herophile was later invented the story of her prophecy to Aeneas: Tib. 2, 5, 67; D.H. 1, 55, 4; Alexandre, p. 25.—In comparison with these different claimants to the name of Herophile (even the Cumaean Sibyl was said to be the same as Herophile) the rest of the Sibyls were hardly able to obtain a real footing in tradition.

[61] The Erythraean Sibyl was dated by Eusebius in Ol. 9, 3 (the absurd addition ἐν Αἰγύπτῳ belongs only to the author of the *Chron. Pasc.* and not to Eus.: Alexandre, p. 80); he dated the Samian in Ol. 17, 1 (it is quite arbitrary to refer this view to Eratosthenes). Acc. to Suid. Σίβυλλα Ἀπόλλωνος καὶ Λαμίας the Erythraean lived 483 years after the fall of Troy; i.e. Ol. 20, 1 (700 B.C.). Herakleides put the Phrygo-Trojan Sib. in the times of Solon and Kyros (to which Epimenides also belongs and to which Aristeas and Abaris were supposed to belong). We can no longer discover or guess at the reasons for these datings. In any case the Chronologists to whom they go back evidently regarded the Sibyls as later than the earliest Pythia at Delphi. Even the Cumaean Sibyl was not to be distinguished

from the Erythraean: [Arist.] *Mirab.* 95, which perhaps comes from Timaeus; Varro ap. Serv. *A.* vi, 36; cf. D.H. 4, 62, 6. In spite of which she is a contemporary of Tarquinius Priscus (this was enough to distinguish the *Cimmeria in Italia* who prophesied to Aeneas from the Cumaean Sibyl: Naev. and Calp. Piso in Varro ap. Lact. 1, 6, 9). Naturally in these chronological straits recourse was had to the favourite device of such accounts—unnatural longevity. The Sibyl is πολυχρονιωτάτη [Arist.]: she lived a thousand years or thereabouts: Phleg., *Macr.* 4 (the oracle of this passage was also known to Plu.; cf. *PO.* 13, 401 B; a similar source inspires Ov., *M.* xiv, 132–53. In this case the Sibyl has already lived 700 years before the arrival of Aeneas, and she will live another 300, which would bring her—by a rather inexact calculation—to about the time of Tarquinius Priscus). In the verses found at Erythrae belonging to a statue of the Sibyl (Buresch, *Woch. Klass. Phil.* 1891, p. 1042; *Ath. Mitt.* 1892, p. 20), the Erythraean Sibyl is said to live 900 years—unfortunately one cannot be sure that this means till the time of the inscr. itself and of the νέος κτίστης of Erythrai in the age of the Antonines who is referred to at the close. If so the Sibyl would have been born about the year 700 B.C. (as in Suid.) or a little earlier. Perhaps, however, the lengthy period refers to the life time of the long since dead Sibyl herself, while the αὖθις δ' ἐνθάδε ἐγὼ ἧμαι of l. 11 f. only applies to the statue. In which case the commencement and end of the Sibyl's lifetime would be unknown.—*Cumaeae saecula vatis* became proverbial: Alexandre, p. 57. Finally the Sibyl was regarded as entirely forgotten by death, as in the story in Petronius 48 (cf. also—probably referring to Erythrai—Ampel., *LM.* viii, 15; *Rh. Mus.* 32, 639).

[62] ρ 383 ff.

[63] The Sibyl is overcome by the *furor divinus* in such a way ut quae sapiens non videat ea videat insanus, et si qui humanos sensus amiserit divinos assecutus sit, Cic., *Div.* ii, 110; cf. i, 34. νοσήματα μανικὰ καὶ ἐνθουσιαστικά of Sibyls and Bakids Arist. *Prob.* 30, 1, 954a, 36. The Sibyl prophesies μαντικῇ χρωμένη ἐνθέῳ, Pl., *Phdr.* 244 B. μαινομένη τε καὶ ἐκ τοῦ θεοῦ κάτοχος, Paus. 10, 12, 2. deo furibunda recepto, Ov., *M.* xiv, 107. There is in her divinitas et quaedam caelitum societas, Plin., *NH.* vii, 119. κατοχὴ καὶ ἐπίπνοια [Just.], *Co. ad. Gr.*, 37, 36 A. So, too, in our collections of Sibylline oracles the S. often speak of their divine frenzy, etc.: e.g. ii, 4, 5; iii, 162 f., 295 f.; xi, 317, 320, 323 f.; xii, 294 f., etc. Frenzy of the Cumaean S.: Vg., *A.* vi, 77 f.—Bakis has his prophetic gift from the Nymphs (Ar., *Pa.* 1071), he is κατάσχετος ἐκ νυμφῶν, μανεὶς ἐκ νυμφῶν (Paus. 10, 12, 11; 4, 27, 4), νυμφόληπτος (cf. θεόληπτος, φοιβόληπτος, πανόληπτος, μητρόληπτος; *Lymphati*: Varro, *LL.* vii, p. 365 Sp., Paul. Fest., p. 120, 11 ff., Placid., p. 62, 15 ff. Deuerl.).

[64] Σίβυλλα δὲ μαινομένῳ στόματι κτλ: Herakleitos ap. Plu., *Pyth. Or.* 6, p. 397 A, *fr.* 12 By. = 92 Diels (the words χιλίων . . . θεοῦ are not H.'s but Plutarch's. Cl. Al., *Str.* 1, 15, p. 358 P. uses only Plu.). To regard Herakleitos' Sibyl as the Pythia (with Bgk., etc.) is absurd apart from the fact that the Pythia is never called Σίβυλλα. It is excluded by the way Plu. introduces the word in this passage, and connects chap. 9 with chap. 6. It is true, though, that Pl. draws a *parallel* between the nature of the Sibyl and that of the Pythia.

[65] Homer knows Kassandra as one of the daughters of Priam and indeed as Πριάμοιο θυγατρῶν εἶδος ἀρίστην, *N* 365; probably that is why she is allotted to Agamemnon as his share of the spoil and why she is slain with him, λ 421 ff. The Κύπρια is the first to tell of her

prophetic skill. Was it the narrative of *Ω* 699 which first suggested to the νεώτεροι the idea of her knowledge of the future ? (In reality that passage alludes rather to the συμπάθεια of the sister and daughter and not to *mantikê*: Sch. B. ad loc.) Her prophetic gifts were elaborated later in many stories : e.g. Bacchyl. xiv, 50 = *fr*. 29 Bgk. (Porph. on Hor. *O*. i, 15). Aesch. represents her as the type of the ecstatic prophetess (φρενομανής, θεοφόρητος, *Ag*. 1140, 1216). As such she is called by Eur. μαντιπόλος βάκχη, *Hec*. 121. φοιβάς 827. τὸ βακχεῖον κάρα τῆς θεσπιῳδοῦ Κασσάνδρας 676. She wildly shakes her head like the Bacchants ὅταν θεοῦ μαντόσυνοι πνεύσωσ' ἀνάγκαι, *IA*. 760 ff.

[66] About the Arcadian Bakis (Kydas or Aletes by name) Θεόπομπος ἐν τῇ θ' τῶν Φιλιππικῶν ἄλλα τε πολλὰ ἱστορεῖ παράδοξα καὶ ὅτι ποτὲ τῶν Λακεδαιμονίων τὰς γυναῖκας μανείσας ἐκάθηρεν, Ἀπόλλωνος τούτοις τοῦτον καθαρτὴν δόντος, Sch. Ar., *Pa*. 1071. The story is closely parallel to that of Melampous and the Proitides, see above, nn. 22–5.

[67] Cf. e.g. Hippocr. π. παρθενίων (ii, p. 528 K. ; viii, 468 L.). Upon their recovery from hysterical hallucinations the women dedicate valuable ἱμάτια to Artemis κελευόντων τῶν μάντεων. This is the regular name for the μάγοι, καθαρταί, ἀγύρται (cf. Teiresias δόλιος ἀγύρτης, S., *OT*. 388 ; Kassandra is accused of being φοιτὰς ἀγύρτρια, A., *Ag*. 1273). Hp. speaks elsewhere also of their manner of healing epilepsy, i, p. 588 K. (vi, 354 L.).

[68] καθαρμοὶ . . . κατὰ τὴν μαντικήν, Pl., *Crat*. 405 AB. The μάντεις are able e.g. to drive away by magic the mist that is so dangerous for the olive-trees : Thphr., *CP*. 2, 7, 5. The μάντεις καὶ τερατοσκόποι, ἀγύρται καὶ μάντεις possess the arts of μαγγανεύματα, ἐπῳδαί, καταδέσεις, and ἐπαγωγαί which compel the gods to do their will, Pl., *Rp*. 364 BC ; *Lg*. 933 CE. These μάντεις correspond in all essentials to the magicians and medicine men of savage tribes. Prophet, doctor, and magician are here united in a single person. A mythical prototype of these Greek " medicine men " is Apis, of whom we hear in Aesch., *Sup*. 260–70. (The μάντεις also officiate as sacrificial priests, esp. where the sacrifice is combined with a special sacrificial *mantikê*—quite unknown to Homer —in which the will of the gods is inquired : Eur., *Hcld*. 401–819 ; *Ph*. 1255 ff. and frequently. Hermann *Gottesdienstl. Alterth*. 33, 9.)

[69] The clearest evidence for this is Hp., *Morb. Sacr*. (vi, 352 L.). See below, n. 81. Assistance in the case of internal diseases is naturally sought in ancient times from magicians, for such diseases arise immediately from the action of a god : στυγερὸς δέ οἱ ἔχραε δαίμων, ε 396 (cf. κ 64), is said of an invalid who lies δηρὸν τηκόμενος. Cf. νοῦσος Διὸς μεγάλου, ι 411. In such cases help is sought from the ἰατρόμαντις (A., *Sup*. 263) who is at once μάντις and τερατοσκόπος and καθαρτής like his divine prototype Apollo : A., *Eum*. 62–3. In a long illness King Kleomenes I of Sparta resorts to καθαρταὶ καὶ μάντεις, Plu., *Ap. Lac*. 11, p. 223 E.

[70] *A* 313 f. ; χ 481 ff. Kathartic practices, however much they may contain a primitive core, were fairly late in attaining popularity in Greece (or in regaining a lost popularity) : as is shown esp. by the all but total absence of any mention of such practices and the superstitions underlying them from Hesiod, *Op*., which otherwise preserves the memory of so much countryside superstition (something rather like it is perhaps to be found in *Op*. 733–6).

[71] Nothing is said in Homer of the purification of the murderer or the homicide : see above, chap. v, n. 166.

[72] Thus at the ἀμφιδρόμια all who have had anything to do with

the μαίωσις, ἀποκαθαίρονται τὰς χεῖρας (Suid. s.v.). But even the child is lustrated: it is carried in the arms of a grown-up who runs with it round the altar and the altar fire: clearly a vestige of the ἀποτροπιασμὸς καὶ κάθαρσις of the child by sacred fire of which so many relics have been observed: see Grimm, p. 625; Tylor, ii, 430 f.—Uncleanness of the pregnant woman until the fortieth day after the child is born: Welcker, *Kl. Schr.* iii, 197–9. At the birth of a child crowns of olive-branches or woollen fillets (ἔρια) were in Attica hung up on the house-door; just as cypress-branches were hung on the doors of houses where a corpse lay (see above, chap. v, n. 39): for kathartic purposes strings of onions (squills) were suspended on house-doors; see below): Hsch. στέφανον ἐκφέρειν. Both are lustral materials. Use of olive branches at καθαρμός: S., *OC.* 483 f.; Vg., *A.* vi, 230. When a mother gives her child that is to be exposed a crown made of olive branches (as in Eur., *Ion*, 1433 ff.), this, too, has an apotropaic purpose as also has the Gorgon's head on the embroidered stuff that also accompanies the child (l. 1420 f.): see on this O. Jahn, *Bös. Blick*, 60. The olive is also sacred to the χθόνιοι (hence its use as a bed for corpses: see above, chap. v, n. 61; cf. τοῖς ἀποθανοῦσιν ἐλαᾶς συνεκφέρουσιν: Artemid. iv, 57, p. 236, 20 H. κοτίνῳ καὶ ταινίᾳ the goddess crowns Chios in his dream and points the man thus dedicated to death to his μνῆμα: Chio, *Epist.* 17, 2). This makes the olive suitable for lustration and ἀποτροπιασμοί. The house in which the child lay was thus regarded as needing "purification". The "uncleanness" felt to exist in this case is clearly expressed by Phot. ῥάμνος· ἀμίαντος ἡ πίττα· διὸ καὶ ἐν ταῖς γενέσεσι τῶν παιδίων (ταύτῃ) χρίουσι τὰς οἰκίας, εἰς ἀπέλασιν δαιμόνων (see above, chap. v, n. 95). It is the neighbourhood of these (chthonic) δαίμονες that cause the pollution.

[73] A., *Pers.* 201 ff., 216 ff.; Ar., *Ra.* 1340; Hp., *Insom.* (ii, p. 10, 13 K. = vi, p. 654 L.); cf. Becker, *Charicles*, p. 133, n. 4 E.T.

[74] Cf. Plu., *Sept. Sap. Conv.* iii, p. 149 D, and on this Wyttenb. vi, p. 930 f.

[75] Purification of houses (χ 481 ff.); e.g. [D.] 47, 71. It was customary to purify οἰκίας καὶ πρόβατα with black hellebore: Thphr., *HP.* 9, 10, 4; Dsc. 4, 149 (hence the superstitious details of its gathering, Thphr., *HP.* 9, 8, 8, and Dsc.). The touching of the house by unholy daimones necessitates purification: Thphr., *Ch.* 28 (16), 15, of the δεισιδαίμων· καὶ πυκνὰ δὲ τὴν οἰκίαν καθᾶραι δεινὸς Ἑκάτης φάσκων ἐπαγωγὴν γεγονέναι.

[76] Presence of a dead body in a house makes the water and fire unclean; "clean" water and fire must then be brought in from elsewhere. See Plu., *QG.* 24 (Argos), p. 297 A (see above, chap. v, n. 38). At a festival of the dead in Lemnos all the fires were put out (as unclean): "clean" fire was sought from Delos, and, after the completion of the ἐναγίσματα brought into the country and distributed. Philostr., *H.* 19, 14, p. 206–8, 7 K.—Alexander was following Greek, as well as Persian, customs when at the burial of Hephaistion he allowed τὸ παρὰ τοῖς Πέρσαις καλούμενον ἱερὸν πῦρ to go out, μέχρι ἂν τελέσῃ τὴν ἐκφοράν, D.S. 17, 114, 4.

[77] "When a Greek saw anyone using expiatory rites, he presumed in that person the will to amend," Nägelsbach, *Nachhom. Theol.*, 363. If this was really so it is strange that we never see this "presumption" expressed in words. We do indeed read that the δεισιδαίμων mortifies himself and ἐξαγορεύει τινὰς ἁμαρτίας αὑτοῦ καὶ πλημμελείας, but in what do these ἁμαρτίαι consist?—ὡς τόδε φαγόντος ἢ πιόντος ἢ βαδίσαντος

ὁδὸν ἣν οὐκ εἴα τὸ δαιμόνιον, Plu., *Superstit.* 7, p. 168 D: merely ritual omissions in fact, not moral transgressions at all. It is the same everywhere in this domain. The conceptions underlying purificatory practice certainly did not correspond to the refined morality of later ages, but they continued in force so long as *kathartikê* remained popular: they are well expressed (though disapprovingly) by Ovid in the well-known lines which we shall, however, do well to recall: omne nefas omnemque mali purgamina causam credebant nostri tollere posse senes. Graecia principium moris fuit: illa nocentis impia lustratos ponere facta putat.—a! nimium faciles, qui tristia crimina caedis fluminea tolli posse putetis aqua, *F.* 2, 35 ff.; cf. Hp. i, p. 593 K., vi, 362 L.

[78] We can only here allude to the remarkable parallel provided by the purificatory and expiatory ritual of India, which is completely analogous to the *kathartikê* of Greece and had a similar origin. Even in details Indian conceptions and procedure answer closely to Greek. They are both as far removed as possible from all idea of quieting a guilt-laden conscience and are directed solely towards effacing, expunging, or expelling an external μίασμα, a pollution arriving from without, a taint arising from contact with a hostile δαιμόνιον conceived as something in the nature of a daimonic fluid. Indian sources are on this point very rich and full: an excellent account of them is given by Oldenberg in his *Religion des Veda* (esp. Fr. tr. 243 ff.; 417 ff.). Greek and Indian practices illuminate each other. It would be a valuable experiment to take the highly elaborated kathartic ritual of the Avesta and compare it with the history and technique of purification and expiation in Greek religion. It would mean renewing Lomeier's old book [*Epimenides s. de lustrat.* Zutphen 1700]: the materials are very scattered and the ground has never been thoroughly gone over since then. By the help also of the "comparative" method of religious study, which in this case is quite justified, it would then be possible to reconstruct a most important fragment of primitive *religio*—a fragment which had become almost entirely forgotten in Homeric times, which then recovered its ancient influence and continued to develop and was even transmitted to the ritual of the Christian church (cf. Anrich, *D. ant. Mysterienw.* 190 f.). We must be careful, however, to shut our ears to the otherwise very convincing people who are so anxious to introduce purely *moral* interests and conceptions into ancient *religio*. Morality is a later achievement in the life-history of the children of men: this fruit did not grow in Eden.

[79] See Appendix v.

[80] What the Greeks meant by μίασμα can be very clearly seen, e.g. in the conversation between Phaidra and her nurse in Eur., *Hp.* 316 ff. Phaidra's distress of mind is not derived from a deed of blood: χεῖρες μὲν ἁγναί she says φρὴν δ' ἔχει μίασμά τι. Does the Nurse think of any *moral* disgrace or defilement of the distressed woman in this φρενὸς μίασμα? Not at all: she only asks, μῶν ἐξ ἐπακτοῦ πημονῆς ἐχθρῶν τινος; in other words by "defilement of the mind" she can only conceive of an enchantment, something from without that comes by ἐπαγωγὴ τινῶν δαιμονίων (see below, n. 108), a stain derived from the polluting neighbourhood of such daimones. This was the general and popular conception. (Taken literally Plato's words also give expression to the popular conception: πολλῶν ὄντων καὶ καλῶν ἐν τῷ τῶν ἀνθρώπων βίῳ, τοῖς πλείστοις αὐτῶν οἷον κῆρες ἐπιπεφύκασιν, αἳ καταμιαίνουσί τε καὶ καταρρυπαίνουσιν αὐτά, *Lg.* 937 D.)

[81] Diseases come παλαιῶν ἐκ μηνιμάτων, Pl., *Phdr.* 244 DE; i.e. from the rage of departed generations of souls or of χθόνιοι, Lob., *Agl.* 635–7. Esp. madness is a νοσεῖν ἐξ ἀλαστόρων, S., *Tr.* 1325, a τάραγμα ταρτάρειον, E., *HF.* 89. Cure of such diseases is undertaken not by doctors but by καθαρταί, μάγοι καὶ ἀγύρται, expiatory priests with magic proceedings—this is well shown by the treatment of the "sacred disease" in Hp., *Morb. Sac.*, p. 587–94 K = vi, 352–64 L. Such people, introducing themselves as magicians in the strict sense (p. 358 L.), use no regular medicinal treatment (356), but operate partly with καθαρμοί and ἐπῳδαί, partly with various prescriptions of abstinence ἁγνεῖαι καὶ καθαρότητες. These last are explained by Hp. on dietetic grounds but the *Kathartai* themselves derived them from τὸ θεῖον καὶ τὸ δαιμόνιον (358). And such they were evidently in intention. The account of such prescriptions given on pp. 354–6 mostly refers to abstentions from plants and animals supposed to be sacred to the underworld. Noticeable also: ἱμάτιον μέλαν μὴ ἔχειν, θανατῶδες γὰρ τὸ μέλαν (all trees with black berries or fruit belong to the *inferi*: Macr. 3, 20, 3). Other superstitions are found with these: μηδὲ πόδα ἐπὶ ποδὶ ἔχειν, μηδὲ χεῖρα ἐπὶ χειρί· ταῦτα γὰρ πάντα κωλύματα εἶναι. The belief is familiar from the story of the birth of Herakles. See Welcker, *Kl. Schr.* iii, 191. Sittl, *Gebärden* 126. (Something of the kind in *P. Mag. Par.* 1052 ff., p. 71 Wess.) The source of the disease was, however, always supposed to be the direct influence of a δαίμων (360–2) which must therefore be averted. Acc. to popular belief it is always God who τὸ ἀνθρώπου σῶμα μιαίνει (cf. p. 362). For this reason the magicians purify, καθαίρουσι, the sick αἵμασι καὶ τοῖσιν ἄλλοισι which are used to purify people μίασμά τι ἔχοντας or on whom a curse has been laid. The καθάρσια are buried or thrown into the sea (καὶ εἰς ἅλα λύματ' ἔβαλλον, *A* 314), or carried away into a deserted mountain district (p. 362). Such καθάρσια are now the resting place of the μίασμα that has been washed off, and so the magician drives εἰς ὀρέων κεφαλὰς νούσους τε καὶ ἄλγη, Orph. *H.* 36, 16. Similarly in India, Oldenberg 495.

[82] *Epôdai* used for stopping the flow of blood, τ 457. Frequently mentioned in later times: particularly used in the magic cure of epilepsy, Hp. vi, 352–4; [D.] 25, §§ 79–80. When houses and hearths are purified by being sprinkled with hellebore συνεπᾴδουσί τινα ἐπῳδήν, Thphr. *HP.* 9, 10, 4 (*comprecationem solemnem* is Pliny's trans., *NH.* 25, 49). Pains of childbirth prevented or alleviated by *epôdai*, Pl., *Tht.* 149 CD. (Much more of the kind in Welcker, *Kl. S.* iii, 64 ff.) The essential meaning of such *epôdai* is regularly an appeal or exorcism addressed to the daimonic creature (clearly an appeal when lions or snakes are appeased in this way: Welcker, iii, 70, 14–15). *Epôdai* accompanying ῥιζοτομία are ἐπικλήσεις of the δαίμων ᾧ ἡ βοτάνη ἀνιέρωται: *P. Mag. Par.* 2973 ff. The meaning of such "conjurings" addressed to diseases—when the daimon is exorcised—is clearly seen in what Plotin. says of the Gnostics: they claimed to heal the sick by means of ἐπαοιδαί, μέλη, ἦχοι, and καθαίρεσθαι νόσων, ὑποστησάμενοι τὰς νόσους δαιμόνια εἶναι, καὶ τὰ τοιαῦτα ἐξαιρεῖν λόγῳ φάσκοντες δύνασθαι, 2, 9, 14.

[83] Clashing of bronze used at ἀποκαθάρσεις to drive away ghosts: see above, chap. v, n. 167; cf. also Macr. 5, 19, 11. Claud. *iv. Cons. Hon.* 149: nec te (like Juppiter) progenitum Cybeleius aere sonoro lustravit Corybas. The noise of bronze has a kathartic effect simply as averting ghosts. In the process of driving out the ghosts at the *Lemuria*, Temesaea concrepat aera, Ov., *F.* 5, 441. Hence (?) χαλκοῦ

αὐδὰν χθονίαν, E., *Hel.* 1346. At eclipses of the sun or moon κινοῦσι χαλκὸν καὶ σίδηρον ἄνθρωποι πάντες (cf. Plu., *Aem.* 17; Juv. vi, 443; Mart. xii, 57, 16 f., etc.) ὡς τοὺς δαίμονας ἀπελαύνοντες, Al. Aphr., *Prb.* 2, 46, p. 65, 28 Id. This is the object of the *crepitus dissonus* at eclipses of the moon: Plin., *NH.* ii, 54; Liv. xxvi, 5, 9; Tac., *A.* i, 28, and cf. Tib. i, 8, 21 f.; *ob strias*: [Aug.] *Sacrileg.* v, 16, with Caspari's refs., p. 31 f.

[84] φόνῳ φόνον ἐκνίπτειν, E., *IT.* 1233. Purgantur <cruore> cum cruore polluuntur . . . Heraclit. (p. 335, 5 Schust. [5 D. = 130 B.]).

[85] A.R. iv, 703 ff. καθαρμοῖς χοιροκτόνοις . . . : A., *Eum.* 283, 449, αἵματος καθαρσίου; cf. Müller, *Aesch. Eum.* 124. Representation of the καθαρμός of Orestes on well-known vase-paintings: *Mon. d. inst.* iv, 48, etc.

[86] The "purification" of the stain of blood in these and similar cases really consisted in a "substitution" sacrifice whereby the anger of the daimones was appeased: so much was, on the whole correctly, observed long ago by Meiners, *Allg. Gesch. der relig.* ii, 137. The μίασμα that clings to the murderer is in fact just the indignation of the murdered man or of the underworld spirits: this is plain in Antiph., *Tet.* 3*a*, 3 (see above, chap. v, n. 176). The thing that makes the son who has not avenged his father's murder "unclean" and keeps him away from the altars of the gods is οὐχ ὁρωμένη πατρὸς μῆνις, A., *Ch.* 293.—In the case of murder or homicide there is not only the contact with the sinister other-world that makes men unclean (this applies to all cases of "pollution"), but, besides this, there is also the anger of the murdered soul itself (and of its protecting spirits). Hence in *this* case, besides καθαρμός, ἱλασμός as well is necessary (see above, chap. v). It is evident, however, that it would be difficult to keep the two processes distinct and that they would easily merge into each other.

[87] The φαρμακοί are put to death at the *Thargelia* of Ionic cities: Hipponax *fr.* 37. In other places on extraordinary occasions, but regularly at the Thargelia in Athens. This is denied by Stengel, *Hermes*, 22, 86 ff., but in the face of definite statements from antiquity general considerations can have no weight. In addition it was only a special mode of execution applied to criminals already condemned to death. (Two men, acc. to Harp. 180, 19: a man and a woman Hsch. φαρμακοί: the variation is explained by Hellad. ap. Phot., *Bibl.*, p. 354a, 3 ff. Bk.) The φαρμακοί serve as καθάρσια to the city (Harp. 180, 19 Bk.): Hippon. *fr.* 4; Hellad. ap. Sch. Ar., *Eq.* 1136. φαρμακός = κάθαρμα, Phot., *Lex.* 640, 8 Pors. The φαρμακοί were *either* burnt (after being put to death) like other propitiatory victims: Tz., *Ch.* v, 736, prob. following Hippon. (the burning of the φαρμ. at Athens seems to be alluded to by Eup. Δῆμ. 120 [i, 290 K.]); *or* stoned: this form of death is implied (in the case of Athens) by the legend of Istros ap. Harp. 180, 23. Analogous customs (indicated by Müller, *Dorians*, i, 345) at Abdera: Ov., *Ib.* 465 f. (which acc. to the Sch. is taken from Call., who evidently transferred to Apollonios the pious wish directed by Hippon. against Boupalos); at Massilia (Petr. *fr.* 1 Bü., where the φαρμακός is either thrown down the cliff or *saxis occidebatur a populo*: Lact. ad Stat., *Th.* 10, 793). Apollonios of Tyana was clearly following ancient custom when he made the people of Ephesos stone an old beggar, who was evidently nothing but the plague-daimon itself, for the purification of the city: καθήρας τοὺς Ἐφεσίους τῆς νόσου, Philostr., *VA.* 4, 10–11. Was the stoning a sort of counter-enchantment? See Roscher, *Kynanthropie*, 38–9.

[88] Among the ingredients of a Ἑκάτης δεῖπνον ἐν τῇ τριόδῳ was an ᾠὸν ἐκ καθαρσίου: Luc., *DM.* 1, 1; or the testicles of a sucking pig that had been used as a victim: D., 54, 39. The ὀξυθύμια, sacrifices to Hekate and the souls of the dead (see above, chap. v, n. 176), are identical with the καθάρματα καὶ ἀπολύματα which were thrown out at the crossroads in the Ἑκαταῖα: Did. ap. Harp. ὀξυθύμια; cf. *EM.* 626, 44. καθάρσια is the name of the purificatory offerings: καθάρματα of the same when they are thrown away: Ammon., p. 79 Valck. The dead bodies of dogs which had been used as victims at the "purification" were afterwards thrown τῇ Ἑκάτῃ μετὰ τῶν ἄλλων καθαρσίων, Plu., *QR.* 68, p. 280 C. Even the blood and water of the purificatory sacrifice, the ἀπόνιμμα, is also dedicated to the dead: Ath. 409 E ff. The fact that the καθάρματα are made over to the invisibly present spirits at the cross roads might be derived also from the necessity for throwing them out ἀμεταστρεπτί (see below, n. 104). Even the Argive custom of throwing the καθάρματα into the Lernaean lake (Znb., iv, 86; Dgn., vi, 7; Hsch. Λέρνη θεατῶν) shows that these kathartic materials are intended as a sacrifice to the underground spirits since the Lernaean lake was an entrance to the underworld (see above, chap. viii, n. 28).

[89] Annual τελετή to Hekate in Aegina reputed to have been founded by Orpheus. Hekate and her καθαρμοί were there regarded as valuable against insanity (for she can remove what she herself has sent): Ar., *Ves.* 122; Lob., *Agl.* 242. This initiation festival lasted on into the fourth century A.D.—Paus. refers to only one other temple of Hekate in Argos: 2, 22, 7.—Indications of a vigorous worship of Hekate in Kos: *GDI.* 3624, iii, p. 345 fin. Hekate was patron-goddess of the city of Stratonikeia: Tac., *A.* iii, 62, Str., 660, and in other cities of Karia (as is known from inscr.). Possibly Hekate is there only a Greek title of a native Karian deity. The ancient cult of the χθόνιοι at the Triopion in Knidos was, however, Greek: Böckh on Sch. Pi., p. 314 f.; *CIG.* i, p. 45.

[90] χθονία καὶ νερτέρων πρύτανις: Sophr. *fr.* 7 Kaib. ap. Sch. Theoc. ii, 12.—She is actually queen in Hades, sharing the throne of Plouton it seems: S., *Ant.* 1199. She is often called χθονία. She is Ἀδμήτου κόρη (i.e. of Hades, K. O. Müller, *Introd. Scient. Myth.* 245): Hsch. She is called ἀδμήτη herself in *H. Mag. Hec.*, Abel, *Orph.*, p. 289. She is the daughter of Euboulos, i.e. Hades: *Orph. H.*, 72, 3 (elsewhere of course she has other origins). As χθονία she is often confused with Persephone (and both, as they are all thus united in several particulars, with Artemis). In the transcript of a metrical inscr. from Budrum (Cilicia) in *JHS.* xi, 252, there appears a Γῇ Ἑκάτῃ. This would certainly be very remarkable but on the stone itself the actual words are τὴν σεβόμεσθ' Ἑκ[άτην]. [But cf. *Tab. Defix.*, p. xiii, a 13.]

[91] Hekate goddess of childbirth: Sophr. *fr.* 7, worshipped in Athens as κουροτρόφος, Sch. Ar., *V.* 804. Samian worship of the κουροτρόφος ἐν τῇ τριόδῳ (i.e. as Hek.), [Hdt.] *V. Hom.* 30; Hes., *Thg.* 450: θῆκε δέ μιν (Hek.) Κρονίδης κουροτρόφον. (Even as early as this κουρ. is the epithet of Hek. and not the name of an independ. feminine daimon which it may have been to begin with, and in isolated cases remained.) Γενετυλλίς goddess of childbirth is said to be ἐοικυῖα τῇ Ἑκάτῃ: Hsch. Γεν. The goddess Eileithyia to whom dogs were sacrificed in Argos is certainly a Hekate (Sokr. ap. Plu., *Q. Rom.* 52, p. 277 B—she was Artemis elsewhere). A consecration to Hekate ὑπὲρ παιδός: inscr. from Larisa, *Ath. Mitth.* xi, 450. Hek. is also a goddess of marriage: as such (ὅτι γαμήλιος ἡ Ἑκάτη, Sch.) she is called upon with Hymenaios

by Kassandra in Eur., *Tr.* 323. Hekate is γαμήλιος simply as χθονία: the χθόνιοι frequently take part in marriage as well as birth: see above, chap. v, p. 64 ff.; Gaia: see Welcker, *Götterl.* i, 327. Offering made πρὸ παίδων καὶ γαμηλίου τέλους to the Erinyes: A., *Eum.* 835.

[92] Hekate present at funerals (rushing πρὸς ἄνδρας νεκρὸν φέροντας, Sophr. *fr.* 7) ἐρχομένα ἀνά τ' ἠρία καὶ μέλαν αἷμα Theoc. ii, 13. χαίρουσα σκυλάκων ὑλακῇ καὶ αἵματι φοίνῳ ἐν νέκυσι στείχουσα κατ' ἠρία τεθνηώτων, *H. Hec.* ap. Hipp., *RH.* iv, 35, p. 102, 64 f. D.-S.—Hekate present at all infamous deeds: see the remarkable formulae ap. Plu., *Superst.* 10, p. 170 B (Bgk., *PLG.*[4] iii, p. 680).—Hek. regarded as devouring corpses (like Eurynomos, etc., above, chap. vii, n. 24): αἱμοπότις, καρδιόδαιτε, σαρκοφάγε, ἀωροβόρε are said of her in the *Hymn. Magic.* 5, ll. 53–4 (p. 294 Ab.). φθισίκηρε should be also read, ib., l. 44 (κῆρες = ψυχαί, see above, chap. v, n. 100); cf. ὠμοφάγοι χθόνιοι, *P. Mag. Par.* 1444. Ἑκάτη ἀκρουροβόρη on a *defixio* from Megara ap. *Tab. Defix.*, p. xiii*a*, l. 7 Wünsch. Probably ἀωροβόρη should be read (Wünsch differently, p. xx*b*).

[93] See above, chap. v, nn. 66, 132.

[94] Medea in E., *Med.* 385 ff.: οὐ γὰρ μὰ τὴν δέσποιναν ἣν ἐγὼ (as magician) σέβω μάλιστα πάντων καὶ ξυνεργὸν εἱλόμην, Ἑκάτην, μυχοῖς ναίουσαν ἑστίας ἐμῆς.—Δήμητρος κόρη is addressed as πυρὸς δέσποινα, in company with Hephaistos, in E., *Phaeth.*, *fr.* 781, 59. Probably Hekate is meant being here as frequently combined or confused with Persephone the daughter of Demeter (cf. *Ion*, 1048).

[95] The pious man cleans and decorates every month τὸν Ἑρμῆν καὶ τὴν Ἑκάτην καὶ τὰ λοιπὰ τῶν ἱερῶν ἃ δὴ τοὺς προγόνους καταλιπεῖν, Theopomp. ap. Porph., *Abs.* ii, 16 (p. 146, 8–9 N.). Acc. to this Hekate and Hermes belong to the θεοὶ πατρῷοι of the house.—Shrines of Hekate before the house-door (Lob., *Agl.* 1336 f.); cf. the sacella of the Heroes in the same place: above, chap. iv, n. 135.

[95a] The late interpolation in Hes., *Th.* 411–52, in praise of Hekate leaves out the uncanny side of her character altogether. Hekate has here become so much the universally revered goddess that she has lost all definite personality in the process. The whole is a telling example of the sort of extension that might be given to a single divinity who had once been the vital cult-object of a small locality. The name of this universally known daimon becomes finally of little importance (for everything is heaped upon one personality). Hence there is little to be learnt of the special characteristics of Hekate from this Hymn. (In any case it is time we gave up calling this Hymn to Hekate "Orphic": the word is even more than usually meaningless and conventional in this case.)

[96] Hekate (ναίουσα at the crossroads, S. *fr.* 492 N.) meets men as an ἀνταία θεός (S. *fr.* 311) and is herself called ἀνταία (*fr.* 311, 368; cf. *EM.* 111, 50, where what precedes is from Sch. A.R. i, 1141). The same adj. applies to a δαίμων that she causes to appear: Hsch. ἀνταία, ἀνταῖος, in this as in most cases with the added sense of hostile. Hek. φαινομένη ἐν ἐκτόποις φάσμασιν, Suid. Ἑκάτην. (from Elias Cret. on Greg. Nz. iv, p. 487 Mg.). She appears or sends apparitions by night as well as by day: Εἰνοδία, θύγατερ Δάματρος, ἃ τῶν νυκτιπόλων ἐφόδων ἀνάσσεις καὶ μεθαμερίων, E., *Ion*, 1048 ff. Meilinoe, a euphemistically (cf. above, chap. v, n. 5) named daimonic creature, either Hekate or Empousa, meets ἀνταίαις ἐφόδοισι κατὰ ζοφοειδέα νύκτα, Orph. *H.* 71, 9. Hek. appears at midday in Luc., *Philops.* 22. In this midday vision she opens the earth and τὰ ἐν Ἅιδου ἅπαντα become visible (c. 24). This reminds us of the story told by Herakl.

Pont. of Empedotimos to whom Plouton and Persephone appeared ἐν μεσημβρίᾳ σταθερᾷ in a lonely spot and the whole world of the spirits became visible (ap. Procl. *in Rp.* ii, 119 Kroll). Lucian is probably parodying that story. Elsewhere in the same pamphlet he gives an absurd turn to a fabulous narrative of Plutarch's (*de An. fr.* 1 Bern. = *Philops.* 25).

[97] See Append. vi.

[98] See Append. vii.

[99] Hekate herself is regarded as having the head of a dog: undoubtedly an ancient conception of her (she has σκυλακώδεα φωνήν, *H. Mag.* 5, 17 Ab.). She is sometimes even a dog herself: Hsch. Ἑκάτης ἄγαλμα, and partic. *AB.* 336, 31–337, 5; Call. *fr.* 100 h, 4. She is identified with Kerberos: Lyd., *Mens.* 3, 8, p. 42 W. She is actually invoked as a dog in *P. Mag. Par.* 1432 ff., p. 80 W.: κυρία Ἑκάτη εἰνοδία, κύων μέλαινα. Hence dogs are sacred to her and are sacrificed to her (earliest witness Sophr. *fr.* 8 Kaib.). The hounds with whom she flies about at night are daimonic creatures like Hekate herself. Porph. (who was specially well informed about such things) said that σαφῶς the hounds of Hekate were πονηροὶ δαίμονες: ap. Eus., *PE.* 4, 23, 7–8. In Lycophron's account (ll. 1174–80) *Hekabe* is represented exactly in this way, i.e. as a daimonic creature who appears to men as a hound (cf. *PLG.* iii, 721 f.). She is transformed by Hekate (Brimo) into one of her train (ἐπωπίδα) who by their nocturnal howling strike terror into men who have neglected to make offering to the goddess.—Dogs occur as symbols of the dead on grave-reliefs?—above, chap. v, n. 105. (Erinyes as hounds; Keres as "Hounds of Hades": A.R. iv, 1665; *AP.* vii, 439, 3 [Theodorid.], etc. Ruhnken, *Ep. Cr.* i, 94.)

[100] See Dilthey, *Rh. Mus.* 25, 332 ff.

[101] The Italian Diana who had long become identical with Hekate remained familiar to the Christianized peoples of the early Middle Ages (allusions in Christian authors: Grimm, pp. 283, 286, 933, 949, 1161 f. O. Jahn, *Bös. Blick*, 108). She was, in fact, the meeting point of the endless mass of superstition that had survived into that time from Graeco-Roman tradition. The nocturnal riding of a mob of women (i.e. "souls" of women) *cum Diana, paganorum dea* is quoted as a popular superstition by the so-called *Canon Episcopi*, which in the controversies on witches was so often appealed to. This document, it seems, cannot be traced back further than Regino (end of ninth century). He seems to have got it out of [Aug.] *De Sp. et Anima* (probably written in the sixth century). It was rescued from oblivion by Burkhard of Wurms, used in the Decretals of Gratian, and became very well known in the Middle Ages. (The passage from Burkhard is printed in Grimm, p. 1741. That the whole is a Canon (24) of the Council of Ancyra, 314 A.D., is, however, only a mistaken idea of Burkhard's.) This belief in the nightly hunt of Diana with the souls may be regarded as a vestige of the ancient idea of Hekate and her nocturnal crew. It was all the more likely to survive in northern countries with their native legends of wild Hunters and the "furious host" with which it could so easily combine. ["Herne the Hunter," *Merry Wives of Windsor*, iv, 4; v, 5.]

[102] ὁκόσα δείματα νυκτὸς παρίσταται, καὶ φόβοι καὶ παράνοιαι καὶ ἀναπηδήσεις ἐκ τῆς κλίνης καὶ φόβητρα καὶ φεύξεις ἔξω, Ἑκάτης φασὶν εἶναι ἐπιβολὰς καὶ ἡρώων ἐφόδους, καθαρμοῖσί τε χρέονται καὶ ἐπαοιδαῖς, Hp., *Morb. Sac.* vi, 362 L.; cf. Plu., *Supers.*, 3, p. 166 A; Hor., *AP.* 454. Hekate is μανιῶν αἰτία, Eust., *Il.*, p. 87, 31 (hence also releases men from madness in the initiations of Aegina, see above, n. 89); cf. ἔνθεος

ἐξ Ἑκάτης, E., *Hip.* 141. Dreams of Hekate, Artemid., 2, 37, p. 139, 1 ff. H. The ἥρωες ἀποπλήκτους ποιεῖν δύνανται: Sch. Ar., *Av.* 1490. The ἥρωες are also the source of nightmares, *Rh. Mus.* 37, 467 n. (like Pan as Ephialtes: Didym. ap. Sch. Ar., *Ves.* 1038—where Εὐάπαν should be read, from εὖα the noise of bleating goats and Πᾶν: Suid. and *CIG.* iv, 8382). The Lamiai and Empousai seem also to have been night-terrors: cf. what is said of their amorous disposition and desire for human blood by Apollonios ap. Philostr. *VA.* 4, 25, p. 145, 18; and what is said of Pan-Ephialtes, ἐὰν δὲ συνουσιάζῃ, Artemid., p. 139, 21 H. General statement: ὀνειρώσσειν comes ἀπὸ δαιμόνων ἐνεργείας Suid. ὀνειροπολεῖν, p. 1124 Gaisf. Seirenes: Crusius, *Philol.* 50, 97 ff.

[103] The "Banquets of Hekate", besides the καθάρματα referred to above (n. 88), included also the specially prepared dishes that were made and put out for Hekate κατὰ μῆνα (Ar., *Plu.* 596) at the τριακάδες (see above, chap. v, n. 88) or else at the νουμηνίαι, Sch. Ar., *Plu.* 594: κατὰ τὴν νουμηνίαν, ἑσπέρας; cf. the offering to Hekate and Hermes at each νουμηνία: Theopomp. ap. Porph., *Abs.* 2, 16, p. 146, 7 N. These banquets of Hek. are meant by Ar., *Plu.* 594 ff., S. *fr.* 668 N.; Plu., *Smp.* 7, 3, p. 709 A.—It is possible that at the turn of the month there was a "purification" of the house, in which case the καθάρσια and the Ἑκάτης δεῖπνα would be again combined.—Ingredients of the offerings to Hek.: eggs and toasted cheese (Sch. Ar.); τρίγλη and μαινάς Ath. 325 B.; flame-cakes (of cheese, πλακοῦντες διὰ τυροῦ, Paus. Lex. ap. Eust. 1165, 14) ἀμφιφῶντες (see Lob., *Agl.* 1062 f.).

[104] The person καθάρματα ἐκπέμψας throws them away ἀστρόφοισιν ὄμμασιν: A., *Cho.* 98–9. The vessel filled with the purificatory offerings was emptied ἐν ταῖς τριόδοις and ἀμεταστρεπτί: Schol. ib. This was regular with καθαρμοί: Theoc. xxiv, 94 ff., and at offerings to the Erinyes: S., *OC.* 490. Even Odysseus is obliged at his sacrifice to the dead ἀπονόσφι τραπέσθαι, κ 528. Medea in collecting her magic juices turns her eyes ἐξοπίσω χερός: S. Ῥιζ. *fr.* 491 N.; A.R. iv, 1315; cf. also Lomeier, *de lustrat.*, p. 455 f. This remained the rule at sacrifices to χθόνιοι and in magic ceremonies which regularly had to do with the underworld. Even Marc. Emp. in giving directions for the cure of φυσικά often enjoins *nec retro respice* e.g. 1, 54, likewise Plin., *NH.* 21, 176; 29, 91. In making an enchantment πορεύου ἀνεπιστρεπτεὶ μηδενὶ δοὺς ἀπόκρισιν, *P. Mag. Lond.*, given in Kenyon *Greek Pap. in B.M.*, i, p. 98. Modern superstition agrees: cf. Grimm, p. 1789, n. 299; cf. nn. 357, 558, 890, 1137. The eye must be turned away from the "furious host": Birlinger, *Aus Schwaben, N.S.* i, 90. The precaution is, however, of primeval antiquity. In the old Indian cult of the dead and worship of formidable deities many of the proceedings must be performed ἀμεταστρεπτί, Oldenberg, 335 f., 487 f., 550, n. 5; 577 f., 580. The reason for the precaution is not hard to see. If the person looked round he would see the spirits engaged in taking possession of the objects thrown to them, which would be sure to bring ill-luck—χαλεποὶ δὲ θεοὶ φαίνεσθαι ἐναργῶς. Hence Odysseus, when he is returning Leukothoë's wimple by throwing it into the sea, must αὐτὸς ἀπονόσφι τραπέσθαι, ε 350. Hence Orpheus must not look back at Eurydike while she belongs to the lower world. (Cf. Hannibal's dream reported after Silenus and Cael. Ant. by Cic., *Div.* i, 49.) οἱ ἐντυγχάνοντες νυκτὸς ἥρωσι διέστρεφον τὰς ὄψεις: Sch. Ar., *Av.* 1493. Very clearly put by Ov., *F.* 5, 437: at the Lemuria the sacrificer throws away the beans aversus . . . nec respicit. umbra putatur colligere et nullo terga vidente sequi. At last when the Manes are

all driven out, *respicit* (444). One of the Pythagorean *σύμβολα*, those invaluable fragments of Greek old wives' wisdom, runs: *ἀποδημῶν τῆς οἰκίας μὴ ἐπιστρέφου· Ἐρινύες γὰρ μετέρχονται* (Iamb., *Protr.*, p. 114, 29 f. Pist.). Here the *reason* for the superstitious practice is clearly shown (cf. also Grimm, p. 1778, n. 14; cf. n. 360): the underworld spirits (wandering over the earth, esp. on the fifth of the month, as in Hes., *Op.* 803) are following the departing person: if he were to turn round he would see them.

[105] Appearance of *εἴδωλα* of the dead: not as in Homer in dreams only, but openly before men's waking eyes. Stories of this go back as far as the poems of the Epic Cycle: cf. appearance of Achilles in the Little Iliad (p. 37 Ki), in the *Νόστοι* (p. 33). How familiar this idea had become by the fifth century may be judged from the frequency of ghosts in the tragedians: A., *Pers. Eum. Prom. Ψυχ.*; S., *Πολυξ.*; cf. *fr.* 795 N.; E., *Hec.*; raising of the spirit of a dead man, *fr.* 912; cf. also the stories of Simonides and the grateful dead (Bgk. on Sim. *fr.* 129); of Pelops and the *εἴδωλον* of Killos (see A. Marx, *Griech. Märchen von dankbaren Thieren*, p. 114 f.).

[106] Spirit-raising at entrances to the underworld at definite *ψυχομαντεῖα* or *νεκυομαντεῖα*: see above, chap. v, n. 23. There were, however, *ψυχαγωγοί* who could compel individual souls to appear at other places as well: E., *Alc.* 1128 f. Such *ψυχαγωγοί* belonging to the fifth century and to be found in Thessaly are spoken of by Plu. ap. Sch. E., *Alc.* 1128. People *τούς τε τεθνεῶτας φάσκοντες ψυχαγωγεῖν καὶ θεοὺς ὑπισχνούμενοι πείθειν, ὡς θυσίαις τε καὶ εὐχαῖς καὶ ἐπῳδαῖς γοητεύοντες* occur in Pl., *Lg.* 909 B. Later literature abounds in such spirit-raisings. Conjuring Hekate to appear was a favourite magic experiment: A.R. iii, 1030 f., etc., recipe for producing this illusion in Hipp., *RH.* iv, 35–6, p. 102 f. D.-S. A *Ἑκάτης ἐπαγωγή* occurs as early as Thphr., *Ch.* 28 (16).

[107] *ἀγύρται καὶ μάντεις* profess *ἐάν τίς τιν' ἐχθρὸν πημῆναι ἐθέλῃ μετὰ σμικρῶν δαπανῶν ὁμοίως δίκαιον ἀδίκῳ βλάψειν, ἐπαγωγαῖς τισι καὶ καταδέσμοις τοὺς θεούς, ὥς φασι, πείθοντές σφισιν ὑπηρετεῖν*, Pl., *Rp.* 364 C. And esp. from *Lg.* 933 AE we get a good idea of the fear that the *μάντεις* and *τερατοσκόποι* generally inspired with their *καταδέσεις ἐπαγωγαί, ἐπῳδαί,* and other *μαγγανεῖαι* (we even hear of wax-figures on house-doors, grave-stones, *ἐπὶ τριόδοις*, as so frequently later, with the same superstitious purpose). Plato himself does not rule out the possibility of such magic incantations: at least they did not conflict with his own daimonic theory: see *Smp.* 203 A. *ἐπαγωγαί* are "evocations" of spirits or gods: see Ruhnk., *Tim.*, p. 115. *ἐπιπομπαί* have the same meaning: see above, chap. v, n. 168. *ἐπιπέμπειν* frequently in this sense in the *Orph. H.* *καταδέσεις, κατάδεσμοι* are the "bindings" whereby the spirit-raiser magically compels the unseen to do his will. Compulsion is regularly found to be necessary: the spirits do not come willingly. The magician by his spells and ceremonies is their master; he exerts over them that *ἀνάγκη* (*ὁ ἐπάναγκος* is frequent in the magical books) or *πειθανάγκη* of which Porph. ap. Eus., *PE.* 5, 8, specially tells us (probably deriving it from Pythagoras of Rhodos). *πείθειν* is Plato's weaker word: the most extreme is *βιαστικαὶ ἀπειλαί*, Iamb. *Myst.* 6, 5 [i.e. Porph. *Ep. Aneb. fr.* 31 Parth.]; cf. *τὸ δεῖνα πράξεις κἂν θέλῃς κἂν μὴ θέλῃς*: refrain in a magic hymn, *P. Mag. Par.* 2252 ff.—Just as in these incantations the *κατάδεσις* affects the gods themselves so in other cases the victim is the unfortunate person whom the magician intends to harm: in this sense we have *καταδέσεις, κατάδεσμοι*, *P. Par.* 336; Orph. *Lith.* 582, and the

devotiones or *defixiones* written on metal tablets which have been found in such numbers in graves; see Gothofred. ad *Cod. Theod.* 9, 16, 3. These are now collected and edited by R. Wünsch, *Defixionum tabellae in Attica repertae* (*CIA.* App.), 1897, with those found outside Attica included in the *Praefatio.* Here we find καταδῶ (καταδίδημι) τὸν δεῖνα his tongue, limbs, mind, etc. (nn. 68, 89, 95, etc.), i.e. a magical disabling, paralysing, fettering of his faculties—and of all his efforts: ἀτελῆ, ἐναντία πάντα γένοιτο, nn. 64, 98. The carrying out of this is entrusted to Hermes χθόνιος or to Hekate (καταδῶ αὐτὸν πρὸς τὸν Ἑρμῆν κτλ.) as the κάτοχοι δαίμονες; cf. nn. 81, 84, 85, 86, 101, 105, 106, 107. Sometimes the promoter of the κατάδεσις says of himself καταδῶ καὶ κατέχω, 109, etc. The *defixio* itself is called ὁ κάτοχος, *Gk. Pap. in B.M.* (Ken.), No. 121, ll. 394, 429 = p. 97–8. καταδεῖν is therefore here = κατέχεσθαι ποιεῖν (= disable him—not make him "possessed") and implies the delivery of the victim into the power of the infernal spirits.—The μάντεις and καθαρταί appear as accomplished weather-magicians in Hp., *Morb. Sac.* vi, 358 L. They are claimed to be able to draw down the moon (an old art of Thessalian witches), make the sun go out, cause rain or drought at will, etc. A γένος of ἀνεμοκοῖται at Korinth was able τοὺς ἀνέμους κοιμίζειν: Hsch. Suid. ἀνεμοκ.; cf. Welcker, *Kl.S.* iii, 63. The claims made by these καθαρταί for themselves were made by later ages on behalf of Abaris, Epimenides, Pythagoras, etc.; Porph., *VP.* 28–9 (Iamb. 135 f.); Empedokles promised them to his own pupils; 464 ff. Mull., *fr.* 111 Diels; and cf. Welcker, *Kl.S.* iii, 60 f.—These are all examples of magical arts from early times; the overwhelming mass of evidence for such proceedings in later ages cannot be mentioned here except as explaining ancient accounts.

[108] Abaris had been mentioned by Pindar (Harp. Ἄβαρις); Hdt. mentions him in iv, 36. There we hear of the arrow which he bore along with him κατὰ πᾶσαν τὴν γῆν and of his complete abstention from food (cf. Iamb., *VP.* 141). The arrow, a σύμβολον τοῦ Ἀπόλλωνος (Lycurg. *fr.* 85, ap. Eudoc., p. 34, 10) is borne by Abaris in his hand—the suggestion of Wesseling, recently revived, that we should in Hdt.'s passage read ὡς τὸν ὀϊστὸς περιέφερε, has been shown to be linguistically impossible by Struve, *Opusc. Crit.* ii, 269. The embellishment of the Abaris story, whereby he (like Musaios) flew through the air on his arrow, is later than Hdt. or than Lyk. (The arrow is presumably the same as the one of which Herak. Pont. tells some strange things; ap. [Eratosth.] *Catast.* 29.) The story sounds rather like Herakleides. See Porph., *VP.* 29; Iamb., *VP.* 91, 136; Him., *O.* 25, 2, 4; Nonn. *D.* 11, 132 f.; Proc. Gaz., *Ep.* 96. Abaris was regarded as ἔνθεος (Eudoc.) as καθαρτής and χρησμολόγος, as driving away pestilences by magic arts (esp. in Sparta, where κωλυτήρια = apotropaic sacrifices, were instituted and a temple of Κόρη σώτειρα founded: Apollon., *Mir.* 4—prob. from Theopomp.: see *Rh. Mus.* 26, 558—Iamb., *VP.* 92, 141; Paus. 3, 13, 2). He is also said to have prophesied earthquakes, pestilence, etc. (Apollon.), and to have given prescriptions against disease and ἐπωδαί (Pl., *Chrm.* 158 CD); was a type of εὐκολίας καὶ λιτότητος καὶ δικαιοσύνης: Str. 301.—The figure of Abaris thus left rather vague in ancient legend was elaborated from two sources: (1) the Athenian cult-legends of the foundation of the *Proërosia*: Harp. Ἄβ., Suid. προηροσία. Sch. Ar., *Eq.* 729; Lycurg. κατὰ Μενεσαίχμου; and (2) the Pythagorean legends. It is in itself very probable that the story in Iamb., *VP.* 91–3, 147, of the meeting between Abaris and Pythagoras goes back to the fabulous "Abaris" of Herakleides

(the story in 215–17 of Abaris and Pythagoras before Phalaris evidently comes from Apoll. Ty.). This was suggested by Krische *de soc. Pythag.*, p. 38, and has been more definitely maintained by Diels, *Arch. f. Gesch. d. Philos.* iii, 468: it cannot, however, be demonstrated absolutely—there is not a scrap of evidence to show that Herakleides did actually make Abaris meet Pythagoras. (*Πυθαγόρας ἐν τῷ πρὸς Ἄβαριν λόγῳ*, Procl. in *Tim.* 141 D, may very possibly, but not *necessarily*, as Diels thinks, refer to the *Abaris* of Herakleides.)—In any case the bringing together of Abaris and Pyth. is a late invention; it is impossible to say whether it could have occurred or did occur as early as the Aristotelian work περὶ τῶν Πυθαγορείων.—In any case, the guiding conception in all this is that Abaris did not belong to the primeval past but came to Greece in the daylight of historical times. Pindar makes this happen κατὰ Κροῖσον τὸν Λυδῶν βασιλέα (prob. about the time of the Σάρδεων ἅλωσις, Ol. 58, 3 = 546): "others" (acc. to Harp.) made it earlier, in Ol. 21 = 696. It is impossible to tell what the reasons were for either of these particular dates. Abaris might still be regarded as a contemporary of Pythagoras by those who, with Eusebios and Nikostratos ap. Harp., put him in Ol. 53 (κατὰ τὴν νγ̄ Ὀλυμπιάδα, for so the figure in Harp. should be read and not γ̄ Ὀλ.; the right reading is preserved from Harp. in Suid. Ἄβ.). This view, however, is not, as Diels thinks, obtained by making Abaris forty years older than Pyth. (The ἀκμή of Pyth. falls in Ol. 62—see *Rh. Mus.* 26, 570—and that, too, is the date—not Ol. 63—given by "Eusebius *Chronica*", i.e. the Armenian. tr. and the MSS. *PEMR* of Jerome.) Perhaps Abaris was regarded as the contemporary of Phalaris whose reign according to one of the versions given by Eusebios began in Ol. 53, or 52, 3. Cf. *Rh. Mus.* 36, 567.

[109] *Ekstasis* of Aristeas: τούτου φασὶ τὴν ψυχήν, ὅταν ἐβούλετο, ἐξιέναι καὶ ἐπανιέναι πάλιν Suid. Ἀριστέας. His body lies as if dead ἡ δὲ ψυχὴ ἐκδῦσα τοῦ σώματος ἐπλάζετο ἐν τῷ αἰθέρι κτλ. Max. Tyr. 16, 2, p. 288 R. (reperimus) Aristeae animum evolantem ex ore in Proconneso corvi effigie, Plin., *NH.* vii, 174 (very similar stories from elsewhere, Grimm, p. 1083 [and Baring-Gould, *Myths of M.A.*]). So, too, the Ἀριμάσπεια said that Aristeas reached the Issedones φοιβόλαμπτος γενόμενος (Hdt. iv, 13); which at least means in some strange way impossible for other men, i.e. in Apolline ecstacy (cf. above, n. 63, νυμφόληπτος, etc.; ἐν ἐκστάσει ἀποφοιβώμενος, *P. Mag. Par.*, p. 63 Wess.). So, too, Max. Tyr. 38, 3, p. 222 ff., makes Aristeas describe how his ψυχή, καταλιποῦσα τὸ σῶμα had reached the Hyperboreans, etc. These accounts are not derived from Hdt. who on the contrary says that Arist. *died* in a fuller's mill at Prokonnesos and that his body then disappeared and was seen by a man at Kyzikos. This would be *translation* of body and soul together *not* ἔκστασις of the soul alone. In this case Hdt. is probably inaccurate. In such cases of translation the point of the story, in fact its whole meaning, lies in the fact that the translated person has not died but that he has vanished without his soul being separated from his body, i.e. without dying; for normally in death the soul alone vanishes. This applies to all the cases of translation referred to in this book (see e.g. the story of the Hero Euthymos: above, chap. iv, n. 116; of Kleomedes, p. 129, above); and also to the legend of Romulus in Plu., *Rom.* 27–8, in which Plu. rightly finds much resemblance with the story of Aristeas as told by Hdt. It applies to the numerous stories of translation which, evidently after Greek models, were told of the Latin and Roman kings (see Preller, *Röm. Mythol.*², p. 84 f., 704). It appears then that

Hdt. has combined two versions of the legend: one acc. to which Aristeas "died" (not only on this occasion but often), i.e. his soul separated itself from his body and had a life of its own; another in which his body and soul were "translated" together without his death. In either version Aristeas might meet with the man in Kyzikos: if he were translated, it would be his vanished body (cf. Romulus' meeting Julius Proculus); but if his soul left his body behind as though lifeless then it would be the soul as εἴδωλον of its body that appeared to the man (as in the cases of Pythagoras and Apoll. Tyan. who were seen at two different places at the same time). This last story seems to be the real and primitive one: it is suggested by the above-mentioned accounts of the ἔκστασις of the soul of Aristeas and it was so understood by the authority (apparently Thpomp.) whom Apollon., *Mirab.* 2, is following.

[110] Hdt. iv, 15, Thpomp. ap. Ath. 13, 605 C: the bronze laurel was set up κατὰ τὴν Ἀριστέα τοῦ Προκοννησίου ἐπιδημίαν ὅτε ἔφησεν ἐξ Ὑπερβορέων παραγεγονέναι. This is not said by Hdt. but is compatible with his account. Acc. to Hdt. Aristeas told the people of Metapontum that they alone of all the Italiots had been visited by Apollo and that he, Aristeas, had been in the god's train in the shape of a raven (sacred to Apollo). This last feature allows us to conclude that Hdt., too, knew of the wanderings made by the soul of Aristeas while his body remained at home as though dead. The raven is clearly the soul of Aristeas: Plin., *NH.* vii, 174.—The ἐπιδημία of Aristeas in Metapontum fell acc. to Hdt.'s own calculation (ὡς συμβαλλόμενος . . . εὕρισκον) 240 years (not 230) after the second ἀφανισμός of Aristeas from Prokonnesos. As Aristeas had in his poem spoken of the beginning of the Kimmerian invasion (Hdt. iv, 13) his first ἀφανισμός cannot have been *before* 681 (the first year of Ardys' reign, when the Kimmerian invasion began acc. to Hdt. i, 15: Prokonnesos was, too, first founded under Gyges: Str. 587). Taking this as a starting point (and it is the earliest admissible terminus) and subtracting 240+7 years (Hdt. iv, 14 fin.) we should arrive at the year 434. This, however, cannot possibly have been meant by Hdt. as the year of the miraculous presence of Aristeas in Metapontum. We seem to have one of Hdt.'s errors of calculation to which he is prone. We cannot indeed make out when exactly he intended to date the various scenes of the Aristeas-story.—In any case, Hdt. never intended to make Aristeas the teacher of Homer, as Bergk following others thinks. He makes Homer's *flor.* about 856: see *Rh. Mus.* 36, 397; and puts the Kimmerian invasion much later. Aristeas could only be regarded as teacher of Homer (Str. 639; Tat. *Gr.* 41) by those who made Homer a contemporary of the Kimmerian invasion, Thpomp. esp.: see *Rh. Mus.* 36, 559.—We do not know what grounds those Chronologists had who made Aristeas contemp. with Kroisos and Kyros and put his *flor.* in Ol. 58, 3 (Suid.). The reason may possibly have been "identification"—this is hardly likely—"or conjunction with Abaris" (Gutschmid ap. Niese, *Hom. Schiffskat.*, p. 49, n.). Unfortunately nothing is known of such a conjunction with Abaris (very problematical conjectures by Crusius in *Myth. Lex.* i, 2814 f.). Possibly those who favoured this view held that the Ἀριμάσπεια had been foisted upon Aristeas; cf. D. H., *Thuc.* 23; π. ὕψους, 10, 4. This work was certainly regarded as having been composed at the time of the Kim. invasion. The historical reality of Aristeas was never doubted in antiquity and in spite of the many legends that gathered about his name there is no need for us to do so. The stories of Aristeas' extremely prolonged lifetime (from the

Kim. invasion to the evidently much later period in which he really lived) appear to have been derived chiefly from fictions in the Ἀριμάσπεια which probably also gave reasons of a mysterious kind for this marvellous extension of his existence. We cannot tell whether Aristeas himself wrote the poem and provided his own halo of marvel or whether someone else, coming later, made use of this name so famous in legend. If there was any basis for the account in Suid. *Πείσανδρος Πείσωνος* fin. we might be justified in attributing the composition of the Ἀριμάσπεια to Aristeas himself. In any case the poem was already in existence at the beginning of the fifth century; it can hardly be doubted that Aeschylus modelled upon it his picture of the griffins and Arimaspoi in *Pr.* 803 ff.

[111] Dexikreon in Samos, Plu., *Q. Gr.* 54.—Polyaratos of Thasos, Phormion of Sparta: Cl. Al., *Str.* i, 21, p. 399 P. Phormion is better known because of his marvellous experiences: Paus. 3, 16, 2–3; Thpomp. ap. Suid. *Φορ.*; see Meineke, *Com.*², p. 1227 ff.—At the end of the above-mentioned enumeration of μάντεις ap. Clem. Al., a certain Ἐμπεδότιμος ὁ Συρακόσιος is given. Varro ap. Serv. on *G.* i, 34, tells of the ecstatic vision of this Empedotimos: after being a quadam potestate divina mortalis aspectus detersus he saw in the sky *inter cetera* three gates and three ways (to the gods and the kingdom of the dead). Varro is evidently quoting the account of some ancient authority not a work of Empedot. himself; but in any case this vision is the source of what Empedotimos had to say about the dwelling-place of the souls in the Milky Way: Suid. Ἐμπεδ., Ἰουλιανός: *Rh. Mus.* 32, 331, n. 1; cf. Damasc. ap. Philop. *in Arist. Meteor.*, p. 117, 10 Hayd. Suid. Ἐμπεδ. calls (probably a guess) the work in which Empedot. gave an account of his visions περὶ φυσικῆς ἀκροάσεως. (Because E. also brought back with him information about the future life, the usual stories about the subterranean chamber, etc., are transferred to him by Sch. ad Greg. Nz., *C.* vii, 286 = Eudocia, p. 682, 15.) Apart from this no one gives us any information about the personality of Emped. except Jul., *Ep.* 295 B., p. 379, 13 ff. H., who tells us how he was murdered but the gods avenged him upon his murderers. This, however, rests upon a confusion (either Julian's or his copyist's) with Ἑρμότιμος whose murderers were punished in the next world acc. to Plu., *Gen. Socr.* 22, p. 592 C. The above-mentioned story of the souls and the Milky Way was also known to Julian (see Suid. Ἰουλ.): his source being Herakleides Pont. (who also probably supplied it to others, e.g. Noumenios ap. Procl. *in Rp.* ii, p. 129 Kroll, Porph., Iamb. ap Stob., *Ecl.* i, p. 378, 12 W., and even earlier, Cicero, *Somn.* 15–16). No older source of this fancy is known: "Pythagoras" mentioned as its authority by Julian, etc., only takes us back again to Herakleides. All that we know up to the present about it suggests the suspicion that the very existence and history of this remarkably little-known "great Empedotimos" may have been a simple *invention* of Herakleides', who may have made use of him in one of his dialogues to add interest and importance to some of his own fancies. But now we come upon something more detailed about the story told by Herakleides of the vision in which Emped. (μετὰ τοῦ σώματος, p. 122, 2) beheld πᾶσαν τὴν περὶ τῶν ψυχῶν ἀληθείαν: Procl. *in Rp.* ii, 119, 21 Kroll. From this passage it is quite clear that Empedotimos is simply a figure in a dialogue by Herakleides, and no more existed in reality than Er the son of Armenios or Thespesios of Soli, or than their prototype Kleonymos of Athens ap. Klearchos of Soli (*Rh. Mus.* 32, 335).

[112] Apollon., *Mirab.* 3 (prob. from Thpomp.); Plin., *NH.* vii, 174; Plu., *Gen. Soc.* 22, p. 592 C (Ἑρμόδωρος—the same copyist's error occurs in Procl. *in Rp.* ii, 113, 24 Kroll); Luc., *Enc. Musc.* 7; Tert., *An.* 2; 44 (from Soranos; cf. Cael. Aur., *Tard.* 1, 3, 5); Or., *Cels.* iii, 3; 32. The same Hermotimos of Klazomenai is undoubtedly the person meant when a Ἑρμότιμος is mentioned among the earlier incarnations of the soul of Pythagoras, even when the country of the person in question is not named (as in D.L. viii, 5 f.; Porph., *VP.* 45; Tert., *An.* 28) or is incorrectly called a Milesian (e.g. in Hipp., *RH.* 1, 2, p. 12 D.-S.). A quite untenable theory about this Hermot. is given by Göttling, *Opusc. Ac.* 211.—Acc. to Plin. the enemies who finally burnt the body of Hermot. (with the connivance of his wife) were the Cantharidae—probably the name of a γένος hostile to Hermot. —There is a remarkably similar story in Indian tradition: see *Rh. Mus.* 26, 559 n. But I no longer suspect any historical connexion between this story and that of Hermot.; the same preconceptions have led in India as in Greece to the invention of the same tale. Similar conceptions in German beliefs: Grimm, 1803, n. 650.

[113] Hence the legend that Apollo after the murder of Python was purified not at Tempe, as the story generally went, but in Krete at Tarrha by Karmanor: Paus. 2, 7, 7; 2, 30, 3; 10, 6, 7 (the hexameters of Phemonoë); 10, 16, 5. The καθάρσια for Zeus were brought from Krete: Orph. *fr.* 183 Ab.; cf. the oracle ap. Oinom. Eus., *PE.* 5, 31, 2; K. O. Müller, *Introd. Scient. Myth.* 98.—Krete an ancient seat of *mantikê*: the Lokrian Onomakritos, teacher of Thaletas, lived in Krete κατὰ τέχνην μαντικήν, Arist., *Pol.* 1274*a*, 25.

[114] See above (pp. 96 f). As one who had been initiated into the orgiastic cult of Zeus in Krete (Str. 468), Epimenides is called νέος Κούρης: Plu., *Sol.* 12; D.L. i, 115. He is called ἱερεὺς Διὸς καὶ Ῥέας in Sch. Clem. Al. iv, p. 103 Klotz.

[115] Legend of the ἄλιμον of E.: H. Smyrn. 18. D.L. i, 114. Plu. 7 *Sap.* 14. He was prepared for it by living on ἀσφόδελος, μαλάχη, and the edible root of a kind of σκίλλα (Thphr., *HP.* 7, 12, 1). All these are sacred to the χθόνιοι (on ασφόδελος, see partic. *AB.* 457, 5 ff., which goes back to Aristarchos; and Hsch. s.v.), and were only eaten occasionally by the poor: Hes., *Op.* 41.

[116] οὗ (Ἐπιμενίδου) λόγος ὡς ἐξίοι ἡ ψυχὴ ὁπόσον ἤθελε χρόνον καὶ πάλιν εἰσῄει ἐν τῷ σώματι, Suid. Ἐπιμεν. This is possibly the meaning of προσποιηθῆναι (λέγεται) πολλάκις ἀναβεβιωκέναι, D.L. i, 114. Epimenides like others μετὰ θάνατον ἐν τοῖς ζῶσι γενόμενος, Procl. *in Rp.* ii, 113, 24 Kr. The story of his prolonged sleep in the cave is an example of a widespread fairy-tale motif; see *Rh. Mus.* 33, 209, n. 2; 35, 160. In the case of Epimenides it has been exaggerated beyond all bounds and attached to him as a sort of popular mode of expressing his long ἐκστάσεις. This cave-sleep is interpreted as a state of *ekstasis* by *Max. Tyr.* 16, 1: ἐν τοῦ Διὸς τοῦ Δικταίου (see above, chap. iii, n. 23) τῷ ἄντρῳ κείμενος ὕπνῳ βαθεῖ ἔτη συχνά (cf. the ψυχή of Hermot. which ἀπὸ τοῦ σώματος πλαζομένη ἀποδημεῖ ἐπὶ πολλὰ ἔτη, Apollon., *Mir.* 3) ὄναρ ἔφη ἐντυχεῖν αὐτὸς θεοῖς κτλ. Thus his ὄνειρος became διδάσκαλος to him, Max. Tyr. 38, 3; cf. Sch. Luc., *Tim.* 6, 110 Rb.

[117] σοφὸς περὶ τὰ θεῖα (δεινὸς τὰ θεῖα, Max. Tyr. 38, 3) τὴν ἐνθουσιαστικὴν σοφίαν, Plu., *Sol.* 12. Epimen. is put among the ἔνθεοι μάντεις, Bakis and the Sibyl, by Cic., *Div.* 1, 34.—Prolonged solitude is a preparation for the business of the ecstatic seer (cf. Plu.'s story of a sort of counterpart to Epimenides, *Def. Or.* 21, p. 421 B). There

is still another fragment remaining from the story of Epim. on this head in the account given by Theopompos (though he makes too rationalistic a use of it): Epim. did not sleep all that time ἀλλὰ χρόνον τινὰ ἐκπατῆσαι, ἀσχολούμενον περὶ ῥιζοτομίαν (which he needed as an ἰατρόμαντις): D.L. i, 112. We cannot help being reminded of the way in which the Angekok of Greenland, after prolonged and profound solitude, severe fasting and concentration of thought, makes himself into a magician (Cranz, *Hist. of Greenland*, p. 194). In the same way the North American Indian stays for weeks in a solitary wood and consciously prepares himself for his visions. At last the real world falls away from him, the imagined world of his visions becomes the real one and seems almost palpable; till finally in complete ecstasy he rushes out of his hiding place. Nor would it be hard to find analogies in the religion of civilized peoples.

[118] Epim. is credited with prophecies of coming events: Pl., *Lg.* 642 D; D.L. i, 114, and also Cic., *Div.* i, 34. On the other hand, Arist., *Rh.* 3, 17, 10, has περὶ τῶν ἐσομένων οὐκ ἐμαντεύετο, ἀλλὰ περὶ τῶν γεγονότων μὲν ἀδήλων δέ which at least means discovering the grounds of an event—grounds known only to the god and the seer; e.g. the interpretation of a pestilence as the vengeance of the daimones for an ancient crime, etc. If only rational explanation were meant there would be no need for a μάντις.

[119] Delos: Plu., *Sept. Sap.* 14, p. 158 A. (There is no need to suppose that there has been any confusion between this μέγας καθαρμός by Epimenides and any other purification of Delos that happens to be better known to us—the Pisistratean or that of the year 426.) Epimenides πόλεις ἐκάθηρεν ἄλλας τε καὶ τὴν Ἀθηναίων, Paus. 1, 14, 4.

[120] The purification of Athens from the Kylonian ἄγος by Epimenides is now further confirmed by the Aristotelian Ἀθ. πολ. 1 fin. This admittedly is not a very strong guarantee of its historical truth; but no strong guarantee is required to dispose of the doubts recently raised as to the historical truth of the story that Athens was purified by Epimenides, and even of Epimenides' very existence. There is no reason at all for such a doubt. The fact that the historical figure of Epimenides has been almost entirely obscured behind the veil of fable and romance gives us of course no right to doubt his existence (or what would be the fate of Pythagoras, Pherekydes of Syros, and of many others?); and further, because some parts of the story of Epim. and his life are fabulous, to doubt the truth of his entirely non-fabulous purification of the Athenians from murder is a monstrous inversion of true historical method.—No exact dating for the purification of Athens is to be derived from the Aristotelian account of the event, as the English ed. (Kenyon) of the Ἀθ. πολ. rightly observes. It certainly does not follow (as e.g. Bauer takes for granted in his *Forsch. zu Arist.* Ἀθ. πολ. 41) that the purification took place *before* the archonship of Drakon (Ol. 39). Furthermore, it is probable that in Plu., *Sol.* 12, everything that comes before τοὺς ὅρους (p. 165, 19, Sint. ed. min.) is taken from Aristotle (though perhaps not directly). In this case Aristotle, too, would be shown to have attributed to Solon the first suggestion that led to the condemnation of the ἐναγεῖς. In Plu., however, Solon is still far from having thoughts of his νομοθεσία, he is still only ἤδη δόξαν ἔχων, c. 12 (not till c. 14 does his archonship begin). Solon's archonship is put by Ἀθ. πολ. in the year 591/0 (c. 14, 1, where we should be careful to avoid arbitrary alteration of the figures); Suid. Σόλων, Eus., *Chron.* also date it in Ol. 47, and the same period is implied by Plu., *Sol.* 14, p. 168, 12. (Ἀθ. πολ.

13, 2, also brings the first archonship of Damasias to 582/1 = Ol. 49, 3: a date to which all other reliable tradition also points). The condemnation of the ἐναγεῖς and the purification of Athens by Epimenides thus took place some considerable time before 591. It is possible that Suid. gives the right date. s.v. Ἐπιμενίδης· ἐκάθηρε τὰς Ἀθήνας τοῦ Κυλωνείου ἄγους κατὰ τὴν μδ̄ Ὀλυμπιάδα (604/1)—that in the Kirrhaian war there was an Ἀλκμαίων general of the Athenians offers no objection: Plu., *Sol.* 11. Suidas' statement has not (as I once thought myself, with Bernhardy) been taken from D.L., nor is it to be corrected acc. to his text. D.L. i, 100, only brings forward the connexion between the purification and the Κυλώνειον ἄγος as the opinion of "some" (which in spite of the vagueness of expression must mean Neanthes ap. Ath. 602 C), while the real reason is said to be a λοιμός, and the purification (as in Eus. *Chr.*) is placed in Ol. 46; i.e. probably 46, 3, the traditional date of Solon's legislation.—Plato, *Lg.* 642 DE, does not conflict with the story of the expiation of the Κυλ. ἄγος by Epimenides: his story that Epimen. was present in Athens in the year 500 and retarded the threatened Persian invasion for ten years is not intended to contest the truth of the tradition of the much earlier purification of Athens by Epimen. ("retarded": so Clem. Al., *Str.* vi, 13, p. 755 P., understood Plato and prob. rightly; we often hear in legendary stories of the gods or their prophets retarding coming events which have been determined by fate; cf. Pl., *Smp.* 201 D; Hdt. i, 91; Ath. 602 B; Eus., *PE.* 5, 35, p. 233 BC; Vg., *A.* vii, 313 ff.; viii, 398 f.; and what Serv. ad loc. reports from the *libri Acheruntici*). How the same man could be living both at the end of the seventh and of the sixth centuries would have troubled Plato not at all—tradition attributed a miraculously long life to Ep. At any rate, it is quite impossible to base the chronology of Ep.'s life on the story in Plato. (It may have been suggested by a forged oracle made ex eventu after 490 and fathered on Epim., as Schultess suggests, *De Epim. Crete*, p. 47, 1877.)

[121] Details of the expiation ceremonies: D.L. i, 111–12; Neanthes ap. Ath. 602 C. It is not the human sacrifice but the sentimental interpretation of Neanth. that Polemon (Ath. 602 F.) declares to be fictitious. They are invariably sacrifices to the χθόνια that Epim. institutes. Thus (as Abaris founded a temple at Sparta for Κόρη σώτειρα) he founded at Athens, evidently as the concluding part of the purification, τὰ ἱερὰ τῶν σεμνῶν θεῶν, i.e. of the Erinyes: D.L. i, 112.

[122] Such a connexion must at least be intended when Aristeas is brought to Metapontum and Phormion to Kroton, both important centres of the Pythagorean society. Aristeas, too, as well as Abaris, Epimenides, etc., is one of the favourite figures of the Pythagoreans: see Iamb., *VP.* 138.

[123] It would certainly be necessary to deny to Epimenides the "Theogony" that the whole of antiquity read and quoted under the name of Epimenides without once expressing a doubt, if the fragments of that Theogony really contained borrowings from the teaching of Anaximenes or, even worse, from the rhapsodical Theogony of Orpheus, as Kern, *de Orphei Ep. Pher. Theog.* 66 ff. maintains. But in the first place a few vague resemblances are not enough to show any connexion between Epimenides and those others. In the second, supposing the connexion proved, Epimenides need not necessarily have been the borrower. In any case, such alleged borrowings do not oblige us to advance the period when Ep. lived from the end of

the seventh to the end of the sixth century. If they really exist then we should rather have to conclude that the Theogony is itself a forgery of a much later date.

[124] The possibility of theoretical activity in the case of these men is often implied in the statements of later writers; e.g. when the name θεολόγος is given to Epimenides (D.S. 5, 80, 4) or Abaris (Apollon., *Mir.* 4); or when Aristeas is called an ἀνὴρ φιλόσοφος (Max. Tyr. 38, 3, p. 222 R.).

[125] Arist., *Meta.* 1, 3, p. 948*b*, 19 f.

[126] See Append. viii.

[127] See above, chap. i, n. 41. Archiloch. *fr.* 12: κείνου κεφαλὴν καὶ χαρίεντα μέλη Ἥφαιστος καθαροῖσιν ἐν εἵμασιν ἀμφεπονήθη. E., *Or.* 40 f.: the slain Klytaimnestra πυρὶ καθήγνισται δέμας and Sch. πάντα γὰρ καθαιρεῖ τὸ πῦρ, καὶ ἁγνὰ δοκεῖ εἶναι τὰ καιόμενα, τὰ δὲ ἄταφα μεμιασμένα. E., *Sup.* 1211: . . . ἵν' αὐτῶν (those who are being buried) σώμαθ' ἡγνίσθη πυρί; cf. ἅγνισον πυρσῷ μέλαθρον, *IT.* 1216. On a grave inscr. from Attica (*Epigr. Gr.* 104): ἐνθάδε Διάλογος καθαρῷ πυρὶ γυῖα καθήρας . . . ᾤχετ' ἐς ἀθάνατους—evidently modelled on ancient ideas; cf. also ib. 109, 5 (*CIA.* iii, 1325). Those, too, who are struck by lightning (see Appendix i) are purified from all earthly taint by the holiest sort of πῦρ καθάρσιον (E., *IA.* 1112; καθαρσίῳ φλογί, E., *Hel.* 869) and go straight πρὸς ἀθανάτους. Iamb., *Myst.* v, 12, also explains how fire τὰ προσαγόμενα καθαίρει καὶ ἀπολύει τῶν ἐν τῇ ὕλῃ δεσμῶν, ἀφομοιοῖ τοῖς θεοῖς, etc.

[128] Cf. also Pl., *Lg.* 677 DE; Plu., *Fac. Orb. Lun.* 25, p. 940 C.

CHAPTER X

THE ORPHICS

The earliest authority who mentions Orphic sects and their practices is Herodotos (ii, 81), who calls attention to the correspondence between certain sacerdotal and ascetic ordinances of the Egyptian priesthood, and the " Orphic and Bacchic " mysteries. The latter, he says, are really Egyptian and Pythagorean, or in other words they were founded by Pythagoras or Pythagoreans upon Egyptian models; and thus, in the opinion of the historian, they cannot have come into existence before the last decade of the sixth century. Herodotos then, either in Athens or elsewhere, had heard during his journeys of certain private societies who by calling themselves after the name of Orpheus, the prototype of Thracian song so well known to legend, recognized the origin of their peculiar cult and creed in the mountains of Thrace, and did honour to Bakchos the Thracian god. The fact that the Greek Orphics did indeed worship Dionysos, the lord of life and death, before all other gods, is clearly shown by the remains of the theological poems that originated in their midst. Orpheus himself, as founder of the Orphic sect, is actually said to have been the founder also of the Dionysiac initiation-mysteries.[1]

This gathering-together in the name of Orpheus for the purpose of offering a special worship to Dionysos was, then, the work of *sects* who, in private association, practised a cult which the public and official worship of the state either did not know of or disdained. There were many such associations, and of very varied character, which kept themselves aloof from the organized religion of the community, and were tolerated by the state.[2] As a rule, they were " foreign gods "[3] who were thus worshipped; and generally by foreigners who thus kept up the special worship of their own homes, though they did not always exclude natives of their adopted country. Now, Dionysos, the god of the Orphic sects, had for a long time ceased to be a foreigner in Greek countries; since his arrival from Thrace he had been refined and matured under the humanizing sun of Greece, until he had become a Greek god, and a worthy associate of the Greek Olympos. It is possible, however, that in this process, the old Thracian god may have seemed to his original worshippers to have lost his real character, and they may on that account have joined together to offer, in separation from the official worship, a special cult in which all the old ideas of the national religion should be preserved unaltered. A secondary wave of influence thus broke upon the long-since-Hellenized god, the Thracian Dionysos in Greece, and *this* wave the official worship either had not the power or lacked the will to assimilate. It was therefore left to special sects who honoured the god after their own private laws. Whether indeed they were *Thracians* who, as in the similar case of the unmodified worship of Bendis,[4] or Kotytto, thus reinstituted their ancient and national worship of Dionysos in Greek countries, we cannot with certainty tell ; but this special cult would certainly not have achieved the importance it did in *Greek* life if it had not been joined by Greek adherents brought up in the native conceptions of Greek piety, who under the name of " Orphics " once more adapted the Thracian god to Greek modes of thought—though this new adaptation differed from the previous assimilation of the god by the official worship of the state. We have no reason for believing that Orphic sects were formed in Greek states before the second half of the sixth century,[5] that critical age of transition when in so many places primitive and mythological modes of thought were developing into a *theosophy*, which in its turn was making an effort to become a philosophy. The Orphic religious poetry is itself clearly marked by this effort—for in Orphism it never became more than an effort and never succeeded in reaching its goal.

The exact point of origin of this combined movement of religion and theosophy, the various steps and manner of its development remain hidden from us. Athens was a centre of Orphism ; it does not therefore follow that Orphism had its origin there, any more than had the multifarious tendencies and activities in art, poetry, and science that at about the same period flowed together, and as though driven by an unseen intellectual current, found their meeting place at Athens. Onomakritos, we are told, the giver of oracles in the court of Peisistratos " founded the secret worship of Dionysos ".[6] This appears to refer to the first founding of an Orphic sect at Athens ; and we meet with the name of Onomakritos among the authors of Orphic poems. But the real authorship of these poems is far more often ascribed to certain men of Southern Italy and Sicily, who can be more or less clearly connected [7] with the Pythagorean societies which were flourishing in those districts about the last decades of the sixth and the first of the fifth centuries.

It seems certain that in Southern Italy at that time, Orphic societies were already in existence—for whom else can these writers have intended their "Orphic" poems? In any case we must take it as certain that the correspondence of Orphic and Pythagorean doctrine on the subject of the soul is not purely accidental. Did Pythagoras when he came to Italy (about 532) find Orphic societies already settled in Kroton and Metapontum, and did he associate himself with their ideas? Or did the "Orphic" sectaries (as Herodotos imagined [8]) owe their inspiration to Pythagoras and his disciples? The various cross-currents of reciprocal influence can no longer be disentangled by us, but if the Pythagoreans were the sole creditors in the bargain we should undoubtedly find the whole body of Orphic doctrine thoroughly permeated with conceptions that belong exclusively to the Pythagorean school. In the wreckage of the Orphic poems, however, except for a few negligible traces of the Pythagorean mystic theory of numbers,[9] we find nothing that must necessarily have been derived by the Orphics from Pythagorean sources.[10] Least of all did they need to derive the doctrine of the migration of souls and its application from this source. It is possible, therefore, that it was the independently developed Orphic doctrine which exerted an influence upon Pythogoras and his adherents in Southern Italy; just as it was a ready-made Orphic teaching (and that, too, perhaps, brought from Southern Italy) with which Onomakritos, the founder of the Orphic sects at Athens, associated himself—about the same time as Pythagoras' similar action in Kroton. It is hardly possible to interpret in any other way the various relations of the Orphics with each other when we learn that at the court of the Peisistratids, in addition to Onomakritos, two other men who had arrived from Southern Italy were active and were counted among the earliest writers of Orphic poems.[11]

§ 2

The Orphics wherever we meet with them in Greek countries always appear as members of a private cult-society who are held together by a specially organized and individual mode of worship. The old Thracian worship of Dionysos in its straining after the infinite conducted its revels under the open sky of night, seeking out deserted mountain-sides and forests where it was farthest from civilization and closest to unspoiled and untrammelled nature. How this cult may have accommodated itself to the narrow limitations of ordinary city-life, it is hard to imagine ;[12] though it is natural to suppose that much of the extravagance that was literal and actual enough in the old northern festival of night was represented in the milder worship of Greece by mere symbol. We have less difficulty in discovering the side of their religious activity which the Orphics, apart from the private worship of the conventicle, revealed to the outer world of the profane. Orpheus himself in the tradition had been not merely the inspired singer but the seer, the magically endowed physician and purification-priest as well,[13] and the Orphics, as his followers, were active, too, in all these directions.[14] In the composition of Greek Orphism the kathartic ideas which had been evolved on Greek soil were combined in a not unnatural alliance with the old Thracian worship of Dionysos. The Orphic priests of purification were preferred to others of their kind by many religious people.[15] But among the inner circles of Orphism the sacerdotal activities of purification and the removal of daimonic hindrances, which were by no means given up, tended rather to produce deeper and broader ideas of purity and of release from the earthly and the transitory. In some such way was evolved that asceticism which in close combination with the Thracian worship of Dionysos gave the peculiar tone to the faith and temperament of the sectaries and gave to their lives their special direction.

The Orphic sect had a fixed and definite set of doctrines ; this alone sufficed to distinguish it both from the official worships of the state, and from all other cult-associations of the time. The reduction of belief to distinct doctrinal formulæ may have done more than anything else to make Orphism a *society* of believers—none of the other *theologi* of the time, Epimenides, Pherekydes, etc., accomplished as much. Without its fundamental religious doctrine Orphism in Greece is inconceivable ; according to Aristotle the " doctrines " of Orpheus were put into poetical form by the founder of the Orphic sect in Athens, Onomakritos.[16] The uncertain accounts given us by the later authorities do not allow us to make out quite clearly [17] what was the extent of Onomakritos' work in the formation or collection of Orphic doctrinal poetry. What is important is the fact that he is distinctly named as the author of the poem called " Initiations ".[18] This poem must have been one of the basic, and in the strictest sense " religious ", writings of the sect ; a poem of this character may very well have had for its central incident the dismemberment of the god at the hands of the Titans—a story which Onomakritos is said to have put into verse.[19]

The religious beliefs and worship of the sect were founded upon the detailed instructions of certain very numerous writings dealing with matters of ritual and theology. These claimed the authority of religious inspiration,[20] and were as a whole supposed to be the work of the primitive Thracian bard, Orpheus, himself. The anonymity which concealed the identity of the real authors of these poems was not, however, very thoroughly preserved; even towards the end of the fourth century there were those who claimed to be able to give with certainty the names of the original authors of the various poems. Strictly canonical authority, such as would at once have reduced to silence every conflicting view or statement, never seems to have belonged to any of these writings. In particular, there were several " Theogonies " [21] —poems which attempted to give expression to the fundamental ideas of Orphic speculation on religious subjects—and in spite of much harmony in general effect they differed considerably from each other in particular mode of expression. They represented ever-renewed and increasingly elaborate attempts to construct a connected doctrinal system for Orphism. With unmistakable allusion to the oldest Greek theological system—that which had been committed to writing in the Hesiodic poem—these Orphic Theogonies described the origin and development of the world from obscure primordial impulses to the clear and distinct variety-in-unity of the organized kosmos, and it described it as the history of a long series of divine powers and figures which issue from each other (each new one overcoming the last) and succeed each other in the task of building and organizing the world until they have absorbed the whole universe into themselves in order to bring it forth anew, animated with one spirit and, with all its infinite variety, a unity. These gods are certainly no longer deities of the familiar Greek type. Not merely the new gods evolved by the creative fancy of Orphism—creatures which had almost entirely lost all distinct and sensible outline under the accumulation of symbolical meaning—but even the figures actually borrowed from the Greek world of divinities are turned into little more than mere personified abstractions. Who would recognize the Zeus of Homer in the Orphic Zeus who after he has devoured the World-God and " taken unto himself the power of Erikapaios ",[22] has become himself the Universe and the Whole? " Zeus the Beginning, Zeus the Middle, in Zeus all things are completed." [23] The concept here so stretches the personality that it threatens to break it down altogether; the outlines of the individual figures are lost and are merged into an intentional "confusion of deities".[24]

Still, the mythical envelope was never quite given up; these poets could not do without it altogether. Their gods did indeed strive to become pure abstractions but they were never quite successful in throwing off all traces of individuality and the limitations of form and matter: the concept never quite broke through the veil of mythology. The poets of the Orphic Theogonies vied with one another in their attempts to make the half-seen and half-conceived accessible alike to the imagination and the reason; and in succession gave varying expression to the same fundamental conceptions until finality was reached as it seems in a poem whose contents are better known to us than the others from quotations made from it by Neoplatonic writers—the Theogonical poem of the four-and-twenty Rhapsodies. Into this poem was poured all the traditional material of mythological and symbolical doctrine, and in it such doctrine achieved its final expression.[25]

§ 3

This combination of religion and quasi-philosophical speculation was a distinguishing feature of the Orphics and of Orphic literature. Religion only entered into their Theogonical poetry in so far as the ethical personalities of the divinities therein described had not entirely faded away into transparent allegories.[26] It was abstract speculation alone which really prevailed there, little respect being paid to religion; and as a result a much greater licence was given to speculative construction.

This abstract speculation, however, reached its climax in a religious narrative of the first importance for the beliefs and cult of the sect. At the end of the series of genealogically connected deities came the son of Zeus and Persephone, Dionysos, who was also given the name of the underworld deity Zagreus.[27] To him, even in infancy, was entrusted the rule of the world by Zeus. But the wicked Titans, urged on by Hera, approached him by a stratagem. They were the enemies of Zeus, and had already been overthrown by Ouranos,[28] but had, it seems, been let loose again by Zeus from Tartaros. They made Dionysos trust them by giving him presents, and while he was looking at his own image in a mirror [29] that they had given him, they fell upon him. He tried to escape them by repeated transformations of shape; finally, in the form of a bull,[30] he was at last overcome and his body torn to pieces which his savage foes thereupon devoured. The heart alone was rescued by Athene, and she brought it to Zeus who swallowed it. From Zeus there sprang the " new Dionysos ", the son of Zeus and Semele, in whom Zagreus came to life again.

The myth of the dismemberment of Zagreus by the Titans was already put into verse by Onomakritos;[31] it continued to be the culminating point of the doctrinal poetry of the Orphics. It occurred not only in the Rhapsodies,[32] but in other versions of the Orphic legend composed in complete independence of these.[33] It is a religious myth in the stricter sense; its *ætiological* character is most marked;[34] its purpose is to explain the religious implication of the ritual dismemberment of the bull-god at the Bacchic nocturnal festivals, and to derive that feature from the legendary sufferings of Dionysos-Zagreus.

But though the legend thus has its roots in the primitive sacrificial ritual of ancient Thrace,[35] in its extended form it belongs entirely to the region of Hellenic thought; and in this combination of the two elements it becomes truly Orphic. The wicked Titans belong entirely to strictly Greek mythology.[36] In this case, as the murderers of the god, they represent the primeval power of evil.[37] They dismember the One into Many parts; by their impiety the One divine being is dispersed into the multiplicity of the things of this world.[38] It is reborn as One in the new Dionysos sprung from Zeus. The Titans—so the legend goes on to relate—who had devoured the limbs of the god were destroyed by Zeus with his lightning flash. From their ashes sprang the race of men in whom, in conformity with their origin, the good derived from Dionysos-Zagreus is mixed with a wicked Titanic element.[39]

With the rule of the new-born Dionysos and the origin of mankind, the series of mythological events in the Orphic poetry came to an end.[40] With the entry of mankind into Creation[41] the existing period of the world begins; the period of world-revolutions is over. The poems now turn to the subject of man and the revelation of his fate, his duty and his purpose in the world.

§ 4

The mixture of the elements that make up the totality of his being in itself prescribes for man the direction that his effort shall take. He must free himself from the Titanic element and, thus purified, return to the god, a fragment of whom is living in him.[42] The distinction between the Titanic and Dionysiac elements in man is an allegorical expression of the popular distinction between body and soul; it also corresponds to a profoundly felt estimate of the relative value of these two sides of man's being. According to Orphic doctrine man's duty is to free himself from the chains of the body in which the soul lies fast bound like the prisoner in his cell.[43] The soul has a long way, however, to go before it can find its freedom; it may not by an act of violence tear its bonds asunder for itself.[44] The death of the body only frees it for a short while; for the soul must once more suffer imprisonment in a body. After leaving its old body, it flutters free in the wind, but a breath of air sends it into a new body again.[45] So it continues its journey, perpetually alternating between an unfettered separate existence, and an ever-renewed incarnation—traversing the great "Circle of Necessity" in which it becomes the life-companion of many bodies both of men and beasts. Thus, the "Wheel of Birth" [46] seems to return ever upon itself in hopeless repetition: in Orphic poetry (and there perhaps for the first time) occurs the despairing thought of the exact repetition of the past; events which have already been lived through once returning again with the convergence of the same attendant circumstances.[47] Thus, Nature, ever reverting to its own beginnings, draws men with it in its senseless revolution round itself.

But the soul has a way open for escape from this perpetual recurrence of all things that threatens to close in upon it; it may hope "to escape from the circle and have a respite from misery".[48] It is formed for blessed freedom, and can at last detach itself from the condition of being it has to endure upon earth—a condition unworthy of it. A "release" is possible; but man in his blindness and thoughtlessness cannot help himself, cannot even, when salvation is at hand, turn himself towards it.[49]

Salvation comes from Orpheus and his Bacchic mysteries; Dionysos himself will loose his worshipper from Evil and the unending way of misery. Not his own power, but the grace of the "releasing gods" is to be the cause of man's liberation.[50] The self-reliance of the older Greece is breaking down; in humility of heart the pious man looks elsewhere for help; he needs the revelation and mediation of "Orpheus the Ruler" [51] in order to find the way of salvation; he must follow his ordinances of salvation with perfect obedience if he is to continue in that way.

It is not only the sacred mysteries themselves, in the form in which Orpheus has ordained them, which prepare for the release; a complete "Orphic life" [52] must be developed out of them. Asceticism is the prime condition of the pious life. This does not mean the practice of the respectable bourgeois virtues, nor the discipline and moral reformation of a man's character; the height of morality is in this case the turning again towards god,[53] and the turning away not merely from the weaknesses and errors of earthly being but from the whole of earthly life itself; renunciation of all that ties man to mortality and the life of the body. The fierce determination with which the Indian penitent tears away his will from life, to which every organ in his body clings desperately—for this, indeed, there was no place among the Greeks, the lovers of life—not even among the world-denying ascetics. Abstention from the eating of flesh was the strongest and most striking species of self-denial practised by the Orphic ascetics.[54] Apart from this, they kept themselves in all essentials uncontaminated by certain things and situations which rather suggested to a religious symbolism than actually indicated in themselves attachment to the world of death and transitoriness. The long-standing ordinances of the priestly ritual of purification were taken up and added to; [55] but they were also raised to a higher plane. They are no longer intended to free men from the effects of daimonic contacts; the soul itself is made pure by them [56]—pure from the body and its polluting association, pure from death and its loathsome mastery. In expiation of "guilt" the soul is confined within the body,[57] the wages of sin is in this case that life upon earth which for the soul is death. The whole multiplicity of the universe, emptied of its innocent and natural sequence of cause and effect, appears to these zealots under the uniform aspect of a correlation between crime and punishment, between pollution and purification. Thus, mysticism enters into the closest alliance with kathartic practices. The soul which comes from the divine and strives to return thither, has no other purpose to fulfil upon earth (and therefore no other moral law to obey); it must be free from life itself and be pure from all that is earthly.

The Orphics, moreover, were the only people who could venture among themselves or before strangers to greet each other with the special name of the "Pure".[58] The first reward of his piety was received by the initiate of the Orphic mysteries in that intermediate region whither men must go after their earthly death. When a man dies, Hermes leads the "deathless soul" into the underworld.[59] Special poems of the Orphic community announced the terrors and delights of the underworld kingdom.[60] What the Orphic mystery-priests vouchsafed to their public upon these hidden matters—outdoing the promises made in the Eleusinian mysteries in coarse appeal to the senses—may have been the most popular, but was certainly not the most original feature of Orphic teaching.[61] In Hades a judgment awaited the soul—it was no instinctive fancy of the people, but the " sacred doctrine "[62] of these sectaries which first introduced and elaborated the idea of compensatory justice in the world of the dead. The impious suffer punishment and purgation in the depths of Tartaros ;[63] those who have not been made pure by the Orphic mysteries lie in the miry Pool ;[64] " dreadful things[65] await " the disdainer of the sacred worship. By a conception that is quite unique in ancient religion, participation in the Orphic ceremonial enables the descendant to obtain from the gods " pardon and purification " for his departed ancestors who may be paying the penalty in the next world for the misdeeds of the past.[66] But for the initiate of the Orphic mysteries himself who has not merely borne the *narthex* but has been a true Bakchos,[67] his reward is that he shall obtain a " milder fate " in the kingdom of the underworld deities whom he has revered on earth, and dwell " in the fair meadows of deep-running Acheron ".[68] The blessed home of refuge no longer lies like the Homeric Elysium upon earth, but below in the world of the Souls, for only the released soul reaches there. There, the initiated and purified will live in communion with the gods of the nether world[69]—we feel that we are listening to Thracian and not Greek conceptions of the ideal when we hear of the " Banquet of the Pure " and the uninterrupted intoxication which they enjoy there.[70]

But the depths restore the soul at last to the light, for its lasting habitation is not below ; it stays there only for the interval which separates death from its next rebirth. For the reprobate this is a time of punishment and purgation—the Orphics could not distress their hearers with the awful and intolerable idea of the *perpetual* punishment of the damned in Hell ; many times over the soul rises again to the light and in continually renewed bodies fulfils the cycle of births. For the deeds of its past life it is recompensed in the next life that it lives, and each man must now suffer exactly what he has done to another.[71] So he pays the penalty for ancient guilt : the " thrice-ancient law "—what thou hast done thou shalt suffer—is thus fulfilled for him in far livelier fashion than it could be in any torments of the shadow-world. So surely also shall the pure be rewarded in future lives by ever-increasing happiness. How exactly the Orphic fancy filled out the individual gradations in the scale of happiness is beyond our knowledge.[72]

But the soul is immortal, and even sinners and the unredeemed cannot perish entirely. Hades and the life on earth holds them in their perpetual round, and this is their punishment. For the soul of the blessed, however, neither Hades nor earthly life can offer the highest crown of happiness. If it has been made pure and spotless in the Orphic mysteries and the Orphic manner of life, it is freed from the necessity of rebirth and withdrawn from the cycle of becoming and perishing. The "purification" ends in a final redemption. The soul mounts upwards from the base level of earthly life, not to become nothing in a final death, for it is now that it first truly begins to live; hitherto it has lain imprisoned in the body like the corpse in the grave.[73] It was death for the soul when it entered into life—now it is free and will no more suffer death; it lives for ever like God, for it comes from God and is itself divine. We do not know whether these theosophists went so far as to lose themsevles in detailed picturing and contemplation of the blissful heights of the divine life.[74] In the remains of their poems we read of stars and the moon as other worlds,[75] perhaps as the dwelling-place of illuminated spirits.[76] But perhaps also the poet allowed the soul to flee from its last contact with mortality without himself desiring to follow it into the unbroken radiance of divinity that no earthly eye can abide.

§ 5

This, then, is the keystone that completes the arch of Orphic religion—the belief in the divine, immortal, and abiding life of the soul for whom union with the body and its desires is a thwarting hindrance and repression—a punishment from which its one desire, as soon as it is awakened to a full knowledge of itself, is to escape in order that it may belong entirely to itself in full enjoyment of its powers. The contrast between these ideas and those of the Homeric world is complete; *there*, the soul released from the body was credited only with a poor, shadowy, half-conscious existence, so that an eternity of godlike being in the full enjoyment of life and its powers was only thinkable if the body and the soul, the twofold self of man, were translated in undissolved communion out of the world of mortality. The Orphic legends about the origin of the human race do not tell us the real source and derivation of the very different beliefs about the soul held by the Orphics; those legends only give expression to the way—and only one of many ways [77]—in which the already established confidence in the divinity of the soul was deducible from what might be considered the oldest historical story of mankind, and how it might be brought into connexion with the Orphic legend of the gods. This persuasion, the belief that a god was living in man and a god that could not be free until he had broken through the prison of the body, was deeply rooted in the worship of Dionysos and the ecstasies belonging to that worship; we cannot be in much doubt that it was taken over ready-made, together with the "enthusiastic" cult of the divinity, and further developed by the Orphic believers. We have already met with traces of this belief even in the Thracian home of the Dionysiac cult; and in what we know of the Thracian form of the religion, traces are not absolutely wanting of an ascetic tendency of living that would easily and naturally arise from such a belief.[78] Even in those Northern countries we found the belief in the transmigration of souls bound up with the religion of Dionysos, and that belief, when it is naïvely held, has as its essential presupposition the idea that the soul, in order to have a complete life, and one that can survive bodily death, must of necessity be united to another body. Even this idea is, however, quite foreign to Orphism. The Orphics retained, in spite of everything, the doctrine of transmigration, and combined it in a strange alliance with their own belief in the divinity of the soul and its vocation to a life of perfect liberty. It is evidently improbable that they invented that doctrine entirely on their own account; the first principles of their creed by no means led necessarily to it. Herodotos [79] asserts distinctly that the doctrine of transmigration came to the Greeks from Egypt; and as a consequence, that it was from Egyptian tradition that the Orphics received it. This assertion has no more to recommend it than any other of Herodotos' many pronouncements as to the Egyptian origin of Greek opinions and legends, and it is even less likely to mislead us in view of the fact that it is by no means certain and not even probable that a belief in transmigration ever really existed in Egypt.[80] This belief has arisen independently in many places on the surface of the earth, without the need of transmission from one place to another; [81] it might easily arise in a country where the belief prevailed that there existed only a limited number of souls of which each one—in order that no earthly body might be without its spiritual guest—must inhabit many perishable life-tenements, and not be bound to any one of them by a real inner necessity. This, however, is a conception common to popular psychology all over the world.[82] If it is still considered more probable that the idea of a migration of the soul through many temporary bodies was not spontaneously evolved by the Orphics, but was received by them from the hands of others, there is yet no reason to reject the most natural assumption—namely, that this also was one of the beliefs that the Orphics took over with the cult of Dionysos from Thrace. Like other mystics,[83] the Orphics took over the belief in transmigration from popular tradition and turned it into a serviceable member of their own body of doctrine.[84] It served them by giving a striking and physical expression to their own conception of the inevitable connexion between guilt and penance, pollution and the refining power of punishment, piety and future blessedness upon which all their religious ethic depended. It was with an exactly similar purpose that they also retained and developed the old Greek idea of a place of the souls in the depths below the earth.

But if they believed in the transmigration of souls, that belief did not with them hold the highest place. There is a realm where the ever free and divine souls have their being, a realm to which the series of lives in earthly bodies is only transitional, and the way to it was pointed out by the saving doctrine of the Orphic mysteries, by the purification and salvation afforded by Orphic asceticism.

NOTES TO CHAPTER X

[1] . . . ὅς ποτε καὶ τελετὰς μυστηρίδας εὕρετο Βάκχου, *AP.* vii, 9, 5 (Damagetos). διὸ καὶ τὰς ὑπὸ τοῦ Διονύσου γενομένας τελετὰς Ὀρφικὰς προσαγορευθῆναι, D.S. 3, 65, 6. εὗρε δὲ Ὀρφεὺς τὰ Διονύσου μυστήρια [Apollod.] 1, 3, 2, 3. (Dionysum) Iove et Luna (natum), cui sacra Orphica putantur confici: Cic., *ND.* iii, 58; cf. Lyd., *Mens.* 4, 51, p. 107 W. Βακχικά an Orphic poem: Suid. Ὀρφεύς (cf. Hiller, *Hermes*, 21, 364 f.), whence *fr.* 3 (Abel); and perhaps *frr.* 152, 167, 169, 168. τὰ Ὀρφικὰ καλούμενα καὶ τὰ Βακχικά are already reckoned as a single class by Hdt. ii, 81.

[2] This is seen in the decree of the Council and people of Athens dealing with the ἔμποροι Κιτιεῖς and their temple of "Aphrodite"—*CIA.* ii, 168 (333/2 B.C.).—That on the other hand such foreign mystery-cults were not always so tolerated (or not without resistance) is shown by the case of Ninos: Dem., *FL.* (19) 281 with Sch.; cf. D.H., *Dinarch.* 11.

[3] θεοὶ ξενικοί, Hsch., see Lob., *Agl.* 627 ff. A nameless θεὸς ξενικός occurs in *CIA.* i, 273 f., 18.—The foundation of such θίασοι for foreign deities (or deities at least not officially worshipped by the city in question) is almost invariably the work of foreigners (many exx. from Rhodos in *BCH.* 1889, p. 364). They are all foreigners, e.g. whose names occur in the decree of the θιασῶται of the Karian Zeus Labraundos, *CIA.* ii, 613 (298/7 B.C.); cf. ib. 614; *SIG.* 726. Merchants from Kition found a cult of their Aphrodite (Astarte) in Athens, just as some Egyptians had a little while before put up τὸ τῆς Ἴσιδος ἱερόν there: *CIA.* ii, 168. The names of foreigners (in addition to Athenians) are very numerous among the ὄνοματα τῶν ἐρανιστῶν of a *collegiun* of Σαβαζιασταί in the Peiraeus (second century B.C.): Ἐφ. Ἀρχ. 1883, p. 245 f. The foreign worship would then begin to receive the support of natives of the host-city (most of them being at first of the poorer classes), and in this way the new religion would gain a footing in its adopted home. (Pure Athenian citizens compose the society of the Dionysiastai in the Peiraeus, second century B.C., *Ath. Mitt.* ix, 288 = *CIA.* iv, 2, 623 d.)

[4] The Bendideia early became a state festival in Athens (even fifth century, *CIA.* i, 210, *fr.* K, p. 93). An allusion in Plato (*Rp.* 327 A), however, shows that the Thracians (who must have introduced the cult of Bendis into Athens, or at least into the Peiraeus, the home of most θίασοι) still kept up a special worship of their goddess in their own manner, side by side with the Hellenized cult. It appears at least as if the worship in its remodelled Greek form seemed to them no longer the right one. (Bendis, too, like Dionysos, is a divinity of both this world and the next: see Hsch. δίλογχον.)

[5] Alleged traces of Orphic influence on special sections of the Iliad (Διὸς ἀπάτη) or the Odyssey are entirely illusory, nor did the Orphic doctrines exert any influence on the Hesiodic *Theogony*. On the other hand, Orphism was itself strongly affected by the primitive Greek theology the fragments of which were put together in the Hesiodic poem.

[6] Ὀνομάκριτος . . . Διονύσῳ συνέθηκεν ὄργια, Paus. 8, 37, 5.

[7] Among the writers of Orphic poems mentioned by (1) Clem. Al., *Str.* 1, 21, p. 397 P. (from Epigenes) and (2) Suidas (from Epigenes and another authority : both Su. and Clem. probably got their information through the mediation of D.H.)—two certain Pythagoreans are named, Brotinos (of Kroton or Metapontum) and Kerkops (not the Milesian). [Abel, *Orphica*, p. 139.] From lower Italy or Sicily come : Zopyros of Herakleia (the same person is probably meant by Iamb., *VP.* 190, 5 N., when he counts Zopyros among the Pythagoreans coming from Tarentum), Orpheus of Kroton, Orpheus of Kamarina (Suid.), Timokles of Syracuse. Pythagoras himself is mentioned among the writers of Orphic poems in the *Τριαγμοί* of [Ion] (at least as early as the beginning of the fourth century). Apart from these the only names of conjectured composers of Orphic poems are : Theognetos *ὁ Θετταλός*, Prodikos of Samos, Herodikos of Perinthos, Persinos of Miletos ; all of whom are unknown to us except Persinos, whom Obrecht not improbably identifies with the court poet of Euboulos of Atarneus mentioned by Poll. ix, 93 (cf. Lob. 359 f. Bgk., *PLG.* iii, 655). In this case he is an Orphic of a much later period.

ὁμολογέουσι δὲ (sc. *Αἰγύπτιοι*) *ταῦτα* (prohibition to bury the dead in woollen clothing) *τοῖσι Ὀρφικοῖσι καλεομένοισι, καὶ Βακχικοῖσι, ἐοῦσι δὲ Αἰγυπτίοισι καὶ Πυθαγορείοισι*, Hdt. ii, 81. There can be no doubt that Hdt. in these words meant to derive the *Ὀρφικὰ καὶ Βακχικά* (the four datives are all neuters, not masc.) from the *Αἰγύπτια καὶ Πυθαγόρεια*, i.e. the Pythagorean ordinances which were themselves derived from Egypt (cf. Gomperz, *Sitzb. Wien. Ak.* 1886, p. 1032). If he had regarded the *Πυθαγόρεια* as entirely independent of the *Αἰγύπτια* (and the *Ὀρφικά* as independent of the Pythag.) he certainly could not have brought them in here. (This answers Zeller, *Ber. Berlin. Ak.* 1889, p. 994, who introduces a comma before *καὶ Πυθ.*)—It is equally impossible (with Maass, *Orpheus*, p. 165, 1895), to connect the *ἐοῦσι δὲ Αἰγυπτίοισι* with *Βακχικοῖσι only* ; it must of necessity go with *τοῖσι Ὀρφικοῖσι* as well ; for it is the whole point of Hdt.'s note to show that the religious usage which he mentions has, like so much else of the kind in Greece wherever it may be found, been borrowed from Egypt, and "is Egyptian". In this he would fail completely if he did not regard the *Ὀρφικά* (and hence also the *Πυθαγόρεια*) as *Αἰγύπτια ἐόντα* and clearly say so. Hdt. certainly has no idea, as Maass would have us believe, of making a generic distinction between *Ὀρφικά* and *Βακχικά* : *Βακχ.* is the name of the genus of which *Ὀρφ.* is the species.—"the *Ὀρφικά*, and the *Βακχικά* in general." Not *all* *Βακχικά* are *Ὀρφικά*. This use of *καὶ* whereby the whole is added subsequently to the part is perfectly regular and legitimate (it may also add the part to the whole as in the cases adduced by Maass, 166 n. : *τὰς Διονυσιακὰς καὶ τὰς Ὀρφικάς*, etc.). Hdt. mentions the *Πυθαγόρεια* last in order to indicate by what intermediate step the Egyptian element in the first-mentioned *Ὀρφικά* was specially assisted —he has further in ii, 123, shown clearly enough that he regarded Pythagoras as one of the pupils of the Egyptians (P. in any case is one of the teachers of immortality there referred to). This is also obvious from his whole attitude.—Hdt.'s opinion does not in any case oblige us to believe in it. He was forced to regard Pythagoras as the earliest author of Orphic doctrine because *his* connexion with Egypt seemed certain (cf. Hdt. ii, 123) while that of the *Ὀρφικοί* themselves was not so : in this way only could Hdt. seem to prove the Egyptian origin of that doctrine.—The priority of the Orphics is often supposed to be proved by the witness of Philolaos (*fr.* 14 D.) ap. Clem. Al., *Str.*

3, 3, p. 518 P. (and cf. Cic., *Hortens. fr.* 85 Or.); it must be admitted, however, that the passage does not prove what it is supposed to do.

[9] *Frr.* 143–51 (cf. Lob. 715 ff.). Here, indeed, Orphic and Pythagorean doctrine are mixed up inextricably. *Fr.* 143 (*Πυθαγορείως τε καὶ Ὀρφικῶς* Syrian.) belongs to the *εἰς τὸν ἀριθμὸν Πυθαγόρειος ὕμνος* which is several times distinctly so called by Proclus. (The *frr.* are in Nauck, Iamb., *VP.*, p. 228, *fr.* iii). *Fr.* 147 (Lyd. *Mens.*) obviously comes from the same (Nauck, p. 234, *fr.* ix). The same is at least highly probable of the *frr.* 144–6, 148–51. Probably what Orpheus says of the number 12 comes from the same *ὕμνος* (ap. Procl. *in Rp.* ii, 131, 10 Kroll). Proclus, however (*in Rp.* 169, 25 K.), also cites ll. 2–5 from the *ὕμνος* (Nauck, *fr.* iii) but this time attributes them to an *εἰς τὸν ἀριθμὸν Ὀρφικὸς ὕμνος*. This Orphico-Pythagorean *ὕμνος* had at any rate nothing to do with the (Rhaps.) Theogony of Orpheus. On the other hand, the words *τετράδα τετρακέρατον*, which acc. to Procl. *in Rp.* 169, 29 K., occurred *μυριάκις* in the *Ὀρφικὴ θεολογία*, come from the Theogony. They were possibly used as a title of Zagreus the *κερόεν βρέφος* (Nonn., *D.* vi, 165): though what is here said by Proclus about the *Διονυσιακὴ* (i.e. of Zagreus) *θεότης*, viz. that it *τετράς ἐστιν*, was applied rather to the four-eyed Orphic *Phanes* by Hermias (*fr.* 64 Ab.).

[10] On the other hand, there is much in Orphic theology and poetry that is taken immediately from the primitive Thracian worship of Dionysos and absent from Pythagorean teaching. This makes it very probable that even such *theologoumena* as are common to Orphism and Pythagoreanism really go back to the fanatical cult of Dionysos, or at least were easily thence derived by religious speculation: in this case the Orphics may well have got them from this original source of mystic lore that was common to both parties and not by the circuitous route of Pythagorean teaching. Orphism remained more closely attached to the common source than did Pythagoreanism, and may for that reason be regarded as somewhat older than its rival and be supposed to have originated independently of it.

[11] Zopyros of Herakleia, Orpheus of Kroton: Tz., *Prol. in Aristoph.* ([p. 20, 28 Kaibel, *Com. Fr.*] Ritschl, *Opusc.* i, 207); Suid. *Ὀρφ. Κροτωνιάτης* (from Asklepiades of Myrlea).

[12] We may not simply take it for granted that the account given in Dem. 18, 259–60, of the nocturnal initiations and the processions by day through the city held by a mystical sect, is intended to describe the secret mysteries of an *Orphic* conventicle (as Lob. does 646 ff., 652 ff., 695 f.). The explanation of the *ἀπομάττειν τῷ πηλῷ* of that passage by reference to the specially Orphic myth of Zagreus and the Titans is arbitrary in itself and hard to reconcile with the language of Demosth. (Harp. and Phot. are responsible for this expl.) Hardly more successful is the derivation of the call *ἄττης ὕης* from the *ἄτη* of Dionysos (Zagreus) on being torn to pieces by the Titans: *EM.* 163, 63. A definite connexion undoubtedly does exist between the *Ὀρφικὰ ὄργια* and the *Σαβάζια καὶ Μητρῷα* (Str. 471) described by Dem.; but the Orphics were never called worshippers of Sabazios nor their god *Σαβάζιος*, and it seems likely that their secret worship was different from the ceremonies of the *Σαβαζιασταί* that Dem. had in view (the latter may have retained more of the primitive barbaric ritual: cf. the ins. given in *Ἐφ. Ἀρχ.* 1883, p. 245 f. = *CIA.* iv, *Supp.* ii, n. 626 b; from the end of second century B.C.).

[13] See Lob., *Agl.* 235 f., 237, 242 f.

[14] To attribute the practical side of Orphism to a late degeneration

of the once purely speculative character of the sect (as many have done) is a very arbitrary proceeding and quite unjustifiable on historical grounds. The fact that a clear description of this activity does not occur before the fourth century (in Plato) does not prove that it did not exist earlier. Apart from this an ὀρφεοτελεστής named Philippos is mentioned by Plu., *Apoph. Lac.* 224 E as a contemporary of King Leotychidas II of Sparta (reigned 491–469). This evidence is not to be so easily set aside, as K. O. Müller, *Introd. Scient. Myth.* 311 ff., would like to do. The Orphic sect from the very beginning derived its strength from its *telestic* and *kathartic* practices.

[15] Thphr., *Ch.* 28 (16).

[16] αὐτοῦ (Ὀρφέως) μὲν εἶναι τὰ δόγματα, ταῦτα δέ φησιν (Aristot.) Ὀνομάκριτον ἐν ἔπεσι κατατεῖναι Arist. π. φιλοσοφίας *fr.* 10 [7] Rose, *Arist. Pseudepig.*

[17] Tatian, *Gr.* 41 (p. 42 Schw.), seems to speak only of *redaction* (συντετάχθαι) of the εἰς Ὀρφέα ἀναφερόμενα among already existing Orphic poems as the work of Onomakritos (in the same way Onomakr. is only the διαθέτης—the arranger not the author—of the χρησμοί of "Mousaios", Hdt. vii, 6). Traces of an external linking-together of the individual poems of Orpheus in a "redaction" are not wanting (cf. the linking-together of the poems of the Epic Cycle or of the corpus Hesiodeum); first of all coming in all probability the greater κρατήρ (as in the enumeration of Clem. Al., *Str.* i, 21, p. 397 P.); see Lob. 376, 417, 469.—Clem. Al., *Str.* i, p. 397 P. (and Eus., *PE.* 10, 11, p. 495 D) is only derived from Tatian, though Onomakr. is here definitely called the *author* of the εἰς Ὀρφέα φερόμενα ποιήματα. Onomakr. seems also to have been simply regarded as the author of the Ὀρφικά in the doxographical excerpt ap. S.E. *P.* iii, 30 = *M.* 9, 361, p. 287 Mutschm.; cf. Gal., *H. Philos.* (*Dox.*, p. 610, 15): Ὀνομάκριτος ἐν τοῖς Ὀρφικοῖς.—On the other hand, in the—admittedly incomplete—enumeration of Orphic poems in Clem. Al., *Str.* i, 21, p. 397 P., not *one* is attributed to Onomakr., and in Suid. Ὀρφεύς he is only given the χρησμοί (no confusion with the χρησμοί of Mousaios is to be suspected here) and the τελεταί. Paus. (8, 37, 5) mentions (without naming them) ἔπη of Onomakr. (cf. Ritschl, *Opusc.* i, 241). Some at least of the poetry going under the name of Orpheus must have been ascribed to Onomakr. by Arist. (*fr.* 10 [7 Teubn.]).

[18] Suid. Ὀρφεύς, 2721 A Gaisf.

[19] Onomakr. εἶναι τοὺς Τιτᾶνας τῷ Διονύσῳ τῶν παθημάτων ἐποίησεν αὐτουργούς, Paus. 8, 37, 5. Lob., p. 335, thinks this refers to the "Theogony": but no authority attributes a single one of the several Orphic Theogonies to Onomakr. as its real author. We should rather be inclined to think of the τελεταί which is distinctly ascribed to Onomakr. and which at least dealt with the practical side of worship: cf. Pl., *Rp.* 364 E–365 A, λύσεις, καθαρμοὶ ἀδικημάτων κτλ. ἃς δὴ τελετὰς καλοῦσιν (but it was not that the mystical βίβλοι were *called* τελεταί as Gruppe, *Gr. Culte u. Mythen*, i, 640, mistakenly supposes: he is otherwise quite right in his protest against Abel's treatment of the τελεταί). They must almost necessarily have dealt with the reproduction of the πάθη τοῦ Διονύσου (as providing the ἱερὸς λόγος to the δρώμενα), and, as the central idea of the orgiastic cult, must have included the most important circumstance of the Orphic τελεταί (see D.S. 5, 75, 4; Clem. Al., *Protr.* ii, 17, p. 15 P.).

[20] One of the poems (perhaps indeed the poem of the ῥαψῳδίαι, and in that case the ἱερὸς λόγος as well) made Orpheus distinctly appeal to a revelation made to him by Apollo: *fr.* 49 (see Lob. 469).

[21] Besides the three Theogonies distinguished by Damascius there were (apart from other more doubtful traces) at least two other variations of the same theme: see *fr.* 85 (Alex. Aphrod.) and *frr.* 37; 38 (Clem. Rom.); cf. Gruppe, i, 640 f.—The series of divine rulers given by "Orpheus" acc. to Nigid. Fig. ap. Serv. *Ecl.* iv, 10 (*fr.* 248 Ab.), conflicts with all the other Theogonies but agrees in some particulars with Lact. i, 13 (*fr.* 243). Still, this remark need not necessarily have been taken from any Orphic "Theogony".

[22] (Zeus) . . . *πρωτογόνοιο χανὸν μένος Ἠρικαπαίου, τῶν πάντων δέμας εἶχεν ἑῇ ἐνὶ γαστέρι κοίλῃ*, *fr.* 120 (from the Rhapsodiai). We are accustomed to read here *χανών* with Zoëga (*Abh.* 262 f.): but *χανών* does not mean "catching up or devouring" [Zo.]; at most it might mean, in bad late-Greek, just the opposite of this—"abandoning" (transitive). Lobeck's explanation (p. 519 n.) is also unsatisfactory. The word may have been originally *χαδών*.

[23] The line occurred in various forms in the Theogonic poem: *frr.* 33 (Plato ?); 46 ([Arist.] *de Mundo*); 123 (Rhapsod).; see Lob. 520–32. It seems certain then (Gruppe's doubts go too far: *Rhaps. Theog.* 704 ff.) that the line appeared in the oldest form of Orphic Theogony and was merely borrowed thence, like so much else that was ancient, by the Rhapsod. Theogony (i.e. the words, *Ζεὺς κεφαλὴ κτλ.* which would be the oldest form, as Gruppe rightly remarks: *κεφαλὴ* = *τελευτή*; cf. Pl., *Ti.* 69 B). Even the writer of the speech *against Aristogeiton A* ([Dem.] 25), an Orphic adherent, appears, as Lob. remarks, to allude to the words in § 8.

[24] *Theokrasia* must have belonged to Orphic theology from the outset: Lob. 614; though the most extreme examples of this may perhaps come from later poems: *frr.* 167; 169 (Macr.); 168 (D.S.); 201 (Rhaps.), etc., being probably derived from the "Little Krater" (*fr.* 160), in which Chrysippos seems to be imitated (Lob. 735 and *fr.* 164), and from the *Διαθῆκαι*, *fr.* 7 (J.M.) a forgery in Judaeo-Christian interests which nevertheless made use of many ancient pieces of Orphic literature (the *ἱερὸς λόγος*: Lob. 450 ff., 454).—Theokrasia is met with even in the orthodox poets of the fifth century, though they did not invent it; the "theologoi" of the sixth century Epimenides and Pherekydes were as familiar with it as were the Orphics; cf. Kern, *de Theogon.* 92.

[25] See Append. ix.

[26] It must have been chiefly the religious significance of the gods which caused the retention of their personalities and prevented them from fading into mere personifications of abstract ideas or elementary powers with which *religion* could have had nothing further to do.

[27] In the statements of the Neoplatonic writers this first Orphic Dionysos is regularly called *Διόνυσος* simply (perhaps also *Βάκχος*: *fr.* 192). Nonnus in recounting the Orphic legend calls him Zagreus: *D.* vi, 165; cf. *Ζαγρέα γειναμένη* (of Perseph.) with clear allusion to Callim. *fr.* 171, *υἷα Διώνυσον Ζαγρέα γειναμένη*. Callim. here, as elsewhere, seems to have in mind the *Orphic* story. Tz. on Lyc. 355 calls the god of the Orphic legend *Διόνυσον τὸν καὶ Ζαγρέα καλούμενον*. *Ζαγρεύς* the great Hunter is a name of the all-absorbing Hades: thus also the *Alkmaionis fr.* 3 Kink. Zagreus is identified with the Dionysos of nocturnal revelry in E., *Kret. fr.* 472, 10 (a reference in *Ba.* 1181 Kirchh.); and see above, chap. viii, n. 28. This Dionysos is regarded as a *χθόνιος* (see Hsch. *Ζαγρεύς*) and this must indubitably have been quite familiar to the poets who made him the son of Persephone: *χθόνιος ὁ τῆς Περσεφόνης Διόνυσος* (Harp. *λεύκη*).

They were as clearly conscious as was Herakleitos of the fact that ὡυτὸς Ἅιδης καὶ Διόνυσος, whereas this consciousness was undoubtedly obscured in the public ceremonial of Dionysos-worship (to which, however, Hcl.'s saying refers). Zagreus-Dionysos was never identified with the Ἴακχος of the Eleusinia (to which Orph. *fr.* 215, l. 2 refers) ; though Dionysos alone was often so identified.

[28] Ouranos casts the Titans into Tartaros : *frr.* 97, 100. Acc. to Procl. (*fr.* 205) and Arn. (196 : prob. not from the Rhaps.) we should be led to suppose that the Titans after they had torn Zagreus in pieces were cast down to Tartaros by *Zeus*. In Arn. this is set down side by side with the statement that the Titans were destroyed by the lightning of Zeus (ἡ Τιτάνων κεραύνωσις, Plu., *Es. Carn.* 1, 7, p. 996 C), though obviously incompatible with the latter statement, as it is also (even more so) with the origin of mankind from the ashes of the Titans which is known not only to Olympiodoros (*ad Phd.*, p. 68 Finckh : Lob. 566), but also to Proclus who got it from the " Rhapsodiai " (as also did Olymp.) : Procl., *in Rp.* ii, 74, 29 ; i, 93 Kroll. It seems from this that Proclus (and perhaps Arn.) in error ascribed the καταταρτάρωσις of the Titans to Zeus instead of to Ouranos.

[29] Nonn. vi, 173 ; O., *fr.* 195. Perhaps Proclus is right in explaining this doubling of the god's figure in the mirror as meaning his entrance upon the μεριστὴ δημιουργία. A reference to a similar explanation of this Διονύσου κάτοπτρον occurs even in Plot. 4, 3, 12 (Lob. 555)—? also in the strange statement made by Marsilius Ficinus as to the crudelissimum apud Orpheum Narcissi fatum (was Zagreus another Narcissus ?) *fr.* 315 ; cf. Plot. 1, 6, 8. The entry of the one origin of the universe into the multiplicity of phenomena is first clearly referred to in the dismemberment of Zagreus, but it would be quite like this symbol-loving poetry to introduce the same motif in a different form with a passing reference earlier in the poem.

[30] Nonn., *D.* vi, 197 ff.

[31] Paus. 8, 37, 5.

[32] Procl., O., *frr.* 195, 198, 199. In any case Nonn. vi, 169 ff. is following the Rhapsodiai.

[33] Callim. and Euphor. knew of the dismemberment of Dionysos by the Titans : Tz. ad *Lyc.* 208 (from the completer version in *EM.*). In any case it is not from the Rhaps. that this legend is also known to D.S. 5, 75, 4 ; Cornut. 30, p. 62, 10 Lang ; Plu., *Es. Carn.* 1, 7, p. 996 C ; *Is. et Os.* 35, p. 364 F ; Clem. Al. (see Orph. *frr.* 196, 200).—A roughly caricatured drawing on a hydria belonging to the early fourth century found at Rhodos and made probably in Attica appears in *JHS.* xi (1890), p. 243 ; where it is said to represent the dismemberment of Zagreus as conceived by Orphics. The picture, however, does not agree at all with the meaning thus attributed to it : the interpretation cannot be the right one.

[34] A true ἱερὸς λόγος, i.e. an account of the origin of ritual acts founded upon myth or legend. (The Orphics had such accounts, e.g. of the prohibition against being buried in woollen clothing : Hdt. ii, 81 fin.)

[35] That the tearing in pieces of the bull in the primitive Thracian manner occurred also in the Orphic ὄργια may perhaps be deduced from the fact that in the legend Orpheus himself is torn in pieces by the Mainads. The priest stands in the place of the god : what the god suffers in the ritual δρώμενα that the priest suffers too. This is frequently met with. Ὀρφεὺς ἅτε τῶν Διονύσου τελετῶν ἡγεμὼν γενόμενος τὰ ὅμοια παθεῖν λέγεται τῷ σφετέρῳ θεῷ, Procl. *in*

Rp. i, 175 Kr. The ancients were fully aware that the bull torn in pieces in the Bacchic orgies represented the god himself (and this not only in Orphic ritual but from the beginning in the Thracian worship): the idea is often expressed (see e.g. Firm. Mat., *Error. P.R.* vi, 5), but nowhere more clearly than in the Orphic ἱερὸς λόγος.

[36] The introduction of the Titans from Hellenic mythology into the Thracian myth is clearly described as the work of Onomakritos by Paus. 8, 37, 5.

[37] *Τιτῆνες κεκομῆται, ὑπέρβιον ἦτορ ἔχοντες, fr.* 102. *ἀμείλιχον ἦτορ ἔχοντες καὶ φύσιν ἐκνομίην, fr.* 97. As early as Hesiod the Titans are hated by their father as δεινότατοι παίδων (*Theog.* 155). Τιτανικὴ φύσις is the evil character that cannot keep an oath: Pl., *Lg.* 701 C; Cic., *Lg.* iii, 5; *impios Titanas*, Hor., *O.* 3, 4, 42.

[38] This explanation of the διαμελισμός of Zagreus is often put forward (though subtilized into a Neoplatonic sense) by those who use the Orphic Rhapsodiai: see Lob. 710 ff. But even Plutarch has something of the sort (*E ap. D.* 9, p. 389 A), and it cannot be doubted that this (apart from its Platonist wrappings) was the meaning of the legend in the mind of its first inventor. Nor can the conception that the separate existence (multiplicity) of things first came into the world by an act of *impiety*, have been strange to the *theologoi* of the sixth century: we must admit this at once on remembering the doctrine of Anaximander that the multiplicity of things which has arisen out of the original one ἄπειρον is in itself an ἀδικία for which it must pay "recompense and punishment" (*fr.* 2 Mull., 9 Diels). Such personification of the processes of nature and the reading of an ethical sense into them, combined as it was with a quietist tendency, was much more likely to have arisen in the fanciful minds of semi-philosophical mystics than to have been given to them by the philosophers.

[39] See the accounts given in Lob. 565 f.: they come from the Rhapsodiai. The fact that the origin of men and the doctrine of Metempsychosis as well were dealt with in the Rhaps. follows from Procl. *in Rp.* ii, 338 Kroll. It must, however, have been from *older* Orphic poetry—at any rate, not from the Rhaps.—that the story was derived by D. Chr. 30, 10 f. Plutarch, too, does at least refer to it: *τὸ ἐν ἡμῖν ἄλογον καὶ ἄτακτον καὶ βίαιον οἱ παλαιοὶ Τιτᾶνας ὠνόμασαν, Es. Carn.* 1, 7, p. 996 C; and possibly Opp., *H.* v, 9–10; Ael. *fr.* 89, p. 230, 19 f. Herch. (Lob. 567 g). Even the words of Xenokrates (*fr.* 20, p. 166 Heinze) seem to allude to this Orphic myth. Thus the Rhapsodiai in this case also were following older Orphic teaching and poetry. Orph. *H.* 37 derives from a later age. What Nic. *Th.* 8 ff. reproduces (mistakenly?) as Hesiodic tradition was perhaps really an echo of Orphic poetry. Was the derivation of Man from the Titans suggested by still earlier fancies such as e.g. meet us in passages like *h. Hom. Ap.* 335 (137) f.: Τιτῆνές τε θεοὶ τῶν ἔξ ἄνδρες τε θεοί τε—? This is not Homeric (for all the Homeric πατὴρ ἀνδρῶν τε θεῶν τε), though possibly it had a different sense from what it had for "Orpheus".

[40] Dionysos is the *last* of the divine rulers of the world: *frr.* 114, 190. Hence δεσπότης ἡμῶν, Procl. *in Crat.*, pp. 59, 114 Boiss. (though Procl. also speaks of e.g. Hermes as ὁ δεσπότης ὑμῶν *in Cr.*, p. 73 B.). Dionysos is the *sixth* ruler; Zeus who came before him being the fifth: *frr.* 113 (85, 121, 122). The order given is: 1 Phanes, 2 Nyx, 3 Ouranos, 4 Kronos, 5 Zeus, 6 Dionysos. This is definitely stated by Syrian.: *fr.* 85 (Proclus follows his master: *frr.* 85, 121), and confirmed by the fragments of the Rhapsodiai: *frr.* 86, 87, 96, 113. It seems, however, as if Plato actually found this order (as Syrian. thought)

in the Orphic Theogony which he read. It is true that as their silence shows the Neoplatonists did not find the verse cited by Plato in the Rhapsodiai as they knew them. (Plato's line is *ἕκτῃ δ' ἐν γενεῇ καταπαύσατε κόσμον ἀοιδῆς*: Plu., *E ap. D.* 15, p. 391 D, has the meaningless *θυμόν* instead of *κόσμον*—did he read *θεσμόν*?) They were right, however, in deducing from the line that the ancient Orphic Theogony referred to by Plato also knew of six generations of the gods (following the Pythagorean *τέλειος ἀριθμός*?) and ended with the sixth generation. The verse was intended doubtless by Plato himself in rather a different sense and he only quotes it humorously (Gruppe differs: *Rhaps. Theog.* 693 f.). This passage therefore provides important evidence of the harmony that existed between the Rhapsodiai and the oldest Orphic Theogony in the general outlines of their construction. It is, of course, quite a different question whether the six rulers in the poem referred to by Plato were the same as those given by the Rhaps.; nor can we tell whether Dionysos there occupied the last place, though the predominance held by Dionysos in Orphic belief makes it very probable that he did.

[41] The authorities who speak of the origin of mankind from the ashes (or the blood) of the Titans (Lob. 565 ff.) express themselves in such a way that we are forced to suppose that they regarded this as essentially the first appearance of men. This, however, cannot be reconciled with what Proclus, as usual following the Rhapsodiai, says of the golden and silver ages of mankind under Phanes and Kronos, which then, and not till then, are followed by the third and last race, *τὸ τιτανικὸν γένος*: see *fr.* 244 and esp. *in Rp.* ii, 74 Kr. *θνητοί* in the reign of Phanes even occurs in the line quoted by Syrian. (*in Ar. Meta.* 935a 22 Us.) *fr.* 85. It is impossible to say whether this improvement upon the Hesiodic legend of the Ages of Mankind actually occurred in an ancient Orphic Theogony (the one used perhaps by Lactant.: O., *fr.* 243, 8; cf. 248), and was thence taken for the Rhapsodiai without being reconciled with the legend of the origin of men from the ashes of the Titans; or whether the two scarcely reconcilable accounts of the origin of men were somehow or other made to agree. (*Fr.* 246 [Plu.] prob. comes from a picture of the long life enjoyed by the earliest generations of men: see Lob. 513. This picture does not necessarily presuppose a series of several *γενεαί before* the Titanic race.)

[42] *μέρος αὐτοῦ (τοῦ Διονύσου) ἐσμέν*, Olymp. (from Orphic doctrine) *in Pl. Phd.*, p. 3 Finckh. *ὁ ἐν ἡμῖν νοῦς Διονυσιακός ἐστιν καὶ ἄγαλμα ὄντως τοῦ Διονύσου*, Procl. *in Crat.*, p. 82 Boiss. The Hellenes are accustomed to make use of the dismemberment, re-integration and resuscitation of Dionysos *εἰς τὸν περὶ τῆς ψυχῆς λόγον ἀνάγειν καὶ τροπολογεῖν*, Orig., *Cels.* 4, 17, p. 21 Lo.

[43] *οἱ ἀμφὶ Ὀρφέα* think that the soul has the body as a *περίβολον, δεσμωτηρίου εἰκόνα*, Pl., *Crat.* 400 C. Certainly Orphic, too (as the Schol. also say), is *ὁ ἐν ἀπορρήτοις λεγόμενος λόγος ὡς ἔν τινι φρουρᾷ ἐσμεν οἱ ἄνθρωποι κτλ.*, Pl., *Phd.* 62 B; see Lob. 795 f.

[44] *fr.* 221 (*Phd.* 62 B with Sch.). The similar saying of Philolaos is, as Plato's manner of recording it shows (*Phd.* 61 E – 62 B) evidently derived from a saying of the Orphic *ἀπόρρητα* (and Philolaos himself appealed to the *παλαιοὶ θεολόγοι τε καὶ μάντιες* in confirmation of the closely connected doctrine of the enclosure of the *ψυχή* in the *σῆμα* of the *σῶμα*: *fr.* 23 Mull. 14 Di.). The doctrine continued to be taught by Pythagoreans: see Euxitheos Pyth. ap. Klearch. in Ath. iv, 157 CD; Cic., *Sen.* 73. It had moreover some root in popular belief and in legal usage: see above, chap. v, n. 33.

[45] According to the Ὀρφικὰ ἔπη καλούμενα, ap. Arist. *de An.* 1, 5, p. 410b, 28 ff.: τὴν ψυχὴν ἐκ τοῦ ὅλου εἰσιέναι ἀναπνεόντων φερομένην ὑπὸ τῶν ἀνέμων. (The ancient commentators add nothing fresh.) ἐκ τοῦ ὁλοῦ means simply "out of space". The ἄνεμοι were regarded as daimonic powers subordinate and related to the Τριτοπάτορες: see above, chap. v, n. 124. We cannot say how this conception was made to square with the other articles of Orphic belief (purgation of souls in Hades, etc.). It is plainly nothing but an attempt at such reconciliation that (following the Rhapsodiai, *fr.* 224) makes the souls that pass in death out of the bodies of *men*, go into Hades, while those that have inhabited the bodies of animals fly about in the wind εἰσόκεν αὐτὰς ἄλλο ἀφαρπάζῃ μίγδην ἀνέμοιο πνοῇσιν. Aristotle knows nothing of any such restriction. Plato (*Phd.* 81 D; rather differently 108 AB) apparently making free use of Orphic ideas regards *all* the μὴ καθαρῶς ἀπολυθεῖσαι ψυχαί as liable to the same fate as that allotted by the Rhapsodiai to the beasts. (Of course it is possible to suppose that the ψυχαί on being released from Hades for a new ἐνσωμάτωσις first of all fly about in the wind round the dwelling places of the living and are then breathed into a new body. This would not prevent there being a predestined conjunction of a particular soul with the particular σῶμα corresponding to its state of purification.)—The establishment in later Orphic poetry of the theory that the ψυχαί dwelt in the air may have been assisted by the philosophic theory of the soaring-up of the πνεύματα into their element the aether (of which more below). This theory, though not first put forward by the Stoics, was specially favoured by them: it almost attained the status of a popularly accepted belief. When the realm of the souls had thus been at least in part transferred to the air, late Orphic poetry began to regard one of the four rivers of the soul-world, Ἀχέρων, as the ἀήρ: *frr.* 155, 156 (Rhaps.). There is no reason to see in all this the traces of a supposed ancient conception in which Okeanos is really a river in the sky (in spite of Bergk's fanciful speculations in *Opusc.* ii, 691–6). The elevation of the soul-kingdom to the sky is in Greek thought invariably the result of comparatively late speculation. We might even ask whether there is not Egyptian influence at work in the transference of Okeanos (= the Milky Way?) to the sky. Such influence would be late of course; but in Egypt the idea of the Nile in the sky was quite familiar.

[46] κύκλος τῆς γενέσεως, *fr.* 226; ὁ τῆς μοίρας τροχός *rota fati et generationis*: see Lob. 797 ff.

[47] οἱ δ' αὐτοὶ πατέρες τε καὶ υἱέες ἐν μεγάροισιν (πολλάκις) ἠδ' ἄλοχοι σεμναὶ κεδναί τε θύγατρες . . . γίγνοντ' ἀλλήλων μεταμειβομένῃσι γενέθλαις, *frr.* 225, 222 (Rhaps.). Here, as Lob. 797 rightly remarks, there is an allusion to the dogma of the recurrence of exactly the same state of things in the world. The doctrine of complete παλιγγενεσία or ἀποκάτασις ἁπάντων (see Gataker ad. M. Ant.[1], p. 385) was closely and indeed indissolubly bound up with the doctrine of the migration of souls. (Illogicality belongs rather to the conception of the break in the circle caused by the secession of individual souls.) It was therefore found among the Pythagoreans to whom it is ascribed by Eudemos *fr.* 51 sp. (see Porph., *VP.* 19, p. 26, 23 ff. N.; used later still in a Pythagorean sense by Synes., *Aeg.* 2, 7, p. 62 f. Krab.). It was borrowed from the Pythagoreans by the Stoa (by Chrysippos esp.), which after its usual fashion pushed the rather bizarre fancy to pedantic extremes. (After the Stoic model is Plot. 5, 7, and perhaps also the *genethliaci* spoken of by Varro ap. Aug., *CD.* 22, 28.) It is at least

probable in the extreme that these ideas were first held by the Orphics and not borrowed by them from the Stoics: there are even traces in Orphic tradition of the great World-year (which is always closely connected with the ἀποκατάστασις τῶν ἁπάντων): Lob. 792 ff.

[48] κύκλου τε λῆξαι καὶ ἀναπνεῦσαι κακότητος were the words Proclus probably had before him: (*fr.* 226) *in Tim.* 330 B. The forms ἂν λήξαι καὶ ἀναπνεύσαι—thus rightly accented here by Schneider—come from Procl. himself, who accommodates the words of the original to the construction of his own sentence. We must therefore *not* write αὖ λῆξαι with Gale and Lob. 800. In this case the subject of the sentence is the praying soul; on the other hand, in the form preserved by Simp., κύκλου τ' ἀλλῦσαι καὶ ἀναψῦξαι κακότητος, the subject is the gods to whom the soul prays; ψυχή being object. In either form the freeing of the soul from the circle is regarded as a grace from the gods.

[49] *fr.* 76. The lines of the *Carm. Aur.* 55 ff. (Nauck, p. 207) are probably modelled on the Orphic οὔτ' ἀγαθοῦ παρεόντος κτλ. The point is: few are they who trouble about the salvation that Orpheus (or Pythagoras) brings them; the ὅσιοι are always a small minority.

[50] *frr.* 208, 226. Διόνυσος λυσεύς, λύσιος, θεοὶ λύσιοι; see Lob. 809 f. and cf. *fr.* 311 (Ficinus).

[51] 'Ορφέα τ' ἄνακτ' ἔχων βάκχευε . . . E., *Hp.* 953 (N.B. ἄναξ not δεσπότης, l. 88).

[52] 'Ορφικὸς βίος, Pl., *Lg.* 782 C; Lobeck, 244 ff.

[53] The Pythagorean ἕπου θεῷ, ἀκολουθεῖν τῷ θεῷ (Iamb., *VP.* 137, from Aristoxenos) might also have been given to the Orphics as their motto.

[54] ἄψυχος βορά of the Orphics: E., *Hp.* 952, Pl., *Lg.* 782 CD; Lob., p. 246. This, too, is the meaning of Ar., *Ra.* 1032, 'Ορφεὺς μὲν γὰρ τελετάς θ' ἡμῖν κατέδειξε φόνων τ' ἀπέχεσθαι, i.e. using slain animals for food. Hor., *AP.* 391 f.: silvestris homines . . . caedibus et victu foedo deterruit Orpheus means to speak not of the ritual vegetarianism of "Orpheus", but of the previous cannibalism of men which Orpheus had put an end to. As this is nowhere else mentioned of Orpheus we might perhaps regard it as mistaken allusion on the part of Horace to the passage of Aristoph. quoted above. It is not, however, impossible that Horace did in fact have in mind some Orphic verse which really reported something like what he himself says of Orpheus. The Orphic fragment [247] ap. S.E., *M.* ii, 31; ix, 15 (Lob., p. 246), may have arisen in the same way; see Maass, *Orpheus*, 77. (The well-known lines of Kritias [S.E., *M.* ix, 54 *fr.* 25 Di.] and Moschion, p. 813 Nauck, can hardly have anything to do with Orphism and should rather be connected with the theories of the Sophists and Demokritos—followed later by the Epicureans—about the gradual evolution of human civilization from miserable and savage origins; and *not* from a "golden age" of which the Orphics too spoke.)

[55] Prohibition to bury corpses in woollen garments: Hdt. ii, 81 (in each case in order that nothing θνησείδιον might cling to the departed). Prohibition against eating eggs: Lob. 251 (eggs are part of the offerings to the dead and the food of the χθόνιοι, and so forbidden: so rightly explained by Lob. 477). It was forbidden in Orphic poetry, as well as Pythagorean, to eat beans: Lob. 251; Nauck on Iamb., *VP.*, p. 231 f.: the reason here, too, being that beans as part of the offerings to the dead, *putantur ad mortuos pertinere* (Fest.); see Lob. 254 and Crusius, *Rh. Mus.* 39, 165. The same or similar reasons are everywhere at work to cause the eating of certain foods to be forbidden

both by the Pythagorean ordinances and in the mystical cult of the χθόνιοι: it is because they are used as offerings to the beings of the lower world, πρὸς τὰ περίδειπνα καὶ τὰς προκλήσεις τῶν νεκρῶν, or even because they have names which, like ἐρέβινθος or λάθυρος, recall ἔρεβος and λήθη: Plu., *QR*. 95, p. 286 E. The purified state requires above all complete separation from anything connected with the realm of the dead and the divinities of the dead.

[56] Cf. *fr*. 208.

[57] The soul is confined within the body (according to those ἀμφὶ Ορφέα), ὡς δίκην διδούσης τῆς ψυχῆς ὧν δὴ ἕνεκα δίδωσιν, Pl., *Crat*. 400 C. The exact nature of this "guilt" of the soul is not explained in our remains of Orphic literature. The point, however, is chiefly that the life within the body is according to their doctrine not in accordance with but contrary to the proper nature of the soul.

[58] συμπόσιον τῶν ὁσίων, Pl., *Rp*. 363 C. ὁσίους μύστας, Orph., *H*. 84, 3; see above, chap. vi, n. 18.

[59] ψυχὰς ἀθανάτας κατάγει Κυλλήνιος Ἑρμῆς γαίης ἐς κευθμῶνα πελώριον *fr*. 224 (it would be vain to look for an example of ἀθάνατος used as adjective to ψυχή in Homer). Hermes χθόνιος leads the souls down into Hades and also upwards again (to fresh ἐνσωματώσεις): Orph., *H*. 57, 6 ff. (For the Pythagorean Hermes see D.L. viii, 31.)

[60] Especially in the κατάβασις εἰς Ἅιδου (Lob. 373; cf. above, chap. vii, n. 3). The descent lay through the chasm at Tainaron: see above, chap. v, n. 23, and cf. Orph., *Arg*. 41.—Other Orphic poems may also have dealt with such matters: πολλὰ μεμυθολόγηται περὶ τῶν ἐν Ἅιδου πραγμάτων τῷ τῆς Καλλιόπης, Jul., *Or*. vii, p. 281, 3 Hertl. [216 D].

[61] λύσεις καὶ καθαρμοί of the living and even the dead carried out by Orphic priests: Pl., *Rp*. 364 E. Reward of the initiated in Hades: cf. the anecdote of Leotychidas II in Plu., *Apophth. Lac*., p. 224 E; and of Antisthenes in D.L. vi, 4. Those who feared the bite of Kerberos or the water-carrying to the leaky cask (see App. iii) sought protection against such things in τελεταὶ καὶ καθαρμοί: Plu., *N.P.Q. Suav. Epic*. 27, p. 1105 B. Hope of immortality for the soul rests on the *Dionysiac* mysteries acc. to Plu., *Cons. ad Ux*. 10, p. 611 D.

[62] It is significant that the belief in a judgment and punishment of ψυχαί is based in [Pl.] *Ep*. vii, 335 A not on popular acceptance or the statements of poets but on παλαιοί τε καὶ ἱεροὶ λόγοι; cf. above, chap. vii, n. 13.

[63] *fr*. 154 (punishment in Hades of those guilty of crimes against their own parents? *fr*. 281).

[64] See above, chap. vii, n. 15.

[65] δεινὰ περιμένει: Pl., *Rp*. 365 A; cf. *fr*. 314 (Ficinus).

[66] *fr*. 208 (Rhaps.) ὄργιά τ' ἐκτελέσουσι (ἄνθρωποι), λύσιν προγόνων ἀθεμίστων μαιόμενοι· σὺ (sc. Dionysos) δὲ τοῖσιν (dat. commodi), ἔχων κράτος, οὕς κ' ἐθέλησθα λύσεις ἔκ τε πόνων χαλεπῶν καὶ ἀπείρονος οἴστρου (of continual rebirth). That this belief in the efficacy of prayers for the "poor souls of the departed" belonged to the earlier stratum of Orphism follows from Pl., *Rp*. 364 BC, E, 365 A, where he speaks of λύσεις τε καὶ καθαρμοί of the Orphics which promised to deliver living *and dead* from the ἀδικήματα αὐτοῦ ἢ προγόνων. (It has been wrongly attempted to fasten the same belief on Plato himself, in the Phaedo.)—For Gnostic and early Christian ideas of the same kind see Anrich, *D. Ant. Mysterienwesen*, 87, 4; 120 n. But even in the Rigveda (7, 35, 4) we may find the thought that the "pious works of the pious" can help others to salvation (Oldenberg, *Rel. d.*

Veda, 289). Religious pietism seems to produce the same effects everywhere.

[67] πολλοὶ μὲν ναρθηκοφόροι κτλ. was an *Orphic* verse. Lob. 809, 813.

[68] *fr.* 154.

[69] ὁ κεκαθαρμένος τε καὶ τετελεσμένος ἐκεῖσε (εἰς Ἅιδου) ἀφικόμενος μετὰ θεῶν οἰκήσει, *fr.* 228 (Pl.).

[70] συμπόσιον τῶν ὁσίων in Hades, μέθη αἰώνιος their reward: Pl., *Rp.* 336 CD (cf. Dieterich, *Nekyia*, 80 n.). Plato there mentions Mousaios and his son (Eumolpos) as authorities for these promises and contrasts with them, by a οἱ δέ, others who made different promises; perhaps referring to other Orphic poems (cf. *fr.* 227). But Mousaios, himself always closely connected in Plato with Orpheus (*Rp.* 364 E, *Prot.* 316 D, *Ap.* 41 A, *Ion*, 536 B), here simply means "Orphic poetry". A literature of essentially Orphic character went under his name. So Plu., *Comp. Cim. et Luc.* 1 seems right in substituting simply τὸν Ὀρφέα for the Μουσαῖος named in Pl.

[71] Pl., *Lg.* 870 DE; then in more detail for a special case but derived from same source: νόμῳ . . . τῷ νῦν δή (i.e. in 870 DE) λεχθέντι 872 DE, 873 A.—The idea of such a religio-juridical *talio* was popular also in Greece: see below (chap. xi, n. 44). Frequently for instance in curses of vengeance the wish is that the doer may suffer exactly the same thing as that which he has done to his victim. Exx. from Soph. (best is *Tr.* 1039 f.) given by G. Wolff in S., *Aias*, 839; cf. A., *Cho.* 309 ff., *Ag.* 1430.—As a Neoplatonic idea: Plot. 3, 2, 13; Porph. and Iamb. ap. Aen. Gaz., *Theophr.*, p. 18 B.

[72] We may, however, suppose that the ideas of the Orphics corresponded with the statements of Empedokles, Plato, etc., about the series of births.

[73] σῶμα—σῆμα is Orphic: Pl., *Crat.* 400 C.

[74] Complete escape from the world of birth and death is distinctly anticipated for the pious Orphic in *fr.* 226, κύκλου τε λῆξαι κτλ. The other and positive side completing this negative promise is not clearly supplied for us by any fragment. (We never even hear distinctly of the return of the individual soul to the one Soul of the World; though certain Orphic myths—probably of late origin—seem to suggest such a doctrine of Emanation and final Remanation.)

[75] *frr.* 1, 81. The moon was regarded as inhabited, like the world, by Pythagoreans too (esp. Philolaos) and also by Anaxagoras.

[76] This at least was the belief of Pythagoreans and later of Platonics: see *Griech. Roman*, 269; Wyttenb. on Eun. *VS.* 117. But the idea occurs as early as in the *Ti.* of Plato, esp. in 42 B. It may have been long familiar to Greek popular belief (as to other peoples; cf. Tylor, ii, 70), and reached Orphics from that source. (Similar though not quite the same is the popular belief ὡς ἀστέρες γιγνόμεθ' ὅταν τις ἀποθάνῃ, Ar., *Pa.* 833 f., which the Greeks shared with all the nations of the earth: cf. "Pythagoras" ap. *Comm. Bern. in Lucan*, 9, 9.)—No opinion can be built upon the statement of Ficinus (*fr.* 321).

[77] Orphic poetry must have varied in its account of what happened to the dismembered limbs of Zagreus-Dionysos. That the Titans tore the god limb from limb seems to have been common to all versions of the Theogonic poem (see nn. 28, 41; p. 341). But whereas according to one account the Titans then devoured the god (except the heart) and from the mixed Titanic and Dionysiac elements of their bodies after they had been destroyed by lightning the race of men had its origin (p. 341); according to others the mangled limbs

of the god were brought by Zeus to Apollo who buried them taking them "on to Parnasos", i.e. at Delphi: see Orph. *fr.* 200 (Clem. Al.) and so, too, Callim. *fr.* 374. The Rhapsodiai gave the first version in detail, but also preserved an account resembling the second (see *frr.* 203, 204: the *ἐνίζειν τὰ μερισθέντα τοῦ Διονύσου μέλη* there refers probably to the reunion of the collected limbs for the purpose of burial and not for the restoration of the dead god to life. This is also possibly the meaning of the *Διονύσου μελῶν κολλήσεις* in Jul., *Chr.*, p. 167, 7 Neum. But Or., *Cels.* 4, 17, p. 21 Lom., speaks of the *reanimation* of Dionysos *συντιθεμένου* after the dismemberment). This second account, where it occurs alone, of course excludes the *Anthropogony* from the Titans' ashes. The second version unmistakably connects itself with the Delphic legend of the grave of Dionysos at the foot of Apollo's tripod (see above, pp. 97 f.) as K. O. Müller observed, *Introd. Scient. Myth.* 242. It does, in fact, accord in this instance, but apart from this it has no connexion whatever with the real Delphic legend about the disappearance of Dionysos into the underworld and his periodic return to this world. (See above, chap. viii, n. 28. The Orphic and Delphic legends are elaborately compared and worked in together as though they were separate fragments of a single whole in Lübbert's book, *de Pindaro theologiae Orph. censore*: Ind. Sch. Bonn. Lib. 1888, p. xiii f.—with shocking results and no intrinsic justification.) Whether this second version was the one put forward by Onomakritos is uncertain. In any case, both accounts are much older than the Rhapsodiai, in which, it appears, they were included side by side and superficially harmonized (—only the limbs of the god *not* devoured by the Titans being buried acc. to this version). Besides these two versions there may have been another *Anthropogony* differing from that given in the first account: the existence of something of the kind is perhaps to be deduced from what the Rhapsodiai themselves have to tell about the golden and silver generations of mankind (see above, n. 41).

[78] Of the Thracian Mysoi *λέγει ὁ Ποσειδώνιος καὶ ἐμψύχων ἀπέχεσθαι* (which Pythagoras is said to have learnt from Zalmoxis, Str. 298) *κατ' εὐσέβειαν, διὰ δὲ τοῦτο καὶ θρεμμάτων· μέλιτι δὲ χρῆσθαι καὶ γάλακτι καὶ τυρῷ, ζῶντας καθ' ἡσυχίαν· διὰ δὲ τοῦτο καλεῖσθαι θεοσεβεῖς τε καὶ καπνοβάτας* (perh. *καπνοβότας* acc. to an ancient conjecture). *εἶναι δέ τινας τῶν Θρᾳκῶν οἳ χωρὶς γυναικὸς ζῶσιν, οὓς κτίστας καλεῖσθαι, ἀνιερῶσθαί τε διὰ τιμὴν καὶ μετ' ἀδείας ζῆν*, Str. 296. The *religious* character of this asceticism is seen in the words *κατ' εὐσέβειαν* and the name *θεοσεβεῖς*; also in the word *ἀνιερῶσθαι*, which are all used of the *κτίσται* as of a monastic order. Jos., *AJ*. 18, 1, 5, says of the Essenes *ζῶσι δ' οὐδὲν παρηλλαγμένως ἀλλ' ὅτι μάλιστα ἐμφέροντες Δακῶν* (i.e. *Θρᾳκῶν, Γετῶν*: *Getae, Daci Romanis dicti*, Plin., *NH*. iv, 80) *τοῖς πολισταῖς καλουμένοις*. In any case the same Thracian ascetics are meant whom Poseidonios (literally translating a Thracian word) calls the *κτίσται*. Thus, they are said like the Essenes to live without women, eat no meat, and in the practice of various other asceticisms live together and have all things in common.—It cannot be certainly decided how old this Thracian asceticism was, its exact connexion with Dionysiac religion, and whether it could or did give any impulse in the direction of asceticism to the Orphics. (Following Hom., *N* 4 ff., many told similar stories of the nomadic Skythoi: see Ephor., *frr.* 76, 78; or of the fabulous Argimpaioi, Hdt. iv, 23; Znb., *Pr.* 5, 25, p. 129, 1, etc. *Griech. Roman*, 203.—*ἀποχὴ ἐμψύχων* occurred also among the Atlantes and certain Indian races: Hdt. iv, 184; iii, 100.)

[79] ii, 123. His words make it plain that the *Greek* teachers of transmigration of souls whom he has in mind (Pherekydes, Pythagoras, Orphics, Empedokles) had no idea of the Egyptian origin of that doctrine (*Rh. Mus.* 26, 556, 1).

[80] The Egyptian monuments show no knowledge of a general transmigration of souls, due to a law of nature or the decree of the gods. We can see very well, however, what it was in Egyptian traditions that might seem like a doctrine of transmigration to Herodotos (cf. Wiedemann, *Erlaüt. zu Herodots 2. B.* p. 457 f.).

[81] It is sufficient to refer to Tylor's collections: ii, 3 ff.—In antiquity the Greeks met with a doctrine of Transmigration, apart from Thrace, among the Keltic races (Caes., *BG.* 6, 14, 5; D.S. 5, 28, 6; cf. Timagenes ap. Amm. Marc. 15, 9, 8). This was the sole reason why Pythagoras was made the pupil of the Gallic Druids: Alex. Polyh. ap. Clem. Al., *Str.* i, p. 355/6 P., etc.

[82] That it was not unnatural for the Greeks also to have the conception of the migration of the soul from its first body to some other suitable second or third body (entry of τῆς τυχούσης ψυχῆς εἰς τὸ τυχὸν σῶμα acc. to Arist.) may be seen from the fact that in Greek popular tales of the transformation of men into beasts the idea regularly prevails that while the body changes in such cases the "soul" remains the same as before. Thus, explicitly in Hom. κ 240 (cf. Sch. there and 329); cf. also Ov., *M.* ii, 485; Nonn., *D.* v, 322 f.; Aesop., *F.* 294 (Halm); [Luc.] *Asin.* 13, 15 init.; Apul., *M.* iii, 26 init.; Aug., *CD.* 18, 18, p. 278, 11 ff. Domb., etc. (In all transformation stories this is regularly implied and gives the point to the story.) This is true from the earliest times onward, down to Voltaire's muleteer who was turned into a mule et du vilain l'âme terrestre et crasse à peine vit qu'elle eut changé de place.)—The beasts also have a ψυχή: e.g. ξ 426.

[83] Brahmins, Buddhists, Manichaean, etc.

[84] A fixed term for "transmigration of souls" does not seem to have been offered by Orphic teaching. It was later called παλιγγενεσία (a term which did not exactly fit the real meaning of the idea): this seems to have been its oldest name (cf. αἱ ψυχαὶ πάλιν γίγνονται ἐκ τῶν τεθνεώτων, Pl., *Phd.* 70 C), and remained its most ceremonious one. "*Pythagoras*" *non* μετεμψύχωσιν *sed* παλιγγενεσίαν *esse dicit*: Serv., *A.* iii, 68. μετενσωμάτωσις is not uncommon (frequent in Hippol., *RH.*, p. 12, 53 D.-S.; 266, etc.). The word most commonly used among ourselves, μετεμψύχωσις, is among the Greeks precisely the least usual; it occurs e.g. in D.S. 10, 6, 1; Gal. iv, 763 K.; Tertul., *de An.* 31; Serv., *A.* vi, 532; 603; Suid. s.v. Φερεκύδης. μετεμψυχοῦσθαι occurs in Sch., A.R. i, 645.

CHAPTER XI

The Philosophers

The Orphic teaching, in which a protracted movement of religion in Greece reached comprehensive expression, might seem almost an anachronism, appearing as it did in an age when a religious interpretation of the world and of mankind was hardly any longer admissible. Eastwards, on the coasts of Ionia, a new view of the world had arisen which, like a youth that has come of age, demanded the right to pursue its course without any guidance from traditional beliefs. The Ionic maritime cities were the meeting-place of all the collected wisdom and experience of mankind; and there all the more serious knowledge and study—both indigenous and of foreign origin—of "Nature", the earth, and the heavenly bodies, was gathered together in the intelligence of those ever-memorable spirits who at that time were laying the foundations of natural science, and of all science in general. This knowledge was now attempting to turn itself into an organized and all-embracing whole. Observation and constructive study combined with an imaginative vision to hazard a picture of the world and reality as a whole. Because it was impossible anywhere in this world to find anything completely and for ever fixed and dead, speculation inevitably pressed forward to the discovery of the undying source of Life, that perpetually fills, moves, and rebuilds this whole, and of the laws according to which it works and necessarily must work.

This was the direction pursued by these earliest pioneers of philosophy; and they pursued it unhampered by any subservience to mythical or religious modes of thought. Where mythology and the theology founded upon it saw a complete history of cosmic events each one of which was the result of the separate and unique action of divine personalities endowed with consciousness and the power of arbitrary choice—there the philosopher saw the play of everlasting forces which could not be completely resolved into the single events of any historical process, for, without beginning or end they had been ever in action, tirelessly fulfilling themselves in accordance with unchanging laws. In such a universe there seemed to be little room left for divine figures created by man after his own image, and worshipped by him as the guiding and supreme powers of the world. And in fact, the foundations were now laid of that tremendous structure of free inquiry, which finally succeeded in weaving out of its treasure new worlds of thought, where even those who had quarrelled or were dissatisfied with the old religion (now inwardly falling into decay for all its outward appearance of being at the most brilliant zenith of its powers) might yet find a refuge if they would not fall back upon sheer nothingness.

And yet Greece never saw a thorough-going opposition and conscious quarrel between science and religion. In a few special cases the religion of the state was forced to recognize its incompatibility with the openly expressed opinions of individual philosophers, and took steps to make its claims to universal supremacy respected. But for the most part, the two streams of influence flowed on side by side for centuries without ever coming into hostile contact. The propagandist temper was completely absent from philosophy from the very beginning. (Even when it appeared later as among the Cynics it produced very little effect on the supremacy of the state religion.) Religion on its side was not represented by any priestly caste which might have been led to take up arms for religion and for what it believed to be its own interest alike. Theoretic contradictions might the more easily remain unobserved when religion depended so little upon fixed dogma or upon a world-embracing whole of opinions and doctrines; while Theology, wherever it accompanied the worship of the gods (εὐσέβεια), which was the real core of religion, was, just as much as philosophy, the business of individuals and their adherents gathered together outside the limits of the official religion of the state. Philosophy (except in a few special and unrepresentative cases) never sought open war with religion—not even with the weakened and diluted religion of the masses. In fact the juxtaposition of philosophy and religion (with theology itself by their side) sometimes went beyond the external conditions of the time, and affected the private intellectual life of certain thinkers. It might seem as if religion and philosophy were not merely different but dealt with different provinces of reality, and thus even strict and philosophically minded thinkers could honestly and without imagining disloyalty to philosophy, adopt particular and even fundamental conceptions from the creed of their fathers, and allow them to grow up side by side and at peace with their own purely philosophical ideas.

§ 2

What the Ionic philosophers in connexion with the rest of their cosmology had to say about the soul of man did not for all its striking novelty bring them into direct conflict with religious opinion. Philosophy and religion used the same words to denote totally different things; it could surprise no one if different things were said about quite different objects.

According to the popular view, which finds expression in Homer, and with which, in spite of their very different estimate of the relative values of body and soul, the religious theory of the Orphics and other *theologi* also agreed—according to this view the "psyche" was regarded as a unique creature of combined spiritual and material nature that, wherever it may have come from, now dwells within man and there, as his second self, carries on its separate existence, making itself felt when the visible self loses consciousness in dream, swoon, or ecstasy (see above, pp. 6 f.). In the same way, the moon and the stars become visible when no longer obscured by the brighter light of the sun. It was already implied in the conception itself that this double of mankind, which could be detached from him temporarily, had a separate existence of its own; it was no very great step from this to the idea that in death, which is simply the permanent separation of the visible man from the invisible, the latter did not perish, but only then became free and able to live by and for itself.

This spiritual being and the obscure manifestations of its existence in the living man, did not attract the observation of the Ionian philosophers. Their thoughts were all for the universe as a whole; they looked for the "origins" (ἀρχαί) of all that is and becomes; for the simple elements of multifarious appearance and for the force which turns the simple into the multifarious while controlling, moving, and giving life to primeval matter. The power of life, the force which can set in motion both itself and all else that without it would be fixed and motionless—this force penetrates all being; where it manifests itself most strikingly in separate individual beings, there it is what these philosophers call the "psyche".

Thought of in this way, the psyche is something quite different from the old psyche of popular belief, idly observing the life and activities of its body, as of some stranger, concentrated in itself, and pursuing its own secret, hidden life. And yet the name given to these very different concepts remained the same. The application of the word "psyche" to the power which gives life and movement to the visible body—man's power of life—might have been suggested to the philosophers by a manner of expression which, though in the strict sense of the words conflicting with Homeric conceptions, is occasionally observable in the Homeric poems, and seems to have become more and more frequent in late times.[1] In more exact language, the " psyche " of these philosophers is a collective expression for all the powers of thought, desire, and will (νόος, μένος, μῆτις, βουλή), and especially for the functions denoted by the untranslatable word θυμός—powers which according to the Homeric and popular partition all belong entirely to the side of the visible man and his body.[2] According to that view, they are all expressions of the body's natural powers of life—though they cannot indeed be awakened to real life before the arrival of the " psyche "—and in Homeric usage are almost the exact opposite of the " psyche ", for they perish at death, while the psyche leaves them behind to wander about in its separate shadow-life.

But the soul, according to the view of the physiologists, has quite a different relation to the totality of life and living, and differs in this respect both from the Homeric psyche and the Homeric θυμός. The same force which manifests itself so strongly, as though specially concentrated there, in the psyche of man, works and rules in all matter as the general source of life that creates and preserves the world. Thus, the psyche loses the special singularity that distinguished it from all the other things and substances in the world, and made it incomparable and unique. Later reporters are wrong in attributing to these Ionic thinkers (for whom vital power and material substance seemed immediately and indissolubly united) the conception of a separate, independent " World-Soul ". Not as emanations from a single Soul of the World did they conceive the separate souls of men ; but neither did they conceive them as simply independent, unique, and entirely incomparable essences. They are expressions of that force which everywhere in all the phenomena of the world produces life and is itself *life*. Attributing spiritual qualities to the primeval source of things, the physiology of the " Hylozoists " naturally could not assume any profound distinction between that source and the " soul ". Deprived in this way of its separateness, the soul acquired a new importance in exchange ; in another sense from that of the mystics and theologians it could still be thought of as something divine, for it was a participator in the one Force which builds and rules the world. It is not the abode of a single daimonic nature, but instead, the very nature of god is alive within it.

The closer its inward connexion with the universal Whole the less, of course, will the soul be able to preserve its individual existence, which was only lent to it while it gave life and movement to the body, when that body, the sign and support of its separateness, is overtaken by death. These earliest philosophers whose view was almost entirely concentrated on the broad outlines of the life of nature as a whole, would hardly have regarded it as part of their task to formulate a deliberate opinion about the fate of the puny individual soul after the death of its body. In no case could they have spoken of an *immortality* of the soul in the same sense as did the mystics who regarded the soul of which they spoke as something which has entered from without into material existence, and as a spiritual essence quite distinct from everything material. The latter were thus able to attribute to the psyche a capacity for separate and continued existence which was inadmissible in the case of a force of movement and sensation completely inhering in matter and in the shaping of matter. And it was such a force which the physiologists called the soul.

Ancient tradition, nevertheless, asserts that Thales of Miletos, whose genius first began the philosophic study of nature, was the first " to call the soul (of man) immortal ".[3] But Thales, who recognized a " soul " also in magnets and plants,[4] and thought of the material stuff and the motive force of the " soul " as inseparable, can only have spoken of the " immortality " of the human soul in the same sense as he might have spoken of the immortality of all " soul-forces " in nature. Like the primal Matter which works and creates by reason of its own natural powers of life, so, too, the universal Force which permeates it [5] is imperishable and indestructible, as it is uncreated. It is entirely and essentially alive and can never be " dead ".

Anaximander said of the " Unlimited " from which all things have been developed by separation, and by which all things are enveloped and directed, that it never grows old, but is immortal and imperishable.[6] This cannot be intended to apply to the human soul as a separate existence ; for like all separate creations out of the " Unlimited " it must " in the order of the time " pay the penalty for the " offence " of its separate existence,[7] and lose itself again in the one primordial matter.

Nor could the third in this series—Anaximenes of Miletos—have differed seriously from Thales in the sense in which he spoke of the soul as " immortal " ; for him it was of the same nature [8] as the one divine [9] primal element of Air that is eternally in movement and produces all things out of itself.

§ 3

In the teaching of Herakleitos of Ephesos the living power of the primal essence—the one [10] and universal, out of which arises through change the many and the particular, which manifests itself in the union, regarded as indissoluble, of matter and motive force—received even greater prominence than with the older Ionians. By them matter itself—described as either limited or not limited in reference to one particular quality—is regarded as self-evidently in motion. For Herakleitos the origin of all multiplicity lies rather in the creative energy of absolute Life itself which is at the same time a definite material substance or analogous to one of the known substances. The idea of *life*, and that form of it which makes its appearance in man, must have been more important for him than for any of his predecessors.

This never-resting force and activity of becoming that has neither beginning nor end, is represented by the Hot and Dry and called by the name of that elementary condition which cannot be thought of as ceasing to move, namely, Fire. The ever-living (ἀείζωον) fire, which periodically kindles itself and periodically goes out (Bywater, *fr.* 20), is formed entirely of movement and livingness. Living belongs to everything ; but living is becoming, changing, becoming something different without cessation. Every appearance brings forth from itself, at the moment of its appearance, the opposite of itself. Birth, life, and death, and fresh birth clash together in a single burning moment, like the lightning (*fr.* 28).

That which thus moves itself in unceasing vitality and has all its being in becoming ; which perpetually changes and " in backward-straining effort " finds itself again—this is something endowed with reason, creative in accordance with reason and " art " ; is Reason (λόγος) itself. In creating the world it loses itself in the elements ; it suffers its " death " (*frr.* 66, 67) when in the " Way downwards " it becomes water and earth (*fr.* 21). There are degrees of value in the elements decided by the relation which they hold towards the moving and self-vivifying fire. But that which in the multiplicity of the phenomena in the world, yet preserves its godlike fiery nature—this is for Herakleitos " psyche ". Psyche is fire.[11] Fire and psyche are interchangeable terms.[12] And so, too, the psyche of man is fire, a part of the universal fiery energy that surrounds it and upholds it, through the "inhalation" of which it maintains itself alive;[13] a portion of the World-Reason by participation in which it is itself rational. In men God is living.[14] But god does not descend into man, as in the teaching of the Theologians, entering as a finite individuality into the vessel of the individual human life. As a united whole he surrounds men with his flood and reaches after and into them, as though with fiery tongues. A portion[15] of his universal Wisdom is living in the soul of man; the "drier", more fiery, nearer to the universal Fire and further from the less living elements he is, the wiser will he be (*frr.* 74, 75, 76). If he sundered himself from the universal wisdom, man would become nothing; it is his business in thinking, as in acting and in moral behaviour, to surrender himself to the One Living essence that "nourishes" him and is the Mind and Law of the world (*frr.* 91, 92, 100, 103).

But the soul itself is also a portion of the universal Fire that in the perpetual variation of its form of being has been encompassed by the body and become entangled in corporeality. Here we no longer have the rigid, unmediated contrast between "Body" and "Soul" such as it appeared from the standpoint of the theologian. The elements of the body, water and earth, have themselves arisen and perpetually arise out of the fire which changes into all other things, and into which everything else changes (*fr.* 22). So it is the soul itself, the creative fire, which *creates* the body. "Soul," i.e. Fire, unceasingly turns itself into the lower elements; there is no contrast between them, and it is but a continual flux of transition.

While it is enclosed in the body the soul is still affected by unceasing change. In this it is like everything else. Nothing in the world can for a single moment preserve the parts which compose it unaltered; the perpetual movement and alteration of its being constitute its life. The sun itself, the greatest fire-body, becomes another sun every day (*fr.* 32). So, too, the soul, though distinct from the body and a self-existing substance, yet is a substance that never remains like itself. In unceasing alteration of its material substance, its contents are perpetually being transposed. It loses its fire of life in the lower elements; it absorbs fresh fire from the living Fire of the universe that surrounds it. There can be no question of the permanent identity of the soul, of the spiritual personality, with itself. What in the unbroken process of upward and downward straining seems to maintain itself as a single person, is in reality a series of souls and personalities, one taking the place of another and ousting and being ousted in turn.

Thus, even while it is in life, the soul is perpetually dying—but to live again ; ever supplementing the departing soul-life or supplying its place with another. So long as it can recruit itself from the surrounding World-Fire, so long the individual lives. Separation from the source of all life, the living and universal fire of the world, would be death for it. The soul may temporarily lose its life-giving contact with the " common world " : this happens in sleep and dreaming which enclose it in their own world (*frr.* 94, 95), and this is already a partial death to it. Sometimes, too, the soul has a tendency to transform itself to a humidity not always made good by fresh fire ; the drunkard has a " moist soul " (*fr.* 73). Finally, there comes the moment when the soul of man cannot any longer repair the loss of the living fire which is taken from it in the perpetual alteration of its matter. Then it dies ; death carries off the last of the series of living fires which in their continuity made up the human soul.[16]

But in Herakleitos' world there is no such thing as death in the absolute sense—an end followed by no beginning, an unconditional cessation of becoming. " Death " is for him only a point where one condition of things gives way to another ; a relative " not-being ", involving death for one but simultaneously bringing birth and life for another (*frr.* 25, [64], 66, 67). Death, just as much as life, is for him a positive thing. " Fire lives the death of earth, and air lives the death of fire ; water lives the death of air, and earth the death of water " (*fr.* 25). The One that is in all things is at once dead and alive (*fr.* 78), immortal and mortal (*fr.* 67) ; a perpetual " death and becoming " agitates it. So, too, the " death " of man must be the exit from one positive state of things, and the entry into another, also positive, condition. Death occurs for man when the " soul " is no longer within him. Only the body is then left ; alone and by itself it is no better than dung (*fr.* 85). But the soul—what becomes of that ? It must have altered ; it was fire, but now it has descended on the " Way downwards " and become water—to become earth after that. So it must happen to all fire. In death the fire in man " goes out " (*fr.* 77). " It is death for the souls to become water " says Herakleitos clearly enough (*fr.* 68).[17] The soul must tread this path at last, and treads it willingly ; change is for the soul its delight and refreshment (*fr.* 83). The soul has then changed itself into the elements of the body, has lost itself in the body.

But it cannot rest permanently in this transformation. "For the souls it is death to become water; for the water it is death to become earth. And yet from earth comes water; and from water, soul" (*fr.* 68). Thus, in the restless up and down of becoming, in the "Way upwards" the soul reconstitutes itself out of the lower elements. But not *that* soul which had formerly animated the particular individual and of whose complete self-identity in the midst of the influx of the Fire-spirit there could be no question even during the life of the body. The inquiry after an individual immortality or even a continued existence of the separate soul could hardly have had any meaning at all for Herakleitos. Nor can he have admitted it under the form of the "transmigration of the soul".[18] It is quite certain that Herakleitos can never have distinctly asserted the changeless persistence of the individual human soul in the midst of the unbroken stream of becoming in which all fixity is nothing but an illusion of the senses. But it is also incredible that, in despite of his own fundamental principles, he even admitted the possibility of this popular view with an indulgence quite foreign to his nature.[19] What could have tempted him to do so? We are told [20] that it was from the mysteries that he adopted this opinion which was one of their most important doctrines. Herakleitos, however, only casts an occasional glance at the mysteries and what might be called their "doctrine" (just as he glanced at other prominent manifestations of the excited religious life of his time [21]); and he does so in order to harmonize their teaching with his own—a result which he achieves rather by imposing an interpretation than by patiently eliciting one. He demonstrates that the mysteries might be harmonized with his own doctrine,[22] which seemed to him able to explain all the phenomena of the world; that contrariwise he ever sought to set his own teaching in harmony with that of the mysteries, or that the latter had shown him the way to his thought, or could ever have tempted him to set foot outside his own self-chosen path—of this there is not a scrap of evidence to be had.

The individual in its isolation has, for Herakleitos, neither value nor importance: to persist in this isolation (if it had been possible) would have seemed to him a crime.[23] The Fire is for him indestructible and immortal as a totality, not as divided into individual particles, but only as the one Universal Mind that transforms itself into all things and draws all things back again into itself. The soul of man has a claim to immortality only as an emanation of this universal Reason, and shares the immortality which belongs to it. So, too, the soul, even when it has lost itself in the elements, finds itself again. Between "want" and "satisfaction" (*frr.* 24, 36), this process of becoming has its perpetual being. A day will come when the Fire will "overtake" everything (*fr.* 26); God will then be utterly by himself—all in all. But that is not the purpose of this world; here change, becoming and passing away will never end. Nor should they end; the "Strife" (*fr.* 43) which has created the world, and ever fashions it anew, is the most inward nature of the All-living which it perpetually stirs to insatiable desire of becoming. For the desire and refreshment of all things is Change (*frr.* 72, 83), the coming and going in the interplay of Becoming.

It is the precise opposite of a quietistic mood that speaks from the whole teaching of Herakleitos. His voice is a trumpet call that grows louder and louder as his lofty and majestic spirit with ever-increasing intensity proclaims prophet-like the last word of wisdom. He knows well that it is only labour that can give meaning to rest, and hunger to satisfaction; only sickness can call forth the desire of health (*fr.* 104). That is the law of the world which binds together the opposing contraries, each of which is engendered from the last, with an inward and complete necessity. He bows before it and assents to it. For him the fixity of the soul in a Blessedness that was without activity and without change—even if such were thinkable [24]—would not have seemed a possible goal of desire.

§ 4

Even before the days of Herakleitos the torch of philosophic inquiry had been borne from the coasts of Ionia to the West by Xenophanes of Kolophon who in a life of adventure had wandered as far as Southern Italy and Sicily. For his fiery temperament the most subtle reflection was turned into life and experience, and the one enduring source of Being to which he ever directed his gaze became the universal Divinity that is all perception and thought, that tirelessly embraces all things in its thought and intelligence, and, without beginning or end, perpetually remains the same with itself. What Xenophanes had to say about this God which for him is the same as the world, became the basis for the elaborated doctrine of the Eleatic school which, in declared opposition to Herakleitos,[25] denied all possibility of movement, becoming, alteration, division of the One into Many, to the one absolute Being that completely and entirely occupies Space, is raised above all development, whether temporal or spatial, and remains perpetually enclosed in itself in absolute self-sufficiency.

For this view the whole multiplicity of things that presses itself upon sense-perception is an *illusion*. Deceptive also is the apparent existence of a multiplicity of animated beings, just as the whole of nature is an illusion. It was not "Nature", the content of actual experience, that provided the starting-point of the philosophy of Parmenides. Without any assistance from experience, simply by the pure logical deductions to be made from a single fundamental concept (that of "Being"), which was to be grasped only by the understanding, this philosophy claimed to arrive at the whole content of its teaching. For the philosophic scientists of Ionia the soul also had been a part of nature and the science of the soul a department of the science of nature; and this inclusion of the psychical within the physical was the peculiarity in their doctrine of the soul which distinguished it from the ordinary popular psychology. When, however, the whole of Nature was to be ruled out of account as a subject of scientific knowledge, the derivation of psychology from physiology had to be given up as well. These *aphysici* [26] were logically debarred from holding any doctrine of the soul.

With a complaisance that is remarkable in view of the uncompromising logical vigour with which they deduced their main theory and based it on abstract, super-sensual knowledge, the Eleatics conceded so much at least to the region of appearance and the pressure of sense-perception that, although they did not deduce from their own fundamental conceptions a physical theory of multifarious appearance and its development, yet, side by side with their rigid doctrine of being, in unjustified and unjustifiable relation with it, they did in fact put forward such a theory. Xenophanes, himself, had already in the same way offered a physical theory of limited and relative validity. Parmenides in the second part of his doctrinal poem, developed, "in deceptive adornment of words," not an authoritative statement of the true nature of being, but "human opinions" of becoming and creation in the world of multiplicity. This, too, must be the standpoint of the physiological doctrines put forward by Zeno of Elea, the boldest dialectician who upheld the doctrine of the motionless All-One. In the course of such a physiology, and with the same implied reservations, the Eleatic philosophers dealt also with the nature and origin of the soul. Their physical doctrine was framed entirely on the lines of the older type of natural philosophy, and they regarded the relation of the spiritual to the corporeal from exactly the same point of view as their predecessors had done. For Parmenides (146 ff. Mull. = *fr.* 16 Diels) the mind (νόος) of man depends for its existence upon the mixture of two ingredients of which everything, including its body, is composed. These ingredients are the " Light " and the " Night " (the Warm and the Cold, Fire and Earth). What is intellectually active is, even in mankind, the " nature of his limbs " ; the character of his thought is determined by the one of the two elements which preponderates in the individual. Even the dead man (because he still has a body) has feeling and sensation : but these powers are deserted by the warm and the fiery and given over to the cold, the dark, and silence. All that is has some capacity of knowledge.[27]—It would be impossible to condemn the " soul " to corporeality more completely than is here done by the bold philosopher of abstract Reason, who at the same time denied so unconditionally all validity to sense-perception. The soul is evidently no longer an independent substance but a mere resultant of material mixture, a function of elements in composition. For Zeno, too, the " soul " in the same way was an exactly equal mixture of the four elementary properties of matter, the Warm, the Cold, the Dry, and the Wet.[28]

It is, therefore, startling, in the face of these utterances, to find that Parmenides also said about the " soul " that the deity that rules the world " at one time, sends it out of the Invisible into the Visible, and at another time back again ".[29] Here, the soul is no longer a condition arising from the mixture of material elements, but an independent being credited with pre-existence before its entry into the " Visible ", i.e. before its entry into the life of the body, and also with a continued existence after its separation from the realm of visibility—and indeed, with a sojourn, several times repeated, in those two worlds. Did Parmenides distinguish between this independently existing soul and the being that perceives in the mixture of the elements and as mind (νόος) thinks, but whose existence is bound up with the elements and the body they together compose ? It is obvious at any rate that in what he says of the psyche, and its alternate life in the visible and the invisible, Parmenides is not speaking as a physiologist, but as an adherent of the Orphic-Pythagorean theosophy. While reserving for himself his knowledge of " Truth " and unalterable Being, he could select as he liked among the " opinions of men " when speaking only hypothetically. In his doctrine as a practical teacher with an ethical purpose in view he preferred to adopt the conceptions of the Pythagoreans with whom he lived in close association.[30]

§ 5

Ionic physiology had fixed its attention on Nature as a whole, and on the phenomena of life displayed in every nook and corner of the universe; man, as a mere ripple on the surface of the ocean of becoming and taking form, was almost entirely neglected. A philosophy that made it its main effort to learn the nature of man, and, still further, with the knowledge so acquired, to show man the way and purpose of his living, had to try other paths.

This is what Pythagoras of Samos did. What he called his "Philosophy"[31] was in essence a practical effort. Plato[32] tells us that Pythagoras was so peculiarly honoured because he discovered a special mode of directing one's life. A distinct way of living, formed on a religious and ethical basis, was his creation. How far his "polymathy",[33] which indubitably contained already the substance of Pythagorean science, may have become a system in his hands, is not distinctly known. What is certain is that in Kroton he formed a society which, together with the strict rules in accordance with which he organized their manner of life for his associates, eventually spread far and wide among the Achæan and Dorian cities of the Italian "great Greece". In this society a profound conception of human life and its purposes was given practical and visible application, and to have brought this about must be regarded as the act and the special service of Pythagoras. The fundamental conception of this way of life, except in so far as it may have contained from the beginning a mystic philosophy of numbers, was by no means the special invention of Pythagoras; the new and potent feature which he introduced was the force of personality which was able to give life and body to the ideal. What was apparently lacking in similar movements in ancient Greece was now provided by a great man who for his followers was a pattern and an example, a leader inspiring imitation and emulation. His personality became a centre to which a whole community was attracted by a sort of inward necessity. Before very long this founder of a community appeared to his followers as a superman, unique and incomparable among all other men. Some lines of Empedokles,[34] who did not himself belong to the Pythagorean society, bear witness to this fact, and to his followers Pythagoras became in memory a saint or even a god in human form, and they related legends of the miracles he had performed. For us it is difficult to form a connected picture or trace the real features of the man beneath the dazzling halo of the saint.

The teaching which enabled him to knit together his followers in a far closer bond of fellowship in living than had been achieved by any Orphic sect, must still in the main have coincided with what in the Orphic doctrine immediately related to the religious life. He too pointed out the way of salvation for the soul and his doctrine of the soul formed the central feature of his philosophy.

So far as our scanty and dubious evidence serves us, the substance of the Pythagorean doctrine of the soul may be stated as follows.

The soul of man, once more regarded entirely as the " double " of the visible body and its powers, is a daimonic immortal being [35] that has been cast down from divine heights and for a punishment is confined within the " custody " of the body.[36] It has no real relationship with the body ; it is not what may be called the personality of the individual visible man : any soul may dwell in any body.[37] When death separates it from the body the soul must first endure a period of purgation in Hades [38] and then return again to the upper world. The souls invisibly swarm about the living ; [39] in the tremulous motion of motes in the sunbeam the Pythagoreans saw the movement of the " souls ".[40] The whole air is full of souls.[41] Upon earth, however, the soul must seek out another body, and this may be repeated many times. So it wanders a long way, passing through many bodies of men and beasts.[42] Very ancient tradition [43] said that Pythagoras himself remembered the earlier incarnations through which his soul had passed (and of which he gave information for the instruction and warning of the faithful). Here, too, the doctrine of the soul's transmigrations took on an edificatory character in a religious and ethical sense. The conditions of the new incarnations and the character of the new lifetime are governed by the performances of the past life. What the soul has done in the past, that it must suffer in its own person when it becomes a man again.[44]

It is thus of primary importance both for the present life and for future incarnations to know and to follow the methods of salvation delivered by Pythagoras to his followers. The society points out the way to its company of the faithful in purifications and initiations, in a " Pythagorean life " [45] entirely organized with the same purpose in view—to " follow the god ".[46] Much of the old ritual symbolism that had been in use for ages must have been incorporated in this Pythagorean asceticism.[47] The theological ethic of asceticism was essentially negative in character, and here, too, it meant nothing more than a protecting of the soul against the attacks of external evil that might come and pollute it.[48] All that matters is to keep the soul pure: no need for moral reformation—only that it be kept free from external evil. The fact of immortality, the soul's perpetuity, stands fast and unalterable; as it was from the beginning so it must ever be and live.[49] To lift it at last altogether from this earthly existence and restore it to a free divine state of being—that, at least, was the final goal.[50]

The practical philosophy of the Pythagorean school is founded upon a conception of the soul as absolutely distinct from "nature", and, in fact, opposed to it. It is thrust into the life of nature, but it is in a foreign world where it preserves its self-enclosed individuality intact and from which it escapes into independence to undergo ever-renewed incarnations. Its origin is supra-mundane, and so, too, when liberated from the shackles of natural life it will one day be enabled to return to a supernatural existence as a spirit.

Not one of these ideas is achieved by a process of scientific thinking. Physiology, the science of the world and all the phenomena of the world could never lead to the conception of the soul's separateness from nature and its life. It was not from Greek science, but neither was it, as ancient tradition would have us believe, from foreign lands, that Pythagoras got his belief in the fallen nature of the soul, descended from supra-mundane heights to this earthly nature, and in its long pilgrimage through many bodies on the completion of which it is to be free at last, through purifications and initiations. He may have owed much to his travels; from his stay in Egypt, perhaps, he may (like Demokritos after him) have derived the stimulus to his mathematical discoveries and much else besides of the "learning" which Herakleitos ascribes to him. His doctrine of the soul, on the other hand, simply reproduces in essentials the fanciful ideas of the old popular psychology, as it had been enlarged and transformed by the *theologi* and the purification priests. Tradition was right in its estimation of his character, when it set him in this company and made him the pupil of Pherekydes of Syros, the *theologos*.[51]

It can hardly be doubted that Pythagoras himself laid the foundations of the Pythagorean science—the doctrine of the creation of the world and perhaps, too, the interpretation of all being and becoming in the world as due to the action and relation of numbers, as the essential basis of all things—all this, at least in elementary outline, must have been handed on by him to his followers. After his death the two sides of his doctrine continued to develop for a period in loose conjunction side by side; the guidance of life by the mystical and religious philosophy (though this, indeed, was hardly capable of further development), and the scientific interest which grew into a fairly elaborate system. Indeed, with the break-up of the Pythagorean society and its bifurcation in the fifth century, the scattered members of the band now brought into touch with the scientific studies of other communities and cut off from the ideal of the Pythagorean life which could only be realized within the limits of the society, were forced to continue their scientific studies in solitude. Pythagorean science, evolving, as it did, a picture of the world as a whole, no less than Ionian physiology deprived the soul of the unique and, indeed, antagonistic relation to nature that Pythagorean theology had given it. Philolaos, conceiving it in a manner strictly conforming to the mathematical and musical theory, called the soul a *Harmony* of contrary elements united together in the body.[52] If, however, the soul is only a binding-together of opposites to unity and harmony, then it must, when death breaks up the conjunction of the united elements, itself pass away and perish.[53] It is difficult to imagine how the older Pythagorean faith in the soul as an independent being dwelling in the body and surviving it—in the immortal soul, in fact—could be accommodated to this conception. Can it be that the two conceptions were not originally intended to be brought into conjunction at all, or were not meant to exclude each other? Ancient tradition spoke of different groups among the followers of Pythagoras who had also different objects, methods, and aims of study; nor shall we be inclined to deny all credibility to this tradition when we observe how little, in fact, Pythagorean science and Pythagorean faith had to do with each other.[54]

And yet we have to admit that the same Philolaos, who described the soul as a harmony of its body, also spoke of the soul as an independent and imperishable being. We may well doubt whether these two contradictory utterances can really come from the same man and apply to the same object; though the same man might really speak in varying language about the one soul if he recognized different *parts* of the soul of which different truths held good; and this was, in fact, first suggested by the Pythagorean school.[55]

§ 6

Empedokles of Akragas did not belong to the Pythagorean school (it lost its external unity in his time); but he approaches Pythagorean doctrine so closely in his opinions and teaching about the soul of man, its problems and destinies, that there can be no doubt about Pythagorean influence upon the formation of his convictions on these points. His many-sided activities also included the study of natural science and he took up the researches of the Ionic Physiologists with zeal and a marked aptitude for the observation and synthesis of natural phenomena. But the roots of his peculiar individuality—the *pathos* which moved and agitated him—lay in a practical activity far removed from scientific investigation and representing a brilliant resuscitation in a very different age of the character and practice of the *mantis*, the purification-priest and magical-physician of the sixth century. The introduction to his "Purifications"[56] gives a picture of his triumphal progress from city to city, crowned with ribbons and garlands, adored as a god and questioned by thousands: "Where is the road to healing?" He intends to give his disciple Pausanias the results of his own experience and to teach him all his remedies for disease and their virtues, the arts of stilling the winds and stirring them up, producing drought or rain, raising the dead from Hades.[57] He himself boasted of being a magician and his pupil Gorgias saw him "do magic".[58] Through him those efforts of the *Kathartes*, the expiation-priest and seer, which an earlier and already distant-seeming time had honoured as the highest form of wisdom, at last achieved a voice and literary expression—an expression given them with the fullest personal experience of the truth of their claims by one who was convinced of their power to control nature and sure of the godlike status of the man who had reached these almost superhuman heights of empire over nature. As a god, an immortal no longer subject to death, he passed through all the land—so Empedokles himself tells us.[59] He may have won credit in many places. He did not, indeed, found an ordered society of disciples and adherents, a sect: this does not seem to have been his intention. But he alone as a unique and unparalleled being, a self-confident personality of the greatest force and weight impressed himself masterfully both as mystic and politician upon the mundane affairs of his contemporaries and pointed the way beyond time and all things temporal to a blessed and divine state as the final goal of human life. He must have made a profound impression upon the men among whom he lived,[60] though he disappeared from their midst like a comet, and left no permanent traces of his presence behind him. Many legends still witness to the astonishment that his appearance among men provoked, more especially those legends that in varying form related his end.[61] They are all expressions of the same belief: that he, as his own verses had foretold, in his departure did not have to suffer death; he had vanished, "translated" body and soul together to an everlasting divine life, as once Menelaos had been and so many great figures of the ancient days, and even a few Heroes of more recent times.[62] Once more the ancient conception shows in this story that it still lives on: immortal life can only be obtained by undissolved union of the psyche with its body. Such a legend hardly did justice to Empedokles' own idea. When he claimed to be a god who would never die he certainly did not mean that his psyche would remain for ever bound to his body. On the contrary, he thought that in "death", as men [63] call it, it would be freed from this last corporeal envelope [64] and never again have to enter into a body, but would live for ever in freedom and divinity. His conception of the conscious after-life of the psyche was as different as it was possible for it to be from the Homeric conception on which that translation legend was based.

Empedokles united in his own person to an astonishing degree the most sober attempts at a study of nature that was scientific according to its lights, and quite irrational beliefs and theological speculations. Occasionally the scientific impulse passes over to influence even the world of his beliefs; [65] but as a rule theology and natural science exist side by side in his mind quite independently. As a physiologist he inherited the already extensive and variously developed stock of ideas belonging to the older generations of inquirers and thinkers. He himself was able to unite conceptions derived from the most different sources into an original whole that satisfied himself at least. Becoming and passing-away, all qualitative change, were denied by him as by the Eleatics, but the permanent substance of Being is for him no single indivisible unity. There are four "roots" of things, the four bodies of elements, which in this division are for the first time clearly distinguished. It is the mixture and separation of the essentially indivisible elements that cause the appearance of becoming and perishing; and those two processes are caused by the two forces—clearly distinguished from the elements—of attraction and repulsion,

Love and Hate, which in the creative process struggle and in turn overmaster each other until at last, in the final victory of one of the two forces, all things are either united or divided; in either case an organic world ceases to exist. The present state of the universe is one in which "Love", the tendency to amalgamation of differences, is prevailing; when this tendency is completed, there will be an absolute levelling-out of all distinction; a result which Empedokles, a quietist in his scientific studies as well, regards as the most desirable end.

In this world, then, that experiences only mechanical movement and change, and from whose evolution Empedokles by an ingenious turn is able to exclude all idea of purpose, there are also to be found souls; or rather psychical powers which grow up entirely within it. Sense-perception is expressly distinguished from the capacity of thought by Empedokles.[66] The former takes place when each of the elements, from the mixture of which the perceiving being has its origin, comes into contact with, and so becomes aware of, the same elements in the object perceived, through the "passages" that connect the interior of the body with the exterior.[67] "Thinking" has its seat in the heart's blood, where the elements and their powers are mixed most equally. Or rather this blood actually *is* thinking and the power of thought; [68] the material substance and its vital functions thus also for Empedokles completely coincide. Plainly, nothing in the nature of a permanent substantial "soul" is here intended by the thinking-power of the "mind", but rather a capacity of bringing together and unifying the individual sense-activities; [69] a capacity no less than the individual powers of sensation bound up with the elements, the senses, and the body.[70] With the varying constitution of the body, they too vary.[71] Both capacities, that of sense-perception, and that of thought, as vital expressions of the matter that is combined together in the organic creature, are present in all organisms; in men, in beasts, and even in plants.[72]

If we give the name of "soul" [73] to the sum of these psychical powers—a name generally reserved for the common permanent substratum of the changing psychical activities—we cannot avoid concluding, in accordance with the logic of this philosopher, that the "soul" must be perishable. With the death and destruction of the individual the elementary parts that go to compose him are disunited, and the soul which in this case is nothing but the highest resultant of that composition, must itself disappear with their dissolution—as it had come into being with their union.[74]

It might seem as if Empedokles himself was as far as possible removed from drawing such conclusions from his own premises. No one speaks more distinctly and forcibly of the spiritual, individual beings that dwell in men and in other creatures of nature as well. They are regarded by him as Daimones fallen to the corporeal world, who have to pass through many different forms of life till they may at last hope for release.

In the introduction to his poem on Nature, he describes, from his own experience, and the information of the Daimones who had once led his soul down to this earthly Vale of Grief,[75] how by an ancient decree of the gods and the compulsion of Necessity, every daimon that has "polluted" itself by drinking the blood or eating the flesh of living beings,[76] or has broken its oath,[77] is banished for a long period [78] from the company of the blessed. It is thrust down to the "Meadow of Disaster", into the realm of contradiction,[79] the cave of misery upon this earth, and must now wander through many "painful ways of life" [80] in changing incarnations. "Thus, I myself was once a boy and also a maiden, a bush, a bird, and a voiceless fish in the salty flood" (ll. 11, 12=*fr.* 117). This daimon that in expiation of its crime must wander through the forms of men, beasts, and even plants, is evidently no other than what popular speech and that of theologians as well called the "psyche", the soul-spirit.[81] In all essentials though perhaps in clearer language, Empedokles merely repeated [82] what the adherents of the doctrine of Transmigration had long told of its divine origin, its fall and penal banishment in earthly bodies. So, too, when as teacher of the means that bring salvation, he tells how more gracious forms and conditions of life may be obtained in the series of births, till at last complete release from rebirth is achieved [83] Empedokles follows in the footsteps of the purification-priests and *theologi* of old. It is a matter of keeping the daimon within us free from the pollutions that bind it fast to the earthly life. To this end the methods of religious purification are most efficacious; Empedokles respects them quite as much as did the old *Kathartai*. It is necessary to keep the internal daimon far removed from every kind of "sin",[84] more particularly from the drinking of blood and the eating of meat which must necessarily involve the murder of kinsmen daimones which are dwelling in the slaughtered beasts.[85] By purification and asceticism (which here again dispenses with a positive form of morality aimed at reforming the man) a gradual process to purer and better births is achieved; [86] in the end the persons thus reborn in a purified condition become seers, poets, doctors, and are the leaders of mankind.[87] Finally, when they have emerged superior even to these highest steps of earthly life, they return to the other immortals, and become themselves gods released from human misery, escaping death, and now indestructible.[88] Empedokles regards himself as one who has reached the last stage,[89] and points out to others the way up to it.

Between what Empedokles the mystic here tells us of the soul that was once living its divine life, but has since been plunged into the world of the elements, though it is not for ever bound to them ; and what Empedokles the physiologist teaches of the psychical powers that dwell in the elements and are bound to the body that is composed of the elements and perish with their dissolution, there seems to be a hopeless contradiction. And yet if we are to grasp the whole truth of what Empedokles means, we must neither leave on one side half of what he says,[90] nor yet by well-meaning interpretation seek to bring the philosopher into harmony with himself,[91] when he clearly speaks with two different voices. The two voices say different things, and yet in the mind of Empedokles, there is no contradiction in what they say, for they are dealing with totally distinct objects. The psychical powers and faculties of feeling and perception which are functions of matter, born in matter, and determined by it, together with the thinking faculty that is no other than the heart's blood of men—these neither make up the character and content of that soul-spirit which dwells in men, beasts, and flowers, nor are they expressions of its activity. They are entirely bound up with the elements and their combination, and in man they are joined to the body and its organs ; they are the powers and faculties of this body, and not of a special and invisible entity, the soul. The soul-daimon is not made out of the elements, nor is it for ever chained to them. It enters as a stranger into this world in which the only permanent component parts are [92] the four elements, and the two forces of Love and Hate ; and it enters it from another world, the world of gods and spirits, to its detriment ; the elements cast it about from one to another " and they all hate it " (*fr.* 115, 12, l. 35 M.). This living soul, with its independent existence, that thus enters into foreign and hostile surroundings, only enters into such earthly creatures as already possess senses, feeling and perception, together with reason or the faculty of thinking, the crowning manifestation of their material union. It is, however, as little identical with these psychical faculties as it is with the mixture of elementary matter or, in the case of men, with the heart's blood. It exists, unmixed and incapable of mixture, *alongside* the body and its faculties which indeed only have life—" what men call life "—(*fr.* 15, 2, l. 117 M.) when united with it. When they are separated from it they fall into dissolution ; not so the soul, which continues its journey and visits other dwelling places, and does not share in their dissolution.

This peculiar dualistic doctrine reflects the two sides of Empedokles' own mental activity. He probably intended in this way to unite the views of both the physiologists and the theologians. To the Greeks, such a twofold division of the inner life may have seemed less surprising than it does to us. The conception of a " soul " that as an independent, unique, and self-contained spiritual being dwells within the body, while the body does not receive its intellectual faculties of perceiving, feeling, willing and thinking from the soul, but exercises these by its own power—this conception agrees at bottom with the ideas of popular psychology that are as a rule described or implied in the Homeric poems.[93] The only difference is that these ideas of poet and populace are elaborated and defined by the speculations of theologians and philosophers. How deeply impressed upon the Greek mind such conceptions, derived eventually from Homer, actually were, can be measured by the fact that a conception of the twofold origin of psychic activity, its twofold nature and sphere of action, closely related to that of Empedokles, is continually recurring in more advanced stages of philosophy. It occurs not merely in Plato, but even in Aristotle, who in addition to the " soul " that directs and expresses itself in the physico-organic nature of man, recognizes another being of divine descent that enters into man "from without", the "mind" (νοῦς) which is separable both from the soul and from the body, and is alone destined to survive the death of the man to which it was assigned.[94] In the doctrine of Empedokles, too, it is a stranger-guest from the distant land of gods that enters into man to give him a soul. This being is indeed far below the " mind " of Aristotle in philosophic importance ; nevertheless, in the introduction of this Stranger into the world composed of the elements and vital faculties, a sense of the absolute uniqueness of spirit, its unlikeness to everything material, its essential distinctness from matter, finds expression, if only in a limited theological fashion.

In the light of such theological considerations, the soul seems also to Empedokles something essentially distinct from its prototype, the Homeric psyche, which after its separation from the body passes to the twilight of a shadowy dream-life. To him, the soul is of divine race, too noble for this world of visibility, and only when it escapes from this world does it seem to him to begin its real and full life. Though confined within the body, it has its separate existence there ; it has no concern with the everyday business of perception and sensation —not even with that of thinking, which is nothing else but the heart's blood. But it is active in the " higher " mode of knowledge, in ecstatic inspiration;[95] to it alone belongs the profound insight of the philosopher who is enabled to pass beyond the limits of mere experience and sense-perception, and behold the totality of the universe in its true nature.[96] To it alone apply all the requirements of ethical and religious systems—duties in this higher sense belong only to the soul ; it is something in the nature of a " conscience ". Its highest duty is to free itself from the unhallowed union with the body, and the elements of this world ; the rules of purification and asceticism refer solely to it.

Between this soul-daimon that yearns after its divine home, and the world of the elements, there exists no inward bond or necessary connexion. And yet, since they have become implicated in each other's existence, a certain parallelism exists between them in character and destiny. In the mechanically moved world, too, the separate and particular phenomena tend back again towards their starting point, the inwardly coherent Unity from which they once took their origin. A day will come when, after all struggle has been done away, " Love " alone will have absolute rule ; and this means for the poet—who in his description even of this world of mechanical attraction and repulsion interpolates half-realized ethical concepts[97]—a state of absolute goodness and happiness. If there is no longer any world, then, until another one is created, no soul-daimon can be bound any more to the individual organisms of a world. Have they then all returned to the blessed communion of the immortal gods ? It appears that not even the gods and daimones (and so not the spirits enclosed in world as " souls ") are regarded by Empedokles as having everlasting life. " Long-living " is the name he repeatedly applies to them ; he never distinctly ascribes *eternal* life to them.[98] They, too, shall for a period enjoy " the happiness of profoundest peace " until, just as the elements and forces are drawn into the unity of the Sphairos, they, too, come together in the unity of the godlike Universal Mind, thence at a new world-creation to appear once more as individual separate being.[99]

§ 7

Empedokles took a fully developed " hylozoic " system (which in itself, with its introduction of the motive forces of Conflict and Love, already betrayed a latent dualism) and attempted to combine with it an extreme form of spiritualist teaching. His attempt illustrates very clearly the observation that a philosophic science of nature in itself could never lead to the establishment of the axiom that the individual " soul " after its separation from the body continues to exist, still less that it is indestructible. Any one who still felt it necessary to assert that axiom could find support for it only by allowing physiology to be either overwhelmed by theological speculation, or else supplemented by it in the manner attempted by Empedokles.

Such an attempt to reconcile the irreconcilable can have found few adherents among those who were accessible to scientific ideas, nor was it likely to tempt the physiological philosophy from the path which it had hitherto followed. Soon after Empedokles, and in essentials hardly influenced by him, Anaxagoras and Demokritos developed those doctrinal systems which were the last products of the independent speculation of Ionia. Demokritos was the founder and completer of the atomic doctrine according to which there exist " in reality " only the indivisible, minutest material bodies —which, while qualitatively indistinguishable, yet differ in shape, position, and arrangement in space as well as in bulk and weight—and empty space. He was obliged to seek for the " soul " (which to the *materialist* may easily present itself as being a separate, substantial, self-existent thing) among those minutest bodies out of which the whole fabric of the world of appearance is built up. The soul is that which confers movement upon the inherently motionless collections of bodies. It is composed of the round and smooth atoms which, in the universal condition of unrest that keeps all the atoms in agitation, are the most easily moved, for they offer least resistance to change of position, and can most easily penetrate others. These atoms compose fire and the soul. It is the soul-atom—one being inserted between every two of the other atoms [100]—which gives these their movement ; and it is from all the soul-atoms uniformly disposed throughout the whole body that the body gets its movement, whence also (though it must be admitted in an unintelligible manner) comes the power of perception, which equally depends on movement, and the thought arising thence, of this same body.

During the life-time of the individual body, the continuance of the soul-atoms is secured by the breathing which continually replaces the smooth soul-particles that are as continually being expelled from the whole atom-complex by the pressure of the surrounding atmosphere. The breathing is always drawing in fresh soul-stuff from the air which is full of floating soul-atoms, and supplies it to the body. A time comes, however, when the breathing refuses this function, and death occurs, which is simply the insufficient supply of these moving and animating atoms.[101] With the coming of death, there is an end to the union of the atoms, whose amalgamation had formed the particular living organism. Neither the soul-atoms nor any of the other atoms are destroyed; they do not alter in kind; but from the loose state of aggregation which even in the living body hardly amounted to an absolute unity to which a single common name could be applied—from this they now escape entirely. It is scarcely possible to see how, on this view of what essentially constitutes mental and vital phenomena, as a mere resultant of the separate and individual activities of individual and disconnected bodies, the unity of the living organism and the spiritual entity could ever come into being. It is even more evident that a unified "soul" could not possibly continue to exist after the dissolution which takes place at death of the atoms that in their union made up the organism. And, in fact, the soul-atoms disperse; [102] they return whence they came into the restless mass of world-stuff. The human individual, in this view of the case, perishes in death entirely.[103] The materials out of which he was shaped and composed are indestructible, and reserved for future construction; but his personality—the invisible personality, the "soul", just as much as the visible—has but a single existence strictly limited to its one appearance in time. The continued existence of the soul after death, an immortality in whatever manner the thing may be conceived, is here for the first time in the history of Greek thought, expressly denied. The Atomist, with the candid precision that distinguishes him, draws the necessary consequences of his premises.

Anaxagoras strikes out a path almost directly opposed to this materialist doctrine. As the first decisive and conscious dualist among Greek philosophers, he takes the material substratum of being, the inexhaustible many of distinctly characterized and distinctly separate "Seeds" of things—which are nevertheless indistinguishably intermingled with each other—and sets over against them a force which he obviously did not mean to derive from them, to which he gives a name usually attached to the faculty of thought in man, and which in any case he thought of as analogous to that faculty.[104] This "Mind", simple, unmixed and unchangeable, is given such titles and adjectives that it is impossible to mistake the effort of Anaxagoras to think of it as something distinct from everything material, and in fact, absolutely immaterial and incorporeal.[105] It is at once power of thought and force of will; at the creation of the world it gives the first circular impulse to the intrinsically motionless lump of matter; the creation of distinct forms in accordance with a conscious purpose is begun by it—though the carrying out of this purpose is indeed to be completed in accordance with pure mechanical laws without the interference of "Mind". This "Mind" that plans and orders but does not make the world, that with the conscious insight of its omniscient wisdom [106] influences matter without being influenced in turn, that moves without being moved; [107] set over against the multiplicity of things as an indivisible unity,[108] "having nothing in common with anything outside itself" [109] but entirely self-contained [110]—how shall we conceive of it otherwise than as an almost personified, transcendent divine power confronting the world of matter as something foreign to it, ruling the world from without by magical, not mechanical, means?

But this transcendent is also completely immanent. Wherever in this world life and independent movement are found, there, too, the mind as the source of life and movement must be active. "Mind rules all that has soul" says Anaxagoras.[111] In saying this he has not indeed asserted the presence of "Mind" within the animated being nor yet identity of nature as between soul and mind. But when we hear that Mind "goes through all things,[112] that in everything there is a part of all things, except of mind, and in some things of mind also", [113] that must imply the penetration of many associations of matter by mind (hardly any longer to be thought of as immaterial) whereby the previously asserted transcendency of mind seems to be given up. At any rate, as such associations in which is "Mind", living and animated beings are regarded. It is in them that "Mind" is present in continual, equal creativeness, though in different degrees; [114] indeed, Mind is or constitutes that very thing that we call the "soul" of a living being.[115] Among these living beings, which exist upon the moon,[116] as well as on earth, are not only men and beasts, but also plants.[117] In all these "Mind" is active; without losing any of its purity or unity, it is mixed with them.[118]

How we are to conceive the omnipotent Mind, whose oneness and self-containedness has been so emphatically asserted, as nevertheless entering simultaneously into the infinity of individual being—that certainly remains obscure. It is clear, however, that having thus derived all animated being from the single World-Mind, Anaxagoras could not speak of the continued existence of individual, self-existent "souls" after the dissolution of the material concretions in which moving and animating "soul-force" had once lived. The view is definitely ascribed to him that separation from the body is also "the soul's death".[119] Nothing, indeed, of the component parts that belong to the whole perishes, and no change in its nature takes place. So "Mind", whose manifestations the "souls" were, maintains itself unaltered and undiminished; but after the dissolution of the united, which "the Hellenes" regard as its destruction,[120] though the component parts of the individual remain, yet not *that* particular mixture in which the peculiarity of the individual was inherent—"Mind" remains, but not the soul . . .

Thus, the first distinct separation of the intellectual thinking principle from the material substance with which it was—not fused, much less identified, but—contrasted in sovereignty and independence, did not lead to the recognition of the indestructibility of the individual spirit.

Shall we say that the mental, self-moved, life-giving principle, whether set over against the material and corporeal or indivisibly united with it, is for the physiologist always something universal—that the essentially real is impersonal? For him the individual, the personality conscious of itself and of the outer world, can be nothing but a manifestation of the universal, whether the latter is regarded as fixed and at rest, or as a living process that untiringly develops itself, recruits itself, and reconstructs itself in ever renewed creations. The only permanent, unchanging reality is the universal, the essential and fundamentally real Nature which appears in all individual things, speaks out of their mouth, and, in reality, only works and lives in them. The individual human soul has its indestructibility only in its identity with the universal that represents itself in it. The individual forms of "appearance", having no independence of their own, cannot permanently abide.

The view that imperishable life belongs to the individual soul could only be reached by a line of thought that took as a fact and held fast to it as something given that the individual spirit is a reality. (Its appearance and disappearance in the midst of the one universe was indeed for the physiologists the true miracle, the problem never satisfactorily solved.) Such a belief in individuality, the belief in an independently existent individual substance that had never had a beginning and could therefore never have an end, was the contribution, however fancifully it might be expressed, of the theologians and the mystics. For them immortality, the power of substantive duration unlimited by time, was extended also to include the individual. The individual soul is for them a self-existent, individual, divine being, indestructible because it is divine.

Greek philosophy underwent many changes in the course of its speculations during the following ages; but exactly in proportion as it, to a greater or lesser degree, accepted theological elements or on the other hand rejected such elements, did it give fundamental support to the view of the soul's immortality, or grudgingly admit it, or absolutely reject it.

NOTES TO CHAPTER XI

[1] ψυχή = "life," "concept of life," in Homer (though not indeed used to denote psychical powers during lifetime): see above, pp. 30, 31. So, too, occasionally in the remains of the Iambic and Elegiac poets of the earliest period: Archil. 23; Tyrt. 10, 14; 11, 5; Sol. 13, 46; Thgn. 568 f., 730; (Hippon. 43, 1 ?). ψυχή = "life" in the proverbial phrase περὶ ψυχῆς τρεχεῖν (see Wessel. and Valck. on Hdt. vii, 57; Jacobs on Ach. Tat., p. 896. ψυχή frequently = "life" in the idiom of the Attic orators (see Meuss, *Jahrb. f. Philol.* 1889, p. 803).

[2] See above, pp. 5, 30. Even the Homeric poems in one case show a slight uncertainty of language and of psychological conception when they use θυμός, the highest and most general of the powers of life dwelling within the visible and living man, in the sense of ψυχή, the double of the man who dwells as a lodger in his body, separate and taking no part in the ordinary business of his life. The θυμός (see above, chap. i, n. 57) is active during the man's lifetime, is enclosed in the midriff (ἐν φρεσὶ θυμός) and when that is overtaken by death is itself overwhelmed (*Ψ* 104): on the arrival of death it leaves the body and perishes—while the ψυχή flies away intact. The distinction is clearly maintained, e.g. in λ 220 f.: "fire destroys the body" ἐπεί κεν πρῶτα λίπῃ λεύκ' ὀστέα θυμός, ψυχὴ δ' ἠύτ' ὄνειρος ἀποπταμένη πεπότηται. θυμός and ψυχή therefore leave the body of the slain man simultaneously (θυμοῦ καὶ ψυχῆς κεκαδών, *Λ* 334, φ 154); but in very different ways. The relation between them becomes, however, interchangeability in the single case when it is said of the θυμός that *it* in death will enter ἀπὸ μελέων δόμον Ἄιδος εἴσω—*H* 131; in reality this could only be said of that very different being, the ψυχή. (When a fainting-fit has passed over we do indeed hear, not that the ψυχή—though this it was that had left the man: see above, chap. i, n. 8—but that ἐς φρένα θυμὸς ἀγέρθη, *X* 475, ε 458, ω 349. This, however, is not a case of θυμός instead of ψυχή, but θυμός is merely an abbreviated form of the whole statement which would be in full: *both* θυμός and ψυχή have now returned into the man; cf. *E* 696. It is a kind of synecdoche.) In the line *H* 131 we really, then, do have θυμός instead of ψυχή, either as the result of a misunderstanding of the real meaning of the two words or merely through an oversight. But never (and this is the most essential point) do we have a case in Homer of the opposite exchange of significance: i.e. of ψυχή used in the sense θυμός (νόος, μένος, ἦτορ, etc.), as meaning the mental power and its activity in the living and waking man. Just this, however, and more than this, the sum and substance of all the mental powers in general, is what the word ψυχή means in the language of the philosophers (except those affected by religious tendencies). They left out of account altogether that spiritual double of mankind whom the popular psychology called the ψυχή, and were thus free to use the word to express the whole psychical content of the human individual. From the fifth century onwards we find the word ψυχή used commonly, and even regularly, in this sense in the vocabulary of non-philosophical poets and prose writers. Only theologians and poets, or philosophers of a theological tendency, continued to use the

word in its ancient and primitive sense. Indeed, when the separation of a spiritual being from the body of a man in death was being spoken of, ψυχή always continued to be the proper word for this sense even in popular language. (An extremely rare example of θυμός in this sense, comparable with *H* 131, is [Arist.] *Pepl.* 61 Bgk. : θυμόν . . . αἰθὴρ λαμπρὸς ἔχει. In the corresponding epigram, *Epigr. Gr.* 41, we have ψυχήν.)

[3] ἔνιοι, among them Choirilos of Samos : D.L. i, 24 (from Favorinus) : *Vors.*[4], i, p. 1, 21.

[4] Arist., *An.* 1, 2, p. 405a, 20 f. "Aristotle and Hippias" ap. D.L. i, 24 ; *Vors.*, p. 2, 1. τὰ φυτὰ ἔμψυχα ζῷα, *Dox.* 438a, 6, b, 1.

[5] Metaphorical language : Θαλῆς ᾠήθη πάντα πλήρη θεῶν εἶναι, Arist., *An.* 1, 5, p. 411a, 8. τὸν κόσμον (ἔμψυχον καὶ) δαιμόνων πλήρη, D.L. i, 27 ; *Dox.* 301b, 2 ; *Vors.* p. 2, 20. Pl., *Lg.* 899 B, is an allusion to the θεῶν πλήρη πάντα (as Krische remarks, *Theol. Lehr. d. Gr. Denker*, p. 37). There is perhaps a half-mocking reference to the words in the saying attributed by anecdotal tradition to Herakleitos : εἶναι καὶ ἐνταῦθα θεούς (i.e. in his own hearth) Arist., *PA.* 1, 5, p. 645a, 17 ff. Hence Herakleitos himself was credited with the opinion of Thales in slightly altered form : πάντα ψυχῶν εἶναι καὶ δαιμόνων πλήρη, D.L. ix, 7 (*Vors.*, p. 68, 29), in the first (and valueless) of the two lists of the doctrines of Herakl. there given.

[6] Arist., *Phys.* 3, 4, p. 203b, 10–14. *Dox.* 559, 18. *Vors.*, p. 17, 35.

[7] Anaximander, *fr.* 2 Mull. *Vors.*, p. 15, 26. That Anaximander declared the soul to be "like air" is an erroneous statement of Theodoret. : see Diels, *Dox.* 387b, 10 (*Vors.* 21, 5).

[8] Anaximenes in *Dox.* 278a, 12 ff. ; b, 8 ff. *fr.* 2 Diels.

[9] Anaxim. calls τὸν ἀέρα θεόν, i.e. it has divine power : *Dox.* 302b, 5 ; 531a, 17, b, 1–2. *Vors.* 24, 18. This at least is to be understood in the same sense in which Anaximander is said to have called τὸ ἄπειρον, τὸ θεῖον (Arist., *Phys.* 3, 4, p. 203b, 13 ; *Vors.*, p. 17, 35).

[10] ἓν πάντα εἶναι, *fr.* 1 (Byw.) ; 50 (Diels).

[11] Arist., *An.* 1, 2, p. 405a, 25 ff. *Vors.* 74, 30. Hkl. is also meant in p. 405a, 5. *Dox.* 471, 2 (Arius Didymus) ; 389a, 3 ff.

[12] Arist., p. 405a, 25 ff. Hkl. *fr.* 68 (36 D.).

[13] S.E., *M.* 7, 127, 129–31. *Vors.* 75, 14 ff.

[14] ὁ θεός is both the Universal Fire, that transforms itself into the world, and at the same time its power (and λόγος : *frr.* 2 [1], 92 [2]) : *fr.* 36 (67). τὸ πῦρ θεὸν ὑπείληφεν, Herakl. : Cl. Al., *Prot.* 5, 64, p. 55 P. [*Vors.* n. 8 A 8]. πῦρ νοερὸν τὸν θεὸν (εἶναι ἐφθέγξατο), Hippol., *RH.* i, 4, p. 10, 57 Mill.—"Zeus" as metaphor for this universal fire (hence οὐκ ἐθέλει καὶ ἐθέλει), the "only wise one" : *fr.* 65 (32).

[15] ἡ ἐπιξενωθεῖσα τοῖς ἡμετέροις σώμασιν ἀπὸ τοῦ περιέχοντος μοῖρα (περιέχ. = the universal Fire) is said of the soul and its reasoning faculty ap. S.E., *M.* vii, 130 ; *Vors.*, p. 75, 19 ; (cf. ἀπορροὴ καὶ μοῖρα ἐκ τοῦ φρονοῦντος, Plu., *Is. et O.* 77, p. 382 B). This is fully Herakleitean in thought if not also in actual form of expression.

[16] That Herakleitos drew the conclusions affecting also the "Soul"—the spiritual man—freely paraphrased in the text, arising necessarily out of his doctrine of the perpetual change in the material substance that excludes all possibility of lasting self-identity in any object (*frr.* 40, 41, 42, 81 = 91, 12, 49 a), is proved especially by the words of Plutarch in the eighteenth chapter of his treatise *de E Delph.* p. 392—a chapter which is entirely based on Herakleitos, who is twice actually cited in it, Not only does ὁ νέος die εἰς τὸν ἀκμάζοντα κτλ., but ὁ χθὲς (ἄνθρωπος) εἰς τὸν σήμερον τέθνηκεν, ὁ δὲ σήμερον εἰς τὸν

αὔριον ἀποθνήσκει. μένει δ' οὐδείς, οὐδ' ἔστιν εἷς, ἀλλὰ γιγνόμεθα πολλοὶ περὶ ἓν φάντασμα κτλ.; cf. *Cons. ad Apoll.* 10, p. 106 E. Herakl. is also the origin of what is said in Plato, *Smp.* 207 D ff.: each man is only apparently one and the same; in reality, even while he is still alive, "he continually suffers a new and different man to take the place of the old and departing one"—and this applies, just as much to the soul as to the body. (Only from the standpoint of Herakleitean doctrine—here adopted in passing by Plato as suiting his chosen method of argument—is the conclusion he reaches justified; the conclusion is that it is only by the perpetual substitution of a new being like the old one that man has immortality, and not by the eternal preservation of his own proper being; for this advantage belongs peculiarly to the divine. This, of course, cannot possibly be understood as the serious teaching of Plato himself.)—The Herakleitean denial of personal identity in men is alluded to by Epicharmos (or a pseudo-Ep. ?) ap. D.L. iii, 11, ll. 13–18; *Vors.*, p. 118–19 (cf. Wytt. ad Plu., *Ser. Num. V.* 559 A = vii, p. 397 f. Ox.; Bernays, *Rh. Mus.* viii, 280 ff.); and cf. Sen., *Ep.* 58, 23.—It is instructive to compare with Herakl.'s doctrine of the instability of the psychic complex the very similar theory of the influx and reflux of the elements of the "soul" as described in the Indian doctrine of Jainism. The soul (in the Indian doctrine) continually transforms, re-arranges, and restores itself, just like the body. See Deussen, *System d. Vedânta*, 330.

[17] The apparently contradictory statement ψυχῇσι τέρψιν, μὴ θάνατον, ὑγρῇσι γενέσθαι ap. Porph., *Antr. Nymph.* 10 (72 By., 77 D.), does not represent the words or real opinion of Hkl., but only of Numenios' (*fr.* 35 Thedinga) arbitrary and personal interpretation of Hkl. doctrine (see Gomperz in *Sitzb. d. Wien. Ak.* 113, 1015 ff.).

[18] A doctrine of transmigration of souls is attributed to Hkl. by Schuster, *Heraklit*, p. 174 ff. (1873). The utterances of Herakleitos there quoted to prove this thesis (*frr.* 78, 67, 123 = 88, 62, 63) do not, however, imply anything of the kind and there is not the slightest indication in the whole of Hkl.'s doctrinal system upon which a theory of the transmigration of the soul might be founded.

[19] To prove that Herakleitos spoke of a continuation of the life of the individual soul after its separation from the body, appeal is made partly to the statements of later philosophers, partly to actual utterances of Herakl. (cf. in particular Zeller, *Greek Phil. to Socr.* ii, 86; Pfleiderer, *Philos. d. Heraklit im Lichte der Mysterienidee*, p. 214 ff.). Platonist philosophers do, of course, attribute to Herakleitos a doctrine of the soul which taught the pre-existence of the individual soul, "its fall in birth," and its departure into a separate life of its own after death (cf. Numenios ap. Porph., *Ant.* 10; Iamb., ap. Stob., *Ecl.* i, 375, 7; 38, 21 ff. W.; Aen. Gaz., *Thphr.*, pp. 5, 7 Boiss.). These accounts, however, are plainly but private and arbitrary interpretations of Herakleitean sayings (μεταβάλλον ἀναπαύεται, κάματός ἐστι τοῖς αὐτοῖς ἀεὶ μοχθεῖν καὶ ἄρχεσθαι) in the light of the conceptions current among those philosophers themselves; they are homiletic, fancifully conceived expositions of very short and ambiguous texts, and can so much the less serve as witnesses of Herakleitos' real opinions since Plotinos (4, 8, 1) openly admits that Herakl. in this matter has omitted σαφῆ ἡμῖν ποιῆσαι τὸν λόγον. Others read into certain Herakleitean utterances the Orphic doctrine of σῶμα—σῆμα, the entombment of the soul in the body (Philo, *Leg. Alleg.* 1, 33, i, p. 65 M.; S.E., *P.* iii, 230), which cannot, however, be seriously supposed to be his teaching. The soul did not for Hkl., any more than for the Pythagoreans or Platonics,

come into existence at birth (substantially) out of nothing (which was the popular idea); it rather, as a portion of the universal fire (the universal psyche) is in existence from eternity. But it certainly does not follow, because later writers insisted on finding in him the idea so familiar to themselves, that Hkl. himself accepted the pre-existence of disembodied separate souls possessing complete and absolute individuality. A few enigmatic and highly picturesque expressions—typical of this philosopher's favourite manner of expressing abstract ideas by clothing them in symbolic imagery—might tempt to such an interpretation. ἀθάνατοι θνητοί, θνητοὶ ἀθάνατοι, ζῶντες τὸν ἐκείνων θάνατον τὸν δὲ ἐκείνων βίον τεθνεῶτες (*fr.* 67 = 62)—that certainly does sound as if Hkl. had meant to speak of the entrance into the human life of individual divine beings (and this was simply substituted in inaccurate quotations of the saying: θεοὶ θνητοί, ἄνθρωποι ἀθάνατοι, etc.; cf. Bernays, *Heraklit. Briefe*, 39 ff.). And yet Herakleitos can only have meant, in conformity with his whole position, that eternal and perishable, divine and human are alike and interchangeable; he has for the moment personified τὸ θεῖον (also called ὁ θεός *fr.* 36 = 67; cf. *fr.* 61 = 102) as individual ἀθάνατοι, but he only means what he says in another place: ταὐτὸ τὸ ζῶν καὶ τεθνηκός (*fr.* 78 = 88), βίος and θάνατος are the same (*fr.* 66 = 48). It seems to me impossible to extract from these words of this 67th fragment (62nd), or from no. 44 (= 53), a doctrine of the ascent to divinity of special great men (with Gomperz, *Sitzb. Wien. Ak.* 1886, p. 1010, 1041 f.). Nor would anything be asserted by such a doctrine about the immortality of such men. The striking phrase ἀνθρώπους μένει τελευτήσαντας ἅσσα οὐκ ἔλπονται (*fr.* 122 = 27) is certainly understood by Cl. Al. as referring to the punishment of the soul after death. But the same Cl. Al., *Str.* 9, v, p. 649 P., is capable of explaining the Herakleitean ἐκπύρωσις (in which Herakl. actually speaks of a κρίσις by fire: *fr.* 26 = 66) as a διὰ πυρὸς κάθαρσις τῶν κακῶς βεβιωκότων. In fact, he is giving to statements torn from their context a meaning that accords with his own knowledge and comprehension. The same sentence (*fr.* 122 = 27) is given a quite different and consolatory sense by Plu. ap. Stob., *Fl.* 120, 8 fin.; cf. Schuster, *Heraklit*, p. 190, n. 1. Herakl. himself need have meant nothing more than the perpetual process of change that "awaits men after death".—Other utterances are no more conclusive for a doctrine of immortality in Hkl. (*fr.* 7 = 18 belongs to quite another context). "Those who have fallen in war are honoured both by gods (whose existence was not denied by Hkl. nor was it necessary that he should) and men," *fr.* 102 = 24; that their reward was anything else but fame—for example, blessed immortality—is not suggested even by Cl. Al. (*Str.* iv, 16, p. 571 P.), and is certainly not to be extracted from H.'s words, *fr.* 126 = 5 (the fool) οὔτι γινώσκων θεοὺς οὐδ' ἥρωας οἵτινές εἰσιν simply shows that Hkl. did not share the popular ideas about gods and Heroes, but supplies nothing positive.—In *fr.* 38 = 98 we have αἱ ψυχαὶ ὀσμῶνται καθ' ᾅδην. Are we really to deduce from this that Herakl. believed in a regular Homeric Hades? ᾅδης is a metaphorical expression for the opposite of the life on earth (just as it is used metaphorically for the opp. of φάος by the Herakleitean [Hippocr.] *de Victu*, 1, 4, p. 632 Kühn = vi, 476 Lit.). For the souls ᾅδης means the ὅδος κάτω and the sense of the dictum is: after disappearing in death the souls when they have travelled on the way downwards through water and earth will at last rise up again through water, and drawing in to themselves pure, dry "fire" will become "souls" again. (ὀσμῶνται is remarkable but not to be altered. ὁσιοῦνται Pfleiderer; but the connexion in which Plu. quotes the saying of Herakl. [*Fac. O. L.* xxviii, p. 943 E] shows that there is no reference to the purification of the souls in Hades, but merely of their nourishment and strengthening by the ἀναθυμίασις of the fiery aether; cf. also S.E., *M.* ix, 73, following Poseidonios. This ἀναθυμιᾶν—and the becoming "fiery" again—is what Hkl. calls ὀσμᾶσθαι.)—From the hopelessly corrupt *fr.* 123 = 63 nothing intelligible can be extracted.—Nowhere can we find clear and unambiguous statements of Herakleitos witnessing to his belief in the immortality of the individual soul; and it would require such statements to make us attribute to Herakleitos a conception that, as everyone admits, is in hopeless contradiction with the rest of his teaching. He says perfectly plainly that in death the soul becomes water; and that means that it, as the soul = fire, *perishes.* If his belief had been anything like that of the mystics (as the Neoplatonists supposed) he must have regarded death—the liberation of the soul from the fetters of corporeality and the realm of the lower elements—as a complete issue of the soul into its proper element, the fire. Whereas, what he teaches is the opposite of this: the soul perishes, becomes water, then earth, and then water again, and finally soul once more (*fr.* 68 = 36). Only in this sense is it indestructible.

[20] e.g. by Pfleiderer, *Philos. d. Heraklit,* etc., p. 209, and frequently.

[21] The Sibyl *fr.* 12 = 92; the Delphic Oracle 11 = 93; Kathartic practices 130 = 5; Bakchoi, etc., 124 = 14.

[22] ὡυτὸς Ἅιδης καὶ Διόνυσος *fr.* 127 = 15 (and to that extent—as being reconcilable with the doctrine of Hkl.—may the Dionysiac mysteries be considered valid: this must be the meaning of the sentence). On the other hand, we have disapproval of the μυστήρια carried out ἀνιερωστί by men: *fr.* 125 = 14 (for the worshippers do not perceive the real meaning of the ceremonies).

[23] In contrast to the Neoplatonic writers who attributed to Hkl. a doctrine of the soul like the Orphico-Pythagorean, the [Plutarchian] account in the *Placita Philos.* is again much nearer the real meaning of Herakleitos; cf. 4, 7 (where the name of Herakleitos has fallen out, as can be seen from Theodoret; see Diels, *Dox.*, p. 392; *Vors.* 76, 1) . . . ἐξιοῦσαν (τὴν ἀνθρώπου ψυχὴν) εἰς τὴν τοῦ παντὸς ψυχὴν ἀναχωρεῖν πρὸς τὸ ὁμογενές. Even this is not quite correct as expressing what Hkl. really thought as to the fate of the soul but it does at least show once more that the contrary views of the Neoplatonists are also only *interpretations,* not evidence.

[24] Ἡράκλειτος ἠρεμίαν καὶ στάσιν ἐκ τῶν ὅλων ἀνῄρει· ἔστι γὰρ τοῦτο τῶν νεκρῶν. *Dox.*, p. 320; *Vors.* 73, 10. στάσις and ἠρεμία could never make a real "life"—not even a blessed life far removed from the world—but are signs of what is "dead", i.e. of what is nowhere to be found in this world, in fact, Nothing.

[25] Parmenides' polemic against Herakleitos: l. 46 ff. Mull.; *fr.* 6, 4 ff. Diels; see Bernays' *Rh. Mus.* vii, 115 (cf. Diels, *Parm.* 68).

[26] Aristotle (acc. to S.E., *M.* x, 46; *Vors.* 142, 33 ff.) ἀφυσίκους αὐτοὺς κέκληκεν, ὅτι ἀρχὴ κινήσεώς ἐστιν ἡ φύσις, ἣν ἀνεῖλον φάμενοι μηδὲν κινεῖσθαι.

[27] Thphr., *Sens.* § 4; *Vors.* 146, 13 f.

[28] γεγενῆσθαι τὴν τῶν πάντων φύσιν ἐκ θερμοῦ καὶ ψυχροῦ καὶ ξηροῦ καὶ ὑγροῦ, λαμβανόντων εἰς ἄλληλα τὴν μεταβολήν, καὶ ψυχὴν κρᾶμα ὑπάρχειν ἐκ τῶν προειρημένων κατὰ μηδενὸς τούτων ἐπικράτησιν, Zeno ap. D.L. ix, 29; *Vors.* 166, 14. The composition out of four elements instead of two as with Parmenides may have been arrived at by Zeno

in imitation of the "four roots" of Empedokles, each of which was distinguished by possessing one of the four qualities θερμόν κτλ. The statement that the ψυχή arises from the *equal* mixture of the four qualities reminds us of Empedokles' account of φρονεῖν (*Vors.* 218, 1 = 220, 23; Thphr., *Sens.* 10, 23). On the other side, Zeno takes over and applies to the ψυχή what the Pythagorean physician Alkmaion said about ὑγίεια (*Vors.* 136, 1; *Dox.*, p. 442; cf. Arist., *An.* 408a, 1): his point of view is almost identical with that of those Pythagoreans who regarded the "soul" as made up out of a ἁρμονία of the Cold, the Warm, etc. (see below). He may have actually got his views from the acquaintance of Pythagorean physiologists (he was regarded as a "Pythagorean": Str. 252).

[29] Simpl. ad Arist., *Ph.*, p. 39 D.; *Vors.* 162, 11; cf. Diels, *Parm.* 109 f. (1897).

[30] Parmenides pupil of Diochaites the Pythagorean and of Ameinias, also as it appears a Pythagorean: Sotion ap. D.L. ix, 21; *Vors.* 138. He was counted a Pythagorean by tradition which, however, was very free with its attributions of this kind. Call. *fr.* 100d, 17; Str. 252; *V. Pyth.* ap. Phot., *Bibl.* 249, p. 439a, 37 Bk.; Iamb., *VP.* 267 (with Sch., p. 190 N.). The Pyth. influence on Parmenides may have been essentially of an ethical nature: εἰς ἡσυχίαν προετράπη ὑπὸ Ἀμεινίου, D.L. ix, 21. *Παρμενίδειος καὶ Πυθαγόρειος βίος* as equivalent: [Ceb.] *Tab.* 2 fin. Str., p. 252, connects the good government of Elea with the Pythagorean influence of Parmenides (and of Zeno). Parmenides law-giver of Elea: Speus. π. φιλοσόφων ap. D.L. ix, 23.

[31] φιλοσοφίαν δὲ πρῶτος ὠνόμασε Πυθαγόρας καὶ ἑαυτὸν φιλόσοφον: D.L., *Proem.* 12 (though the rest is from the fictitious dialogue of Herakl. Pont. see Cic., *TD.* v, 8–9).

[32] Pl., *Rp.* 600 AB.

[33] πολυμαθίη, ἱστορίη of Pythag.: Herakl. *frr.* 16, 17 = 40, 129. παντοίων τὰ μάλιστα σοφῶν ἐπιήρανος ἔργων is said of Pythag. by Emped. (429 Mull.) *fr.* 129, 3.—The Pythagorean account of the construction of the world was known to Parmenides at the beginning of the fifth century and imitated by him in several points: Krische, *Theol. Lehren d. gr. D.* 103 ff. (To what extent Parmenides in other respects controverted Pythag. doctrine—as has been recently asserted of him—may be left undecided.) Fanciful speculations about numbers are attributed to Pythag. himself by Aristot., *MM.* 1182a, 11 ff.; *Vors.* 347, 3.

[34] Emped. 427 ff. Mull.; *fr.* 129 Diels. That this *praeconium* does really refer to Pythag. (as Timaeus and others supposed) and not to Parmenides (as the undefined οἱ δέ of D.L. viii, 54, thought) appears to be proved by l. 4 ff., which allude to a remarkable power of ἀνάμνησις which was certainly attributed by legend to Pythag., never to Parmenides.

[35] ψυχαί filling the whole air, not distinguished from δαίμονες and ἥρωες, Alex. Polyh. ap. D.L. viii, 32; *Vors.*[4] i, xliv (who in this section of his account—§§ 31 ff.—is giving *older* Pythagorean ideas. Poseidonios expresses the same ideas; but it does not therefore follow that he got them from the Stoics. Poseid. borrowed and elaborated many Pythagorean views). More subtly expressed: the soul is ἀθάνατος because it is eternally in motion like τὰ θεῖα πάντα, the moon, sun, stars, and heaven; Alkmaion ap. Arist., *An.* 405a, 29 ff.; *Vors.* 133, 40; cf. Krische, 75 f. The perpetual movement of the ψυχαί was one of the older Pythag. beliefs: it is expressed in the old fable (known already to Demokritos) of the motes in the sunbeam,

which, in their continual agitation, are, or enclose, swarming souls (see below, n. 40). In Alkmaion's treatment of the doctrine there is the additional idea that the soul of man ἔοικε τοῖς ἀθανάτοις. The derivation of its immortality and divinity from its origin in the World-soul (this is often said to be a Pythagorean doctrine: Cic., *ND.* i, 27; *Sen.* 78; D.L. viii, 28; S.E., *M.* ix, 127) does indeed suggest Stoic pantheism in the form of its expression but in substance it may very well go back to the older Pythag. teaching. (The genuineness of the frag. [21 D.] of Philolaos ap. Stob., *Ecl.* i, 20, 2 ff.; *Vors.* 318, 13, remains, however, dubious.) The idea that the soul and νοῦς of man came to him from an impersonal θεῖον, an all-pervading ἐν τῷ παντὶ φρόνησις, must have been widespread even in the fifth century. It finds expression in Xen., *M.* 1, 4, 8–17; 4, 3, 14, where it is certainly not an original fancy of Xenophon's, but must have been derived by him from somewhere or other (not from Socrates, however, nor Plato).

[36] ἐν φρουρᾷ, Pl., *Phd.* 62 B. This is traced back to Pythag. belief (though he misinterprets the meaning of the word φρουρά) by Cic., *Sen.* 73; cf. the Pythagorean Euxitheos ap. Ath. 157 C; *Vors.* 315, 19. See Böckh, *Philol.* 179 ff. (Philolaos *fr.* 15 [16 Mull.] speaks of the World-soul or God who holds and contains all things ἐν φρουρᾷ without mentioning the human soul: see Böckh, p. 151.) The comparison of life in the body to a φρουρά may very well be Pythagorean; nor is this presented by the fact that it is also Orphic (see above, chap. x, n. 43). This comparison implies the conception of the earthly life as a punishment. διά τινας τιμωρίας the soul is enclosed in the body: Philolaos *fr.* 14 (23) appealing to παλαιοὶ θεολόγοι τε καὶ μάντιες (cf. Iamb., *VP.* 85, ἀγαθὸν οἱ πόνοι . . . ἐπὶ κολάσει γὰρ ἐλθόντας δεῖ κολασθῆναι).—Espinas in *Arch. f. Ges. d. Philos.* viii, 452, interprets the ἐν φρουρᾷ of Pl., *Phd.* 62, as = "in the cattle-pen" or "sheep-fold"; the idea of God as the Shepherd of man would then be vaguely present even here (cf. *Plt.* 271 E; *Criti.* 109 B). It remains, however, to be proved (to begin with) that φρουρά is ever used in the sense of σηκός or εἱρκτή.

[37] Arist., *An.* 1, 3, p. 407b, 22 ff.

[38] οἱ ἐν τῷ ταρτάρῳ terrified by thunder acc. to Pythag. belief: Arist., *An. Po.* 94b, 32 ff.; σύνοδοι τῶν τεθνεώτων in the depths of the earth, Ael., *VH.* iv, 17 (perhaps from Arist. π. τῶν Πυθαγορείων). Description of the condition of things in Hades given in the Pythagorean Κατάβασις εἰς ᾅδου. As in the case of the Orphics this purgation and punishment in the spirit-world must have belonged to the parts of the Πυθαγόρειοι μῦθοι that were quite seriously believed.

[39] ἐκριφθεῖσαν (out of the body) αὐτὴν (τὴν ψυχὴν) ἐπὶ γῆς πλάζεσθαι ἐν τῷ ἀέρι ὁμοίαν τῷ σώματι (being a complete εἴδωλον of the living): Alex. Polyh. ap. D.L. viii, 31.

[40] Arist., *An.* 1, 2, 4, p. 404a, 16 ff.; *Vors.* 357, 1; many called the ἐν τῷ ἀέρι ξύσματα themselves "souls", others τὸ ταῦτα κινοῦν. This may rest on a real popular belief which, however, has already been partially elevated to a philosophical standing: the souls are compared to what is evidently itself in perpetual agitation (Arist., l. 19 f.). This was undoubtedly Pythagorean (and old Ionic) teaching: see Alkmaion ap. Arist., *An.* 405a, 29 ff.; *Vors.* 133, 40. (Statement of *Dox.* 386a, 13 ff., b, 8 ff., is more doubtful.)

[41] D.L. viii, 32; *Vors*[4]. i, p. xliv.

[42] That the Pythagoreans believed in the entry of the soul into the bodies of animals also is implied in the satirical verses of Xenophanes

(*fr.* 6) ap. D.L. viii, 36. All probability suggests that this was the reason for the injunction to abstain from flesh food among the older Pythagoreans themselves (and with Empedokles). (S.E., *M.* ix, 127 ff., however, drags in the " World-Soul " in a moment of untimely Stoicism. S.E.'s own quotation from Empedokles shows that the latter at any rate derived the ἀποχὴ ἐμψύχων simply from the fact of Metamorphosis, and not at all from the ψυχῆς πνεῦμα which rules in all life; though this last is attributed to him by S.E.)

[43] See Appendix x.

[44] According to the Pythagoreans τὸ δίκαιον is nothing else than τὸ ἀντιπεπονθός, i.e. ἅ τις ἐποίησε ταῦτ' ἀντιπαθεῖν: Arist., *EN.* 5, 5, p. 1132b, 21 ff.; *MM.* 1194a, 29 ff. (also given with fanciful numerical expression, *MM.* 1182a, 14; Sch. Arist. 540a, 19 ff.; 541b, 6 Br.; [Iamb.] *Theol. Arith.*, p. 28 f. Ast). This definition of justice was simply taken over by the Pythagoreans from popular sayings such as the verse of Rhadamanthys ap. Arist., *EN.* about the δράσαντι παθεῖν and similar formulae: see collection in Blomfield's Gloss. in A., *Cho.* 307; Soph. *fr.* 229 P. Compensatory justice of this kind we may suppose was manifested in the rebirths of men (in this respect the P. went beyond the commonplace sense of that τριγέρων μῦθος): we may assume this without further hesitation if we remember the completely analogous application of this conception by the Orphics (above, chap. x, n. 71).

[45] Πυθαγόρειος τρόπος τοῦ βίου, Pl., *Rp.* 600 B.

[46] ἀκολουθεῖν τῷ θεῷ, Iamb., *VP.* 137 (following Aristoxenos); *Vors.* 362, 32; ἕπου θεῷ Pythagoras ap. Stob., *Ecl.* ii, p. 49, 16 W. See Wyttenb. on Plu., *Ser. Num. Vind.* 550 D.

[47] Ancient testimony ascribes to the Pythagoreans: abstinence from flesh-food or at least from the flesh of such animals as are not sacrificed to the Olympians (the ἀνθρώπου ψυχή does not enter into the θύσιμα ζῷα in transmigration: Iamb., *VP.* 85; *Vors.* 359, 13); from eating fish, particularly τρίγλαι and μελάνουροι, and beans; from using linen clothing (or being buried in it: Hdt. ii, 81); and a few other forms of abstinence and measures assuring ritual purity. The whole apparatus of ritual ἁγνεία is ascribed to the older Pythagoreans by Alex. Polyh. ap. D.L. viii, 33. This, as a general statement is certainly correct. It is customary to say that it began among the degenerate Pythagoreans after the break up of the Italian society (so esp. Krische, *De Soc. a Pythag. cond. scopo politico*, Gött., 1831). But when Aristoxenos, the contemporary of the later, scientifically-minded Pythagoreans, denies all such superstitious ideas and regulations to the original Pythagoreans, his evidence really applies only to those Pythagorean *scholars* with whom he was acquainted and who seemed to him to have preserved the real spirit of the older Pythagoreanism much more truly than the ascetic (and in any case degenerate) Pythagoreans of the same period. Everything, however, goes to show that the strength of the surviving community as it had been founded by Pythagoras lay in the religious and mystical elements of its doctrine; and that what was oldest in Pythagoreanism was what it had in common with the faith and religious discipline of the Orphics. To this side belongs what we learn from tradition of the older Pythagorean asceticism. Much, then, that is of early Pythagorean origin (though certainly combined with other and later elements) is to be found in many of the ἀκούσματα or σύμβολα of the Pythagoreans, esp. in those of them (and they are numerous) that give directions of a ritual or merely superstitious kind. A fresh collection, arrangement and

explanation of these remarkable fragments would be very useful: Göttling's purely rationalist treatment of them does them less than justice. (Corn. Hölk, *De acusmatis s. symbolis Pythag.*, Diss. Kiel. 1894.)

[48] Efforts in a more positive direction may perhaps be seen in the practice of the musical form of *κάθαρσις* which Pythag. and the Pythagoreans used in accordance with an elaborate system: cf. Iamb., *VP.* 64 ff., 110 ff.; Sch. V. on *X* 391; also Quint. 9, 4, 12; Porph., *VP.* 33, etc.—What Aristoxenos has to say about Pythagorean ethics, moralistic *parainesis* and edification—most of it of a purely rationalist kind—can scarcely be said to have historical value.

[49] Good formulation of Pythag. belief ap. Max. Tyr. 16, 2, i, 287 R.: *Πυθαγόρας πρῶτος ἐν τοῖς Ἕλλησιν ἐτόλμησεν εἰπεῖν, ὅτι αὐτῷ τὸ μὲν σῶμα τεθνήξεται, ἡ δὲ ψυχὴ ἀναπτᾶσα οἰχήσεται ἀθανὴς καὶ ἀγήρως. καὶ γὰρ εἶναι αὐτὴν πρὶν ἥκειν δεῦρο.* i.e. the life of the soul is not only endless but without beginning; the soul is immortal because it is timeless.

[50] The withdrawal of the soul from the *κύκλος ἀνάγκης* and its return to an emancipated existence as a bodiless spirit was never so clearly held in view for the "Pure" by the older Pythagorean tradition as it was among the Orphics (and by Empedokles). It is, however, hardly thinkable that a system which regarded every incarnation of the soul as a punishment and the body as its prison or its tomb should never have held out to the true *βάκχοι* of its mysteries the prospect of a full and permanent liberation of the soul, at last, from corporeality and the earthly life. Only so could the long chain of deaths and rebirths reach a final and satisfactory conclusion. Eternally detained in the cycle of births the soul would be eternally punished (this is e.g. the idea of Empedokles: 455 f., *fr.* 145 D.); and this cannot have been the real conclusion of the Pythagorean doctrine of salvation. Claud. Mamertus, *de An.* 2, 7 [*Vors.* 320, 12], gives it as a doctrine of Philolaos [*fr.* 22] that the (pure) soul after its separation from the body leads a "bodiless" life in the "Universe" (the *κόσμος* situated above the *οὐρανός*): see Böckh, *Philol.* 177. Apart from this the only evidence for the withdrawal of the soul is late: *Carm. Aur.* 70 f. (making use of the Empedok. verses, *fr.* 112, 4 f. = 400 Mull.), Alex. Polyh. ap. D.L. viii, 31 (*ἄγεσθαι τὰς καθαρὰς* [*ψυχὰς*] *ἐπὶ τὸν ὕψιστον* "in altissimum locum" Cobet: but an ellipse of *τόπον* is hardly admissible. *ὁ ὕψιστος* = the highest God would be a Hebraic form of expression, nor can it be a possible one here for Alex. Polyh.—we should also, with this meaning of *ὕψιστος*, expect *πρὸς τ. ὕ.* ad superiores circulos bene viventium animae, secundum philosophorum altam scientiam, Serv., *A.* vi, 127—should we then supply *ἐπὶ τὸν ὕψιστον* <*κύκλον*>? Or perh. *ἐπὶ τὸ ὕψιστον*?)—An escape of the souls after the expiry of their *περίοδοι* must have been known as a Pythagorean belief to Luc., *VH.* ii, 21. (Vergil, too, is speaking in a Pythagorean sense, *A.* vi, 744, pauci laeta arva [Elysii] tenemus.—i.e. for ever without renewed *ἐνσωμάτωσις*—see Serv., *A.* vi, 404, 426, 713. It is true the line is out of its right place, but there can be no doubt that it reproduces the words and the—in this section Pythagorean—opinion of Vergil.) The idea that the cycle of births is never to be broken cannot be regarded as Pythagorean nor even as Neopythagorean. (A few isolated later accounts of Pythag. doctrine; e.g. D.L. viii, 14 (from Favorinus), Porph., *VP.* 19, and also the cursory description in Ov., *M.* xv—with a good deal of foreign matter added—speak of the Pyth. doctrine of soul-transmigration without also referring to the possibility of *κύκλου λῆξαι*; but they are not meant to deny that

possibility but merely leave it unmentioned as unnecessary in the context.) There seems to be no example of a Greek doctrine of transmigration that did not also include a promise to the ὅσιοι or the φιλόσοφοι that they would be able to escape from the cycle of births (at least for a world-period: as Syrian. took it, though probably not Porph.). Such a promise, as the consummation of the promises of salvation therein made, could only be dispensed with in the case of a doctrine of transmigration in which being born again was itself regarded as a *reward* for the pious (as in the teaching which Jos., *BJ.* 2, 8, 14, attributes to the Pharisees). By Greek partisans of the doctrine of Metempsychosis rebirth upon earth is always regarded as a punishment or at any rate a burden, not as a desirable goal for the life of the soul. We must therefore presume that the promise of escape from the cycle of rebirth was made also by the oldest Pythagorean teaching as the final benefit of its message of salvation. Without this completing touch Pythagoreanism would be like Buddhism without the promise of a final attainment of Nirvâna.

[51] Pythagoras is called the pupil of Pherekydes as early as Andron of Ephesos (before Theopompos): D.L. i, 119; *Vors.* ii, 199, 18. Pherekydes was regarded as "the first" who taught the immortality of the soul (Cic., *TD.* i, 38) or more correctly metempsychosis (Suid. Φερεκ.); cf. Preller, *Rh. Mus.* (N.F.), iv, 388 f. A hint of such teaching must have been found in his mystical treatise (cf. Porph., *Antr.* 31; *Vors.* ii, 204, 12—Gomperz is rather too sceptical, *Gk. Thinkers*, i, 542). This teaching seems to have been the chief reason which tempted later writers to make the old *theologos* into the teacher of Pythagoras, the chief spokesman of the doctrine of the soul's transmigrations.—It is, however, an untenable theory that Pherek. illustrated his doctrine of transmigration by the example of Aithalides. What the Sch. on A.R. i, 645 [*Vors.* ii, 204, 24], quotes from "Pherekydes" about the alternate sojourn of the ψυχή of Aithalides in Hades and on earth, does not come from Pherekydes the *theologos* (as Göttling, *Opusc.* 210, and Kern, *de Orph. Epim. Pherec.*, pp. 89, 106, think) but without the slightest doubt from the genealogist and historian; this is the only Pherekydes who is used by the Sch. of Ap. Rh., and he is used frequently. Besides this, the way in which the different statements of the various authorities used in this Scholion are distinguished, shows quite clearly that Pherekydes had only spoken of Aithalides' alternate dwelling above and below the earth, but *as still being* Aithalides, and not as metamorphosed by the series of births into other personalities living upon earth. Pherekydes was obviously reproducing a Phthiotic local-legend in which Aithalides as the son of (the chthonic ?) Hermes alternately lived on and below the earth, as an ἑτερήμερος—like the Dioscuri in Lacedaimonian legend (λ 301 ff.: in that passage and generally in the older view—as held by Alkman, Pindar, etc.—*both* the Dioscuri change their place of abode together: it is not till later that the variant arose acc. to which they alternate with each other: see Hemst. *Luc.* ii, p. 344 Bip.). It was Herakleides Pont. who first turned the alternate sojourning of Aithalides into death and resurrection (he also made Aithalides one of the previous incarnations of Pythagoras: see Appendix x); but as a *different* person, so that A. thus became an example of metempsychosis. It is not hard to see why Aithalides was chosen as one of the previous incarnations of P., nor how the old miracle-story, preserved to literature by Pherekydes, was thus transformed to suit its new purpose. Plainly Pherekydes did *not* say that Hermes

also gave Aithalides the power of memory after his death (otherwise the statement to this effect in Sch. A.R. would have stood under the name of Pherek.); and the privilege was rather meaningless until after Herakleides' narrative. Perhaps it was Her. who first added this touch to the story. Ap. Rh. follows him in this point (i, 643 ff.), but not—or not plainly, at least: 646 ff.—in what Herakleides had invented about the metempsychosis of Aithalides.

[52] Macr., *Som. Scip.* 1, 14, 19, attributes this view to Pythagoras and Philolaos, being certainly correct in the case of the latter; since the opinion that the soul is a κρᾶσις and ἁρμονία of the warm and the cold, the dry and the wet, which go to make up the body, is given by Simmias in Pl., *Phd.* 86B, as a tradition that he has received and not an invention of his own. But what else can this mean than a tradition handed down in Thebes by his teacher Philolaos (*Phd.* 61 D)? (Hence Ἁρμονίας τῆς Θηβαϊκῆς, 95 A.) It is true that Claud. Mam. *de An.* ii, 7, only attributes to Philolaos the doctrine that the soul is *bound up* with the body "in eternal and incorporeal harmony" (*convenientiam*): which would imply an independent substance of the soul side by side with that of the body. But this must have been a misunderstanding of the real meaning of Philolaos. Aristoxenos, too, can only have got his doctrine of the soul as a harmony from his Pythagorean friends. Perhaps, too, this was the influence which suggested to Dikaiarchos his view that the "soul" is a ἁρμονία τῶν τεσσάρων στοιχείων (*Dox.*, p. 387), and indeed τῶν ἐν τῷ σώματι θερμῶν καὶ ψυχρῶν καὶ ὑγρῶν καὶ ξηρῶν, as Nemes., *Nat. Hom.*, p. 69 Matth., tells us—thus exactly resembling Simmias in Plato (unless indeed the passage in Nemes. is a mere reminiscence of Plato strayed here by accident). See also chap. x, n. 27.

[53] See Pl., *Phd.* 86 CD. Pre-existence of the soul impossible if it is only an ἁρμονία of the body: 92 AB.

[54] It was in itself almost unavoidable that a community founded like the Pythagorean mainly on a mystical doctrine but not ill-disposed to scientific studies, should, as it was extended (and still followed practical aims) split up into two parties: an inner circle of qualified teachers and scholars, and one or more groups, outside and attached to them, of lay members for whom a special teaching suited for popular comprehension would be provided. Thus the inner circle of Buddhism, the Bikshu, was surrounded by the common herd of "worshippers"; and the same can be seen in Christian monastic organizations. A division, then, of the followers of Pythagoras into Akousmatikoi and Mathematikoi—Pythagoreioi and Pythagoristai—etc., is not in itself at all incredible.

[55] The division of the soul, or the δυνάμεις of the soul, into the λογικόν and the ἄλογον was made, before Plato, by Pythagoras—so we might have learnt, αὐτοῦ τοῦ Πυθαγόρου συγγράμματος οὐδενὸς εἰς ἡμᾶς σωζομένου, from the writings of his followers, acc. to Poseidonios ap. Galen, *de Plac. Hipp. et Pl.* 5, p. 459 Müll. = v, 478 K.; cf. also 425 K. (*Vors.* 34, 23). From Poseidonios evidently comes the same opinion in Cic., *TD.* iv, 10. And, in fact, a fragment of Philolaos π. φύσεως, *fr.* 13 Diels (*Theol. Ar.*, p. 20, 35 A.), gives a division of the ἀρχαὶ τοῦ ζῴου τοῦ λογικοῦ, which depends upon the idea that the highest living organism contains within itself and makes use of all the lower organisms as well (νοῦς in the head, ἀνθρώπου ἀρχά—ψυχὰ καὶ αἴσθησις in the heart, ζῴου ἀρχά—ῥίζωσις καὶ ἀνάφυσις in the navel, φυτοῦ ἀρχά—σπέρματος μεταβολά and γέννησις in the αἰδοῖον, ξυναπάντων ἀρχά). Then in the psychical region we have a division between the λογικόν

and the ἄλογον according to their nature and "seat" in man (λογικόν being made up of reasoning power, νοῦς, specific to man, and sense-perception, αἴσθησις, which also belongs to the other ζῷα, while the ἄλογον = ῥίζωσις καὶ ἀνάφυσις and resembles the αἴτιον τοῦ τρέφεσθαι καὶ αὔξεσθαι, or the φυτικόν, a part of the ἄλογον τῆς ψυχῆς in Arist., *EN*. 1, 13, p. 1102a, 32 ff.). This evidently represents an attempt at a division of the soul into λογικόν and ἄλογον, such as Poseidonios must have found carried out by other Pythagoreans. A clear distinction between φρονεῖν (ξυνιέναι) and αἰσθάνεσθαι was made by the Pythag. physician Alkmaion, whose division was at least different from and more profound than that of Empedokles (with whom he is contrasted by Thphr., *Sens*. 25; *Vors*. 132, 20). Empedokles did indeed distinguish between thinking and perceiving, but thinking (νοεῖν) was only a σωματικόν τι ὥσπερ τὸ αἰσθάνεσθαι and to this extent ταὐτόν with it (Arist., *An*. 3, 3, p. 427a, 21). Alkmaion cannot, therefore, have made ξυνιέναι σωματικόν. These Pythagoreans were on the way to separating from the soul as a whole a separate, thinking soul that required no sense-perception for its thought, the νοῦς. To this latter alone would divinity and immortality be ascribed, as in later philosophy (and thus *Dox*. 393a, 10, though unhistorically and prematurely, gives τὸ λογικὸν [τῆς ψυχῆς] ἄφθαρτον as a doctrine of "Pythagoras").—It is certainly difficult to see how Philolaos' doctrine of the distinction between the ἀνθρώπου ἀρχά, the νοῦς—an element of the soul belonging exclusively to men—and the ζῴου ἀρχά (confined to αἴσθησις and ψυχά, power of life) could possibly be reconciled with the older Pythagorean doctrine of the soul's transmigration. Acc. to that belief the soul wanders through the bodies of animals as well as men, and the idea implies the view that the *same* soul could inhabit animals as well as men; that, in fact, πάντα τὰ γενόμενα ἔμψυχα are ὁμογενῆ (Porph., *VP*. 19; cf. S.E., *M*. ix, 127). Philolaos, on the contrary, holds that the soul of man is differently constituted from the souls of animals—the latter lack νοῦς (it is not merely that its efficacy is hindered in animals by the δυσκρασία τοῦ σώματος as is said wrongly to be the opinion of Pythag. by *Dox*. 432a, 15 ff.). The same difficulty arises again in the case of Plato's doctrine of transmigration.—Alkmaion who ascribes ξυνιέναι to man alone seems not to have held the transmigration doctrine.

[56] 401 ff. Mull.; *fr*. 112, 5 Diels.

[57] 462 ff. *fr*. 111.

[58] Satyros ap. D.L. viii, 59; *Vors*. 195, 26.—Especially famous was his feat of driving away adverse winds from Akragas (cf. *fr*. 111, 3); see also Welcker, *Kl. Schr*. iii, 60–1.—The asses' skins with which Emped. kept the north winds away from Akragas were at any rate intended as *apotropaic* materials—magic means of driving away spirits. In the same way protection against hail and lightning is obtained by hanging up the skin of a hyena, a seal, etc. (see *Geop*. i, 14, 3–5; i, 16, and Niclas' notes there). These skins ἔχουσι δύναμιν ἀντιπαθῆ: Plu., *Smp*. 4, 2, 1, p. 664 C.—Other magic charms against hail—the χαλαζοφύλακες, Plu., *Smp*. 7, 2, 2, p. 700 F; Sen., *NQ*. 4b, 6.

[59] . . . ἐγὼ δ' ὑμῖν θεὸς ἄμβροτος, οὐκέτι θνητός, πωλεῦμαι μετὰ πᾶσι τετιμένος κτλ. 400 f. (*fr*. 112, 4 f.).

[60] A late echo is to be found in the inspired lines of Lucretius in praise of Empedokles, i, 717 ff.

[61] The well-known story of Empedokles' leap into the crater of Mt. Aetna—intended by his complete disappearance to call forth the belief that he had not died (Luc., *DM*. xx, 4), but had been *translated*

alive—is a parody of a serious translation legend and presupposes the existence of one. The parodists' version was contradicted early by Empedokles' follower, the physician Pausanias: D.L. viii, 69 (this does not come from the fabulously conceived narrative of Herakleides Pont. It does not follow, from the epigram quoted by D.L. viii, 61, *fr.* 156; *AP.* vii, 508, that Paus. died before Emped.; the authorship of that ep. is uncertain and in any case it is not very worthy of credit). The seriously intended legend must then have arisen soon after the disappearance of Empedokles: it was founded upon the fact that no one did know where Emp. had died (θάνατος ἄδηλος, Timaeus ap. D.L. viii, 71), or could point to the grave which covered his remains. (This is expressly stated by Timaeus, who, in other respects, contradicts the translation-fable as well as the story of the leap into Mt. Aetna: D.L. viii, 72. In the face of this no importance need be attached to what some one—Neanthes apparently—states ap. D.L. viii, 73; that there was a grave of Emped. at Megara.) Free elaboration was given to the translation story by Herakleides Pont. π. νόσων: D.L. viii, 67-8 (in return, his philosophic rivals contemptuously applied a malicious story of feigned translation to Herakleides himself, who in this way wished to legitimize his own claim to be god or Hero: D.L. v, 89 ff. From other sources comes Suid. Ἡρακλ. Εὐθύφρονος; cf. Marx, *Griech. Märchen v. dankb. Thieren*, p. 97 ff.). All kinds of stupid variations of the story of Empedokles' end ap. D.L. viii, 74.

[62] See above, chap. ii, and p. 129.

[63] Cf. 113 ff.; *fr.* 9.

[64] σαρκῶν χιτών, 414, *fr.* 126.

[65] His treatment of the woman who seemed to be dead (ἄπνους, D.L. viii, 60) has quite the appearance of a psychophysical *experiment*; one, however, that was intended to prove the correctness of precisely the irrational side of his doctrine of the soul.

[66] γυίων πίστις is distinguished from νοεῖν in v. 57 (*fr.* 4, 13), and νόῳ δέρκεσθαι from δέρκεσθαι ὄμμασιν in 82 (*fr.* 17, 21); cf. οὔτ' ἐπιδερκτα τάδ' ἄνδρασιν οὔτ' ἐπακουστά, οὔτε νόῳ περίληπτα, 42 f. (*fr.* 2, 7).—Elsewhere it is true that Emped. (who throughout avoids prosaic exactitude in the use of technical terms) uses νοῆσαι as simply = sense-perception following epic idiom: e.g. 56 (*fr.* 4, 12; but it is not quite correct to say that Emped. τὸ φρονεῖν καὶ τὸ αἰσθάνεσθαι ταὐτό φησι, as Arist. declares: *An.* 427a, 22).

[67] 378 ff.; *fr.* 109: γαίῃ μὲν γὰρ γαῖαν ὀπώπαμεν, etc. (ὁρᾶν is here used in its widest sense, εἶδος ἀντὶ γένους, and = αἰσθάνεσθαι. Thus, νόῳ δέρκεσθαι in 82 [17, 21] = αἰσθάνεσθαι, and very commonly words denoting one of the modes of perception are used instead of those of another εἶδος, or for the whole γένος of αἴσθησις. Lob., *Rhemat.* 334 ff.).

[68] 372 ff. Mull.; *fr.* 105: αἵματος ἐν πελάγεσσι . . . τῇ τε νόημα μάλιστα κυκλίσκεται ἀνθρώποισιν· αἷμα γὰρ ἀνθρώποις περικάρδιόν ἐστι νόημα.—The blood is the seat of τὸ φρονεῖν· ἐν τούτῳ γὰρ μάλιστα κεκρᾶσθαι τὰ στοιχεῖα, Thphr., *Sens.* 10, 23 f.

[69] A kind of συγγυμνασία τῶν αἰσθήσεων as the physician Asklepiades defines the idea of the ψυχή (*Dox.* 378a, 7).—It resembles what Arist. calls the πρῶτον αἰσθητήριον.—This function which Emped. calls φρονεῖν would probably be the ἑνοποιοῦν of the perceptions which Aristot. found wanting in Emp. (*An.* 409b, 30 ff.; 410a, 1-10; b, 10).

[70] τὸ νοεῖν is σωματικὸν ὥσπερ τὸ αἰσθάνεσθαι, Arist., *An.* 427a, 26.

[71] Arist., *Metaph.* 1009b, 17 ff.

[72] 298 Mull.; *fr.* 110, 10: πάντα γὰρ ἴσθι φρόνησιν ἔχειν καὶ νώματος αἶσαν. The πάντα must be understood quite literally; for it is the

elements in which the powers of perception inhere (ἕκαστον τῶν στοιχείων ψυχὴν εἶναι is the opinion attributed to Emped. by Arist., *An.* 404b, 12). But elements are present in the mixture of all things, and thus stones, etc., have φρόνησις and a "portion of mind" in them (though the statement that it is αἷμα that first produces φρόνησις will not square with this: Thphr., *Sens.* 23). Emped. attributed complete sensation and perception to plants, and even gave them νοῦς and γνῶσις (without blood ?): [Arist.] *Plant.* 815a, 16 ff.; b, 16 f. That is why they, too, are capable of harbouring fallen daimones.

[73] Emped. himself does not use the word ψυχή at all in the fragments that have been preserved to us; and it is hardly probable that he himself would have used the term of the psychical faculties of the body even if he regarded these as gathered together to a substantive unity. Later authorities, on the other hand, in their accounts of the doctrine of Emped. give the name of ψυχή precisely to these "somatic" intellectual faculties; thus Arist., *An.* 404b, 9 ff.; 409b, 23 ff.: αἷμά φησιν εἶναι τὴν ψυχήν, Gal., *Hipp. et Pla.* 2 = v, 283 K.; cf. Cic., *TD.* i, 19; Tert., *An.* 5.

[74] 113–19 Mull.; *frr.* 11, 15, do not (as Plu., *adv. Col.* 12, p. 1113 D, understood them) teach the pre-existence and persistence after death of the psychic powers within the world of the elements, but merely speak of the indestructibility of the elements that are the component parts of the human body, even when the latter has suffered dissolution.

[75] ἄτης λειμών, *fr.* 121, 4 (21 Mull.; cf. 16) is the name given by Empedokles to the earth; and not to Hades (as has been supposed), of which—as an intermediate place of purgation between two births—there is nowhere any mention in his verses. That the ἀτερπὴς χῶρος (*fr.* 121, 1) to which Emped. is cast down, the realm of Φόνος κτλ. (*fr.* 121) and the Ἄτης λειμών, all refer to the *earth*, ὁ ἔγγειος τόπος, τὰ περὶ γῆν, is expressly stated by Themistios, *Or.* 13, and Hierocl. *in C. Aur.* 24 (*fr.* 121), p. 470 Mull. [*FPG.* i]; Synes. also implies it (*Ep.* 147, p. 283 C; *Prov.* i, 89 D); the same is distinctly implied for *fr.* 121, 4, and by Jul., *Or.* vii, 226 B; Philo, ii, p. 638 M.—Procl., *in Crat.*, p. 103 Boiss., connects *fr.* 121, 3, αὐχμηραί τε νόσοι καὶ σήψιες ἔργα τε ῥευστά immediately with *fr.* 121, 2, and both lines acc. to him apply to τὰ ὑπὸ τὴν σελήνην; i.e. not to any kind of underworld but to the region of the earth (cf. Emp. ap. Hippol., *RH.* i, 4; *Vors.* 210, 27; *Dox.* 559). The idea that Hades is being spoken of in these lines is a view peculiar to moderns who have misunderstood the poet and set aside the clear testimony of Themistios and the rest. Maass, *Orpheus*, 113, speaks as though the interpretation in favour of Hades rested upon a tradition which I "contradicted". On the contrary, that interpretation is itself contradicted by definite tradition and by common sense (for Emp. falls from Heaven to earth and not, please God, to Hades!). The view is quite baseless (though Maass himself finds in the ἔργα ῥευστά of *fr.* 121 [20 M.]—the inconstant, transitory works of men upon earth—a support for his Hades-view: these "fluid works" or things are, he thinks, nothing else but the stream of filth, the σκὼρ ἀείνων, in Hades of which pious invention rumoured: certainly an ingenious interpretation). Emp. is, in fact, the first to regard this earthly sojourning as the real Hell—the ἀσυνήθης, ἀτερπὴς χῶρος (*fr.* 118, 121, 1, the latter a parodying reminiscence of λ 94)—an ἄντρον ὑπόστεγον (*fr.* 120) filled with all the plagues and terrors of the original Hades (121). Stoics and Epicureans (see below) took up the idea after him and elaborated it in detail. The daimones that are shut up in this life here below—a ζωὴ ἄβιος (*fr.* 2, 3)—are as if dead:

frr. 125 (?), 35, 14. The Orphic idea of the σῶμα-σῆμα (see above, p. 345) was thus thoroughly and energetically carried out. (Macr., *in S. Scip.* 1, 10, 9 ff., attributed the idea that the *inferi* are nothing else but the material world of earth to the old *theologi* (§ 17) who, he says, lived *before* the development of a philosophic science of nature.)

[76] 3 Mull.; *fr.* 115, 3: εὖτέ τις (τῶν δαιμόνων) ἀμπλακίῃσι φόνῳ φίλα γυῖα μιήνῃ. He means βρῶσις σαρκῶν καὶ ἀλληλοφαγία as Plu. paraphrases it, *Es. Carn.* 1, p. 996 B (for this must always imply acc. to Emp. the "murder" of a spirit of the same race: *fr.* 136). Even for God it is a crime to taste of a meat ("blood")-offering and, in fact, there were only bloodless offerings made in the Golden Age (which was described by Emp. not in the Φυσικά—the principle of which work denied that there had ever been such a period—but in some other poem in which he left his philosophic doctrine out of account; perhaps the Καθαρμοί): 420 ff. M; *fr.* 128, 3 ff.

[77] *fr.* 115, 4. The earth then becomes the place of their banishment and punishment for gods that have broken their oath. This is a version of the impressive picture in Hes., *Th.* 793 ff. *Dei peierantes* were punished for nine years (cf. Hes., *Th.* 801) in Tartaros: Orpheus (not Lucan in his "Orpheus") ap. Serv., *A.* vi, 565. (To this also alludes the poet from whose elegiac verses came the frag. ap. Serv., *A.* vi, 324: τοῦ [sc. Στυγὸς ὕδατος] στυγνὸν πῶμα καὶ ἀθανάτῳ: this is probably how the words should be read.) So that instead of the "underworld" or Tartaros, the world is for Emp. the worst place of sorrows. From Emp. is derived the conception that the realm of the *inferi* is our world, that inhabited by men, and that there is no other, nor any need of another ᾅδης—a conception often alluded to and improved upon by Stoic and other semi-philosophers (esp. clear in Serv., *A.* vi, 127, often only in allegorical sense: Lucr. iii, 978 ff. [See also Bevan, *Stoics and Sceptics*, p. 107.]).

[78] 30,000 ὧραι: which means probably "years" (hardly "seasons" as Dieterich, *Nekyia*, 119, takes it). The figure 30,000 has no special meaning (e.g. 300 periods of a life-time each): it is merely a concrete phrase for "innumerable" (and is frequent: Hirzel, *Ber. sächs. Ges. d. Wiss.* 1885, p. 64 ff.). This enormous period of time is the divine counter-part, as measured by divine standards of time, of the μέγας ἐνιαυτός, the *ennaëteris* during which the earthly murderer had to fly from the land of his violent deed. The fiction of Emp. clearly shows the influence of this expiation of murder by ἀπενιαυτισμός.

[79] *fr.* 121 (22 ff.).

[80] ἀργαλέας βιότοιο κελεύθους . . . *fr.* 115, 8 (8).

[81] Emp. does not even use the word ψυχή of these δαίμονες confined within corporeality. They are so named, however, regularly and without qualification by the later authors who quote verses from the *Prooimion* of the Φυσικά, Plutarch, Plotinos, Hippolytos, etc.

[82] Peculiar to Emp. is the attempt to give actual details of the crimes for which the spirits are condemned to ἐνσωμάτωσις; and also the extension of metempsychosis to plants (which is occasionally attributed, but by late authorities only, to the Pythagoreans as well).

[83] The entirely unpurified seem not to have been condemned to everlasting punishment in Hades, of which in general he shows no knowledge, by Emp. (as by the Pythagoreans sometimes). He merely, it seems, threatens them with ever-renewed rebirth upon earth and the impossibility of τὸ κύκλου λῆξαι (until the complete ascendency of φιλία). This appears to be the meaning of *fr.* 145 (455 f.) from the way in which Cl. Al., *Protr.* ii, 27, p. 23 P., cites the lines.

[84] As we may paraphrase—though indeed here, too, only with reservations—the κακότης and κακότητες of Emp. *fr.* 145 (454 f.).

[85] *frr.* 136–7, 128, 9 f. (424, 440). Very remarkable in a thinker of such an early period is what is said (*fr.* 135) about the πάντων νόμιμον which forbids κτείνειν τὸ ἔμψυχον.—Apart from this we have other vestiges of *kathartic* rules: purification with water drawn from five springs: *fr.* 143 (see Append. v); abstention from the eating of beans (*fr.* 141) and of laurel leaves (*fr.* 140). The laurel is sacred as a magic plant, together with the σκίλλα (see App. v) and ῥάμνος (see above, chap. v, n. 95). Cf. *Gp.* 11, 2, etc. Its special sacredness gives the laurel its importance in the cult of Apollo. Emp. (like Pythagoras) seems to have paid special honour to Apollo: it appears from something that is said ap. D.L. viii, 57, that he wrote a προοίμιον εἰς Ἀπόλλωνα: the exalted conception of a divinity that is pure φρὴν ἱερή in abstraction from all sense-perception, elaborated by Emp. in *frr.* 133–4, was regarded by him as applying particularly περὶ Ἀπόλλωνος (Amm. in Arist., *Interpr.* 249, 1 ed. Brand. 135a, 23).

[86] In fanciful ways: *fr.* 127 (lion, laurel), 448 Mull.

[87] *fr.* 146 (457) πρόμοι being used probably with intention as a vague term: regal power would hardly have seemed to possess special merit to the democratically minded Emp. He hardly knew it in any form but the tyrannis and to this he showed himself an energetic opponent (even though the violent language of Timaeus, the enemy of tyrants, is not to be taken quite literally). He himself was offered royal power, but he refused it with contempt as one who was πάσης ἀρχῆς ἀλλότριος: Xanthos and Arist. ap. D.L. viii, 63; *Vors.* 196, 10. He might all the same (and rightly) regard himself in political matters, too, as one of the πρόμοι; it is plain that in the enumeration of those who were εἰς τέλος born as μάντεις τε καὶ ὑμνοπόλοι καὶ ἰητροί, καὶ πρόμοι ἀνθρώποισιν ἐπιχθονίοισι πέλονται, and were never to be born again, he includes himself especially, and, in fact, takes himself as the model of this last and highest stage upon earth. He himself was all these things simultaneously.

[88] *frr.* 146–7 (459 ff.) ἔνθεν ἀναβλαστοῦσι θεοὶ τιμῇσι φέριστοι, ἀθανάτοις ἄλλοισιν ὁμέστιοι, ἔν τε τραπέζαις (read ἔν τε τράπεζοι—a tmesis, = ἐντράπεζοί τε)· εὔνιες ἀνδρείων ἀχέων, ἀπόκηροι, ἀτειρεῖς.

[89] Emped. perhaps described himself as "god" also in *fr.* 23, 11 (144) ἀλλὰ τορῶς τοῦτ' ἴσθι (he is speaking to Pausanias), θεοῦ πάρα μῦθον ἀκούσας. See Bidez, *Biogr. d'Emp.*, p. 166 (1894)—unless these words would be better taken as an abbreviated comparison (with omission of ὡς): "as certainly as if you had received these words from a god."

[90] As Plu. is inclined to do: *Exil.* xvii, p. 607 D.

[91] As several modern critics have attempted to do.

[92] *fr.* 17, 30 (92).

[93] See above, chap. i, pp. 4 ff.

[94] As late again as Plotinos, who speaks of the διττὸν ἐν ἡμῖν: the σῶμα which is a θηρίον ζωωθέν and the ἀληθὴς ἄνθρωπος distinct from it, etc. (1, 1, 10; 6, 7, 5).

[95] At any rate Emp. spoke of the ekstasis, the *furor* which is an *animi purgatio* and to be entirely distinguished from that which is produced by *alienatio mentis* (φρονεῖν ἀλλοῖα, *fr.* 108): Cael. Aur., *Morb. Chron.* i, 5, p. 25 Sich. = *Vors.* 223. A special ἐνθουσιαστικόν in the soul as its θειότατον (part): Stoics (and Plato) acc. to *Dox.* 639, 25. A special organ of the soul which effects the union with the divine, being the ἄνθος τῆς οὐσίας ἡμῶν, is mentioned in Proclus (Zeller, *Phil. d. Griech.*[2] iii, 2, 738).

[96] τὸ ὅλον, the whole reality of Being and Becoming in the world, cannot be comprehended by man through his senses nor even with νοῦς: *fr.* 2 (36–43). But Empedokles has in his own persuasion grasped it; he is situated σοφίης ἐπ' ἄκροισι (*fr.* 4, 8), αὐτὴν ἐπαγγέλλεται δώσειν τὴν ἀλήθειαν (Procl., *in Ti.* 106 E). Proclus declares that the words σοφίης ἐπ' ἄκροισι—and this is a further point—are meant to apply to Emped. himself. (I do not quite understand Bidez' doubts about what is said here, and in what follows: see *Archiv. f. Gesch. d. Phil.* ix, 205, 42.) Whence, then, did the poet obtain this knowledge of the truth since it is revealed neither to the senses nor to the νοῦς? At any rate, the ψυχοπομποὶ δυνάμεις (Porph., *Antr.* 8), who conducted his soul-daimon out of the region of the gods, say to the soul (*fr.* 2, 8): σὺ δ' οὖν ἐπεὶ ὧδ' ἐλιάσθης (i.e. " since you have been cast up here—on the earth "—not " since you have so desired it ", as Bergk, *Opusc.* ii, 23, explains: which would be a distorted idea expressed in distorted language)—πεύσεαι οὐ πλέον ἠὲ βροτείη μῆτις ὄπωπεν (thus with Panzerbieter, for ὄρωρε). According to this we must suppose that his more profound knowledge (insight into the μῖξίς τε διάλλαξίς τε μιγέντων of the elements, together with knowledge of the destiny and purpose of the soul-daimones, etc.), which he cannot have got on earth or in his earthly body must have been brought with him out of his divine past-life. This knowledge is then peculiar to the daimon (or ψυχή in the older sense) that is buried in the body; and Emp. presumably owes it to an ἀνάμνησις of his earlier life (a faculty that is only rarely active). From what other source could he have got his knowledge of his previous ἐνσωματώσεις (*fr.* 117)? He has even farther and more profound knowledge than he dares communicate—*fr.* 4 (45–51), and says quite plainly that he is keeping back in piety a last remnant of wisdom that is unsuited for human ears (to this extent the authorities—ἄλλοι δ' ἦσαν οἱ λέγοντες—of S.E., *M.* vii, 122—have rightly understood him).—The belief in a miraculous power of ἀνάμνησις that goes beyond the present life of the individual may have been derived by Emp. from Pythagorean doctrine or mythology. Emp. himself follows the legend of the Pyth. school and attributes such a power of recollection to Pythagoras: ὁππότε γὰρ πάσῃσι . . . *fr.* 129 [430 ff.]. See Append. x. The eager development—indeed, the cult—of the μνήμη in Pythagorean circles is well known. The invention of the myths describing the fountain of Mnemosyne in Hades may also be Pythagorean (see below). Throughout the various ἐνσωματώσεις of the soul it is the undying μνήμη that alone preserves the unity of personality which (as the ψυχή) lives through all these transformations and is bound together in this way. It is evident how important this idea was for the doctrine of transmigration (it occurs also in the teaching of Buddha). Plato, like Empedokles, seems to have got the idea of an ἀνάμνησις reaching beyond the limits of the present life from the Pythagoreans: he, then, it is true, developed the idea in connexion with his own philosophy to unexpected conclusions (cf. further, Dieterich, *Nekyia*, 122).

[97] φιλία is for him (not indeed in his words but in his intention as Arist. understood him): αἰτία τῶν ἀγαθῶν, τὸ δὲ νεῖκος τῶν κακῶν, *Metaph.* 985a, 4 ff.; 1075b, 1–7. Hence the ἠπιόφρων Φιλότητος ἀμεμφέος ἄμβροτος ὁρμή (*fr.* 35) is contrasted with Νεῖκος μαινόμενον (115, 14), οὐλόμενον (17, 19), λυγρόν (109). The σφαῖρος in which only φιλία prevails while νεῖκος is completely vanquished, is called μονίῃ περιήγεϊ γαίων, *fr.* 27, 28.

[98] θεοὶ δολιχαίωνες (*frr.* 20, 12, 23, 8). Exactly the same is said of the δαίμονες οἶτε βίοιο λελόγχασι μακραίωνος (115, 5). In the face of these expressions, so definitely setting a period to the lifetime of the gods, we must suppose that the epithets which Emp. applies to himself—he is to be in the future θεὸς ἄμβροτος οὐκ ἔτι θνητός, 112, 4—are merely intended to assert that he shall not die any more in his incarnation as a man (the same thing must be meant when those who are delivered from the circle of rebirth are called ἀπόκηροι, ἀτειρεῖς (147); the gods are only called ἀθάνατοι by traditional convention). Plutarch also, *Def. Or.* 16, p. 418 E, distinctly states that the δαίμονες of Emp. eventually die. That the gods (but not τὸ θεῖον itself) were liable to extinction had already been the opinion of Anaximander and Anaximenes. Acc. to Emp. the individual δαίμονες would be reabsorbed into the universal divinity, the σφαῖρος (just as the individual deities of the Stoics are reabsorbed at the world-conflagration into Zeus who is alone indestructible). [=ll. 131, 141, 461, 460 M.]

[99] Emp., *frr.* 133, 134 (389–96), speaks of a supersensual divinity that is entirely φρὴν ἱερή: he gives to this divinity the name of Apollo, but the description is said to apply περὶ παντὸς τοῦ θείου. Hipp., *RH.* vii, 29, p. 386 D.-S., refers the description to the σφαῖρος. The σφαῖρος, in which no νεῖκος is left was called by Emp. ὁ θεός, ὁ εὐδαιμονέστατος θεός (Arist., *An.* i, 5, 410b, 5–6; *Metaph.* ii, 4, 1000b, 3). It is, however, certain that Emp. would not have regraded the σφαῖρος as pure φρὴν ἱερή. It appears, in fact, that in the σφαῖρος, in which everything is together and united, even the divine power thought of as supersensual is brought to a close. In the world-state of multiplicity caused by νεῖκος divinity seems to be regarded as separate from the elements and the forces. "Furious conflict" (115, 14) then attacks even the divinity and divides it against itself; hence the origin of individual δαίμονες as a self-caused division of the divine, a desertion from the One θεῖον—the individual δαίμονες are φυγάδες θεόθεν (115, 13). These individual δαίμονες are entangled in the world from its origin until at last, having become purified, they rise again to the heights of divinity; and when all individuality is again fused into one by φιλία they return once more into the universal divinity in order with it to enter into the σφαῖρος.—Thus we may perhaps reconstruct the Empedoklean fantasy. His lines do not supply sufficient evidence for the complete reconstruction of his picture of the perpetually recurring process. We should naturally expect a certain obscurity to cling to this attempt to fuse together physiology and theology.

[100] Lucr. iii, 370–3.

[101] All that is essential on the subject of Demokritos' doctrine of the soul is to be found in Arist., *An.* i, 2, p. 403b, 31–404a, 16; 405a, 7–13; i, 3, p. 406b, 15–22; *Resp.* iv, p. 471b, 30–472a, 17.—The air is full of the particles which Demokritos calls νοῦς and ψυχή: *Resp.* 472a, 6–8 [*Vors.* ii, 36]. The atoms hovering in the air become visible as "motes in the sunbeam"; of these some are the soul-atoms (this must be the meaning of *An.* 404a, 3 ff.; Iamb. ap. Stob., *Ecl.* i, p. 384, 15 W., is only drawing upon Arist.). This is a modification of the opinion held by the Pythagoreans (mentioned also by Arist. 404a, 16 ff.) that the motes in the sunbeam are "souls" (see above, chap. x, n. 34). Inhalation of the world-stuff as a condition of life in the individual is imitated from Herakleitos (see S.E., *M.* vii, 129).

[102] The soul acc. to Dem. ἐκβαίνει μὲν τοῦ σώματος, ἐν δὲ τῷ ἐκβαίνειν διαφορεῖται καὶ διασκεδάννυται, Iamb. ap. Stob., *Ecl.* i, p. 384, 16 f. W.

[103] Dem. φθαρτὴν (εἶναι τὴν ψυχήν) τῷ σώματι συνδιαφθειρομένην, *Dox.* 393a, 8 [*Vors.* A 109]. Since the disruption of the soul-atoms is not effected at a single blow death may, in consequence, sometimes be only apparent; i.e. when many but not all the soul-particles have escaped. For this reason also, with the possible re-assemblage of the soul-atoms, ἀναβιώσεις of the apparently dead may occur. Cases of this kind seem to have been treated in the work περὶ τῶν ἐν Ἅιδου: see Procl., *in Rp.* ii, 113, 6 Kr.; D.L. ix, 46; it is counted among the most famous, or at least the most popular of Dem.'s writings in the anecdote ap. Ath. 168 B; cf. [Hp.] *Ep.* 10, 3, p. 291 Hch. [ix, 322 Lit.]; *Vors.* 55 C, 2. This view of the retention of vitality, of course, only applies to the period immediately following the (apparent) death (it is fairly correctly represented by [Plu.] *Plac. Ph.* 4, 4, 4 [*Dox.* 390], it was probably attributed to Dem. on account of a similar observation made by Parmenides; see above, p. 373). Nevertheless, out of it grew up the assertion, which was then attributed to Dem., that in fact τὰ νεκρὰ τῶν σωμάτων αἰσθάνεται: e.g. Alex. Aph. in Arist., *Top.* 21, 21; [*Vors.* ii, 38, 8]; Stob., *Ecl.* i, p. 477, 18 W. In the case, at least, of those that are really "dead", i.e. of bodies that have been deserted by all the soul-atoms, Dem. certainly never taught the presence of αἴσθησις: against the vulgarization of his opinions that would attribute such a view as this to him (as Epicurus himself did) the *Democritici* spoken of by Cic. (*TD.* i, 82) made their protest.—The work περὶ τῶν ἐν Ἅιδου can certainly not have confined itself to considerations of a purely physical nature; otherwise Thrasyllos (D.L. ix, 46) could not have classified it among the ἠθικὰ βιβλία of Dem. [*Vors.* ii, 19]. It is, indeed, difficult to imagine what from Dem.'s point of view there could have been to say about "the things in the Underworld". It is hardly possible to suppose (as Mullach, *Dem. fr.*, pp. 117–18, and Heyne do) that Dem. would think himself obliged either to answer or to parody the fabulous inventions of the poets about the realm of shadows. It is difficult to be certain that Dem. was really the author of the work: the forgery of later times was particularly fond of turning the most clear-headed of materialists into a mage and a jack-of-all-trades. (Dem.'s observations of the possibility of ἀναβιοῦν is in part at least the origin of the writing π. τ. ἐν ᾅδου; it is also responsible for the anecdote that makes him promise to the Persian king that he will restore his dead wife to life again, etc.—a variation of an ingenious story widely spread both in the East and the West. See my Lecture on Greek Novel-writing: *Verh. der Philologenvers. zu Rostock*, 1875, p. 68 f.)—The "fragmenta moralia" of Dem. are with rare exceptions (e.g. Mull. *frr.* 7, 23, 48, 49, etc. = 146, 159, 147, 127 D.) wholesale fabrications of the feeblest kind. One of them, however (119 Mull., 297 D.), agrees at least with what Dem. may very well have said about the punishments in Hell (though in rather different words—he was incapable of quite such a monstrosity as μυθοπλαστέοντες, which sounds very late Greek. Vain efforts have been made to justify this μυθοπλαστέω by reference to the older μυθοπλάστης. But μυθοποιός, ὁδοφύλαξ, ἀργυροκόπος, etc., are also old, and it is no secret that verbs derived by further extension from such composite verbal nouns are mostly late formations: thus μυθοποιέω, ὁδοφυλακέω, ἀργυροκοπέω, and again πετροβολέω, ἱεροφαντέω, τεκνοκτονέω, etc.). In another of these *falsa* no echo even of Dem.'s thought is to be found: *fr. moral.* 1 Mull. [171 D.] ψυχὴ οἰκητήριον δαίμονος.

[104] Dem., whose inquiries set out from the study of inorganic nature,

was led to predicate a mechanical obedience to law in organic nature as well. Anaxagoras starting from the study of organic nature and in particular of man, its highest development, derived from that study the concept of purpose—purpose consciously undertaken and carried out—and this idea affected his outlook upon the whole of nature, including inorganic nature. This teleological system, regarded as of universal application, is made by him to depend on a Being modelled upon the human mind, the only source, in fact, from which he could have derived his experience of action carried out in accordance with pre-arranged purpose.

[105] Cf. here and on what follows, Heinze, *Ber. d. Sächs. Ges. d. Wiss.* 1890, pp. 1 ff.

[106] *νοῦς* must be omniscient if it *γνώμην περὶ παντὸς ἴσχει* (*fr.* 6 M. = 12 D.). It has organized (*διεκόσμησε*) not only what was and is but also what is to be: *frr.* 6, 12 [12, 14 D.].

[107] Arist., *Ph.* 256b, 24 ff.

[108] *ὁ γὰρ νοῦς* (of Anaxag.) *εἷς*: Arist., *Metaph.* 1069b, 31. On the other hand, *χρήματα ἄπειρα πλῆθος*: Anaxag. *fr.* 1.

[109] *'Αναξαγόρας φησὶ τὸν νοῦν κοινὸν οὐθὲν οὐθενὶ τῶν ἄλλων ἔχειν.* Arist., *An.* i, 2, p. 405b, 19 ff.; cf. iii, 4, p. 429b, 23 f.

[110] Anaxag. *fr.* 6 [12]: *τὰ μὲν ἄλλα <πάντα> παντὸς μοῖραν μετέχει, νόος δέ ἐστι ἄπειρον καὶ αὐτοκρατὲς καὶ μέμικται οὐδενὶ χρήματι, ἀλλὰ μοῦνος αὐτὸς ἐφ, ἑωυτοῦ ἐστι.* (*ἄπειρον* does not seem to supply the required opposition to what preceeds: ? *ἁπλόον*. Anaxag. used the word of *νοῦς* acc. to Arist., *An.* 405a, 16; 429b, 23. Zeller also suggests *ἁπλόον*, *Archiv f. G. d. Philos.* v, 441.)

[111] *ὅσα ψυχὴν ἔχει, καὶ τὰ μέζω καὶ τὰ ἐλάσσω, πάντων νόος κρατέει· καὶ τῆς περιχωρήσιος τῆς συμπάσης νόος ἐκράτησε, ὥστε περιχωρῆσαι τὴν ἀρχήν*, *fr.* 6 [12]. This *κρατεῖν* at the beginning of the *περιχώρησις* cannot at any rate take place by the inter-mixture of *νοῦς* in the *σπέρματα* or by the entry of *νοῦς* into these. Because *νοῦς* is both *ἀπαθής* and *ἀμιγής*, it *κρατοίη ἂν ἀμιγὴς ὤν*, Arist., *Ph.* 256b, 27; cf. 429a, 18. Does this also apply to *νοῦς* when it *τῶν ψυχὴν ἐχόντων κρατέει*? And yet in this case it appears to be divided, as *μείζων* or *ἐλάττων* in each case, in the *ζῷα*.—No one can help being reminded here of the insoluble *aporiai* raised in Aristotle's own doctrine of the active *νοῦς* which, in this case too, is *ἀπαθής, ἀμιγής, χωριστός* from the body; is also deprived of all attributes of individuality (which reside entirely in the lower psychical powers) and thus appears as a common divine spirit. And yet it is said to be a *μόριον τῆς ψυχῆς*, present *ἐν τῇ ψυχῇ*, dwelling inside the body yet having nothing in common with it, and in any case is thought of as an individual mind. In the case of Anaxagoras the same *aporiai* apply also to the nourishing, feeling, desiring, and moving soul (as it is called by Arist.); for all the "parts" of the soul are included almost indistinguishably by him under the conception of *νοῦς*.—The difficulty of reconciling the unity and inward continuity of the spiritual (immaterial, that cannot be thought of as divided)—with its individuation and distribution into the multiplicity of souls, is one which repeatedly occurs in Greek philosophy.

[112] *διὰ πάντων ἰόντα*, Pl., *Crat.* 413 C.

[113] *ἐν παντὶ παντὸς μοῖρα ἔνεστι πλὴν νόου· ἔστι οἷσι δὲ καὶ νόος ἔνι*, *fr.* 5 [11].

[114] *νόος δὲ πᾶς ὅμοιός ἐστι καὶ ὁ μέζων καὶ ὁ ἐλάσσων*, *fr.* 6 [12].

[115] Arist., *An.* i, 2, p. 404b, 1–7: Anaxag. often gives *τὸν νοῦν* as *τὸ αἴτιον τοῦ καλῶς καὶ ὀρθῶς· ἑτέρωθι δὲ* (he says) *τοῦτον εἶναι τὴν ψυχήν· ἐν ἅπασι γὰρ ὑπάρχειν αὐτὸν τοῖς ζῴοις, καὶ μεγάλοις καὶ μικροῖς*

καὶ τιμίοις καὶ ἀτιμοτέροις (in which case the νοῦς that dwells within all the ζῷα cannot be any longer regarded as ὁ κατὰ φρόνησιν λεγόμενος νοῦς). Anaxag. had expressed himself indistinctly: ἧττον διασαφεῖ περὶ αὐτῶν (i.e. the relation between νοῦς and ψυχή). Cf. 405a, 13 f. In the sense of the words as used by Anaxagoras νοῦς and ψυχή were simply identified by Plato: *Crat.* 400 A.

[116] D.L. ii, 8 [*Vors.* 375]. Acc. to Anaxag. the moon has οἰκήσεις (ἀλλὰ καὶ λόφους καὶ φάραγγας). *Fr.* 10 [4] probably refers to the men and other ζῷα in the moon (to whom yet another moon gives light). Anaxag. τὴν σελήνην γῆν φησὶν εἶναι (i.e. an inhabitable heavenly body like the earth), Pl., *Ap.* 26 D; cf. Hippol., *R.H.* i, 8, 10, p. 22, 40 D.-S.—We are reminded of the Orphico-Pythagorean fantasies about life on the moon (see above, chap. x, n. 76).

[117] Anaxag. counted the plants as ζῷα and ascribed emotions to them: ἥδεσθαι καὶ λυπεῖσθαι [Arist.] *Plant.* 815a, 18. Like Plato and Demokritos Anaxag. also regarded plants as ζῷα ἔγγεια: Plu., *QN.* 1, 911 D.

[118] In spite of its entry into χρήματα, νοῦς is yet said to remain "unmixed" and unaffected by them: αὐτοκράτορα γὰρ αὐτὸν ὄντα καὶ οὐδενὶ μεμιγμένον πάντα φησὶν αὐτὸν κοσμεῖν τὰ πράγματα διὰ πάντων ἰόντα, Pl., *Crat.* 413 C. We thus have at the same time διὰ πάντων ἰόντα and denial of mixture which is reiterated in stronger and stronger language. Thus νοῦς even so remains still ἐφ' ἑωυτοῦ (εἰ μὴ γὰρ ἐφ' ἑωυτοῦ ἦν, ἄλλῳ τέῳ ἐμέμικτο ἄν· μετεῖχε δὲ ἂν ἁπάντων χρημάτων εἰ ἐμέμικτό τεῳ· ἐν παντὶ γὰρ παντὸς μοῖρα ἔνεστι κτλ. So perhaps we should read *fr.* 6 [12] restoring a completed syllogism. In the traditional text the clause εἰ ἐμέμικτό τεῳ is superfluous and in the way). It takes no particle of the others into itself.

[119] [Plu.] *Plac. Phil.* 5, 25, 2 (Aët., *Dox.* 437; *Vors.* 397, 18), in the chap. πότερον ἐστὶν ὕπνος καὶ θάνατος ψυχῆς ἢ σώματος; Anaxag. taught: εἶναι δὲ καὶ ψυχῆς θάνατον τὸν διαχωρισμόν. Nothing else can be meant by the words—the theme of the chapter alone shows it—than: the death of the soul (as well as of the body) occurs with its separation (from the body). τὸν διαχωρισμόν is subject and εἶναι τῆς ψυχῆς θάνατον predicate of the sentence (not the other way round as Siebeck seems to think: *Ges. d. Psychol.* i, 285). The violent alteration proposed by Wyttenbach (*de immort. animi*, Opusc. ii, 597 f.) has not the smallest justification: εἶναι δὲ καὶ τὸν θάνατον ψυχῆς διαχωρισμὸν καὶ σώματος. There could have been no reason at all in appealing specially to Anaxagoras for a confirmation of the popular conception of death (it would be nothing more). Further, in this particular connexion such a definition of death is quite out of place; since the theme of the chap. is only to ask the question whether death also affects the soul, not what it is. ψυχή here must mean the individual soul, not the νοῦς which is the basis of the individual souls. Anaxag. made the individual soul perish at death—so much is certain. It must be admitted that we cannot say for certain whether the Placita are referring to an actual utterance of Anaxag. or are only drawing conclusions from his teaching.

[120] *fr.* 17 [17].

CHAPTER XII

THE LAY AUTHORS

Theology and Philosophy, each in its own way attempting to go beyond inadequate popular belief, could only very gradually transcend the limits of those narrow communities within which their influence was first felt and reach the circles in which that popular belief held sway. During the earliest successes of the theological and philosophical spirit hardly a voice was raised that might have suggested that the belief in the imperishability and divine nature of the human Soul, of the inherence of all things spiritual in one imperishable, fundamental substance, might become something more than a mystery known to the wise and illuminated, and enter into the convictions of the people and the unlearned. " After the death of the body, the Image of Life remains alive ; for that alone is descended from the gods "—such is the announcement of Pindar. But for all the confidence with which, as though anticipating no contradiction, he here proclaims the view of the soul's immortality and bases it upon its divine nature, such an opinion can at that time have been no more than the persuasion of isolated communities formed and instructed in that particular doctrine. It cannot be merely accidental,[1] that in the fragments which have come down to us of the lyric and semi-lyric (elegiac and iambic) poetry—poetry intended for a wide and unspecialized public and expressing feelings and ideas in language that all could understand—hardly a trace appears of that enhanced conception of the worth and nature of the Soul. Reflexion does not linger over such dark subjects ; whenever they are illuminated for a passing moment, we discern the outlines of those figures from the spirit world just as the Homeric imagination had given them shape.

Life and light are only to be found in this world ;[2] Death, to which we are all " owing ",[3] leads the soul into a realm of nothingness.[4] Inarticulate, voiceless, the dead man lies in the grave like a statue.[5] Upon earth, and not in any shadowy hereafter, is completed that judgment[6] which divine Justice passes upon the criminal himself, or upon his descendants in whom something of him still lives on. It is the lack of such descendants that forms the bitterest pang, as he goes down to Hades, of the man who passes childless out of this life.[7]

More distinctly and bitterly, in this age of advancing civilization and growing sensibility, sounds the wail over the pain and affliction of life, the obscurity of its ways, and the uncertainty of its outcome.[8] Silenos, the prophetic wood-spirit, so went the ancient legend, when captured by King Midas in his rose-gardens at Bermios earned his release with the judgment of melancholy wisdom that the Greek was never tired of repeating in ever-varying forms—not to be born is the best thing for men, but having been born, let him pray that he may return as soon as possible to the kingdom of Night,[9] and of Hades.[10] The cheerful enjoyment of life is no longer so sure of itself as once it had been in the days of its naïve confidence ; and yet there is no substitute attempted, no compensatory hereafter in a next world of justice and untroubled happiness. We rather hear the opinion expressed that rest is the greatest of all earthly blessings ; and rest is brought by Death. Nevertheless there is little demand for consolation ; a robust and virile sense of life that can put up with whatever may befall of evil or hardship in healthy indifference, is in the air, and speaks to us from many a page of this poetic legacy with unpretending veracity. No attempt is made to smooth over the hardship and cruelty of life. Man's power is small, his efforts go unrewarded, one necessity after another besets his short life ; over all alike hangs the shadow of inevitable death. All things come at last to the awful chasm—the bravest virtue and the highest authority in the world.[11] Yet life is good and death an evil ; else, why do the blessed gods not die ? asks Sappho[12] with feminine naiveté ; though indeed, her life's path had lain through the deepest valley of the shadow. Even the dead man, if he wishes to be preserved from utter nothingness, must depend upon the world of the living as the only place of reality ; the fame of his virtues and his deeds is all that outlasts his death.[13] Perhaps some dim perception of that fame reaches even to the dead.[14] They themselves are for the living as though they had passed into nothingness ; we should not, thinks a poet, give them another thought after we have buried them.[15]

Here even the time-honoured conventions associated with the cult of souls seem to be perversely cast aside. In general, the poet with his wide-ranging observation of mankind had small occasion to be reminded of the cult of the soul that the narrow circles of family or city offered to their dead, or of the conceptions thereby encouraged of the continued life enjoyed by the departed. The omission is supplied by the Orators of the fifth and fourth centuries and by what they say—and do not say—of the state of things hereafter. The greatest period of lyric poetry was by that time already fading into the past, and yet whoever wished in speaking before a citizen assembly to meet with general agreement and understanding was still obliged to refrain from speaking of the blessed immortality, the eternity and divinity of the soul. The Orators [16] never pass beyond the conceptions of the survival, power, and rights of the souls of the departed which were called forth and maintained in existence by the cult of the soul. The continued existence of the souls in the next world is not called in question ; but the opinion that the souls still preserve their consciousness and have any knowledge of what happens on this earth is only expressed with the most cautious avoidance of definiteness.[17] What—apart from the sacrificial offerings of their relatives—still binds the dead to the life upon earth, is little more than the fame accorded to them among the living.[18] Even in the elevated language of solemn funeral orations the consolations offered to the survivors omit all mention of any enhanced state of being, any thought of immortal life in fully-conscious blessedness, that might belong now to the glorious departed.[19] Such high visions and hopes for the future were still, it appears, as little necessary or demanded for the comfort of the people as they had been in the times of the great wars of liberty.[20] The beloved dead who had given their lives for their country in those wars, as well as many others of the time whom death had overtaken, were the recipients of the epitaphs composed by Simonides the master of brilliant and condensed inscriptions. Nevertheless, not once does he vouchsafe a word that might point forward to a land of blessed immortality for the departed. There is a vestige of life still remaining for the dead—but it is in this world : the memory of the living and their own great name honoured by after generations is all that can prolong their existence.

It seems like an echo from another world when (about the middle of the fifth century) Melanippides the dithyrambic poet addresses a god in the words : " Hear me Father, marvel of all mortal men, Thou that rulest over the *everliving Souls.*" The words must be addressed to Dionysos ; [21] for such as entered into the magic circle of his nightly festival those visions of the imperishability of the human soul and its divine power acquired reality. Such wisdom received but partial assent from those who lived unaffected by the conceptions of isolated sects of the theologically or philosophically minded.

§ 2

A peculiar position is taken up by Pindar. Two contrasted views of the nature, origin, and destiny of the soul seem to be combined in his mind with equal claim to authority.

In the Victory Odes allusions predominate which imply an agreement with the popular view expressed in the sayings of poets and the presuppositions of the cult of souls and the worship of Heroes. After its separation from the body, the soul disappears into the underworld.[22] The piety and affectionate memory of relatives and descendants remains as a link between the dead and the living ; [23] whether the soul itself is still conscious of any connexion with the world of the living seems uncertain.[24] Its power is over and done with—it is certainly no condition of blessed happiness into which it has entered. Only the glorious name, the fame that is honoured in song, rewards the great deeds of the virtuous after death.[25]

An exalted state of being, after their departure from this earth, is attributed to the *Heroes* alone. The belief in the existence, importance, and power of these illuminated spirits holds complete sway ; [26] it emerges in lively reality from the words and narrations of the poet throughout all his work. Moreover, the ancient conception—in reality rendered untenable by the belief in Heroes—that only with the undivided union of body and soul is complete life imaginable, is discernible in many allusions and stories of Translation that imply that conception. Amphiaraos, the most illustrious of those who have been translated to everlasting life, is specially dear to the heart of the Theban poet, and is glorified more than once in the language of unaffected faith in such miracles.[27] But, further, even when death has occurred in the meantime, elevation to a higher life remains possible—even beyond the heights of the " Hero ". Semele lives for ever, though she died under the crash of the thunder-bolt.[28] The barrier between men and gods is not insuperable ; we can distantly approach the immortals not only in greatness of mind, but in bodily vigour.[29] One mother gave birth to both races, though the gulf between them is indeed a deep one ; man is nought—a shadow's dream-image ; for the gods the brazen heavens remain for ever as an unconquerable stronghold.[30] Only a miracle of divine interference with the lawful and normal course of nature, can raise the individual soul to the everlasting life of the gods and Heroes.

Such visions as these could be indulged in by one who still

kept his feet firmly fixed upon the ground of popular belief. And yet side by side with them in Pindar's works are to be found descriptions of quite another order in which is expressed, with elaborate fullness and dogmatic exactitude, a complete doctrine of the nature, destiny, and fate of the soul; passages in which, in spite of some little poetic licence in detail, a well ordered and, in the main, consistent whole is pictured.

The Soul, the "Image of Life", the other Self of the living and visible man, sleeps while the limbs of man are active; when the individual is asleep it shows him dream-visions of the future.[31] This psyche[32] which during the waking and conscious hours of the man is itself lying in the darkness of unconsciousness, is far from being the totality of mental powers gathered together in a single creature, or at any rate, in a single concept, such as the philosophers as well as the everyday use of the word at that period understood by the name "psyche". Here, again, the name once more denotes the double of mankind dwelling within the living man such as it was known to primeval popular belief and to the Homeric poems. A theological meaning has, however, been added to it. This "Image" of man, we are told, "is alone descended from the gods," and with this the *reason* also is discovered why the soul-image alone after the destruction of the body by death remains alive.[33]

Derived from the gods and therefore eternally exempt from destruction, everlasting and immortal, the soul is none the less condemned to finiteness; it dwells within the mortal body of man. This is the result of the "ancient guilt" of which, quite in the manner of theological poetry, Pindar also speaks.[34] After the death of the body it is to await in Hades the stern sentence that "One" shall pronounce over its earthly deeds.[35] For the condemned there is in store "affliction past beholding"[36] in deep Tartaros, "where the slow rivers of murky night spit out endless darkness," and forgetfulness encloses the victims.[37] The just enter into the subterranean places of bliss where the sun gives them light when he has set upon earth.[38] In flowery meadows they enjoy an existence of resplendent idleness, such as only the Greek imagination, nourished amid the artistic surroundings of Greek life, could describe without falling into emptiness and futility.

But the soul has not even so found its last resting place. It must again give life to a body and not until it has completed upon earth a third faultless life can it hope for an end of its earthly course of being.[39] The conditions of each new life upon earth depend upon the degree of purity that the soul has achieved in its previous lifetimes. When at last the Queen of the Underworld considers that its " ancient guilt " has been atoned for she sends forth the souls after the ninth year [40] of their last sojourn in Hades once more to live in the upper world, this time in happiness. Here they pass through one more lifetime as kings, mighty men of valour, and Wise Men.[41] Then at last they escape from the necessity of earthly rebirth. As " Heroes " they are honoured among men ; [42] and they have therefore entered into a state of higher being which the popular belief of Pindar's time ascribed not only to the souls of the great ancestral figures of the past, but also to many who had departed hence in more recent times after a life of valour and service.[43] Now they are beyond the reach of Hades as much as of the world of men. Faith seeks them in " Islands of the Blest " far out in Okeanos ; thither, to the " Citadel of Kronos " they travel on the " Way of Zeus " [44] and enjoy, in company with the great ones of the past, under the protection of Kronos [45] and his assessor Rhadamanthys, a life of bliss for ever undisturbed.

Such conceptions of the origin, fortunes, and ultimate destiny of the soul, the more they diverge from commonly held opinions, the more certainly must they be regarded as being part of the private and real persuasion of the poet himself. The poet, who on other occasions when he makes passing and casual reference to the things of the next world accommodates himself to the traditional view, gives himself up willingly to such hopes and aspirations where the circumstances of his song provided an opportunity of dealing at length with such matters—especially in hymns of mourning for the dead. He may have paid attention in such poems to the special opinions of those who were to be the first hearers of his song. Theron, the ruler of Akragas, to whom was dedicated the second Olympian Ode of Victory that deals so fully with the hope of bliss to come, was an old man whose thoughts might well be occupied with the life after death.[46] In this case, therefore, we may presume perhaps the special interest of the person whose praises are sung in these reflections that lead so far away from the commonly accepted view of the Soul.[47] But that Pindar, proud and self-willed, conscious of special knowledge and proud of that consciousness, should have given expression to strange doctrine so foreign to popular ideas simply out of complaisance to another's will, and in subserviance to another man's belief—that is quite unthinkable. It is rather the substance of what he believes himself and has achieved by his own struggles that in a solemn hour he reveals for a moment to like-minded friends.

The different elements out of which Pindar has composed his special view are not hard to distinguish. He is following theological doctrine in what he tells of the divine origin of the soul, its wanderings through several bodies, the judgment in Hades, the special place assigned to the just, and that of the wicked. But it is layman's theology that he is propounding; it does not bind itself to a single unalterable formula, and betrays throughout that its exponent is a poet. Pindar, throughout the whole of his poetic activity, combines the office of singer with that of professional teacher, more especially where he has to speak of the things of an invisible divine world. But for all his didactic professionalism he remains the poet, for whom as depository and trustee of the Myth it is out of the question to abandon the traditional, whether in legend or belief. His task is to keep pure what has been handed down to him, to make it more profound, perhaps to supplement and complete it, but with all this to justify it. Thus, poetic legend and popular belief enter even into his theologian's doctrine of the Soul; the Islands of the Blest, the elevation of man to Hero—these were things he could not give up.

From what particular direction Pindar's theological interests may have come to him we cannot say with precision or certainty. Orphic as well as Pythagorean doctrines may have come to his notice in Sicily whither he made repeated visits after 477 B.C.[48] For both sects this country was the original nursery and breeding ground.

There, too, the poet may perhaps have (even at that date) met with certain varieties of the Orphic mystical doctrine which, like his own views, were intermingled with elements taken from conventional mythology. Examples of this type of Orphic mysticism allied with foreign elements are the verses which, inscribed upon gold tablets, were found not long ago in graves near the ancient Sybaris.[49] Three of these poems begin with phrases that are common to them all, and imply the same underlying conceptions; after that they part company and represent two different views. The soul of the dead person[50] thus addresses itself to the Queen of the lower world, and the other gods of the depths below: "I draw near to you purified and born of pure parents."[51] It belongs then to a mortal who, like his parents before him, has been "purified" in the sacred mysteries of a religious association.[52] It claims also to be descended from the blessed race of the deities of the lower world.[53] "Lightning robbed me of life," so one of the versions goes on,[54] "and so I escaped from the Circle, the burdensome, the grievous." In these words purely Orphic belief is expressed: the Soul has now at last escaped entirely from the "Circle of Births",[55] and it enters as it tells us "with speedy feet into the wished-for precinct",[56] and buries itself in the bosom of the Queen of the Underworld.[57] It is the latter, probably, who at the end greets the liberated soul with the words: "Fortunate and to be called Blessed art thou; now shalt thou be, instead of a mortal—*a god.*"

Much less exalted are the hopes expressed in the other two versions of the mystic document—two versions that resemble each other in most essentials. Here the soul asserts that it has done penance for unrighteous deeds; now it appears before the revered Persephoneia to implore her graciously to send it to the dwelling places of the pure and the holy.[58]

How are we to explain the discrepancy? It would indeed be possible to explain the more restrained version as that of a sect whose members were less confident of their own divine origin and of the necessary return of the soul at last to its enfranchised divine state. It is much more probable, however—since in fact the presupposition of the divine nature of the soul and its kinship with the divine is really made in both cases and with the same words—that we here have to do with the beliefs of one and the same sect, and that the varying heights of felicity aspired to correspond to different stages of the process of redemption. He who through participation in the sacred mysteries has atoned for the ancient guilt, can be admitted by the goddess into the paradise of the blest in the midst of Hades. But he must still, in subsequent rebirths upon earth first complete the cycle before he can be fully released from rebirth and become once more what he was at the beginning, entirely a god. The dead man of the first tablet has reached the final goal of his pilgrimage; the other two have only reached an intermediate resting place.[59] Another inscription, found in a grave of the same neighbourhood,[60] by its use of a mystic formula [61] appended also to the first version of the above-mentioned poems, reveals itself as an expression of faith deriving from the same sect. Among a variety of disconnected instructions and appeals to the dead,[62] strung together with no particular arrangement, it contains the following statement: "a *god* hast thou become instead of a mortal." This then always remained the crowning point of the salvation promised by the sect.

In the cult and beliefs of this sect which thus with divided voice speaks to us in these verses, the worship of the ancient Greek divinities of the Underworld (among whom Dionysos is not this time included) was fused with the boldest conception belonging to the Dionysiac mysteries: the confident assurance that the divine nature of the soul must in the end break through, purified and triumphant over the earthliness that obscured it. Pindar in another, but not very different, way has brought the same elements into conjunction. One would indeed like to be able to estimate the influence which his doctrine, which lay so close to his own heart, may have exercised on the hearers and readers of his poems. He was at once something more and something less than a theological teacher. Never again among the Greeks did the blessed life of the sanctified soul receive such majestic expression, clothed in such ample and resplendent diction, as that which poured so freely from the heart of this richly gifted poet. But though the poet may have touched the heart of his hearer and tempted his imagination to stray along the path laid out for him, yet it cannot have been easy (and perhaps the greatness of the poet's triumph almost made it harder) permanently to mistake the magic gleam of poetry for the sunlight of reality. One may doubt whether the poems in which Pindar recounted his dreams of future blessedness can have found many hearers in whom they awakened not merely æsthetic satisfaction, but belief in the literal truth of the teaching, in the reality of those beautiful, dim, haloed figures.

§ 3

But perhaps by the expression of such doubts we do less than justice to the influence which a Greek poet might exercise upon the minds and dispositions of his hearers. Greek popular opinion was very much inclined to place the poet on a pedestal to which his modern representative would hardly care to aspire, and to which at any rate he could never attain. The purely artistic value and importance of a poem did not seem to be impaired by the demand that it should at the same time instruct and edify. The poet was to be the teacher of his people in an age when, in the conditions of Greek life, the people had no other instructor. He was to be a teacher in the highest sense of all when, speaking in the language of the most exalted poetry, he dealt with the doubts and certainties of religion and the relationship between religion and morality. In these matters he could supplement out of the wealth of his own far-reaching reflection what was lacking in the public morality of the time through the absence of an official, authoritative religious Book. By giving them intelligible and memorable expression, together with greater cohesion and unity, he could strengthen the foundations of the common stock of moral ideas that had been evolved in the course of social and city life. He might also expand and give greater depth to the ideas of popular morality, tempering them in the fire of his own more rigorous thought and interpreting and refining them from the heights of a more elevated understanding of the divine. What he thus gave back to the people stamped with the impress of his own very personal temperament and outlook, no longer remained the casual opinion of a single individual, but took root in suitably constituted minds and became for many a valued possession, an enduring addition to their consciousness.

It was not until the rise in later times of a fully developed philosophy extending its range of interpretation to the whole of life that poetry was deprived of its special office of instructress to the aspiring minds among the people.[63] Poetry had always been willing to exercise this function, but never so decidedly or with such fully conscious purpose as in the times of transition at the beginning of which Pindar lived—the transition from an unsophisticated faith in the traditional view of all things visible and invisible to a fresh stabilization of belief secured by, and resting upon, philosphic conviction. The need felt for the readjustment or verification of the ancestral or traditional forms of belief was vividly awakened, and it was still only poetry that could extend the light of its teaching to illuminate the minds of whole classes of the population. The influence of the poets must have increased in proportion as the numbers increased of those who were ready to receive the special bounty which they were able to offer. But if the influence wielded by Pindar, the Pan-Hellenic poet of the great Festivals, as the teacher of his people was, as we have seen, considerable, a very wide field indeed for the propagation of fruitful ideas lay open to the Attic tragedians in the huge concourse of the people which flocked together to hear their creations—a multitude which seemed all the greater for being confined within a narrower space. The poets themselves frequently allow it to be seen how seriously they regarded themselves as the teachers of their public, and the people admitted their claims. All men expected and demanded instruction from the word of the poet—the highest instruction from the highest poetry.[64] We shall not be much mistaken if we believe that the opinions and reflections to which Aeschylus, Sophokles, and not least Euripides, gave utterance in their tragic drama did not remain the sole property of those in whose minds they had first arisen.

§ 4

The Attic Tragedy of the fifth century must of its own accord, even if the conscious purpose of the dramatists had not tended in the same direction, have developed into an artistic product based on psychological interest. The real theatre of that drama must inevitably have become the interior of its hero's mind.

The tragic poet attempted something hitherto unknown. The characters and events of ancient legend or history which had passed shadowlike before the minds of the hearers or readers of all earlier poetry, at the mercy of those hearers' own private and variously limited imagination—these same events and characters were now to take form and body and appear visibly before the eyes of all beholders alike in equal clearness. What had hitherto seemed a dream-vision of the imagination now visibly presented itself to the eyes of the beholder, unchanging, precise, independent of the limitations of intellect among the audience, a concrete and self-moving object of waking perception. Thus reawakened to a palpable and fully realized life, the myth was seen in a new light. What in it was mere incident became subordinated to the personality of the man who plays his part in these events before our eyes, and whose importance and content is not exhausted in the single particular action. The old legend in becoming drama has undergone an extension both spatial and temporal, and even in externals the plot that unfolds itself in a series of momentary acts plays the least part in the story. The speeches and counter-speeches of the hero and the other actors who take part in the story were bound to take up the greater part of the time. Motives of action, expressed, debated and fought out in words, become more important than their eventual outcome in passionate deed or mortal woe. With the advance of artistic skill the intellect seeks to grasp the permanent outlines of the character that in the given circumstances can be moved by particular motives to particular acts. Thus, the complete materialization of the myth leads to its complete spiritualization. The eyes and mind of the beholder are directed less to the external events—these, being familiar from the ancient legend, could awaken little curiosity—and more to the inward meaning and import of what the hero does and suffers.

And it was here that the dramatic poet was faced with his special and peculiar problem. What was to happen in his drama was settled out of hand by the course of the ancient legend (in a few cases by the course of historical events) and the lines along which his invention must move were planned out for him in advance. To give life to the personages of the drama, motivation and justification to the events of the drama—that was his particular business. But in this he was thrown entirely upon his own resources. Even if he could he was not permitted to derive the inner motive forces of the action from the real modes of feeling and thinking that had belonged to the distant past in which the myth had first been conceived. Such motives would have remained unintelligible to the audience, and his play would have been stillborn. But on the other hand, how was he to make plausible and intelligible to the vastly different mentality and changed feelings of the age in which he lived actions which really sprang from the habits and moral ideas of a long since vanished age? It is open to him (if he is not content to be a mere annalist simply stringing together bare events) to take the actual incident given him by the mythical legend and set over against it the actor in the story whose emotions are those of a modern man, and upon whose shoulders the burden of the event is laid; he may represent this opposition as beyond reconciliation, and so lead to the most simple and overwhelming of tragic conflicts. This simple opposition of character and destiny which places both the poet and his hero—another Hamlet—in a position of direct hostility to the mythological background can, however, never become the rule. It is the business of the poet as far as possible to assimilate and make his own the spirit that actually called forth the dark and cruel legend of the past, while yet remaining true to the mode of perception proper to his own time. He must manage to leave undisturbed the full primitive sense of the mythical story and bring it about that by its marriage with the spirit of a later age its meaning is not destroyed but deepened. He is committed to the search for an adjustment between the mental attitudes of an older and a newer age.

Such an adjustment came most easily to Aeschylus and satisfied the needs of his temperament. As one who had grown to manhood in the Athens of the period before the Persian wars his own character had its roots in ancient and traditional modes of thought. These he built up under the guiding influence of his own special ways of thinking and feeling into a new and loftier whole: to corroborate this whole, which appeared to him as a law of the moral world, by reference to typical examples taken from mythology—examples chosen by him with deliberate care to serve as subjects of his dramatic poetry—this was one of the chief aims of his art. To the plot in its moral—nay, its religious—sense, all his thoughts are directed; the characters of the actors themselves are only illuminated from the standpoint of this special interest; their wider, independent existence outside the life of the drama which completely envelopes them is not meant to draw attention to itself. He himself gives us the right, in studying his plays, to leave out of sight for a moment the representational aspect of the particular and the personal—all that in fact makes them essentially works of art—in order to observe more closely the under-current of generalized belief which we may reasonably call the ethic and theology of the poet.

Behind the living tissue of his artistic creation Aeschylus allows us to perceive pretty clearly the firm outlines of his own ethical and religious convictions. He fuses together elements prescribed to him from without with that which was dictated by his own spirit. What is prescribed to him by legend—which he allows to run its full course, in strictly dramatic form and by preference as a trilogy, a form in this case uniquely adapted to the subject—is a history that deals with the continued operation of the forces of evil and suffering upon several generations of a family, persisting from father to son and from son to son's son. The belief also in such interconnexion of human destinies is prescribed to him from without. That the sins of the ancestors were visited upon their descendants here upon earth was an ancient article of faith especially strong in Attica.[65] What Aeschylus contributes on his part is the unswerving conviction that the son and grandson of the sinner are punished for their *own* sin too. Suffering is punishment,[66] and suffering would not have overtaken Oedipus, nor the sons of Oedipus, if Laïos had been the only guilty one—if their own sin had not deserved punishment.

And yet it does not lie within their power to choose whether the guilt shall be theirs or not: they cannot escape the deed of sin. How, we may ask, can a guilty deed be necessitated, imposed upon the guilty one by the decree of a higher power, and yet at the same time the *fault* of the doer of the deed, as though he had acted of his own free will?

The question is a perplexing and a formidable one, and it was by no means unnoticed by the poet. Behind the external apparatus of myth he finds himself faced by the problem of the freedom or determination of man's will, which, as civilization and culture advance, feels itself morally responsible for every decision. He finds a way out of the difficulty in the view that it is not merely the deed of wickedness itself, but the conscious decision that leads up to the deed that arises out of the family inheritance of crime. The conscious choice and decision, though regarded as necessary, seemed to demonstrate fully the personal guilt and responsibility of the doer.[67] The cloud of evil that proceeds from the deed of the ancestor casts a dark shadow also over the minds of his son and his son's son. Not from his own mind or character does the will to do wrong take its origin. The noble, pure and resolute Eteokles, the model of intelligent manhood, the shield and protection of his people, falls in a moment, a victim to ominous destiny; his clear-sighted spirit is darkened, he gives himself up—his better self—for lost,[68] and rushes upon his doom with awful resolve. The "sins derived from his ancestors"[69] drive him on. Then, and not till then, is the full measure of penance at last paid for the crime done by the ancestor;[70] his descendants are his representatives, and become guilty on his behalf and then, for their own guilt as well as his, they suffer retribution. Divinity, or a spirit of vengeance sent with a divine mission, drives the victims burdened with the inheritance of crime to the criminal deed. The divine guidance is actuated no longer, as in ancient and undying popular belief, by personal desire of vengeance, anger or malice,[71] but by divine justice, acting with "just deceit",[72] that the measure of guilt may be fulfilled, and that the divine will to justice may have a means to complete satisfaction. The evil Spirit of the House assists Klytaimnestra to conceive the thought of murdering her husband:[73] God himself guides and urges forward Orestes to the act of matricide which he plans and carries out with fully conscious purpose—a crime that is also a duty. To the poet the old ideas of the duty of avenging murder are a very living reality. The right to worship and cult possessed by the souls, their claim to vengeance when they have been violently done to death, their ghostly influence exerted upon the life and destinies of their immediate kinsfolk upon whom the duty of taking vengeance rests—all these things are for him not the obsolete fancies of an older generation but true and awful realities.[74] Whole dramas, the Choephorai and the Eumenides, for instance, would appear as a meaningless beating of the air if they were not animated and made significant by unaltered faith in the right and the might of the souls, the reality and potency of the daimonic counsel, the Erinyes,[75] who appear on behalf of the murdered mother. And now at last light breaks through the dark and clouded sky of awful imagination : where Duty and Crime have become inextricably confused, divine grace, though yielding nothing of its rights, finds at last a solution.

All these things, however—conflict and solution, crime and its expiation in ever-renewed crime and the suffering that arises thence—fulfil themselves in *this* world. Guilt is avenged always upon earth. The " other " world is by no means an indispensable link in this chain of conceptions and fancies : the poet's view is rarely turned in that direction. Speculation upon the state of the soul after death, upon a blessed life in the kingdom of the spirits,[76] does not interest him. Only such portions of the eschatological imaginings of the theologians as might serve the purposes of moral inspiration or support, found favour with the poet. There are occasional allusions to the judgment that, in Hades, " another Zeus " holds over the deeds of earthly life,[77] but they remain dark and vague. It is not explained in what relation this judgment in Hades stands to the complete equivalence of guilt and destiny that, here upon earth, Zeus and Moira bring to completion in the person of the criminal himself and, after his death, of his descendants. Side by side with the allusions to the judgment in the underworld implying the complete consciousness of the dead, stand expressions that call up a picture of the senseless, twilight existence of the souls in Hades like that described in Homer.[78] The poet, to whom every feature of the beliefs derived from the cult of the souls about the relations of the departed to the life of the dwellers on earth was intensely and vividly real, never cared to fix his attention for long upon the nature and condition of the dead in their separate other-world existence. In fact his chosen work of giving a moral significance and deeper meaning to popular and ancient faith was wholly derived from this faith itself ; and so also was the lofty and consistent idea of divinity which fills the background of his picture of life. The generation which had fought at Marathon, in spite of a profounder and even more sombre meditation upon life and destiny, could still dispense almost entirely with the assistance of the theological doctrines of the sects who sought refuge from the dark and austere realities of this unsatisfying world in thoughts of an imagined hereafter.

§ 5

Towards the great problems of dramatic philosophy—the problems of the freedom or compulsion of the will, the guilt and destiny of man—Sophokles took up a position that differed essentially from that of his great predecessor. A maturer and calmer self-abandonment to the observation of life and its difficulties made him less able to rest content with simple or sweeping solutions of the complexities ; made him seek out other and more various modes of understanding. The individual man, stamped with the unique impression of his peculiar being, with him becomes more fully detached from the background of omnipotent might and universal law. The individual finds within himself the rules of his behaviour, the causes of his success, or his tragic failure. No petty, egotistical motive inspires the action of Antigone or Elektra : they are obedient to the old, unwritten laws of the gods. But the force that leads them to obey is derived solely from the special fashion and impulse of their own hearts. No one else could do what they do, suffer what they suffer. We realize the necessity and justification of what they do and suffer solely from the contemplation of the strength and weakness of their own characters as displayed for us in the action that takes place upon the stage. Indeed, the length to which Sophokles, in the "Elektra", goes in the suppression of such universally recognized and binding motives as those derived from the duty of vengeance and the rights of injured souls, may well cause surprise. The special and individual case must for him carry its own justification within itself, and in fact it receives such justification so completely from the character and behaviour of the actors in the drama that, unlike the hero of Aeschylus' tragedy, Orestes needs to have no qualm of doubt in the performance of his deed, and suffers no remorse after the murder of the wicked murderess. Once again as in the Homeric story, with Orestes' "righteous deed of blood",[79] the circle of calamity is complete : no Erinys rises from the earth to demand his overthrow.[80]

So, too, when the suffering and calamity that befalls the mortal hero comes not from his own conscious decision and exercise of will, but from obscure decrees of fate it is still the special character of the hero which not only demands the greater part of our attention, but entirely conditions and sufficiently explains the course of events. The same misfortune might overtake another man, but neither its inward nor its outward effects would be the same as they are for Oedipus or Aias. Only tragically extreme characters can have a tragic fate.

And yet, in these as in other tragedies, what gives the first impulse and direction to the course of the story does not arise from the will or character of their heroes. The mind of Aias is not free but subject when he performs the deed that sends him to his death. Oedipus, Deianeira take vengeance upon themselves for the deeds of horror that they have brought about without knowing what they did. Notwithstanding the fact that the interest of the "Philoktetes" centres so completely round the vividly contrasted characters of Philoktetes, Neoptolemos, and Odysseus, yet the situation which brings them into opposition is one which it was beyond the power or the purpose of man to bring about or to hinder. An obscure destiny plunges man into suffering, drives him to actions in the face of which easy and ready-made judgments about "guilt" and the relation between suffering and desert are silenced. It is not inherited family crime that here forces the son and the grandson to deeds that can hardly be called their own. The poet, it is true, knows of these conceptions [81] that play so large a part in the poetry of Aeschylus, but they are mere historical tradition to him, not vital motives of his drama. Nor is it mere irrational chance, or impersonal fate working by necessity and without passion that directs the mind and guides the hand of the actor in his bondage. Clearly or obscurely moving about in the background of events the will of a divine power can be discerned that, inevitable as fate,[82] guides the deeds and the fate of men in accordance with its own purpose.

The divine purpose brings to maturity a plan in which the individual man and his destiny are mere instruments. To make plain the premeditated character of this purposeful direction of human affairs is the object of the prophetic anticipations of the future, the divine oracles and prophecies of seers of which we hear so much in the plays. If this divine purpose should involve the fatal act, the undeserved suffering of the individual, then that purpose will be fulfilled though human happiness may be destroyed in the process, and though pain, crime, agony, and violent death may overwhelm the mortal individual. The well-being of the individual does not enter into the question where the intentions of a divinity that sees far beyond this puny existence are concerned. An honest, simple-minded, good-hearted man, without deceit or fault, like Philoktetes, is abandoned for many long years to every kind of suffering in order that he may not interfere prematurely in the development of the war against Troy with the magic weapons that are in his possession.[83] He is an involuntary martyr for the good of the whole community. In order that Herakles may be released from this life at the precise moment of time that has been fixed by divine foreknowledge,[84] Deianeira, the most devoted and womanly character in the whole of the Attic drama, must out of the goodness of her heart and the love she bears to her husband send him to the most awful of deaths and then perish herself. Simply because such is the will of heaven [85] must Oedipus, unknowing and blameless, slay his father, marry his mother, and plunge himself into the deepest depth of misery.

Thus, out of the darkness, the hand of divine superiority guides the destinies of humanity, the will and behaviour of men, according to its own purposes. The problematical in human life, the disparity between personal guilt and personal suffering, which daily experience brings before our eyes, seemed to the poet to be rendered more intelligible by this conception. He preaches dutiful submission to these dispensations of a higher power. He himself is one of the pious, in the specific sense of the word,[86] for whom to perceive the will of the gods is sufficient to call forth adoration of the gods; who feel no need that this mighty will should justify itself to human ideas of morality and goodness.[87] It may be right to call this will a holy will; but there is no need for it to prove itself such at the bar of human judgment. Nor does such piety find itself disturbed in its worship when, in order to assert the divine prerogative over humanity (whose first duty it is to recognize the limits of what is allowed and possible for it), divine inhumanity and cold lust of vengeance manifest themselves so clearly as in the Athene of the "Ajax".[88] It gives the measure of the peculiar and unique character of Sophoklean art and the Sophoklean attitude to life—a quite personal character not to be explained on abstract grounds—that this attitude of awed submissiveness in matters of religion could exist side by side with the strong appreciation and justification of the unfettered action of free individuality. Rarely—only once or twice in the plays—is a cry of pain wrested from the lips of one of these uncomplaining victims of a purpose not their own.[89] As a rule, the eye shuns to behold, the judgment to criticize, the ultimate reasons of divine action. It is partly artistic restraint no doubt, but religious discretion, too, makes the poet leave such things in semi-obscurity.[90] The majesty of divine power remains for the most part in the background and does not mingle familiarly with men or too notoriously interfere with human destiny.[91]

But the individual who with his sufferings must serve a purpose that is not his own, Humanity that lives under such bitter laws—what elevating and consoling thoughts are awakened by the contemplation of their fate. The poet employs all the resources of his overwhelming art to secure the profoundest sympathies of his hearers for the undeserved sufferings of the victim, for the delusions of well-intentioned but limited vision that must always stray from the goal at which it aims. The moral of the play is not lost even on the sufferer's foe as he beholds the error and guilt of the noble but misguided heart.[92] What thus overwhelms the strong and the wise, the good and the well-meaning, through no fault of their own, may descend upon any member of the human family. Thus the destinies of men are allotted. The lament over the vanity and the sorrow of life, its brief happiness, and the uncertainty of its joy, is poured forth in memorable lines.[93] They end on a note of resignation which gives the keynote of the poet's own character; but there is a bitterness which remains behind.

It might have been supposed that one who thus abandoned all attempt to reconcile the worth and actions of men with their fate upon earth, would feel all the more need, for his own satisfaction and that of others, to prove the existence of a divine justice that should restore the balance in a future state of being. But the poet shows little sign of any such need. Thoughts of what may happen after death are never of very great moment to him. They never distinctly affect the behaviour of those whose deeds or suffering fill his plays.[94]

When, however, light is thrown for a passing moment on the unknown land beyond the grave the scene that imagination reveals hardly differs at all from the picture that had once been present to the minds of the Homeric singers. The place that is in store for the departed is Hades,[95] the unlovely country of the dead,[96] whither the Soul flits powerless, shadowlike, little more than a nothing,[97] feeling no joy but no pain either;[98] where it enters upon a state of insensibility that the grief-stricken sufferer on earth often longs for as a much-desired haven of rest.[99] Plouton, Persephone, all the deities of the earth below,[100] there rule over the departed. But it is not grace nor kindliness that prevails there—only Justice: Hades demands equal justice for all.[101]

Pious veneration of the gods continues also in the other world,[102] and for the rest we hear nothing of either reward or punishment or of a final supplementing in the land of the Souls of the inadequacy of the justice that fulfils itself on earth.

But though departed into Hades the dead have still a claim upon the upper world and on those who still are living there. Together with the Homeric picture of the lower world is united the cult of the souls and the ideas, connected with that cult, of the continued life of the dead. The next of kin owe to the departed the ceremonious burial that is the first expression of their pious solicitude for his soul's welfare.[103] In two plays the "Ajax" and the "Antigone", the love and loyalty of the survivors is obliged to fight for this right of the dead in desperate encounter with earthly authority and even with the sacrifice of their own devoted lives. Such instances serve to bring out clearly the fact that it is no empty convention or tradition that is thus defended and carried through to the end. Nor does the completion of the burial mark the end of the dead man's relations with the upper world: even after that he may be benefited by offerings made at his grave.[104] Information of what happens on earth may penetrate to the dead; [105] and he himself, under the protection of the underworld spirits and of their assessor Dikê, who take cognizance of his claims,[106] may interfere in the affairs of the living as a "Curse-spirit" upon those who disregard his wishes,[107] by sending threatening dream-visions upon his foes,[108] and as a very present help and unseen ally to his friends in their hour of need.[109]

As to an eternity of bliss awaiting the soul, the god in man, after its final release from the shackles of the body, the poet knows as little of such as he does of an eternity of damnation for the wicked. Only the quite special state of grace which is enjoyed by those who have been purified in the mysteries of the goddesses at Eleusis receives mention by him [110]: he is frequently disposed to think of this supreme expression of Attic worship with patriotic pride.[111] But it is only a minority of the good who thus achieve by the grace of the goddesses a privileged "life" in the kingdom of shadows. One and only one is lifted by the divine grace clear of the human fate of annihilation, and in the Grove of the Erinyes the sorely-tried Oedipus is translated without seeing death out of this earthly life.[112] So living a reality to this poet of ancient piety is the conviction that the divine miracle of translation [113] is a literal truth, that he is even ready to make this strange circumstance serve as the sole aim and purpose of a whole drama: a miracle which all the other scenes serve not so much to prepare as simply to postpone, and thus heighten the expectancy with which the event is awaited. It is not supreme virtue that secures an immortality for Oedipus which others also who showed an equal degree of goodness might possibly attain. He reveals himself to us as an innocent sufferer indeed,[114] but also as obdurate in his rash and violent nature, vindictive, stubborn, and self-willed, not ennobled but rather brutalized by his sufferings.[115] Nevertheless, divine power elevates him to the state of immortal *Hero* less almost for the sake of the satisfaction and bliss to himself as in order that he may be the saviour of the Attic land, the country of humanity and kindness that has taken into its protection[116] the unfortunate one, and desires to preserve for ever his power of blessing.[117] Just as once it had pleased divine power to overwhelm the innocent victim in a sea of crime and suffering, so now it pleases the same divine power to raise the sufferer, without any new or special merit on his side, to a fate of superhuman bliss.[118] In his case a divine miracle occurs, into the ultimate reasons for which it is not profitable to inquire.

In his views, so far as he allows us to see them, of the things of the next world, Sophokles differs not at all from those who still saw life and worshipped the gods as their fathers had done before them. The great poet of human, tragic destiny, the profound student of the divine government of this mournful world, was unwilling to set by the side of it a brighter and more comforting picture of a spirit world of the imagination. In this, too, he is modest and will not say much—he knows no more of these matters, and in no other fashion, than " any other honest citizen of Athens ".[119]

§ 6

In the course of a long life Sophokles was able to make himself complete master of his art and grow up into strong and generous manhood without the guidance or support of either theological or philosophical learning. Theology he did not care to seek out in its hiding place, the obscurity of isolated sects. Philosophy, in the period of his impressionable youth, had not yet reached Athens, and when he had attained riper years his noble simplicity of temper had little to gain or to fear from the meditated wisdom or folly of the younger generation. In serene detachment he passed on his way through all the press and clamour of the market place.

The moving impulse which since the end of the sixth century had collected together at Athens all the intellectual forces of Greece for a final expansion of their capacity now began, in the middle of the fifth century, to take hold of philosophy as it had long since done literature and the fine arts. Athens saw the last representatives of Ionian physiology gathered together within her walls. Some, like Anaxagoras, took up their residence there for a long period, and left the impress of their teaching upon the foremost minds of the city. The others who paid briefer visits were those who in conscious opposition to the recent trend of thinking, stoutly upheld the older principles of philosophic Monism or Hylozoism, such as Diogenes of Apollonia or Hippon of Samos; or who sought like Archelaos to reconcile the old and the new Ionic doctrine. Besides these, Athens was a headquarters of the wandering exponents of the newest wisdom, the Sophists. Nowhere did unfettered discussion find such cultivated appreciation of its daring; nowhere was such an eager welcome given to the dialectical word-play that, seeming to be an end in itself, was destined to become the most fruitful nursery of native Athenian philosophy. All traditional beliefs and customs that had not their origin or their justification in reflexion were already doomed as soon as they, together with every conventional view of life and the world, were deprived of their natural protection of unchallenged self-evidence by the cold scrutiny of the sovereign tyrant Dialectic. The Sophists, those skirmishers of a new and as yet unrecognizable philosophy, scattered and put to flight the old guard of positive and doctrinal wisdom, but to the individual, who was bidden to depend upon his own resources, they offered stimulus to reflection in abundance but no permanent foothold in the shifting sands of opinion. It would be but a final assertion of the principle that there are no principles if by any chance the Sophists themselves should for a moment speak in the language of edification and, for example, lend the support of their eloquence to certain articles of doctrine that provided a positive teaching as to the nature and life of the soul.[120]

If Sophokles remained quite unaffected by this whole movement which reached its flood tide in Athens, Euripides was drawn completely into its current. He sought out philosophers and sophists personally and in their writings. His was a spirit that urgently desired to know the truth and he followed every available guide to knowledge and wisdom for a stage upon their journey. But he was never able to continue permanently in any one direction; in the restlessness and bewilderment of search and experiment he is the true son of his age.

His philosophical and sophistical leanings were sufficiently marked to make it impossible for him to accept any part of the belief or tradition of his countrymen without trial. So far as it is possible within the limits of dramatic art, he instituted an unsparing and unhesitating criticism of all accepted things, and in the process felt himself immeasurably superior to the wit and wisdom of the past. And yet he never satisfied himself. He could never rest content with a merely negative position, for all onesidedness was foreign to his nature. The tremendous honesty of his nature made it impossible for him to admit that element of frivolity which made the sophistic movement and the dialectical negation of all certainty so simple and attractive, and at the same time took away half its sting. But he could take nothing easily; and so with all his sophistic enlightenment he was never happy. The pupil of the Sophists would hear every other side as well; there were even moments when he longed to take refuge in the restful narrowness of old and traditional piety. But it was not given to him to settle down in any fixed set of opinions; all his convictions were provisional, mere hypotheses adopted for the purposes of experiment. Afloat on a changeful sea, he let himself be driven hither and thither by every wind of intellectual excitement or artistic necessity.

When all convictions were involved together in a state of perpetual change and instability, the conception of the nature and being of the soul and its relation to the powers of life and death could not alone remain in fixed and dogmatic certainty.

Where the content and character of the fable chosen as the subject of his drama demand it, the poet frankly adopts the popular view of the nature and destiny of the departed soul, its power and claim upon the worship of the survivors upon earth. In the fairy-tale play of the "Alcestis" the whole apparatus of popular belief plays its part; the God of Death and his awful office, the dwelling of the dead in the underworld, are spoken of as facts and creatures of experience and reality.[121] The elaborate funeral ceremonies owed to the dead are treated with the utmost seriousness and precision.[122] A whole drama, the "Suppliant Women", has as its real subject, or at least as its ostensible motive, the religious importance of a ritual burial,[123] nor is there any lack of isolated passages in which the importance of burial and the honour paid to graves is stressed.[124] The survivors on earth give pleasure to the dead by offerings at their graves,[125] and in this way obtain their goodwill and can count upon their support.[126] Power and honour belong not only to the great ones of antiquity translated to a higher state of being; [127] not only "Heroes" can extend their influence beyond their graves and affect the course of earthly events: [128] from the soul of his murdered father, the son expects assistance and succour in his time of need. The dread creatures of antique faith, the Erinyes, exact vengeance for the murdered mother.[129]

But at this point it becomes apparent that the poet only associates himself for his own purposes with this circle of ancient and sanctified popular fancy—so long in fact as it suits the tone that he wishes to give to the drama and its characters. The Erinyes are excellent material for the play—that in reality their horrid figures only exist in the imagination of the mentally diseased is clearly asserted in the "Orestes".[130] The whole series of beliefs and demands—murder ever calling forth fresh murder in accordance with the sacred duty of vengeance, the Erinyes, the bloodthirsty patrons of the murdered victim who leaves no proper avenger behind him—all these have ceased to have any validity for him: The "animal and bloodthirsty" part of these figures of ancient belief call forth the loathing of the poet living in the days of organized justice and humaner manners.[131] He does not believe in the souls' right to blood; the ancient legends which depend on this right are an abomination to him. In fact, he only seems to have written his plays about them in order, by the manner of his presentation, to have his revenge upon this material that was almost unavoidably thrust upon him by the tradition of the tragic stage. The duty of the living to offer a cult to the departed souls becomes doubtful in its turn. The seriousness with which that cult is sometimes handled in the plays is compromised by such reflections as these: it is certain that it matters little to the dead whether rich offerings are placed in their graves or not; such things only satisfy the idle vanity of the living; [132] honour and dishonour are of no further consequence to the dead.[133] How should they be, if the departed no longer feel either pleasure or pain, are nothing at all, as is repeatedly declared even in the middle of the "Alcestis"? [134]

It is evident that only from an arbitrarily adopted point of view do the picturesque creations of popular belief in the soul and of the cult of souls seem real to the poet; apart from this they disappear from his mind like the creatures of a dream.[135] The teachings of the theologians supplied him with no real substitute for popular faith; at the most they were a momentary and passing stimulus. No doubt he did not shut his eyes completely to these manifestations of the spiritual life of his time. His plays contain allusions to Orphic poetry and he joins the asceticism of the Orphics to the cold virtue of his Hippolytos.[136] The thought that the soul has fallen from a higher state of being and is enclosed within the body like the dead man in his coffin takes captive his imagination for a moment. " Who knows then whether life is not a kind of death," so that in death the soul awakes to its real life ? [137] The gloomy view of human destiny upon this earth to which the poet so often gives expression, might seem to hint at a consolation to come in a more satisfactory hereafter ; but the poet has no longing for the consolation offered by the theologians. Among the many and various reflections of the poet upon the reality that may reveal itself when the curtain is drawn aside by death, we never meet with the conception that lies at the bottom of the assurances made by the theologians —the conception that the spiritual individual is certain of its immortality because in its individuality it is of divine nature and is itself a god.[138] True, he is the author of the bold saying so often quoted and varied in later times, that God is nothing else but the mind that dwells in men.[139] But this makes no allusion to the theological doctrine of the multiplicity of individual gods or daimones banished into the life of men ; it rather implies a semi-philosphic doctrine of the soul in which one may perceive for the first time the expression of a permanent conviction on the part of the poet.

In quite inapposite contexts Euripides sometimes introduces passing allusions to a philosophical view of the world and humanity, that is the more certainly to be regarded as the private conviction of the poet himself as the utterances fail to correspond fully with the character of the person in the play who makes them, and do not arise necessarily from the dramatic situation. Everything in the world has had its origin from Earth and " the Aether of Zeus " ; the Earth is the maternal womb from which the Aether brings everything to birth.[140] Both constituents combine to produce the multiplicity of appearance ; they are not fused together nor are they to be derived from a single common original element ; [141] they remain in dualistic contrast side by side.[142] It was probably the dualism of this cosmological fancy that reminded the ancients of Anaxagoras ; but these statements cannot be regarded as simply a poetical version of the doctrine of Anaxagoras ; [143] for they derive the multiplicity of matter and things from the simple element of " Earth " from which they arise only by a process of change and transformation, while in the "seedmixture" of Anaxagoras, the unchangeable seeds of all things only separate themselves out from the whole and give rise by mechanical reassemblings to all the perceived appearances of the world. The "Aether" of Euripides in its relations with the "Earth" is besides being the active partner also the intellectual and animated element. The isolation of such an element from the rest of matter does indeed remind us of the procedure of Anaxagoras. But the poet's Aether is still an element though it may be penetrated by mind and animated by spirit; it is not a mental being standing over against all the other elements in essential distinctness like the *Nous* of Anaxagoras. The fact that it is the element of the Aether, i.e. the dry and hot air, in which intellectual capacity is said to inhere, may be regarded as having been borrowed from Diogenes of Apollonia, a philosopher who was held in considerable estimation at Athens at that time, and who was well known to Euripides.[144] In his doctrine, the air (which indeed, in contrast to the view of Euripides, produces all other things simply out of itself) is expressly identified with the "Soul" and is itself described as "having understanding".[145]

This view of the elementary forces and constitution of the universe, made up as it is from philosophical suggestions of a scarcely reconcilable character, in which the dualistic tendency is in fact finally predominant, suggests itself to the poet whenever in an exalted mood he speaks of the final destiny of the human soul. The soul on its separation from the body will depart to join the "Aether". But in such conceptions it is not always the imagination of the philosopher-poet that finds expression. On this subject it is accompanied or replaced by a more popular view that only distantly resembles it, but which led to the same result. When we hear now and again of the Aether, the luminous atmosphere above the clouds, as being the *dwelling place* of the departed souls,[146] the view—more theological than philosophic in its character—seems to be implied that after death the liberated soul will float upwards to the seat of the gods[147] which has long ceased to be situated upon Olympos, but is in "heaven" or in this same Aether. This, too, was the meaning of a saying traditionally ascribed to Epicharmos the comic-poet of Sicily who was himself versed in philosophy. In this saying the pious man is assured that for him death will bring no evil for his "mind" will dwell permanently in "heaven".[148] This conception, which appears so frequently in later epitaphs, must have been familiar to popular imagination at Athens at an early period; at least in the grave-epigram officially dedicated by the state to the memory of the Athenians who fell in the year 432 before Poteidaia, we find the belief expressed (as a commonly received opinion) that the souls of these brave men have been received by the "Aether" just as the earth has received their bodies.[149] Such official use implies a commonly accepted opinion and the fundamental ideas of the popular cult of the souls might have led to similar results. From the beginning popular belief had regarded the psyche, which got its name from the air or breath, as closely akin to the winds, the mobile air and its spirits. It would not be difficult for the idea to arise that the soul, as soon as it was free to decide for itself what should become of it, should go to join the elemental spirits that are its kinsfolk. Perhaps this, too, is what Epicharmos means when on another occasion he says that in death when the united are parted asunder each returns whence it came, the body to earth, but the soul up to the heights—its name, in which allusion is made to its perpetual mobility, being now after the example of Xenophanes derived from the breath of the wind, the moving air (πνεῦμα), a usage which became very common in later times.[150]

But perhaps the use of such a name is an indication that this poet also regards the soul as standing in a close relation and kinship with the Aether that is destined to receive it after its release from the body; so that from this side, too [151]—in addition to the more popular conception just mentioned—Euripides may have received a hint for his peculiar version of the physiological theory of Diogenes. In his view the soul participates in the nature of the Aether. But it is more important to notice that the Aether participates in the nature and true reality of the soul; it possesses life, consciousness and power of thought. They both belong to one family. The Aether according to the poet—and here the speculations of Anaximenes as revived by Diogenes are unmistakable [152]—is a true vital atmosphere, an all-embracing psychic element, so that it becomes, not a mere vehicle of mind, but the All-Mind itself. The concept is even condensed and half-personified, it is called by the name of the highest divine power, Zeus,[153] and the poet as though speaking of a personal god, calls it "immortal".[154] The human mind, too, as akin to the universal god and the All-Mind, appears, as it had been in the teaching of Diogenes,[155] as a part of this God, this universal Mind. God is the mind, and the mind and understanding in us is God—so the poet clearly asserts.[156] In death, when the separation of the mind from its earthly elements takes place, the Pneuma of man will "not indeed live", as it had done in the separate existence of the individual man, but it will "preserve an immortal consciousness", entering into the immortal Aether and fusing itself with the All-living and the All-thinking.[157] None of the physiologists who conceived the same idea of an immortality excluding the personal immortality of the individual, of the universal spirit of life in mankind, has expressed his meaning with such distinctness as this philosophic layman.

The poet may have wished to remain permanently upon the sublime heights of this Pantheistic vision; but he must, in his peculiar all-embracing spirit that never held fast to any one view with enduring persistence, have experienced too often the truth of the saying of Protagoras that every statement calls forth its equally legitimate opposite,[158] to have become an unswerving adherent of any single opinion. Death, and whatever may reveal itself after death, is beyond the experience of any man.[159] It may be that complete disappearance into nothingness follows death; that the dead man becomes simply nothing.[160] It may be that in the permanence of the human race the great name and the renown of glorious deeds lives on undying.[161] Whether there may remain besides a vestige of life in a spirit world, who can tell? Perhaps such a thing is hardly even to be wished.[162] It is just what makes death such a comforting thing, that it puts an end to all feeling and therefore to all pain and every care. We should not lament over our fate if, like the harvests that follow each other in the course of the years, one generation of men after another flowers, fades, and is carried off. So it is ordered in the course of Nature, and we ought not to be dismayed by anything that is rendered inevitable by her laws.[163]

NOTES TO CHAPTER XII

[1] The learned and more particularly the philosophers of later ages paid special attention to utterances of the older poetry that gave expression to belief of a spiritualist tendency. Just as they selected and preserved passages from Pindar (and from Melanippides in the case soon to be mentioned), which bore witness to an advanced view of the soul, so they must also have given us similar passages from other melic or from iambic and elegiac poets—if such passages had existed. They must, for example, have been absent from the θρῆνοι of Simonides which were famous as the models of this kind of poetry. And so with all the rest.

[2] Hades puts an end to all pleasure for every man; hence the warning that man should enjoy his youth upon earth: Thgn. 973 ff.; cf. 877 f., 1191 ff., 1009 f.; Sol. 24; Thgn. 719 ff.

[3] θανάτῳ πάντες ὀφειλόμεθα—an ancient saying often repeated; cf. Bergk on Simon. 122, 2; Nauck on Soph., *El.* 1173 [Blaydes ad loc.].

[4] Hades himself plays the part of Thanatos and carries off the souls to the lower world. Thus as early as Semon. i, 13 f., τοὺς δ' Ἄρει δεδμημένους πέμπει μελαίνης Ἀΐδης ὑπὸ χθονός. In metaphorical language Ἅιδης for θάνατος is quite regular from the time of Pindar onwards. This, in turn, lent support to the use of the name of Ἅιδης instead of the *personified* Θάνατος. So esp. in Pi., *O.* ix, 33–5; cf. besides, *Epigr. Gr.* 89, 3–4. τόνδε . . . μάρψας Ἅιδης οἱ σκοτίας ἀμφέβαλεν πτέρυγας; cf. 201, 2; 252, 1–2. (And therefore in Eur., *Alc.* 261, we should not alter the πτερωτὸς Ἅιδας who is named instead of Thanatos—not even in favour of the otherwise ingenious βλέπων . . . ᾆδαν.)

[5] δηρὸν ἔνερθεν γῆς ὀλέσας ψυχὴν κείσομαι ὥστε λίθος ἄφθογγος Thgn. 567 f.—the condition of things in Hades is regarded exactly as in the Homeric pictures: Thgn. 704–10.

[6] See esp. Sol. 13, 29 ff.; Thgn. 731–42; 205 ff.

[7] Mimn. ii, 13: ἄλλος δ' αὖ παίδων ἐπιδεύεται, ὧντε μάλιστα ἱμείρων κατὰ γῆς ἔρχεται εἰς Ἀΐδην. Without children there can be no assurance that the cult of the soul will be carried on. But we may well believe that the attaching of so much importance to offspring was assisted by the natural human belief that the man who left children behind him on earth did not completely perish in death (hence ἀειγενές ἐστι καὶ ἀθάνατον ὡς θνητῷ ἡ γέννησις as in Plato, *Smp.* 206 E). This alone gives a meaning and a reason for the widespread belief among the Greeks that the wicked man who is punished after his death in his children and children's children himself feels that punishment.

[8] Semon. 1; 3. Mimn. 2. Sol. 13, 63 ff.; 14. Thgn. 167 f.; 425 ff. We may also add here the expressions of resignation, Hdt. vii, 46; i, 31.

[9] Νυκτὸς θάλαμος [Ion] *fr.* 8, 2.

[10] On the story of Midas and Silenos see *Griech. Roman*, p. 204 f. As to the ancient and often repeated maxim ἀρχὴν (or πάντων) μὲν μὴ φῦναι ἐπιχθονίοισιν ἄριστον κτλ., see Bgk., *Opusc.* ii, 214; *PLG*[4]. ii, p. 155 f. Nietzsche, *Rh. Mus.* xxviii, 212 ff. (whose view that the

beginning ἀρχὴν . . . is old and original—but not his involved explanation of this—has been fully confirmed by the finding of the primitive form of the ἀγών: Mahaffy, *On the Flinders Petrie Papyri*, i, p. 70).

[11] Simon. *fr.* 39; 38.

[12] *fr.* 137.—Usener, *Götternamen*, 229, 13, says of Sappho that "she was possessed by the belief that as a poetess she would live again after her death among the gods, and would therefore become a *heroine*; see *frr.* 68 and 136". But from these fragments of Sappho no such belief can be extracted without first reading into them a good deal that they do not say.

[13] Of the man who has fallen in glory on the battlefield Tyrtaios says, 12, 31 f.: οὐδέ ποτε κλέος ἐσθλὸν ἀπόλλυται οὐδ' ὄνομ' αὐτοῦ, ἀλλ' ὑπὸ γῆς περ ἐὼν γίγνεται ἀθάνατος (i.e. in renown upon earth). Thgn. says to his Kyrnos, 243 ff., in your lifetime my songs will make you famous καὶ ὅταν δνοφερῆς ὑπὸ κεύθεσι γαίης βῇς πολυκωκύτους εἰς Ἀίδαο δόμους, οὐδέποτ' οὐδὲ θανὼν ἀπολεῖς κλέος ἀλλὰ μελήσεις ἄφθιτον ἀνθρώποις αἰὲν ἔχων ὄνομα . . . ; cf. Aesch., *Epigr.* iii, 3 (241 Bgk. = 449 Di.), ζωὸν δὲ φθιμένων πέλεται κλέος.

[14] Even in Hades the dead perceive χθονίᾳ φρενί if they themselves or the ἀρεταί of their descendants upon earth are praised: Pi., *P.* v, 98; cf. *O.* viii, 81 ff.; xiv, 20 ff.; [Ion] *Anth. Pal.* vii, 43, 3 (to Eurip.), ἴσθι δ' ὑπὸ χθονὸς ὤν, ὅτι σοι κλέος ἄφθιτον ἔσται κτλ.—In the expressions collected by Meuss, *Jahrb. f. Philol.* 1889, p. 812 f., from the fourth century orators there only remains a very faint recollection of such a belief.

[15] Semon. 2, τοῦ μὲν θανόντος οὐκ ἂν ἐνθυμοίμεθα, εἴ τι φρονοῖμεν, πλεῖον ἡμέρης μιῆς.—Stes. 51 ἀτελέστατα γὰρ καὶ ἀμάχανα τοὺς θανόντας κλαίειν. 52, θανόντος ἀνδρὸς πᾶσ' ἀπόλλυται ποτ' ἀνθρώπων χάρις.

[16] This emerges at once if we review the material collected by H. Meuss upon "the conceptions appearing in the Attic orators of existence after death": *Jahrb. f. Philol.* 1889, pp. 801–15. For the cult of the soul and all that attaches to it the orators are our most authoritative witnesses and as such are frequently examined in the sections of this book that deal with the subject.

[17] εἴ τινες τῶν τετελευτηκότων λάβοιεν τρόπῳ τινὶ τοῦ νῦν γιγνομένου πράγματος αἴσθησιν and frequently in this style: cf. the passages quoted by Westermann on D., *Lept.* (20), 87; cf. also Lehrs, *Pop. Aufs.* 329 ff. The question is always whether the dead are capable in any way of apprehending what goes on in this world. The continued life of the dead is never doubtful but rather implied throughout; for without such implication *no* possibility whatever would be left for that εἰ—.

[18] See Nägelsbach, *Nachhom. Theol.* 420. Meuss, p. 812.

[19] This is well brought out by Lehrs, *Pop. Aufs.* 331. But the statement holds good in an even more precise and exclusive sense than he there gives it. The words of Hyper., *Epit.* xiii, § 39, deal simply with the existence in Hades of those who have died for their country (with some traditional embellishments: see above, chap. vii, n. 5)—this much can hardly ever have been expressly doubted or denied by any orator. But it is wrong to say (as Lehrs does: p. 331) that Hyp. expresses, though in other words, what was afterwards laid down by [D.H.] *Rhet.* vi, 5, as proper "for such funeral speeches" (no, only for *private* funerals—which is quite another matter). It is true that the advice there given is to say that the soul is ἀθάνατος and now dwells

"with the gods". But it never enters into the head of Hyp. to say any such thing (nor in the frag. of the speech preserved by Stob., *Fl.* 124, 36). In fact, the precept of this sophistic writer (still more the advice given by Men. Rhet., *de Encom.* 414, 16 ff.; 421, 16 ff. Sp.) rather reveals the enormous contrast between the style of the sophistic funeral oratory of a later period and the real characteristics of the old Attic funeral orations: a difference founded upon the difference of sentiment manifested by the public that listened to such speeches in two different ages. Even the statements of [Dem.] *Epit.* (60) 34 (πάρεδροι τοῖς κάτω θεοῖς together with the ἀγαθοὶ ἄνδρες of earlier times ἐν μακάρων νήσοις) betray sophistic colouring though falling far short of the excesses of Ps.-D.H. and Men. Rhet.

[20] The only thing ἀγήραντος about those who have fallen in the wars of freedom is their εὐλογίη Simon. 100, 4; cf. 106, 4 (with Bgk.'s note). 99, 3–4 οὐδὲ τεθνᾶσι θανόντες ἐπεί σφ' ἀρετὴ καθύπερθεν κυδαίνουσ' ἀνάγει δώματος ἐξ 'Αΐδεω (which is imitated in the epitaph of Thrasymachos the Kretan οὐδὲ θανὼν ἀρετᾶς ὄνυμ' ὠλέσας, ἀλλά σε Φάμα κυδαίνουσ' ἀνάγει δώματος ἐξ 'Αΐδα, *BCH.* 1889, p. 60).

[21] κλῦθί μοι ὦ πάτερ, θαῦμα βροτῶν, τᾶς ἀειζώου μεδέων ψυχᾶς, Melanipp. 6. The words θαῦμα βροτῶν (modelled on the θαῦμα βροτοῖσι of Homer) can refer only to Dionysos (of the gods who enter into the question here): Διώνυσος, χάρμα βροτοῖσιν, Ξ 325. Further, it is natural to think of Dionysos in the work of a dithyrambic poet.

[22] The dead man ἀμφ' 'Αχέροντι ναιετάων, Pi., *N.* iv, 85. This is the general assumption: e.g. *P.* xi, 19–22; *O.* ix, 33–5; *I.* viii, 59 f.; *fr.* 207 Bgk.

[23] ἔστι δὲ καί τι θανόντεσσιν μέρος κὰν νόμον ἐρδόμενον· κατακρύπτει δ' οὐ κόνις συγγόνων κεδνὰν χάριν, *O.* viii, 77 ff.

[24] Something of the kind is adopted for the moment, e.g. in *O.* xiv, 20 ff.; viii, 81 ff. A real belief in such a possibility appears perhaps most clearly in *P.* v, 98 ff.

[25] For him who dies fighting for his country there is in store—not blessedness but only Fame, *I.* vii, 26 ff. He who comes καλὰ ἔρξαις ἀοιδᾶς ἄτερ εἰς 'Αΐδα σταθμόν has little reward for his pains (his reward would, in fact, have been just the praise given in the ἀοιδά), *O.* x, 91 ff., cf. *N.* vii, 30–2.

[26] A strange expression is the δαίμων γενέθλιος of *O.* xiii, 105 (in the same poem we also have Ξενοφῶντος δαίμων 28, which in this case at least is something more than "destiny", otherwise the normal meaning of δαίμων in Pindar, cf. *P.* v, 123, *I.* vii, 43). It almost seems as if it were intended to describe the ancestor spirit that brings good luck to the house like the *genius generis* or ἥρως συγγενείας (see above, chap. v, n. 132).

[27] Amphiaraos, *O.* vi, 14; *N.* ix, 24 ff.; x, 8 f. (Amph. from his underground cavern sees the fighting in the war of the Epigonoi, *P.* viii, 39–56. There is no suggestion that the 'Επίγονοι inquire at his oracle—as Dissen supposes; with this the ὧδ' εἶπε μαρναμένων 43 is inconsistent.)—Ganymedes translated to eternal life, *O.* i, 44; x, 104 f. Apart from this there are temporary translations to the gods or from one place on earth to another, *O.* i, 36 ff.; ix, 59; *P.* ix, 5 ff.; *I.* viii, 20 f.

[28] *O.* ii, 27 ff.

[29] ἀλλά τι προσφέρομεν ἔμπαν ἢ μέγαν νόον ἤτοι φύσιν ἀθανάτοις, *N.* vi, 4 f.

[30] σκιᾶς ὄναρ ἄνθρωπος, *P.* viii, 95. ἓν ἀνδρῶν ἓν θεῶν γένος, ἐκ μιᾶς δὲ πνέομεν ματρὸς ἀμφότεροι· διείργει δὲ πᾶσα κεκριμένα δύναμις,

ὡς τὸ μὲν οὐδέν, ὁ δὲ χάλκεος ἀσφαλὲς αἰὲν ἕδος μένει οὐρανός, *N.* vi, 1 ff.

[31] *fr.* 131 Bgk.

[32] Pindar in these lines speaks only of the αἰῶνος εἴδωλον; but that by this he means the ψυχή is obvious in itself and is stated by Plutarch, who preserves the lines, *Cons. ad Apoll.* 35, p. 120 D (περὶ ψυχῆς λέγων; cf. *Rom.* 28).—ψυχή in Pindar sometimes stands for what is otherwise called καρδία or φρήν, "heart" or "disposition" e.g. *P.* i, 48; iv, 122; *N.* ix, 39; *I.* iv, 53b, and *O.* ii, 77, and prob. also *P.* iii, 41; "disposition," *N.* ix, 32. The word is sometimes (as in Homer) equivalent to ζωή, *P.* iii, 101, ψυχὰν λιπών. It simultaneously = "life" and the *alter ego* dwelling within the living man, *O.* viii, 39, ψυχὰς βάλον; cf. *N.* i, 47. But the poet knows also the full meaning of ψυχά in the older idiom and belief. Entirely in the manner of Homeric usage ψυχά denotes the spiritual double of mankind, which survives the man himself, in those instances where the ψυχή of the dead is said to be still in existence: ψυχὰν κομίξαι, *P.* iv, 159; *N.* viii, 44 f.; σὺν Ἀγαμεμνονίᾳ ψυχᾷ (is Kassandra sent into Hades), *P.* xi, 20 f. Persephone ἀναδιδοῖ ψυχὰς πάλιν (out of Hades), *fr.* 133, 3 (Bgk.); *I.* i, 68, ψυχὰν Ἀΐδᾳ τελέων (in death).—ψυχαί is also used in the old idiomatic sense in *fr.* 132, 1: which is, however, spurious.—ψυχά in Pindar never denotes the psychical powers of the living man inclusive of the intellect, much less the intellect, νοῦς, alone.

[33] καὶ σῶμα μὲν πάντων ἕπεται θανάτῳ περισθενεῖ, ζῶον δ' ἔτι λείπεται αἰῶνος εἴδωλον· τὸ γάρ ἐστι μόνον ἐκ θεῶν, *fr.* 131 (96 Boeckh).

[34] οἶσι δὲ Φερσεφόνα ποινὰν παλαιοῦ πένθεος δέξεται—*fr.* 133. What is meant is undoubtedly the ancient "guilt" of the soul for which Perseph. receives satisfaction. This guilt can only be called a πένθος if she who accepts the satisfaction is regarded as herself grief-stricken by the guilty dead; if, in fact, the deed has been the occasion of mourning for Persephone. That this can apply to the goddess of the underworld is startling, but it cannot be got rid of by artificial interpretation (as Dissen would like to get rid of it). Pindar follows throughout the analogy of the ancient procedure of expiation in the case of blood-guiltiness. But this procedure seems to be familiar with the idea that, apart from the ἀγχιστεία of the murdered man, the underworld gods themselves (as guardians of the Souls) are immediately injured by the deed and stricken by grief and must receive satisfaction on their own account. Hence in certain legends (typificatory of ritual) the murderer not only has to fly from the land but to undergo servitude to the χθόνιοι: Apollo, especially after the slaying of Python, has to serve Ἄδμητος, i.e. Hades for an *ennaëteris* (more on this subject below, n. 40). Thus, the guilty soul banished from its proper home serves a "great year" under Persephone, and this is the ποινά that it pays.

[35] *O.* ii, 63–5. Everything here refers to judgment and compensation *in Hades.* In the words θανόντων μὲν ἐνθάδ' αὐτίκ' ἀπάλαμνοι φρένες ποινὰς ἔτισαν the ἐνθάδε cannot possibly belong to the ποινὰς ἔτισαν, as Aristarchos supposed, so that the words should refer to the punishment in the course of a new birth upon *earth* of crimes committed in Hades (in itself a remarkable conception). θανόντες alone would not be put for θανόντες καὶ ἀναβεβιωκότες, and we can only understand by the word those who after a life-time upon earth have died and are now spending their time below in the underworld. Moreover, it is hardly likely (as Ty. Mommsen reminds us *adnot. crit. ad Olymp.* 24) that the exposition of the "knowledge of the future" (62) on the part of

a man still living upon earth would *begin* with what may happen to man, not after his death, but in a second appearance upon earth that is to fall to his lot later on. We must first of all be told what happens after the conclusion of the present condition of life, viz. that upon earth. Finally, the use of αὐτίκα is quite satisfactory if it refers to the judgment in Hades that follows immediately after death; while it is meaningless in Aristarchos' interpretation (hence Rauchenstein writes αὖτις—a mere conjecture and a superfluous one). The view that the μὲν—δέ of 63–4 necessitates Aristarchos' explanation is not convincing (as Lübbert thinks, *Ind. Schol. Bonn. hib.* 1887, p. xviii—incidentally he quite unjustifiably introduces specifically Platonic fancies into Pindar, p. xix). The θανόντων μέν of 63 is not answered till ὅσοι δ' ἐτόλμασαν . . . 75, just as the αὐτίκα of 63 does not receive its contrast till we come to what happens much later—after the life on earth has been thrice repeated—described in 75 ff. The δέ of 64 and 67 are subordinate (not adversative) to what is introduced by the μέν of 63 and they continue the thought. The ἐνθάδε of 63 might indeed, in accordance with an otherwise correct usage, be connected with ἀπάλαμνοι φρένες, as it is by one of the Scholiasts: "the φρένες which have committed crimes here upon earth." But ἀπάλαμνος does not mean *sceleratus, impius* (nor does it in the passages adduced for this meaning by Zacher, *Diss. Halens.* iii, 237: Thgn. 281; Sim. v, 3). The ἀπάλαμνοι φρένες are simply equivalent to the ἀμενηνὰ κάρηνα of Homer, and are a very suitable expression for the ψυχαί of the dead (though not indeed for the ψυχαί of the reborn as Aristarchos would have it). No alternative remains save to connect θανόντων and ἐνθάδε: simulac mortui sunt hic, s. decedunt hinc (Dissen). The sentence τὰ δ' ἐν τᾷδε . . . must then either be a more exact description of what has been stated generally just before in ποινὰς ἔτισαν (and this is Mommsen's view supported by one Schol.), or else be subordinated—together with its contrasted ἴσαις δὲ . . . 67 ff. —to ποινὰς ἔτισαν. ποινά in Pindar means regularly compensation, whether expiation for evil deeds or reward for good (cf. *P.* i, 59; *N.* i, 70b). If we might suppose that by a brachylogy not beyond possibility in Pindar ποινὰς ἔτισαν is put for ποινὰς ἔτισαν καὶ ἐδέξαντο, then the sense might be: after death the souls receive at once recompense for their actions—and *then* follows the division of the bad 64 ff., and the good 67 ff. But we may perhaps rest content with Mommsen's explanation.

[36] *O.* ii, 74.

[37] Plu., *de Lat. Viv.* 7, p. 1130 C after citing the lines of Pindar *fr.* 130 (95) adds: (the rivers of Erebos) δεχόμενοι καὶ ἀποκρύπτοντες ἀγνοίᾳ καὶ λήθῃ τοὺς κολαζομένους. This *might* possibly be an addition made by Plu. on his own account—he had frequently spoken of εἰς ἄγνοιαν αὑτὸν ἐμβαλεῖν, etc., in his war against the Epicurean λάθε βιώσας and here the same thing appears again from Erebos. But the words are more probably a paraphrase from Pindar. At any rate, what is said in Plu. about the μνῆμαι καὶ λόγοι of the εὐσεβεῖς in clear contrast with the λήθη of the ἀσεβεῖς, comes from Pindar: this is shown by the allusions of Aristid. i, p. 146, 1 Dind. From this parallel it is also clearly proved that the λήθη does not refer (as Lehrs, *Pop. Aufs.* 313 thinks) to the forgetfulness of the κολαζόμενοι in the minds of the living, but forgetfulness of their previous life by the κολαζόμενοι themselves. Accordingly we are to suppose that Pindar assigns retention of memory and complete consciousness only to the good in Hades, as their special privilege (cf. the position of Teiresias in κ 494), while the punishment

of the wicked is enhanced by λήθη (cf. above, chap. vii, n. 21). Not to have fallen a victim to λήθη in Hades—not to have drunk the waters of Lethe—is occasionally alluded to in poetico-religious utterances of later times as a special privilege of the good, e.g. *Epigr. Gr.* 204, 11 (first century B.C.); 414, 10. Λήθης and Μνημοσύνης πήγη in Hades (as in the sanctuary of Trophonios at Lebadea, Paus. 9, 39, 8): *Epigr.* 1037 (cf. above, chap. vii, n. 21; chap. xi, n. 96; and see also below).

[38] τοῖσι λάμπει μὲν μένος ἀελίου τὰν ἐνθάδε νύκτα κάτω, *fr.* 129. In this naive conception, what Helios only threatens to do in Homer, δύσομαι εἰς 'Αΐδαο καὶ ἐν νεκύεσσι φαείνω, he does in reality and regularly during the earthly night. The same idea must be referred to in *O.* ii, 61 ff., ἴσον δὲ νύκτεσσιν αἰεὶ ἴσον ἐν ἁμέραις ἅλιον ἔχοντες (so Boeckh)—the ἐσθλοί live in the χῶρος εὐσεβῶν in Hades: they have by night and day the same sun (as we: the ἀπονέστερον of 62 also implies this), that is to say, just as much of the sun as we have on earth only in reverse order of time. The sun only shines upon the εὐσεβεῖς below; μόνοις γὰρ ἡμῖν ἥλιος καὶ φέγγος ἱλαρόν ἐστι sing the initiated in Hades in Ar., *Ran.* 454 f. (but it is the *same* sun which shines upon them as shines on us, φῶς κάλλιστον ὥσπερ ἐνθάδε 155. solemque suum sua sidera norunt is a subtlety of later excogitation). Helios shining by night in Hades occurs again in the late Greek Hymn εἰς Ἥλιον (*Orph.*, p. 291 Ab.), v. 11, ἣν γαίης κευθμῶνα μόλῃς νεκύων τ' ἐπὶ χῶρον. *Epigr. Gr.* 228b, 7–8, Λητογενές, σὺ δὲ παῖδας ἐν ἡρώεσσι φυλάσσοις, εὐσεβέων ἀεὶ χῶρον ἐπερχόμενος.

[39] *O.* ii, 75 ff.

[40] *fr.* 133 ἐνάτῳ ἔτεϊ. What is meant is beyond all question "after the expiration of an *ennaëteris*" (period of 99 months, i.e. 8 years and 3 intercalary months), a period which besides being familiar as a cycle of religious festivals (Apolline specially but not exclusively) also occurs in the ancient procedure of atonement for murder as the period of self-banishment and servitude in a foreign land undergone by the murderer. Apollo after slaying Python serves μέγαν εἰς ἐνιαυτόν (i.e. an ennaëteris) in the house of Admetos (i.e. the god of the lower world) and then returns purified (Müller, *Dorians*, i, 338); in the same way Herakles serves Eurystheus (at least a trace of this is found in [Apollod.] 2, 5, 11, 1; see Müller, *Dorians*, i, 445).—After the murder of Iphitos Herakles has to serve as bondsman to Omphale (peculiar in this case is the combination of this species of atonement for murder with the buying-off of the relatives of the murdered man [Apollod.] 2, 6, 2, 5; D.S. 4, 31, 5). At the end of this period of service he is once more "pure" (ἁγνὸς ἦν S., *Trach.* 258).—Kadmos after slaying the dragon and the Σπαρτοί serves Ares (the chthonic ?) for an ἐνιαυτός of eight years [Apollod.] 3, 4, 2, 1; Müller, *Orchomen.* 213.—Hippotes after the murder of Mantis has to fly the country δέκα ἔτη [Apollod.] 2, 8, 3, 3.—On the analogy of this custom the gods, too, who have broken an oath sworn by the Styx are banished nine years from the rest of the Olympians (and confined to Hades, since menial service of the χθόνιοι is the essential idea of all such ἀπενιαυτισμός), Hes., *Th.* 793 ff.; Orph. *fr.* 157. With a reminiscence of this expiatory banishment Pindar makes the souls at the conclusion of their earthly pilgrimage (which is itself a banishment) undergo a final period of penance in Hades for an ennaëteris, at the end of which the ποινή for the ancient crime is regarded as completely paid off.—The life on earth and the period in Hades which follows is regarded as an exile of the souls (on account of serious crime).—Such an idea was most natural if the real home of the soul was thought of as being

a divine (not earthly) country; the idea occurs quite clearly in Empedokles (certainly uninfluenced by the brief allusions of Pindar); see above, chap. xi, n. 75.

[41] *fr.* 133. The similarity to the promises made by Emped. *fr.* 146 (457 f.) is immediately apparent, but is not to be explained by imitation of Pindar by Emped., but simply by the similarity of imaginative outlook which led to similar results in the two cases.—Elevation to the rank of Hero is the reward which next awaits the man who is born a king, according to this view. Very remarkable is the manner in which Pindar, *O.* ii, 58–62, effects the transition to his eschatological statement: the man who possesses πλοῦτος ἀρεταῖς δεδαιδαλμένος knows the future, viz. what we are then told about the fate of the soul hereafter. This assertion, which seems to attribute to the virtuous Great Man at once a higher and a profounder knowledge, is perhaps best explained by the allusions of *fr.* 133. He who has reached this highest stage of earthly happiness must deduce from that very circumstance that for him now it is fated after another death to become a Hero. He therefore knows that everything, indeed, happens that is related in ll. 63–74, but that before him in particular lies that which follows in ll. 75 ff.; and this is to be regarded as the real import of what the man in question "knows", 62, while the rest, 63–74, is only added for the sake of completeness. Theron, therefore—for it is he who is alluded to throughout—may be assured beforehand that after death he will be gathered to the Heroes. This is what Pindar means to say here, or at least to give the συνετοί to understand 91 ff. As a matter of historical fact Theron was worshipped with ἡρωϊκαὶ τιμαί after his death, D.S. xi, 53, 2.

[42] *fr.* 133. There is according to Dissen a contradiction between *fr.* 133 and *O.* ii, 75 ff.: in the latter three periods of life on earth are necessary before the final departure, in *fr.* 133 only two. This variation would be got rid of if we could adopt the interpretation given by Ty. Mommsen, *adnot. crit. Olymp.* 30, and assert that in *O.* ii also Pindar only speaks of two earthly lives with a single residence in Hades intervening. But the words ἐς τρὶς ἑκατέρωθι μείναντες, 75–6, can hardly bear any other interpretation than "three times on each of the two sides" (not: "on both sides—once on that side, twice on this side: total three times"). At the same time there is nothing in *fr.* 133 to prevent us taking the same number of lives (three as a minimum) to be implied there too. We are not there told that the birth as kings, etc., must always be the one to follow the first birth: in this case also two earlier lives may have gone before.

[43] See above, chap. iv, § 8.

[44] ἔτειλαν Διὸς ὁδὸν παρὰ Κρόνου τύρσιν, *O.* ii, 77. What exactly is to be understood by the "way of Zeus" was presumably clearer to the συνετοί versed in the mythology of mysticism for whom Pindar is here writing, than it is to us. It must mean (as Boeckh supposes) the way which Zeus treads in order to reach that Island, far to the West in Okeanos, inaccessible as the Land of the Hyperboreans to ship or traveller on foot; it is a special ἀθανάτων ὁδός like that which leads to Homer's grotto of the Nymphs, ν 112. Acc. to Bergk, *Opusc.* ii, 708, it is "certain" that Pindar means the Milky Way. Along this the gods travel to the house of Zeus, Ovid, *M.* i, 168; and Orpheus in the same way *fr.* 123, 17 Ab., speaks of the θεῶν ὁδοὶ οὐρανιώνων in the heavens. But the souls could only be made to travel along the Milky Way if their habitation was placed in the sky as it often was later. So, as Bergk points out, following Lob., *Agl.* 935,

the Empedotimos of Herakld. Pont. calls the Milky Way ὁδὸς ψυχῶν τῶν ᾅδην τὸν ἐν οὐράνῳ διαπορευομένων ap. Philop. in Arist., *Mete.*, p. 117, 10 Hayd.; see above, chap. ix, n. 111. But Pindar situates his μακάρων νῆσος in the Ocean (78): it is difficult to see how the souls could arrive there on the Milky Way from the place where they find themselves after death. (We may surely acquit Pindar of the later fancies about an Okeanos in the heavens.) Q.S. iii, 761 ff. (cited by Tafel) knows of a special way belonging to the gods which leads from heaven down to the Ἠλύσιον πεδίον. But the way by which the souls reach the μακάρων νῆσος does not, like that way, begin in heaven. We should rather think of some way only passable for gods and spirits leading from the inhabited world over the pathless Ocean to the latter's "sources" far in the West.

[45] In *O.* ii, 84–5, it is certainly Kronos who is meant (as Didymos took it, though he gave an absurd interpretation of the passage) and not Zeus as Aristarchos imagined. The exceedingly corrupt and (owing to the intrusion of glosses) unmetrical lines are beyond certain restoration: the emendations of the Byzantine scholars give the required sense.—What happened to the incorrigibly wicked? In accordance with the theory of the soul's Transmigration two alternative views as to their fate were possible: they might be regarded as passing from body to body unceasingly (Empedokl.) or as doing penance by suffering eternal punishment in Hell (as with Plato and others). The circumstances in which he alludes to these matters do not give Pindar any special occasion to declare himself for either view. He has only to speak of the final condition of the just; the fate of the ἀσεβεῖς is left in semi-obscurity. Something about the matter is, however, said in *fr.* 132: ψυχαὶ ἀσεβέων hover under the vault of heaven that covers the earth (γαίᾳ either corrupt or grammatically bad Greek), while the pious above the vault of heaven (ἐπουράνιοι) sing to the "Great Blessed One". Everything in this is un-Pindaric, the inadequacy and even incorrectness of the language (μολπαῖς ἐν ὕμνοις), the unconcealed monotheism of the phrase μάκαρα μέγαν, the conception of the souls as having nothing else to do than sing to the One God, the whole idea that these blessed ones dwell "in heaven". This last is an idea familiar to Greeks of a later period, nor is the division of souls into ὑπουράνιοι and ἐπουράνιοι unknown to them; cf. *Epigr. Gr.* 650, 9 ff. But Pindar cannot have written anything of the kind. It is even doubtful whether Clem. Al. who, *Str.* iv, 640 P., names as the author of the lines τὸν μελοποιόν, meant Pindar by the words: Theodoret. (*Gr. Aff. C.* viii, 599 C), who attributes the second half of the frag. to Pindar, had no other source but the same Clem. Al. But it may be doubted whether the whole is to be attributed to any Greek of the older faith. It has quite the appearance, as Zeller, *Socr. and Socratics*, p. 24, n. 3, strikingly suggests, of one of those *Jewish* forgeries in which Jewish monotheism and the ideas connected with it were to be fathered upon Greek antiquity. Welcker, *Kl. Schr.* v, 252 ff.; *Götterl.* i, 741 f., defends the *fr.* (and most unconvincingly connects the ψυχαὶ ὑπουράνιοι and ἐπουράνιοι of the *fr.* with the quite different δαίμονες ἐπιχθόνιοι and ὑποχθόνιοι of Hes., *Op.* 123 and 141). He thinks he can defend the genuineness of the lines (which had already been declared spurious by Dissen) by pointing to the words of Horace about Pindar's θρῆνοι (*O.* iv, 2, 21): flebili sponsae iuvenem raptum plorat, et vires animumque moresque aureos educit in astra nigroque invidet Orco. Even supposing that this referred to the transport of the souls to the stars the witness of Horace thus given would only

remove a single difficulty from a passage that has other overwhelming difficulties in profusion. But Horace says nothing of the transport of the "Soul" to the heavenly regions. *vires, animus, mores,* all these together refer not at all to the ψυχή but to the ἦθος and the ἀρεταί of the dead. Pindar, Horace means, rescues the *memory* of the nature and merits of the youth from decay: only the fame which the poet secures for him is under discussion. *educit in astra* and *invidet Orco* mean nothing more than: he rescues the memory of the dead from oblivion, exactly as in the epitaph quoted above, n. 20: οὐδὲ θανὼν ἀρετᾶς ὄνυμ' ὤλεσας ἀλλά σε Φάμα κυδαίνουσ' ἀνάγει δώματος ἐξ 'Αΐδα. Thus, it is least of all to be concluded from Horace's words that Pindar transported the souls of the εὐσεβεῖς into the heavens (rather that in the θρῆνοι—as much as anywhere else: see above, n. 25—Pindar sometimes only recognizes the immortality of fame: of that alone does Horace speak).

[46] *O.* ii celebrates the victory which Theron had won at Olympia in *Ol.* 76, but was probably written some time after that victory. Theron died *Ol.* 77, 1, or 76, 4.

[47] Sicily was rich in cults of χθόνιοι, in which Gelon, Hieron and their ancestors were hierophants, Hdt. vii, 153; Pi., *O.* vi, 95. So, too, Akragas the city of Theron (and the home of Empedokles which also is not without its importance) was Φερσεφόνας ἕδος, Pi., *P.* xii, 2, having been given by Zeus to Persephone on her marriage, Sch. Pi., *O.* ii, 16 (as also had, in addition to other cities, Pindar's native city Thebes, Euphorion, *fr.* 48; cf. Eur., *Phoen.* 684 ff. Theron's family traced its descent from Eteokles the son of Oedipus). It is very possible that the hopes of a blessed immortality of the soul such as were fostered in many ways in the cult of the χθόνιοι and particularly in that of Persephone, should have been familiar to Theron from such a cult and attractive to him.

[48] The theological character of much of Pindar's work makes knowledge of mystic doctrine not surprising in him. In *fr.* 137 he speaks of the Eleusinia (to which he otherwise owes nothing). In *fr.* 131, though the words are unfortunately most corrupt and probably contain lacunae as they have been transmitted, he speaks of the "releasing Initiations", ὀλβία δ' ἅπαντες αἶσα λυσίπονον τελετάν—this is the form of the words required by the metre (dactylo-epitritic), and thus (not τελευτάν) they appear in Plu., *Cons. Apoll.* 35, p. 120 D, and also in cod. Vatic. 139 (which I have collated).

[49] *IG.* xiv = *IG. Sic. et It.*, 641, 1–2–3. [Harrison-Murray, *Prolegom.* 661 ff.; *Vors.* 66 B, 18, 19.]—The inscription of the oldest of these poems belongs to the fourth century B.C. The verses can, however, be cited here because the original or rather the two originals upon which the poems are modelled were older than the oldest of the three surviving inscr. (which itself shows serious corruption of the primitive text); and nothing prevents us from supposing that the original forms of these verses go back to the fifth century.—The common ancestor of versions 2 and 3 is not derived from version 1, even in the parts in which it agrees with that version, but from a still older original.—Acc. to Dieterich, *Nekyia* 128 f., 135 f., the lines are taken from a poem of *Orpheus'* descent to Hades; but of this they themselves offer not the slightest suggestion.

[50] The feminine ἔρχομαι ἐκ καθαρῶν καθαρά—and also νῦν δ' ἱκέτις ἥκω (though this indeed is metrically impossible) *IG.* xiv, 641, 2, l. 6—refers probably to the ψυχή and not to the sex of the dead person as though a woman were speaking in all three cases. Moreover, in

No. 1, 9, Persephone speaks as though to a man ὄλβιε καὶ μακαριστέ, θεὸς δ' ἔσῃ ἀντὶ βροτοῖο.

[51] l. 1, ἔρχομαι ἐκ καθαρῶν καθαρά, χθονίων βασίλεια. This is certainly the right punctuation (and is given by the editors), and not Hofmann's ἐκ καθαρῶν, καθαρὰ χθ. β. "Pure and born of the pure" (referring to the immediate parents of the dead: more distant ancestry would be expressed by ἀπό); cf. κάκιστος κἀκ κακῶν, etc. (Nauck on Soph., *OT.* 1397; *Ph.* 874); ἀγαθοὶ ἐξ ἀγαθῶν ὄντες, Andoc., *M.* 109.

[52] The parents are καθαροί, the soul of the dead καθαρά, simply as being "purified", "sanctified", in τελεταί of the χθόνιοι. In the same way, elsewhere, the Mystai are ὅσιοι "the pure": see above, chap. vi, n. 18.

[53] καὶ γὰρ ἐγὼν ὑμῶν γένος ὄλβιον εὔχομαι εἶμεν—so in all three versions.

[54] ἀλλά με μοῖρ' ἐδάμασσε καὶ ἀστεροπῆτα κεραυνῶν (particip.): so in the original to which the readings of three versions point, as restored by O. Hofmann in *GDI.* 1654. ἀστεροβλῆτα is in No. 1—this might simply = ἀστεροποβλῆτα, but it may only have been substituted by mistake for ἀστεροπῆτα (= ἀστεροπητής of Homer). The line in this form occurs in No. 1, 4. Versions 2 and 3 have εἴτε με μοῖρ' ἐδάμασσ' εἴτ' ἀστεροπῆτα κεραυνῶν. But the dead had no *choice* between natural death (for this is what μοῖρα must mean as contrasted with death by the thunderbolt) and death by being struck by lightning; one or other of the two (or more) forms of death must in actual fact have occurred. In this embarrassment—for death by lightning is not a very frequent occurrence—the ancient verse was altered in such a way that it might refer also to one who had died a natural death. The attempt was indeed not a great success. Originally death by lightning can alone have been mentioned (as in No. 1) and the original form of the lines must have referred to someone who had actually perished in this way. The dead person was then immediately regarded as sanctified simply on account of the method of his death; he became a ἱερὸς νεκρός translated to a higher and continued life: see above, chap. ix, n. 127, and Appendix i. This is the only interpretation of the lines which gives any point to the introduction here of this peculiar manner of death—one who has been thus translated out of life will certainly now be θεὸς ἀντὶ βροτοῖο.

[55] κύκλος τῆς γενέσεως, rota fati, etc. Lob., *Agl.* 798 ff.

[56] ἱμερτοῦ δ' ἐπέβαν στεφάνου ποσὶ καρπαλίμοισι, Δεσποίνας δ' ὑπὸ κόλπον ἔδυν χθονίας βασιλείας, No. 1, 6–7. The στέφανος will probably be the sacred precinct, the enclosure that surrounds the realm of Persephone, as Dieterich, *De hymn. Orph.* 35, very plausibly suggests.

[57] See Appendix xi.

[58] ὥς με πρόφρων πέμψῃ ἕδρας ἐς εὐαγέων. The ἕδραι εὐαγέων correspond to the χῶρος εὐσεβῶν of other poets and mythologists. But the strange phrase does also contain an allusion to the fact that this paradise of the "pure" is specially reserved for the initiates of the mysteries. The εὐαγής, the man untouched by any ἄγος, is ὅσιος (ὅσιος ἔστω καὶ εὐαγής law ap. And., *M.* 96): εὐαγεῖν = ὁσιοῦν in an ins. from Ialysos in Rhodos, *IGM. Aeg.* i, 677. Ordinary non-religious language also preserves the original meaning of the word: it frequently means (in contrast to σκοτώδης and the like) "bright, pure, clean" (and in places, too, where it is customary to insert without good reason εὐαυγής, following the ex. of Hemsterh. on Eur., *Suppl.* 662).

[59] The similarity with the stages of the reward given to the good in Pindar is obvious: χῶρος εὐσεβῶν in Hades; then and not till then

escape from the underworld and from human life as well. The only difference is that in Pi. the soul's final end is to become a ἥρως while here it becomes θεός.

[60] *IG.* xiv, 642.

[61] id. 641, 1, v. 10, ἔριφος ἐς γάλ' ἔπετον. 642, 4, θεὸς ἐγένου ἐξ ἀνθρώπου. ἔριφος ἐς γάλα ἔπετες. The conjunction of the two phrases in 642 shows that " As a kid I fell into the milk " is a condition of " I became a God ". We may certainly recognize in the phrase a σύνθημα or σύμβολον of the Mystai like those usual in other secret initiatory rites—ἐκ τυμπάνου ἔφαγον κτλ., Lob. 23 ff.—which refer to performance of symbolical actions in the initiation ceremonies. The precise sense of *this* σύνθημα cannot be made out (Dieterich's efforts, *H. Orph.*, p. 35, have not succeeded in clearing up the matter).

[62] Worth remarking is the instruction ἀλλ' ὁπόταμ ψυχὴ προλίπῃ φάος ἀελίοιο, δεξιὸν εἰσιέναι πεφυλαγμένος εὖ μάλα πάντα (this or something like it may have been the original form of the lines which have been thrown into confusion by the intrusion of the explanatory words δεῖ τινα). Then at the conclusion (ὦ) χαῖρε χαῖρε, δεξιὰν ὁδοιπορῶν λειμῶνάς τε ἱεροὺς καὶ ἄλσεα Φερσεφονείας. (καί : this and nothing else is probably concealed by the KAT of the inscription—καί long before a vowel in 3rd thesis is even in Homer not unheard of.) Here at a comparatively early date we meet with the legend of the Two Ways at the entrance to the underworld, of which that to the right leads to the χῶρος εὐσεβῶν, the left to the place of punishment of the ἄδικοι. It may derive from the fancies of South Italian mystic sects. δεξιόν and ἀριστερόν in the Pythagorean table of Opposites—and in *oionistike* for a long time before that—mean the same as ἀγαθόν and κακόν (Arist., *Metaph.* 1, 5, p. 986a, 24 ; cf. Iamb., *VP.* 156).—The Y Pythagoreum denoted the parting of the ways of life to the right (to virtue) and to the left (vice) : Serv., *A.* vi, 136 ; cf. O. Jahn, *Pers.*, p. 155 f. Plato transferred the Two Ways to the underworld probably following Pythagorean example, *Rp.* 614 C ; cf. τὼ ὁδώ, *Gorg.* 524 A ; *divorso itinere*, Cato ap. Sall., *C.* 52, 13, in a Platonist passage. To the right the fountain of Mnemosyne, to the left that of Lethe—grave-tablet from Petelia : *Epigr. Gr.* 1037 = *IG.* xiv, 638. The Two Ways in the underworld (of which that to the right hand regularly leads to salvation) are also spoken of by the ποιητής whose lines are quoted by Hippol., *RH.* 5, 8, p. 164, 80 D.-S. (perhaps " Orpheus " as Dieterich, *Nek.* 193 thinks) ; cf. also Verg., *A.* vi, 540 ff., Hegesipp., *AP.* vii, 545, and the Jewish forgery under the name of Philem., Mein. 4, 67, 6 f. (ii, p. 539 K.).—*Three* Ways in the world of the spirits, which he takes as being in the sky, are seen by the Empedotimos of Herakld. Pont. (see above, chap. ix, n. 111) : Serv., *G.* i, 34. Plutarch also alludes to *three* Ways in the underworld, *Lat. Viv.* vii, p. 1130, for in giving his quotation from Pindar's θρῆνος *fr.* 129–30 he suddenly, without having previously said anything about the other two Ways, speaks of the τρίτη τῶν ἀνοσίως βεβιωκότων καὶ παράνομων ὁδός which leads into Erebos. We should suppose that he found these three Ways in Pindar whom he is making use of throughout the passage. Three Ways would seem natural to one who knew of three classes of souls ; the εὐσεβεῖς and the ἀσεβεῖς having in between them those who have not strayed seriously from either side of the middle way of ordinary morality and deserve neither reward nor severe punishment. To these then was probably allotted, instead of the bliss or sorrow of the two other classes, the indifferent state of the Homeric εἴδωλα καμόντων. So at least it appears from Lucian, *Luct.* 7–9. A similar triple

division occurs in a popular form ap. D.H. viii, 52 ad fin.: (1) a place of punishment, a kind of Tartaros; (2) τὸ λήθης πεδίον (which is here the indifferent state); (3) the αἰθήρ which is the dwelling-place of the Blessed. Verg., too, has three classes, but he places the middling characters in the *limbus infantium*, beyond which the road first divides towards Elysium and Tartarus. Did Pindar then anticipate these and incidentally—he need not have been logically consistent about it—introduce such a triple division of the souls?

[63] Plato's violent attacks on poets and poetry—in which nevertheless acc. to his own account οὐδὲν σπουδῆς χαρίν, ἀλλὰ παιδιᾶς ἕνεκα πάντα δρᾶται—show once more clearly enough that in his time the old Greek view of the poets as the true *teachers* of their age was by no means a thing of the past. It was precisely as teachers, whether rightly or wrongly so regarded, that they seemed to him dangerous and worth opposing.

[64] Aristophanes is only formulating popular opinion—and in unusually naive language—when he says *Ran.* 1030 ταῦτα γὰρ ἄνδρας χρὴ ποιητὰς ἀσκεῖν σκέψαι γὰρ ἀπ' ἀρχῆς ὡς ὠφέλιμοι τῶν ποιητῶν οἱ γενναῖοι γεγένηνται κτλ. And again 1053 ff. where he is referring particularly to tragic dramatists, ἀποκρύπτειν χρὴ τὸ πονηρὸν τόν γε ποιητήν, καὶ μὴ παράγειν μηδὲ διδάσκειν. τοῖς μὲν γὰρ παιδαρίοισιν ἔστι διδάσκαλος ὅστις φράζει, τοῖς ἡβῶσιν δὲ ποιηταί.

[65] This idea is alluded to as early as *Δ* 160 ff. Then Hes., *Op.* 282 ff. It is established for Hdt.; cf. i, 91, vi, 86. Further examples collected by Nägelsbach, *Nachhom. Theol.* 34 f. Thgn. 205 ff., 731 ff., is particularly definite. Among Attic authors; cf. Sol., *fr.* 13, 29 (ἀναίτιοι ἔργα τίνουσιν); E., *Hipp.* 831 ff., 1378 ff. (where note τὸν οὐδὲν ὄντ' ἐπαίτιον), *fr.* 980; [Lys.] 6, 20; Lycurg. 79. It is briefly alluded to as a commonly held opinion by Isoc. 11, 25; cf. Lys., *fr.* 53 Th. The case of Diagoras of Melos the ἄθεος may also be remembered; cf. above, chap. vii, n. 16.—This idea of the punishment of the son for the deeds of the father receives its justification acc. to Plu., *Ser. Nu. Vi.* 16, 559 D (quite in accordance with primitive ideas) in the unity that belongs to all the members of the same γένος—so that in the person of the son it is the father himself, though he may be dead, who is also punished. The idea arises from the deeply ingrained feeling of the unity, solidarity, and continuity of the ancient family cult-circle pre-supposed by the cult of souls. (This is primitive and meets us, e.g. in India as well: "release us from the wrongs that our fathers have done; take away the sins of that we ourselves have committed" is the prayer to Varuna in the Rigveda, 7, 86, 5. τὰ ἐκ προτέρων ἀπλακήματα are transferred also to the next generation "like a pestilence-breeding substance", Oldenberg, *Rel. d. V.* 289. Elsewhere the conception emerges that the guilty ancestor lives again in the descendant and is punished in his person: Robinsohn, *Psychol. d. Naturv.* 47.)

[66] It is precisely on this point, namely, that evil does not befall men without their own fault, that the Chorus, i.e. the poet, of the *Agamemnon* (757), acknowledges δίχα δ' ἄλλων μονόφρων εἰμί.

[67] In this way, too, the Stoics saved the responsibility of men for their own deeds in spite of the unavoidable εἱμαρμένη. The deeds would not have come to fruition if the personal συγκατάθεσις of the man had not been added to the original necessary cause conditioning the acts. The συγκ., though not itself "free", yet always remains ἐφ' ἡμῖν and makes us responsible: Cic., *Fat.* 18; Nemes. *Nat. Hom.*, p. 291 Matth.

[68] Clearly so from l. 689 onwards.

[69] τὰ γὰρ ἐκ τῶν προτέρων ἀπλακήματά νιν πρὸς τάσδ' (τὰς 'Ερινύας) ἀπάγει, *Eum.* 934.

[70] Only when Eteokles and Polyneikes have fallen in single combat ἔληξε δαίμων, *Sept.* 956.

[71] This idea is quite common in Homer (Nägelsbach, *Hom. Theol.* 70 f., 320 f.), and in later times reappears frequently in the case of such authors as always, or on occasion, express popular ideas : Thgn. Hdt. esp. Eur. (cf. *Fr. Trag. Adesp.* 4, 55 N.), and the orators: see Nägelsbach, *Nachhom. Th.* 54 ff., 332 f., 378.

[72] ἀπάτης δικαίας οὐκ ἀποστατεῖ θεός, *fr.* 301 S. This, too, must be the meaning of other expressions in which the poet refers less plainly to the righteous purpose of divine deception : *Pers.* 93 ff., 742 ; *frr.* 156, 302 (cf. also *Suppl.* 403 f.).—Aristoph. makes his Clouds speak quite in accordance with the Aeschylean ideas, *Nub.* 1458 ff. This grim idea must, in fact, have had considerable success and spread beyond the stage. Falsehood and deception for a good end presented no difficulty to the mind of the Greeks (even as applied to their gods). Hence Sokrates (in Xen.), Plato, and certain Stoics could quite openly approve of and recommend such falsehoods (and the author of the Διαλέξεις, c. 3 in defending the same theory also appeals to the lines of Aesch.).

[73] *Ag.* 1497–1508. Here there is a clear opposition between the popular view which attributed all guilt to an ἀλάστωρ tempting to crime (a reminiscence of which appears in Soph., *El.* 197 ff.), and the more elevated conception of the poet who holds fast to the view that though the ἀλάστωρ may contribute to the result the agent of the evil deed is not ἀναίτιος.

[74] The dead man stands in need of the cult paid by his surviving kinsfolk, *Cho.* 484 (his grave a βωμός, *Cho.* 106 ; χοαὶ γαμήλιοι for him, 486 f.). As an appeasement of his easily aroused wrath χοαὶ νερτέρων μειλίγματα, *Cho.* 15. The dead man is still conscious of events both past and present upon earth: φρόνημα τοῦ θανόντος οὐ δαμάζει πυρὸς μαλερὰ γνάθος, *Cho.* 324 f. In the song of awakening addressed to the departed and the invocations sung by Electra and the Chorus in *Cho.* the soul of Agamem. is similarly regarded as fully alive and accessible to the callers (though, indeed, ἐξ ἀμαυρᾶς φρενός 157) and addressed accordingly (cf. 139, 147 f., 156 f., 479 ff. ; *Pers.* 636). It is even expected that his soul, invisibly present in the upper world, will take an active share in the work of vengeance : ἄκουσον ἐς φάος μολών, ξὺν δὲ γενοῦ πρὸς ἐχθρούς, *Cho.* 459 ; cf. 489. So, too, Orestes, *Eum.* 598, hopes in his extremity of need that ἀρωγὰς ἐκ τάφου πέμψει πατήρ. More especially the murdered man has a right to be avenged by his ἀγχιστεῖς (οὐδ' ἀπ' ἄλλων, *Cho.* 472) and Apollo himself has commanded Orestes to take such vengeance, *Cho.* 269 ff., etc. Dread results of neglecting this duty, *Cho.* 278–96 (possibly an interpolated passage, but still an extension of the words of A. himself 271 ff. in a sense thoroughly in consonance with popular belief).

[75] The Erinyes only avenge the murder of a blood-relation and not therefore when one of a married pair is murdered by the other, *Eum.* 210–12, 604 ff. But the opinion emerges that they are particularly charged with the vengeance of a *mother* who has been murdered by her son (rather than a father who has suffered the same fate), 658 ff., 736 ff. (Reminiscences of such a view in S., *El.* 341 ff., 352 ff. ; E., *Orest.* 552 ff., *fr.* 1064.) This may possibly be an old popular belief (not fully understood by A. himself) which need not, however (as is often

supposed), depend upon an ancient system of " matriarchy " for which there is no other evidence in Greece. It is simply explained by the fact that the father has plenty of men still living among his kinsfolk who will avenge him (even against his own son), whereas the mother who is separated from her *own* family can expect no avenger from that side, while in the family of her husband there will be nobody yet old enough to take vengeance on her own son. For this reason it is for her most particularly and necessarily that the daimonic avengers of murder must intervene, and they are the Erinyes, who are always thought of as only active where no earthly avenger is available. —Of course, it could never be denied that there exists also *πατρὸς εὐκταίαν 'Ερινύν*, *Sep.* 783.

[76] *δαίμων, θεός, δῖος ἀνάκτωρ, ἰσοδαίμων βασιλεύς* are titles given only to the dead Persian king, *Pers.* 620, 633, 644, 651. They are, however, probably intended to characterize Persian and not Greek beliefs (the Greek king, too, is still a king in Hades, but not a *δαίμων*, *Cho.* 355–62).

[77] *κἀκεῖ δικάζει τἀμπλακήμαθ', ὡς λόγος, Ζεὺς ἄλλος* (cf. *Ζῆνα τῶν κεκμηκότων* 158) *ἐν καμοῦσιν ὑστάτας δίκας*, *Suppl.* 230 f. ; cf. 414 ff.—*μέγας γὰρ "Αιδης ἐστὶν εὔθυνος βροτῶν ἔνερθε χθονός, δελτογράφῳ δὲ πάντ' ἐπωπᾷ φρενί*, *Eum.* 273 ff. Not even in Hades do the Erinyes let the murderer go, *Eum.* 340. The punishment in Hades seems to be regarded as merely supplementary to the (perhaps delayed) punishment of crime on earth *ῥοπὴ δ' ἐπισκοπεῖ δίκας ταχεῖα τοὺς μὲν ἐν φάει, τὰ δ' ἐν μεταιχμίῳ σκότου μένει χρονίζοντας ἄχη, τοὺς δ' ἄκρατος ἔχει νύξ*, *Cho.* 61 ff.

[78] *τοὺς θανόντας εἰ θέλεις εὐεργετεῖν εἴτ' οὖν κακουργεῖν, ἀμφιδεξίως ἔχει τῷ μήτε χαίρειν μήτε λυπεῖσθαι νεκρούς*, *fr.* 266. This does, not, however, agree with *Cho.* 324 f., or with the frequently occurring expressions which presuppose consciousness and feeling (and so also *χαίρειν* and *λυπεῖσθαι*) in the dead. Consistency in such matters must not, in fact, be looked for in a non-theological poet. The *ψυχή* of the dead man a shadow without the sap of life, *fr.* 229. Death a refuge from earthly suffering, *fr.* 255. The speedy death which the Chorus wish for themselves, *Ag.* 1449 ff., brings with it *τὸν ἀεὶ ἀτέλευτον ὕπνον* and therefore a condition of unconsciousness if not of complete nothingness.—The shadow of Dareios takes his leave of the Persian nobles in the foll. words : *ὑμεῖς δέ, πρέσβεις, χαίρετ', ἐν κακοῖς ὅμως ψυχὴν διδόντες ἡδονῇ καθ' ἡμέραν, ὡς τοῖς θανοῦσι πλοῦτος οὐδὲν ὠφελεῖ*, *Pers.* 840 ff. This view of life is perhaps intended to have an Oriental colouring (like the epitaph of Sardanapalus which is rightly quoted in illustration of this passage) ; the reason given *ὡς τοῖς θανοῦσι κτλ.* is perhaps to be similarly explained.

[79] *ἔνδικοι σφαγαί*, 37. Orestes is to his father's house *δίκῃ καθαρτὴς πρὸς θεῶν ὡρμημένος* 70.

[80] One reason why no Erinys pursues Orestes after he has murdered his mother is, indeed, the fact that Sophokles is treating the " Elektra " in isolation as an independent drama and could not therefore introduce a fresh thread of interest at the end, if he was to bring it to a satisfactory conclusion. But the mere fact that he could so arrange matters shows that for him, in contrast with Aeschylus, the belief in the veritable reality of the Erinys and the necessary perpetuation of the idea of vengeance in the family was already obscured and almost obsolete. The ancient family blood-feud is less important to him than the rights of the separate and independent individual.

[81] Casual allusions, *El.* 504 ff. ; *OC.* 965 ; *Ant.* 856 ; and cf. 584 ff., 594 ff.

[82] οὐ γὰρ ἴδοις ἂν ἀθρῶν βροτὸν ὅστις ἄν, εἰ θεὸς ἄγοι, ἐκφυγεῖν δύναιτο, *O.C.* 252. ὅταν δέ τις θεῶν βλάπτῃ, δύναιτ' ἂν οὐδ' ἂν ὁ σθένων φυγεῖν, *El.* 696 f. αἴσχη μέν, ὦ γυναῖκες, οὐδ' ἂν εἷς φύγοι βροτῶν ποθ' ᾧ καὶ Ζεὺς (as the one who rules and ordains everything, cf. *El.* 175 ; *O.C.* 1085) ἐφορμήσῃ κακά · νόσους δ' ἀνάγκη τὰς θεηλάτους φέρειν, *fr.* 619 N.

[83] *Phil.* 191–200.

[84] It is fixed long before by an oracle : 821 ff. ; 1159 ff. It is not exactly overpowering violence or heaven-sent madness that drives Deianeira to carry out the prophecy ; it is rather an obscure force that transforms her purest intentions to an evil result. She herself is completely innocent : ἥμαρτε χρηστὰ μωμένη.

[85] The reason for this will of the gods is not revealed to us, either in *OT.* or in the subsequent treatment given in *OC.* The only thing that is made quite clear there is the complete innocence of Oedipus : as to the meaning of the divine purpose that has plunged him into such deeds of horror the sufferer can only say θεοῖς γὰρ ἦν οὕτω φίλον, τάχ' ἄν τι μηνίουσιν εἰς γένος πάλαι (964 f.). This is a passage in which modern interpretation of the ancients finds the "upholding of the moral order in the world" clearly expressed as a motive of divine will.

[86] καὶ γὰρ ἦν τῶν θεοσεβεστάτων, Sch., *El.* 831.

[87] *fr.* 226 N., σοφὸς γὰρ οὐδεὶς πλὴν ὃν ἂν τιμᾷ θεός. ἀλλ' εἰς θεόν σ' ὁρῶντα, κἂν ἔξω δίκης χωρεῖν κελεύῃ, κεῖσ' ὁδοιπορεῖν χρεών. αἰσχρὸν γὰρ οὐδὲν ὧν ὑφηγοῦνται θεοί.

[88] Aias has angered the goddess because he has boasted that he could do without her help. Thus he has drawn upon himself ἀστεργῆ θεᾶς ὀργήν, 776. The goddess makes him insane that he may recognize τὴν θεῶν ἰσχὺν ὅση, 118. Thus, her superior power is shown and the folly of men who despise that power. But as for showing that the revengeful act of the goddess has any sort of moral purpose or meaning behind it, the pious poet makes no such attempt.—The interpolation of ideas more familiar in modern times does not make it any easier to understand the peculiar character of such antique εὐσέβεια and δεισιδαιμονία. The same kind of fearful awe of the gods which we find here, runs through the whole of Herodotos' historical writing (Hdt. was not without reason a friend of Sophokles) and meets us again in the character of Nikias and to a large extent in Xenophon, too. Thuc. and, on the whole, Eurip. (for he varies) calmly ignore it or else violently reject it. Its nature is shown (better than in the more usual εὐσέβεια) by the phrase ἡ πρὸς τοὺς θεοὺς εὐλάβεια which also occurs : [D.] 59 (*Neaer.*) 74.

[89] *Trach.* 1266 f. ; 1272 (where, however, there remains a suspicion that the traditional text may be unsound) ; *fr.* 103 N. Parallels occur also in *Phil.*

[90] There exists a region of divine mystery that is not to be fathomed : οὐ γὰρ ἂν τὰ θεῖα κρυπτόντων θεῶν μάθοις ἄν, οὐδ' εἰ πάντ' ἐπεξέλθοις σκοπῶν, *fr.* 833 ; cf. *OT.* 280 f. and πολλὰ καὶ λαθεῖν καλόν, *fr.* 80 N.

[91] The behaviour of Athene in the prologue of the *Aias* is an exception.

[92] Odysseus beholding the insane Aias : ἐποικτίρω δέ νιν δύστηνον ὄντα καίπερ ὄντα δυσμενῆ, ὁθούνεκ' ἄτῃ συγκατέζευκται κακῇ, οὐδὲν τὸ τούτου μᾶλλον ἢ τοὐμὸν σκοπῶν · ὁρῶ γὰρ ἡμᾶς οὐδὲν ὄντας ἄλλο πλὴν εἴδωλ' ὅσοιπερ ζῶμεν, ἢ κούφην σκιάν, *Ai.* 121 ff.

[93] ἰὼ γενεαὶ βροτῶν κτλ. *OT.* 1186 ff. ; ὅστις τοῦ πλέονος μέρους χρῄζει . . . *OC.* 1211–38 ; cf. *frr.* 12, 535, 536, 588, 859, 860.

[94] Nor is Antigone affected by such motives as might appear from a casual or isolated study of such lines as *Ant.* 73 ff. The whole play

shows that Antig. throughout follows the *ἄγραπτα κἀσφαλῆ θεῶν νόμιμα* and the instincts of her own nature, without paying any attention to what may happen to her on earth and without a side glance at what may be the result in the world below of her "pious crime".

[95] We often have *ἐν Ἅιδου κεκευθότων* (*Ant.* 911) *μυχοὺς κιχεῖν τοῦ κάτω θεοῦ* (*Ai.* 571) and other phrases = "be dead" (cf. to be an *οἰκήτωρ* of Erebos, *Ai.* 395 ff. Hades seems to be called *πανδόκος ξενόστασις fr.* 252). The confusion of the idea of a kingdom of Hades with that of the grave is shown in the not infrequent expression *ἐν Ἅιδου, παρ' Ἅιδῃ κεῖσθαι, El.* 463; *OT.* 972; *Ph.* 861; *φίλη μετ' αὐτοῦ κείσομαι φίλου μέτα, Ant.* 73; cf. *fr.* 518.

[96] *τὸν ἀπότροπον Ἅιδαν, Ai.* 608; *fr.* 275.

[97] The dead man a *σκιά, Ai.* 1231. *σποδὸς καὶ σκιὰ ἀνωφελής, El.* 1159a. *μηδέν, El.* 1166; *Ai.* 1231.—In spite of this, in the Homeric manner, a definite shape and a measure of semi-conscious existence is presumed in the shades in Hades: *OT.* 1371 ff.—Doubt: *εἴ τις ἔστ' ἐκεῖ χάρις, El.* 356.

[98] *θανόντων οὐδὲν ἄλγος ἅπτεται, OC.* 955. *τοῖς γὰρ θανοῦσι μόχθος οὐ προσγίγνεται, Tr.* 1173. *τοὺς γὰρ θανόντας οὐχ ὁρῶ λυπουμένους, El.* 1170. (All three lines are denied to Soph. by the latest criticism.)

[99] *Ph.* 797 f.; *Ai.* 854; *OC.* 1220 ff.; *fr.* 631 (cf. A., *fr.* 255; *Fr. Tr. Adesp.* 360. *λιμὴν κακῶν ὁ θάνατος*, a commonplace of later moralists: see Wyttenb. Plu., *Mor.* vi, p. 720, was taken over from tragedy).—The converse *fr.* 64, 275.

[100] Collectively *οἱ νέρτεροι, οἱ νέρτεροι θεοί, OC.* 1661; *Ant.* 602. Hades in particular is often mentioned, and also *Πλούτων*: *Ἅιδης στεναγμοῖς καὶ γόοις πλουτίζεται, OT.* 30; *fr.* 251. *ὁ παρὰ τὸν Ἀχέροντα* (*τὰν Ἀχέροντος ἀκτάν, Ant.* 812. *ἀκτὰν ἑσπέρου θεοῦ, OT.* 177) *θεὸς ἀνάσσων, El.* 184. Persephone and Aidoneus, *OC.* 1556 ff. Erinyes, Thanatos, Kerberos: *OC.* 1568 ff. *πομπαῖος Ἑρμῆς χθόνιος, Ai.* 832; and see *El.* 110 ff., etc.—*Ἅιδης* (here as often = *Θάνατος*) desires to devour men: *δαίσασθαι, El.* 542, f.—a popular conception or at least popular language: see above, chap. vii, n. 25.

[101] Hades *ὅς οὔτε τοὐπιεικὲς οὔτε τὴν χάριν οἶδεν, μόνην δ' ἔστερξε τὴν ἁπλῶς δίκην, fr.* 703, i.e. the justice of absolute equality (for all earthly distinctions have passed away): *ὅ γ' Ἅιδης τοὺς νόμους ἴσους ποθεῖ, Ant.* 519.

[102] *ἡ γὰρ εὐσέβεια συνθνήσκει βροτοῖς* (it dies when the man dies to whom it belonged: i.e. it follows him, or his *ψυχή*, into the lower-world. No textual corruption need be assumed here), *κἂν ζῶσι κἂν θάνωσιν οὐκ ἀπόλλυται, Ph.* 1443 f.

[103] Without ritual burial the dead man is *τῶν κάτωθε θεῶν ἄμοιρος ἀκτέριστος ἀνόσιος νέκυς, Ant.* 1070 f.

[104] *ἐντάφια οἷα τοῖς κάτω νομίζεται, El.* 326. *κτερίσματα*, 434, 931. *λουτρά*, 84, 434 (cf. above, chap. v, nn. 106, 107), *ἔμπυρα*, 405. *χοαί*, 440.—*El.* 452, prayer is made to the dead that he "shall help us and Orestes" *ὅπως τὸ λοιπὸν αὐτὸν ἀφνεωτέραις χερσὶν στέφωμεν ἢ τὰ νῦν δωρούμεθα* (at present only a lock of hair and a girdle, 448 ff.).—Offerings to the dead made by foes and even the approach of such persons to the neighbourhood of the grave is displeasing and hateful to the departed who lies therein: *El.* 431 ff., 442 ff.; *Ai.* 1394 f. (cf. above, chap. v, n. 109). In this case as in the cult of the soul generally the presence of the dead man in the grave, or else in its immediate neighbourhood, is presupposed—not his departure into an inaccessible land of the dead. The latter view, retained from Homeric

poetry, is generally allowed to remain incongruously side by side with the former.

[105] *El.* 1066 ff.

[106] The god of the underworld is οὐκ ἀπερίτροπος of the murdered man: *El.* 182 f. Hence all the gods and spirits of the lower world are summoned to take vengeance for the murder of Agamemnon: *El.* 110–16. We hear of Δίκη ἡ ξύνοικος τῶν κάτω θεῶν as the patron of the dead in their claim to justice: *Ant.* 451.

[107] Herakles in giving his last commands to Hyllos finally threatens the latter: εἰ δὲ μή, μενῶ σ' ἐγὼ καὶ νέρθεν ὤν, ἀραῖος εἰς ἀεὶ βαρύς, *Tr.* 1201 f.; cf. *fr.* 367; see above, chap. v, n. 148.

[108] Elektra thinks that Agamemnon himself may have sent the δυσπρόσοπτ' ὀνείρατα to Klytaimnestra: *El.* 459 f. (There is no reason for altering the traditional text here—with Nauck—to make the gods the senders of the dreams instead of the dead man. ἥρωες, too, can send nocturnal visions of terror: see above, chap. ix, n. 102.) Here Elektra supposes that by sending such harbingers of his wrath the unavenged victim of murder has signified his readiness to assist in the taking of vengeance. This makes perfectly good sense and is the only interpretation that suits the context of Elektra's admonitions to her sister.

[109] ἀρωγός, *El.* 454. ζῶσιν οἱ γᾶς κάτω κείμενοι. παλίρρυτον γὰρ αἷμα ὑπεξαιροῦσι τῶν κτανόντων οἱ πάλαι θανόντες, *El.* 1419 f. "The dead man brings death to the living," Nauck on *Tr.* 1163.

[110] *frr.* 753, 805.

[111] *OC.* 1049 ff., 680; *fr.* 736.

[112] Oedipus does not die but vanishes (is seen no more, 1649); the depths of the earth open and receive him: 1661 f., 1681. What is meant is *translation* without death as in the case of Amphiaraos, etc. The poet only hints at the miracle in intentionally vague words—but they cannot refer to anything but translation. ὤλετο 1656, and ἔθανε are therefore only inaccurate expressions to describe his departure (see also above, chap. iii, n. 2). The Messenger of 1583 f. refuses, however, to give a distinct answer to the question of the Chorus ὄλωλε γὰρ δύστηνος; he will only hint that Oedipus has indeed ὄλωλε (1580), but has not simply died—he has instead been translated out of earthly life. The corrupt ὡς λελοιπότα κεῖνον τὸν ἀεὶ (this was already what the Alexandrians read) βίοτον ἐξεπίστασο may not therefore be altered simply into τὸν αἰνόν, τὸν ἄβιον βίοτον. It may perhaps have originally been something like τὸν ἔνθα, τὸν ἐν γῇ, τὸν ἀνδρῶν βίοτον (cf. Medea to her children ἐς ἄλλο σχῆμ' ἀποστάντες βίου, E., *Med.* 1039. A dead woman ὑποκεχώρηκε αἰφνίδιον τοῦ καθ' ἡμᾶς βίου. Ins. from Amorgos, *BCH.* 1891, p. 576, ll. 9–10).

[113] A distinct act of precaution against disbelief in such a miracle: *OC.* 1665 f. (cf. ἔρρει δὲ τὰ θεῖα, *OT.* 906 ff.; which refers esp. to the belief in the Oracle of Loxias, a matter of great importance to Soph.).

[114] The innocence of Oedipus and the fact that the awful crimes committed by him have been done in ignorance and against his will θεῶν ἀγόντων, is stressed in order that his elevation to the position of *Heros* may not seem to be an honour done to a guilt-stained criminal. But the poet does not attribute positive virtues to him even in *OC.*—far less in fact than in *OT.*

[115] One has only to read the play without preconceived ideas to see that this passionate and savage old man, pitilessly heaping dreadful curses on his sons, gloating vindictively over the coming misfortunes

of his own country, is quite ignorant of the "deep peace from the gods" or the "illumination of the pious sufferer" which conventional literary interpretation has been anxious to ascribe to him. The poet is not one to gloss over the harsh realities of life with trite phrases of vapid consolation, and he has clearly perceived that the usual effect of unhappiness and misery upon men is not to "illuminate" but to enfeeble and vulgarize them. His Oedipus is pious (he was that from the beginning in *OT.* as well), but he is made savage, ἠγρίωται, exactly like Philoktetes in his misery (*Ph.* 1321).

[116] Humanitarianism of Athens and her king: 562 ff., 1125 ff.

[117] It is emphasized over and over again that the settlement of Oedipus on Attic soil is meant to bring about the salvation of the Athenians and the discomfiture of the Thebans (Apollo's oracle has thus decreed it): 92 f., 287 f., 402, 409 ff., 576 ff., 621 ff. The whereabouts of the valuable possession must therefore be kept secret (as frequently with the graves of Heroes: see above, chap. iv, n. 38); 1520 ff. This elevation of Oedipus to be the σωτήρ of Attica (459 f.) is evidently what makes the interest and importance for the poet of the whole mystery which he relates.

[118] νῦν γὰρ θεοί σ' ὀρθοῦσι, πρόσθε δ' ὤλλυσαν, 394. The gods now feel ὤραν τινά for Oedipus, 386. After many πήματα πάλιν σφε δαίμων δίκαιος αὔξοι (ἄν), 1565 f. It is, in fact, an act of kindness after a long period of ill-usage: there is a reversal of fortune, but there is no reward or indemnification given in recognition of a just claim. It is all *grace*.

[119] In this, too, ὡς ἄν τις εἷς τῶν χρηστῶν Ἀθηναίων (Ion ap. Ath. 13, 604 D).

[120] Prodikos is, acc. to Welcker, *Kl. Schr.* ii, 497 ff., responsible for most of the theories propounded in the Ps.-Platonic *Axiochus* on the subject of the ἀθανασία τῆς ψυχῆς, *Ax.* 370 B ff., the tendency of the soul to the heavenly αἰθήρ (366 A), and even of the Platonizing fantasy at the end about the fate of the departed (371–2). Prodikos, if we adopted this attribution, would become less the "forerunner of Sokrates" (as Welcker calls him) than the forerunner of Plato. There is, however, no real reason to attribute to him any more share in that document than is asserted distinctly in it. The brief and carelessly composed pamphlet consists of a medley of the conventional ingredients of the usual λόγοι παραμυθητικοί loosely strung together. To Prod. is assigned: the disquisition on the troubles of life in all its stages 336 D–367 E; and the saying ὅτι ὁ θάνατος οὔτε περὶ τοὺς ζῶντάς ἐστιν οὔτε περὶ τοὺς μετηλλαχότας κτλ., 369 B (cf. Buresch, *Leip. Stud.* ix, 8–9). These two passages put together would establish as the opinion of Prodikos just the opposite of what Welcker wishes to ascribe to him. He would show himself as a true πεισιθάνατος (—ἐξ ἐκείνου θανατᾷ μου ἡ ψυχή, 366 C), who would make death a mere exit into a state of unconsciousness after the troubles of life, and thus seem an absolute nonentity. But the piece is in reality quite without authority; it apparently puts forward the name of Prodikos, who is so often stated in Plato to have been the "teacher" of Sokrates, merely in order to have a definite authority (like the fabulous Gobryes later on) for what the author does not wish to represent Sokrates as saying on his own account. One of the sayings attributed to the imaginary Prodikos, ὅτι ὁ θάνατος . . . is, however, only too clearly a simple appropriation of Epicurus' aphorism, ὁ θάνατος οὐδὲν πρὸς ἡμᾶς κτλ. (p. 61, 6 Usen.; cf. p. 227, 30; 391. Heinze also points this out, *Ber. sächs. Ges. d. Wiss.* 1884, p. 332). The other passage (366 D ff.) agrees suspiciously

with what Teles (p. 38 Hens.) has to say on the same subject apparently in entire dependence on Krates the Cynic. It seems extremely probable that the author of the *Axiochus* also had Krates before him or even Teles (as Wyttenbach already suggested, Plu., *Mor.* vi, p. 41); and that he attributes what he has thus borrowed from extraneous sources to "Prodikos" by a fiction that never came amiss to the composers of such dialogues.—It follows then that what Prodikos really said about the soul and its destiny is unknown to us; cf. on this recently much-discussed subject: Brinkmann, *Rh. Mus.* 51, 444 ff.

[121] In the Prologue Thanatos at once describes his claims and his office. He has to receive the departed and cut off the lock of hair from the forehead (75 f. probably as a sign that the dead enter into the possession of the underworld deities: in Verg., *A.* iv, 698 f. Proserpina in the same way dedicates the dead to Orcus). He then leads them to Hades, 871. He comes in person to the grave and enjoys the offerings laid there, 844 ff., 851 f. (like the dead man himself on other occasions, see above, chap. v, n. 108). Properly speaking he is only the servant of Hades; but just as the word ᾅδης was already common as = θάνατος, so Thanatos himself is also actually called Ἅιδης (268, see above, n. 4); only as identical with Hades can he be called ἄναξ νεκρῶν, 843; cf. δαιμόνων κοίρανος, 1140.—In the underworld are Charon ὁ ψυχοπομπός, 361, 254 ff., 458 f., and Kerberos, 360. Hades and Hermes χθόνιος receive the dead. εἰ δέ τι κἀκεῖ πλέον ἔστ' ἀγαθοῖς Alkestis will have the seat of honour next to Persephone: 744 ff. By the living who survive she is regarded on account of her incomparable virtue as μάκαιρα δαίμων and her grave is not the abode of a dead woman but a place of worship, 995–1005. Such facile elevation to the rank of "Heroine" was supposed to be characteristic of Thessaly and Eurip. may in this also have intended to give his poem a touch of Thessalian local colour. (δαίμων as an intermediate stage between θεοί and ἄνθρωποι; so frequently in Eur., e.g. *Tro.* 55–6; *Med.* 1391; is this the meaning of the μέσον in *Hel.* 1137 ?)—Thoroughly in keeping with popular belief is χαῖρε κἀν Ἅιδου δόμοις εὖ σοι γένοιτο, 626 f. (such a χαῖρε is the last word with which ὡς νομίζεται one addresses the dead ἐξιοῦσαν ὑστάτην ὁδὸν, 609 f.). Similar also (but really implying the conception of the dead as resting in the grave and not in Hades) is: κοῦφά σοι χθὼν ἐπάνωθε πέσοι, 463.

[122] The funeral dirge, 86 ff.; κόσμος buried with the dead, 618 ff.; mourning ceremonies: the manes of the horses are cut short; no sound of flute or lyre is to be heard in the town for twelve months, 428 ff. (πένθος ἐτήσιον is usual, 336). These extreme observances are probably taken from the mourning customs of the Thessalian dynastic families.

[123] Burial of the dead in accordance with νόμος παλαιὸς δαιμόνων, *Suppl.* 563; νόμιμα θεῶν, 19; a general Hellenic custom, 526 f.—Burial of Polyneikes in spite of Kreon's prohibition: *Phoen.* and probably Ἀντιγόνη.

[124] τοῖς γὰρ θανοῦσι χρὴ τὸν οὐ τεθνηκότα τιμὰς διδόντα χθόνιον εὐσεβεῖν θεόν, *Ph.* 1320 f. ἐν εὐσεβεῖ γοῦν νόμιμα μὴ κλέπτειν νεκρῶν, *Hel.* 1277. The honour of the grave more important even than good fortune upon earth, *Hec.* 317 f. Lament over the dishonouring of the grave of Agamem., *El.* 323 ff. Request for the burial of Astyanax, *Tro.* 1133 ff., of Orestes, *IT.* 702 ff., of Makaria, *Hcld.* 588 ff. The shade of the murdered Polydoros prays especially for burial, *Hec.* 47 ff. (31 f., 796 f.). He is an example of the wandering of the ἄταφοι upon the upper earth; he ἄθαπτος ἀλαίνει, *Tro.* 1084 (see above, p. 163, and Append. vii).—Funeral ceremony for those who have

been drowned at sea, *Hel.* 1057 ff., 1253 ff.; though there the idea is only used as an excuse for the intrigue.

[125] χοαί for the dead, e.g. *Or.* 112 ff., *El.* 511 ff.; *IT.* 159 ff.

[126] χοαί make the dead εὐμενῆ towards the givers of the offering, *Or.* 119. The children call upon the soul of the murdered father to help them, *El.* 676 ff., in the belief that πάντ' ἀκούει τάδε πατήρ, 684. The soul of the dead man hovers above the living observing everything, *Or.* 674 ff. Invocation of the dead (striking both hands on the ground: see above, chap. iii, n. 10), *Tro.* 1305 f. Expectation that the dead thus called on will σῶσαι his friends, *Or.* 797, or help them, *El.* 679. Calling upon the departed in Hades ἄρηξον, ἐλθὲ καὶ σκιὰ φάνηθί μοι, *HF.* 494 (though with the qualification εἴ τις φθόγγος εἰσακούσεται θνητῶν παρ' Ἅιδῃ, 490).

[127] Translation miracles are touched upon by the poet with obvious pleasure; cf. transl. of Kadmos and Harmonia, *Bac.* 1330 ff., 1338 ff.; of Peleus, *Andr.* 1257 ff.; of Helen, *Or.* 1629 ff.; of Herakles, *Hcld.* 910; of Menelaos (in unmistakable sarcasm), *Hel.* 1676 ff. So, too, in the spurious conclusion to the *IA.* there is a translation of Iphigeneia, 1583 ff. (πρὸς θεοὺς ἀφίπτατο, 1608).

[128] Eurystheus buried in the temple of Athene Pallenis will bring safety to Athens and evil to her enemies: *Hcld.* 1026 ff. Eurysth. says σοὶ μὲν εὔνους καὶ πόλει σωτήριος μέτοικος ἀεὶ κείσομαι κατὰ χθονός, 1032 f.; i.e. he will become a ἥρως σωτήρ of the land (just as Oedip. was to become σωτήρ for Attica, S., *OC.* 460, and Brasidas Heros σωτήρ of the Amphipolitans, Thuc. 5, 11, 1). Heroic cult of Hippolytos, *Hip.* 1423 ff., *fr.* 446.

[129] The Erinyes are spoken of (apparently with real belief) in *IT.* 79 ff. and elsewhere.

[130] *Or.* 258 f., not very different, *IT.* 288–94.

[131] τὸ θηριῶδες τοῦτο καὶ μιαιφόνον, *Or.* 524. Orestes instead of committing murder himself should have brought his father to justice, *Or.* 500 f. Agamemnon himself if he could have been asked would not have desired this bloody vengeance, *Or.* 288 ff. It is only Apollo's unwise counsel that has led Orestes to the murder of his mother, *El.* 971 ff., 1296 f.; *Or.* 276 ff., 416, 591. After the deed Orestes does indeed feel remorse but no *religious* terrors, *El.* 1177 (in spite of which there is much about the pursuing Erinyes of his mother). How completely this whole series of ideas, the duty of vengeance, etc., has lost its meaning for the poet, is to be felt more especially in the sophistical frigidity with which the subject is treated in an ἀγών between Tyndareos and Orestes, *Or.* 491–604, and in the hair-splitting of the speech of Orestes himself, 932 ff.

[132] δοκῶ δὲ τοῖς θανοῦσι διαφέρειν βραχύ, εἰ πλουσίων τις τεύξεται κτερισμάτων· κενὸν δὲ γαύρωμ' ἐστὶ τῶν ζώντων τόδε, *Tro.* 1248 ff.

[133] *fr.* 176.

[134] οὐδὲν ἔσθ' ὁ κατθανών, *Alc.* 381. The dead are οἱ οὐκέτ' ὄντες 322. τοῖς (the dead) μὲν γὰρ οὐδὲν ἄλγος ἅψεταί ποτε, πολλῶν δὲ μόχθων εὐκλεὴς ἐπαύσατο, 937 f. But even fame is nothing to the dead. Admetos says to his father in the scurrilous dialogue θανεῖ γε μέντοι δυσκλεής, ὅταν θάνῃς. To which the old man unconcernedly replies κακῶς ἀκούειν οὐ μέλει θανόντι μοι (725 f.).

[135] It might seem simpler to regard all the utterances of persons in the plays which correspond to conventional beliefs as being merely dramatic expressions of the character's own (orthodox) view, and in no sense put forward by the poet as his own opinion. And certainly the separate and independently acting persons of the drama can only

speak and act in accordance with their own proper conceptions and springs of action—not in accordance with the poet's. But in the antique drama this complete detachment of the creatures of the dramatic imagination from their creator, the poet of the drama, only holds good in a limited sense. The ancient dramatists exercised their office of judge much more vigorously than the greatest of the moderns. The course of his play showed clearly what acts and characters the poet disapproved of, but also which opinions he sanctioned and which he did not. We have only to remember the attacks of Oedipus and Iokaste upon the judgments of the gods in *OT.* (or the story of Sen., *Ep.* 115, 14; Eur. *fr.* 324). Accordingly we may take it that such utterances of dramatic characters as are not supplied with practical or spoken corrective are among those of which the poet did not disapprove. Euripides so very frequently puts words into the mouth of his characters which can only express his own moods or opinions that we may also assume that when their language harmonizes with traditional belief then, too, the most subjective of the tragedians is for the moment expressing his own view. Thus, for example, we cannot doubt that the strain of piety running through the whole of the *Hiketides* (subjection of φρόνησις to God's wisdom, 216 ff., submission to the guidance of the gods, 592 ff., and to Zeus' government of the world, 734 ff.), and especially the whole-hearted elaboration of the picture of Theseus as a model of εὐσέβεια, represent the actual opinion of the poet at that particular period (he clearly speaks of himself, 180–3). At other times, too (apart from the *Bacchae*), though generally for a short time only, he shows vague aspirations towards orthodoxy.

[136] *Alc.* 968 ff.; *Hipp.* 952 ff.—Asceticism of the *mystai* of Zeus and Zagreus of the Mountain Mother and the Kouretes: *Κρῆτες*, *fr.* 472.

[137] *Polyid. fr.* 638; *Phrixos, fr.* 833. It is usual (cf. Bergk, *Gr. Litt.* 3, 475, 33) to see here a reminiscence of Herakleitos. But the latter's ἀθάνατοι θνητοί, θνητοὶ ἀθάνατοι, ζῶντες τὸν ἐκείνων θάνατον, τὸν δὲ ἐκείνων βίον τεθνεῶτες (*fr.* 67 Byw. 62 D.) is clearly intended to express the view that "death" and "life" are purely relative concepts; that death (of the one, i.e. Fire) and life (of the other, i.e. Water or Earth) are simultaneously present in the same object (see also *frr.* 68, 78 = 36, 88). According to this view it would be strictly true that life on earth is not more life than it is death; but that is certainly not what Eurip. means to say. Philo and Sext. Emp. are mistaken in attributing to Herakl. the Orphic doctrine of the "death" of the soul which takes place when it is enclosed in the σῶμα, as its σῆμα (see above, chap. xi, n. 19). But it is precisely this Orphic doctrine that is present to the mind of Eurip. (and Plato, *Gorg.* 492 E, 493 A, brings it into immediate connexion with the verses of E.). He is speaking of the true "death" of the soul in the life of the body and of its release to a real (and not a merely relative) life after death; and thinks that "life" has no claim to the distinguishing name (cf. ὃ δὴ βίοτον καλέουσι Emped. 117 Mull. = *fr.* 15 D.).

[138] *Palingenesia* is alluded to once only and in jest as a desirable reward for the virtuous, *HF.* 655–68; cf. M. Ant. xii, 5.

[139] ὁ νοῦς γὰρ ἡμῶν ἐστιν ἐν ἑκάστῳ θεός, *fr.* 1018.

[140] *fr.* 839 (*Chrysipp.*) fully physical in *fr.* 898, 7 ff.—*fr.* 1023 *Αἰθέρα καὶ Γαῖαν πάντων γενέτειραν ἀείδω.* Cf. *fr.* 1004.

[141] *fr.* 484 (*Μελαν. ἡ σοφή*)—*ὡς οὐρανός τε γαῖά τ' ἦν μορφὴ μία κτλ.* Here, too, the poet is speaking of a mere initial association of the elements afterwards to be parted, but thought of as always from the

beginning independent—there is no derivation of both from a single common original element, or of one out of the other. Eurip. may really have been thinking here of the ὅμου πάντα χρήματα ἦν of Anaxagoras (as the ancient authorities supposed), esp. as, with Anax. also, out of the general conglomeration *two* masses, ἀήρ and αἰθήρ, first emerge (though in this case νοῦς is not included in the αἰθήρ as it is with Eurip.). Here, too, then the usual dualism of the Euripidean cosmogony is preserved. For the rest this *fr.* 484 allows us to perceive that in spite of all his physiological tendencies Eurip. can never quite get rid of the *mythical* element in his cosmogonical events. The reason why Ouranos and Gaia in particular recommend themselves to him as elemental forces (and κοινοὶ ἁπάντων γονεῖς, *fr.* 1004) was that these figures had long been set at the beginning of the world and of the gods by cosmogonical *poetry* (αἰθήρ is simply the more physiological term for what is half-personified as Οὐρανός). This probably explains why matter (or at least the more solid forms of matter as distinguished from the αἰθήρ the λεπτότατον πάντων χρημάτων) is for him included in the description " earth ". In this he is not following the old physiologists, none of whom had called " earth " the original matter—at least not earth alone (see Ilberg, *Quaest. Pseudohippocrat.*, p. 16 ff., 1883). " Earth " as describing the merely material, matter deserted by spirit, may have come to him from popular usage. As early as *Ω* 54 the body deserted by soul and life is called κωφὴ γαῖα (cf. Eur. *frr.* 532; 757, 5). Thus for the poet the contrast between γῆ and αἰθήρ almost amounts to that between " matter " and " mind ", except that he either could not or would not think of a " mind " without any material substratum and that for this reason his αἰθήρ still preserves a remnant of matter.

[142] This is esp. clear in *fr.* 839, 8 ff. In the disruption of the elements out of which πάντα are composed each of the two, γῆ and αἰθήρ, preserves itself undiminished and unmixed. θνῄσκει δ' οὐδὲν τῶν γιγνομένων διακρινόμενον δ' ἄλλο πρὸς ἄλλου μορφὴν ἰδίαν ἀπέδειξεν (restores itself in its independent being). Whereupon we feel ourselves irresistibly reminded of the saying of Anaxagoras—οὐδὲν γὰρ χρῆμα γίνεται οὐδὲ ἀπόλλυται, ἀλλ' ἀπ' ἐόντων χρημάτων συμμίσγεταί τε καὶ διακρίνεται, καὶ οὕτως ἂν ὀρθῶς καλοῖεν τό τε γίνεσθαι συμμίσγεσθαι καὶ τὸ ἀπόλλυσθαι διακρίνεσθαι, *fr.* 17 Mull. [and D.].

[143] That it was not Anaxagoras, or at least not he alone, who gave the decided direction to the philosophic ideas of Eurip. has rightly come to be held of late. We do not find a trace in Eurip. of the separation of νοῦς from matter, at least not in the form in which Anaxagoras understood it. For E. the mind is bound to one of the two primal elements and quite foreign to the other, the earth. Thus he arrives at a dualism indeed, but in quite a different sense from that of Anaxag. Dümmler, *Proleg. zu Platons Staat* (Progr. Basel, 1891), p. 48, points out reminiscences in Eurip. of Diogenes of Apollonia—but it is not true to say that the poet's views show the " closest kinship " with the monistic system of Diog., or with any Monism.

[144] *Tro.* 884 ff. The air, called by the name of Zeus, and identical with the νοῦς βροτῶν, can only be taken from the doctrine of Diog.: Diels, *Rh. Mus.* 42, 12.

[145] Diog. Apoll., *frr.* 3, 4, 5 Mull. (= 8, 3, 4 D.). The soul is ἀὴρ θερμότερος τοῦ ἔξω, ἐν ᾧ ἐσμεν, though it is colder than the air which is παρὰ τῷ ἡλίῳ, *fr.* 6 [5]. The soul is therefore more akin to the αἰθήρ than to the ἀήρ (αἰθήρ and ἀήρ were at that time often confused: e.g. in E., *fr.* 944, αἰθήρ instead of ἀήρ).

[146] *Suppl.* 1140 αἰθὴρ ἔχει νιν ἤδη κτλ. Elektra expects to find her dead father in the Aither, *El.* 59. Of a dying man, πνεῦμ' ἀφεὶς εἰς αἰθέρα, *fr.* 971 (differently, *Or.* 1086 f.) ; cf. also *Suppl.* 531–6 (imitated from Epicharm.), where again the αἰθήρ is only spoken of as the abode, and not as the original and consubstantial element of the soul.

[147] αἰθὴρ οἴκησις Διός, Eur., *fr.* 487 (*Melanip.*).

[148] Epich., *fr.* 7, p. 257 Lor. [= *fr.* 265 Kaibel].

[149] *CIA.* i, 442, αἰθὴρ μὲν ψυχὰς ὑπεδέξατο, σώ[ματα δὲ χθὼν] τῶνδε. . . .

[150] συνεκρίθη καὶ διεκρίθη, κἀπῆλθεν ὅθεν ἦλθεν πάλιν, γᾶ μὲν ἐς γᾶν, πνεῦμ' ἄνω· τί τῶνδε χάλεπόν ; οὐδὲ ἕν, Epich. ap. Plu., *Cons. ad Apoll.* 15, 110 A ; Epich., *fr.* 8 [245 Kaib.]. πνεῦμα as a general name for the ψυχή occurs also in Epich., *fr.* 7 [265]. No earlier authority is to be found for this usage that became so common later (under Stoic influence) than Xenophanes who πρῶτος ἀπεφήνατο ὅτι ἡ ψυχὴ πνεῦμα (D.L. ix, 19). Epicharm. may have been actually following Xenophanes (whose writings he knew : Arist., *Meta.* iii, 5, 1010a, 6) in this use of the word. Eurip. then did the same, *Suppl.* 533. πνεῦμα is the name given to the ἀήρ in so far as it is in *motion.* (ὑποληπτέον, εἶναι σῶμα τὸν ἀέρα) γίνεται δὲ πνεῦμα κινηθείς. οὐθὲν γὰρ ἕτερόν ἐστι πνεῦμα ἢ κινούμενος ἀήρ : Hero, μηχαν. σύστ., p. 121 (ed. Diels = i, p. 6, ed. Schmidt) after Straton. The soul is called a πνεῦμα just because the soul is that which has continual movement from its very nature (and is the principle of movement) : as such it had already been regarded by Alkmaion (and later by Plato), and even before that by Pythagoras (see above, chap. xi, n. 40) ; in a different way by Herakleitos and Demokritos also. The universal ἀήρ and the Soul-πνεῦμα, if we give the terms their proper meaning, are to be thought of as being of the same nature, so that the ἀήρ, too (still more the αἰθήρ as a higher ἀήρ), is psychical and animated by soul. That at least was how Diogenes of Apollonia regarded it. (ἀήρ = the outer air, πνεῦμα the air which is inside men's bodies : [Hp.] *de Flatib.* 3 [vi, 94 L.], a section taken from Diog. Ap.)

[151] Numerous references in Eurip. to verses of Epicharm. are pointed out by Wilamowitz, *Eurip. Herakles*, i, 29. The fact that Eurip. knew the poems of Epich. and valued them for their philosophic contents is clearly made out by Wilamowitz' study. But he goes on to assert that all the allusions of Eurip. refer only to the (or one of the) forgeries in the name of Epicharm., of which many were known in antiquity. The reason alleged for this statement—" Euripides never quotes comedies "—is merely a petitio principii. It may be that Eurip. does not " quote " contemporary Attic comedy, but whether he maintained the same attitude to the brilliantly original comic poet of Sicily, whom Aristotle and even Plato (*Gorg.* 505 E and esp. *Tht.* 152 E) were not ashamed to notice, is the very point at issue ; nothing is gained by unproved denial of this main premiss.—Moreover, it would be a most unusual species of forger that preferred to publish gems like νᾶφε καὶ . . . (imitated by Eurip.) or νόος ὁρῇ—under another man's name. The fragments of the Πολιτεία, which is really a forgery fathered on Epicharmos (ap. Clem. Al., *Str.* v, p. 719 P. = Lor., p. 297), are of a very different character.

[152] Archelaos makes a less satisfactory model for Eurip. here. Arch. in his reconciliation of the doctrines of Anaxagoras and Diogenes did not separate νοῦς from the mixture of the material elements (or from the ἀήρ), but he distinguished between them, while for the poet αἰθήρ and mind are the same.

[153] αἰθήρ = Zeus. *fr.* 941. αἰθὴρ . . . Ζεὺς ὃς ἀνθρώποις ὀνομάζεται, *fr.* 877. Hence the αἰθήρ is κορυφὴ θεῶν, *fr.* 919.—In the same way for Diog. Ap. the air is god (Cic., *ND.* i, 29) and Zeus (Philod., *Piet.* c. 6b, p. 70 Gomp. ; *Dox.* 536).—In E., *fr.* 941 : τὸν ὑψοῦ τόνδ' ἄπειρον αἰθέρα καὶ γῆν πέριξ ἔχονθ' ὑγραῖς ἐν ἀγκάλαις the αἰθήρ is not put instead of ἀήρ (for τὸν ὑψοῦ only suits αἰθήρ in its proper sense), but the two are combined under the one word (ὑγραῖς ἐν ἀγκάλαις could not be said of the αἰθήρ in the strict sense), just as the ἀήρ of Diogenes includes the αἰθήρ (for the hot ἀὴρ παρὰ τῷ ἡλίῳ, *fr.* 6 [5 Diels] is, in fact, the αἰθήρ, and so, too, essentially, is the warm ἀήρ in our bodies).

[154] —εἰς ἀθάνατον αἰθέρ' ἐμπεσών, *Hel.* 1016.

[155] ὁ ἐντὸς ἀὴρ (which alone αἰσθάνεται—not the senses) μικρὸν μόριον ὢν τοῦ θεοῦ, Diog. ap. Thphr., *Sens.* 42.

[156] The living air, or Zeus, is νοῦς βροτῶν, *Tro.* 886. And vice versa, the νοῦς in each one of us is no other than God, *fr.* 1018.

[157] ὁ νοῦς τῶν κατθανόντων ζῇ μὲν οὔ, γνώμην δ' ἔχει ἀθάνατον, εἰς ἀθάνατον αἰθέρ' ἐμπεσών, *Hel.* 1013 ff.—Ambiguity attaches to the passages in which a dying person is said to depart εἰς ἄλλο σχῆμα βίου (*Med.* 1039), ἐς ἄλλας βιότου μορφάς (*Ion*, 1068), to ἕτερον αἰῶνα καὶ μοῖραν (*IA.* 1508). It is possible that in each case a personal existence continued in a land of the dead is understood—but if they mean no more than that they are remarkably pregnant in form. In reading them (esp. *Med.* 1039) one is reminded of the remarkable lines of Philiskos (pupil of Isocr.) ap. [Plu.] *Vit. X Or.*, p. 243, 60 West. τῷ γὰρ ἐς ἄλλο σχῆμα μεθαρμοσθέντι καὶ ἄλλοις ἐν κόσμοισι βίου σῶμα λαβόνθ' ἕτερον—said of the dead Lysias. But here the idea of metempsychosis seems really to be involved, which it can hardly be in the case of Eurip.

[158] Eur. adopts it for himself, *fr.* 189 (*Antiope*), and confirms it by so many λόγων ἅμιλλαι in which he allows the most contradictory opinions about a single subject to be given equally plausible expression.

[159] ἀπειροσύνη ἄλλου βιότου, etc. *Hip.* 191–7. τὸ ζῆν γὰρ ἴσμεν, τοῦ θανεῖν δ' ἀπειρίᾳ πᾶς τις φοβεῖται φῶς λιπεῖν τόδ' ἡλίου, *fr.* 816, 10 f. (*Phoinix*).

[160] The dead man is γῆ καὶ σκιά—τὸ μηδὲν εἰς οὐδὲν ῥέπει, *fr.* 532 ; cf. 533, 534. τὸ μὴ γενέσθαι τῷ θανεῖν ἴσον · ὥσπερ οὐκ ἰδοῦσα φῶς the dead woman knows nothing of herself or her sufferings, *Tro.* 636–44 (a locus often initiated in " consolations " : *Axioch.* 365 D, Plu., *Cons. ad Apoll.* 15, p. 110 A).

[161] φήμη τὸν ἐσθλὸν κἂν μυχοῖς δείκνυσι γῆς, *fr.* 865. ἀρετὴ δὲ κἂν θάνῃ τις οὐκ ἀπόλλυται, ζῇ δ' οὐκέτ' ὄντος σώματος, *fr.* 734 ; cf. *Andr.* 772. At the sacrifice of Makaria the chorus in *Hcld.* 621 ff. can only offer as consolation the fame which awaits her—οὐδ' ἀκλεής νιν δόξα πρὸς ἀνθρώπων ὑποδέξεται.

[162] Makaria voluntarily going to meet her death—εἴ τι δὴ κατὰ χθονός · εἴη γε μέντοι μηδέν. εἰ γὰρ ἕξομεν κἀκεῖ μερίμνας οἱ θανούμενοι βροτῶν οὐκ οἶδ' ὅποι τις τρέψεται · τὸ γὰρ θανεῖν κακῶν μέγιστον φάρμακον νομίζεται, *Hcld.* 592 ff. ; cf. *fr.* 916.

[163] *fr.* 757 (the metaphor of ll. 5 ff. is employed for homiletic purposes by Epictet. ii, 6, 11–14) ; *Andr.* 1270 ff.

CHAPTER XIII

PLATO

The belief in human immortality, construed in a theological or philosophical sense, had at this time hardly penetrated to circles of ordinary lay folk. Socrates himself, when it came to such inquiries into the unknowable, never claimed to provide an answer that differed from that which would be given by the majority of his fellow citizens out of the accumulated wisdom of their ancestors. Where in the pages of Plato he is allowed to give undisguised expression to his natural and homely vigour—in the *Apology*—he shows little anticipation of an immortal life of the soul. Death, he thinks, either brings complete unconsciousness to men, like a dreamless sleep, or else it means the transition of the soul to another life in the realm of the Souls—a realm which, to judge by his allusions, has much more resemblance to the Homeric Hades than to any of the visionary countries imagined by theologians or theologically minded poets.[1] Both possibilities he accepts with complete equanimity, trusting in the righteousness of the controlling gods,[2] and he looks no further. How should he know with certainty where everyone was ignorant ? [3]

With a like absence of concern it is possible that the majority of the cultured (who were just beginning to separate themselves from the rest of the community) left unsettled the problem of the Unknown.[4] Plato assures us that it was in his time a widespread belief of the populace that the outgoing soul-breath of the dying was caught up by the winds—especially if its exit took place in stormy weather—and was dispersed, blown away, into nothing.[5] In other ways, too, we may suppose that the orthodox Greek, when death approached, allowed his fancy to picture what might await his soul on the other side of death's threshold.[6] But it is certain that the belief in an unending life of the soul—a life with no end because it had no beginning—was not among these thoughts. Plato himself lets us see how strange such a conception was even to those who were capable of following and understanding a philosophical discussion. Towards the end of the long dialogue upon the best kind of State his Sokrates asks Glaukon with apparent irrelevance " are you not aware that our soul is *immortal* and never perishes ?" Whereupon, we are told, Glaukon looked at him in astonishment and said, "No, in truth, of that I was not aware: can you then assert any such thing ?" [7]

The idea that the soul of man may be everlasting and imperishable seemed thus a paradoxical freak to one who was no adept in the theological doctrine of the soul. If in later times the case was altered, no one contributed more effectually or more permanently to bring that change about than the great thinker and poet who established the theological conception of personal immortality in the very heart of philosophy and then gave back the idea strengthened and made more profound to its parent theology, while he himself extended the influence of that idea far beyond the bounds of school or sect by the far-reaching power of his own unaging writings which belong, not to the schoolroom, but to the greatest achievements of literature whether of Greece or of mankind. It is beyond calculation what power has been wielded since their first appearance by the Platonic dialogues in the confirmation, dissemination, and precise definition of the belief in immortality—a power that with all its alteration in the passage of the centuries has maintained itself unbroken into our own times.

§ 2

Plato had not always given his assent to the belief in immortality. At any rate, it must have remained very much in the background of his thoughts and his belief in the days when he still regarded the world from the point of view of a slightly more developed Socraticism. Not only at that period (in the *Apology*) does he make his Sokrates go to his death without the most distant approach to a belief in the undying vitality of his soul, but also in the first sketch of his Ideal State—a sketch made while the influence of the Socratic view of life still prevailed with him—the belief in immortality is omitted and even excluded.[8] It seems as if Plato did not reach the higher conception of the nature and value of the soul, its origin and destiny reaching out beyond all temporal limitation, until the great change which came over his philosophy had been completed. The world of ever-changing Appearance manifesting itself to the senses in perpetual flux and efflux—this in its inessential, unseizable unreality he abandoned to the criticisms of Herakleitos. But above it, in accordance with his own deepest longings and, as it seemed, implied as its real object by the Socratic search itself after conceptual knowledge, stood a world of unchangeable Being without beginning or end, to which all the appearances of this lower world owed such reality as they possessed. " Being " itself, the totality of the Ideas, remained uncontaminated with " Becoming " and passing away; remained the highest goal and supreme aim standing high above all that aspired to it, or felt a longing for its complete and unlimited fullness.[9] This everlasting reality holds itself aloof from the stream of appearance and is not to be grasped within that stream; it is not manifested in the deceitful ever-changing perception of the senses, nor yet in the Opinion that is based upon them; it can only be apprehended, without any assistance from the senses, by the pure intuition of the Reason.[10] This world of everlasting self-identical Being exists outside the thought and knowledge of man, but it first reveals itself to man in the activity of his own thinking;[11] and at the same time there is revealed to him a higher power than the mere capacity to abstract the unsubstantial general conceptions from the multiplicity of experience—a power that is the highest capacity of the soul, enabling it to voyage out beyond all experience and with infallible knowledge[12] to soar of its own independent power upwards to a transcendental world of permanent and essential reality. The highest capacity that belongs to man, the soul of his soul, is not enclosed within this world that surrounds his senses in its restless flood. Like the objects that are the last goal of its study the soul itself is raised to where it can for the first time find a form of activity worthy of its natural powers. It achieves a new distinction, a priestlike dignity, as an intermediary between the two worlds to both of which it belongs.

The soul is a pure spiritual essence; it contains nothing within it that is material, nothing of the " place " where Becoming is shaped into a distant resemblance to Being.[13] It is incorporeal and belongs to the realm of the " invisible ", which in this immaterialist doctrine counts as the most real of all, more real than the most solid matter.[14] It is not one of the Ideas; on the contrary it seems to partake in one of the Ideas—that of Life—only as other appearances share in their Ideas.[15] But it stands nearer to the whole world of the everlasting Ideas than anything else that is not itself an Idea; of all the things in the world it is " most like " to the Idea.[16]

But it has also a share in Becoming. It cannot simply remain with the Ideas in unaltered other-world transcendence. It has its origin indeed in that other world beyond Appearance. It *was* from the beginning, uncreated[17] like the Ideas and like the Soul of the World to which it is akin.[18] It is " older than the body " [19] to which it must link itself; it does not come into being at the same time as the body, but is only drawn down from its spiritual state of being into the realm of matter and becoming. In the *Phaedrus* this " fall into birth " appears as the necessary result of an intellectual " fall " which takes place within the soul itself.[20] In the *Timaeus*, however, with its study of the general life of the whole world-organism, the animation of the living creature has now to be explained as arising out of the plan—not from a failure of the plan—of the Creator.[21] The soul thus seems to be destined from the beginning to give life to a body. It is not only the knowing and thinking element in a world of inanimate things, it is also the source of all movement. Itself in motion from the beginning it bestows the power of movement upon the body with which it is associated; without it, there would be no movement in the world, and no life either.[22]

But though enclosed within the body it remains a stranger to the body. On its side it has no need of the body and is not conditioned by it. It remains independently associated with it as its mistress and leader.[23] Even in their united existence there is a great gulf fixed between the soul and all that is not soul; [24] body and soul never fuse into one, however closely they may be bound up with each other. And yet the body and its impulses have the power to influence profoundly the immortal being that dwells within it. By its union with the body the soul can be made unclean; " diseases " such as folly and unrestrained passion come to it from the body.[25] It is not beyond the reach of change like the Ideas, to which it is akin without being of their nature; on the contrary, it can degenerate entirely. The evil influences of the body penetrate to its inmost being; even in its everlasting, immaterial, spiritual nature it can derive something " corporeal " [26] from such a sinister partnership.

It is bound to the body by influences of a lower kind which attach themselves to the pure power of knowledge that alone is proper to it. At the outset of his speculations Plato, like other thinkers before him,[27] had thought of the different capacities of the soul, alternately in conflict or alliance with each other, as " parts " of unequal rank and value, bound up together within the soul of man.[28] Even in the previous life of the soul, in the other world, the reasoning power of the soul is, according to the *Phaedrus*, already coupled with " Temper " and " Desire "; it is these in fact which drag down the soul into the realm of the material; and the three parts still remain indissolubly united in the everlasting life which awaits the soul after its release from the body.

But in proportion as the philosopher extends and elevates his conception of the soul, and as he becomes more convinced of its eternal destiny and vocation to a life of unending blessedness in a realm of unchangeable being, the more impossible does it seem to him that this candidate for immortality in the realm of the everlasting Forms can be a composite amalgam of elements capable of being resolved again by division and analysis [29]—that the reasoning faculty can be for ever united with Effort and Desire, which perpetually threaten to drag it downwards into materiality. The soul in its true and original nature is now for him simple and indivisible.[30] Only with its enclosure in the body does the everlasting, thinking soul, whose tendency is towards the eternal, acquire impulses and desires [31] that have their origin in the body and belong to the body,[32] that only adhere to the soul during the period of its earthly life, that with their separation from their immortal associate will pass away, since they are themselves mortal and such as perish with the body.

The soul, to which sense-perception,[33] feeling, emotion, and desire are only added from outside, is in its own imperishable nature nothing but pure capacity of thought and knowledge—with which indeed the power to will that which is conceived in thought, seems to be directly associated. It is destined for the "other" world, for the intuition and undistorted reflection in its consciousness of the immaterial essences. Banished to this earth amid the restless change and alteration of all being, and not uninfluenced by the forces of bodily life, it must endure a brief exile here.[34] Not unscathed does it leave behind it, in death, its ill-assorted companion, the body.[35] Then it goes into an intermediate region of bodiless existence in which it must do penance for the misdeeds of its life on earth, and free itself from their effects.[36] After that it is driven away once more into a body and transported to a fresh life upon earth, the character of which it chooses for itself in accordance with the special nature that it had evolved in its earlier incarnation upon earth.[37] Though no organic connexion exists between them, yet there is a certain "symmetry" [38] between the individual soul and the body that is lent to it.

Thus, the soul lives through a series of earthly lives [39] of the most varied character; it may even sink so low as the animals in the course of its incarnations.[40] Its own merits, the success or failure of its conflict with the passions and desires of the body, decide whether or not its lives shall lead it upwards to a nobler type of existence. Its task is plain : it must *free* itself from its impure companions, sensual Lust and the darkening of the powers of Reason. If it can succeed in this it will find once more the " way upwards " [41] which at last leads it into complete immunity from renewed incarnation and brings it home again into the kingdom of everlasting untroubled Being.

§ 3

It is evident that in what he thus, clothing philosophy in the language of poetry, says of the origin, destiny, and character of the soul, which though beyond time is yet placed within time, and though beyond space is yet the cause of all movement within space—that in all this Plato is following in the track of the *theologians* of earlier times. Only in the poetry and speculative thought of *theologi*, not in any physiologists' doctrine, did he find the conception, imaginatively expressed and pointing in the direction which he also followed, of a multiplicity of independent souls whose existence had been from all time and was not first begun in the material world with the creation of a living organism ; of souls enclosed in the corporeal as though in a foreign, hostile element, which survive their association with the body, passing through many such bodies and yet preserving themselves intact after the destruction of each of those bodies, immortal, endless (for they are without beginning),[42] and alive from the very beginning of Time. The souls, moreover, have life as distinct, complete, and indivisible personalities, not as mere dependent emanations of a simple common Source of all life.

The theory of the eternity and indestructibility of the individual souls, of the personal immortality of the souls, is difficult to reconcile with more specifically Platonic doctrine—with the doctrine of the Ideas.[43] And yet it is undeniable that from the moment that he first adopted this theory—and adopted it, too, precisely in connexion with the philosophy of the Ideas—he adhered to it steadfastly and without deviating from its essential meaning. The process by which he arrived at it is not to be found in the " proofs " by which he attempts in the *Phaedo* to establish the truth of the soul's immortality in which he himself already believed. Those proofs in reality do not prove what they are intended to prove (and what considered as a fact of experience is unproved and as an axiom necessary to thought is beyond proof) ; they cannot therefore be the reasons that led the philosopher to hold his conviction. He has in fact borrowed this article of his faith from the creeds which already contained it. He himself scarcely conceals the fact. As authority for the main outlines of the soul's history as given by himself he refers us almost apologetically, and as though excusing himself for not providing a philosophical proof, to the *theologi* and priests of the mysteries.[44] And he himself becomes the philosophical poet, completely and without concealment, when in imitation of the poetry of edification he, too, gives a picture of the soul's sojourn in an intermediate station of its pilgrimage or describes the stages of its earthly existence [45] that lead the soul down even to the animal.

For such mythological expressions of the inexpressible the philosopher himself claims no more than symbolical truth.[46] He is fully in earnest, however, with the fundamental conception of the soul as an independent substance that enters from beyond space and time into the material and perceptible world, and into external conjunction with the body, not into organic union with it; that maintains itself as a being of spiritual essence in the midst of the flux and decay of the material world, though at the same time its pure brightness is overshadowed through this conjunction and must purify itself from the effects; that *can* disentangle itself,[47] even to the extent of complete severance from the embrace of the material and the perceptible. All that is essential in this conception he derives from the theologians, but he brings it into close relationship with his own philosophy which depends upon a conviction of the absolute opposition between Being and Becoming, and upon the dualistic division of the world into matter and mind—a dualism that applies also to the relations of soul and body and throughout the whole realm of Appearance. The soul which stands half-way between the unity and unchangeability of Being and the ever-varying multiplicity of matter has in this realm of fragmentary and subordinate validity, into which it is temporarily exiled, the power to reflect the Ideas and represent them in its own consciousness clear and unfalsified. The soul in its complete independence of sense-perception and of concepts derived from the senses is alone able to pursue the "Quest of Reality".[48] In this pursuit the body with which it is associated is nothing but a hindrance and a serious one. The soul has a hard struggle against the tendencies of the body in spite of its independence and aloofness. Just as, in the creation of the universe, matter, though not a cause is at least a subordinate cause which by its influence and exigencies gives various hindrances [49] to the " Mind " that shapes and orders the world, so, too, the soul finds in this ephemeral and inconstant Matter, with its stirring and tumultuous unrest, a serious obstacle to its own proper activity. This is the evil, or the cause of evil,[50] which must be overthrown in order that the mind may win its way to freedom and final rest and security in the realm of pure Being. Plato often speaks of the *katharsis*, the purification, after which man must strive.[51] He takes both the word and the idea from the theologians, but he gives it a higher meaning while yet preserving unmistakably the analogy with the *katharsis* of the *theologi* and mystery-priests. It is not the pollution which comes from contact with sinister *daimones* and from all that belongs to them, that is to be avoided, but rather the dulling of the power of knowledge and of willing what is known (regarded as a simultaneously created power) due to the world of the senses and its fierce impulses.[52] Man's effort must be directed not so much to ritual purity, as to the preservation of his knowledge of the eternal from eclipse through the deceptive illusions of the senses; towards the concentration and gathering together of the soul within itself; [53] its withdrawal from contact with the ephemeral as the source of pollution and debasement.

Thus, even in this philosophic reinterpretation of ritual abstinence in terms of a spiritual release and emancipation, the effort after " purity " retains its *religious* sense. The world of the Ideas, the world of pure Being, to which only the pure soul can attain,[54] is a world of divinity. The " Good " as the highest of the Ideas, the loftiest pattern, the supreme aim to which all Being and Becoming tend, which is at the same time more than all the Ideas—the first cause of all Being and all knowledge—is also God.[55] The soul for which, in its desire and longing for the full being of the Idea, the knowledge of the " Good " is the " supreme science ",[56] enters hereby into the closest communion with God. The " turning away " of the soul from the many-coloured image to the sun of the highest Idea, is itself [57] a turning towards the divine, towards the luminous source of all Being and Knowing.

Thus exalted, philosophic inquiry turns to *enthousiasmos*.[85] The way which leads upwards from the lower levels of Becoming to Being, is discovered by means of *dialectic*, which in its " comprehensive view " [59] is able to unite the distracted ever-moving flood of multifarious Appearance into the ever-enduring unity of the Idea which is reflected in Appearance. Dialectic travels through the whole range of the Ideas, graduated one above the other, till it reaches the last and most universal of the Ideas. In its upward course it passes by an effort of sheer logic through the whole edifice of the highest concepts.[60] Plato is the most subtle of dialecticians; he almost carries subtlety to excess in his eager pursuit of every intricacy of logic—and of paralogism. But he combined to a remarkable degree the cold exactitude of the logician with the enthusiastic intensity of the seer; and his dialectic, after its patient upward march step by step from concept to concept, at last soars to its final goal in a single tremendous flight, in which the longed-for realm of the Ideas reveals itself in a moment of immediate vision. So the Bacchant in his ecstasy saw divinity suddenly plain, and so too in the nights consecrated by the mysteries the *epoptês* beheld the vision of the Goddesses in the torch-lit glare of Eleusis.[61]

To this loftiest height whence a view is obtained of "colourless, formless Being, beyond the reach of every contact", inaccessible to sense-perception, it is dialectic that shows the way; and dialectic now becomes a way of salvation in which the soul finds once more its own divine nature and its divine home. The soul is closely akin to godhead and like it [62]—it is itself something divine. The reason in the soul is divine,[63] and comprehends everlasting Being immediately by its power of thought. "If the eye were not sunlike, it could never see the sun"; [64] if the mind were not akin by nature to the good,[65] the highest of the Ideas, it could never comprehend the Good, the Beautiful, and all that is perfect and eternal. In its power of recognizing the eternal the soul bears within itself the surest proof that it is itself eternal.[66]

The "purification" by means of which the soul gets rid of [67] the defacement that has overtaken it during its earthly life reveals again the divine in man. Even on earth the philosopher is thus rendered immortal and godlike.[68] As long as he can continue in a state of pure intellectual knowledge and comprehension of the everlasting, for so long is he living, already in this life, "in the Islands of the Blest." [69] By expelling all traces of the corruptible and the mortal in and about himself, he is more and more to "become like God"; [70] so that when it is at last set free from this earthly existence, his soul may enter into the divine, the invisible, the pure, the eternally self-identical, and as a disembodied mind remain for ever with that which is its kin.[70a] At this point, language that can only make use of physical imagery becomes totally inadequate.[71] A goal is set before the soul that lies outside all physical nature, beyond time and space, without past or future, an ever-present *now*.[72]

The soul can escape out of time and space and find its home in eternity, without at the same time losing its own self in the General and Universal that stands above time and space. We must not inquire what sort of personality and individual distinctness can yet remain with the soul when it has cast off all effort, desire, sense-perception, and everything related to the world of change and multiplicity, to become once more a pure mirror of the eternal. Nor must we ask how it is possible to think of a spirit removed above space and time and all the multiplicity of matter and yet personal and separate in its personality.[73] For Plato the Souls live on as they had been in the beginning—individual beings conscious of themselves in a time that has no end and is beyond all time. He teaches a personal immortality.

§ 4

There is an " other-worldly " tone in this philosophy, and its doctrine of the soul. Far beyond the world in which life has placed man lies the realm of pure Being, the good, the perfect, and the unspoilt. To reach that realm at last, to free the mind from the unrest and illusion of the senses, to be rid of the desires and emotions that would " nail " [74] it down here below, to sever its connexion [75] with the body and bodily things—that is the soul's highest duty. The only reason why it is banished into this world is that it may all the more completely separate itself from the world. To die—to be dead inwardly to all that is visible, material, physical—that is the goal and the fruit of philosophy.[76] " To be ready and fit to die " is the hall-mark of the complete philosopher. For such, philosophy is the deliverer that frees him for all time from the body [77]—from its desires, its restlessness, its wild passions [78]—and gives him back again to the eternal and its silence.

To be pure, to be free from evil, to die already in this temporal world—these are the oft-repeated exhortations which the philosopher addresses to the immortal soul. Ascetic morality here again demands from man what is essentially a quite negative proceeding. But this denial of the world is only a step leading on to the most supremely positive behaviour. *Katharsis* is only the gateway to philosophy ; and it is philosophy which teaches man how to reach what alone is positive, the only true and unconditional Being ; instructs him how to reach the clear and perfect understanding of the only permanent good and how to merge himself utterly in that good.[79] The soul of the thinker yearns after Reality ; [80]

death is for it not merely the annihilation of the chains of the body that impede it, but a very positive "acquisition of intellectual knowledge" [81] to which it is urged on by its proper nature—which is therefore also a fulfilment of its proper task. So the turning aside from the physical and the ephemeral is at the same time and without transition a turning towards the eternal and the divine. The flight from the things of this world is in itself an entry into that other world, and a becoming like to the divine.[82]

But the true realities are not to be found in this world. To grasp them plainly in its thought—to recover the untroubled vision of its spiritual eye—the soul must divest itself entirely of all the stress and distraction of the earthly. For this mundane world, the mirage that encompasses the senses, the philospher has nothing but denial. Because it gives no foothold for true knowledge the whole world of Becoming has no independent value for his science. The apprehension of that which is never more than relative, which simultaneously manifests contrary qualities in itself, can only serve as stimulus and invitation to the search for what is absolute.[83] In this realm of doubtful shadows the soul finds nothing but obscure reminders of that which it had once beheld plainly. The beauty of the physical world which is apprehended by the noblest of the senses, the eye, serves indeed to recall to the soul's memory the Beautiful-in-itself, of which that other is but a pale copy, and to disclose to the soul what is really its own property, what it had brought with it ready made from an earlier existence beyond the bounds of all matter.[84] But the observation of beauty here below must lead beyond itself at once and conduct the mind out of the world of mere appearance to the pure forms of the Ideal world. The process of Becoming tells us nothing about the nature of Being; the thinker learns nothing from this source—in fact he learns no *new* knowledge or wisdom of any kind in this world; he only recovers what he had before and always possessed in latent form.[85] The treasure, however, lies beyond the limits of this world. He must turn away his gaze from the shadow-figures upon the wall of the cave of this world, and direct it towards the sun of eternity.[86] He is placed in this world of perpetual change; to it his senses and his understanding are directly referred; and yet he must disdain and rise superior to, and flee from, all that this world offers, giving himself up immediately and entirely to the unseen, and taking flight from this world to that where he will become like God, and be purified and justified by the power and might of his knowledge.[87]

Earthly life as it actually is will remain strange to him, and he a stranger in earthly life,[88] despised as a fool for his inaptitude in earthly affairs by the great majority of those who are so versed in such things.[89] He has something higher to think about—the salvation of his own soul. He will not live for the community, but for himself, and his real task.[90] Human interests seem to him hardly worth troubling about,[91] the state itself hopelessly corrupt, founded as it is upon deception and passion and injustice. At the same time, he himself of course would be the real statesman,[92] the leader who could guide his fellow citizens to their true salvation—acting not as the servant of their lusts, but as a doctor who gives help to the sick.[93] It is " not ships and harbours and walls and taxes and such trivialities " [94] that he would give the city, but justice and health and everything else which after this life can stand before the stern judgment of the other world.[95] This would be the best mode of life,[96] and he could show them the way to it ; no worldly power or greatness can do as much—none of the great statesmen of the past, Themistokles, Kimon, and Perikles, understood anything of all this ; all their efforts were nothing but blind error and wandering.[97]

At the climax of his life and of his philosophical development Plato completed an ideal picture of the State, drawn in accordance with the principles and the requirements of his own philosophy. It rests upon a broad foundation—the multitude of its inhabitants divided strictly into classes that in themselves and their manner of life are to display, like a beacon that can be seen afar, the virtue of Justice. At one period this had seemed to include all that was necessary for the completion of the ideal State ; but now, far above that level, pointing upwards into the lofty *aether* above the earth, a final consummation reveals itself to him, to which all mere mundane things serve but as support and furtherance. A small minority of the citizens, the philosphers, form this last pinnacle of the building. Here on earth and in this state that is organized in conformity with justice, they will serve the state, as in duty bound and not for their own satisfaction, and take part in government.[98] As soon as duty is fulfilled they will return to the supramundane contemplation which is the aim and content of their whole life's activity. To provide a place where these contemplatives may live, where they may be educated for their vocation, the highest there is ; to allow *dialectic* as a form of living to take its place in the activity of worldly civilization as an object of men's effort [99]—to bring about all this the Ideal State is built up step by step. The bourgeois social virtues and their firm establishment and interconnexion, which had once seemed the real and sufficient reason for the erection of the whole edifice of the state—seen from this elevation, these no longer retain their independent importance. "The so-called virtues" all pale before the highest capacity of the soul, which is the mystic beholding of the eternal.[100] The chief mission of the perfect wise man is no longer to fulfil his obligations to the others that stand without. To make his own inner life fit and ready for self-emancipation is now his real and immediate task. Mysticism aims at a personal salvation such as the individual can only obtain for himself. Good works are no longer necessary when the mind has no further connexion with earthly life and conduct. When it comes to dealing with practical earthly affairs he who possesses the highest virtue will have all these others added unto him.[101] Virtue belongs to him; it is his real condition of being; but the particular virtues he will rarely need to use.

This lofty pinnacle is accessible to but a few. God alone and a small [102] company of mortals are able to approach in pure thought to the everlasting Reality, the sole object of certain, plain and unchanging Knowledge. The majority of men can never become philosophers.[103] And yet, according to this philosophy, the crown of all life belongs to the philosopher. This is no religion for the poor in spirit. Science—the supreme knowledge of the highest Being—is a pre-condition of salvation. To know God is to become like God.[104] It is easy to see why such a message of salvation could not attract a wider community of believers. It could not have done so without being false to its own nature. To a few lofty spirits among mankind, it offers a reward that beckons from eternity. Freedom from life in the corruptible body is the prize it offers; that and a never-ending union with true Reality—a return to what is everlasting and divine. A symbol of what the philosopher has achieved after his death will be provided by the community by whom the departed will be honoured as a Daimon.[105]

Such then is the ideal vision of a civilization in which the belief in the soul's immortality and its vocation to an everlasting life in the kingdom of the gods was held with profound and serious conviction. The belief in immortality here becomes the corner-stone of a building, the architect of which regards all earthly things as only valid for the moment, and therefore of profound unimportance. For him only the Heaven of the spiritual world with its everlasting laws and patterns seriously matters. He discards without a regret the whole of Greek culture as it had expressed itself in state and society, custom and art—an art that will last as long as humanity itself. He demands an aristocracy, and an aristocracy measured by a standard of what is the " best " that was quite beyond the reach of any possible human society even though it were as deeply impregnated with aristocratic ideas as Greek society always was. And the final aim and ideal sought by this organization of life on earth was to be the superseding of all earthly life . . .

The mind of Plato, equally ready to receive as to give, was not likely to become immobilized for ever in a mystic rapture of vision. Even when he had finished the *Republic* he did not cease to reshape his system at many points and in many directions, while some special problems were taken up again for further and repeated study. Even a second sketch of a political system was left behind by him in which he sought to lay down rules for the guidance of life among the multitude who are still regarded as completely shut out from the realm of the everlasting Forms. To this end the highest aims of human endeavour are almost left out of sight and practical rules for reaching the attainable " better " are supplied for the benefit of the majority. He had learnt resignation at many points. Nevertheless, the profound conviction of all his thoughts remained unchanged; the claims that he put before the world and mankind remained essentially the same. For this reason after generations have not been mistaken in seeing in him the priestly man of wisdom, who with warning finger points the immortal spirit of man on its way from this feeble world upwards to the everlasting life.

NOTES TO CHAPTER XIII

[1] Pl., *Ap.* c. 32 f. (40 C ff.).
[2] *Ap.* 41 C D.
[3] *Ap.* 29 A B, 37 B.
[4] Xen., *Cyrop.* 8, 7, 17, makes the dying Kyros justify his faith that the soul survives the body rather on the lines of popular belief and the cult of souls than from would-be-philosophical considerations (§ 20; see above, chap. v, n. 178). In spite of this he allows the question to remain undecided—as though of little importance—whether, in fact, the soul then leaves the body and lives on or whether *μένουσα ἡ ψυχὴ ἐν τῷ σώματι συναποθνήσκει*, § 21. In either eventuality he will after death *μηδὲν ἔτι κακὸν παθεῖν*, § 27.—Arist., *SE.* xvii, p. 176b, 16, *πότερον φθαρτὴ ἢ ἀθάνατος ἡ ψυχὴ τῶν ζῴων, οὐ διώρισται τοῖς πολλοῖς*—in this question they *ἀμφιδοξοῦσι*.
[5] Pl., *Phd.* 70 A, 77 B, 80 D. This belief of the *πολλοί* and *παῖδες* looks indeed much more like a piece of superstition than a denial of the continued life of the *ψυχή* (in which light Pl. represents it). We have already met with the soul as a wind-spirit more than once: when it leaves the body the other wind-spirits carry it off and away with themselves (cf. above, chap. i, n. 10), esp. when a high wind is blowing (cf. the German popular belief that when a man hangs himself a storm arises: Grimm, p. 635: cf. Mannhardt, *Germ. Myth.* 270 n. In other words, the "furious host", the personified storm-spirits—Grimm, p. 632; cf. Append. vii—come and carry away with them the poor unquiet soul).
[6] Cf. Pl., *Rp.* 330 D E. There is more about these matters in the speech against Aristogeiton, [D.] 25, 52–3. In spite of the popular form in which it is put such an opinion is not to be claimed at once as a popular and generally held belief: the author of this speech is a follower of Orpheus, a fact which he himself betrays in § 11.
[7] Pl., *Rp.* 608 D.
[8] It is probable that in the *Πολιτεία* two essentially distinct stages of Platonic doctrine are found side by side with only an external bond of union, and that in particular what is said in Bk. v, 471 C ff., to the end of Bk. vii about the *φιλόσοφοι*, their education and position in the state (and outside politics), is an extraneous addition to the completed picture of the *καλλίπολις* which is given in Bks. ii—v, 471 C: an afterthought not originally included in the plan of the whole book and not anticipated in the beginning of it. This seems to me to emerge unmistakably from a careful and unprejudiced study of the whole work and to have been completely demonstrated by Krohn and Pfleiderer. That Plato himself regarded the first sketch of an ideal state as a separate work (which may even have been actually published separately: Gellius, 14, 3, 3), is shown by the beginning of the *Timaeus*. Here—with the implication of quite a different staging of the dialogue and a different introduction from what we now read in *Rp.*, Bk. i, c.1—ii, c. 9—we have an exact recapitulation of the subject of the inquiry in the *Πολιτεία* from ii, 10, 367 E, to v, 460 C, with the definite statement (19AB) that thus far and no farther had the discussion gone "yesterday". The stages in which the whole work was composed seem then to be divisible as follows: (1) Sketch of the state of the

φύλακες (in brief) embodied in a dialogue between Sokrates, Kriton, Timaios, Hermokrates, and another companion: in subject matter agreeing (apart from the introduction) substantially with *Rp.* ii, 10, 367 E, to v, 460 C. (2) Continuation of this sketch in the story of ancient Athens and the people of Atlantis. Its completion is transferred elsewhere because in the meantime the Πολιτεία itself has been extended and into the empty framework of the *Τίμ.* thus left available the account of the creation of the world given by Timaios is very loosely inserted: the frame-narratives of the Τίμαιος and Κριτίας never being completed. (3) Continuation of the first sketch (still virtually along the lines originally laid down) in *Rp.* v, 460 D–471 C (in which 466 E ff. is a brief account of the behaviour of the state in time of war—a substitute for the longer and more detailed statement on the same subject in *Tim.* 20 B f.), and in viii, ix (the greater part), and x, second half (608 C ff.). (4) Finally the whole work receives its crown and completion in a section that was, however, not foreseen in the older parts of the design, for it disturbs part of that original design's independence and validity and does more than merely supplement it—the introduction of the φιλόσοφοι and their special type of "virtue", v, 471 C–vii fin.; ix, 580 D–588 A; x, part 1 (to 608 B).—Then came the final editing of the whole: insertion of the new introduction, i, 1–ii, 9 (not necessarily left until the completion of the whole); necessary bringing into harmony of the divergent elements by a few excisions, qualifications, etc.; and probably a literary revision and polishing of the whole book.—The whole thus finally produced reveals its origin clearly enough in the outgrowing of a first plan and its replacement by a second that has naturally suggested itself in the course of the author's own continued development. At the same time Plato could claim that the whole edifice, in spite of much extension and rebuilding in a different style of architecture, should be considered as a unity in the form in which he finally left it (as a noteworthy monument, too, of his own alteration of view). He himself in the sublimest moments of his mystic flight in Bks. vi and vii in no sense rejects the groundwork of the καλλίπολις of ii–v (though not, indeed, designed originally as such), but merely reduces it to the position of a substructure which remains a necessary and sole foundation even for the mystic pinnacle and preserves its absolute validity for the great majority of the citizens who inhabit the καλλίπολις (for the φιλόσοφοι are still regarded as very few in number) for whom it is a school for the exhibition of political virtue.—In the first sketch, then, there is no trace of a doctrine of immortality that can be properly so called, and the popular belief in a continued life of the soul after death has for Plato, at this stage at least, no serious weight or importance. The φύλακες are not to trouble about what may follow death (iii, 1 ff.); the main purpose in view is to show that δικαιοσύνη is its own reward, and the rewards which are anticipated for it after death are only ironically alluded to (ii, 363 CD; cf. 366 AB); Sokrates means to do without such hopes (366 E ff.). The ἀθανασία ψυχῆς is only introduced as a paradox in x, 608 D (in the continuation of the first sketch) for which proof is sought; whereupon the importance of the question as to what may await the soul after death emerges (614 A ff.) as well as the necessity of taking thought not for this short life but ὑπὲρ τοῦ ἅπαντος χρόνου (608 C), of which nothing had been said or could have been said in iii–v. Finally in vi–vii the indestructibility of the soul is implied in its sublimest form. It is evident that Plato's own views on these matters had undergone changes in the course of time, and that these changes are reflected in the various strata of the Πολιτεία even after its final editing. (Cf. Krohn, *Platon. Staat*, p. 265; Pfleiderer, *Platon. Frage*, p. 23 f., 35 ff., 1888.)

[9] The Appearance βούλεται, ὀρέγεται, προθυμεῖται εἶναι what its Idea *is*: *Phd.* 74 D, 75 AB. The Ideas are thus teleological causes like the divine νοῦς of Aristotle which, unmoved itself, κινεῖ ὡς ἐρώμενον (just as matter has a desire for form, potentiality for actuality). Plato it is true did not keep to this method of illustrating rather than explaining the relation between the Appearance and the unmoved Idea.

[10] νοήσει μετὰ λόγου περιληπτόν, *Tim.* 27 D. οὗ οὔποτ' ἂν ἄλλῳ ἐπιλάβοιο ἢ τῷ τῆς διανοίας λογισμῷ, *Phd.* 79 A. αὐτὴ δι' αὑτῆς ἡ ψυχὴ τὰ κοινὰ φαίνεταί περὶ πάντων ἐπισκοπεῖν, *Tht.* 185 D.

[11] The *prius* in the case of man is really the perception of his own mental activity in νόησις μετὰ λόγου as being a process essentially different from δόξα μετ' αἰσθήσεως ἀλόγου. It is inference from the former alone that leads to the conclusion that the νοούμενα exist: *Tim.* 51 B–52 A. It is the Ideas that we grasp in abstract thought: αὐτὴ ἡ οὐσία ἧς λόγον δίδομεν καὶ ἐρωτῶντες καὶ ἀποκρινόμενοι, *Phd.* 78 D.

[12] The ἐπιστήμη which διαλεκτική alone can give (*Rp.* 533 DE) is ἀναμάρτητος (*Rp.* 477 E).

[13] Of the three εἴδη or γένη—the ὄν, the γιγνόμενον and the ἐν ᾧ γίγνεται (the χώρα), of *Tim.* 48 E f., 52 ABD—the third at any rate is quite foreign to the soul. Like the World-Soul (*Tim.* 35 A), along with which it is "mixed" (41 D), the individual soul also is a middle term between the ἀμερές of the Idea and the κατὰ τὰ σώματα μεριστόν, having a share in both.

[14] True, unalterable Being belongs only to the ἀειδές and therefore also to the soul: *Phd.* 79 A f.

[15] *Phd.* c. 54–6 (105 B–107 B).

[16] ὁμοιότερον ψυχὴ σώματός ἐστι τῷ ἀειδεῖ (and that = τῷ ἀεὶ ὡσαύτως ἔχοντι), *Phd.* 79 B. τῷ θείῳ καὶ ἀθανάτῳ καὶ νοητῷ καὶ μονοειδεῖ καὶ ἀδιαλύτῳ καὶ ὡσαύτως κατὰ ταὐτὰ ἔχοντι ἑαυτῷ ὁμοιότατον ψυχή, 80 AB.

[17] ἀγένητον, *Phdr.* c. 24, 245 D (ἀΐδιος simply, *Rp.* 611 B). The creation of the souls in *Tim.* is only intended to represent the origin of the spiritual from the δημιουργός (not the coming into being of the soul *in time*): see Siebeck, *Ges. d. Psychol.* i, 1, 275 ff. Still, it remains impossible to say whether Plato whenever he speaks of the pre-existence of the soul always means that the soul existed without beginning.

[18] As to the relation of the individual soul to the soul of the universe, neither the mythical account in *Timaeus* nor the briefer allusion in *Phileb.* 30 A allows us to conclude that the soul of our body is "taken from" the soul of the σῶμα τοῦ παντός. In reality the fiction of a "World-Soul" is intended to serve quite other purposes than the derivation of the individual soul from a single common source.

[19] *Tim.* 34 C; *Lg.* 891 A–896 C.

[20] Acc. to the account in *Phdr.* 246 C, the soul suffers its downfall into the earthly existence if ὁ τῆς κάκης ἵππος, i.e. the ἐπιθυμία in the soul, tends towards the earth—247 B. It must, therefore, be the result of the preponderance of the appetitive impulses. This, however, can only happen if the λογιστικόν of the soul has become too weak to drive the soul-chariot any longer as its duty was. Hence the supporting wings, i.e. the νόησις, of the soul-horse fall off. It is thus a weakening of the cognitive part of the soul that causes its downfall into materiality (just as it is the measure of their capacity for knowledge that determines

the character of the ἐνσωμάτωσις of the souls, and their return to the τόπος ὑπερουράνιος is equally determined by their recovery of the purer form of knowledge: 248 C ff., 249 AC). Thus it is not, as in Empedokles, a religio-moral transgression that leads to the incarnation of the souls, but a failure of intellect, an intellectual fall in sin.

[21] The soul is, acc. to the account in *Tim.*, created in order that by animating and governing a body, it may complete the sum of creation: without the ζῷα the οὐρανός (the universe) would be ἀτελής, *Tim.* 41 B ff. Acc. to this teleological motivation of the being and the ἐνσωμάτωσις of the soul, this latter, the ἐνσωμάτωσις, would have belonged to the original plan of the δημιουργός and there would be no purpose in the creation of the souls (by the δημιουργός and the inferior gods) unless they were destined to the animation of the ζῷα and conjunction with σώματα. But it is obviously inconsistent with all this that the *object* of the soul's endeavour should be to separate itself as soon as possible and as completely as possible from the body and everything material in order to get back again to immaterial life without any body—42 BD. This is a relic of the original *theological* view of the relation between body and soul. In *Phd.* (and usually in Plato) it displays itself unconcealed; but it was far too closely bound up with the whole of Plato's ethic and metaphysics not to make its illicit appearance even when as in *Tim.* he wished to keep the physiological side to the fore.

[22] *Phdr.* 245 C–246 A. The soul is τὸ αὐτὸ κινοῦν, and indeed continually, ἀεικίνητον, it is τοῖς ἄλλοις ὅσα κινεῖται πηγὴ καὶ ἀρχὴ κινήσεως (the body only *seems* to move itself, but it is really the soul within which moves it—246 C). If the soul were to perish, πᾶς οὐρανὸς πᾶσά τε γένεσις would be at a standstill. The conception of the "soul" as the ἀεικίνητον was already well and long established in Plato's time (see above, chap. xii, n. 150). In the form in which he introduces it here (as a proof of the imperishability of the soul) he may have modelled his conception on that of Alkmaion (Arist., *An.* 405a, 29): see Hirzel, *Hermes*, xi, 244. But Plato here and throughout *Phdr.* is speaking of the individual soul (ψυχή collective singular). So too in *Lg.* 894 E ff., 896 A ff. (λόγος of the soul: ἡ δυναμένη αὐτὴ αὑτὴν κινεῖν κίνησις. It is the αἰτία and the issue of all movement in the world, the source of life; for life belongs to that which αὐτὸ αὑτὸ κινεῖ 895 C.) As distinguished from the ψυχὴ ἐνοικοῦσα ἐν ἅπασι τοῖς κινουμένοις we do not hear of the (double) World-Soul until 896 E. There is in fact κίνησις in plenty in the world besides that of the animated organisms.

[23] *Phd.* 93 B (c. 43) and often.

[24] ψυχή on the one side, πᾶν τὸ ἄψυχον on the other. *Phdr.* 246 B and so generally.

[25] *Tim.* 86 B ff. (c. 41).—In brief: κακὸς ἑκὼν οὐδείς, διὰ δὲ πονηρὰν ἕξιν τινὰ τοῦ σώματος καὶ ἀπαίδευτον τροφὴν (education of the soul) ὁ κακὸς γίγνεται κακός, 86 E.

[26] τὸ σωματοειδὲς ὃ τῇ ψυχῇ ἡ ὁμιλία τε καὶ ξυνουσία τοῦ σώματος . . . ἐνεποίησε ξύμφυτον κτλ. *Phd.* 81 C, 83 D.

[27] Pythagoreans, see above (chap. xi, n. 55); hardly Demokritos (*Dox.*, p. 390, 14). The trichotomy can exist very well side by side with the dichotomy (which also appears) into λογιστικόν and ἀλόγιστον, the last being simply divided again into θυμός and ἐπιθυμία.

[28] In the first sketch of the *Republic* (ii–v). Here it is admittedly bound up with the three classes or castes of the state, but it has not been invented for the benefit of these classes. On the contrary, the

trichotomy of the soul is original and the division of the citizen body into three parts is derived and explained from it; cf. 435 E.—The view that Plato was never quite serious about the threefold division of the soul but always spoke of it as something semi-mythical or as a temporarily adopted hypothesis, will not appear plausible on an unprejudiced study of the passages in the Platonic writings that deal with the threefold division of the soul.

[29] *Rp.* x, 611 A–E (c. 11), shows clearly that the reason which made Plato abandon his conception (given in the first sketch of the *Rep.* and still maintained in the *Phaedrus*) of the natural trichotomy of the soul into parts or divisions was the consideration of its immortality and vocation to intercourse with the θεῖον καὶ ἀθάνατον καὶ ἀεὶ ὄν.—The emotions and passions by which the soul is "fettered" ὑπὸ τοῦ σώματος, explain its tendency to clothe itself in another body after death, *Phd.* 83 C ff. If the emotions and passions were indissolubly linked to the soul the latter could never escape from the cycle of rebirths.—On the other hand, if only the λογιστικόν, as the only independently existing side of the soul, goes into the place of judgment in the other world there would seem to be no reason that should tempt this simple uncompounded soul to renewed ἐνσωμάτωσις, a process which implies materiality and desire. (This difficulty troubled Plotinos too.) Plato takes into view the possibility of an inner corruption of the pure and undivided intellectual soul which makes a future state of punishment and purgatory possible and intelligible and explains the existence (until a complete return to purity is achieved) of a tendency or constraint to renewed ἐνσωματώσεις even without a permanent association with the θυμοειδές and the ἐπιθυμητικόν.

[30] τῇ ἀληθεστάτῃ φύσει the soul is μονοειδές, *Rep.* x, c. 11 (611 B, 612 A). Hence it is τὸ παράπαν ἀδιάλυτος ἢ ἐγγύς τι τούτου, *Phd.* 80 B.

[31] The intellect-soul ἀθάνατον ἀρχὴν θνητοῦ ζῴου is the creation of the δημιουργός; the other faculties of the soul, θυμός, ἐπιθυμία (and αἴσθησις therewith), ψυχῆς ὅσον θνητόν (*Tim.* 61 C), are all added to the soul at the moment of its union with the body by the subordinate deities: *Tim.* 41 D–44 D; 69 A–70 D (c. 14, 15, 31). The same idea appears in *Rp.* x, 611 BC. τὸ ἀειγενὲς μέρος τῆς ψυχῆς is distinguished from the ζωογενές: *Polit.* 309 C.

[32] τὸ σῶμα καὶ αἱ τούτου ἐπιθυμίαι, *Phd.* 66 C. The soul moved by passion suffers ὑπὸ σώματος, 83 CD. In death the soul is καθαρὰ πάντων τῶν περὶ τὸ σῶμα κακῶν καὶ ἐπιθυμιῶν, *Crat.* 404 A.

[33] *Tim.* 43 C. It is only as a result of this violent and contradictory excitement through the physical perception of Becoming that the soul *becomes* ἄνους (which is orginally foreign to it) ὅταν εἰς σῶμα ἐνδεθῇ θνητόν, 44 A. (It will in time become ἔμφρων once more and can become wise, 44 BC. In the case of the animals, which can be inhabited by the same soul, it will remain always ἄφρων—one may suppose.)

[34] . . . σμικρὸν χρόνον, οὐδὲν μὲν οὖν πρὸς τὸν ἅπαντα (χρόνον). *Rp.* 498 D.

[35] In accordance with popular thought (but obviously also in perfect seriousness and without any special concession) death is regarded as τῆς ψυχῆς ἀπὸ τοῦ σώματος ἀπαλλαγή, *Phd.* 64 C; *Gorg.* 524 B. Hence, it usually happens that the soul μηδέποτε εἰς Ἅιδου καθαρῶς ἀφικέσθαι, ἀλλ' ἀεὶ τοῦ σώματος ἀναπλέα ἐξιέναι, *Phd.* 83 D. (—ἀεὶ, i.e. with the exception of the few complete φιλόσοφοι that do not need further purification in Hades, and this is, in fact, the doctrine of the *Phd.* itself; cf. 114 C, 80 E, 81 A.)

[36] Purgatory, punishment and rewards in the other world: *Gorg.*

523 ff.; *Rp*. x, c. 13 ff., 614 A ff. (vision of Er, son of Armenios in the continuation of the first version of the πολιτεία); *Phd.* 110 B–114 C. We must not here go into the details of the individual myths in which it is still perhaps possible to distinguish what parts Plato has taken out of ancient poetry and popular legend and what comes from theological and particularly Orphic doctrinal poetry—or even (*Rp*. x) from Oriental fables—and how much he has added independently on his own account. (A few remarks will be found in G. Ettig, *Acherunt.*, *Leipz. Stud.* xiii, 305 ff.; cf. also Döring, *Arch. Ges. Phil.* 1893, p. 475 ff.; Dieterich, *Nekyia*, 112 ff.) He usually distinguishes three classes among the souls (only apparently two in *Phdr*. 249 A): those who are affected with curable faults, the hopelessly and incurable guilty (who are condemned to *eternal* punishment in Tartaros without rebirth: *Gorg*. 525 C ff.; *Rp*. 615 D; *Phd.* 113 E); and, thirdly the ὁσίως βεβιωκότες, δίκαιοι καὶ ὅσιοι. This is the system of *Gorg*. 525 BC, 526 C; *Rp*. 615 BC. (With these come also the ἄωροι, 615 C, who neither deserve punishment nor reward—of them Er said ἄλλα, οὐκ ἄξια μνήμης. Perhaps older theologians had already concerned themselves with these, not being satisfied with the fate assigned by popular mythology to the ἄωροι—see Append. vii—it would have been a natural subject for the professional attention of these Schoolmen of popular superstition.) In *Phd.* 113 D ff. the question is even more minutely dealt with. Here we have (1) οἱ μέσως βεβιωκότες (che visser' senz' infamia e senza lode), (2) οἱ ἀνιάτως ἔχοντες, (3) οἱ ἰάσιμα ἡμαρτηκότες, (4) οἱ διαφερόντως ὁσίως βεβιωκότες, and (5) the élite of these ὅσιοι, the real philosophers, οἱ φιλοσοφίᾳ ἱκανῶς καθηράμενοι—these are not born again. To the other classes are assigned their appropriate purgation, reward or punishment. Here classes 2, 3, and 4 correspond to the three classes of *Rp*. and *Gorg*. (which may perhaps be modelled on the divisions popularized by older theological poetry—see above, chap. xii, n. 62). Novelties are the μέσως βεβιωκότες and the true philosophers. For these last the abode upon the μακάρων νῆσοι (*Gorg*. 526 C), or, what comes to the same thing, upon the surface of the earth (*Phd.* 114 BC), is no longer sufficient. They go ἐς μακάρων τινὰς εὐδαιμονίας (115 D), which means that they are really freed entirely from temporal existence and enter into the unchanging "Now" of eternity. (As far as the complete escape of the φιλόσοφοι is concerned the account in *Rp*. x, c. 13 [614 A–615 C] does not contradict that of *Phd.* The only reason why this is not mentioned in *Rp*. is that these absolutely enfranchized souls could not appear upon the λειμών there mentioned: 614 E.)—Of these various accounts that of *Phd.* seems to be the latest. In *Lg*. there is yet another indefinite allusion to the necessity of undergoing a judgment after death: 904 C ff.

[37] *Choice* of their new state of life by the souls in the other world, *Rp*. 617 E ff.; *Phdr*. 249 B. The purpose of this arrangement is made clear by *Rp*. 617 E: αἰτία ἑλομένου· θεὸς ἀναίτιος (cf. *Tim.* 42 D). It is, in fact, a theodicy and at the same time secures the complete responsibility of every man for his own character and deeds (cf. 619 C). There is no idea of founding a determinist theory upon it.—The choice is guided by the special character of the soul (which it has developed in its previous life) and its tendencies (cf. *Phd.* 81 E; *Lg*. 904 BC). For the same reason there is no choice on the occasion of the soul's first ἐνσωμάτωσις (*Tim.* 41 E): after that, in later births, a definite descent in well-marked stages *in peius*, can be observed, each conditioned by the degree of corruption attaching to the soul (*Tim.* 42 B ff.).

All of which can very well co-exist with a choice of its own fate by the soul conditioned by its own nature.

[38] ξυμμετρία, *Tim.* 87 D.

[39] At least three (as in Pi., *O.* ii, 75 ff.), acc. to *Phdr.* 249 A. Between each two births there is an intervening period of 1,000 years (*Rp.* 615 A; *Phdr.* 249 AB). This cuts away the ground from such myths as that of the various "lives" of Pythagoras (see Append. x).

[40] Incarnation in animals, *Phdr.* 249 B; *Rp.* 618 A, 620 ff.; *Phd.* 81 E; *Tim.* 42 BC. That this part was any less seriously meant than any other part of his doctrine of metempsychosis is not in the least suggested by Plato himself. Acc. to *Tim.* 91 D–92 B, *all* the animals have souls that had once inhabited the bodies of men (see Procl., *in Rp.* ii, 332 Kroll; he is trying to harmonize *Tim.* and *Phdr.*). In fact, the idea that a man's soul might inhabit an animal was precisely the great difficulty in Plato's doctrine of the soul. If, as is said in *Phdr.* 249 BC, a real animal-soul cannot enter into a human body because it does not possess νόησις or the power of "dialectic" which constitutes the essential part of the human soul's activity, how can a real human soul enter into an animal's body when it is obvious that as an animal it can make no use of its νόησις? (For this very reason many Platonists—those who were not satisfied with ingenious or artificial interpretations: cf. Sallust., *de Dis* 20; Procl., *in Tim.* 329 DE—denied the entrance of the human soul into animals; cf. Aug. *CD.* x, 30, and partic. Nemes., p. 116 Matth. Lucr. iii, 760, already seems to have such Platonists in mind.) The λογιστικόν of the soul seems to be absent from animals or to be present but undeveloped as in children: *Rp.* iv, 441 A B (or does it remain permanently bound in ἀφροσύνη? see above, this chap., n. 33. Just such a theory put forward by exponents of μετεμψύχωσις who would make the ψυχή always the same but not always equally active, is attacked by Alex. Aphr., *de An.*, p. 27 Br.). But acc. to the later doctrine of Plato the λογιστικόν comprises the whole contents of the soul before it enters a body; if the animals do not possess it then they do not strictly speaking possess a soul (θυμός and ἐπιθυμία in themselves are not the soul; they are only added to the soul when it first enters into a body). It seems certain that Plato adopted the view that the soul migrates into the bodies of animals from the theologians and Pythagoreans, while he still believed that the soul was not pure power of thought but also (as still in *Phdr.*) included θυμός and ἐπιθυμία in itself. Later, because it was difficult to do without the migration-theory of the soul on account of its ethical importance, he allowed the idea to remain side by side with his reorganized and sublimated doctrine of the soul. (On the other hand, metempsychosis into plants—which are certainly also ζῷα, though they only have τὸ ἐπιθυμητικόν, *Tim.* 77 B—was never adopted by him from Empedokles; cf. Procl., *in Rp.* ii, 333 Kr., and for the same reason: this idea was unimportant and indifferent from an ethical point of view.)

[41] τὴν εἰς τὸν νοητὸν τόπον τῆς ψυχῆς ἄνοδον, *Rp.* 517 B.

[42] ἐπειδὴ δὲ ἀγένητόν ἐστι, καὶ ἀδιάφθορον αὐτὸ ἀνάγκη εἶναι, *Phdr.* 245 D—the ancient argument from the fact that the individual soul (and of this Plato is speaking) has no beginning to the conclusion that its life can have no end.

[43] This much may be conceded to Teichmüller's observations. "The individual, and the individual soul, is not an independent principle but only a resultant of the compounding of the Idea and the principle of Becoming"—though this is not how Plato regards the

matter; hence in Plato—"the individual is not eternal (i.e. not necessarily), and the eternal Principles are not individual", *Stud. z. Ges. d. Begr.*, p. 115, 142 (1874). But all that Teichmüller has to say under this head is in reality only a *criticism* of the Platonic doctrine of the soul and does not help us to determine what exactly that doctrine was. Plato speaks always of the immortality, i.e. the eternity, of the individual soul; nowhere does he confine indestructibility to the "common nature" of the soul; and this fact is not even remotely explained by appealing as Teichmüller does to an alleged "orthodoxy" to which Plato is supposed to be accommodating his words. If from no other passage we should be obliged to conclude definitely from *Rp.* 611 A that Plato believed in the existence of a plurality of souls and in their indestructibility: *ἀεὶ ἂν εἶεν αἱ αὐταί (ψυχαί). οὔτε γὰρ ἄν που ἐλάττους γένοιντο μηδεμιᾶς ἀπολλυμένης, οὔτε αὖ πλείους.* Here the predicate of the first sentence is indubitably *εἶεν* only: it is affirmed that always the same souls will exist, not that *αἱ αὐταὶ εἶεν* ("the souls are always the same ones") as Teichmüller supposes, *Platon. Frage*, 7 ff., and it is asserted with all possible plainness that the plurality of individual souls, of which a definite number exist, is indestructible.

[44] E.g. appeal made to *τελεταί, παλαιοὶ λόγοι ἐν ἀπορρήτοις λεγόμενοι*, and particularly to Orphic doctrine, in those places where he is speaking of the inward difference between the soul and all that is corporeal, of the soul's "death" in earthly life, of its enclosure in the *σῶμα* as its *σῆμα* in punishment of its misdeeds—of punishment and purification after death in *Ἅιδης*, of the migration of the soul, its imperishability, dwelling of the pure in the neighbourhood of the gods (*Phd.* 61 BC, 63 C, 70 C, 81 A, 107 D ff.; *Gorg.* 493 A; *Crat.* 400 BC; *Men.* 81 A; *Lg.* 870 DE, 872 E). This also is the origin of the tendency to compare the highest philosophical activity, or the beholding of the Ideas before all time, with the *ἐποπτεῖαι* of the mysteries: *Phdr.* 250 B; cf. Lob., *Agl.* 128.

[45] Nine (an ancient sacred number) stages from the *φιλόσοφος* downwards to the *τύραννος*, *Phdr.* 248 DE.

[46] This is frequently stated in individual myths; cf. also *Phd.* 85 CD.

[47] *Phdr.* 250 C (*ὄστρεον*); *Rp.* 611 CD (Glaukos).

[48] *τὴν τοῦ ὄντος θήραν*, *Phd.* 66 C (*ὅταν αὐτὴ καθ' αὑτὴν πραγματεύηται ἡ ψυχὴ περὶ τὰ ὄντα*, *Tht.* 187 A. *αὐτῇ τῇ ψυχῇ θεατέον αὐτὰ τὰ πράγματα*, *Phd.* 66 D).

[49] *ξυναίτια*, *Tim.* 46 C ff. *νοῦς καὶ ἀνάγκη*, 47 E ff. (*ὁ θεός* is *πολλῶν ἀναίτιος*, namely *τῶν κακῶν*, *Rp.* 379 AC).

[50] The *σῶμα* with which the soul is bound up is a *κακόν*, *Phd.* 66 B (*δεσμοί* of the soul, 67 D). The *κακά* in the world are regularly said to come from matter until in *Lg.*, side by side with the *ἐνεργέτις ψυχή* of the world, there appears an evil World-Soul that works evil.

[51] Particularly in *Phd.*, *καθαρεύειν—κάθαρσις—οἱ φιλοσοφίᾳ ἱκανῶς καθηράμενοι* in contrast with the *ἀκάθαρτοι ψυχαί*, 67 A ff., 69 BC, 80 E, 82 D, 108 B, 114 C. Katharsis of the soul through dialectic *Soph.* 230 C ff. Express allusion to the analogous requirement of *κάθαρσις* by *οἱ τὰς τελετὰς ἡμῖν καταστήσαντες*, *Phd.* 69 C.

[52] *κάθαρσις εἶναι τοῦτο ξυμβαίνει, τὸ χωρίζειν ὅ τι μάλιστα ἀπὸ τοῦ σώματος τὴν ψυχὴν καὶ ἐθίσαι αὐτὴν καθ' αὑτὴν πανταχόθεν ἐκ τοῦ σώματος συναγείρεσθαί τε καὶ ἀθροίζεσθαι, καὶ οἰκεῖν κατὰ τὸ δυνατὸν καὶ ἐν τῷ νῦν παρόντι καὶ ἐν τῷ ἔπειτα μόνην καθ' αὑτήν, ἐκλυομένην ὥσπερ ἐκ δεσμῶν ἐκ τοῦ σώματος*, *Phd.* 67 C. Thus *δικαιοσύνη* and

ἀνδρεία, and more particularly φρόνησις, are καθαρμός τις, 69 BC. λύσις τε καὶ καθαρμός of φιλοσοφία, 82 D.

[53] φιλοσοφία teaches the soul εἰς αὑτὴν ξυλλέγεσθαι καὶ ἀθροίζεσθαι and to ἀναχωρεῖν from the ἀπάτη of the senses ὅσον μὴ ἀνάγκη αὐτοῖς χρῆσθαι, *Phd.* 83 A.—ἐὰν καθαρὰ ἡ ψυχὴ ἀπαλλάττηται . . . φεύγουσα τὸ σῶμα καὶ συνηθροισμένη αὐτὴ εἰς αὑτήν, 80 E, 76 C.

[54] . . . καθαροὶ ἀπαλλαττόμενοι τῆς τοῦ σώματος ἀφροσύνης . . . γνωσόμεθα δι' ἡμῶν αὐτῶν πᾶν τὸ εἰλικρινές, μὴ καθαρῷ γὰρ καθαροῦ ἐφάπτεσθαι μὴ οὐ θεμιτὸν ᾖ, *Phd.* 67 AB.

[55] For the ἀγαθόν, ἡ τοῦ ἀγαθοῦ ἰδέα, αἰτία both of ἀλήθεια and of ἐπιστήμη but identical with neither (they are only ἀγαθοειδῆ) and ἔτι μειζόνως τιμητέον—cause of the γιγνωσκόμενα and not only of γιγνώσκεσθαι, of both εἶναι and οὐσία, οὐκ οὐσίας ὄντος τοῦ ἀγαθοῦ ἀλλ' ἔτι ἐπέκεινα τῆς οὐσίας πρεσβείᾳ καὶ δυνάμει ὑπερέχοντος—see *Rp.* vi, c. 19 (508 A ff.), 517 BC. Here τὸ ἀγαθόν, as the reason and active cause of all Being is itself placed beyond and above Being (as it is regularly with the Neoplatonics) and identified with Godhead (the θεῖος νοῦς, *Phil.* 22 C) ; this last is, however, in *Tim.* set side by side with the Ideas, of which τὸ ἀγαθόν is now the highest.

[56] ἡ τοῦ ἀγαθοῦ ἰδέα μέγιστον μάθημα, *Rp.* 505 A.

[57] The περιαγωγή of the soul, *Rp.* vii init.

[58] The philosopher, ἐξιστάμενος τῶν ἀνθρωπίνων σπουδασμάτων καὶ πρὸς τῷ θείῳ γιγνόμενος, ἐνθουσιάζων λέληθε τοὺς πολλούς, *Phdr.* 249 D.

[59] ὁ γὰρ συνοπτικὸς διαλεκτικός, *Rp.* 537 C. εἰς μίαν ἰδέαν συνορῶντα ἄγειν τὰ πολλαχῇ διεσπαρμένα (and again κατ' εἴδη τέμνειν what is unified)—this is the business of the διαλεκτικός, *Phdr.* 265 D. ἐκ πολλῶν αἰσθήσεων εἰς ἓν λογισμῷ ξυναιρούμενον (ἰέναι), *Phdr.* 249 B.

[60] Gradual ascent of dialectic upwards to αὐτὸ ὅ ἐστιν ἀγαθόν, *Rp.* 532 A f., 511 BC, 534 B ff.—to αὐτὸ τὸ καλόν, *Smp.* c. 28–9 (211 B). Its aim is ἐπαναγωγὴ τοῦ βελτίστου ἐν ψυχῇ πρὸς τοῦ ἀρίστου ἐν τοῖς οὖσι θέαν, *Rp.* 532 C.

[61] The philosophic ἐρωτικός at the end of the dialectic ascent ἐξαίφνης κατόψεταί τι θαυμαστὸν τὴν φύσιν καλόν κτλ., *Smp.* 210 E—exactly as in the τέλεα καὶ ἐποπτικὰ μυστήρια, 210 A. ὁλόκληρα καὶ ἁπλᾶ καὶ εὐδαίμονα φάσματα μυουμενοί τε καὶ ἐποπτεύοντες ἐν αὐγῇ καθαρᾷ, *Phdr.* 250 C.—it is a visionary and a suddenly acquired apprehension of the world-order, not one obtained in discursive thought. We may compare the way in which Plotinos, with a recollection of such Platonic passages, describes the arrival of ἔκστασις—ὅταν ἡ ψυχὴ ἐξαίφνης φῶς λάβῃ κτλ. (5, 3, 17 ; cf. 5, 5, 17).

[62] The soul ἔοικε τῷ θείῳ, *Phd.* 80 A. It is ξυγγενὴς τῷ τε θείῳ καὶ ἀθανάτῳ καὶ τῷ ἀεὶ ὄντι, *Rp.* 611 E—συγγένεια θεία of men ; *Lg.* 899 D. The eternal and immortal is, as such, divine. The real *Ego* of man, the ἀθάνατον, ψυχὴ ἐπονομαζόμενον, after death goes παρὰ θεοὺς ἄλλους, *Lg.* 959 B.

[63] The θεῖον, ἀθανάτοις ὁμώνυμον, part of the soul is ἀθάνατος ἀρχὴ θνητοῦ ζῴου, *Tim.* 41 C, 42 E. The φρόνησις of the soul (its " wing " *Phdr.* 246 D) τῷ θείῳ ἔοικεν, *Alc.*[1] 133 C.—In *Tim.* 90 A C this κυριώτατον τῆς ψυχῆς εἶδος is actually called the δαίμων which man has ξύνοικον ἐν αὑτῷ.

[64] The eye is ἡλιοειδέστατον τῶν περὶ τὰς αἰσθήσεις ὀργάνων, *Rp.* 508 B.—Goethe is alluding either to these words or to the phrase of Plotinos taken from them, 1, 6 (περὶ τοῦ καλοῦ), 9.

[65] ἐπιστήμη καὶ ἀλήθεια are both ἀγαθοειδῆ, *Rp.* 509 A—the soul something θεοειδές, *Phd.* 95 C.

[66] From the φιλοσοφία of the soul and from the question ὧν ἅπτεται καὶ οἵων ἐφίεται ὁμιλιῶν its real nature can be discerned as one which is ξυγγενὴς τῷ θείῳ καὶ ἀθανάτῳ καὶ τῷ ἀεὶ ὄντι, *Rp.* 611 DE ; *Phd.* 79 D. With the ξυγγενές of the soul we achieve contact with the ὄντως ὄν, *Rp.* 490 B. If the Ideas are everlasting, so must our soul be, *Phd.* 76 DE. By its power of φρονεῖν ἀθάνατα καὶ θεῖα the ἀνθρωπίνη φύσις has itself a share καθ' ὅσον ἐνδέχεται (i.e. with νοῦς) in ἀθανασία, *Tim.* 90 BC. This thinking "part" of the soul πρὸς τὴν ἐν οὐρανῷ ξυγγένειαν ἀπὸ γῆς ἡμᾶς αἴρει, ὡς ὄντας φυτὸν οὐκ ἔγγειον ἀλλ' οὐράνιον, *Tim.* 90 A.

[67] λύειν τὴν ψυχὴν from the body and from sense-perception, *Phd.* 83 AB, 65 A, 67 D. λύσις and καθαρμός of the soul by φιλοσοφία, *Phd.* 82 D. λύσις καὶ ἴασις τῶν δεσμῶν (of the body) καὶ τῆς ἀφροσύνης, *Rp.* 515 C.

[68] θεῖος εἰς τὸ δυνατὸν ἀνθρώπῳ γίγνεται—said of the true philosopher, *Rp.* 500 D ; ἀθάνατος, *Smp.* 212 A. The φιλόσοφος is perpetually in contact with the ὂν ἀεί and the θεῖον, which last is with difficulty recognizable by the eyes of τῆς τῶν πολλῶν ψυχῆς, *Soph.* 254 A.—καί μοι δοκεῖ θεὸς μὲν (as e.g. Empedokles called himself) ἀνὴρ οὐδαμῶς εἶναι, θεῖος μήν· πάντας γὰρ ἐγὼ τοὺς φιλοσόφους τοιούτους προσαγορεύω, *Soph.* 216 B (where θεῖος is used in quite a different sense from that it has in other passages where Plato speaks of χρησμῳδοὶ καὶ θεομάντεις as θεῖοι, *Men.* 99 C, and of the insight and virtue of the unphilosophic as coming θείᾳ μοίρᾳ ἄνευ νοῦ).

[69] *Rp.* 519 C, 540 B.—τῆς τοῦ ὄντος θέας, οἵαν ἡδονὴν ἔχει, ἀδύνατον ἄλλῳ γεγεῦσθαι πλὴν τῷ φιλοσόφῳ, *Rp.* 582 C (cf. *Phileb.*).

[70] The flight ἐνθένδε ἐκεῖσε produces ὁμοίωσιν θεῷ κατὰ τὸ δυνατόν, *Tht.* 176 B. ὁμοιοῦσθαι θεῷ, *Rp.* 613 A (τὸ κατανοουμένῳ τὸ κατανοοῦν ἐξομοιῶσαι, *Tim.* 90 D).

[70a] The soul that has through philosophy become completely "pure" is withdrawn from the cycle of Rebirth and from the whole material world. Even as early as *Phdr.* the souls of the φιλοσοφήσαντες after a third ἐνσωμάτωσις are exempt for the remainder of the περίοδος of 10,000 years, while the real and unwavering (ἀεί) philosopher remains *for ever* free from the body. That at least must be the meaning of 248 C–249 A. The subject is then treated in more detail in *Phd.* : Release of the φιλοσοφίᾳ ἱκανῶς καθηράμενοι for ever from life in the body (ἄνευ σωμάτων ζῶσι τὸ παράπαν εἰς τὸν ἔπειτα χρόνον, 114 C)—entry of the pure soul to its kin (εἰς τὸ ξυγγενές, 84 B) and its like (εἰς τὸ ὅμοιον αὐτῇ, τὸ ἀειδές, 81 A), and εἰς θεῶν γένος, 82 B—and to the τοῦ θείου τε καὶ καθαροῦ καὶ μονοειδοῦς ξυνουσία, 83 E. Still more mythologically expressed—*Tim.* 42 BD (ὁ τῶν κακῶν καθαρὸς τόπος *Tht.* 177 A). Throughout we have the release theory of the theologians re-expressed in a philosophical and more elevated manner (Orphic : μεμυημένοι, *Phd.* 81).

[71] . . . οὐ ῥᾴδιον δηλῶσαι . . . , *Phd.* 114 C.

[72] To the ἀΐδιος οὐσία, τὸ ἔστι μόνον κατὰ τὸν ἀληθῆ λόγον προσήκει *Tim.* 37 E.

[73] It is true that not until it becomes associated with the body does the soul, by obtaining αἴσθησις, ἐπιθυμία, θυμός, and all the other faculties that bring it into touch with Becoming and Changing, obtain what can strictly be called its individual personality. The perfectly adequate comprehension in thought of the ever-Unchanging by the bodiless and free soul would have no individualized content. We must not, however (with Teichm., *Pl. Fr.* 40), conclude from this that Plato knew nothing of an immortality of the individual and of

individuality. He did not distinctly raise the question of the seat and origin of individuality in the souls. He is content to suppose that a plurality of individual souls was living before their entanglement with Becoming, and to conclude from this that in eternity, too, after their last escape from *γένεσις*, the same number of individual souls will still be living. Numerical distinctness (which affects in a scarcely intelligible manner the spaceless and immaterial) has to do duty with him for qualitative distinctness which would alone be able to account for the self-consciousness of this plurality. Acc. to the picture given in *Tim.* c. 14 (41 D ff.) the souls created by the *δημιουργός* are evidently all alike (hence also is *γένεσις πρώτη τεταγμένη μία πᾶσιν*, 41 E), and only when they are in the *σῶμα*, and bound up with mortal portions of soul, do they react in different ways to what affects them from without—and so become different. (This is so, however, in the pre-existent period, too, acc. to *Phd.*: but in that account *θυμός* and *ἐπιθυμία* are also bound up with the soul in pre-existence.) The influence of the lower soul-partners and of the *τροφὴ παιδεύσεως* (*Tim.* 44 B) makes the *λογιστικά* also of the souls differ among themselves. This acquired individual characterization, the fruit of differing *παιδεία καὶ τροφή*—something quite the reverse of the "common nature" of "soul" in general which Teichmüller supposes to be meant here: *Stud.* 143—is taken with it by the soul to the place of judgment, i.e. Hades, *Phd.* 107 D. When, however, by the best *τροφὴ παιδεύσεως* it has become completely pure and free from all the trammels of the physical and perishable and departs into bodiless existence in the *ἀειδές*—then in truth all individual distinctness has been dissolved out of it. Still, it must endure for ever as a self-conscious personality; for that this is what Plato meant cannot be doubted.

[74] *Phd.* 83 D.

[75] *χωρίζειν ὅτι μάλιστα ἀπὸ τοῦ σώματος τὴν ψυχήν*, *Phd.* 67 C. *ἀναχωρεῖν*, 83 A (quite in the manner of genuine mysticism—it is the "separateness" of the man who is to behold god, of which Eckhart speaks).

[76] *Phd.* 64 A ff., 67 E.

[77] *Phd.* 114 C.

[78] *τοῦ σώματος πτόησις καὶ μανία*, *Crat.* 404 A.

[79] *τῷ ξυγγενεῖ πλησιάσας καὶ μιγεὶς τῷ ὄντι ὄντως*, *Rp.* 490 B.

[80] The soul *ἐῶσα χαίρειν τὸ σῶμα καὶ καθ' ὅσον δύναται οὐ κοινωνοῦσα ὀρέγεται τοῦ ὄντος*, *Phd.* 65 C. In the same way the Appearance yearns after the Idea; see above, this chap., n. 9.

[81] *τῆς φρονήσεως κτῆσις*, *Phd.* 65 A ff.

[82] *πειρᾶσθαι χρὴ ἐνθένδε ἐκεῖσε φεύγειν ὅτι τάχιστα. φυγὴ δὲ ὁμοίωσις θεῷ κατὰ τὸ δυνατόν*, *Tht.* 176 AB.

[83] *Rp.* 523 A–524 D.

[84] Beyond all other things it is the *κάλλος* of the world of Appearance that awakes the memory of that which has once been seen in the world of Ideas: *Phdr.* 250 B, 250 D ff.; *Smp.* c. 28 ff. (210 A ff.). Plato gives a peculiar reason for this, but in reality it is due to a vigorous re-emergence of the fundamental artistic sense—the aesthetic element in his philosophic speculation and enthusiasm—which the thinker had so violently suppressed in obedience to his theory that the *αἰσθήσεις* and all the arts are merely imitations of deceptive imitations of the only true Reality.

[85] Not *μάθησις*—only *ἀνάμνησις*, *Phdr.* 249 BC; *Men.* c. 14 ff. (80 D ff.); *Phd.* c. 18 ff. (72 E ff.). (This theory occurs regularly in Plato in close connexion with the theory of the soul's migrations;

and it appears that he did as a matter of fact derive it from the anticipations and suggestions of earlier teachers of metempsychosis : see above, chap. xi, n. 96.)

[86] *Rp.* vii init.

[87] ὁμοίωσις δὲ θεῷ δίκαιον καὶ ὅσιον μετὰ φρονήσεως γενέσθαι, *Tht.* 176 B.

[88] εἰς ἀγορὰν οὐκ ἴσασι τὴν ὁδόν κτλ., *Tht.* 173 D ff.

[89] *Tht.* 172 C–177 C. The philosopher is unskilled in the life of the everyday world and its arts, and is quite indifferent towards them. Commonplace people, if he is at any time drawn into the affairs of the market place or the law courts, regard him as εὐήθης, ἀνόητος, γελοῖος. Sometimes δόξαν παράσχοιντ' ἂν (οἱ ὄντως φιλόσοφοι) ὡς παντάπασιν ἔχοντες μανικῶς, *Soph.* 216 D ; *Rp.* 517 A—passages from the later writing of Plato. Even as early as *Phdr.* 249 D ἐξιστάμενος τῶν ἀνθρωπίνων σπουδασμάτων καὶ πρὸς τῷ θείῳ γιγνόμενος νουθετεῖται ὑπὸ τῶν πολλῶν ὡς παρακινῶν κτλ.

[90] ἰδιωτεύειν ἀλλὰ μὴ δημοσιεύειν is the injunction made to the philosopher, *Ap.* 32 A ; at least, in πόλεις as they are *Rp.* 520 B. After death comes the reward ἀνδρὸς φιλοσόφου τὰ αὑτοῦ πράξαντος καὶ οὐ πολυπραγμονήσαντος ἐν τῷ βίῳ, *Gorg.* 526 C. ὥσπερ εἰς θηρία ἄνθρωπος ἐμπεσών the true philosopher will ἡσυχίαν ἔχειν καὶ τὰ αὑτοῦ πράττειν, *Rp.* 496 D.

[91] τὰ τῶν ἀνθρώπων πράγματα μεγάλης μὲν σπουδῆς οὐκ ἄξια, *Lg.* 803 B.

[92] *Gorg.* 521 D. ὁ ὡς ἀληθῶς κυβερνητικός, *Rp.* 488 E (cf. also *Men.* 99 E, 100 A).

[93] Not διάκονος καὶ ἐπιθυμιῶν παρασκευαστής but rather an ἰατρός, *Gorg.* 518 C, 521 A ; cf. 464 B ff.

[94] *Gorg.* 519 A. All these worldly matters seem to him φλυαρίαι : just as all the Appearances in the world of Becoming are for him but φλυαρίαι, Rp. 515 D.

[95] *Gorg.* c. 78 ff. (522 B ff.).

[96] οὗτος ὁ τρόπος ἄριστος τοῦ βίου, *Gorg.* 527 E—(this is the real subject of the *Gorg.*, viz. ὅντινα χρὴ τρόπον ζῆν, 500 C, and not the nature of ῥητορική—and it is this which gives its special emotional tone to the dialogue).

[97] *Gorg.* 515 C ff., 519 A ff. Summary : οὐδένα ἡμεῖς ἴσμεν ἄνδρα ἀγαθὸν γεγονότα τὰ πολιτικὰ ἐν τῇδε τῇ πόλει, 517 A.

[98] οὐχ ὡς καλόν τι ἀλλ' ὡς ἀναγκαῖον πράττοντες, *Rp.* 540 B.

[99] It is now the σκοπὸς ἐν τῷ βίῳ—inaccessible to the ἀπαίδευτοι—οὗ στοχαζομένους δεῖ ἅπαντα πράττειν, *Rp.* 519 C.

[100] The ἄλλαι ἀρεταὶ καλούμεναι (even including σοφία regarded as practical shrewdness : *Rp.* 428 B ff.) as ἐγγὺς οὖσαι τῶν τοῦ σώματος become of secondary importance compared with the virtue of φρόνησις, i.e. of dialectic and the contemplation of the Ideas, *Rp.* 518 DE. This alone is θειότερον, something μεῖζον than those bourgeois virtues, *Rp.* 504 D—philosophy stands high above δημοτική τε καὶ πολιτικὴ ἀρετή, ἐξ ἔθους τε καὶ μελετῆς γεγονυῖα ἄνευ φιλοσοφίας τε καὶ νοῦ, *Phd.* 82 BC.—This, too, rightly understood, is the real point of the inquiry in *Meno.* Explicitly, indeed, the dialogue only concerns itself with that ἀρετή which is commonly so regarded and is based on ἀληθὴς δόξα, coming into existence by instinct (θεία μοῖρα) ; which, however, to the philosopher is not ἀρετή in the proper sense of the word ; that name he would only give to ἐπιστήμη, the only sort of knowledge that can be learnt and acquired as a permanent possession, depending as it does upon the doctrine of the Ideas. To ἐπιστήμη he this time only makes distant allusion.

[101] *Rp.* vii, c. 15 (535 A, 536 D); cf. vi, c. 2, 5 (485 B, 487 B; 489 D, 490 E).

[102] *καὶ τοῦ μὲν (δόξης ἀληθοῦς) πάντα ἄνδρα μετέχειν φατέον, νοῦ δὲ θεούς, ἀνθρώπων δὲ γένος βραχύ τι*, *Tim.* 51 E.

[103] *φιλόσοφον πλῆθος ἀδύνατον εἶναι*, *Rp.* 494 A. *φύσεις* of a completely philosophical kind, *πᾶς ἡμῖν ὁμολογήσει ὀλιγάκις ἐν ἀνθρώποις φύεσθαι καὶ ὀλίγας*, *Rp.* 491 B.

[104] "That into which I sink myself—that becomes one with me: when I think on Him I *am* as God that is the Fount of Being"—the true mystic note. For the mystics, knowledge of an object is real oneness with the thing known; knowledge of God is union with God.

[105] *Rp.* 540 B.

CHAPTER XIV

THE LATER AGE OF THE GREEK WORLD

PART I

PHILOSOPHY

Plato and the Platonic account of the nature, origin, and destiny of the soul closes a period. It marks the end of that theological and spiritualist movement to the force and significance of which nothing bears clearer witness than the fact that it could have such a conclusion. After this point its development ceases—at least it disappears from the surface of Greek life: like one of those Asiatic torrents with which the ancients were familiar it buries itself underground for a long stretch of its course, only to reappear eventually, with all the greater effect, far away from the place of its origin. Even Plato's own school almost immediately after the death of its master and directing spirit turned its attention in a direction quite other than that which he had given it.[1] To have retained the Platonic outlook would have made his pupils even more isolated in their very different age than Plato himself had been in his own.

Greece entered upon a new and final phase of her development. The ominous breakdown of the older political fabric at the end of the fourth century might have seemed likely to put an end to the natural vitality of the Greek peoples. With the conquest of the East by Macedonians and Greeks, however, new tasks were set before that people and with the new task they acquired new faculties. The *polis*, indeed, the purest expression of Greek constructive ability, could not be restored to life. Such of the old and narrow city-republics as had not perished completely in that stormy period only languished in a stagnant peace. Rare, indeed, are the exceptions in which (as particularly in Rhodos) a more vigorous and independent life asserted itself. The new and swollen cities of the Macedonian Empire, with their motley populations drawn from many nationalities, could not make good the loss. The Leagues in which Greece seemed to be making an effort to find a political organization of a wider compass soon broke down under the effects of inward corruption and external violence. Even in its deepest and most essential character the old national spirit of Greece, which had drawn its strength from its clear-cut individuality, seemed to be suffering damage through the unlimited extension eastwards and westwards of Greek life. It did not cease to be an immeasurable advantage to be a Greek, but a Greek now meant anyone who had a share in the one thing that still distinguished and characterized the Greeks, namely, Greek culture—and Greek culture was no longer confined to a single nation. It was no fault of this Greek humanism that not a single one of the vast populations of the East (and in the West at last Rome stood alone) was able to make their own this culture so generously offered to the whole world, so that there, too, all should become *Greek* who were capable of becoming free human beings. Nevertheless, from all countries and nationalities uncounted multitudes of *individuals* entered into the circle of this extended Hellenism. The way was open for all who could live without the need of a way of life and thinking modelled strictly upon national lines: for the culture which now united all Greeks and Greek communities was based upon science—and science knows nothing of national frontiers.

The science which could thus present itself as the guiding principle of such a large and heterogeneous mass of cultured people, must at any rate have reached a condition of stability if not of completely rounded finality. After all the stir and controversy of the previous centuries it had at last arrived at a period of contented enjoyment of its own resources: the long drawn-out struggle, the restless years of search were now held to have borne fruit. In philosophy at least there was a distinct slackening of the insatiable zeal and boldness of individual thinkers in posing new questions and wresting answers or in seeking for fresh solutions to old problems. A few great systems, formulated in accordance with the fixed tenets of the various schools of thought, still offered a refuge to those who demanded fixity and definition in their opinions; for centuries they kept up their special traditions without serious alteration until they, too, fell in pieces at last. A greater measure of independence and variety was displayed by the special sciences which since they had now been completely released for the first time from the leading-strings of philosophy proceeded to develop freely in accordance with their own principles. Art, too, was by no means devoid as yet of originality and attractiveness, and in spite of the overwhelming achievements of the past refused to be driven into a position of subservience and imitation. But it was no longer, in conjunction with the peculiar customs and manners of a people, the mistress and dispenser of wisdom and knowledge of the world. Art becomes a plaything and an incidental diversion: it is science that determines the general character and content of culture. But this scientifically minded culture shares in the natural temper of all science. Science has its feet firmly planted in life itself: it keeps men's minds actively employed in this world: it has small temptation to leave the firm ground of what is knowable and can never be too well known, to voyage out into the region of the intangible which can never be a subject of scientific inquiry. A cool rationalism, a calm adherence to the intelligible and thinkable, without any leanings to the gloomy terrors of a mysterious world of the unknown—such is the temper that marks the science and culture of the Hellenistic age and marks it more distinctively than any other period of Greek culture. Such mysticism as was still vigorous and effective kept itself timidly in the background at this time; in the everyday world it is rather the direct contrary of mysticism that we are made aware of: the unlovely results of the prevailing rationalism, a bleak reasonableness, a knowing and prosaic common sense such as stares dully at us from the pages of Polybios' History as the point of view of the narrator himself and of those of whom he writes. It was no age of heroes or of the heroic. A weaker and more delicate generation holds the field. The breakdown of political life and the disappearance of its obligations made it more possible than it had ever been before for the individual to lead his own life in his own way.[2] And he makes the most of his freedom, his culture, the treasures of an inward, private life enriched with all the brilliance and charm of an old and perfected civilization. All the past had thought and laboured on his behalf; he is not idle, but he is busy without ever being in a hurry, enjoying his heritage and taking his ease in the cooling sunlight of the long drawn-out autumn of Greek life. And he is little concerned to inquire what may follow when this brilliant, many-coloured world that surrounds him shall have vanished from his gaze. This world is all in all to him. The hope or fear of immortality has little effect upon the educated people of the age.[3] Philosophy to which in one form or another they are all more or less closely attached teaches them according to its particular mood to cherish that hope or calmly to set it on one side: in none of the popular sects had the doctrine of the eternity or imperishable nature of the soul any serious significance as the central doctrine of a system. Natural science ruled the day, while theology remained in the background and could only obtain a doubtful hearing (if it was even listened to at all) for its proclamation of the divine origin and everlasting life of the souls.

§ 2

At the outset of this period, and illuminating a long stretch of it with the light of his genius, stands the figure of Aristotle. In what this master *di color' che sanno* had to say of the soul's nature and destiny two voices are distinctly audible. The soul, he instructs us, is that which in a living and organic physical body brings the potentially existing to actual existence. It is the *form* to the body's matter, the culmination of the capacities of independent life residing in the particular body. Bodiless and immaterial itself, it is not the outcome of the mixture of the various parts of the body ; it is the cause, not the resultant, of the vital functions of its body which exists for the soul's benefit as its " instrument ".[4] It dwells within a natural organism and though it is itself unmoved it moves that organism as the source of its growth and nourishment, of its desires and locomotion, of its feeling and perceiving ; while in the higher organisms it acts as the combination of all these faces. It is as little to be thought of as separate from the body—its own body—as the power of vision is in separation from the eye or as its shape from the moulded waxen image.[5] Theoretically, indeed, it is possible to distinguish between body and soul, but actually and in the animated organism they cannot be distinguished. When the living creature dies the matter of which it was composed loses it special adaptation to a purposeful organism, and this adaptation was its life ; without it there can be no independent " Substance " (οὐσία).[6] The Form, the functional power of the once living organism, its " soul ", has no longer any independent existence.

This is the voice of Aristotle the physicist when he is speaking from the standpoint of a physical doctrine which includes the study of the soul " in so far as it occurs not without matter ".[7] Aristotle the metaphysician takes us further. In the soul of man, besides the vital powers of the organized individual, there lives a spiritual being of more than natural character and origin, the " Mind "—" that in us which thinks and conceives ".[8] This thinking mind is not bound to the body and its life.[9] It does not come into being with the creation of the human organism which is completed by the addition of Mind. It has no beginning and was uncreated from eternity:[10] it enters into man at his creation "from without".[11] Even while it lives within the body it remains unmingled with the body and its powers and uninfluenced by them.[12] Enclosed within itself it lives its separate life as something quite other than the "soul" (of which it is nevertheless called a "part"[13]) and separated from it by a gulf. Comparable with the God of Aristotle's world it transcends what might be called its "little world",[14] the living human organism. It influences that organism without being influenced in turn. It is akin to God; it is called the "divine" in man.[15] Its activity is the same as that of God.[16] God—pure substance, unlimited, highest, everlasting actuality—is absolute and perpetually operant thinking.[17] All practical activity, doing and creating, is far removed from God.[18] So, too, the "Mind" is entirely occupied in thinking (though here there is some alternation perhaps between the potential and the actual).[19] It grasps, in an intuition of the intellect that is beyond failure and error,[20] the "unmediated" first principles, the first and highest concepts, immediately certain and not deducible from still higher concepts, from which all knowledge and philosophy is derived.[21]

In its association with the body and its "soul" this thinking Reason lives as "the ruling"[22] element over both—not, however, as the "realization" of this particular individual creature. The Mind is indeed said to be that which the individual man "is",[23] and without the addition of Mind the man could not exist; but the special and personal character belonging to the individual is not to be found in this reasoning Mind.[24] Mind is totally devoid of distinguishable qualities and is identical in every case where it appears; it is invariably foreign to the separate and individual character of the man to whom it is added, and hardly seems to be *his* peculiar property.

When death occurs the thinking "Mind" is not involved in the destruction which overtakes the human organism with which it was associated. Death does not affect it. Like everything that is without beginning it is indestructible.[25] It returns again to its separate existence. Like the great World-Mind, God, and in company with it—for it has not sprung from God and does not merge again into God—the individual Mind of man continues in unending life.[26] It disappears now into impenetrable darkness. The separate existence of the Mind is beyond not merely our perception but our conceiving as well—persisting for itself alone, Mind has no mental activity, no memory and no consciousness; indeed, it is impossible to say what special qualities or activity can be attributed to it beyond the simple predicate of existence, of being.[27]

In the doctrine of this thinking Mind which is associated with the human soul "from without" and never merges into it, of its pre-existence from eternity, its kinship with God and its imperishable life after its separation from the human organism—in all this Aristotle preserves a mythological element taken from the dogmatic teaching of Plato.

There was a time when he had been a complete Platonist precisely in his doctrine of the soul. In his youth, like other members of the Academy, he had yielded [28] to the fascination of clothing in artistic and perfected language brilliant fantasies about the origin, nature, and destiny of the soul—the divine daimon [29] inhabiting the mortal frame of man. Later, however, it seemed inconceivable to him that "any soul may inhabit any body".[30] He could only conceive of the "soul" of the individual man as a realization of the life of this entirely distinct and physical organism, to which it is indissolubly bound as the purpose and form of the particular instrument. All the vital powers as well as appetite, perception, memory, and reflective thought, appeared to him merely as the modes of activity manifested by the animated body which is itself unthinkable apart from its "soul". And yet he still preserved a relic of the old dualistic opposition between the body and the independent substantial soul—the same conception of the soul, in fact, as that which Plato had himself, in the later period of his philosophical development, alone retained. This was as the contemplative Mind which is occupied in apprehending the highest truths in intellectual intuition; and this mind is, according to Aristotle, not to be included in the "soul", but to be separated from it as a special being that has descended from the heights of divinity and has been coupled with the soul from without and for its limited period of life. The origin of this conception of a reduplicated soul is plain: it is derived from memories of Plato and beyond that from theological doctrine which was itself in the last resort but a spritualized restatement of primeval popular fancies of the psyche that dwells in the living body. But though he took over the doctrine he did not take over the special sense that the theologians had given to it: he omitted both the conclusions they drew and the exhortations they based upon it. We hear no more of the "purification" of the divine Mind within mankind. It has nothing impure or evil in it nor can any breath of pollution affect it from without. The effort towards the "other world" of purity, the denial and rejection of its earthly partner the living body, are foreign to the "Mind" of Aristotle.[31] It has no impulse to "deliverance" or self-emancipation; it knows of no peculiar task that points beyond this world. The presence of this "separable" Mind in the living man is an assured fact, and nothing more: no purpose in life is deducible from it. The fact itself seemed to be evident from the power that man possesses of grasping immediately a highest form of knowledge that is beyond demonstration, not as the result of the mental activity of his soul, for the apprehension is prior to the soul, but by means of a higher spiritual faculty, a special intellectual being that seemed to proclaim its presence and existence within man in this way. It is thus by way of a theory of knowledge not of a theological doctrine that we arrive at the distinction between "Mind" and "Soul". But the doctrine thus reasserted was in reality nothing but the old doctrine of the theologians. This "Mind", too, seems to the thinker to be a being akin to God. The pure contemplative existence, a life consisting in the contemplation of the final objects of intuition is counted as a privilege of the divine and of all divine beings, as the true purpose of vital energy and of its manifestation; and in the description of this state the sober reserve of his lecture style seems to be uplifted and almost illuminated with the warmth and brilliance imparted by a genuine glow of personal experience.[32] This pure activity of contemplation, finding its deepest satisfaction in itself, belongs to the divine in man—to the Mind; its whole life lies in this. This activity, however, the Mind performs and finishes in this life, while it is united with the body and the body's "soul". There is nothing left that can be thought of as forming the content of the life and activity of the Mind in its separate existence after the completion of its period of life on earth. Mind and the man with whom it is associated can hardly have a very urgent desire for that emancipation in "another world" which is thus left blank and without content for our thought. The thought of immortality cast in this form could no longer possess any real value or ethical significance for man.[33] It arises from a logical deduction, from metaphysical considerations, not from a demand of the spirit. It lacks not only the distinctness that might have appealed to the senses and given direction to the imagination, but the power (or the intention) of playing a leading part in the conduct or direction of life on this earth. There is no inspiration in this doctrine—not even for the philosopher, though it was to him and his activity and his efforts that the picture and panegyric of " Mind ", the philosopher in man, had really referred.

It was quite possible to abide by the teaching and philosophy of Aristotle, directed as it was to the observation and interpretation of the things of this world, while abandoning the advanced post of the doctrine of Mind—that Being which has sunk to the level of this world from the other world of divinity, which separates itself, with the death of man, once more to everlasting divine life though hardly to a continuation of individual existence. On this point in particular free discussion of the master's teaching maintained itself in his school: some, and by no means the weakest, of Aristotle's successors denied altogether and in every form the doctrine of immortality.[34]

§ 3

The dogmatic teaching of the Stoics on the subject of the human soul is closely bound up with the materialistic pantheism by means of which they explained all the phenomena of life, of being and becoming upon earth. God is All, and divinity is nothing outside this " all ", which forms the world: the Universe is God. God is thus not only the matter but the form, the life and the power of the world. Divinity is the original matter, the etherial Fire, the fiery " breath " which maintains itself or changes and in innumerable metamorphoses creates the world. God is also what supplies a purpose to this world and is the purposeful force—the reason and law of the world. The universal deity which is thus at once matter, mind, and formative principle sends out from itself at varying periods the multiplicity of Appearance and then again at another time takes back the multifarious and the divided into the fiery unity of its own breath of life. Thus, in everything that has shape, in everything that lives and moves, the content and the unifying form is God: he is and works as their " state " in inorganic things, as " nature " in plants, as " irrational soul " in the other living things, as rational and thinking soul in man.[35]

The soul of man, thus endowed with reason, is a fragment of the divine,[36] and is itself divine like everything else in the world but in a purer sense than all other things. It has remained closer to the first and original essence of the divine, conceived as "creative fire" (πῦρ τεχνικόν), than the earthly fire which has lost much of its original purity and refinement. It is closer [37] than the lower matter that in all its changeful forms degenerates progressively as it gets farther and farther away from the divine fire by gradual loss of the tension (τόνος) that had once been living and active in the primeval fire; closer even than the material of its own body in which it dwells and rules. As something essentially distinct from the body, then, the individual soul comes into being among the elements of its body when that body is conceived, and it develops its full nature after the birth of the individual.[38] But even in its individual, separate existence it remains incompletely detached from the universal life that is present in it; it remains subject to the "universal Law" of the world, which is God, and fast bound by "fate", the "destiny" (πεπρωμένη, εἱμαρμένη) which decrees the course of their existence for the totality of all Life and the individual lives.[39] Nevertheless, the soul has its special gifts and special task—it is capable of self-determination and is responsible for its own decisions and acts. Though it is a pure emanation from the universal Reason and bound down to no irrational elements, it has the power of irrational choice and can resolve upon what is evil. Though they have all sprung from one and the same original source the individual souls are of very different character, intellect, and propensity of will. Unreason in thought, will, and conduct is common in the world; those who have real insight are few; in fact, the Wise Man, the man who keeps his own will in complete harmony with the universal and divine direction of the world, is but a picture of imaginary perfection, *naturæ humanæ exemplar*, never fully and perfectly realized in actual life.

Ethical interests demanded the freedom and independence of the moral personality and its will, which can only fulfil the requirements of duty by self-mastery and the overthrow of base impulses; but this independence was in conflict with the essential principles of Stoic metaphysics. The Stoics taught that the world (and the soul included in it) is only the necessary self-development of a single and absolute Being that excludes all independent and separate multiplicity. Nor could they recognize any principle of Evil, an anti-rational principle answering to the purity of divine power, working evil and suggesting it, and making the individual capable of wilful disobedience to the laws of all-embracing divinity. Pure pantheism, uniting God and the world in indissoluble unity, cannot imagine a real conflict between humanity and divinity ; it cannot postulate a principle of Evil through the overthrow of which a lost unity with God is to be restored. Pantheism makes no claims of an ethical or religious kind. The ingenuity of the Stoic doctors was exercised in vain in the attempt to find a way out of this dilemma.[40]

From the very origin of the school two tendencies were discernible in the teaching of the Stoa, derived as that teaching was from such different sources. On the one hand, the ethical doctrine of the Cynics, to whom the Stoics owed the greater part of their practical teaching, threw the individual back upon his own resources and made everything depend upon the determination of his own will. It thus pointed in the direction of the most self-sufficient individualism—to an ethical atomism. The physical doctrine derived from Herakleitos, on the other hand, merged the individual completely into the omnipotence and omnipresence of the All-One ; and therefore, as its ethical counterpart, demanded that this relation of the individual to the universal Logos of the world should find expression in a life lived completely *ex ductu rationis*, in unconditional abandonment of the individual will to the Universal Mind that is the World and God.[41] In actual fact it was Cynicism that had the profounder influence in ethical matters. The universal Law and order of the world, embracing both universe and individual in its absolute decrees, threw its net too widely to be able to answer closely enough to the needs of narrow and individual existence. No practical ethics could possibly unite this distant and final aim with the individual man in a single nexus of ordered self-determination. The intermediate link between the universe and its laws, on the one hand, and the individual with his private will, on the other, had formerly been the Greek *polis* with its law and custom. But it was a cosmopolitan age, and for the Stoics as well as for the Cynics before them the city-state had lost most of its educative force. The individual saw himself more and more left to his own devices and forced to depend upon his own strength—his life had to be ordered on self-erected standards and guided by self-found rules. Individualism, which gave its tone to the age more decisively than in any past period of Greek life, began to win a footing even in this pantheistic system. The " Wise Man " who is a law to himself in perfect self-determination,[42] and feels himself bound only to those like himself,[43] is individualism's fairest flower.

But the soul, thus elevated to a height where it was capable of much that was impossible for or only incompletely within the reach of its weaker sisters, began more and more to seem like something rather different from a mere dependent offshoot of the One divine power that is the same everywhere. It is, in fact, regarded as an independent, divine, and self-enclosed creature in those passages where in Stoic literature, as in the older literature of the theologians, the soul is called a "daimon"—the daimon dwelling within the individual man, and given to him as his associate.[44] Death, too, is regarded by this professedly monist system as a separation of soul from body[45] in accordance with what was really a naive or a conscious spiritualism. In death, then, this soul-essence whose independence had been so marked even in life, does not perish with the body—it does not even lose itself again in the One from which it had taken its origin. An infinitely extended individual life is indeed not attributed to the individual souls: only God, the one Soul of the World, is eternally indestructible.[46] But the souls which have arisen by separation from the one and all-embracing divinity, survive the destruction of their bodies: until the final dissolution, in the Conflagration that will make an end of the present period of world-history, they persist in their independent life; either all of them (as was the older teaching of the school) or, as Chrysippos, the master of Stoic orthodoxy, taught, the souls of the "Wise" only, while the others have been lost in the general life of the Whole some time previously.[47] The stronger ethical personality is held together in itself for a longer time.[48]

From the point of view of physical science and materialist doctrine[49] it was also hard to see why the soul, composed of pure fire-breath, which even in life had held the body together and had not been held together by the body,[50] should disappear at once when that body was disintegrated. As it had once held the body together, so it might well and all the more easily hold itself together now. Its lightness carries it upwards into the pure air under the moon, where it is fed by the breath that rises upwards and where there is nothing that can put an end to it.[51] An "underworld" region like that of popular imagination and theological teaching, was expressly denied by the Stoics.[52] Their imagination preferred to exercise itself in an imaginary extension of life in the Aether, which was their region of the souls ;[53] but as a rule it appears that such flights of fancy were avoided. The life of the souls after death—that of the wise as well as of the unwise—remained indistinct and without content [54] in the imagination of those whose life was still upon earth.

Thus, the doctrine of the soul-personality and its continued existence (never simply expanded into personal immortality), which was in reality not required by the metaphysical principles of Stoicism, and could indeed hardly be reconciled with them, had in fact no serious significance for the general intention and substance of Stoicism—least of all for Stoic ethics and conduct of life. The philosophy of Stoicism is directed to the study of life; not of death. In this life on earth and only here can the purpose of human endeavour —the reproduction of divine wisdom and virtue in the human spirit—be fulfilled in manful contest with contrary impulses, fulfilled, that is, in so far as such a thing is possible for lonely and isolated fragments of divinity.[55]

But virtue is sufficient in itself for the attainment of happiness—a happiness which loses nothing through the brevity of its duration and to which nothing would be added by the prolongation of its span.[56] Nothing in the doctrine of Stoicism points man, or the Wise Man, to another world beyond the life of the body and outside this earthly theatre of conflict and duty, for the fulfilment of his being and his task.

§ 4

The limited doctrine of immortality which, as we have seen, was not an essential part of the teaching of Stoicism, began to be called in question as soon as the rigid dogmatism of the school was subjected to the too-searching criticism of other schools of thought. In the clash of opinions Stoicism began to be doubtful of the absolute validity of its own teaching. The boundaries of orthodox doctrine once so firmly drawn now became more fluid ; exchange and even compromise became common. Panaitios, the first writer among the pedantic professors of Stoicism to achieve a wider popularity for his writings, became the teacher and friend of those aristocratic Romans who found in Greek philosophy the impulse to a humanism that the barren soil of Rome could never have produced unaided. And Panaitios differed in more than one point from the strict orthodoxy of the older Stoicism. For him the soul is formed of two distinct elements [57]—it is no longer simple and undivided, but compounded of "Nature" and "Soul" (in the narrower sense).[58] In death these two elements separate and change into other forms. The soul having had its origin at a particular point in past time now perishes in time. Being capable of grief and subject to the destructive influence of the emotions it falls a victim at last to its own pains. Panaitios, while remaining a Stoic, taught the dissolution of the soul, its death and simultaneous destruction with the death of the body.[59]

His pupil Poseidonios, who as a writer possessed an even greater influence than Panaitios with the great majority of cultivated readers who belonged to no special school of thought, returned to the older Stoic doctrine of the simple and undivided nature of the soul as fiery breath. He distinguished three faculties but not three separate and independent elements in the human soul, and as a consequence of this view had no further need to believe in the dissolution of the soul into its component parts at death. He also denied the origin of the individual soul in time, from which the doctrine of its destruction in time had seemed to follow by a logical necessity. He returned to the old theological idea of the pre-existence of the soul, its life since the beginning of the created world; and could therefore go on to assert its continued existence after death—at least till the time of the next destruction of the World at the hands of omnipotent Fire.[60]

It was not an inward and private necessity that led to this transformation of the old teaching of the School. Doubts and criticisms levelled at it from outside—from the Sceptics in particular—had necessitated the change. While some gave up the struggle, others sought refuge in a re-arrangement of the figures of the dialectical game and by the introduction of fresh characters.[61] Immortality might be abandoned to criticism or reaffirmed in either case with equal indifference. The Platonic and poetic version of Stoicism provided by Poseidonios may have found a wider response among the readers of a highly cultivated society who felt the need of a doctrine of immortality more as a satisfaction to the artistic fancy than from any deeper or more temperamental causes. Cicero, the most eloquent representative of the Hellenized Roman culture of the time, may perhaps give us a picture of the refined and æsthetic partiality with which these ideas were taken up. In the *Dream of Scipio* and the first book of the *Tusculans*, he gives an account, mainly based on Poseidonios, of the belief then held of a continued life of the soul in the divine element of the Aether.[62]

§ 5

Stoicism had a long and vigorous life. More than ever during the first and second centuries of our era did it fulfil its real task of acting as a practical guide to conduct, not as a mere museum of dead erudition. It made good its claim to provide its adherents with the autonomous freedom and independence of a mind at peace with itself, whose virtue was proof against the tribulation and failure of life, and not corrupted by its plenty. It was not always blind imitation of a literary fashion or the love of displaying virtuous paradoxes that attracted the noblest of the higher Roman aristocracy to the doctrines of Stoicism. Not a few of them guided their lives in accordance with its principles and even died for their convictions. Not entirely " without tragic emotion ", as the Stoic Emperor would prefer it, but at any rate with conscious and deliberate purpose—not in mere unreasoning stubborness [63]—did these Stoic martyrs go to their death. Nor was it the unquestioned certainty of a continued life in a higher existence that made them so ready to give up life upon this earth.[64] Each in the special manner dictated to him by his own temperament and the circumstances of his life, they still speak to us, these leaders of Roman Stoicism—Seneca the philosophic director of the world's conscience, Marcus Aurelius the Emperor, and those instructors and patterns of the aspiring youth of Rome, Musonius and Epictetus. The eager and unswerving effort of these wise men to educate themselves to the attainment of freedom and peace, of purity and goodness of heart, wins our admiration—not least in the case of Seneca in whom the struggle for self-mastery and philosophic calm must have been a continual war with his own too-receptive and imaginative nature. But just as they looked for no supernatural helper and redeemer but trusted to the power of their own spirit for the assurance of success, so they required no promise of a future crowning of their labours in an after-life of the soul. The whole scope of their endeavour lies within the limits of this world. The old Stoic belief in the continued life of the individual soul until the annihilation of all separate creation in the World Conflagration [65] is regarded at the best as one possibility among many [66]—it is perhaps but a " beautiful dream ".[67] But whether death is a transition to another form of being or a complete termination of individual life—to the wise man it is equally welcome, for he measures the value of life not by the number of its years but by the richness of its content. At bottom Seneca is inclined to the view that death is the end of all things for man, after which "everlasting peace" awaits the restless spirit.[68]

The Stoic Emperor is uncertain whether death is a dissipation of the elements of the soul (as the atomists teach) or whether the mind survives in a conscious or an unconscious existence that must yet disappear eventually in the life of the Whole. All things are in perpetual flux—so the Law of the universe has willed it—nor shall the human personality maintain itself untouched and unchanged. But even supposing that death is a "putting out" of his small individual candle, the wise man is not afraid: to the melancholy that is the prevailing mood of his gentle, pure, and high-strung character Death, the annihilator, seems to beckon like a friend.[69]

The tougher spirit of the Phrygian slave and freedman needed no conviction of personal survival to enable him to face the battle of earthly life with courage and intrepidity. What has been made must be unmade: without hesitation and without regret the wise man gives himself up to the laws of the rationally-ordered universe in which the present must make way for the future—not indeed to be lost entirely, but to be changed and to merge its individuality, its unimportant self in new manifestations of the creative stuff of Life. The Whole does not perish, but its parts change and alter their relations among themselves.[70] The pantheistic principles of the school which had been taken over from Herakleitos and which made it permanently inconceivable that the diminutive individual spark of life could achieve a lasting separation from the central fiery mass, had become a settled conviction. The passionate abandonment of the personal, short-lived self to the everlasting Whole and One had become a fixed habit of mind. No longer did it seem intolerable that the individual existence should pass away after a brief span of life; it was possible to remain a Stoic and yet assert expressly, like Cornutus the teacher of Persius, that with the death of its body there is an end, too, of the individual soul.[71]

§ 6

The atomist doctrine renewed by Epicurus demanded in the most emphatic manner of its adherents that they should abandon the belief in personal survival.

For the atomist the soul is corporeal, a compound made

up of the most mobile of the atoms which form the plastic elements of air and fire. It occupies all parts of the body, and is held together by the body, while at the same time, and in spite of this, holding itself in essential distinctness from the body.[72] Epicurus also speaks of the "Soul" as a special and enduring substance within the body, a "part" of the corporeal, not a mere "harmony" resulting from the association of the parts of the body.[73] He even speaks of two parts or modes of manifestation in the "soul": the irrational, which holds the whole body in its sway as its vital force, and the rational, situated in the breast, which exercises will and intelligence and is the last and most essential source of life in living things, without the undivided presence of which death occurs.[74] *Anima* and *animus* (as Lucretius calls them), distinct but not separable from one another,[75] come into being in the embryo of man and grow to maturity, old age and decay, together with the body.[76] If death occurs it means that the atoms belonging to the body are separated and the soul-atoms withdrawn—even before the final dissolution of the body, the separable "soul" disappears. No longer held together by the body, it is blown away in the wind, it disappears "like smoke" in the air.[77] The soul, this soul that had animated the individual man, is no more.[78] The material elements of which it was composed are indestructible; it is quite possible that they may at some future time combine together with the life-stuff to produce new life and consciousness of exactly the same kind as had once been joined together in the living man. But, if so, it will be a new creature that thus comes into being: the original man has been annihilated by death; there is no bond of continuous consciousness uniting him with the fresh creation.[79] The vital forces of the world are continuous, undiminished, indestructible, but in the formation of the individual living creature they are only lent temporarily, for this occasion and for a brief period, after which they are withdrawn for ever from the particular creature. *Vitaque mancipio nulli datur, omnibus usu.*

After his death the individual is unaffected by the fate of his inanimate body; [80] nor should he be troubled by the thought of what may happen to the atoms of his soul. Death does not concern him at all; for he only is when death is not; where death is, he is no longer there.[81] Sensation and consciousness have left him at the dissolution of body and soul; what he cannot possibly feel affects him no longer. Epicurean maxims are never tired of driving home this proposition: death is nothing to us.[82] From every possible direction, from abstract principle and practical experience in actual life, Lucretius labours to demonstrate the truth of this view [83] as ardently as other philosophers seek to prove its opposite. Physical science has no more valuable service to render than that of convincing us of its truth.[84] Just as the wisdom of Epicurus has no other purpose than to protect man, of all creatures the one most sensitive to pain, from distress and anguish—and even pleasure is but the removal of pain—so more particularly, in putting an end to the fear of death and the craving after unceasing life, it serves this finite life itself,[85] that is committed to us once and for all and never repeated.[86] If a man has once succeeded in realizing that he will cease to be in the very moment of death's coming, he will neither be oppressed with terror at the threatened loss of self-consciousness nor will the terrors of eternity [87] or the fabulous monsters of the spirit-world below the earth [88] darken his existence by casting their dark shadow over all his life.[89] He will devote himself to life without repining, neither fearing death nor seeking it.[90]

He alone—the ideal Wise Man of the Epicurean faith—will know how to live as the true artist of his own life; [91] he will not waste the precious time in vain preparations for the future,[92] but will cram every moment to the full so that his brief span of existence will have all that a long life could give. Long life, in fact, even life without an end, would not make him any happier or any richer. What life has to offer it has already offered—anything further must only be a repetition of what has gone before: *eadem sunt omnia semper.*[93] The Wise Man has no reason even to look for an eternity of life.[94] In his own personality, in this present "now", he possesses all the conditions necessary to happiness. The very transience of this supreme happiness to which mortality can attain makes it seem the more valuable to him. To the development and the enjoyment of this, the only life that belongs to him he will devote himself exclusively. In ethical matters, too, the atomist doctrine holds good. There is no such thing in nature as an essential community of human beings—still less of humanity—there are only individuals.[95] In associations entered into by free and unforced choice the individual may attach himself to the individual as one friend to another; but the political societies that men have invented and set up among themselves have no obligations for the Wise Man. He is himself the centre and indeed the whole circumference of the world surrounding him. State and society are valuable, and indeed only exist for the protection of the individual and to make it possible for him under their enfolding care to develop his own personality in freedom.[96] The individual, on the other hand, does not exist for the state, but for himself. "It is no longer necessary to save the Hellenes or to win crowns of victory from them in contests of wisdom."[97] Such is the decision reached with a sigh of relief by a civilization that has attained the highest point of its development and is now overcome by a lassitude in which it no longer sets itself new tasks, but takes its ease as age may be permitted to do. In its lassitude it no longer hopes, and in all honesty no longer cares, to extend the period of its existence beyond the limits of this earthly life. Calm and untroubled it sees this life, dear though it may once have been, fade away, taking its leave and sinking into nothingness without a struggle.

NOTES TO CHAPTER XIV

PART I

[1] At first the philosophy of Plato's old age lived on in spirit in the Academy. Just as his pupils carried on his Pythagorean speculations about numbers, reduced his imaginative suggestions as to a daimonic nature intermediate between that of God and man to pedantic system, and elaborated the theological strain in his thought to a gloomy and burdensome *deisidaimonia* (witness esp. the *Epinomis* of Philippos of Opos and in addition all that we know of Xenokrates' speculations)—so too they retained and respected for a time the Platonic doctrine of the soul and the ascetic tendency in his ethical teaching. For Philippos of Opos the aim of all human endeavour is a final and blessed emancipation from this world (which, however, is only possible for a few of those who are, in his special manner, "wise"—973 C ff., 992 C). He is a mystic for whom this earth and its life fall away into nothing: all serious interest is confined to the contemplation of divine things such as are revealed in mathematics and astronomy. Again, the Platonic doctrine of the soul, in its mystic and world-renouncing sense, lies at the bottom of the fabulous narratives of Herakleides Pontikos (in the *Ἄβαρις*, *Ἐμπεδότιμος*, etc.). This, too, accounts for the youthful attempts in this direction of Aristotle himself (in the *Εὔδημος* and probably also in the *Προτρεπτικός*). This side of his doctrine was as it seems systematized from the standpoint of the latest stage of Platonism by Xenokrates in particular. It may be merely accident that we do not hear very reliably of anything indicating an ascetic tendency or an "other-worldly" effort after emanicipation of the soul in connexion with Xenokrates. Krantor (in his much-read book *περὶ πένθους*) was already capable of employing the Platonic doctrine of the soul and the imaginative fancies that could be attached to it simply as a literary adornment. And before him his teacher Polemon betrays a turning aside from the true Platonic mysticism. With Arkesilaos the last vestige of this whole type of thought disappears completely.

[2] *τοῖς ἐλευθέροις ἥκιστα ἔξεστιν ὅ τι ἔτυχε ποιεῖν, ἀλλὰ πάντα ἢ τὰ πλεῖστα τέτακται*, Arist., *Meta*. 1075a, 19 (in maxima fortuna minima licentia est, Sall., *C*. 51, 13). Freedom in *this* sense indeed was a thing of the past.

[3] Not that such hopes or fears were entirely absent. The reader will remember the case of Kleombrotos of Ambrakia (Call., *Ep*. 25), who by reading the *Phaedo* of Plato (and completely misunderstanding the meaning of the prophet, as not unfrequently happens) was led to seek an immediate entrance into the life of the other world by a violent break with this one—and committed suicide. This is an isolated example of a mood to which Epiktetos bears witness as common in his own much later time—the desire felt by many young men of ardent temperament to escape from the distracted life of humanity and return as quickly as possible to the universal life of God by the destruction of their own individual existence: Epict. 1, 9, 11 ff. But in the earlier period such violent manifestations of other-worldly fanaticism were of rare occurrence. Hedonism was

capable of leading to the same result as we may see from the Ἀποκαρτερῶν of Hegesias the Cyrenaic, called ὁ πεισιθάνατος, whom Cicero mentions together with this same Kleombrotos: *TD.* i, 83–4.

[4] τὸ σῶμά πως τῆς ψυχῆς ἕνεκεν (γέγονει), as ὁ πρίων τῆς πρίσεως ἕνεκα—and not vice versa: *PA.* 1, 5, 645b, 19.

[5] The ψυχή is related to the body as ὄψις is to the eye, i.e. as the effective power residing in the ὄργανον (not like ὅρασις, the individual act of vision). It is the πρώτη ἐντελέχεια of its body *de An.* ii, 1, 412a, 27. There is no σύνθεσις of σῶμα and ψυχή; they are simply "together" like the wax and the ball formed out of the wax: *Top.* 151a, 20 ff.; *GA.* 729b, 9 ff.; *de An.* 412b, 7.

[6] ἀπελθούσης γοῦν (τῆς ψυχῆς) οὔκετι ζῷόν ἐστιν, οὐδὲ τῶν μορίων οὐδὲν τὸ αὐτὸ λείπεται, πλὴν τῷ σχήματι μόνον καθάπερ τὰ μυθευόμενα λιθοῦσθαι, *PA.* 641a, 18.

[7] *Meta.* 1026a, 5: περὶ ψυχῆς ἐνίας θεωρῆσαι τοῦ φυσικοῦ, ὅση μὴ ἄνευ τῆς ὕλης ἐστίν.—οὐδὲ γὰρ πᾶσα ψυχὴ φύσις, ἀλλά τι μόριον αὐτῆς, *PA.* 641b, 9. The subject of τὸ κεχωρισμένον of the soul is studied by ὁ πρῶτος φιλόσοφος: *de An.* 403b, 16.

[8] λέγω δὲ νοῦν, ᾧ διανοεῖται καὶ ὑπολαμβάνει ἡ ψυχή, *de An.* 429a, 23.

[9] The νοῦς and its θεωρητικὴ δύναμις ἔοικε ψυχῆς γένος ἕτερον εἶναι καὶ τοῦτο μόνον ἐνδέχεται χωρίζεσθαι, καθάπερ τὸ ἀΐδιον τοῦ φθαρτοῦ, τὰ δὲ λοιπὰ μόρια τῆς ψυχῆς οὐκ ἔστι χωριστά κτλ., *de An.* 413b, 25.

[10] There can be no doubt that Aristotle's opinion was that νοῦς was uncreated and existed without beginning from eternity: see Zeller, *Sitzb. Berl. Ak.* 1882, p. 1033 ff.

[11] θύραθεν ἐπεισέρχεται into the man as he is being made, *GA.* 736b, 28; cf. ὁ θύραθεν νοῦς, 744b, 21.

[12] νοῦς is ἀπαθής, ἀμιγής, οὐ μέμικται τῷ σώματι—it has no physical ὄργανον, *de An.* iii, 4. οὐδὲν αὐτοῦ (τοῦ νοῦ) τῇ ἐνεργείᾳ κοινωνεῖ σωματικὴ ἐνέργεια, *GA.* 736b, 28.

[13] μόριον τῆς ψυχῆς, *de An.* 429a, 10 ff. ψυχὴ οὐχ ὅλη, ἀλλ' ἡ νοητική, 429a, 28. ἡ ψυχὴ . . . μὴ πᾶσα ἀλλ' ὁ νοῦς, *Meta.* 1070a, 26.

[14] The ζῷον a μικρὸς κόσμος, *Phys.* 252b, 26.

[15] νοῦς, θειότερόν τι καὶ ἀπαθές, *de An.* 408b, 29.—τὸν νοῦν θεῖον εἶναι μόνον, *GA.* 736b, 28 (737a, 10). εἴτε θεῖον ὂν εἴτε τῶν ἐν ἡμῖν τὸ θειότατον, *EN.* 1177a, 15. νοῦς is τὸ συγγενέστατον to the gods, 1179a, 26.—τὸ ἀνθρώπων γένος ἢ μόνον μετέχει τοῦ θείου τῶν ἡμῖν γνωρίμων ζῴων ἢ μάλιστα πάντων, *PA.* 656a, 7.

[16] ἔργον τοῦ θειοτάτου τὸ νοεῖν καὶ φρονεῖν, *PA.* 686a, 28.

[17] *Meta.* Λ 7, 9.

[18] *EN.* 1178b, 7–22; *Cael.* 292b, 4 ff.

[19] So too ἐπικαλύπτεται ὁ νοῦς ἐνίοτε πάθει ἢ νόσῳ ἢ ὕπνῳ, *de An.* 429a, 7.

[20] θιγγάνειν is the term often applied to the activity of νοῦς, i.e. a simple and indivisible act of apperceiving the ἀσύνθετα. This act not being composite (of subject and predicate), like judgment, leaves no room for error: the act simply occurs or does not occur—ἀληθές or ψεῦδος does not enter into the question with it. *Meta.* 1051b, 16–26 (θιγεῖν, 24–5), 1027b, 21.

[21] τὰ ἀληθῆ καὶ πρῶτα καὶ ἄμεσα καὶ γνωριμώτερα καὶ πρότερα καὶ αἴτια τοῦ συμπεράσματος, *An. Po.* i, 2. This ἀμέσων ἐπιστήμη ἀναπόδεικτος (72b, 19) belongs to νοῦς. There is only a νοῦς—not an ἐπιστήμη (as being a ἕξις ἀποδεικτική, *EN.* 1139b, 31)—τῶν ἀρχῶν, τῆς ἀρχῆς τοῦ ἐπιστητοῦ, *EN.* vi, 6. Thus also νοῦς is ἐπιστήμης ἀρχή, *An. Po.* 100b, 5–17. τῶν ἀκινήτων ὅρων καὶ πρώτων νοῦς ἐστὶ καὶ οὐ λόγος, *EN.* 1143b, 1 (cf. *MM.* 1197a, 20 ff.).

[22] τὸ κύριον, *EN*. 1178a, 3, and frequently. νοῦς δοκεῖ ἄρχειν καὶ ἡγεῖσθαι, 1177a, 14. It rules esp. over ὄρεξις (as ἡ ψυχή does over the σῶμα), *Pol*. 1254b, 5 (cf. *EN*. 1102b, 29 ff.).

[23] A man is called ἐγκρατής or ἀκρατής, τῷ κρατεῖν τὸν νοῦν ἢ μή· ὡς τούτου ἑκάστου ὄντος, *EN*. 1168b, 35. δόξειε δ' ἂν καὶ εἶναι ἕκαστος τοῦτο (νοῦς), 1178a, 2. τῷ ἀνθρώπῳ δὴ (κράτιστον καὶ ἥδιστον) ὁ κατὰ τὸν νοῦν βίος, εἴπερ τοῦτο μάλιστα ἄνθρωπος (here only in so far as the possession of νοῦς distinguishes men in general from the other ζῷα), 1178a, 6.

[24] Cicero makes a distinction of this kind between *ratio* and *animus*, *Off*. i, 107 (after Panaetius): intellegendum est, duabus quasi nos a natura indutos esse personis; quarum una communis est ex eo quod omnes participes sumus rationis . . .; altera autem quae proprie singulis est tributa.

[25] ἅπαντα τὰ γινόμενα καὶ φθειρόμενα φαίνεται, *Cael*. 279b, 20. τὸ γενόμενον ἀνάγκη τέλος λαβεῖν, *Ph*. 203b, 8. But ἅπαν τὸ ἀεὶ ὂν ἁπλῶς ἄφθαρτον. ὁμοίως δὲ καὶ ἀγένητον, *Cael*. 281b, 25. εἰ τὸ ἀγένητον ἄφθαρτον καὶ τὸ ἄφθαρτον ἀγένητον ἀνάγκη καὶ τὸ "ἀΐδιον" ἑκατέρῳ ἀκολουθεῖν, καὶ εἴτε τι ἀγένητον, ἀΐδιον, εἴτε τι ἄφθαρτον, ἀΐδιον κτλ, *Cael*. 282a, 31 ff. Thus too νοῦς (ἀπαθής) as uncreated is everlasting and imperishable (see Zeller, *Sitzb. B. Ak*. 1882, p. 1044 f.). It belongs to the imperishable οὐσίαι, which as such are τίμιαι καὶ θεῖαι, *PA*. 644b, 22 ff.

[26] ὁ νοῦς ὑπομένει at the separation, *Meta*. 1070a, 25–6. More strictly this applies to the νοῦς ἀπαθής (ποιητικός). While the νοῦς παθητικός (whose relation to the νοῦς ποιητικός remains most obscure) is φθαρτός, we hear of the νοῦς ποιητικός that it is χωρισθεὶς μόνον τοῦτο ὅπερ ἐστί, καὶ τοῦτο μόνον ἀθάνατον καὶ ἀΐδιον, *de An*. 430a, 10–25.

[27] *de An*. 408b, 18 ff.: νοῦς οὐ φθείρεται, nor ὑπὸ τῆς ἐν τῷ γήρᾳ ἀμαυρώσεως . . . τὸ νοεῖν καὶ τὸ θεωρεῖν μαραίνεται (in old age) ἄλλου τινος ἔσω φθειρομένου (? nothing perishes within τὸ νοεῖν—read ἐν ᾧ as in l. 23 and understand: ἄλλου τινὸς ἐν ᾧ τὸ νοεῖν = ὁ νοῦς, ἔνεστι, i.e. the whole living man), αὐτὸ δὲ ἀπαθές ἐστιν (just as νοῦς is always ἀναλλοίωτον, even its νόησις is no κίνησις, and the λῆψις τῆς ἐπιστήμης makes no ἀλλοίωσις for it. *de An*. 407a, 32; *Ph*. 247a, 28; b, 1 ff.; 20 ff.), τὸ δὲ διανοεῖσθαι (thinking and judging) καὶ φιλεῖν ἢ μισεῖν οὐκ ἔστιν ἐκείνου πάθη, ἀλλὰ τοῦδε τοῦ ἔχοντος ἐκεῖνο, ᾗ ἐκεῖνο ἔχει. διὸ καὶ τούτου φθειρομένου οὔτε μνημονεύει οὔτε φιλεῖ, οὐ γὰρ ἐκείνου ἦν, ἀλλὰ τοῦ κοίνου (that which had once been associated with the νοῦς), ὃ ἀπόλωλεν· ὁ δὲ νοῦς ἴσως θειότερόν τι καὶ ἀπαθές ἐστιν. In its separate existence νοῦς has no memory—this at least is meant by οὐ μνημονεύομεν, *de An*. 430a, 23, however we may be inclined to interpret the rest of the sentence.

[28] Particularly in the *Εὔδημος* (*frr*. 31–40 [37–44]), probably also in the *Προτρεπτικός*.

[29] For this must be the meaning of *fr*. 36 = 44 (*Εὔδ*.)—the δαίμων is the soul itself; cf. 35 [41].

[30] *de An*. 407b, 13–26; 414a, 19–27.—And yet it must be admitted that the νοῦς of Aristotle is itself a τυχόν within another τυχόν—not indeed as a separate entity with *any* qualities set in a fortuitous vessel of perhaps discordant qualities that do not fit it (which acc. to the *Πυθαγόρειος μῦθος* was true of the ψυχή in the σῶμα)—but at any rate set within an animated individual with quite definite qualities as a stranger, itself devoid of all definite quality and therefore not capable of having a character specially fitting that individual in which it is placed. Thus, after all, the Aristotelian μῦθος about the νοῦς betrays its origin from the μῦθοι of old theology.

[31] It is only as an argumentum ad hominem that the view is suggested on one occasion, that βέλτιον τῷ νῷ μὴ μετὰ σώματος εἶναι (καθάπερ εἴωθέ τε λέγεσθαι καὶ πολλοῖς συνδοκεῖ), *de An.* 407b, 4.

[32] *EN.* x, 7–9.—δοκεῖ ἡ φιλοσοφία θαυμαστὰς ἡδονὰς ἔχειν καθαριότητι καὶ τῷ βεβαίῳ. εὔλογον δὲ τοῖς εἰδόσι τῶν ζητούντων ἡδίω τὴν διαγωγὴν εἶναι, 1177a, 26. The σοφός requires no σύνεργοι (as the σώφρων and the ἀνδρεῖος do), and is αὐταρκέστατος in himself. The activity of νοῦς is the most valuable as being θεωρητική and because παρ' αὐτὴν οὐδένος ἐφίεται τέλους. A sufficiently long life of the theoretic activity of νοῦς is τελεία εὐδαιμονία ἀνθρώπου—indeed, this is no longer an ἀνθρώπινος βίος, but rather κρείττων ἢ κατ' ἄνθρωπον—a θεῖος βίος as νοῦς θεῖόν τι ἐν ἀνθρώπῳ ὑπάρχει. Therefore man must not ἀνθρώπινα φρονεῖν but ἐφ' ὅσον ἐνδέχεται ἀθανατίζειν (be immortal already in this life) καὶ πάντα ποιεῖν πρὸς τὸ ζῆν κατὰ τὸ κράτιστον τῶν ἐν αὐτῷ (1177b, 31 ff.). This τελεία εὐδαιμονία, as a θεωρητικὴ ἐνέργεια, brings the thinkers near to the *gods* whose life does not consist in πράττειν (not even virtuous) or ποιεῖν but in pure θεωρία, and this can be so with the life of man (alone among the ζῷα) ἐφ' ὅσον ὁμοίωμά τι τῆς τοιαύτης (θεωρητικῆς) ἐνεργείας ὑπάρχει (1178b, 7–32). Nowhere do we meet with so much as the shadow of an idea that the εὐδαιμονία of the θεωρητικὸς βίος can only become τελεία in " another " world, or is conceivable as existing elsewhere than in the life on earth. The only condition for τελεία εὐδαιμονία that is made is μῆκος βίου τέλειον (1177b, 25)—nothing lying outside or beyond this life. The θεωρητικὸς βίος has its complete and final development here upon earth.—τέλειος βίος is mentioned as necessary for the obtaining of εὐδαιμονία, *EN.* 1100a, 5 ; 1101a, 16. But εὐδαιμονία is completely confined within the limits of earthly life ; to call a dead man εὐδαίμονα would be παντελῶς ἄτοπον, for he lacks the ἐνέργεια which is the essence of εὐδαιμονία—only a mere shadow of sensation can belong to the κεκμηκότες (almost the Homeric conception) 1100a, 11–29 ; 1101a, 22–b, 9.—Since it is impossible for the individual to enjoy an unending permanence and share in τὸ ἀεὶ καὶ θεῖον, it follows that the continuation of the individual after death consists only in the continuance of the εἶδος—not of the αὐτό (which perishes) but only of the οἷον αὐτό which persists in the series of creatures propagated on earth : *de An.* 415a, 28–b, 7 ; *GA.* 731a, 24–b, 1. (Borrowed from the observations of Plato, *Smp.* 206 C–207 A ; cf. also *Lg.* 721 C, 773 E ; Philo, *Incor. Mund.* 8, ii, p. 495 M., after Kritolaos.) It was much easier for Aristotle to take this conception seriously than it was for Plato with his particular outlook : only for the passing requirements of his dialogue does Plato adopt the Herakleitean view and expand it : see above, chap. xi, n. 16.

[33] οἶμαι δὲ τοῦ γινώσκειν τὰ ὄντα καὶ φρονεῖν ἀφαιρεθέντος οὐ βίον ἀλλὰ χρόνον εἶναι τὴν ἀθανασίαν, Plu., *Is. et Os.* i, fin., p. 351 E. Origen (*Cels.* iii, 80, p. 359 Lom.) draws a clear distinction between the ἀθανασία τῆς ψυχῆς of Platonic doctrine and the Stoic ἐπιδιαμονὴ τῆς ψυχῆς on the one hand—and this Aristotelian doctrine of the τοῦ νοῦ ἀθανασία : οἱ πεισθέντες περὶ τοῦ θύραθεν νοῦ ὡς ἀθανάτου (θανάτου Edd.) καὶ μόνου (καινοῦ Edd.) διαγωγὴν (= βίον) ἕξοντος (—this is how the passage should be read).

[34] Theophrastos discussed (by the method of ἀπορίαι fashionable with the school) the obscurities and difficulties inherent in the doctrine of νοῦς, particularly of the reduplicated νοῦς, the ποιητικός and the παθητικός. True to his character, however, he adheres to the fixed dogma of his school of the νοῦς χωριστός which ἔξωθεν ὢν καὶ ὥσπερ

ἐπίθετος is ὅμως σύμφυτος with man and being ἀγέννητος is also ἄφθαρτος: *Frag.* 53b, p. 226 ff.; 53, p. 176 Wim. (θεωρία belongs to νοῦς, θιγόντι καὶ οἷον ἀψαμένῳ, and is therefore without ἀπάτη, *fr.* 12, § 26. The νοῦς is κρεῖττόν τι μέρος [τῆς ψυχῆς] καὶ θειότερον, *fr.* 53. To the νοῦς and its θεωρία we must suppose the κατὰ δύναμιν ὁμοιοῦσθαι θεῷ to refer—for this is the teaching of Thphr. also: Jul., *Or.* vi, p. 185 A.) Nowhere is there any indication that for him the immortality of νοῦς had the slightest importance for this life and its conduct. Nor has it any in the ethical doctrine of the very theologically inclined Eudemos. Here the aim of life—the ἀρετὴ τέλειος which is καλοκἀγαθία—is said to be ἡ τοῦ θεοῦ θεωρία which is carried on by the νοῦς, τὸ ἐν ἡμῖν θεῖον, 1248a, 27; in this process it is best ἥκιστα αἰσθάνεσθαι τοῦ ἄλλου μέρους τῆς ψυχῆς, 1249b, 22. For the sake of τὸ γνωρίζειν man wishes ζῆν ἀεί, 1245a, 9—but upon earth and in the body: there is no thought of the other world. (This would have been quite natural and to be expected of this semi-theological thinker who, e.g. speaks quite seriously of the separability of νοῦς from the λόγος—the ἄλλο μέρος τῆς ψυχῆς—in bodily life and of its higher intuition in *enthousiasmos* and veracious dreaming: 1214a, 23; 1225a, 28; 1248a, 40.)—To this first generation of Peripatetics belong also Aristoxenos and Dikaiarchos who did not recognize *any* peculiar substance of the "soul" apart from the "harmony" brought about by the mixture of bodily material. Dik. ἀνῄρηκε τὴν ὅλην ὑπόστασιν τῆς ψυχῆς: Atticus ap. Eus., *PE.* xv, 810 A. Aristox. and Dik. nullum omnino animum esse dixerunt Cic. *TD.* 1, 51; 21; 41, etc.; Dik. (in the Λεσβιακοὶ λόγοι) expressly controverted the doctrine of immortality, *TD.* i, 77. (It remains very remarkable that Dik. who naturally knew nothing of a *separabilis animus, TD.* i, 21, nevertheless, believed not merely in *mantic* dreams—that would be just intelligible, ἔχει γάρ τινα λόγον, Arist., *P. Nat.* 462b ff.—but also in the prophetic power of ἐνθουσιασμός, Cic., *Div.* i, 5; 113; *Dox.* 416a, which invariably presupposes the dogma of a special substance of the "soul" and its separability from the body.)—Straton "the naturalist" (*d.* 270), for whom the soul is an undivided force, inseparable from the body and the αἰσθήσεις, gave up completely the belief in the νοῦς χωριστός of Aristotle: he cannot possibly have held any doctrine of immortality in any form or under any limitations.—Then follows the period of pure scholarship when the Peripatetic school almost gave up philosophy. With the return to the study of the master's writings (from the time of Aristonikos) they gained a new lease of life. The problems of the parts of the soul, the relation of νοῦς to the soul (and to the νοῦς παθητικός) were discussed once more. It became more and more common, however, to set aside the νοῦς θύραθεν ἐπεισιών (cf. the definition of the soul given by Andronikos ap. Galen π. τ. τῆς ψυχῆς ἠθῶν, iv, 782 f., K.; Themist., *de An.* ii, 56, 11; 59, 6 Sp.). This meant the denial of immortality (which belonged to νοῦς only): e.g. by Boëthos: Simp., *de An.* p. 247, 24 ff. Hayd. [*Sto. Vet.* iii, 267 Arn.]. A different view again, and one which even went beyond Aristotle, was held by Kratippos, the contemporary of Boëthos: Cic., *Div.* i, 70; cf. 5; 113. Alexander of Aphrodisias the great ἐξηγητής absolutely banished the νοῦς ποιητικός from the human soul. (This is the divine νοῦς, which is perpetually νοῦς and νοητὸν ἐνεργείᾳ, and that, too, already πρὸ τοῦ νοεῖσθαι by the ὑλικὸς νοῦς of man. It enters into the latter θύραθεν—though not locally, for it is incapable of change of place, p. 113, 18 f.—with the individual act of νοεῖν by the νοῦς ὑλικός, but it never becomes a μόριον καὶ δύναμίς τις τῆς ἡμετέρας ψυχῆς: Alex. *de An.*, p. 107–9; p. 90 Br.). For him νοῦς is χωριστός and ἀθάνατος, ἀπαθής, etc., whereas the human soul exactly like the εἶδος of its σῶμα from which it is ἀχωριστός perishes at death together with its νοῦς ὑλικός, completely: συμφθείρεται τῷ σώματι, *de An.*, p. 21, 22 f.; p. 90, 16 f. The individual soul thus perishes: the imperishable νοῦς had not communicated itself to the individual. —The indestructibility of the individual νοῦς of man (and this was indubitably what Aristotle himself taught), a doctrine derived not from experience but from pure logical inference, had in reality no serious significance for the general teaching of the Peripatetics so long as they preserved their independence. Finally, indeed, they too were swallowed up in the ferment of Neoplatonism.

[35] ἕξις, φύσις, ἄλογος ψυχή, ψυχὴ λόγον ἔχουσα καὶ διάνοιαν, Plu., *Virt. Mor.* 451 BC and A. Through all these and all things in which these are—διήκει ὁ νοῦς, D.L. vii, 138 f. [ii, p. 192 Arn.].

[36] Our soul an ἀπόσπασμα of the ἔμψυχος κόσμος, D.L. vii, 143 [ii, 191 Arn.]. We often find the soul of man called an ἀπόσπασμα τοῦ θεοῦ (Διός), θεία ἀπόμοιρα, ἀπόρροια (see Gataker on M. Ant., pp. 48, 211; Ed. 1652)—and often even θεός (see Bonhöffer, *Epiktet u. d. Stoa*, p. 76 f.).

[37] (ἡ ψυχὴ) ἀραιότερον πνεῦμα τῆς φύσεως καὶ λεπτομέρεστερον . . . Chrysipp. ap. Plu., *Stoic. Rep.* 41, p. 1052 F [ii, 222 Arn.]. "Nature" is πνεῦμα that has become moist, soul the same πνεῦμα which has remained dry (Galen. iv, 783 f. K. [p. 218 Arn.]).

[38] The βρέφος is created as a φυτόν, and only afterwards becomes a ζῷον by περίψυξις (derivation of ψυχή hence!). Chrysipp. ap. Plu., *Stoic. Rep.* 1052 F [p. 222 Arn.]. Thus comes ἐκ φύσεως ψυχή, Plu., *Prim. Frig.* ii, p. 946 C.

[39] It would almost be possible to employ the semi-Stoic language of Philo to describe the soul as conceived by this Stoic Pantheism: τῆς θείας ψυχῆς ἀπόσπασμα οὐ διαιρετόν (τέμνεται γὰρ οὐδὲν τοῦ θείου κατ' ἀπάρτησιν, ἀλλὰ μόνον ἐκτείνεται), *Q. Det. Pot. Insid.*, 24, i, p. 209 M. But in orthodox Stoic doctrine the idea prevails that the individual ἀποσπάσματα are completely detached from the universal θεῖον—but at the same time without denial of ultimate connexion with the "All" and the "One".

[40] Acc. to the older Stoical doctrine as systematized by Chrysippos the soul is absolutely simple and unified, having sprung from the universal Reason of God which contains no ἄλογον. Its impulses (ὁρμαί) must on this view be rational just as much as its willed decisions (κρίσεις): it is affected from without by φύσις, which, being itself a development of the highest reason, God, can only be good and rational. It is quite impossible to conceive how, on the principles of the older Stoicism, erroneous judgment or excessive and evil impulses could arise. ἡ τῆς κακίας γένεσις is rendered unintelligible as Poseidonios maintains in opposition to the subtle observations of Chrysipp. on this head (see Schmekel, *Phil. d. mittl. Stoa*, p. 327 ff.).

[41] ἀκολούθως τῇ φύσει ζῆν (but our φύσεις are μέρη τῆς τοῦ ὅλου), i.e. in harmony with the κοινὸς νόμος ὅσπερ ἐστὶν ὁ ὀρθὸς λόγος ὁ διὰ πάντων ἐρχόμενος, ὁ αὐτὸς ὢν τῷ Διί, καθηγεμόνι τούτῳ τῆς τῶν ὅλων διοικήσεως ὄντι, Chrysipp. ap. D.L. vii, 87–8 [iii, 3 Arn.]. This obedience to the rational order and governance of the world—the *deum sequere*, Sen., *VB.* 15, 5; *Ep.* 16, 5; ἕπεσθαι θεοῖς, Epict. i, 12, 5, etc.—is more often regarded as a passive attitude of self-abandonment adopted consciously and with συγκατάθεσις: χρῶ μοι λοιπὸν εἰς ὃ ἂν θέλῃς. ὁμογνωμονῶ σοι, σός εἰμι κτλ., Epict. ii, 16, 42. θέλε γίνεσθαι τὰ

γινόμενα ὡς γίνεται, καὶ εὐροήσεις (this sounds very like "make God's will your own will"), *Ench.* 8. Much the same idea occurs already in the lines of Kleanthes ἄγου δέ μ' ὦ Ζεῦ καὶ σύ γ' ἡ Πεπρωμένη κτλ. [i, 118 Arn.]. But such "affirmation of the universe", understood in the full pantheistic sense (cf. Kleanthes τὴν κοινὴν μόνην ἐκδέχεται φύσιν ᾗ δεῖ ἀκολουθεῖν, οὐκέτι δὲ καὶ τὴν ἐπὶ μέρους, D.L. vii, 89 [i, 126 Arn.]), could not lead to an ethical teaching of active character and concrete substance.

[42] The σοφός is μόνος ἐλεύθερος· εἶναι γὰρ τὴν ἐλευθερίαν ἐξουσίαν αὐτοπραγίας, D.L. vii, 121. Laws and constitutions do not apply to him: Cic., *Ac. Pri.* ii, 136.

[43] Enemies and strangers are μὴ σπουδαῖοι to one another—πολῖται καὶ φίλοι καὶ οἰκεῖοι οἱ σπουδαῖοι μόνον. Zeno, ἐν τῇ Πολιτείᾳ, ap. D.L. vii, 32–3 [i, 54 Arn.].

[44] ὁ παρ' ἑκάστῳ δαίμων which one must keep in harmony πρὸς τὴν τοῦ τῶν ὅλων διοικητοῦ βούλησιν, D.L. vii, 88, after Chrysipp. [iii, 4 Arn.]. In the later Stoic literature, the only part of it which has come down to us, we often hear of this δαίμων of the individual—sacer intra nos spiritus (Sen., Epict., M. Ant.: see Bonhöffer, *Epiktet*, 83). It is generally spoken of in language that seems to regard it as something *separable* from the man or his soul, including the ἡγεμονικόν; Zeus παρέστησεν ἐπίτροπον ἑκάστῳ τὸν ἑκάστου δαίμονα καὶ παρέδωκε φυλάσσειν αὐτὸν αὐτῷ κτλ., Epict. i, 14, 12. ὁ δαίμων ὃν ἑκάστῳ προστάτην καὶ ἡγεμόνα ὁ Ζεὺς ἔδωκεν, M. Ant. v, 27. ἀνάκρινον τὸ δαιμόνιον, Epict. iii, 22, 53 (one can ask questions of it, as Sokrates did of his δαιμόνιον, as something other and different from oneself). This δαίμων then does not seem to be simply identifiable with the "soul" of man like the daimon in man of which the *theologians* speak. It is conceived and spoken of in language that suggests rather the "protecting spirit" of a man as known to popular belief (cf. now Usener, *Götternamen*, 294 ff.). ἅπαντι δαίμων ἀνδρὶ συμπαρίσταται εὐθὺς γενομένῳ μυσταγωγὸς τοῦ βίου, Menand. 550 K. (where the idea of *two* daimonic partners in the life of man is already rejected: Eukleides Socr. had spoken of such, cf. Censor., *DN.* iii, 3, and in a different way again Phocyl., *fr.* 15). Plato himself speaks (with a λέγεται) of the δαίμων ὅσπερ ζῶντα εἰλήχει (and guides the departed soul into Hades): *Phd.* 107 D. The idea, however, must have been much older: it appears fairly clearly expressed in Pindar's words, *O.* xiii, 28 (Ζεῦ πάτερ), Ξενόφωντος εὔθυνε δαίμονος οὖρον, where the transition to the meaning "fate" for the word δαίμων has not yet been completed. Later (with the Tragedians and other poets) this use became very common, but even then still presupposes the belief in such personal daimonic partners in the life of man: the use would have been quite impossible otherwise. (δαίμων = πότμος, Pi., *P.* v, 121 f., and already in Thgn. 161, 163. When Herakleitos says ἦθος ἀνθρώπῳ δαίμων, *fr.* 121 By., 119 D. he uses δαίμων in the sense of fortune in life. The word means both ἦθος and condition of life at the same time in Pl., *Rp.* 617 E, οὐχ ὑμᾶς δαίμων λήξεται, ἀλλ' ὑμεῖς δαίμονα αἱρήσεσθε, where the derivation of the metaphorical use of the word δαίμων from a belief in a special daimon belonging to the individual man can still be seen plainly. See also [Lys.] *Epit.* (2), 78. But the metaphorical use comes as early as Θ 166, πάρος τοι δαίμονα δώσω = πότμον ἐφήσω.)—The personal existence of the daimon is still far removed from all danger of such abstraction in a very remarkable case: in Halikarnassos Poseidonios and his ἔκγονοι decide that on the first day of the month they will offer Δαίμονι ἀγαθῷ Ποσειδωνίου . . . κριόν (*Gr. Ins. in Br. Mus.*

iv, 1, n. 896, p. 70, l. 35. The inscr. seems to date from the third century B.C.). Here then offering is made to the ἀγαθὸς δαίμων (see above, chap. v, n. 133) of the *living*, just as offering was made on birthdays, and at other times also, to the *genius* of Romans ; ἀγ. δ. is here clearly equivalent to *genius*. Apollo whose advice had been sought at his oracle had expressly enjoined (ib., l. 9) . . . τιμᾶν καὶ ἱλάσκεσθαι καὶ ἀγαθὸν δαίμονα Ποσειδωνίου καὶ Γόργιδος (the latter, P.'s mother, seems to have been already dead : l. 34).—This special δαίμων attached to individuals with whom it can be contrasted (as Brutus can be with his δαίμων κακός : Plu., *Brut.* 36) is distinct from the individual's ψυχή, though it is natural to suppose that it may have arisen from the projection of the ψυχή—conceived as very independent—outside the man himself, in which it would again resemble the Roman *genius*. (The daimonic φύλακες of Hesiod [cf. above, p. 67 ff.], belong to quite a different range of ideas.) At any rate the Stoics had this analogous popular conception in mind when they spoke of the παρ' ἑκάστῳ δαίμων as something different from the man himself and his ἡγεμονικόν. They use it, however, only as a figure of speech. The δαίμων of the individual really means for them "the original, ideal personality as contrasted with the empirical personality" (as Bonhöffer very rightly puts it : *Epikt.* 84)—the character the man already *is* ideally but must *become* actually (γένοι' οἷος ἐσσί . . .). Thus the δαίμων is distinct from the ψυχή (διάνοια) and yet identical with it. It is a semi-allegorical play upon the idea of the δαίμων as individual genius and at the same time as crown or summit of the human personality—just as Plato had used the word already incidentally, *Tim.* 90 A. Finally—for the Stoics did not seriously wish to establish the existence of an independent protecting deity that enters man from without and rules over him—the ἡγεμονικόν is the same as the δαίμων. Thus in M. Ant. iv, 27, the δαίμων is completely identical with the ἀπόσπασμα Διός, and the ἑκάστου νοῦς καὶ λόγος (cf. also iii, 3 fin. ; ii, 13 ; 17 ; iii, 7, τὸν ἑαυτοῦ νοῦν καὶ δαίμονα). The fact, however, that this ἀπόσπασμα τοῦ θεοῦ can be called a δαίμων bears witness to a tendency to conceive the soul-spirit as something independent and more cut off and separated from the common and original source of divinity than was possible for Stoic pantheism of the stricter sort (to which the terms ἀπόσπασμα, ἀπόρροια τοῦ θεοῦ were more apt). A decided approximation was thus made to the theological idea of the "soul" as an individual daimon which persists in its separate existence. To this view Poseidonios went over completely : he regards the individual δαίμων that lives in man as συγγενὴς ὢν τῷ τὸν ὅλον κόσμον διοικοῦντι (Pos. ap. Gal. v, 469), and no longer as the dependent ἀπόσπασμα of the latter, but as one of many independent and individually characterized spirits that have lived from all time in the air and enter into man at birth. (See Bonhöffer, *Epikt.* 79–80, and also Schmekel, *Phil. d. mittl. Stoa*, 249 ff., 256.)

[45] ὁ θάνατός ἐστι χωρισμὸς ψυχῆς ἀπὸ σώματος . . . Chrysipp. ap Nemes., *NH.*, p. 81 Matth. ; Zeno and Chrysipp. ap. Tert., *An.* 5 [ii, 219 Arn.].

[46] Everything comes into being and perishes, including the gods, ὁ δὲ Ζεὺς μόνος ἀΐδιός ἐστι, Chrysipp. ap. Plu., *Sto. Rep.* 38, p. 1052 A ; *Comm. Not.* 31, p. 1075 A ff. [ii, 309 Arn.].—ἐπιδιαμονή but not ἀθανασία of the human soul [ib., 223].

[47] Κλεάνθης μὲν οὖν πάσας (τὰς ψυχὰς) ἐπιδιαμένειν (λέγει) μέχρι τῆς ἐκπυρώσεως, Χρύσιππος δὲ τὰς τῶν σοφῶν μόνον, D.L. vii, 157.

A statement often repeated without mention of the two authorities: Arius Did. ap. Eus., *PE*. 15, 20, 6, p. 822 A (the ψυχαὶ τῶν ἀφρόνων καὶ ἀλόγων ζώων perish immediately with the death of the body, C) and others [ii, 223 Arn.]. Chrysippos' doctrine comes also in Tac., *Agr*. 46, si ut sapientibus placet non cum corpore extinguuntur magnae animae (αἱ μεγάλαι ψυχαί, Plu., *Def. Or*. 18, p. 419 f.); cf. omnium quidem animos immortalis esse sed fortium bonorumque divinos, Cic., *Leg*. ii, 27, not quite accurately put.

[48] The ἀσθενεστέρα ψυχή (αὕτη δέ ἐστι τῶν ἀπαιδεύτων) perishes sooner, ἡ δὲ ἰσχυροτέρα, οἷα ἐστὶ περὶ τοὺς σοφούς remains μέχρι τῆς ἐκπυρώσεως, [Plu.] *Plac. Phil*., 4, 7 ap. *Dox*. 393a.

[49] The predominance of the materialistic point of view is remarkable in those *Stoici* who acc. to Seneca, *Ep*. 57, 7, existimant animum hominis magno pondere extriti permanere non posse et statim spargi, quia non fuerit illi exitus liber (which reminds us of the popular belief that the soul of one who has died in a high wind εὐθὺς διαπεφύσηται καὶ ἀπόλωλεν, Pl., *Phd*. 70 A, 80 D, see above, chap. xiii, n. 5).

[50] οὐ τὰ σώματα τὰς ψυχὰς συνέχει ἀλλ' αἱ ψυχαὶ τὰ σώματα, ὥσπερ καὶ ἡ κόλλα καὶ ἑαυτὴν καὶ τὰ ἐκτὸς κρατεῖ, Poseidon. ap. Ach. Tat., *Isag*., p. 133 E Petav., borrowed from Arist. (*de An*. 1, 5, 411b, 7), but a thoroughly Stoic idea as contrasted with Epicurean doctrine (see Heinze, *Xenokrates*, 100 f.).

[51] S.E., *M*. ix, 71–3. The naive but quite plain statements go back to Poseid. as has often been pointed out (e.g. by Corssen, *de Pos. Rhod*., p. 45, 1878, and others). So, too, do the similar remarks in Cic., *TD*. i, 42. Poseid. does not appear to be uttering heterodox opinions in this case, so far as we can see.

[52] —καὶ γὰρ οὐδὲ τὰς ψυχὰς ἔνεστιν ὑπονοῆσαι κάτω φερομένας. λεπτομερεῖς γὰρ οὖσαι εἰς τοὺς ἄνω μᾶλλον τόπους κουφοφοροῦσιν, S.E., *M*. ix, 71. This physical reason was in itself enough to make it impossible for the Stoics to believe in a subterranean region of the souls: οὐδεὶς Ἅιδης, οὐδ' Ἀχέρων, οὐδὲ Κωκυτός κτλ., Epict. iii, 13, 15. It is the regular Stoic doctrine: see Bonhöffer, *Epikt*. 56 f.; cf. Cic., *TD*. i, 36 f.; Sen., *C. ad Marc*. 19, 4. When Stoics speak occasionally of *inferi* or ᾅδης as the abode of the souls, they are only using metaphorical language. When the word is not a mere conventionalism, they mean the regions nearer the earth, the cloud regions and lower levels of the air, ὁ παχυμερέστατος καὶ προσγειότατος ἀήρ (Corn., *ND*. 5, p. 4, 17 L; other exx. in Heinze, *Xenokr*. 147, 2). Here the "unwise" souls (the moister, less buoyant ones) are supposed to remain after death (*circa terram* as Tert., *An*. 54 says, alluding to Stoic doctrine—and this is obviously where the *inferi* mentioned at the end of the same chapter are situated). This ἀήρ (distinguished from the higher regions of the air) = ᾅδης, must have been what Zeno referred to when he spoke of the *loca tenebrosa* where the souls of the unwise have to expiate their folly (quoted and varied by Lact., *Inst*. 7, 7, 13, in a Platonic sense [i, 40 Arn.]).

[53] Abode of the souls in the air: S. E., *M*. ix, 73; Cic., *TD*. i, 42–3, both probably after Poseid. Cf. sapientum animas in supernis mansionibus callocant (Stoici), Tert., *An*. 54. Generally: εἰς τὸν ἀέρα μεθίστασθαι said of the departed souls, M. Ant. iv, 21. ἐν τῷ περιέχοντι . . . διαμένειν τὰς τῶν ἀποθανόντων ψυχάς, Ar. Did. ap. Eus., *PE*. xv, 822 A [ii, 225 Arn.]. (Gradual ascent to ever higher regions, Sen., *C. ad Marc*. 25, 1—hardly orthodox Stoic doctrine).—The conception may possibly belong to the older Stoicism, and may underlie the opinion of Chrysipp.: σφαιροειδεῖς—as fiery μετέωρα—τὰς ψυχὰς

μετὰ θάνατον γίνεσθαι, ap. Eust., *Il.* 1288, 10 f. [224 Arn.]. Poseid. seems to have worked it out further, probably making use also of Pythagorean and Platonic fancies to which he was distinctly inclined. The Pythagoreans had fancies about the souls hovering in the air (see above, chap. xi, n. 35), of the sun and moon as places where the souls lived (chap. x, n. 76). Acc. to Poseid. the souls inhabit τὸν ὑπὸ σελήνην τόπον (S.E., *M.* ix, 73) as suitable for divine but not perfect creatures. It is the souls who are meant when people speak of δαίμονες (S.E. § 74), or ἥρωες (Stoic in this use D.L. vi, 151 [ii, 320 Arn.]); cf. *heroes et lares et genii*, Varro using Stoic language (ap. Aug., *CD.* vii, 6, p. 282, 14 Domb.). The whole air is full of them: Pos. ap. Cic., *Div.* i, 64. Something very similar given as Pythag. doctrine by Alex. Polyh. ap. D.L viii, 32: see above, chap. xi, n. 35. But Poseidonios (esp. if he is really the source of the Ciceronian *Somn. Scip.*) seems to have emulated more particularly the imaginative efforts of Herakleides Pont. and his story of Empedotimos' vision (see above, chap. ix, n. 111). Herakl. contributed largely to popularizing the idea that the souls inhabit the air and giving it shape; the interest with which his fancies were studied is shown by the quotations from his book so common from Varro down to Proclus and Damascius. He must have been led to make the souls, on being freed from the body, float upwards (and occupy the stars or the moon—which are inhabitable heavenly bodies: *Dox.* 343, 7 ff.; 356a, 10) by the view—just as the Stoics after him were—that the soul is an αἰθέριον σῶμα (Philop.)—φωτοειδής, a *lumen*, Tert., *An.* 9. In this he is following an idea that had been common in the fifth century (held by Xenophanes, Epicharmos, Eurip.: see above, p. 436 ff.), and had even attained popular vogue. This idea from the very first led to the conclusion that the soul, when ready for it, enters εἰς τὸν ὅμοιον αἰθέρα and ascends to the upper regions (of the aether). Herakleides carried this idea further and embellished it with philosophical and astronomical fancies. (On another occasion he seems to have denied substance and consistency to individual "souls": Plu., *Mor.* v, p. 699 Wytt.—a view to which his doctrine of the ὄγκοι might easily have led him.) Poseidonios then took up this idea of Herakl. In this way, or at least not uninfluenced by this semi-philosophical literature, the belief in the abode of the "souls" in the aether attained the popularity that grave inscriptions witness for it (see below, ch. xiv, 2, n. 135).

[54] Cicero, following Poseid., imagines a blissful observation of the earth and the stars by the souls in the air: *TD.* i, 44–7 (cf. Sen., *C. ad Marc.* 25, 1–2); and similarly in *Somn. Sci.*; in both cases the idea certainly comes from Herakl. Pont.

[55] ἀπόσπασμα τοῦ θεοῦ [i, 36 Arn.].

[56] A frequently repeated Stoic dogma (stated with particular fullness by Senec., *Ep.* 93): see Gataker on M. Ant. (iii, 7), p. 108–9. The happiness of the (Stoic) wise man does not require μῆκος βίου τέλειον as Aristot. had maintained (see above, n. 32). In this point Stoic and Epicurean doctrine fully agreed: magni artificis est clusisse totum in exiguo: tantum sapienti sua, quantum deo omnis aetas patet (Sen., *Ep.* 53, 11, and see below, n. 92).

[57] Acc. to Panaitios there are *duo genera* in the soul which he calls *inflammata anima* (Cic., *TD.* i, 42). It is at any rate very probable that Panaitios (and Boëthos—roughly contemporary with Pan.: see Comparetti, *Ind. Stoic.*, p. 78 f.—acc. to Macr., *in S. Scip.* 1, 14, 20) regarded the soul as compounded of two elements, *aer et ignis*, not

as a single and uncompounded πνεῦμα ἔνθερμον as the older Stoa had taught (see Schmekel, *Philos. d. mittl. Stoa*, 324 f.).

[58] φύσις and ψυχή: Pan. ap. Nemes., *NH.*, p. 212 Matth. This clearly shows a tendency to a psychological dualism: Zeller, *Stoics and Epicureans*, p. 542 f. What further suggestions were made by Pan. about the division of the soul remains very problematical. The only more precise statement is Cicero's, *TD.* i, 80 (speaking of Pan.), aegritudines iras libidinesque semotas a mente et disclusas putat.

[59] Panaitios denied not merely the immortality but even the διαμονή of the soul after death: Cic., *TD.* i, 78–9. Two reasons are there given: everything that has come into being (like the soul of man at birth) must also perish—the Aristotelian principle: see above, n. 25; what can feel pain (as the soul does) must become diseased and what is diseased must eventually perish. (Here the distruction of the soul from its own inward decay is asserted—not from the effect of external force at the world conflagration, the periodic occurrence of which Pan. at least called in question.) Acc. to Schmekel (*mittl. Stoa*, p. 309) it follows from Cic., *TD.* i, 42, that Panaitios also added a third argument: that the soul being composite must suffer the dissolution of its parts in death which change into other elements. This does not indeed at all follow from the passage, but such a view would almost have been inevitable with Panaitios' doctrine of the soul and had already been suggested by Karneades in his polemic against the indestructibility of the divine and of every ζῷον—an argument to which Pan. on the whole yielded.

[60] Poseidonios distinguished in the human soul not three parts but three δυνάμεις μιᾶς οὐσίας ἐκ τῆς καρδίας ὁρμωμένης (Gal. v, 515), namely, the Platonic three, the λογιστικόν, θυμοειδές, ἐπιθυμητικόν (Gal. v, 476). The last two are the δυνάμεις ἄλογοι (they only give φαντασίαι the special forms taken by their impulses: Gal. v, 474, 399). The πάθη are not judgments nor the consequences of judgment but the motions (κινήσεις) of these δυνάμεις ἄλογοι (Gal. v, 429; cf. 378). In this way alone is it possible to understand how passion or wrong-doing can arise in man; it is because soul is not (as Chrysipp. had taught) pure reasoning power (cf. also Gal. iv, 820). There exists then in man an ἄλογον καὶ κακόδαιμον καὶ ἄθεον in addition to the δαίμων συγγενὴς τῷ τὸν ὅλον κόσμον διοικοῦντι: Gal. v, 469 f. How, indeed, this is possible when the soul is a single οὐσία and in its nature nothing but divine πνεῦμα it is difficult to say.—Pos. too was quite ignorant of an evil principle in the world, not the divine or contrary to the divine principle. The ethical teaching of Stoicism had always contained a dualism which is here transferred to the physical doctrine where it was originally unknown. From the time of Pos. there is an ever growing tendency to emphasize the contrast (which was, however, always familiar to the older Stoics as well) between "soul" and "body", the *inutilis caro ac fluida*, Pos. ap. Sen., *Ep.* 92, 10. In view of this contrast the "soul" too is no longer said to come into being with the body or with the physical conception of the individual (cf. γεγονέναι τὴν ψυχὴν καὶ μεταγενεστέραν εἶναι [τοῦ σώματος], Chrysipp. ap. Plu., *Sto. Rep.* 1053 D [ii, 222 Arn.]), but rather to have been living before that, in the separate life of the divine. It is nowhere expressly or authoritatively stated that Poseidonios held the "pre-existence" of the "soul"; but that view has been rightly attributed to him, fitting in as it does with his other ideas, and because it is often introduced and taken for granted in those passages where

Cicero or Seneca are following Pos. (see Corssen, *de Pos. Rhod.*, p. 25 ff. But we may not read the doctrine of pre-existence into S.E., *M.* ix, 71, as Heinze, *Xenok.* 134, 2, does). If the soul-δαίμων was in existence before its incarnation it can presumably only enter the body with the conception of the individual life θύραθεν, *tractus extrinsecus* as Cic. puts it, *Div.* ii, 119 ; a passage obviously related (as Bonhöffer, *Epikt.* 79 remarks) to the statement in *Div.* i, 64, where he is speaking of the *immortales animi* of which the air is full—and there Pos. is mentioned by name as the authority. From its pre-existent life in the air the " soul " enters into man. The multitude of individual bodiless souls—not only the one impersonal soul-substance of the world—were thus living before their ἐνσωμάτωσις, and the Stoic pantheism thus turns into a rather questionable " pandaemonism ". On the other hand, Poseidonios in opposition to his teacher, Panaitios, adheres to the doctrine of the periodic extinction of all life in the one Soul of the World, the original Fire : cf. *Dox.* 388a, 18 ; b, 19. Holding this view he cannot very well have put the origin of each of the individual soul-daimones before the beginning of the particular world-period in which they live. Nor can the survival of the souls after their separation from the body be prolonged beyond the next ἐκπύρωσις (which makes Cicero's *immortales animi* inexact : *Div.* i, 64, after Pos.). Thus, although the survival which Panaitios had denied is reaffirmed it does not go beyond the qualified doctrine of immortality which the older Stoics had held. At the same time Pos. could hold, with Chrysipp. and other Stoics, that there was a περιοδικὴ παλιγγενεσία (M. Ant. xi, 1) after the world-conflagration and even that each individual man of the previous world-period would be restored again in precisely the same place (Chrysipp. ap. Lact., *Inst.* 7, 23, 3, etc. ; ii, 189 Arn. ; cf. the Orphico-Pythagorean fantasy : above, chap. x, n. 47). But this would not amount to an ἀθανασία for the individual : the individual life has been interrupted and is separated from its ἀποκατάστασις by a long interval of time.—There is no satisfactory reason for assigning to Pos. the belief in a series of μετενσωματώσεις of the soul—as Heinze does, *Xen.* 132 ff.—though such an idea would not have been hard to arrive at, even while holding fast to the doctrine of the final ἐκπύρωσις. But the dubious accounts given by many δοξογράφοι of Stoic teaching on the question of the μεταγγισμὸς ψυχῶν need not necessarily refer to Poseidonios : nor are we bound to draw this conclusion because they reappear in Plutarch. Plu. does indeed here and there follow Poseidonios, but he never hesitates to add Platonic ideas or fancies of his own invention, a fact which makes it most risky to attempt to fix an exact source for any particular detail in his variegated mosaic.

[61] Schmekel (*Phil. d. mittl. Stoa*, 1892) maintains convincingly that Panaitios was led to his view of the nature and fate of the soul chiefly by the polemic of Karneades against the dogmatic philosophers and particularly the Stoics. It is less certain that Poseidonios and his heterodox views are influenced by respect for Karneades. It is certain, however, that Pos. differs from Chrysipp., and still more from Panaitios. There is thus an indirect connexion between him and Karneades, to whose criticisms Panaitios had in the most essential points given way.

[62] That Pos. is being used in the first book of *Tusc. Disp.* is admitted on all hands (as to the extent of that use conjecture may indeed be various). It is at least very possible in the case of *Somn. Scip.* (see Corssen, *Pos.* 40 ff.).—The attraction of such theories of immortality

remained an aesthetic one with Cicero (and probably among all the cultured of his age and social circle). Where he is not speaking rhetorically or in pursuance of a literary pose—in his letters esp.—he shows no trace of the conviction that he defends at other times with so much ardour (see Boissier, *Rel. rom. d'Aug. aux Ant.* i, 58 f.).

[63] *οὐ κατὰ ψιλὴν παράταξιν, ἀλλὰ λελογισμένως καὶ σεμνῶς* though not always quite *ἀτραγῴδως* (M. Ant. xi, 3).

[64] Julius Kanus when condemned to death by Gaius only attempts to *enquire* whether there is any truth in the belief in immortality: Sen., *Tr. An.* 14, 8–9. De natura animae et dissociatione spiritus corporisque inquirebat Thrasea Paetus, before his execution, with his instructor Demetrius the Cynic: Tac., *A.* xvi, 34. They have no firm conviction in these matters that might serve to explain or account for their heroism (Cato reads the *Phaedo* before his suicide: Plu., *Cat. min.* 68, 70).

[65] nos quoque felices animae et aeterna sortitae says the soul of her father to Marcia: Sen., *C. ad Marc.* 26, 7, in antiqua elementa vertemur at the *ἐκπύρωσις*.

[66] Sen., *Ep.* 88, 34.

[67] *bellum somnium*, Sen., *Ep.* 102, 2.

[68] Where Seneca admits more positive conceptions of a life after death he never goes beyond a fortasse, si modo vera sapientium fama est (*Ep.* 63, 16); a deliberate concession to the consensus hominum (*Ep.* 117, 6) or the opiniones magnorum virorum rem gratissimam promittentium magis quam probantium (*Ep.* 102, 3). Following the conventional style of consolatory discourses he gives such expressions a more vivid turn in the *Consolationes*: e.g. *Marc.* 25, 1 ff.; *Helv.* 11, 7; *Polyb.* 9, 8. But even there the idea of *personal* immortality hardly seems to be taken seriously. In the same pieces death is commended simply as putting an end to all pain, and, in fact, to all sensation: *Marc.* 19, 4–5. In death we become again as we were before being born, *Marc.* 19, 5; cf. *Ep.* 54, 4, mors est non esse. id quale sit iam scio. hoc erit post me quod ante me fuit; and *Ep.* 77, 11, non eris: nec fuisti. So that whether death is a *finis* or a *transitus*, (*Prov.* 6, 6; *Ep.* 65, 24), it is equally welcome to the wise man who has made the most of his life, however short it may have been. Whether he goes then to the gods or whether on the other hand nothing is left of the mortal creature after death aeque magnum animum habebit (*Ep.* 93, 10); cf. nunquam magis divinum est (pectus humanum) quam ubi mortalitatem suam cogitat, et scit in hoc natum hominem ut vita defungeretur cet., (*Ep.* 120, 14); ipsum perire non est magnum. anima in expedito est habenda (*QN.* 6, 32, 5); to be ready is everything.—Of the old Stoic dogmas the only one that seems to remain certain for Seneca is that of *παλιγγενεσία* at the new creation of the world, *Ep.* 36, 10-11: mors intermittit vitam, non eripit: venit iterum qui nos in lucem reponat dies; but that is not in any way a consolation: multi recusarent nisi oblitos reduceret. Consciousness ceases with the coming of death in this world-period.

[69] It is very rarely that the utterances of the Emperor on the subject of what happens after death resemble those of a convinced Stoic of the old school. The souls are all parts of the one *νοερὰ ψυχή* of the world which though extended over so many individual souls yet remains a unity (ix, 8; xii, 30). After death the individual soul will survive for a period in the air until it is merged into the universal soul *εἰς τὸν τῶν ὅλων σπερματικὸν λόγον* (iv, 21). This implies the survival of the personal self for an undefined period, but it is

not a fixed conviction of M. Ant. As a rule he allows the choice between σβέσις ἢ μετάστασις, i.e. immediate extinction and merging of the individual soul (Panait.) or its removal into a temporary abode of the souls in the air (αἱ εἰς τὸν ἀέρα μεθιστάμεναι ψυχαί, iv, 21; cf. v, 53). Or else the choice is between σβέσις, μετάστασις (both in agreement with the Stoic doctrine of the ἕνωσις of the soul) or σκεδασμός of the soul-elements, in case the atomists are right (vii, 32; viii, 25; vi, 24)—a dilemma which really comes down to σκεδασμός or σβέσις (= ληφθῆναι εἰς τοὺς τοῦ κόσμου σπερματικοὺς λόγους); and μετάστασις falls out. This is probably the meaning also of x, 7: ἤτοι σκεδασμὸς στοιχείων ἢ τροπή (in which τὸ πνευματικόν disappears εἰς τὸ ἀερῶδες) and τροπή only of the last πνευματικόν that man preserves in himself: for here (at the end of the chapter) the identity of the individual soul with itself is given up in the Herakleitean manner (see above, p. 370). Sometimes the choice is presented between ἀναισθησία or ἕτερος βίος after death (iii, 3) or αἴσθησις ἑτεροία in an ἀλλοῖον ζῷον (viii, 58). This is no allusion to metempsychosis (in which the envelope into which the soul goes is another but its αἴσθησις does not become ἑτεροία): it means the turning of the *soul-pneuma*, exhaled in death, to new forms of life united to the previous forms by no identity of soul-personality. In this case we can indeed say τοῦ ζῆν οὐ παύσῃ: but there can be no idea of the survival of the personal ego. ἡ τῶν ὅλων φύσις exchanges and redistributes its elements; all things are changing (viii, 6; ix, 28). The Emperor never seriously thinks of the survival of personality; he seeks rather to inquire why things are as they are; but he never doubts that as a matter of fact even the noblest of mankind must also "go out" completely with death (xii, 5). Everything changes and one thing perishes to make way for another (xii, 21); and so each man must say to himself μετ' οὐ πολὺ οὐδεὶς οὐδαμοῦ ἔσῃ (xii, 21; viii, 5). The wise man will say it with calmness: his soul is ἕτοιμος ἐὰν ἤδη ἀπολυθῆναι δέῃ τοῦ σώματος . . . xi, 3. Living among men to whom his way of thought is strange (ἐν τῇ διαφωνίᾳ τῆς συμβιώσεως) he sighs at times θᾶττον ἔλθοις, ὦ θάνατε . . . ix, 3; cf. Bonhöffer, *Epikt. u. d. Stoa*, 59 ff.

[70] I shall die without resisting God εἰδὼς ὅτι τὸ γενόμενον καὶ φθαρῆναι δεῖ. οὐ γάρ εἰμι αἰὼν ἀλλ' ἄνθρωπος, μέρος τῶν πάντων ὡς ὥρα ἡμέρας· ἐνστῆναί με δεῖ ὡς τὴν ὥραν καὶ παρελθεῖν ὡς ὥραν, Epictet. ii, 5, 13. The present must make way for the future ἵν' ἡ περίοδος ἀνύηται τοῦ κόσμου, ii, 17–18; iv, 1, 106. Death brings with it not complete destruction, οὐκ ἀπώλειαν, but τῶν προτέρων εἰς ἕτερα μεταβολάς, iii, 24, 91–4. But the personality of the now living individual does indeed perish completely in death.—Cf. Bonhöffer, *Epiktet*, 65 f.; cf. also the same author's *Ethik des Epiktet*, p. 26 ff., 52 (1894).

[71] Cornutus ap. Stob., *Ecl.* i, 383, 24–384, 2 W.

[72] The ψυχή a σῶμα (the only ἀσώματον is empty space which is merely a passage way for the σώματα), D.L. x, 67 [p. 21 Us.]. It is a σῶμα λεπτομερές, παρ' ὅλον τὸ ἄθροισμα (i.e. of atoms to a body) παρεσπαρμένον, προσεμφερέστατον δὲ πνεύματι θερμοῦ τινα κρᾶσιν ἔχοντι, D.L. x, 63. Cf. Lucr. iii, 126 ff.; more precise is iii, 231–46. It is the ἄθροισμα which τὴν ψυχὴν στεγάζει, D.L. x, 64. vas quasi constitit eius, Lucr. iii, 440, 555.

[73] Lucr. iii, 94 ff., 117 ff.

[74] The ἄλογον ὃ ἐν τῷ λοιπῷ παρέσπαρται σώματι, τὸ δὲ λογικὸν ἐν τῷ θώρακι, Sch. D.L. x, 67 (p. 21 Us.), *fr.* 312, 313 Us. *anima* and *animus*, Lucr. iii, 136 ff. The *anima*, though it is diminished

when the man loses his limbs (in which it inheres), yet allows him to remain alive. The *animus*, however, *vitai claustra coercens*, must not be diminished otherwise the *anima* escapes as well and the man dies: Lucr. iii, 396 ff. The *animus* with its perceptions is more independent of *anima* and *corpus* than they are of it: Lucr. iii, 145 ff.

[75] Lucr. iii, 421–4.

[76] Lucr. iii, 445 ff.

[77] The soul διασπείρεται, λυομένου τοῦ ὅλου ἀθροίσματος and cannot retain any αἴσθησις apart from its ἄθροισμα, D.L. x, 65–6. The winds disperse it: Lucr. iii, 506 ff. καπνοῦ δίκην σκίδναται, Epicur. *fr.* 337. *ceu fumus*, Lucr. iii, 446–583.

[78] radicitus e vita se tollit et eicit, Lucr. iii, 877.

[79] Lucr. iii, 854–60; 847–53.

[80] οὐδὲ ταφῆς φροντιεῖν (τὸν σοφόν) *fr.* 578. Cf. Lucr. iii, 870 ff. The way in which the body, deserted by its soul, is buried or disposed of is of no consequence: Phld., *Mort.*, p. 41–2 Mekl.

[81] D.L. x, 124–5.

[82] ὁ θάνατος οὐδὲν πρὸς ἡμᾶς, τὸ γὰρ διαλυθὲν ἀναισθητεῖ, τὸ δὲ ἀναισθητοῦν οὐδὲν πρὸς ἡμᾶς, Ep., *Sent.* ii; D.L. x, 139 (p. 71 Us.). Frequently repeated: see Usen., p. 391 f.

[83] dolor and morbus, leti fabricator uterque, affect the soul too, Lucr. iii, 459 ff., 470 ff., 484 ff. Nothing that can be broken up into parts can be eternal; 640 ff., 667 ff. The chief argument: quod cum corpore nascitur, cum corpore intereat necesse est, Ep., *fr.* 336. (They are identical in part with the arguments which Karneades directed against the theory of the eternity and indestructibility of the highest ζῷον, God. Karn. must have got them from Epicurus.)

[84] Cf. Ep., *Sent.* xi, p. 73 f. Us.

[85] To be able to see μηδὲν πρὸς ἡμᾶς εἶναι τὸν θάνατον, ἀπόλαυστον ποιεῖ τὸ τῆς ζωῆς θνητόν, οὐκ ἄπειρον προτιθεῖσα χρόνον ἀλλὰ τὸν τῆς ἀθανασίας ἀφελομένη πόθον, D.L. x, 123; cf. Metrod. (?), ed. Körte, p. 588, col. xvi.

[86] γεγόναμεν ἅπαξ, δὶς δὲ οὐκ ἔστι γενέσθαι κτλ. hence *carpe diem*! *fr.* 204; see also *fr.* 490–4. Metrod. *fr.* 53 K.

[87] D.L. x, 81.

[88] Against the fear of torment and punishment in the underworld: *fr.* 340–1, cf. Lucr. iii, 1011 ff. (torments such as those fabled of Hades exist in *this* world: iii, 978 ff.). Cf. the letter of the Epicurean Diogenes, *Rh. Mus.* 47, 428 . . . φοβοῦμαι γὰρ οὐδὲν (sc. τὸν θάνατον) διὰ τοὺς Τιτυοὺς καὶ τοὺς Ταντάλους οὓς ἀναγράφουσιν ἐν Ἅιδου τινές, οὐδὲ φρίττω τὴν μύδησιν (μήδησιν the stone) κτλ.

[89] metus ille foras praeceps Acheruntis agendus, funditus humanam qui vitam turbat ab imo, omnia suffundens mortis nigrore neque ullam esse voluptatem liquidam puramque reliquit, Lucr. iii, 37 ff.

[90] D.L. x, 126. ridiculum est currere ad mortem taedio vitae, *fr.* 496.

[91] artifex vitae, Sen., *Ep.* 90, 27.

[92] —σὺ δὲ τῆς αὔριον οὐκ ὢν κύριος ἀναβάλλῃ τὸν καιρόν· ὁ δὲ πάντων βίος μελλησμῷ παραπόλλυται . . . *fr.* 204.

[93] Negat Epicurus ne diuturnitatem quidem temporis ad beate vivendum aliquid afferre, nec minorem voluptatem percipi in brevitate temporis quam si sit illa sempiterna, Cic., *Fin.* ii, 87; cf. Ep., *Sent.* xix (p. 75 Us.). χρόνον οὐ τὸν μήκιστον ἀλλὰ τὸν ἥδιστον καρπίζεται (ὁ σοφός): D.L. x, 126.—quae mala nos subigit vitai tanta cupido, Lucr. iii, 1077. eadem sunt omnia semper, 945.

[94] ἡ διάνοια . . . τὸν παντελῆ βίον παρεσκεύασεν καὶ οὐδὲν ἔτι τοῦ ἀπείρου χρόνου προσεδεήθη, *Sent.* xx (p. 75 Us.).
[95] οὐκ ἔστι φυσικὴ κοινωνία τοῖς λογικοῖς πρὸς ἀλλήλους.—*sibi quemque consulere, fr.* 523. Aloofness from ταῖς τῶν πληθῶν ἀρχαῖς *frr.* 554, 552, 9.
[96] οἱ νόμοι χάριν τῶν σοφῶν κεῖνται, οὐχ ὅπως μὴ ἀδικῶσιν, ἀλλ' ὅπως μὴ ἀδικῶνται, *fr.* 530.
[97] οὐκέτι δεῖ σῴζειν τοὺς Ἕλληνας, οὐδ' ἐπὶ σοφίᾳ στεφάνων παρ' αὐτοῖς τυγχάνειν . . . Metrod. *fr.* 41.

CHAPTER XIV

PART II

POPULAR BELIEF

Philosophic teaching and the philosophic outlook were at this time by no means confined exclusively to the narrow circles dominated by particular schools. Never more widely or more effectively than in this Hellenistic period did philosophy in one shape or another provide the basis and common medium of a culture that no one of moderate wealth and leisure would willingly be without. Such ideas as educated people of the time generally possessed, dealing in a more connected and definite form with the things of this life and existence that lie beyond the scope of immediate perception, were all drawn from the teaching of philosophy. To a certain extent this is true also of the current views as to the nature and destiny of the soul. But in the region of the unknowable philosophy can never entirely replace or suppress the natural—the irrational beliefs—of mankind. Such beliefs were in their natural element in dealing with such subjects. They influenced even the philosophically enlightened and their authority was supreme with the many who in every age are incapable of understanding the disinterested search for knowledge. Even in this supreme period of universal philosophic culture, popular beliefs about the soul still remained in force, unmodified by the speculations or the exhortations of philosophers.

They had their roots—these beliefs—not in any form of speculative thought but in the practice of the Cult of Souls: and that Cult, as it has been described [1] for an earlier stage of Greek life, still went on unaltered and with undiminished vigour. This may be asserted with confidence, though we can produce no very important evidence from the literature of this later period. The character and content of that literature is such that we should hardly expect to find such evidence in it. But for the most part the literary evidence from which we were able to illustrate the Cult of Souls in an earlier period may be taken to apply equally to the age with which we are now dealing. Even in its final years Lucian's pamphlet *On Mourning* bears express witness to the survival of the ancient and sanctified usages in their fullest compass. We hear again of the washing, anointing, and crowning of the dead, the ceremonious lying-in-state upon the bier, the violent and extravagant lament over the dead body, and all the traditional customs that are still in full force. Last comes the solemn interment of the body—the articles of luxury burnt together with the corpse of the dead man or buried with him in the grave—articles that had once belonged to him and which he is supposed to enjoy even in death—the feeding of the helpless soul of the dead with libations of wine and burnt-offerings—the ritual fasting of the relatives only broken, after three days, in the Banquet of the Dead.[2]

The dead man must not be deprived of a single one of "the customary things"—only so can his well-being be fully secured.[3] The most important of these is the solemn interment of the body. This is carried out not only by the family of the dead man, but in many cases also by the society to which he may have belonged.[4] In these times when the cities sought to make up for the loss of more serious interests in their life by an often touching care for the immediate and the insignificant, deserving citizens were frequently honoured with elaborate funeral processions in which the municipality took part; [5] the city fathers would then probably decree that representatives should be sent to the survivors and commissioned to express the sympathy of the city in their loss and distract their minds from their grief by a speech.[6]

The ritual act of burial, the object of so much pious zeal, was the very reverse of the indifferent matter that philosophy loved to represent it.[7] The sanctity of the place where rests the dead is also a matter of great importance, not only for the dead man himself but for the rest of the family which desires to be still united in the life of the spirit world, and so inhabits a common burial-ground (generally outside the city, very rarely within,[8] but sometimes, even yet, actually inside the house).[9] The founder of a family-grave desires the members of it to be joined together in the same grave for at least three generations.[10] Those who have a right to be buried there take steps—religious and legal or municipal—against the profanation of this family tomb and sanctuary by the burying in it of strangers or the pillaging of the vault—a practice that became increasingly common in the final period of the antique world.[11] There are innumerable grave-notices threatening money penalties in accordance with the ancient law of the city, to be paid into the public treasury by those who violate the peace of the grave.[12] No less common are the inscriptions which place the grave and its sanctity under the protection of the underworld deities, invoking at the same time the most shocking curses—torments and calamities both temporal and eternal—against profaners of the holiness of the tomb.[13] Especially the inhabitants of certain districts of Asia Minor, only very superficially Hellenized, give themselves free rein in the accumulation of such violent execrations. In their case the dark superstitions of ancestral and native worship of gods or spirits may have infected the Hellenes also—it is often the Greeks who become barbarian rather than the barbarians who are Hellenized in the history of Greek relations with these stubborn and barbarous native populations.[14] But even in lands where the Greek population has maintained itself without admixture such execrations are occasionally to be found in graves.

As time went on and the sanctity and peace of the grave began to be more and more seriously threatened, measures of all kinds were taken for its protection. The grave is no mere chamber of corruption: the souls of the dead dwell there,[15] and therefore is it holy; as a sanctuary it becomes completely sanctified when it has received the last member of the family, and is enclosed for ever.[16] The family so long as it lasts continues to pay the regular Soul-Cult to its ancestors;[17] sometimes special foundations ensure the payment for ever[18] of the Soul-Cult of which the dead have need.[19] Even those whose burial place lies far away from the graves of their own family[20] are not entirely deprived of benevolent care and cult.

The pre-supposition of all Cult of Souls—that the dead survive to enjoy at least a gloomy sepulchral existence in their last resting-place—is everywhere vividly implied. It speaks to us with archaic simplicity from those gravestones upon which the dead, as though still accessible to the sounds of the human voice and able to understand the words of the living, are addressed with the customary words of greeting.[21] Sometimes the dead man himself is provided with a similar greeting which he is supposed to address to the passers-by[22]—between him, confined to his grave, and the others who still walk about in the daylight a dialogue takes place.[23] The dead man is not entirely cut off from the affairs of the upper world. He feels an access of fresh life when he is called by the name that he had once borne in his life-time, and the memory of which is now preserved only by his gravestone. His fellow-citizens call upon him three times by name at his burial;[24] but even in the grave he is capable of hearing the precious sound. On a gravestone at Athens [25] the dead man enjoins upon the members of the actors' guild to which he had belonged to call upon his name in chorus whenever they pass by his grave, and to gladden him with the sound of hand-clapping, to which he had been accustomed in life. At other times the passer-by "kisses his hand" [26] to the dead man; a gesture which denotes the honour paid to a Hero.[27] The soul is not merely alive; it belongs now, as primitive and age-long belief expressed it, to the Higher and Mightier Ones.[28] Perhaps this exaltation of the wrath and power of the dead is the meaning of the custom by which the dead are called the Good, the Honest (χρηστοί). This usage must have become established at an early period,[29] but it is not until these later days that it is first employed as an addition to the simple words of greeting addressed to the dead on gravestones. In this use it is not uniformly current: it is rare in Attica (at least, on graves of natives of that country); whereas in Boeotia, Thessaly, and the countries of Asia Minor it is frequent and almost universal.[30] In fact it is natural to suppose [31] that this mode of address, originally a euphemistic title addressed to the ghosts of the dead who were conceived as quite capable of acting in a manner the very reverse of that attributed to them by the word, was intended to suggest the power belonging to the personality so addressed as one who has risen to a higher form of existence—and to venerate him with becoming awe.[32]

§ 2

The conception of the departed spirit as one who has been raised to a higher state of dignity and power receives clearer and more conscious expression where the departed one is called a Hero.

This class of intermediate beings standing on the border line between mankind and godhead—the world of the Heroes—was in no danger of extinction at this period of Greek religious belief. The attitude of mind that could think of certain special souls as withdrawn from the limitations of visible existence and raised to a higher spiritual state remained still vigorous and was even able to give birth to new conceptions.

In its original and proper sense the name *Heros* never indicated an independent and self-sufficient spirit. *Archegetes*, "leader" or "originator", is his real and distinctive title. The *Heros* stands at the beginning of a series, taking its origin from him, of mortal men for whom he is the leader and " ancestor ". The genuine Heroes are the ancestors, whether real or imaginary, of a family or a house ; in the " Heroes ", after whom they wish to be called, the members of a society, a clan, or even a whole race honour the *archegetai* of those groups. They are always men of power and influence, prominent and distinguished from other men, who are regarded as having thus entered into the life of Heroes after their death. And even in later times the Heroes of a more recent elevation, though they may no longer be the leaders of a train of descendants taking their origin from them, are yet regarded as distinguished from the people who worship them by their peculiar virtue and dignity. To become a *Heros* after death was a privilege reserved for a few great and uncommon personalities who even in their lifetime were not as other men were.

The companies of these old and specially chosen Heroes did not suffer the fate of forgetfulness which would have been their second and real death. The love of country and city, undying among the Greeks, attached itself in reverent memory to the illuminated spirits of the past who had once protected and defended their native land. When Messene was refounded in the fourth century the Heroes of the country were solemnly called upon to become inhabitants of the city as they had been before—more particularly Aristomenes, the never-forgotten champion of Messenian freedom.[33] Even at Leuctra he had appeared in the melée of the fight, doing battle for the Thebans.[34] Before the battle, Epameinondas had secured the favour of the Heroines of the place, the daughters of Skedasos, by means of prayer and sacrifice.[35] These were events of the last heroic age of Greek history, but the cult and memory of the local Heroes of the Greek countries survived into a much later age. Leonidas was worshipped by the people of Sparta for many centuries,[36] and the champions of the Persian Wars, the saviours of Hellas, were worshipped by their remote descendants.[37] Even in imperial times the inhabitants of the island of Kos still worshipped those who had fallen to secure their freedom centuries before.[38] Such individual cases allow us to see what was the general rule : the memory and cult of a Hero lived on as long as the community remained in existence whose duty it was to maintain his worship. Even those Heroes—a class by themselves—who have secured their immortality through their fame in ancient poetry [39] still retained their cult undiminished. The heroic figure of Hektor still preserved life and reality for his worshippers in the Troad or at Thebes.[40] Even in the third century of our era the district of Troy and the neighbouring coasts of Europe still kept fresh the memory and the cult of the Heroes of Epic renown.[41] Of Achilles, who had a special fate, we must speak in another connexion.[42]

Nor did less splendid figures vanish from the memory of their narrower associations of worshippers. Autolykos the founder of Sinope retained his cult even in the time of Lucullus.[43] At a quite late period the relics of the specially popular Heroes of the Pan-Hellenic games were still the subject of many superstitions [44] that bear witness to their continued influence. Heroes to whom healing powers were ascribed continued to do works of healing and to be worshipped, and their number was even extended.[45] Mere local spirits, whose very names had been forgotten, nevertheless lost none of the honour that came to them from their beneficent miracles; such were, for instance, that Philopregmon of Poteideia who was celebrated by a late poet,[46] or the Hero Euodos of Apollinopolis in Egypt who dispensed "good journey" to those who honoured him in passing by his monument.[47]

But all Heroes were not yet reduced to such casual salutations from occasional passers-by. In many places [48] the regular festivals and sacrifices to Heroes still survived—even human sacrifice was still sometimes made to spirits who were held capable of special exhibitions of power.[49] In a few cases the festivals of Heroes are the chief feasts in the annual calendar of a city.[50] The names of Heroes quite as much as of Gods were used in oath-taking [51] at treaties made by Greek cities so long as they retained their independence. Foundations were dedicated to the honour of Gods and Heroes together.[52] Cult associations called themselves after the Heroes they met to worship.[53] Special priests of certain Heroes were regularly appointed.[54] Even in the second century, in his book of travels, Pausanias is able to inform us of not a few Heroes whose cult, as he distinctly says, had gone on unbroken in their cities down to his own day.[55] The annual festival of the Heroes who had fallen at Plataea was still celebrated with the greatest pomp in the time of Plutarch, who describes every detail of its archaic ceremonial.[56] And at Sikyon, at the same time, the Heroic festival of Aratos, the founder of the Achæan League, was still celebrated, though here the centuries had robbed the occasion of many of its former glories.[57]

In all such ceremonies it was to a single and definite spirit-personality that the devotion of men was offered. Each of them received the cult that was due to him by the terms of some old-established and sanctified foundation. Nothing was further from men's minds than the loose and vague conception, expressed sometimes by ancient writers, that *all* brave men of the past or all outstanding individuals of whatever time are to be regarded forthwith as Heroes.[58] It was still clearly and consciously felt that elevation to the rank of Hero was not a privilege that belonged as a matter of course to any particular class of mankind, but, wherever it occurred, was essentially a ratification of quite exceptional worth and influence displayed already in the lifetime of the Hero. Following this conception even the Hellenistic age added to the number of the Heroes by drawing upon the great men of the present. A little earlier Pelopidas and Timoleon had been honoured in this way, and now the figures of Leosthenes, Kleomenes, and Philopoimen were raised to heroic glory.[59] Even Aratos, the very incarnation of the sobriety of a too matter-of-fact age, at the end of a life devoted with ardour but without enduring success to the service of his country, was supposed by his countrymen to have passed over in a mysterious manner into the realm of heroic semi-divinity.[60]

As in these cases whole populations honoured individuals so also did narrower and much humbler associations, even in this rationalist age, elevate their helpers and protectors to the rank of Hero and honour them as such. The slaves of Kos thus honoured their former comrade and leader Drimakos; [61] at another place there was a Hero who protected all refugees who took shelter with him; [62] at Ephesos there was a Hero who had been a simple shepherd.[63] At the time of Augustus, a benefactor of his city, Athenodoros, the philosopher, had been made a Hero by grateful Tarsians after his death.[64] It sometimes happens that a Hero of the distant past may find himself confused with a descendant of the same name whom his contemporaries put in the place of his own ancestor and worship in his stead.[65]

So little were men grown out of the ideas centred round the cult of Heroes that, accustomed to the ever-increasing adoration of the "Mightier and Better", every age was eager to add to their number from the men of the present. They did not always wait for the death of the individual so honoured before beginning to address him as *Heros*; even in his lifetime he must enjoy a foretaste of the honour that was destined to be his after his departure from this life. Thus, Lysander was saluted as a Hero after his victory by the Greeks whom he had liberated from the despotism of Athens; and in the Hellenistic age many a fortunate army commander or mighty king received the same honour. Of the Romans Flamininus the friend of the Greeks was the first to receive it.[66] This misapplication of the cult of Heroes to the living then became still further extended.[67] It may be that sometimes it was a real feeling of unusual merit that fired the impulsive temperament of the Greeks; but in the end the custom became almost a meaningless convention: even private individuals were thus called Hero in their lifetime[68] and heroic honours—even the foundation of annual athletic games—were granted to living persons almost indiscriminately.[69]

And at last when it was necessary to honour an individual whom the love and passionate regret of a monarch elevated to the rank of Hero after his death then, indeed, the age could hardly do enough in the hyperbole of pomp and ceremony. The funeral honours paid to the dead Hephaistion are an extravagant example of this.[70]

If in such cases the limits between the worship of a Hero and the adoration of a god seemed almost to have disappeared, we still have evidence of individual cases in which the survivors, without actually naming them Heroes, offer to their much-loved dead a memorial cult that hardly falls short of full heroic honours.[71] Nor is it only in such cases as these that we perceive the signs of a tendency to exalt the Cult of Souls everywhere and to approximate it to the worship of ancestors in the ancient Cult of Heroes. It emerges clearly enough, for all the brevity of their language, from the multitude of epitaphic inscriptions in which members of simple citizen families are addressed with the title of *Heros*. At any rate, it betokens an increase in the importance and dignity of the dead when a tombstone expressly announces that an individual citizen has been "heroized" by the city after his death. And this is what not infrequently happened—early in Thera and later on in many other places as well.[72] The same conclusion must be drawn when we hear of associations declaring a dead member to be a *Heros*;[73] or when a society recognizes a dead man as *Heros* on the formal motion of an individual.[74] Families, too, become accustomed to giving the name to those of their number that have died before the rest; and a son will thus speak of his father, parents of a son, and a wife of her husband—either informally or by a formal declaration naming the dead one as *Heros.*[75] A higher and mightier form of existence after death must be imagined for the departed when he is thus distinguished so explicitly from the ordinary multitude of the dead—still more so in those cases when the dead man, elevated to a mystic communion with higher forms of life, loses his own name and receives in exchange that of a Hero of long-standing honour, or even that of a God.[76]

In every case that is known to us, the "heroizing" of a dead person by the city or a society or the family is carried out entirely on the independent authority of those bodies. The Delphic Oracle, without whose deciding voice it was hardly possible in early times for the company of the elect to receive any addition,[77] was, in these days when the prestige of the oracle had sunk almost to nothing, no longer applied to for its sanction. The consequence was hardly avoidable that the licence thus accorded to corporations and families should widen still further the bounds of the Heroes' kingdom. In the end, these boundaries broke down entirely. There were cities and countries where it became the custom to apply the title of "Hero" as an epithet of honour belonging to all the dead without distinction. It seems that this extension of "heroizing" to all the dead first became common in Boeotia,[78] though here it was not quite universal—Thespiai was an exception.[79] Thessalian grave-inscriptions give the fullest evidence for the heroizing of the dead of every age and description. But the custom spread to every country populated by Greeks; [80] only Athens is less unrestrained [81] in the bestowal of the title of Hero upon the dead—a title which retained no more of the old and essential meaning of the word (which perhaps survived longest in Athens) than to say that the dead were really now dead.[82]

In spite of such indiscriminate application the name "Hero" still continued to be something of a title of honour. An honour, indeed, that was thus accorded to everyone without distinction was in danger of becoming the reverse of an honour. But isolated phrases of a naive and popular character make it clear that a difference was still felt to exist between the "Hero" and those who were not honoured with this distinguishing epithet.[83] When the name of Hero was thus applied to all the dead, not in exceptional cases but as a rule, the glory and distinction of which the idea of the "Hero" was thus deprived must have fallen in some measure upon the individual dead, if they and the Heroes could meet on common ground. Thus, even the dissipation of the heroic honour and its indiscriminate application to all the dead is in reality but another indication of the fact that even in the decline of the ancient world the power and dignity of the departed soul had not declined too, but had, on the contrary, grown greater.

§ 3

The souls of the departed show their power and the fact that they are still alive more particularly in the effect that they have on this life and on the living. For the purposes of the Cult of Souls they are regarded as confined to the region of the inhabited earth; they continue in the grave or near it, for a time or permanently, and can therefore be reached by the offerings or the prayers of their living relatives. There can be no doubt that at this time men still believed, as they had done since the earliest times, in a kindly relationship between the family and its departed members, an exchange in which offerings were made at the grave by the living and blessings vouchsafed by the Unseen. It is true, however, that we only have imperfect records of such calm and comfortable family belief in the survival of the departed and of the part they continue to play in the daily life of their descendants.

But there is a more sinister variety of intercourse with the souls or spirits of the dead. They sometimes appear unsought to the living; they can be compelled by the force of magic to use their powers in the service of the living. Both these possibilities apply more particularly to those unquiet souls whom fate or their own hands have deprived of life violently and before their time; to those who have not been consigned to the peace of the grave by ceremonious burial.[84] The enlightened of the time do indeed refuse to believe in ghosts and haunting spirits of the dead that wander without rest about the place of their tragic fate, and make their presence disagreeably felt by the living.[85] But the populace, even in such enlightened days, gave the fullest credence to stories in which the existence of a spirit-world seemed to reveal its sinister reality, trespassing at times upon the world of the living. Regular folk-tales of spectral apparitions, vagrant ghosts of unfortunate souls, vampire-like spirits of the grave,[86] are preserved to us in some numbers—chiefly such as appealed to a perverted philosophy, the *insaniens sapientia* of an outworn age, as seeming to confirm its fancies of an invisible world between heaven and earth. In Lucian's *Lover of Lies* the grey-beard philosophers entertain each other in portentous seriousness with such communications from the spirit world.[87] Plutarch himself is quite seriously convinced of the reality of some ghostly appearances.[88] Philosophy, which at this time was going back to Plato, found in its system of demonology a means of making such old wives' tales intelligible and credible to itself.

Finally, the time arrives when the violent and arbitrary interference with the unseen world—sorcery and spirit-raising—becomes a part of orthodox philosophy. The popular imagination of the Greeks did not have to wait for instruction from their barbarian neighbours, who had reduced the irrational to a system, before they could believe in the summoning of spirits from the deep. Magic in this sense was of extreme antiquity in Greece.[89] But in the fusion and intermixture of Greeks with barbarians which marked the Hellenistic age similar and cognate superstitions from all the corners of the earth met together and acquired strength from their union. It was foreign sources rather than Greek which chiefly contributed to swell the turbid and noxious stream of sorceries and spirit-raisings, the practical application of an irrational theory of the nature and being of the soul in separation from the body. The lofty heaven of the old Greek gods was beginning to grow dim before the troubled vision of this later age; more and more their place was taken by a mob of idols and an obscure rabble of lesser devils. In this chaotic medley of Greek and barbarian demonology the companies of unquiet souls and ghosts of the dead easily found a place. The ghost was no longer an alien when the Gods themselves had become ghostly. When both Gods and spirits have to answer to the spells of the sorcerer the souls of the dead are seldom left in peace.[90] We possess some relics of the art of spirit-raising in the Græco-Egyptian magic books; and we can now see with our eyes specimens which illustrate the practical outcome of this delusion in the magic charms and exorcisms that were scratched on tablets of lead or gold and placed in the graves—as the natural abode of the spirits which were to be compelled—where they have been found in considerable quantities in modern times. Among the sinister influences that are thus conjured to do the work of vengeance, punishment, or destruction upon the conjurer's enemy, the unquiet souls of the dead are also regularly mentioned. To them is attributed the power and the will to intervene with malevolence and obstruction in the life of men, no less than to the other spiritual powers of heaven and hell in company with whom they are summoned.[91]

§ 4

The Cult of Souls for all its expansion gave no assistance to the picturing of what might be the condition of the departed souls independently of their connexion with the living. Those who troubled themselves about such matters and sought further information were obliged to have recourse, if not to the systems of theologians and philosophers, then to the imaginative accounts and pictures of ancient poetry and legend.

The idea of a distant realm of the souls into which the strengthless shadows of those who had departed this life disappeared had not lost its hold on the popular imagination even of these later ages—difficult as it might be to reconcile[92] such an idea with the pre-suppositions of cultus with its customary worship and sustenance of the souls confined within the grave. The belief in a distant kingdom of the dead could not but continue to be current among men for whom the Homeric poems remained the earliest manual and school-book in the hands of youth and the source of instruction and entertainment to every age. The passionate indignation with which philosophers of the Stoic as well as the Epicurean faith attacked the beliefs resting on the teaching of Homer cannot be explained except by supposing that Homer and his picture had remained a guiding force with the masses who were uninstructed in philosophy. And, in fact, ancient writers use language which shows that the ancient conception of Hades was by no means discarded but on the contrary was still vigorously alive among the populace.[93]

As to what might go on down below and the general appearance of the underworld—these were questions that the invention of theological and semi-philosophic fancy, each according to its special lights and preconceptions, strove to answer in eager competition.[94] But such attempts to picture the condition of things in the kingdom of the souls—attempts which reached their highest point in the elaborate chiaroscuro of Vergil's Hades—remained the exercises of ingenious fancy and rarely pretended to be anything else. A distinct and authoritative popular system of belief on these points was scarcely possible when the orthodox religion of the state formally and dogmatically rejected everything of the kind.

It would, indeed, have been more natural if in connexion with the idea of the congregation of souls enclosed in the kingdom of the underworld deities a belief in a compensatory justice to be found in this after-life of the dead, had grown up and obtained popular currency. The oppressed and needy who feel themselves deprived of their share in this world's goods think only too easily that somewhere there must be a place where they too will some day enjoy the fruits that others alone are allowed to pluck upon earth—and place that " somewhere " beyond the boundaries of this world and of reality. Pious belief in the gods expects to obtain the prize, so often denied upon earth, in a realm of the spirit. If indeed such a conviction of a compensatory justice to come [95]—reward of the virtuous and punishment of the wicked in a hereafter—was really more widely and seriously held in this age than it had been before,[96] then the cult of the underworld deities as it was practised in the mysteries of the states and the various religious societies must have contributed in a large degree to bring this about. And contrariwise, the belief that the punishing and rewarding omnipotence of the gods would be felt in a hereafter must have brought an unbroken stream of adherents to those mysteries which in fact offered their help and mediation in the life to come. Those only could imagine that they had detailed knowledge of the enigmas that lie beyond the reach of all experience, who could surrender themselves entirely to the dogmatic teaching of a closed sect. We may in fact take leave to doubt whether the gruesome pictures of a place of torment in Hades, with its undying punishment in devouring flames, and the similar fancies that later authors sometimes express, were in reality anything more than the private imaginations with which exclusive and superstitious conventicles sought to terrorize their members.[97] The charming pictures of a " Land of Arrival " to which death sends the much-tried children of men, may have been more widely accepted. Homer, the universal instructor, had stamped them upon men's memories. For the poet the Elysian plain had been a place situated upon the surface of the earth to which the occasional favour of the gods was able to translate a few of their dearest favourites, that they might there enjoy, without seeing death, unending bliss.[98] In imitation of the Homeric fancy, the poetry of the following ages had imagined the translation of many other Heroes and heroic women of the legendary past to a secret life of bliss in Elysium or in the Islands of the Blest.[99] Later fancy, which saw in Elysium the Land of Promise to which all men who had lived in a manner pleasing to the gods would be taken after their death,[100] now placed its Elysium or Islands of the Blest in the interior of the earth beyond the reach of all save disembodied souls. In later times this became the currently accepted view, but the subject remained undefined and subject to variation. Men must still, in fact, have imagined The Isles of the Blest, the abode of privileged spirits, to be situated upon the surface of the earth (though, indeed, far away beyond the limits of the discovered countries of the globe), when attempts could be made to find the way there and to bring back news to the living. The attempt attributed to Sertorius was only the most famous of such voyages of discovery.[101] Why, indeed, should these magic Isles remain for ever undiscovered upon the borders of the inhabited world that yet offered so wide a field for discovery, when everybody knew of the island in the Black Sea, often visited by living men, where Achilles, the supreme example of miraculous translation, lived for ever in perpetual enjoyment of his youth? For centuries the island of Leukê, the separate Elysium of Achilles and a few select among the Heroes, was visited and reverenced with religious awe.[102] Here men thought they could discern in immediate perception, and in actual physical contact, something of the mysterious existence of blessed spirits. The belief in the possibility of miraculous translation to an eternity of unbroken union of body and soul, thus palpably and visibly substantiated, could not completely die even in this prosaic age. The educated did indeed find this conception so strange and unintelligible that when they come to speak of translation legends of the past they profess themselves unable to say what exactly the ancients had supposed to occur when such miracles took place.[103] But the populace, which finds nothing easier to believe in than the impossible, once more naively accepted the miracle. Did not the examples of Amphiaraos and Trophonios plainly establish the fact of translation to underground retreats? And to them as being still alive in their caves beneath the earth a cult was offered until an advanced period.[104] The translation of beautiful youths to everlasting life in the kingdom of the nymphs and spirits was the subject of many folk-tales.[105] Even in contemporary life the miracle of translation seemed not altogether impossible.[106] When the kings and queens of the Macedonian empire of the East began to receive divine honours in imitation of the great Alexander himself, it was not long before men ventured to affirm that at the end of his earthly existence the Divine Ruler everywhere does not die but is merely "carried away" by the gods and still lives on.[107] It is the peculiar property of divinity, as Plato clearly expresses it,[108] to live for ever in the indivisible unity of body and soul. A court-bred theology could the more easily make such demands upon the belief of subject peoples in the Semitic East, and possibly in Egypt too, because native [109] legends had already told of the translation to immortal life of individual men dear to the gods and akin to the gods in nature; just as similar stories became common in Italian legends too,[110] though possibly only under the influence of Greek models. Indeed, quite apart from obsequious courtliness, Greeks and half-Greeks were quite capable of entertaining the idea[111] that the darlings of their fancy, such as Alexander the Great, had not suffered death but had been translated alive to the realm of imperishable physical existence. This is shown clearly enough by the success which attended the appearance, in Moesia at the beginning of the third century A.D., of another Alexander. This imposter travelled from land to land with a great train of Bacchants, and everywhere men believed in his identity with the great monarch.[112] A little earlier they had believed with equal credulity in the reappearance upon earth of the Emperor Nero,[113] who, it was thought, had not died but had merely disappeared. When Antinous, the beautiful youth beloved by the Emperor Hadrian, sank and disappeared in his watery grave he was at once regarded as a god who had, in fact, not died but had been translated.[114] The miraculous translation of Apollonios of Tyana is reported with the utmost seriousness;[115] like the other marvels and mysteries in the strange and enigmatic existence of this prophetic figure, it found believers enough.[116]

But such unbroken continuance of the united life of body and soul, begun upon earth and carried on in a mysterious abode of bliss (the oldest form taken by the idea of human immortality in the Greek mind), was never attributed to more than a few specially favoured and specially gifted individuals. An immortality of the human soul as such, by virtue of its nature and composition—as the imperishable force of divinity in the mortal body—never became a real part of the belief of the Greek populace. When approximations to such a belief do occasionally find expression in popular modes of thought, it is because a fragment of theology or of the universally popular philosophy has penetrated to the lower strata of the uninstructed populace. Theology and philosophy remained the sole true repositories of the belief in the immortality of the soul. In the meeting together and conjunction of Greek and foreign ideas in the Hellenized Orient it was not Greek popular tradition but solely the influence of Greek philosophy, that, finding favour even outside the limits of Greek nationality, communicated to foreign nations the arresting concept of the divine, imperishable vitality of the human soul—upon the impressionable Jewish people, at least, it had the profoundest and most deeply penetrating influence.[117]

§ 5

All the various modes of conceiving the life enjoyed by the soul after the death of the body, as they had been explored, modified, and developed in the course of centuries, were admitted on an equal footing to the consciousness of the Greeks in this late period of their maturity. No formulated body of religious doctrine had by a process of exclusion and definition given the victory to any one conception at the expense of the others. But where so much was permitted and so little proscribed it is still possible to ask how these various formulations of belief, expectation, and hope stood in relation to each other. Were any more popular and more readily received than others? To answer this question it is natural to suppose that we have only to turn to the numerous inscriptions from the gravestones of the people. Here, especially in these later times, individuals give unhampered expression to their own feelings and thus reveal the extent and character of popular belief. But information derived from this source must be carefully scrutinized if it is not to lead to misconception.

If we pass in imagination through the long rows of streets in which the Greeks placed the memorials of their dead, and read the inscriptions on the tombstones—they now form part of the accumulated treasures of Greek Epigraphy—the first thing that must arrest our attention is the complete silence maintained by the enormous majority of these inscriptions with regard to any hope—however formulated—or any expectation of a life of the soul after death. They content themselves with recording the name of the dead, adding only the name of the father and (in the case of a foreigner) the country of the deceased. At the most, the custom of some localities may add a "Farewell". Such stubborn silence cannot be satisfactorily explained simply on the grounds of an economy practised by the surviving relatives of the deceased (though in some cases a municipal regulation against wordy inscriptions may have given countenance to such economies).[118] The very silence of this people that was never at a loss for words to express its meaning whether in verse or in prose, is in itself expressive. Where so little need was felt to give utterance to hopes of comfort, such hopes cannot have been of very vital consequence or matters of much assurance. Men rescued from forgetfulness only what had been the exclusive property of the individual—his name: the appellation which had distinguished him from all others in his lifetime and has now become the barest and emptiest envelope of the once living personality. Inscriptions in which precise hopes of a future life are expressed form a very small proportion of the great mass of epitaphic records. And of these very few again are in prose. Not as simple records of plain and authentic fact do such provisions and announcements of a blessed and hoped-for futurity present themselves. They need the artistic pomp and circumstance with which poetic fancy and extravagant affection clothe their inspired voyagings beyond the region of cold and matter of fact reality. This is certainly significant. Even among the poetic epitaphs the majority allude only to the life which the deceased has now done with, looking back upon the circumstances of his life—his fortunes and activities and character; giving expression, often with the most convincing sincerity, to the regret and dependence of the survivors; fixing attention exclusively upon things of this world. Wherever, at last, allusion is made to a future life, the tendency is rather to let fancy roam far beyond the limits of experience and sober reflexion to a vague and visionary land of promise. Such lofty aspirations needed more than any others the elevated language of verse. But we should run the risk of falling into grave error if we concluded from the preponderance of such aspirations among the metrical epitaphs that these were the normal views of the city folk who were their contemporaries.

The simple and archaic conception which perpetuates the old Homeric attitude and views without a complaint or a regret the disappearance of the soul of the departed into Erebos, is of the rarest occurrence among these sepulchral verses.[119] More commonly we have the prayer that the departed may " rest in peace ", expressed in the traditional formula [120]—a formula that really refers to the dead man lying in his grave but also contains a further allusion to the " soul " that has departed to Hades.[121] The idea is not yet dead that there is a realm of the souls which receives the departed—Hades, the world ruled over by the Underworld deities, the "Chamber" of Persephone, the seat of primeval Night.[122] Here a state of semi-conscious existence is conceived to prevail, under the empire of "Forgetfulness", drinking of which[123] the consciousness of the soul is darkened. Here "the majority"[124] are assembled, and the dead man is visited by the reassuring thought that he may greet once more the souls of those who have gone before him.[125]

But sterner conceptions also occur. There is occasional reference to a judgment[126] that separates the souls in the world below, dividing them into two and sometimes three[127] classes in accordance with the deserts which they have earned on earth. There is no lingering over the pains of the damned,[128] in the description of which the theological imagination had indulged so frequently. A more simple-minded fancy did not need such pharisaical satisfaction in the misfortunes of sinners in order to heighten its own assurance of superiority. There is no trace of a sentiment of penitence and terror indulged in for its own sake. The soul hopes to come by its rights;[129] to reach the "Blessed", to arrive at the Isles or the Island of the Blest—to Elysium, the abode of Heroes and demi-gods.[130] Such hopes are very commonly expressed, but as a rule only in a brief phrase of confidence and hope. We rarely meet with any elaborate or alluring picture of the abode of the blessed.[131] That abode is generally placed within the limits of the underworld kingdom of the souls,[132] and such anticipations, when particularized, refer commonly to a "Place of the Good", which in various forms is represented as the hoped-for dwelling-place of future life.[133]

But we also meet with the view that the company of the good is entirely removed from the region of underworld darkness.[134] For many individuals the hope is expressed or the certainty announced that after death they will have their dwelling in the sky—in the shining *Aether*, among the stars. This belief in the elevation of the disembodied soul to the regions above the earth is so frequently repeated in various forms in this late period that we must suppose that among those who entertained precise conceptions of the things of the next world this was the most popular and widely held conviction.[135] This belief that the soul rises to the neighbourhood and even the community of the heavenly deities[136] has its origin both in religious aspiration and in philosophy. Its roots, indeed, stretch back to a much earlier period [137] and we may suppose that even in these later days it was derived from and very largely supported by the popular conception, disseminated by Stoic writers, of a living " breath ", which composes the human soul, and its effort upwards to the heavenly regions.[138]

But such language is in many cases plainly nothing more than a conventional formula which has already lost all vital significance; it rarely goes further than the expression of a hope that the soul will mount upwards to the heavenly heights. Very occasionally, in the adjective " immortal " [139] applied to the soul (which only sleeps in death),[140] we may detect the influence of mixed philosophical and theological ideas. We soon come to an end of the inscriptions which give expression to the doctrines of theology and of theologically minded philosophy as to the divine nature of the soul, its brief pilgrimage through earthly life and destined return to its true home in a divine incorporeal existence.[141] There is no certain mention of a belief in the transmigration of souls.[142] Of the specifically Platonic doctrine or its influence there is scarcely a trace.[143]

Another type of belief derives its strength not from the teachings of philosophers but from the usage and popular practice of religion. This is the belief of those who hope to be conducted after death to a blessed life by the special care of a god, presumably the god to which in their life-time they have offered particular devotion. Such a god will lead them by the hand, they hope, and conduct them into the land of bliss and purity. One who has thus " obtained a god as his leader " [144] may face the future with equanimity. Together with Hermes the " messenger of Persephoneia ",[145] Persephone herself is most frequently mentioned among these conducting deities.[146] Perhaps in this we may see a reminiscence of the hopes awakened and cherished in the Eleusinian and other related mysteries [147]—hopes otherwise expressed on these tombstones with striking rarity. On the epitaph—certainly a late composition—of a Hierophant of Eleusis who " goes to the Immortals ", the dead man is made to commend, as a mystery revealed by the gods, the ancient opinion illustrated by stories like that of Kleobis and Biton [148] " that death not only brings no evil to mortals, but is rather a blessing ".[149] A gloomy philosophy has in these latter days of the old religion and worship of the gods taken hold of the mysteries themselves and given them an attitude of hostility to human life that was not originally theirs.[150] We are reminded of the mysteries again when we find prayers or promises that the dead shall not drink of the water of forgetfulness in the realm of the souls, but shall be given the "cold water" to drink by the God of the lower world; that he shall be refreshed at the spring of Mnemosyne, the bath of immortality, and so preserve intact his memory and consciousness, the necessary conditions of full and blessed life.[151] Here there appears to be a reference to the promises made by particular secret cults in which the departed has specially recommended himself to the powers of life and death. This must plainly be the case when, instead of the Greek Aidoneus, there is mention of Osiris, the Egyptian Lord of Souls. "May Osiris give you the cold water" is a common prayer expressed in a formula that is of frequent and significant occurrence in late epitaphs.[152] Of the numerous secret cults of these later times that promised a blessed immortality to their adherents, there is but infrequent mention in the grave-inscriptions: occasionally at the most there is an allusion to the special favour, reaching even beyond the grave, which belongs to the initiated in the mysteries of Mithras.[153]

No doubtful promises, but real and practical experience forms the basis of the belief of those to whom the dead has appeared visibly in a dream to assure them that his "soul" has not been annihilated by death.[154] The oldest proof of the continued existence of the soul remains in force the longest. The pupil hopes for something higher from the master whom death has taken away from his sight: he prays to him that, as he had once in life, so he will now continue to stand by his side, assisting him in the pursuance of his profession as a physician—"Thou canst, for now thou hast a more divine part in life."[155]

Expectations of an energetic after-life of the departed soul, expressing themselves in many forms, are widely current; but such expectations never achieve a unified, dogmatic form. Nor was anyone forbidden to cherish for himself and inscribe upon his grave-stone, unorthodox opinions of every kind—even though they should point to the very opposite of such expectations.[156]

A dubious "If" precedes on many epitaphs the anticipation of a conscious life of the dead in full possession of the senses, or a reward of the dead in accordance with their deserts: "if anything yet remains below". Such phrases are of very frequent occurrence.[157] Indeed the doubt itself is set aside when it is distinctly asserted that after death nothing of the man remains alive. All that men say of Hades and its terrors or its consolations is the fabled invention of poets; darkness and nothingness is all that awaits us below.[158] The dead turns to ashes or to earth; [159] the elements out of which he was created take back what is their own.[160] Life is only lent to man and in death he restores the loan again.[161] In death he pays tribute to nature.[162] The bitter outcry of the survivors against death, the savage beast of prey, loveless and pitiless, that has snatched away their dearest from their side, shows small hope of the preservation of the vanished life.[163] Grief and complaint, say others, are vain both for the dead and for the living; no man returns; the parting effected by death is for ever.[164] Only submission is left.[165] "Take comfort, child, no man is immortal"—so runs the conventional phrase current among the populace and inscribed by many upon the graves of their vanished dead.[166] "Once I was not, then I was, and now I am no more: what more is there to be said?"—so speaks the dead from more than one gravestone, addressing the living who is soon to suffer the same fate.[167] "Live," he cries to the living, "for there is nothing sweeter granted to us mortals than this life in the daylight." [168] A last thought reverts once more to the life that has been left behind on earth. The body dies, personality vanishes, nothing is left alive on earth but the memory of the deeds and virtue of the departed.[169] But there is a continuance in the life of others, more vital than in the empty sound of fame, achieved by him who leaves behind him on earth children and children's children. There are many who, in these later ages too, are content, in the true spirit of Antiquity, with this blessing and desire no other consolation for their own annihilation.[170]

§ 6

But such reassertions of the antique temper were of rarer and rarer occurrence. The ancient world to which it had given such toughness and energy of purpose was on its death-bed. With the end of the third and the beginning of the fourth century it enters upon its last agony; a general failure of nerve had long threatened the loosely bound masses that shared in the Græco-Roman civilization. In the general atrophy that beset its old age the vigorous blood of the genuine and unadultered Greek and Roman stocks was flowing but feebly. Now the universal process of decay sets in irresistibly. It was its own inherent weakness that made the attacks of outside forces so ominous to the old world. In the West the old order vanished more swiftly and submitted more completely to the new forces, than in the Hellenized East. It was not that the old civilization was any less rotten in the East than in the West. The enfeebled hand and the failing mind betray themselves in every utterance—in the last spasms of vital energy that inspired the art and literature of moribund Greece. The impoverishment of the vital forces out of which Greece had once brought forth the flower of its special and characteristic spirit makes itself felt in the altered relation of the individual to the whole, and of the totality of visible life to the shadowy powers of the unseen world. Individualism has had its day. No longer is the emancipation of the individual the object of man's endeavour; no longer is he required to arm himself against all that is not himself, that is outside the region of his free will and choice. He is not strong enough, and should not feel himself strong enough, to trust to the self-conscious strength of his own intelligence. Authority—an authority that is the same for all—must be his guide. Rationalism is dead. In the last years of the second century a religious reaction begins to assert itself and makes itself felt more and more in the period that follows. Philosophy itself becomes at last a religion, drawing its nourishment from surmise and revelation. The invisible world wins the day over the meagre present, so grievously bound down by the limitation of mere experience. No longer does the soul await with courage and calmness whatever may be hidden behind the dark curtain of death. Life seemed to need something to complete it. And how faded and grey life had become[171]—a rejuvenation upon this earth seemed to be out of the question. All the more complete, in consequence, is the submission that throws itself with closed eyes and eager yearning upon another world, situated now far beyond the limits of the known or knowable world of the living. Hopes and a vague longing, a shrinking before the mysterious terrors of the unknown, fill the soul. Never in the history of the ancient world is the belief in an immortal life of the soul after death a matter of such burning and exacerbated ardour as in these last days when the antique civilization was preparing itself to breathe its last.

Hopes of immortality, widely espoused by the masses and fed rather on faith than on reflexion, sought satisfaction in the brilliant ceremonial of religions that easily outshone the simple worship of every day officially undertaken by the city. In these new rites the worshippers united in the secret cult seemed to be placed more directly in the hands of the gods; and, above all, a blessed existence hereafter was assured to pious believers. In these days the ancient and hallowed mysteries of Eleusis awake to a new life and remain in vigorous activity till nearly the end of the fourth century.[172] Orphic conventicles must have attracted worshippers for ages; [173] the Hellenized Orient was familiar with many such orgiastic cults.

In the mixed populations of the East the new religions proved more attractive to the Greeks, too, than their old worship of the gods of Greece. Clear and definite obligations, fixed commandments and dogmas, holding the weak and frail individual in their stronger embrace, seemed to belong more peculiarly to these foreign worships than to the old beliefs of Greece. Rigid and unalterable maintenance of primitive ideas and practices seemed to give the former the stamp of sacred and certain knowledge. From all men they demanded perfect submission to the God and his priests; perfect renunciation of the world, conceived as dualistically opposed to the divine; the purging away of the contamination of its lusts by purifications and sanctifications, ceremonial expiations and asceticisms. By these means the faithful prepared themselves for the highest reward that piety could conceive; an unending life of bliss far away from this unclean world in the realm of the holy and the consecrated. To the belief in a blessed immortality these foreign mysteries contributed their much desired support; and the populace welcomed their message of salvation with all the greater eagerness since their varied and impressive ceremonial contrasted so strikingly with the plain and homely worship of the Greek gods. In the symbolism of these exotic cults men seemed to discern a mysterious and secret knowledge; and to the divine figures illuminated by such a halo were easily attributed strange and magical powers beyond belief or experience. The cult of the Egyptian deities had long been familiar both in the East and in the West, and they maintained and extended their influence down to the last days of the ancient religions. The Phrygian deities, the Thraco-Phrygian cults of Sabazios, Attis, and Kybele, and the Persian worship of Mithras were later comers, but they, too, took equally firm root and spread over the whole extent of the empire.[174]

The higher culture of these last centuries, having become credulous and avid of marvels, no longer looked with contempt upon the means of salvation and sanctification which had once been left almost entirely to the lower orders of the population. The most cultivated and educated people of these times used their culture and their education simply to justify everything mysterious and incomprehensible in itself—even when it was expressed in the most physical symbolism. The newly awakened religious interest of the populace had coincided with a return on the part of philosophy to the teaching of Plato ; a teaching which itself tended towards religion. Platonism had invaded the doctrine of other schools at many points, and it had already acquired a new home for itself in the restored Academy, where once an un-Platonic Scepticism had overthrown the teaching of the master. Now a new Platonism comes forward and overwhelms all the other schools of philosophy. Absorbing the doctrines of Aristotle and Chrysippos (which it fancied it could reconcile with Platonism), it weaved them into its own special teaching so that the whole presented a subtle and far-reaching system of thought. The speculative system of Neoplatonism, into which the old age of Greece, in spite of its weariness, contrived to introduce so much profundity, spirit, and ingenuity (together with a luxuriant mass of scholastic folly), fills the history of the last centuries of Greek thought. Its fundamental tendency is, once more, a turning away from the life of nature, and a determined invasion of a transcendent world of pure spirit ; and it was by this tendency that it satisfied the needs of its time. The Sole and First Cause, lying beyond all being and continually expressing itself in creative emanations, yet never troubled or impaired in its perfect and eternal transcendency ; the development, in an unbroken process from this One, of the world of thinking, of the Ideas and pure thought preserved in it—the world of Spirit and the world of Matter—until at last, in longing and desire,[175] all things created return to the origin of all Being : to describe and express all this is the single theme, persisting throughout all variations, of this philosophy. The whole fabric of reality, the interplay of cause and effect, depends upon the inherence of the thing caused in its Cause from which it takes its origin and to which it returns at last. That which in the evolution of nature takes its origin from the One, and degenerates more and more completely, in the darkness and corruption of Matter, as it gets further away from its source—now becomes Man and seeks in morality and religion a conscious return to the pure and everlasting and unfailing One. The divine does not descend to earth and man must reach upwards to the divine heights in order to unite himself with the One that is before all multiplicity. This union can be brought about by the pure exercise of the human reason, but also in the mysterious harmony of the individual life with the First Cause that is beyond all reason in the ecstasy that is above all rationality. It can be achieved when at last the whole series of rebirths has been passed through, whereupon the pure soul, the divine in man, enters into the divinity of the Whole.[176]

To fly from the world—not to work within the world to produce something better—is the teaching and injunction of this last Greek philosophy. Away from all separate, divided Being, upward towards the uninterrupted glory of the One divine life, the soul wings its way. The world, this visible world of matter, is fair, says Plotinos, for it is the work and image of the divine, present and working in it. A last gleam of the departing sunlight of Greek sensibility seems to break through the words in which Plotinos rejects the Christian-Gnostic hatred of the world.[177] The ugly, he says, is strange and contrary to God as well as to Nature.[178] But the soul must no longer rest in the world of created beauty.[179] The soul is so profoundly conscious of its derivation from the suprasensual, of its divinity and eternity, that it must rise above all created being and reach out to the One that was before the world and remains for ever outside the world.[180]

This philosophy, profoundly estranged though it was from the old Greek attitude to life with its enjoyment of the world, nevertheless felt itself called upon to oppose the rising tide of the new and irresistible religion. It took under its protection the ancient Greek culture and the ancient faith that was so inseparably bound up with that culture. Its most convinced supporters, with the last of the Emperors of the old faith at their head, threw themselves whole-heartedly into the fray. And before them rode the Genius of ancient Hellas, and the old beliefs of Greece. But when the battle had been fought and lost it became apparent to all the world that it was a corpse that rode before the exalted combatants, like the body of the dead Cid Campeador fastened upon his horse and leading his hosts against the Moors. The ancient religion of Greece, and with it the whole civilized life of the Greek world, faded and died at that discovery, and could not be recalled to life. A newer faith, very differently endowed and having power to crush the heavily laden soul and point it upwards in absolute submission to the divine compassion, held the field. The new world that was coming into being had need of it.

And yet—was Greece quite extinguished and dead for ever? Much—only too much—of the philosophy of its old age lived on in the speculative system of the Christian faith. And in the whole of modern culture so far as it has built itself upon

Christianity or by extension from it, in all modern science and art, not a little survives of Greek genius and Greek inspiration. The outward embodiment of Hellas is gone; its spirit is imperishable. Nothing that has once been alive in the spiritual life of man can ever perish entirely; it has achieved a new form of existence in the consciousness of mankind—an immortality of its own. Not always in equal measure, nor always in the same place, does the stream of Greek thought rise to the surface in the life of mankind. But it is a river that never quite runs dry: it vanishes, to reappear; it buries itself to emerge again. *Desinunt ista, non pereunt.*

NOTES TO CHAPTER XIV

PART II

[1] See above, chap. v, p. 162 f.

[2] Lucian 50, *De Luctu*: washing, anointing, crowning of the dead body, πρόθεσις: c. 11. Violent dirge-singing over the dead, 12; accompanied by the αὐλός, 19; and led by a special singer θρηνῶν σοφιστής, 20. Special lament by the father, 13. The dead is before them with jaws tied up and so secured against unsightly gaping, 19 fin. (a stronger form of the Homeric σύν τε στόμ' ἐρείδειν, λ 426). For this purpose narrow bands are drawn round the chin, cheeks, and forehead of the dead man. We sometimes see them represented on vases depicting a lying-in-state, and they have also been found sometimes in graves in which case they have been made of metal (gold or lead): see Wolters, *Ath. Mitth.* 1896, p. 367 ff. ἐσθής, κόσμος (even including horses and slaves) burnt or buried in company with the dead for his pleasure, 14. ὀβολός given to the dead, 10. The dead fed by χοαί and καθαγίσματα, 9. The gravestone crowned; sprinkled with ἄκρατος; burnt offering, 19. περίδειπνον after a three days' fast, 24.

[3] From a rather earlier period we hear that it is a bad thing to be dead μὴ τυχόντα τῶν νομίμων—it is an infamous deed for the son to deny his father τὰ νομιζόμενα after death; Din., *Aristog.* viii, 18; cf. [D.] 25, 54.—The dead man says with satisfaction πάνθ' ὅσα τοῖς χρηστοῖς φθιμένοις νόμος ἐστὶ γενέσθαι τῶνδε τυχὼν κἀγὼ τόνδε τάφον κατέχω, *Epigr. Gr.*, 137; cf. 153, 7–8.

[4] ὁμόταφοι are mentioned among other associations as occurring in a Solonian law: *Digest.* 47, 22, 4. These would probably be special *collegia funeraticia* (at any rate societies of which the exclusive or essential bond of union consisted in ὁμοῦ ταφῆναι—and not, therefore, any of the ordinary θίασοι or any "gentilician association" as Ziebarth thinks, *Gr. Vereinswesen*, p. 17 [1896]). There are also traces (but not very frequent) of common burial grounds belonging to θίασοι; e.g. in Kos, *Inscr. Cos*, 155–9. ἐρανισταί bury their dead member, *CIA.* ii, 3308; συμμύσται do the same, *Ath. Mitt.* ix, 35. A member contributes as ταμίας of the *collegium* out of his own means, for the benefit of dead members of an ἔρανος, εἰς τὴν ταφήν, τοῦ εὐσχημονεῖν αὐτοὺς καὶ τετελευτηκότας κτλ., *CIA.* ii, 621 (about 150 B.C.). Another ταμίας δέδωκεν τοῖς μεταλλάξασιν (θιασώταις) τὸ ταφικὸν παραχρῆμα ins. from Attica, third century B.C. *CIA.* iv, 2, 623b; cf. ib., 615b, l. 14–15; Rhod. inscr. in *BCH.* iv, 138. Dionysiastai, Athenaistai in Tanagra ἔθαψαν τὸν δεῖνα: *GDI.* 960–2 (*IG. Sept.* i, 685–9). The Iobakchai in Athens (third century A.D.) offer a crown and wine at the burial of a member: *Ath. Mitt.* 1894, 261, l. 158 ff. οἱ θίασοι πάντες and even οἱ ἔφηβοι καὶ οἱ νέοι, ὁ δῆμος, ἡ γερουσία erect the monument, *CIG.* 3101, 3112. (Teos) συνοδεῖται bury together the members of their σύνοδοι, *IPE.* ii, 60–5. A gymnasiarch also undertakes τῶν ἐκκομιδῶν ἐπιμέλειαν, *Inscr. Perg.* ii, 252, l. 16; noteworthy also is ii, 374 B, l. 21–5. A few more exx. are given by E. Loch, *Zu d. griech. Grabschriften* (*Festschr. Friedländer*, 1895), p. 288.

[5] δημοσία ταφή frequently. Resolution πανδημεὶ παραπέμψασθαι τὸ σῶμα τοῦ δεῖνος ἐπὶ τὴν κηδείαν αὐτοῦ, inscr. of Amorgos, *BCH.* 1891, p. 577 (l. 26); p. 586 (l. 17 ff.). Resolution of the council and people of Olbia (first century B.C.): when the body of a certain deserving citizen who has died abroad is brought into the city, all workshops are to close, the citizens wearing black shall follow his ἐκφορά; an equestrian statue of the dead man to be erected and every year at the ἱπποδρομίαι of Achilles the golden crown granted to the dead man to be proclaimed, etc.: *IPE.* i, 17, 22 ff.—Honour paid to a dead man by granting a golden crown, *CIG.* 3185; cf. Cic., *Flac.* 75. This example comes from Smyrna, where such honours were particularly common: see Böckh on *CIG.* 3216. Frequent on Asia Minor inss.: ἁ πόλις sc. στεφανοῖ, ἔθαψεν, τὸν δεῖνα. ὁ δᾶμος τῷ δεῖνι, sc. ἀνέθηκε, on graves: see esp. G. Hirschfeld, *Greek Inscr. in Brit. Mus.* iv, 1, p. 34. More ap. Loch, op. cit., p. 287.

[6] This seems to have been particularly common in Amorgos: cf. *CIG.* 2264b; four inss. from Amorgos, *BCH.* 1891, p. 574 (153–4 B.C.), 577, 586 (242 B.C.), 588 f. The Council of the Areopagos and the people of Athens decree the erection of a statue in honour of a young man of rank (T. Statilius Lamprias) who has died πρὸ ὥρας in Epidauros, and also the dispatch of envoys to παραμυθήσασθαι ἀπὸ τοῦ τῆς πόλεως ὀνόματος his parents and his grandfather Lamprias. In the same way the citizens of Sparta send an embassy of sympathy and consolation to other relatives of the same youth (first century A.D.), *Fouil. d'Epidaur.* i, 205–9, pp. 67–70. Honorific decree of council and people of Corinth for the same person, *'Εφ. 'Αρχ.*, 1894, p. 15. ψηφίσματα παραμυθητικά of two Lydian cities at the death of a man of rank (first century A.D.), *Anz. Wien. Ak.*, Phil. Hist. Cl., 16th Nov., 1893 (n. 24) = *Ath. Mitt.* 1894, p. 102 f.; cf. Paros, *CIG.* 2383 (the council and people decree the erection of a stutue to a dead boy ἐπὶ μέρους παραμυθησόμενοι τὸν πατέρα); Aphrodisias in Karia, *CIG.* 277b, 2775b–d; Neapolis, *CIG.* 5836 = *IG. Sic. It.* 758.—The grounds of consolation, so far as they are alluded to, are regularly independent of any theological teaching: φέρειν συμμέτρως τὰ τῆς λύπης εἰδότας ὅτι ἀπαραίτητός ἐστιν ἡ ἐπὶ πάντων ἀνθρώπων μοῖρα and the like (φέρειν τὸ συμβεβηκὸς ἀνθρωπίνως, *F. d'Epid.* i, 209). We are reminded of the παραμυθητικοὶ λόγοι of the philosophers which are literary expressions of these consolations—the philosophers in fact were expected *ex officio* to offer such consolations to the mourners, cf. Plu., *Superst.* 186 C; D. Chr. 27, § 9 (ii, 285 Arn.).

[7] In spite of any brevity in the narrative the fact of ritual burial is regularly alluded to (as an important circumstance) in the romance of Xen. Eph. and in the *Historia Apollonii*: *Griech. Roman*, 391, 3; 413, 1.

[8] At Athens his friend vainly tries to obtain burial *intra urbem* for the murdered Marcellus: quod religione se impediri dicerent; neque id antea cuiquam concesserunt (while in Rome people were occasionally buried in the city in spite of the prohibition of the XII tables: Cic., *Lg.* ii, 58): Servius to Cicero, *Fam.* 4, 12, 3 (45 B.C.). There it was permitted uti in quo vellent gymnasio eum sepelirent and finally his body was cremated and the remains buried in nobilissimo orbis terrarum gymnasio, the Academy. ἐνταφὰ καὶ θέσις τοῦ σώματος ἐν τῷ γυμνασίῳ (of an aristocratic Roman) in Kyme: *GDI.* 311. To a living benefactor of that city συνεχωρήθη καὶ ἐνταφῆναι (in the future) ἐν τῷ γυμνασίῳ, *CIG.* 279b (Aphrodisias in Karia). As a special mark of honour paid to a benefactor of the city it is permitted that his body in oppidum introferatur (into Smyrna: Cic., *Flac.* 75), ἐνταφὰ κατὰ πόλιν καὶ

ταφὰ δημοσίᾳ, ἐνταφὰ κατὰ πόλιν ἐν τῷ ἐπισαμοτάτῳ τοῦ γυμνασίου τόπῳ, Knidos, *GDI.* 3501, 3502 (time of Augustus). The city buries a youth γυμνάδος ἐν τεμένει, *Epigr. Gr.* 222 (Amorgos).—Ulpian, *Dig.* 47, 12, 3, 5, implies the possibility that lex municipalis permittat in civitate sepeliri.

[9] σῆμα, i.e. probably grave and monument, of Messia set up by her husband in his own house: *Epigr. Gr.* 682 (Rome).

[10] Thus *Inscr. Perg.* ii, 590, ζῶν ὁ δεῖνα κατεσκεύασε τὸ μνημεῖον τῇ ἰδίᾳ μάμμῃ . . . καὶ τῷ πάππῳ, ἑαυτῷ, γυναικί, τέκνοις, ἐκγόνοις ἀνεξαλλοτρίωτον ἕως διαδοχῆς κτλ. Similar directions, ib., n. 591, and frequently. The series includes the old and traditional circle of the ἀγχιστεῖς: see above, chap. v, nn. 141 and 146 (where μέχρι ἀνεψιαδῶν παίδων should be read).

[11] There was even a Solonian law against violation and plunder of tombs: Cic., *Lg.* ii, 64. The specially invented word τυμβωρύχος shows that such practices were frequent at a quite early period; cf. σημάτων φῶρα, Herond. v, 57. Complaint on account of the rifling of a tomb: Egypt. papyr. of 127 B.C., *Notices et extraits*, xviii, 2, p. 161 f. Frequent rescripts of emperors of the fourth century against the profanation of graves, *Cod. Theod.* ix, 17. But even emperors of second and third centuries had to deal with the subject: *Dig.* 47, 12, and cf. Paul., *Sent.* 1, 21, 4 ff.; *sepulchri violati actio*, Quint., *Decl.* 299, 369, 373. Grave-thieves were a favourite character in romance: e.g. ap. Xen. Eph., Chariton and others. Epigram of Greg. Naz. on the subject of looted graves, *Anth. Pal.* viii, 176 ff. From the fourth century the Christians in particular seem to have been a danger to heathen burial places (cf. Gothofred., ad *Cod. Theod.* iii, p. 150 Ritt.)—in fact, ecclesiastics were specially given to grave-robbery: *Novell. Valentin.* 5 (p. 111 Ritt.), Cassiod., *Var.* iv, 18; *bustuarii latrones* (Amm. Marc. 28, 1, 12), were then frequent. An Egyptian anchorite had at an earlier period become latronum maximus et sepulchrorum violator: Rufin., *Vit. Patr.* 9 (p. 446b Rossw.).

[12] Inscrr. indicating such sepulchral penalties are rare on the mainland of Greece, common in Thrace and the Greek cities of Asia Minor, but most frequent of all in Lykia. Most of them belong to the Roman period, but also appeal occasionally to τὸν τῆς ἀσεβείας νόμον of the city (cf. also Korkyra, *CIG.* 1933); or refer to the ἔγκλημα τυμβωρυχίας as though it were a local process of law which had perhaps been confirmed by an Imperial ordinance (ὑπεύθυνος ἔστω τοῖς διατάγμασι καὶ τοῖς πατρίοις νόμοις, inscr. from Tralles: see Hirschfeld, p. 121). They therefore cannot be simply borrowed from the Roman custom, but belong to the old law of the country esp. in Lykia where a similar prescription has been found dating from the third century B.C.: *CIG.* 4529; see Hirschfeld, *Königsb. Stud.* i, pp. 85–144 (1887)—doubt is thrown on the legal validity of the penal clauses in such inscrr. by J. Merkel, *Festg. f. Ihering*, p. 109 ff. (1892).

[13] Curses directed against those who bury unauthorized persons in a grave or damage the monument are rare in European Greece: e.g. Aegina, *CIG.* 2140b; Thessaly, *BCH.* xv, 568; Athens, *CIA.* iii, 1417–28; among these is a Thessalian grave, 1427; a Christian, 1428; 1417–22 are set up by Herodes Atticus to Apia Regilla and Polydeukion (cf. K. Keil, Pauly-Wiss. i, 2101), but his coquetting with the cult of the χθόνιοι proves nothing for the common opinion of his fellow citizens. Sepulchral curses are particularly common in inss. from Lykia and Phrygia; also Cilicia, *JHS.* 1891, p. 228, 231, 267; a few also from Halikarnassian graves; Samos, *CIG.* 2260.—The

grave and its peace are placed under the care of the underworld deities in these inss.: παραδίδωμι τοῖς καταχθονίοις θεοῖς τοῦτο τὸ ἡρῷον φυλάσσειν κτλ., *CIA*. iii, 1423–4. Cf. also a Cretan inscr. *Ath. Mitt.* 1893, p. 211. Whoever introduces a stranger into the grave or damages the grave ἀσεβὴς ἔστω θεοῖς καταχθονίοις (thus in Lykia, *CIG*. 4207; 4290; 4292), ἀσεβήσει τὰ περὶ τοὺς θεούς τε καὶ θεὰς πάσας καὶ ἥρωας πάντας (from Itonos in Phthiotis, *BCH*. xv, 568). ἁμαρτωλὸς ἔστω θεοῖς καταχθονίοις, *CIG*. 4252b, 4259, 4300e, i, k, v, 4307, 4308; *BCH*. 1894, p. 326 (n. 9)—all from Lykia. (The formula occurs already in a Lyk. inscr. of 240 B.C.; *BCH*. 1890, p. 164: ἁμαρτωλοὶ ἔστωσαν—the archons and citizens who neglect to offer the yearly sacrifice to Zeus Soter—θεῶν πάντων καὶ ἀποτινέτω ὁ ἄρχων κτλ., which thus corresponds exactly with the oldest Lyk. inscr. with sepulchral penalty, *CIG*. 4259). ἔστω ἱερόσυλος θεοῖς οὐρανίοις καὶ καταχθονίοις, *CIG*. 4253 (Pinara in Lykia). This must mean: he shall be regarded as having transgressed the *law* against ἀσέβεια, ἱεροσυλία (cf. οἱ νόμοι οἱ περὶ ἱεροσύλου, Teos, *SIG*. 523, 51), τυμβωρυχία, having at the same time offended against the gods (see Hirschfeld, op. cit., p. 120 f.). More particular is another Lyk. ins.: ἁμαρτωλὸς ἔστω θεῶν πάντων καὶ Λητοῦς καὶ τῶν τέκνων (as the special gods of the country), *CIG*. 4259, 4303, (iii, p. 1138), 4303 e[3] (p. 1139). In Cilicia ἔστω ἠσεβηκὼς ἔς τε τὸν Δία καὶ τὴν Σελήνην, *JHS*. xii, 231. Phrygian: κεχολωμένον ἔχοιτο Μῆνα καταχθόνιον, *BCH*. 1886, p. 503, 6; cf. ἐνορκιζόμεθα Μῆνα καταχθόνιον εἰς τοῦτο μνημεῖον μηδένα εἰσελθεῖν, *Amer. School at Athens* iii, 174. The same is intended by the peculiarly Phrygian denunciation ἔστω αὐτῷ πρὸς τὸν θεόν, πρὸς τὴν χεῖρα τοῦ θεοῦ, πρὸς τὸ μέγα ὄνομα τοῦ θεοῦ, *CIG*. 3872b (p. 1099), 3890, 3902 f.o., 3963; *Amer. School* iii, 411; *BCH*. 1893, p. 246 ff. That these are Christian formulae—as Ramsay, *JHS*. iv, p. 400 f., supposes—is hardly likely. Equally unlikely in the case of 3902r (Franz rightly protests against the idea): ἔσται αὐτῷ πρὸς τὸν ζῶντα θεόν (the same occurs again in a decisively non-Christian sense: *BCH*. 1893, p. 241) καὶ νῦν καὶ ἐν τῷ κρισίμῳ ἡμέρᾳ (κρίσις apparently = death in *CIG*. 6731, from Rome, which, considering the words ἄγαλμά εἰμι Ἡλίου, can hardly be Christian). τῆς τοῦ θεοῦ ὀργῆς μεθέξεται, *CIA*. iii, 1427. Obscure threat: οὐ γὰρ μὴ συνείκῃ . . ., *CIG*. 2140b (Aegina). The profaner of graves is cursed in more detail: τούτῳ μὴ γῆ βατή, μὴ θάλασσα πλωτή, ἀλλὰ ἐκρειζωθήσεται παγγένει (the ἀραί on the inss. of Herod. Att. agree so far at least in intention, *CIA*. iii, 1417–22). πᾶσι τοῖς κακοῖς πεῖραν δώσει, καὶ φρείκῃ καὶ πυρετῷ καὶ τεταρταίῳ καὶ ἐλέφαντι κτλ., *CIA*. iii, 1423–4 (similar curse on a lead tablet from Crete: *Ath. Mitt.* 1893, p. 211). The first half of this imprecation represents the regular formula in such ἀραί and ὅρκοι—μὴ γῆ βατή κτλ.; cf. Wünsch, *Defix.*, p. vii, and a Jewish-Greek inscr. from Euboea: Ἐφ. Ἀρχ., 1892, p. 175; it occurs also in *CIG*. 2664, 2667 (Halikarnassos); 4303 (p. 1138 Phrygia). δώσει τοῖς καταχθονίοις θεοῖς δίκην, 4190 (Cappadocia). ὄρφανα τέκνα λίποιτο, χῆρον βιόν, οἶκον ἔρημον, ἐν πυρὶ πάντα δάμοιτο, κακῶν ὕπο χεῖρας ὄλοιτο, 3862, 3875, 400 (Phrygia). These are all peculiarly and originally *Phrygian*; something similar seems to occur in inss. in the Phrygian language: see *Ztschr. vergl. Sprachf.* 28, 381 ff.; *BCH*. 1896, p. 111 ff. Phrygian, too, is the curse οὗτος δ' ἀώροις περιπέσοιτο συμφοραῖς, *Epigr. Gr.*, p. 149, *Amer. Sch. Ath.* ii, 168—i.e. may his children die ἄωροι. (More plainly τέκνων ἀώρων περιπέσοιτο συμφορᾷ, *BCH*. 1893, p. 272.) Sometimes the additional phrase is found καὶ μετὰ θάνατον δὲ λάβοι τοὺς ὑποχθονίους θεοὺς τιμωροὺς καὶ κεχολωμένους,

CIG. 3915 (Phrygian). Besides the common imprecations we also have θανόντι δὲ οὐδὲ ἡ γῆ παρέξει αὐτῷ τάφον, 2826 (Aphrodisias in Karia); μήτε οὐρανὸς τὴν ψυχὴν αὐτοῦ παραδέξαιτο, *Am. Sch. Ath.* iii, 411 (Pisidia). Barbarous in the extreme is an inscr. from Cilicia (*JHS.* 1891, p. 267): ἕξει πάντα τὰ θεῖα κεχολωμένα καὶ τὰς στυγερὰς Ἐρεινύας καὶ ἰδίου τέκνου ἥπατος γεύσεται.—With these grave-imprecations we may compare also the threats uttered against those who shall neglect the directions for the honouring of King Antiochos of Kommagene who lies buried in his ἱεροθέσιον (ib, 13; iiib, 3: hence correct ἱεροθύσιον in Paus. 4, 32, 1) on the Nemrud Dagh: εἰδότας ὅτι χαλεπὴ νέμεσις βασιλικῶν δαιμόνων, τιμωρὸς ὁμοίως ἀμελίας τε καὶ ὕβρεως, ἀσέβειαν διώκει καθωσιωμένων τε ἡρώων ἀτειμασθεὶς νόμος ἀνειλάτους ἔχει ποινάς. τὰ μὲν γὰρ ὅσιον ἅπαν κουφὸν ἔργον, τῆς δὲ ἀσεβείας ὀπισθοβαρεῖς ἀναγκαί (iiia, 22 ff., *Ber. Berl. Akad.* 1883).

[14] From the point of view of religion, at any rate, it is true, though with considerable reservations, that most of the Greeks and Macedonians scattered over Asia and Egypt in *coloniae*, in Syros Parthos Aegyptios degenerarunt, Liv. 38, 17, 11–12. The only non-Greek nation (apart from the Romans) which learnt anything from the Greeks or from the semi-religious Greek philosophy was the Jewish—at once the most stubborn and the most pliable of them all.

[15] At a quite late period, in order to explain the impiety of grave-robbing, Valentinian says (following the libri veteris sapientiae quite as much as Christian teaching) licet occasus necessitatem mens divina (of man) non sentiat, amant tamen animae sedem corporum relictorum et nescio qua sorte rationis occultae sepulchri honore laetantur (*Nov. Valent.* v, p. 111 Ritt.).

[16] After the reception of the last person who has a right there ἀποιερῶσθαι τὸν πλάταν, ἀφηρωΐσθαι τὸ μνημεῖον, *CIG.* 2827, 2834. κορακωθήσεται, i.e. it will be finally shut up: 3919.

[17] ἐπεὰν δὲ τοῖς καμοῦσιν ἐγχυτλώσωμεν, Herond. v, 84 (i.e. at the end of the month: festival of the dead at the τριακάδες, see above, chap. v, n. 88. ἡμέρας ληγούσης καὶ μηνὸς φθίνοντος εἰώθασιν ἐναγίζειν οἱ πολλοί, Plu., *Q. Rom.* 34, p. 272 D). Offerings to the dead at the grave: see besides Luc., *Charon*, 22.

[18] Epikteta: see above, chap. v, n. 126. Traces of a similar foundation on an inscr. from Thera ap. Ross, *Inscr. Gr.* 198 (ii, p. 81).—Otherwise the son will perhaps offer to his father τὴν ταφὴν καὶ τὸν ἐναγισμόν (*CIG.* 1976, Thessalonike; 3645 Lampsakos)—τὸ ἡρῷον κατεσκεύασεν εἰς αἰώνιον μνήμην καὶ τῇ μετὰ θάνατον ἀφωσιωμένῃ θρησκείᾳ (*CIG.* 4224d, iii, p. 1119 Lykia). A dead man has left the council of a city a sum of money for a στεφανωτικόν (*CIG.* 3912, 3916 Hierapolis in Phrygia); i.e. in order that his grave may be crowned every year from the interest of the money: 3919. Another man leaves money to a society to celebrate his memory yearly by holding a εὐωχία with οἰνοποσία illumination and crowns: 3028 Ephesos. An annual feast in honour of a dead man's memory on his γενέθλιος ἡμέρα: 3417 Philadelphia in Lydia (this is the proper day for a feast of the dead: see above, chap. v, n. 89). Annual memorial in the month Ὑακίνθιος for a dead ἀρχιερανιστής in Rhodos, ἀναγόρευσις of his crowns of honour and crowning of his μνημεῖον, regular ἀναγόρευσις τᾶν τιμᾶν ἐν ταῖς συνόδοις (of the ἔρανος) καὶ ταῖς ἐπιχύσεσιν (second century B.C.), *IGM. Aeg.* i, 155, l. 53 ff., 67 ff. Another foundation, in Elatea (*BCH.* x, 382), seems to have been much more elaborate in intention and to have included the sacrifice of a bull, as well as εὐωχία and an ἀγών.

[19] *τάφος, δευόμενος γεράων*, inscr. from Athens (second century A.D.): *Ath. Mitt.* 1892, p. 272, l. 6. *θέλγειν ψυχὴν τεθνηκότος ἀνδρός* by libations at the grave: *Epigr. Gr.* 120, 9–10.

[20] The *ἀπόταφοι*: this is the name given to those *ἀπεστερημένοι τῶν προγονικῶν τάφων*, *EM.* 131, 44. They even had a burial place of their own: *ἀποτάφων τάφων* on a marble vase from Rhodos, *IGM. Aeg.* i, 656.

[21] This *χαῖρε* repeats the last farewell which accompanied the removal of the body from the house (Eur., *Alc.* 626 f.). Cf. *χαῖρέ μοι ὦ Πάτροκλε καὶ εἰν 'Αΐδαο δόμοισιν*, the words with which Achilles (Ψ 179) addresses his dead friend lying upon the funeral pyre. So too on tombstones *χαῖρε* must be intended to suggest the continued sympathy of the survivors and the appreciation by the dead of that sympathy. Does it also imply veneration of the departed as *κρείττων*? Gods and Heroes were also addressed with this word: cf. *χαῖρ' ἄναξ 'Ηράκλεες*, etc.—The passer-by calls out *χαῖρε*: *χαίρετε ἥρωες. ὁ παράγων σε ἀσπάζεται*, *Ath. Mitt.* ix, 263; and cf. *Epigr. Gr.* 218, 17–18; 237, 7–8; cf. Loch, op. cit., 278 f.

[22] *χαίρετε* is said by the dead man to the living: Böckh on *CIG.* 3775 (ii, p. 968); cf. *χαιρέτω ὁ ἀναγνούς*, *IG. Sic. et It.* [*IG.* xiv] 350.

[23] *χαίρετε ἥρωες. χαῖρε καὶ σὺ καὶ εὐόδει*, *CIG.* 1956 (more given by Böckh, ii, p. 50; see also on 3278); *Inscr. Cos*, 343; *IG. Sic. et It.* 60, 319; *BCH.* 1893–4, 242 (5), 249 (22), 528 (24), 533 (36); specially noteworthy is p. 529 (28), *Λεύκιε Λικίνιε χαῖρε. κὲ σύ γε ὦ παροδεῖτα* "*χαίροις ὅτι τοῦτο τὸ σεμνὸν | εἶπας ἐμοὶ χαίρειν εἵνεκεν εὐσεβίης*". To call upon the dead is an act of *εὐσέβεια*.

[24] At the burial of a woman who is being given a public funeral *ἐπεβόασε ὁ δᾶμος τρὶς τὸ ὄνομα αὐτᾶς*, *GDI.* 3504 (Knidos; in the time of Trajan). In the same way the name of the *ἥρως* was called out three times at a sacrifice in his honour: see above, chap. iv, n. 62.

[25] Tombstone of Q. Marcius Strato (circ. second century A.D.), *Ath. Mitt.* 1892, p. 272, l. 5 ff. *τοίγαρ ὅσοι Βρομίῳ Παφίῃ τε νέοι μεμέλησθε, δευόμενον γεράων μὴ μαρανεῖσθε τάφον ἀλλὰ παραστείχοντες ἢ οὔνομα κλεινὸν ὁμαρτῇ βωστρέετ' ἢ ῥαδινὰς συμπαταγεῖτε χέρας.* Those who are thus charged answer, *προσεννέπω Στράτωνα καὶ τιμῶ κρότῳ.*

[26] Often represented on Attic *lekythoi*: Pottier, *Les lécythes blancs*, p. 57.

[27] The gods and their statues are honoured in this way: Sittl, *Gebärden*, p. 182.

[28] *βελτίονες καὶ κρείττονες*, Arist., *Eudem. fr.* 37 [44].

[29] *χρηστοὺς ποιεῖν* euphemism for *ἀποκτιννύναι* in a treaty between Tegea and Sparta: Arist., *fr.* 542 [592]. They *become χρηστοί* only after death. This ancient and evidently popular expression gives far stronger grounds for believing that *χρηστός* was applied to the dead than does the passage from Thphr., *Ch.* x, 16 (xiii, 3), for the opposite view (the *περίεργος* writes on a tombstone that a dead woman and her family *χρηστοὶ ἦσαν*, from which Loch concludes that the word really "denotes a quality of the living and not of the dead", op. cit., 281). It is possible at the same time that those who used such words did not mean anything special by their *χρηστὲ χαῖρε*, and at any rate only thought of it as a vague adjective of praise. But that was not its real meaning.

[30] *χρηστὲ χαῖρε* and the like, with or without *ἥρως*, are very commonly met with on epitaphs from Thessaly, Boeotia, the countries of Asia Minor (and Cyprus as well: cf. *BCH.* 1896, pp. 343–6; 353–6). On

Attic graves the use of the title χρηστός seems to be confined to foreigners and those mostly slaves (see Keil, *Jahrb. Phil.* suppl. iv, 628; Gutscher, *Att. Grabinschr.* i, p. 24; ii, p. 13).

[31] With Gutscher, op. cit., i, 24; ii, 39.—From the fact that in Attica this word does not seem to be given to natives no conclusion is to be drawn as to the opinions held by the Athenians about their dead (as though they thought of them with less respect). The word was simply not traditional in this sense in Attica. On the other hand, the word μακαρίτης was specifically Attic as applied to the dead (see above, ch. vii, n. 10), and this provides unmistakable evidence that the conception of the dead as "blessed" was current also in Attica.

[32] χρηστῶν θεῶν, Hdt. viii, 111.—ὁ ἥρως (Protesilaos), χρηστὸς ὤν, ξυγχωρεῖ that people should sit down in his τέμενος: Philostr., *Her.* p. 134, 4 Ks.—Other modes of address intended to mollify the dead are ἄλυπε, χρηστὲ καὶ ἄλυπε, ἄριστε, ἄμεμπτε, etc. χαῖρε (cf. *Inscr. Cos*, 165, 263, 279, and Loch, op. cit., 281).

[33] Paus. 4, 27, 6.

[34] Paus. 4, 32, 4.

[35] Paus. 9, 13, 5–6. Sacrifice (ἐντέμνειν) of a white mare to the Heroines: Plu., *Pelop.* 20–2. The same thing is briefly referred to in Xen., *HG.* 6, 4, 7; see also D.S. xv, 54. Detailed account of the fate of the maidens ap. Plu., *Narr. Amor.* 3; Jerome, *a. Jovin.* i, 41 (ii, 1, 308 D Vall.).—αἱ Λεύκτρου θυγατέρες, Plu., *Herod. Mal.* ii, p. 856 F.

[36] Λεωνίδεια in Sparta (*CIG.* 1421) at which there were "speeches" about Leonidas (even in Sparta not a surprising circumstance at this late period), and an ἀγών in which only Spartiates might take part: Paus. 3, 14, 1.—ἀγωνισάμενοι τὸν ἐπιτάφιο[ν Λεωνίδου] καὶ Πανσανί[ου καὶ τῶν λοι]πῶν ἡρώω[ν ἀγῶνα], *CIG.* 1417.

[37] At Marathon: crowning and ἐναγισμός at the πολυάνδρειον of the Marathonian Heroes carried out by the *epheboi*: *CIA.* ii, 471, 26. Cf. more generally Aristid. ii, p. 229 f. Dind. Nocturnal fighting of the ghosts there: Paus. 1, 32, 4 (the oldest prototype of the similar legends told, in connexion with the story of the battle between the dead Huns and Romans, by Damasc., *V. Isid.* 63).

[38] ἄνδρας] ἐθ' ἥρωας σέβεται πατρίς κτλ., *Inscr. Cos*, 350 (beginning of Empire).

[39] Speaking of the Attic tragedians, D. Chr. thinks (15, p. 237 M. = ii, 235 Arn.) οὓς ἐκεῖνοι ἀποδεικνύουσιν ἥρωας τούτοις φαίνονται ἐναγίζοντες (οἱ Ἕλληνες) ὡς ἥρωσιν, καὶ τὰ ἡρῷα ἐκείνοις ᾠκοδομημένα ἰδεῖν ἔστιν. But this is only true in a very limited and qualified sense.

[40] Ἕκτορι ἔτι θύουσιν ἐν Ἰλίῳ, says Luc. (expressly speaking of his own times), *D. Conc.* 12. Apparition of Hektor in Troad: Max. Tyr. 15, 7, p. 283 R. Miracles worked: Philostr., *Her.* pass. Hekt. in Thebes: Lyc. 1204 ff.

[41] In the Ἡρωικός Philostratos gives plenty of evidence of this. Most of what he says about the Heroes of the Trojan war is entirely without traditional basis, but not all of it; and especially where he speaks (in the first part of the dialogue) of the appearances and displays of power attributed in his own day to the Heroes he is far from inventing. (His powers of invention are exercised particularly in what he says about the events of their lives where he is expanding or correcting Homer.) Acc. to Philostr. (*Her.* 681, p. 149, 32 ff. Kays., 1871) ὁρῶνται—at least by the shepherds of the Trojan plain—the figures of the Homeric champions (gigantic in size, pp. 136–40 [667]; φαίνονται in full armour,

p. 131, 1). Hektor in particular appears, works miracles, and his statue πολλὰ ἐργάζεται χρηστὰ κοινῇ τε καὶ ἐς ἕνα, pp. 151–2. Legend about Antilochos, p. 155, 10 ff. Palamedes appears, p. 154. On the south coast of the Troad opposite Lesbos he has an ancient temple in which θύουσιν to him ξυνιόντες οἱ τὰς ἀκταίας οἰκοῦντες πόλεις, p. 184, 21 (see also *V. Ap.* iv, 13). Sacrifice to Palamedes as a Hero, 153, 29 ff.—*Mantic* power attributed to the ἥρωες, 135, 21 ff. ; 148, 20 ff. (to Odysseus in Ithaca, 195, 5 ff.). Hence Protesilaos in particular, who appears at Elaious in Thrac. Chers. to the vineyard-keeper into whose mouth Philostr. puts his story, has so much to say even about what he had not himself seen or experienced. Protes. is still fully alive (ζῇ, 130, 23) ; like Achilles (in Leuke, etc.) he has his ἱεροὶ δρόμοι ἐν οἷς γυμνάζεται (131, 31). A vision of Protes. appearing to an enemy makes him blind (132, 9). (To meet a Hero often blinds a mortal, cf. Hdt. vi, 117, and the case of Stesichoros and the Dioskouroi.) He protects his protégé's fields from snakes, wild beasts, and everything harmful : 132, 15 ff. He himself is now ἐν Ἅιδου (when he is with Laodameia), now in Phthia, and now in the Troad (143, 17 ff.). He appears about midday (143, 21, 32 ; cf. Append. vi). At his ancient oracle at Elaious (mentioned already by Hdt. ix, 116, 120 ; alluded to by Philostr., p. 141, 12) he dispenses oracles more particularly to the champions of the great games, the heroes of the age (p. 146, 13 ff., 24 ff., 147, 8 ff., 15 ff. ; famous contemporaries are mentioned : Eudaimon of Alexandria, victor at Olympia in Ol. 237, and Helix well-known from the Γυμναστικός). He heals diseases, esp. consumption, dropsy, ophthalmia, and ague, and he helps people in the pains of love (p. 147, 30 ff.). Prot. also gives oracles in his Phthiotic home Phylake (where he pays frequent visits), 148, 24 ff.—It is the regular series of miraculous performances normally attributed to the ἥρωες of older legends, that Protesilaos carries out here.—On Mt. Ismaros in Thrace Maron (Εὐανθέος υἱός, *Od.* ι 197) appears and ὁρᾶται τοῖς γεωργοῖς to whom he sends rain (149, 3 ff.). Mt. Rhodope in Thrace is haunted (οἰκεῖ) by Rhesos, who lives there a life of chivalry, breeding horses, practising his weapons, and hunting ; the woodland animals offer themselves willingly as sacrifices at his altar ; the *heros* keeps the plague away from the surrounding κῶμαι (149, 7–19).—The legendary details from Philostratos here selected for mention may be taken as really derived from popular tradition (cf. also W. Schmid, *D. Atticismus*, iv, 572 ff.).

[42] Again in 375 A.D. Achilles preserved Attica from an earthquake (Zosim. iv, 18) ; in 396 he kept Alaric away from Athens ; ib., v, 6.

[43] Plu., *Lucull.* 23 ; App., *Mithr.* 83. Lucullus was Roman enough to carry off from the inhabitants of Sinope their much-honoured statue of Autolykos, to which the elaborate cult was principally attached : ἐτίμων Autol. ὡς θεόν. ἦν δὲ καὶ μαντεῖον αὐτοῦ, Str. 546.

[44] See above, chap. iv, nn. 119–20.—*Heroon* of Kyniska (sister of Agesilaos) in Sparta as victor at Olympos : Paus. 3, 15, 1.

[45] Hero-physicians : see above, chap. iv, § 10. Our knowledge of the cult and activity of these Heroes is chiefly derived from evidence from later times. — An evidently late creation is the Hero Neryllinos in the Troad, of whose worship, healing, and prophetic powers Athenag., *Apol.* 26, has something to say (Lob. *Agl.* 1171). ὁ ξένος ἰατρός, Toxaris, in Athens : Luc., *Scyth.* 1 ; 2. (The special name of the ξένος ἰατρός may be Lucian's invention, but not what he tells us of his cult.) There was a permanent cult of Hippokrates in Kos in the time of Soranos : the Koans offered sacrifice to him (ἐναγίζειν) annually on his birthday

(see above, chap. v, n. 89): Soran. ap. Anon., *V. Hipp.* 450, 13 West. (miracle at the tomb of Hipp. in Larisa: ib., 451, 55 ff.). The doctor in Luc., *Philops.* 21, makes an elaborate sacrifice (something more than *ἐναγίζειν*) annually to his bronze statue of Hipp.—A good story thoroughly in the manner of popular folk-lore is that told of Pellichos the Corinthian general who was also worshipped as giving help in sickness and the magic tricks that he (simply as *ἥρως*) was able to play on the Libyan slave who had stolen the gold pieces which used to be offered to him: Luc., *Philops.* 18–20.

[46] *Anth. Pal.* vii, 694 (*Ἀδδαίου*, probably the Macedonian).

[47] *CIG.* 4838b (see above, chap. iv, n. 60). The name expresses the idea: *εὐόδει* was the greeting which the dead man returned to the traveller, *CIG.* 1956.

[48] Another example: bulls are still sacrificed in Megara in the fourth century A.D. officially by the city to the Heroes who had fallen in the Persian wars, *IG. Sept.* i, 53.

[49] At the monument of Philopoimen, Plu., *Philop.* 21.

[50] *ἐν τοῖς Ἡρωϊκοῖς καὶ ἐν ταῖς ἄλλαις ἑορταῖς*—in Priansos and Hierapytna in Crete (third century B.C.), *CIG.* 2556, 37. Annual festival of the *Ἡρῷα*, in which were held *εὐχαριστήριοι ἀγῶνες* for Asklepiades and those who had fought with him in one of the city's wars. A decree honouring the grandsons of this Asklep. has been found at Eski-Manyas near Kyzikos: *Ath. Mitt.* 1884, p. 33.

[51] In taking an oath they swore by the gods *καὶ ἥρωας καὶ ἡρωάσσας* (Dreros in Crete): Cauer, *Delect.*[1] 38 A, 31 (third century B.C.). Treaty between Rhodos and Hierapytna (second century B.C.), Cauer, 44, 3: *εὔξασθαι τῷ Ἁλίῳ και τᾷ Ῥόδῳ καὶ τοῖς ἄλλοις θεοῖς πᾶσι καὶ πάσαις καὶ τοῖς ἀρχαγέταις καὶ τοῖς ἥρωσι, ὅσοι ἔχοντι τὰν πόλιν καὶ τὰν χώραν τὰν Ῥοδίων . . .* Oath of citizenship from Chersonnesos (third century), *Sitzb. Berl. Akad.* 1892, p. 480: *ὀμνύω . . . ἥρωας ὅσοι πόλιν καὶ χώραν καὶ τεύχη ἔχοντι τὰ Χερσονασιτᾶν.*—Similar exx. from earlier times: see above, chap. iv, n. 4 (and cf. Din., *Dem.* 64: *μαρτύρομαι . . . καὶ τοὺς ἥρωας τοὺς ἐγχωρίους κτλ.*).

[52] e.g. inscr. from Astypalaia *BCH.* 1891, p. 632 (n. 4): Damatrios son of Hippias dedicates a fountain and trees *θεοῖς ἥρωσί τε . . . ἀθλοφόρου τέχνας ἀντιδιδοὺς χάριτα.*—A grave is dedicated *θεοῖς ἥρωσι*, *CIG.* 3272 (Smyrna), i.e. probably *θ. καὶ ἥρωσι* (cf. *θεοῖς δαίμοσι*, 5827, etc.).

[53] Collegia of *ἡρωισταί*: Foucart, *Assoc. relig.* 230 (49), 233 (56). *CIA.* ii, 630. In Boeotia, *Ath. Mitt.* 3, 299 = *IG. Sept.* i, 2725.

[54] e.g. inscr. on one of the seats in the theatre at Athens: *ἱερέως Ἀνάκοιν καὶ ἥρωος ἐπιτεγίου*, *CIA.* iii, 290.

[55] *διαμένουσι δὲ καὶ ἐς τόδε τῷ Αἴαντι παρ' Ἀθηναίοις τιμαί, αὐτῷ τε καὶ Εὐρυσάκει*, Paus. 1, 35, 3 (*Αἰάντεια* in Salamis in first century B.C., *CIA.* ii, 467–71). *ἐναγίζουσι δὲ καὶ ἐς ἡμᾶς ἔτι τῷ Φορωνεῖ* (in Argos), 2, 20, 3. *καί οἱ* (Theras) *καὶ νῦν ἔτι οἱ Θηραῖοι κατ' ἔτος ἐναγίζουσιν ὡς οἰκιστῇ*, 3, 1, 8. He also bears witness to the still surviving cult of Pandion as Hero in Megara, 1, 41, 6; Tereus in Megara, 1, 41, 9; Melampous in Aigosthena, 1, 44, 5; Aristomenes in Messenia, 4, 14, 7; Aitolos in Elis (*ἐναγίζει ὁ γυμνασίαρχος ἔτι καὶ ἐς ἐμὲ καθ' ἕκαστον ἔτος τῷ Αἰτωλῷ*, 5, 4, 4; cf. the *γυμνασίαρχος* who looks after the *ἐκκομιδαί*: above, this chap., n. 4); Sostratos the *ἐρώμενος* of Herakles in Dyme, 7, 17, 8; Iphikles in Phenea, 8, 14, 9; the boys slain at Kaphyai, 8, 23, 6–7; the four lawgivers of Tegea, 8, 48, 1; the *Εὐσεβεῖς* in Katana, 10, 28, 4–5.—Of course, it does not follow that when Paus. mentions other very numerous Heroes without so

expressly saying that their cult still survived, he means that those cults had died out.

[56] Plu., *Aristid.* 21.

[57] Aratos received from the Achaeans after his death θυσίαν καὶ τιμὰς ἡρωικάς in which he may take pleasure himself εἴπερ καὶ περὶ τοὺς ἀποιχομένους ἔστι τις αἴσθησις, Polyb. 8, 14, 8. He was buried at Sikyon, as οἰκιστὴς καὶ σωτὴρ τῆς πόλεως, in a τόπος περίοπτος called the Ἀράτειον (cf. Paus. 2, 8, 1 ; 9, 4). Sacrifice was made to him twice a year, on the day when he had freed Sikyon, 5th Daisios, the Σωτήρια, and on his birthday; the former was carried out by the priest of Zeus Soter, the latter by the priest of Aratos. They included: Hymn by the Dionysiac τεχνῖται, procession of παῖδες and ἔφηβοι in which the *gymnasiarchoi*, the *boule* wearing crowns, and the citizens took part. Of all this only δείγματα μικρά still survived in Plutarch's time, αἱ δὲ πλεῖσται τῶν τιμῶν ὑπὸ χρόνου καὶ πραγμάτων ἄλλων ἐκλελοίπασιν, Plu., *Arat.* 53 (σωτήρ: cf. epigram in c. 14).

[58] πάντες ἥρωας νομίζουσι τοὺς σφόδρα παλαιοὺς ἄνδρας, καὶ ἐὰν μηδὲν ἐξαίρετον ἔχωσι, δι' αὐτὸν οἶμαι τὸν χρόνον. But only a few of them have regular τελετὰς ἡρώων: D. Chr. 31, p. 335 M. [i, 243 Arn.]. omnes qui patriam conservarint, adiuverint, auxerint become immortal: Cic., *Som. Sci.* 3, which also goes too far.

[59] Pelopidas, Timoleon, Leosthenes, Aratos become Heroes: see Keil, *Anal. epigr. et onom.* 50–4. Kleomenes Plu., *Cleom.* 39. Philopoimen, *Philop.* 21. ἰσόθεοι τιμαί annual sacrifice of a bull and hymns of praise to Philop. sung by the νέοι: D.S. 29, 18; Liv. 39, 50, 9; *SIG.* 289. See Keil, op. cit., 9 ff.

[60] In Sikyon Aratos is held to be the son of Asklepios who had visited his mother in the form of a snake: Paus. 2, 10, 3; 4, 14, 7–8 (favourite form of stories of divine parentage: see Marx, *Märchen v. dankb. Thieren*, 122, 2).

[61] The very charming and characteristic story of Drimakos, the leader and law-giver of the δραπέται in Chios, is told by Nymphodoros (ap. Ath. vi, c. 88–90), as having happened μικρὸν πρὸ ἡμῶν. He had a ἡρῷον in which he was honoured under the name of ἥρως εὐμενής (by the δραπέται with the firstfruits of their plunder). He frequently appeared to masters to whom he revealed the οἰκετῶν ἐπιβουλάς.

[62] Hsch. Γαθιάδας· ἥρωος ὄνομα, ὃς καὶ τοὺς καταφεύγοντας εἰς αὐτὸν ῥύεται [καὶ] θανάτου.

[63] Pixodaros, a shepherd of Ephesos, discovered in a strange fashion a very excellent kind of marble, a discovery which he communicated to the authorities (for use in temple-building). He was made a Hero and renamed ἥρως εὐάγγελος: sacrifice was made to him officially every month, *hodieque*, Vitruv. x, 2.

[64] Luc., *Macrob.* 21 (for Athenod. see *FHG.* iii, 485 f.).—In Kos an *exedra* in the theatre was dedicated to C. Stertinius Xenophon (court-physician to the Emp. Claudius) ἥρωι, *Inscr. Cos*, 93.—In Mitylene there was even an apotheosis of the historian Theophanes (the friend of Pompeius: cf. Γν. Πομπήιος Ἱεροίτα υἱὸς Θεοφάνης with full name, *Ath. Mitt.* ix, 87): Tac., *A.* vi, 18. Θεοφάνης θεός on coins of the city, and cf. Σέξστον ἥρωα, Λεσβῶναξ ἥρως νέος, etc., on the same city's coins (Head, *Hist. Num.* 488).

[65] On a *stele* in Messene there was a portrait of a certain Aithidas of the beginning of the third century B.C.; instead of whom a descendant of the same name is worshipped: Paus. 4, 32, 2. In the market place of Mantinea stood a *heroon* of Podares who had

distinguished himself in the battle of Mant. (362). Three generations before Paus. visited the place the Mantineans had altered the inscription on the *heroon* and dedicated it to a later Podares, a descendant of the original one, who lived in the Roman period: Paus. 8, 9, 9.

[66] Cf. Keil, *Anal. Epigr.* 62.

[67] Cult paid to king Lysimachos in his lifetime in Samothrake, *SIG.* 190 (*Archaol. Unters. auf. Samoth.* ii, 85, n. 2). "Heroizing" of Diogenes *phrourarchos* of Demetrios; in 229 B.C. he was bribed by Aratos to lead the Macedonian garrison out of Attica: see Köhler, *Hermes*, vii, 1 ff.—ὑπὲρ τᾶς Νικία τοῦ δάμου υἱοῦ, φιλοπάτριδος, ἥρωος, εὐεργέτα δὲ τᾶς πόλιος, σωτηρίας a dedication θεοῖς πατρῴοις, *Inscr. Cos*, 76. This is a decree made in the lifetime of the *heros* (or why σωτηρίας?), who is probably identical, as the editors suggest, with Nikias, tyrant of Kos in the Strabo's time: Str. 658; Perizonius on Ael., *VH.* i, 29.

[68] ἥρως applied to a living person occasionally on inss. of the Imperial age, *CIG.* 2583, Lyttos, Crete; 3665 ἡρωίς, living, Kyzikos second century; *Ath. Mitt.* vi, 121 (Kyzikos again) ἱππαρχοῦντος Κλεομένους ἥρωος also certainly living.

[69] When Demetrios Poliorketes conquered and rebuilt Sikyon in 303 the inhabitants of the city which is now called "Demetrias" offer to him while still alive, sacrifice, festival, and annual ἀγῶνες as κτίστῃ (ἀλλὰ ταῦτα μὲν ὁ χρόνος ἠκύρωσεν): D.S. 20, 102, 3. Later this frequently occurred: Marcellea, Lucullea, etc., are well known. But the matter did not stop there. The inhabitants of Lete in Macedonia in the year 117 B.C. decree to a prominent Roman, besides other honours, τίθεσθαι αὐτῷ ἀγῶνα ἱππικὸν κατ' ἔτος ἐν τῷ Δαισίῳ μηνί, ὅταν καὶ τοῖς ἄλλοις εὐεργέταις οἱ ἀγῶνες ἐπιτελῶνται (*Arch. des miss. scientif.* 3e série, iii, p. 278, n. 127). This implies that *all* εὐεργέται were by custom offered such games at this time.

[70] D.S. 17, 115. Alexander after inquiry at the oracle of Ammon commanded that he should be worshipped as ἥρως (the oracle having granted in his case ἐναγίζειν ὡς ἥρωι, but not ὡς θεῷ θύειν): Arrian, *An.* 7, 14, 7; 23, 6; Plu., *Alex.* 72 (an ἡρῷον was immediately set up to him in Alexandria Aeg.: Arr. 7, 23, 7). This did not prevent the superstition and servility which flourished together in Alexander's empire from occasionally worshipping Heph. as Ἡφαιστίων θεὸς πάρεδρος.—D.S. probably only exaggerates the truth: 17, 115, 6; cf. Luc., *Calumn.* 17–18. (The new *heros* or god immediately gave proof of his power by appearances, visions sent in dreams, ἰάματα, μαντεῖαι, ib. 17.)—Elaborate pomp at the funeral of Dem. Poliork.: Plu., *Demetr.* 53.

[71] Cf. the Testament of Epikteta and other foundations mentioned above, this chap., n. 18, and chap. v, n. 126. Or cf. the elaborate arrangements which Herodes Atticus made for the funeral, etc., of Regilla and Polydeukes (but ἥρως Πολυδευκίων is only said in the weakened sense in which ἥρως had been current for a long time): collected by Keil in Pauly-Wiss. i, 2101 ff. The extravagant manifestations of grief that Cicero offered to the memory of his daughter were modelled on Greek originals (and upon the certainly Greek auctores qui dicant fieri id oportere: *Att.* 12, 81, 1). In *Att.* 12 he gives an account of their architectural side; he frequently calls the object that he meditates an ἀποθέωσις; cf. *consecrabo te* (*Consol. fr.* 5 Or.).—Cf. the Temple-tomb of Pomptilla, who like another Alkestis died instead of her husband, whom she followed into exile as far as Sardinia: her death was caused by breathing in the breath of the sick man. Her

temple is at Cagliari in Sardinia, and is adorned with many inss. in Latin and Greek: *IG. Sic. et It.* 607, p. 144 ff. (first century A.D.).

[72] ὁ δᾶμος (occasionally also ἁ βουλὰ καὶ ὁ δᾶμος) ἀφηρώϊξε—Thera, *CIG.* 2467; Ross, *Inscr. Gr. Ined.* 203 ff. (and sometimes outside Thera: Loch, *Zu d. gr. Grabschr.* 282, 1) ὁ δᾶμος ἐτίμασε (τὸν δεῖνα) . . . ἥρωα. Cf. also (Thera) *Ath. Mitt.* xvi, 166; *Epigr. Gr.* 191–2.

[73] φροντίσαι δὲ τοὺς ὀργεῶνας (the members of a *collegium* of Dionysiasts) ὅπως ἀφηρωισθεῖ Διονύσιος καὶ ἀνατεθεῖ ἐν τῷ ἱερῷ παρὰ τὸν θεόν, ὅπου καὶ ὁ πατὴρ αὐτοῦ, ἵνα ὑπάρχει κάλλιστον ὑπόμνημα αὐτοῦ εἰς τὸν ἅπαντα χρόνον, inscr. of Peiraeus, second century B.C.; *CIA.* iv, 2, n. 623e, 45 ff. In Argos a guild, apparently of tanners, puts up an inscr. τῷ δεῖνι, κτίστᾳ ἥρωι, *CIG.* 1134.

[74] Like that Naulochos whom Philios of Salamis saw three times in a dream appearing in company with Demeter and Kore. The city of Priene thereupon ordered that he should be worshipped (ἥρωα σέβειν, *Epigr. Gr.* 774).

[75] Κάρπος τὰν ἰδίαν γυναῖκα ἀφηρώϊξε (Thera) *CIG.* 2471. From the same place come many more exx. of ἀφηρωίζειν by members of a family: 2472b–d, 2473; cf. Ἀνδροσθένην Φίλωνος νέον ἥρωα . . . ἡ μήτηρ (Macedonia) *Arch. miss. scient.* iii, 1876, 295, n. 130.—This is probably how we should understand the matter when in sepulchral epigrams one member of the family addresses or refers to another as ἥρως: *Epigr. Gr.* 483, 510, 552, 674.—But ἥρως συγγενείας, *CIA.* iii, 1460, must have a fuller sense than the otherwise usual ἥρως. It distinguishes a true ἀρχηγέτης. Prob. this is also the meaning of Χαρμύλου ἥρωος τῶν Χαρμυλείων, *GDI.* 3701 (Kos). Something more than simple ἥρως is also probably intended by the language of the Pergamene inscr. (specially distorted to suit the ἰσοψηφία) *Inscr. Perg.* ii, 587, Ἰ. Νικόδημος, ὁ καὶ Νίκων (αφιγ) ἀγαθὸς εἶεν ἂν ἥρως (αφιγ).

[76] It is true that it is difficult to find certain exx. of the identification of a dead man with an already existing and honoured *heros* of another name. Of the various examples generally quoted for this perhaps the only relevant is the Spartan inscr. Ἀριστοκλῆς ὁ καὶ Ζῆθος, *Ath. Mitt.* iv, *tab.* 8, 2. Identification with a god is of frequent occurrence: cf. imagines defuncti, quas ad habitum dei Liberi formaverat (uxor), divinis percolens honoribus: Apul., *M.* viii, 7. (Cf. Lob., *Agl.* 1002, who also thinks of the example given in the Πρωτεσίλαος of Eur.; but the resemblance is only a distant one.) The dead man as Βάκχος, *Epigr. Gr.* 821; Διονύσου ἄγαλμα, ib. 705; cf. the dead man of *CIG.* 6731, ἄγαλμά εἰμι Ἡλίου. Many similar exx. of the representation of the dead in accordance with the types of Dionysos, Asklepios, Hermes are given by Ross, *Archäol. Aufs.* i, 51; Deneken in Roscher, *Lex.* i, 2588.

[77] See above, chap. iv, p. 128 ff.

[78] See Keil, *Syll. Inscr. Boeot.*, p. 153.

[79] In Thespiai the inss. do not show the addition of ἥρως to the name of the dead until Imperial times: see Dittenberger on *IG. Sept.* i, 2110, p. 367.

[80] Many exx. of ἥρως, ἥρως χρηστὲ χαῖρε, etc., are collected and arranged by Deneken in Roscher's *Lex.* s. *Heros*, i, 2549 ff. See also Loch, *Gr. Grabschr.*, p. 282 ff.

[81] As Keil has already observed, loc. cit. [n. 78].—At any rate ἡρωίνη still preserves its full sense when the council and people of Athens, in the first century A.D., so describe a woman of position after her death, *CIA.* iii, 889. Or again, when the Athenian as well as the

Spartan decree calls P. Statilius Lamprias expressly ἥρως (see above, n. 6)—*Fouilles d'Epid.* i, n. 205–9.

[82] It is curious how, much later, in Christian times, ὁ ἥρως is applied to one who has recently died (exactly synonymous with ὁ μακαρίτης): cf. ὁ ἥρως Εὐδόξιος, ὁ ἥρως Πατρίκιος, Ἰάμβλιχος in *Schol. Basilic.*

[83] ὕπνος ἔχει σε μάκαρ . . . , καὶ ζῇς ὡς ἥρως καὶ νέκυς οὐκ ἐγένου, *Epigr. Gr.* 433; where it is evident that the ἥρως is something more living than the mere νέκυς. ἀσπάζεσθ' ἥρωα, τὸν οὐκ ἐδαμάσσατο λύπη (i.e. who has not been made nothing by death), ib., 296. The husband τιμαῖς ἰσόμοιρον ἔθηκε τὰν ὁμόλεκτρον ἥρωσιν, 189, 3. The title ἥρως still has a stronger and deeper sense in inss. such as *CIG.* 1627 (referring to a descendent of Plutarch's) and 4058 (. . . ἄνδρα φιλόλογον καὶ πάσῃ ἀρετῇ κεκοσμημένον εὐδαίμονα ἥρωα). Cf. Orig., *Cels.* 3, 80, p. 359 Lom.: οἱ βιοῦντες ὥσθ' ἥρωες γενέσθαι καὶ μετὰ θεῶν ἕξειν τὰς διατριβάς. In 3, 22, p. 276, he distinguishes between θεοί, ἥρωες, ἁπαξαπλῶς ψυχαί (the soul can divina *fieri* et a legibus mortalitatis educi, Arnob. ii, 62; cf. Corn. Labeo ap. Serv., *Aen.* iii, 168).

[84] ἄωροι, βιοθάνατοι, ἄταφοι see Append. vii.—θάπτειν καὶ ὁσιοῦν τῇ Γῇ, significantly, Philostr., *Her.* 714, p. 182, 9 f. K.

[85] Plu., *Dio*, 2: some say that only children and women and foolish men see ghosts, δαίμονα πονηρὸν ἐν αὐτοῖς δεισιδαιμονίαν ἔχοντες. Plu. on the other hand thinks that he can confound the unbelieving by pointing to the fact that even Dio and Brutus had seen φάσματα shortly before their death.

[86] Cf. the story of Philinnion and Machates in Amphipolis: Phleg., *Mirab.* 1. Procl. *in Rp.*, p. 64 Sch. [ii, p. 116 Kr.; see Rohde in *Rh. Mus.* 32, 329 ff.]. The Erinyes in Aesch. are conceived as vampire-like: *Eum.* 264 f.; see above, chap. v, n. 161.—Souls of the dead as nightmare, ἐφιάλτης, *incubo* oppressing a man's enemy: Soran. ap. Tert., *An.* 44; Cael. Aurel., *Morb. Chron.* 1, 3, 55 (*Rh. Mus.* 37, 467, 1).

[87] The Φιλοψευδής is a genuine treasure-house of typical narratives of apparitions and sorceries of every kind. δαίμονας ἀνάγειν καὶ νεκροὺς ἑώλους ἀνακαλεῖν is a mere bagatelle, according to these sage doctors, to the magician: c. 13. An example is given of this conjuration of the dead (the seven-months dead father of Glaukias): 14. Appearance of the dead wife of Eukrates whose golden sandals they had forgotten to burn with her: 27 (see above, chap. i, n. 51). As a rule the only haunting ghosts are αἱ τῶν βιαίως ἀποθανόντων ψυχαί not those of the κατὰ μοῖραν ἀποθανόντων as the learned Pythagorean instructs us, c. 29. Then follows the story of the ghost of Corinth (30–1), which must be taken from a widely known ghost-story, as it agrees completely in its circumstances with the story told with such simple candour by Pliny (*Ep.* vii, 27). δαίμονάς τινας εἶναι καὶ φάσματα καὶ νεκρῶν ψυχὰς περιπολεῖν ὑπὲρ γῆς καὶ φαίνεσθαι οἷς ἂν ἐθέλωσιν (29) is the fixed conviction of these philosophers. The living too can sometimes catch a glimpse of the underworld: 22–4. A man's soul can be detached from his body and go down to Hades, and afterwards, again reunited to his body, relate its adventures. Thus the soul of Kleodemos, while his body lay in fever, is taken down to the lower world by a messenger but then sent back again since he had been taken by mistake for his neighbour, the smith Demylos: 25. This edifying narrative is certainly intended as a parody of the similar story told in good faith by Plu. *de An. fr.* 1, preserved

ap. Eus., *PE*. 11, 36, p. 563. It is certain that Plu. did not simply invent such a story; he may perhaps have found it in some older collection of miraculous ἀναβιώσεις such as, for example, Chrysippos did not disdain to make. The probability that Plu. got this story of mistaken identity from a collection of folk-tales is made all the likelier since the same story occurs again in a popular guise. Of a similar character is what Augustine has to say on the authority of Corn. Labeo: *Civ. Dei* 22, 28 (p. 622, 1–5 Domb.). Augustine himself, *Cur. pro Mort.* 15, tells a story exactly like that of Plu. (about Curma the *curialis* and Curma the *faber ferrarius*), which, of course, is supposed to happen a little before his time in Africa; and once more at the end of the sixth century Gregory the Great introduces a vision of Hell by the same formula: *Dial.* 4, 36, p. 384 AB Migne. The inventive powers of ghoststory-tellers is very limited: they keep on repeating the same few old and tried motifs.

[88] Plu., *Dio*, 2, 55; *Cimon*, 1; *Brut.* 36 f., 48.

[89] Cf. above, chap. v, n. 23; chap. ix, nn. 105 ff.

[90] ψυχὰς ἡρώων ἀνακαλεῖν among the regular arts of the magician, Cels. ap. Orig., *Cels.* 1, 68, p. 127 Lomm.

[91] See Append. xii.

[92] And in consequence we sometimes have the most surprising confusion of the two states of being. Lucian, e.g. (in *D. Mort.* frequently, cf. 18, 1; 20, 2, and *Necyom.* 15, 17; *Char.* 24) speaks of the dead in *Hades* as skeletons lying one upon another, Aiakos allowing them each one foot of earth, etc. (The Romans have the same confusion of ideas: nemo tam puer est, says Sen., *Ep.* 24, 18, ut Cerberum timeat et tenebras et larvalem habitum nudis ossibus cohaerentium. Cf. Prop. iv, 5, 3, Cerberus. . . ieiuno terreat ossa sono, etc.) There is also a confusion between the grave and Hades in such expressions as μετ' εὐσεβέεσσι κεῖσθαι: *Epigr. Gr.* 259, 1; σκῆνος νῦν κεῖμαι Πλουτέος ἐμμελάθροις, 226, 4; cf. above, chap. xii, n. 95. Such a mixture of ideas was all the more natural seeing that "Αιδης also occurs as a metaphor for τύμβος (see below, n. 135).

[93] ὁ πολὺς ὅμιλος οὓς ἰδιώτας οἱ σοφοὶ καλοῦσιν, Ὁμήρῳ καὶ Ἡσιόδῳ καὶ τοῖς ἄλλοις μυθοποιοῖς περὶ τούτων πειθόμενοι, τόπον τινὰ ὑπὸ τὴν γῆν βαθὺν "Αιδην ὑπειλήφασι κτλ., Luc., *Luct.* 2 (continued to c. 9). Plu., *Suav. Viv.* 27, 1105 AB, thinks that οὐ πάνυ πολλοὶ are afraid of Kerberos, having to fill broken pitchers and the other terrors of Hades, as being μητέρων καὶ τιτθῶν δόγματα καὶ λόγους μυθώδεις. And yet as protection against these things people are always seeking τελετὰς καὶ καθαρμούς.

[94] See *Griech. Roman*, 261, Ettig *Acheruntica* (*Leipz. Stud.* 13, 251 ff.).

[95] Man hopes that after death he will see τοὺς νῦν ὑβρίζοντας ὑπὸ πλούτου καὶ δυνάμεως κτλ. ἀξίαν δίκην τίνοντας, Plu., *Suav. V.* 28, 2, 1105 C. Reversal of earthly situation in Hades: τὰ πράγματα ἐς τοὔμπαλιν ἀνεστραμμένα· ἡμεῖς μὲν γὰρ οἱ πένητες γελῶμεν, ἀνιῶνται δὲ καὶ οἰμώζουσιν οἱ πλούσιοι, Luc., *Catapl.* 15; cf. *DM.* 15, 2; 25, 2: ἰσοτιμία, ἰσηγορία in Hades and ὅμοιοι πάντες. aequat omnes cinis; impares nascimur, pares morimur, Sen., *Ep.* 91, 16—a favourite commonplace: see Gataker on M. Ant. vi, 24, p. 235 f.

[96] How far indeed this really happened is of course not to be answered decisively. The Celsus against whom Origen wrote his polemical treatise looks at the matter from the popular point of view on the whole. (He is no Epicurean as Orig. supposes; but neither in fact is he a professional philosopher of any kind, but rather

an ἰδιώτης with inclinations to philosophy of all sorts and esp. to the semi-Platonism current at the time.) He distinctly says μήτε τούτοις (the Christians) εἴη μήτ' ἐμοὶ μήτ' ἄλλῳ τινὶ ἀνθρώπων ἀποθέσθαι τὸ περὶ τοῦ κολασθήσεσθαι τοὺς ἀδίκους καὶ γερῶν ἀξιωθήσεσθαι τοὺς δικαίους δόγμα (ap. Orig., *Cels.* 3, 16, p. 270 Lomm.).—On the other hand, it is significant of the temper of the very "secular" Graeco-Roman society which was at the head of affairs at the end of the last century B.C., that Cicero at the end of his work, *de Nat. Deor.* (iii, 81 ff.), in discussing the various means of obtaining a balance between desert and punishment, virtue and reward, in the circumstances of human life, never even mentions the belief in a final balance and recompense after death. (He only mentions among other things the visiting of the sins of the father upon his descendents on earth—90 ff.—that old Greek belief [see above, chap. xii, n. 65] which really excludes the idea of an after life.) Between the days of Cic. and those of Celsus ideas had changed. We know this from innumerable indications; even the next world was looked at in quite a different light in the second century A.D. from what it had been two centuries earlier.

[97] τιμωρίαι αἰώνιοι ὑπὸ γῆν καὶ κολασμοὶ φρικώδεις are expected after death by many (while others regard death as merely an ἀγαθῶν στέρησις): Plu., *Virt. Moral.* 10, 450 A. Horrible tortures in the κολαστήριον in Hades, fire, scourging, etc.: Luc., *Necyom.* 14 (carried still further in Plu.'s pictures of Hades, *Gen. Soc.* and *Ser. NV.*). Fire, pitch, and sulphur belong to the regular apparatus of this place of torment; already in *Axioch.* 372 A, sinners are scorched by burning torches ἀϊδίοις τιμωρίαις (cf. Lehrs, *Popl. Aufs.* 308 ff.). How far such horrors really represented popular belief it is difficult to say for certain (they became quite familiar to Christian writers on Hell from classical tradition: cf. Maury, *Magie et l'astrol. dans l'antiq.* 166 ff.). But Celsus, for example, though he himself believes in the punishments of Hell (Orig., *Cels.* 8, 49, p. 180) only appeals in confirmation of his belief to the teaching of ἐξηγηταὶ τελεσταί τε καὶ μυσταγωγοί of certain (not precisely defined) ἱερά: 8, 48, p. 178; cf. above, chap. vii, § 2; chap. x, n. 62.

[98] See above, chap. ii, § 1.

[99] Peleus, Kadmos, Achilles in the Islands of the Blest: Pi., *O.* ii, 86 ff. (Peleus and Kadmos the supreme examples of εὐδαιμονία: *P.* iii, 86 ff.). In Eur., *Andr.* 1254 ff. Thetis promises to Peleus immortal life Νηρέως ἐν δόμοις. An ancient poem must have spoken to this effect of Kadmos (and of Harmonia his wife); both are transported μακάρων ἐς αἶαν Eur., *Ba.* 1338 f.; ποιηταί and μυθογράφοι ap. Sch. Pi., *P.* iii, 153 (this would be after their "death" in Illyria where their graves were shown, and the snakes of stone into which they had been changed: see Müller on Scylax, 24, p. 31). Achilles and Diomedes are νήσοις ἐν μακάρων acc. to the *skolion* on Harmodios: *Carm. pop. fr.* 10 Bgk. (Thus we often hear that Achilles is in the Is. of the Blest or in the Ἠλύσιον πεδίον which was regularly identified with them—cf. Ἠλύσιος λειμών in the μακάρων νῆσος: Luc., *Jup. Conf.* 17; *VH.* ii, 14—e.g. Pla., *Smp.* 199 E; A.R. iv, 811; [Apollod.] *Epit.* v, 5. His special place of abode the island of Leuke is also a μακάρων νῆσος and an older invention than the common Is. of the Blest of which we first hear in Hes., *Op.* 159 ff. Diomedes in the same way after his ἀφανισμός enjoyed immortal life in the island named after him in the Adriatic: Ibyc. ap. Sch. Pi., *N.* x, 12; Str. 283–4, etc.; but the *skolion* transferred him to the common dwelling-place of the blessed Heroes.) Achilles, sometimes in Leuke, sometimes on the Is.

of the Blest, is accompanied by his wife Medea (in Elys.: Ibyc. Simon. Sch. A.R. iv, 814; A.R. iv, 811 ff.) or Iphigeneia who had once been betrothed to him (in Leuke: Ant. Lib. 27 after Nikand.; different version by Lycophr. 183 ff.) or Helen (Paus. 3, 19, 11–13; Conon, 18; Sch. Pl., *Phdr.* 243 A; Philostr., *Her.* 211 ff. Kays.).—Alkmene after her *body* had vanished from the sight of those who were bearing the coffin (cf. Plu., *Rom.* 28) was translated to the μακάρων νῆσοι: Ant. Lib 33 after Pherecyd.—Neoptolemos is transported ἐς ἠλύσιον πεδίον μακάρων ἐπὶ γαῖαν, Q.S. iii, 761 ff.—Among the other Heroes there Agamemnon is also implied: Artemid. v, 16.—In all these fabulous accounts the Is. of the Blest (Elysion) remain invariably the abode of special and chosen Heroes (Harmodios' translation there in the *skolion* is no exception; nor is Lucian's jesting reference, *VH.* ii, 17). It was only later imagination that, under the influence of theology, made this kingdom of bliss the common dwelling-place of almost all the εὐσεβεῖς.

[100] Fortunatorum memorant insulas quo cuncti qui aetatem egerint caste suam conveniant, Plaut., *Trin.* 549 f. Menand. Rh., *Encom.* 414, 16 ff. Sp., recommends the use in a παραμυθητικὸς λόγος of the words: πείθομαι τὸν μεταστάντα τὸ ἠλύσιον πεδίον οἰκεῖν (—and even καὶ τάχα που μᾶλλον μετὰ τῶν θεῶν διαιτᾶται νῦν); cf. p. 421, 16–17 Sp. And much later, χάριν ἀμείψασθαι αὐτὸν εὔχομαι τοὺς θεούς, ἐν μακάρων νήσοις ἤδη συζῆν ἠξιώμενον, Suid. Ἀντώνιος Ἀλεξανδρεύς (410 B Gaisf.) from Damascius.

[101] Sertorius: Plu., *Sert.* 8–9; Sall., *H.* 1, *fr.* 61, 62; Flor. 2, 10 (Hor., *Epod.* 16, 39 ff.). Some even thought that they had found (cf. Phoen. legends: *Gr. Roman* 215) the μακ. νῆσ. off the west coast of Africa: Str. i, p. 3; iii, 150; Mela, iii, 10; Plin., *NH.* vi, 202 ff.; Marcellus, *Αἰθιοπ.* ap. Procl., *in Tim.*, p. 54 F, 55 A, 56 B, etc. Islands inhabited by spirits in the north: Plu., *Def. Or.* 18, p. 419 F; *fr.* vol. v, 764 ff. Wytt. Procop., *Goth.* iv, 20 (the μακάρων νῆσοι are in the middle of the African continent acc. to Hdt. iii, 26; in Boeot. Thebes, Lyc. 1204 with Sch.). Ps. Callisth. makes Alex. the Great reach the land of the Blest, ii, 39 ff. There may have been many such fables which have been parodied by Lucian in *VH.* ii, 6 ff., where he and his company ἔτι ζῶντες ἱεροῦ χωρίου ἐπιβαίνουσιν (ii, 10). It was always natural to hope that at the *Antipodes* (cf. Serv., *A.* vi, 532) such a land of the Souls and the Blest might some day be discovered—as indeed many have thought they *had* discovered it in the progressive geographical discovery of the Middle Ages and modern times.

[102] Leuke, to which already in the *Aithiopis* Achilles had been translated, was originally a purely mythical place (see above, p. 65), the island of the pallid shades (like the Λευκὰς πέτρη of *Od.* ω 11, at the entrance of Hades; cf. κ 515. It is the same rock of Hades from which unhappy lovers cast themselves down to death, ἀρθεὶς δηὖτ' ἀπὸ Λευκάδος πέτρης κτλ. Anacr. 17, etc. [cf. Dieterich, *Nek.* 27 f.]. λεύκη, the white poplar, as the tree of Hades, was used to make the garlands of the Mystai at Eleusis; cf. λευκὴ κυπάρισσος at the entrance of Hades, *Epigr. Gr.* 1037, 2).—It was probably Milesian sailors who localized this island of Achilles in the Black Sea (there was a cult of Ach. in Olbia and in Miletos itself). Alc. already knows of the champion as ruling over the country of the Scythians: *fr.* 48b, ἐν Εὐξείνῳ πελάγει φαεννὰν Ἀχιλεὺς νᾶσον (ἔχει), Pi., *N.* iv, 49. Then Eur., *Andr.* 1259 ff.; *IT.* 436 ff.; finally Q.S. iii, 770 ff. Leuke was particularly identified with an uninhabited islet rising with its white limestone cliffs out of the sea at the mouth of the Danube:

Κέλτου πρὸς ἐκβολαῖσι, Lyc. 189 (probably the Istros is meant but the latest editor simply substitutes *Ἴστρου πρὸς ἐκ.*—a far too facile conjecture).—It stood, more exactly, before the *ψιλὸν στόμα*, i.e. the most northerly mouth of the river (the Kilia mouth): Arrian, *Peripl.* 20, 3 H.; [Scylax] *Peripl.* 68 prob. means the same island; cf. Leuke, *εὐθὺ Ἴστρου*, Max. Tyr. 15, 7. It has been proposed to identify it with the " snake island " which lies more or less in the same neighbourhood: see H. Koehler, *Mém. sur les îles et la course cons. à Achille*, etc., Mém. acad. S. Petersb. 1826, iv, p. 599 ff. It was only by a confusion that the long sandy beach at the mouth of the Borysthenes, called *Ἀχιλλέως δρόμος*, was identified with Leuke (e.g. by Mela, ii, 98; Plin., *NH.* iv, 93; D.P. 541 ff.); legends of Achilles' epiphanies may have been current there too (as in other islands of the same name: Dionys. of Olbia ap. Sch. A.R. ii, 658); the Olbiopolitai offer a cult to *Ἀχιλλεὺς Ποντάρχης* there: *CIG.* 2076–7, 2080, 2096b–f (*IPE.* i, 77–83). But as a settled abode of Achilles only Leuke was generally recognized (there was a *δρόμος Ἀχιλλέως* there as well: Eur., *IT.* 437; Hesych. *Ἀχίλλ. πλάκα*; Arr. 21—hence the confusion mentioned above). Strabo's remarks on the subject are peculiar (vii, 306 f.). He distinguishes the *Ἀχ. δρόμος* (which had already been mentioned by Hdt. iv, 55) from Leuke altogether; and he places that island not at the mouth of the Istros but 500 stades away at the mouth of the Tyras (Dniester). But the place where sacrifice and worship was made to Achilles, as the abode of his spirit, was definitely fixed; and this was, in fact, the island at the mouth of the Danube (*κατὰ τοῦ Ἴστρου τὰς ἐκβολάς*, Paus. 3, 19, 11), of which Arr. 23, 3, gives an account based partially on the evidence of eye-witnesses (p. 399, 12 Müll.). It was an uninhabited, thickly wooded island only occupied by numerous birds; there was a temple and a statue of Ach. on it, and also an oracle (Arr. 22, 3), which must have been an oracle taken by casting or drawing lots (for there were no human intermediaries) which those who landed on the island could make use of for themselves. The birds—which were perhaps regarded as incarnations of the Heroes, or as handmaidens of the " divinity of light " which Achilles was, acc. to R. Holland, *Heroenvögel in d. gr. Myth.* 7 ff., 1896—the birds purify the temple every morning with their wings, which they have dipped in the water: Arr., p. 398, 18 ff. Philostr., *Her.* 746, p. 212, 24 Kays. (Cf. the comrades of Diomedes changed into birds on his magic island: Iuba ap. Plin., *NH.* x, 127—another bird miracle: ib., x, 78). No human beings dared to live on the island, though sailors often landed there; they had to leave before nightfall (when spirits are abroad): Amm. Marc. 22, 8, 35; Philostr., *Her.* 747, p. 212, 30–213, 6. The temple possessed many votive offerings and Greek and Latin inss. (*IPE.* i, 171–2). Those who landed there sacrificed the goats which had been placed on the island and ran wild. Sometimes Ach. appeared to visitors; at other times they heard him singing the Paian. In dreams too he sometimes appeared (i.e. if a person happened to sleep—there was no Dream-oracle there). To sailors he gave directions and sometimes appeared like the Dioskouroi (as a flame ?) on the top of the ship's mast (see Arr., *Peripl.* 21–3; Scymn. 790–6; from both these is derived Anon., *P. Pont. Eux.* 64–6; Max. Tyr. 15, 7, p. 281 f. R.; Paus. 3, 19, 11; Amm. Marc. 22, 8, 35. (The account in Philostr., *Her.* 745, p. 211, 17–219, 6 Kays., is fantastic but uses good material and is throughout quite in keeping with the true legendary spirit—esp. in the story also of the girl torn to pieces by ghosts: 215, 6–30. Nor is it likely that

Phil. himself invented the marvellous tale laid precisely in the year 163–4 B.C.). Achilles is not regarded as living quite alone here: Patroklos is with him (Arr. 32, 34; Max. Tyr. 15, 7), and Helen or Iphigeneia is given him as his wife (see above, n. 99). Leonymos of Kroton, sixth century B.C., meets the two Aiantes and Antilochos there: Paus. 3, 19, 13; Conon 18; D.P. (time of Hadrian) says (545): κεῖθι δ' Ἀχιλλῆος καὶ ἡρώων φάτις ἄλλων ψυχὰς εἱλίσσεσθαι ἐρημαίας ἀνὰ βήσσας (which Avien., *Des. Orb.*, misunderstands and improves on: 722 ff.). Thus the island, though in a limited sense, became a true μακάρων νῆσος—insula Achillea eadem Leuce et Macaron appelata, Plin., *NH.* iv, 93.

[103] Cic., speaking of the "translations" of Herakles and Romulus, says non corpora in caelum elata, non enim natura pateretur . . . (ap. Aug., *CD.* 22, 4); only their animi remanserunt et aeternitate fruuntur, *ND.* ii, 62; cf. iii, 12. Plu., *Rom.* 28, speaks in the same way of the old translation stories (those of Aristeas, Kleomedes, Alkmene, and finally Romulus)—it was not their bodies which had disappeared together with their souls, for it would be παρὰ τὸ εἰκός, ἐνθειάζειν τὸ θνητὸν τῆς φύσεως ἅμα τοῖς θείοις (cf. *Pelop.* 16 fin.); cf. also the Hymn (represented as ancient) of Philostr. dealing with the translated Achilles: *Her.* 741, p. 208, 24 ff. K.

[104] Celsus and Plutarch both know and describe the ancient cult and oracular power of Amphiaraos (only at Oropos now) as still in existence; the same applies to that of Trophonios (like that of Amphilochos also in Cilicia). An inscr. from Lebadeia (first half third century A.D.) mentions a priestess τῆς Ὁμονοίας τῶν Ἑλλήνων παρὰ τῷ Τροφωνίῳ, *IG. Sept.* i, 3426.

[105] Ἀστακίδην τὸν Κρῆτα, τὸν αἰπόλον, ἥρπασε νύμφη ἐξ ὀρέων καὶ νῦν ἱερὸς Ἀστακίδης (he has become divine, i.e. immortal): Call., *Ep.* 24. Of a similar character is the legend of Hylas: ἀφανὴς ἐγένετο, Ant. Lib. 26; and of Bormos among the Maryandynoi (νυμφόληπτος Hesych. Βῶρμον, ἀφανισθῆναι Nymphis, *fr.* 9). The Daphnis legend is another example, and even the story of Odysseus and Kalypso, who detains him in her cave and would like to make him immortal and ageless for ever, is in reality based on such legends of the Nymphs. (Even the name of the Nymph in this case indicates her power: to καλύπτειν her mortal lover, i.e. ἀφανῆ ποιεῖν.) Only in this case the spell is broken and the ἀπαθανάτισις of the translated lover is never carried out. For other exx. of legends of the love of Nymphs for a youth see *Griech. Roman*, 109, 1; a Homeric ex. in Z 21 of the νηὶς Ἀβαρβαρέη and Boukolion the son of Laomedon. The idea that a person translated by the nymphs did not die but lived on for ever, remained current: cf. inscr. from Rome, *Epigr. Gr.* 570, 9–10: τοῖς πάρος οὖν μύθοις πιστεύσατε· παῖδα γὰρ ἐσθλὴν ἥρπασεν ὡς τερπνὴν Ναΐδες, οὐ θάνατος. And again, n. 571: Νύμφαι κρηναῖαί με συνήρπασαν ἐκ βιότοιο, καὶ τάχα που τιμῆς εἵνεκα τοῦτ' ἔπαθον.

[106] In the extravagant and fanatical worship of Dionysos that was transplanted from Greece to Italy and Rome in the year 186 B.C. the miracle of translation was carried out in a very practical fashion (belief in its possibility was evidently firmly established). Machines were prepared upon which those whose disappearance was to be effected were bound; they were then transferred by the machine *in abditos specus*; whereupon the miracle was announced: *raptos a dis homines istos*: Liv. 39, 13. This only becomes intelligible in the light of such legends of the translation of mortals, body and soul, to immortality, of which we have been speaking.

107 Plainly so in the case of Berenike the consort of Ptolemy Soter: Theoc. 17, 46. Theocritus addresses Aphrodite: σέθεν δ' ἕνεκεν Βερενίκα εὐειδὴς Ἀχέροντα πολύστονον οὐκ ἐπέρασεν, ἀλλά μιν ἁρπάξασα πάροιθ' ἐπὶ νῆα κατελθεῖν κυανέαν καὶ στυγνὸν ἀεὶ πορθμῆα καμόντων, ἐς ναὸν κατέθηκας, ἑᾶς δ' ἀπεδάσσαο τιμᾶς (as θεὰ πάρεδρος or σύνναος: cf. *Inscr. Perg.* i, 246, 8). Cf. also Theoc. 15, 106 ff. As a rule, however, this idea is not so definitely expressed (though it is plainly implied that translation is the normal way in which deified princes depart this life, in the story indignantly rejected by Arrian, *Anab.* 7, 27, 3, that Alexander the Great wanted to throw himself into the Euphrates ὡς ἀφανὴς ἐξ ἀνθρώπων γενόμενος πιστοτέραν τὴν δόξαν παρὰ τοῖς ἔπειτα ἐγκαταλείποι ὅτι ἐκ θεοῦ τε αὐτῷ ἡ γένεσις συνέβη καὶ παρὰ θεοὺς ἡ ἀποχώρησις—which is the regular and ancient idea of translation, exhibited e.g. in the story of Empedokles' end: see above, chap. xi, n. 61: and Christian pamphleteers transferred the fable to Julian and his end). The Roman Emperors also allowed such conventional miracles to be told of themselves, in which at least they were imitating the practice of the Hellenistic monarchs and the "consecration" fables usual at their death (they do not die but μεθίστανται ἐξ ἀνθρώπων, μεθ. εἰς θεούς, *SIG*[1]. 246, 16; *Inscr. Perg.* i, 249, 4; inscr. from Hierapolis given by Fränkel, ib. i, p. 39a). That the god is *translated*, his whole personality *in caelum redit*, is implied as occurring at the death of an Emperor on the coins of consecration, in which the translated is represented as being carried up to heaven by a *Genius* or a bird (e.g. the eagle which was set free at the *rogus* of the emperor: D.C. 56, 42, 3; 74, 5, 5; Hdn. 4, 2 fin.): see Marquardt, *Röm. Staatsverw.* 3, 447, 3. Nor were there lacking people who maintained on oath that they had actually witnessed the translation of the emperor body and soul to heaven, as had once happened to Julius Proculus and Romulus. Thus at the end of Augustus' life: D.C. 56, 46, 2, and that of Drusilla: 59, 11, 4. Sen., *Apocol.* 1. It was the official and only recognized manner in which a god can leave this life.

108 *Phdr.* 246 CD. πλάττομεν . . . θεόν, ἀθάνατόν τι ζῷον, ἔχον μὲν ψυχήν, ἔχον δὲ σῶμα, τὸν ἀεὶ δὲ χρόνον ταῦτα ξυμπεφυκότα. In acc. with the will of the δημιουργός body and soul in the gods remain joined together (though in itself τὸ δεθὲν πᾶν λυτόν. It is to this that Klearch. alludes ap. Ath. 15, 670 B, ὅτι λυτὸν [λύεται the MSS.] μὲν πᾶν τὸ δεδεμένον): hence they are ἀθάνατοι, *Tim.* 41 AB.

109 Hasisatra, Enoch: see above, chap. ii, n. 18. Moses, too, was translated acc. to later legend, and Elijah (cf. after the battle of Panormos Hamilcar disappears and for that reason is worshipped with sacrifice: Hdt. vii, 166–7). In Egypt too: D.S. 1, 25, 7, speaks of the ἐξ ἀνθρώπων μετάστασις, i.e. translation, of Osiris (for the expression cf. Κάστωρ καὶ Πολυδεύκης ἐξ ἀνθρώπων ἠφανίσθησαν, Isoc., *Archid.* (6), 18, etc., frequently).

110 Stories of the disappearance (non comparuit, nusquam apparuit = ἠφανίσθη) of Aeneas and Turnus, King Latinus, Romulus and others: Preller, *Röm. Myth.*[2], pp. 84–5; 683, 2; 704. Anchises: Procop., *Goth.* iv, 22 fin.

111 So too Caesar in deorum numerum relatus est non ore modo decernentium sed et persuasione volgi, Suet., *Jul.* 88.

112 D.C. 79, 18.—It is natural to suppose that some prophecy of the return of the great Macedonian was current and encouraged the attempt to turn the prophecy into a reality and predisposed people to believe in it. This at least is what happened in the case of Nero

and the false Fredericks of the middle ages. This seems to have been at the back of the superstitious cult of Alexander particularly flourishing just at that time (cf. the story told of the family of the Macriani by Treb. Poll. *xxx Tyr.* 14, 4–6). Caracalla (Aur. Vict., *Epit.* 21; cf. Hdn. 4, 8; D.C. 77, 7–8) and Alexander Severus actually regarded themselves as Avatars of Alexander reborn and incarnated in themselves (the latter was first called Alexander at his elevation to the principate, certainly *ominis causa*, and was supposed to have been born, on the anniversary of Alexander's death, in A.'s temple: Lamprid., *Al. Sev.* 5, 1; 13, 1, 3, 4. He paid special honour to Alex., and as we are expressly told by Lamp. 64, 3, se magnum Alexandrum videri volebat).

[113] The Christian anticipation of the return of Nero (as Antichrist) is well known: he was supposed to have disappeared and not to have died. They based their expectation, however, on a widespread belief of the populace which the various Ψευδονέρωνες who actually appeared turned to their advantage (Suet., *Ner.* 57; Tac., *H.* i, 2; ii, 8; Luc., *Indoct.* 20).

[114] This was the idea lying behind the deification of Antinous commanded by the Emperor; as may be seen from the connexion in which Celsus speaks of the matter (ap. Orig., *Cels.* 3, 36, p. 296 Lomm.): he mentions the disappearance of Ant. in the same context as the translation of Kleomedes, Amphiaraos, Amphilochos, etc. (c. 33–4).—The language in which the deification of Ant. is spoken of on the obelisk at Rome gives no precise idea of what happened: see Erman, *Mit. arch. Inst. röm. Abt.* 1896, p. 113 ff.—In this case, then, we have a translation effected by a river-god: cf. the water-nymphs mentioned above, n. 105. In the same way Aeneas disappeared into the river Numicius: Serv., *Aen.* xii, 794; Sch. Veron., *Aen.* i, 259; D.H. i, 64, 4; Arnob. i, 36; Ov., *M.* xiv, 598 ff.; Liv. i, 2, 6. cf. the fable of Alex. the Great's translation into a river: n. 107. Euthymos in the same way vanished into the river Kaikinos (supposed to be his real father: Paus. 6, 6, 4): see above, chap. iv, n. 116.

[115] Philostr., *V. Ap.* viii, 29–30 (not indeed from Damis as Ph. himself definitely asserts; but certainly from sincere accounts derived from the various adherents of Apoll.—none of the facts in the biography are Phil.'s own invention). Apoll. either died in Ephesos or disappeared (ἀφανισθῆναι) in the temple of Athene at Lindos or disappeared in the temple of Diktynna in Crete and ascended to heaven αὐτῷ σώματι (as Eus. *adv. Hierocl.* 44, 408, 5 Ks. rightly understands it). This was the legend generally preferred. His ἀφανισμός was confirmed by the fact that no grave or cenotaph of Apoll. was to be found: Philostr. viii, 31 fin. The imitation of the legends about the disappearance of Empedokles is obvious.

[116] τοῦ Ἀπολλωνίου ἐξ ἀνθρώπου ἤδη ὄντος, θαυμαζομένον δὲ ἐπὶ τῇ μεταβολῇ καὶ μηδ' ἀντιλέξαι θαρροῦντος μηδένος ὡς οὐκ ἀθάνατος εἴη, Philostr. viii, 31. Then follows a miracle vouchsafed to an unbelieving Thomas to whom Apoll. himself appears.

[117] Pre-existence of the soul, return of the souls of the good to their home with God, punishment of the wicked, complete ἀθανασία of all souls as such—all this belongs to the wisdom of Solomon. The Essene doctrine of the soul as described by Jos., *BJ.* 2, 8, 11, is also thoroughly Greek; it belongs to the Stoico-Platonic teaching (i.e. the Neopythagorean variety): see Schwally, *Leben n. Tode n. Vorst. alt. Israël*, p. 151 ff., 179 ff. [1892]. The *carmen Phocylideum* is the work of some Jewish author who obscurely mixes up

Platonic ideas with those of Greek theologians (cf. 104 where Bgk., *PLG.* ii, p. 95, rightly defends the MSS. θεοί against Bernays), and of the Stoics (108)—adding also ideas derived from the Jewish doctrine of the resurrection (115 at least is completely Greek: ψυχὴ δ' ἀθάνατος καὶ ἀγήρως ζῇ διὰ παντός). In Philo's doctrine of the soul everything comes from Platonic or Stoic sources.

[118] e.g. in Sikyon as it appears: Paus. 2, 7, 2.

[119] Perhaps in *Epigr. Gr.* ed. Kaibel (which will be referred to in this section as *Ep.*), 35a, p. 517; but this belongs to the fourth century B.C. A late example (in prose), *IG. Sic. et It.* 1702.

[120] γαῖαν ἔχοις ἐλαφράν, *Ep.* 195, 4; cf. 103, 9; 538, 7; 551, 4; 559, 3; *IG. Sic. et It.* 229; Rhodian inscr., *IGM. Aeg.* i, 151, 3–4 (first–second century A.D.): ἀλλὰ σύ, δαῖμον, τῇ φθιμένῃ κούφην γαῖαν ὕπερθεν ἔχοις.—Eur. already has something similar: *Alc.* 463; see above, chap. xii, n. 121.

[121] The confusion of ideas is evident, e.g. in *Ep.* 700, κοῦφον ἔχοις γαίης βάρος εὐσεβίης ἐνὶ χώρῳ, cf. 222b, 11–12.—The real meaning of such wishes is indicated by Luc., *Luct.* 18; the dead son says to his mourning father, δέδιας μή σοι ἀποπνιγῶ κατακλεισθεὶς ἐν τῷ μνήματι.

[122] Φερσεφόνης θάλαμος, θάλαμοι, *Ep.* 35, 4; 50, 2; 201, 4; 231, 2; *Anth. Pal.* vii, 507–8 "Simonides". φθιμένοις ἀέναος θάλαμος, *Ep.* 143, 2. δόμος Νυκτός, *AP.* vii, 232. (We need not hesitate to use the grave-epigrams in the *Anthology* side by side with the actual sepulchral inss. The former are sometimes the models of the latter, sometimes modelled upon actual epitaphic inscriptions, but always closely related to the more literary epitaphs.)

[123] Λήθης πανσίπονον πόμα, *Ep.* 244, 10. ἦν καταβῇς ἐς πῶμα Λήθης, 261, 20. (Νύξ, λήθης δῶρα φέρουσ' ἐπ' ἐμοί, 312.) Μοῖραι καὶ Λήθη με κατήγαγον εἰς 'Αΐδαο, 521. (Cf. *AP.* vii, Λήθης δόμοι, 25, 6; Λήθης λιμήν, 498; Λήθης πέλαγος, 711, 716.) Λάθας ἤλυθον εἰς λιμένας, Mysian inscr. *BCH.* xvii (1894), p. 532, n. 34.

[124] οἱ πλείους = the dead (like the Latin *plures*: Plaut., *Trin.* 291; Petron. 42): ἐς πλεόνων in Hades, *Ep.* 373, 4; *AP.* vii, 731, 6; xi, 42. Already in Ar., *Eccl.* 1073: γραῦς ἀναστηκυῖα παρὰ τῶν πλειόνων. Call., *Epigr.* 5 (cf. Boisson. on Eunap., p. 309). Ancient oracle ap. Polyb. 8, 30, 7: μετὰ τῶν πλεόνων = τῶν μετηλλαχότων (Tarentum). Even in the present day: 'στοὺς πολλούς, Schmidt, *Volksl. d. Neugr.* i, 235.

[125] *Ep.* 266, μὴ μύρου, φίλ' ἄνερ, με· καὶ αὐτὸς ἐκεῖ γὰρ ὁδεύσας εὑρήσεις τὴν σὴν σύγγαμον Εὐτυχίην. Cf. 558, 5 ff.; 397, 5. Phrygian inscr., *Papers American School*, iii, 305 (n. 427): a father addressing his dead son καὶ πολὺ τερσανέω τότε δάκρυον ἥνικα σεῖο ψυχὴν ἀθρήσω γῆν ὑποδυσάμενος.

[126] εἰ δέ τις ἐν φθιμένοις κρίσις, ὡς λόγος ἀμφὶ θανόντων, *Ep.* 215, 5. A mother boasts of the piety of her son to Rhadamanthys: 514, 5 (cf. 559, 3 f.). So too, in *AP.* vii there is little mention of a judgment (596 Agathias).

[127] The division of the dead into two classes is implied where the pious departed is said to be about to dwell ἐν μακάρεσσιν, etc. But the distinct separation of the dead into two or three classes [see above, chap. xii, n. 62] is rare in the sepulchral inscr.: *Ep.* 650, 9 ff., is an exception (but there one company is ἐπιχθονίη, the other in the *aither*—a Stoic idea).—A peculiar arrangement, implying the three classes, is given in [Socr.] *Epist.* 27, 1 (they are in the τόπος εὐσ. and ἀσεβῶν in Hades, and in the *aither*): τοῦ εἴτε κατὰ γῆν ἐν εὐσεβῶν χώρῳ ὄντος

εἴτε κατ' ἄστρα (*ὅπερ καὶ μάλα πείθομαι*) *Σωκράτους*.—The same again in *AP*. vii, 370 (Diodor.) *ἐν Διὸς* (i.e. in Heaven) *ἢ μακάρων*.

128 There is perhaps no reference in the grave-inss. to the punishment of the *ἀσεβεῖς*, and scarcely any in *AP*. vii (but cf. 377, 7 f. Erykios).

129 *ψυχὴ δ' ἐς τὸ δίκαιον ἔβη*, *Ep*. 502, 13 ; i.c. to the place to which it justly belongs.

130 *ναίεις μακάρων νήσους θαλίῃ ἐνὶ πολλῇ*, *Ep*. 649, 2 ; 366, 6 ; 648, 9. *νῆσον ἔχεις μακάρων*, 473, 2 ; 107, 2 ; *AP*. vii, 690, 4. *μακάρων πεδίον*, *Ep*. 516, 1–2. *Ἠλύσιον πεδίον*, 414, 8 ; 150, 6. *πεδία Ἠλύσια*, 338, 2 ; 649, 3. *χῶρος ἠλύσιος*, 618a, 8. *μετ' εὐσεβέων ἐσμὲν ἐν Ἠλυσίῳ*, 554, 4.—*ναίω δ' ἡρώων ἱερὸν δόμον, οὐκ Ἀχέροντος · τοῖον γὰρ βιότου τέρμα σοφοῖσιν ἔνι*, *Ep*. 228, 7–8. *ἡρώων χῶρον ἔχοις φθίμενος*, 539, 4. *Λητογενές, σὺ δὲ παῖδας ἐν ἡρώεσσι φυλάσσοις, εὐσεβέων ἀεὶ χῶρον ἐπερχόμενος*, 228b, 7 (p. 520). *ᾤχετ' ἐς ἡμιθέους*, 699 (*σοὶ μὲν ἕδρη θείοισι παρ' ἀνδράσι*, *AP*. vii, 659, 3).

131 Description of the charms of the *μακάρων νῆσοι* and the Elysian fields where *οὐδὲ ποθεινὸς ἀνθρώπων ἔτι βίοτος*, *Ep*. 649. More elaborate in the poem of Marcellus on Regilla the wife of Herodes Att. : *Ep*. 1046 (she is *μεθ' ἡρῴνησιν ἐν μακάρων νήσοισιν, ἵνα Κρόνος ἐμβασιλεύει*, 8–9 ; Zeus had dispatched her thither with soft breezes, *ἐς ὠκεανόν*, 21 ff. Now she is *οὐ θνητή, ἀτὰρ οὐδὲ θέαινα* but a Heroine, 42 ff. In the *χορὸς προτεράων ἡμιθεάων* she serves as an *ὀπάων νύμφη* of Persephone, 51 ff.).

132 Clearly e.g. the place where Rhadamanthys holds sway in Hades, *Ep*. 452, 18–19.

133 The *χῶρος εὐσεβέων* clearly indicates Hades : *Ἀίδεω νυχίοιο μέλας ὑπεδέξατο κόλπος, εὐσεβέων θ' ὁσίην εὔνασεν ἐς κλισίην*, *Ep*. 27, 3–4 ; cf. inscr. from Rhodos, *IGM. Aeg*. i, 141, of an old schoolmaster — *εὐσεβῶν χῶρος* [*σφ' ἔχει*] · *Πλούτων γὰρ αὐτὸν καὶ Κόρη κατῴκισαν, Ἑρμῆς τε καὶ δᾳδοῦχος Ἑκάτη, προσφ*[*ιλῆ*] *ἅπασιν εἶναι, μυστικῶν τ' ἐπιστάτην ἔταξαν αὐτὸν πίστεως πάσης χάριν*.—Not infrequently Elysion and the place of the *εὐσεβέες* are identified : e.g. *Ep*. 338, *εὐσεβέες δὲ ψυχὴν* (sc. *ἔχουσι*) *καὶ πεδίων τέρμονες Ἠλυσίων. τοῦτο σαοφροσύνης ἔλαχον γέρας, ἀμβροσίην δὲ* (the immortality of her *soul*) *σώματος ὑβριστὴς οὐκ ἐπάτησε χρόνος*. *ἀλλὰ νέη νύμφῃσι* (thus the stone : *Ath. Mitt*. iv, 17) *μετ' εὐσεβέεσσι καθῆται*.—If there is a judgment in Hades *οἰκήσεις εἰς δόμον εὐσεβέων*, *Ep*. 215, 5–6. Kore conducts the dead *χῶρον ἐπ' εὐσεβέων*, 218, 15–16. *κἄστιν ἐν εὐσεβέων ἣν διὰ σωφροσύνην*, 569, 12. *εὐσεβέων χῶρος*, 296. *εὐσ. δόμος*, 222, 7–8. *εὐσεβέων ναίοις ἱερὸν δόμον*, *IPE*. ii, 298, 11. *ψυχὴ δ' εὐσεβέων οἴχεται εἰς θάλαμον*, *Ep*. 90 (*CIA*. ii, 3004). *εὐσ. εἰς ἱεροὺς θαλάμους*, 222b, 12. *εὐσ. ἐν σκιεροῖς θαλάμοις*, 253, 6. *ἐσθλὰ δὲ ναίω δώματα Φερσεφόνας χώρῳ ἐν εὐσεβέων* 189, 5–6. *μετ' εὐσεβέεσσι κεῖσθαι, ἀντ' ἀρετῆς*, 259. *θῆκ' Ἀίδης ἐς μυχὸν εὐσεβέων*, 241a, 18. *εὐσεβίης δ' εἵνεκεν εὐσεβέων χῶρον ἔβη φθίμενος*, *Ath. Mitt*. xi, 427 (Kolophon). Late Roman inscr., *IG. Sic. et It*. 1660 : a wife says of her dead husband *περὶ οὗ δέομαι τοὺς καταχθονίους θεούς, τὴν ψυχὴν εἰς τοὺς εὐσεβεῖς κατατάξαι*.

134 The *χῶρος μακάρων* in the sky : *ψυχὴ δ' ἀθανάτων βουλαῖς ἐπιδήμιός ἐστιν ἄστροις καὶ ἱερὸν χῶρον ἔχει μακάρων*, *Ep*. 324, 3–4. *καὶ ναίεις μακάρων νήσους . . . αὐγαῖς ἐν καθαραῖσιν, Ὀλύμπου πλησίον ὄντως*, 649, 2, 8. The *ἠλύσιον πεδίον* outside the *φθιμένων δόμοι*, 414, 8, 6. Sometimes both the heavenly abode of the blessed and the Islands of the Blest occur together : [Luc.] *Dem. Enc*. 50.

Demosth. is after his death either in the *μακάρων νήσοις* with the Heroes, or else in the *οὐρανός* as an attendant daimon on *Ζεὺς Ἐλευθέριος*.

[135] *ψυχὴ πρὸς Ὄλυμπον ἀνήλλατο*, *Ep*. 646a, 3. *ψυχὴ δ' ἐν Ὀλύμπῳ*, 159, 261, 11. *ἦλθεν δ' εἰς Ἀίδαο δέμας, ψυχὴ δ' ἐς Ὄλυμπον*, *AP*. vii, 362, 3. (*Ἀίδης* here = the grave as often ; so too in *Ep*. 288, 4–5, *ψυχὴ . . . ἐς αἰθέρα . . . ὀστέα εἰς Ἀίδην ἄτροπος εἷλε νόμος*.) *μετὰ πότμον ὁρῶ φάος Οὐλύμποιο*, *AP*. vii, 678, 5.—*ψυχὴν δ' ἐκ μελέων οὐρανὸς εὐρὺς ἔχει*, *Ep*. 104b, 4. *ἦτορ δ' οὐρανῷ μετάρσιον*, 462, 6. *ψυχή μοι ναίει δώματ' ἐπουράνια*, 261, 10 (and frequently in this poem in various forms). *ἐς οὐρανίας ἀταρποὺς ψυχὴ παπταίνει σῶμ' ἀποδυσαμένη*, *AP*. vii, 337, 7 ; cf. also 363, 3 ; 587, 2 ; 672, 1 and ix, 207–8. *αἰθὴρ μὲν ψυχὰς ὑπεδέξατο*, *Ep*. 21 (fifth century B.C., see above, chap. xii, n. 149). *Εὐρυμάχου ψυχὴν καὶ ὑπερφιάλους διανοίας αἰθὴρ ὑγρὸς ἔχει*, 41 (fourth century B.C. but the *αἰθήρ* is not " moist "—*αἰθὴρ λαμπρὸς ἔχει* is the more primitive version of the phrase given in the corresponding epigr. of the *Πέπλος*. The *ἀήρ* would be *ὑγρός* : *τὴν ψυχὴν ἀπέδωκεν ἐς ἀέρα*, *Ep*. 642, 7). *ψυχὴ μὲν ἐς αἰθέρα καὶ Διὸς αὐλάς*, 288, 4. *ψυχὴ δ' αἰθέριον κατέχει πόλον*, 225, 3. *ἐς αἴθρην ψυχὴ ἔβη ἐμέθεν*, 325, 5.—*ψυχὴ δ' ἀθανάτων βουλαῖς ἐπιδήμιός ἐστιν ἄστροις*, *Ep*. 324, 3. From Thyatira, *BCH*. 1887, p. 461 : *θάψεν δ' ἀδελφὸς Ἀρχέλαος σῶμ' ἐμόν, ψυχὰ δέ μευ πρὸς ἄστρα καὶ θεοὺς ΕΣΙ* (read *ἔβη*). One company of the souls *τείρεσσι σὺν αἰθερίοισι χορεύει· ἧς στρατιῆς εἷς εἰμι*, *Ep*. 650, 11–12 (Diogenes) *νῦν δε θανὼν ἀστέρας οἶκον ἔχει*, *AP*. vii, 64, 4.

[136] *ψυχὴ δ' ἐκ ῥεθέων πταμένη μετὰ δαίμονας ἄλλους ἤλυθε σή, ναίεις δ' ἐν μακάρων δαπέδῳ*, *Ep*. 243, 5–6. *καί με θεῶν μακάρων κατέχει δόμος ἆσσον ἰόντα, οὐρανίοις τε δόμοισι βλέπω φάος Ἠριγενείης*, 312, 6.—*τὴν σύνετον ψυχὴν μακάρων εἰς ἀέρα δοῦσα, πρόσθεν μὲν θνητή, νῦν δὲ θεῶν μέτοχος*, 654, 4–5.—*ἀλλὰ νῦν εἰς τοὺς θεούς* *IG. Sic. et It.* 1420. *ὡς δὲ φύσις μὲν ἔλυσεν ἀπὸ χθονός, ἀθάνατοι μὲν αὐτὸν ἔχουσι θεοὶ σῶμα δὲ σηκὸς ὅδε*, *AP*. vii, 570 ; 61, 2 ; 573, 3–4.

[137] See above, chap. xii, p. 436 ff.

[138] See above, p. 500 f. *πνεῦμα*, *Ep*. 250, 6 ; 613, 6 ; *πνεῦμα λαβὼν δάνος οὐρανόθεν τελέσας χρόνον ἀνταπέδωκα* (cf. *πνεῦμα γάρ ἐστι θεοῦ χρῆσις θνητοῖσι*, *Carm. Phoc.* 106). 156, 2 : *πνοιὴν αἰθὴρ ἔλαβεν πάλιν, ὅσπερ ἔδωκεν* (third century B.C. ; see Köhler on *CIA*. ii, 4135).—This conception having become popular frequently occurs in the theological poetry of later times : e.g. *χρησμός* ap. Stob., *Ecl.* 1, 49, 46, i, p. 414 W. : *τὸ μὲν (τὸ σῶμα) λυθέν ἐστι κόνις, ψυχὴ δὲ πρὸς αἴθρην σκίδναται, ὁππόθεν ἦλθε, μετήορος εἰς αἰθέρ' ἁπλοῦν* (read *αἰθέρ' ἐς ἁγνόν*). Oracle of Apoll. Tyan. ap. Philostr., *VA*. viii, 31 : *ἀθάνατος ψυχὴ . . . μετὰ σῶμα μαρανθὲν . . . ῥηιδίως προθοροῦσα κεράννυται ἠέρι κούφῳ*.

[139] *ψυχὴν δ' ἀθάνατον κοινὸς ἔχει θάνατος*, *Ep*. 35, 6 (*CIA*. ii, 3620, fourth century B.C.). *IG. Sic. et It.* 940, 3–4 : *ἀθανάτη ψυχὴ μὲν ἐς αἰθέρι καὶ Διὸς αὐγαῖς πωτᾶται.* ib. 942 : *. . . ἐνθάδε κεῖμαι, οὐχὶ θανών· θνήσκειν μὴ λέγε τοὺς ἀγαθούς* (from Call., *Epigr*. 11, *τᾷδε Σάων . . . ἱερὸν ὕπνον κοιμᾶται. θνάσκειν μὴ λέγε τοὺς ἀγαθούς*).—*οὐκ ἔθανες, Πρώτη, μετέβης δ' ἐς ἀμείνονα χῶρον*, *Ep*. 649.

[140] This retains its full and original meaning (as in Call., *Epigr*. 11) ; cf. *Ep*. 559, 7, *λέγε Ποπιλίην εὕδειν ἄνερ· οὐ θεμιτὸν θνήσκειν τοὺς ἀγαθούς, ἀλλ' ὕπνον ἡδὺν ἔχειν.* More often as a mere conventional phrase : 433 ; 101, 4 ; 202, 1 ; 204, 7 ; *σ' ἐκοίμισεν ὕπνος ὁ λήθης*, 223, 3 ; 502, 2 ; *AP*. vii, 29, 1 ; 30, 2 ; 260.

[141] *Ep*. 651 : *θνητὸν σῶμα . . . τὸ δ' ἀθάνατον ἐς μακάρων ἀνόρουσε*

κέαρ · ψυχὴ γὰρ ἀείζως ἣ τὸ ζῆν παρέχει καὶ θεόφιν κατέβη . . . σῶμα χιτὼν ψυχῆς (cf. Emp. 414 M. = *fr.* 126 D., *σαρκῶν περιστέλλουσα χιτῶνι* sc. *τὴν ψυχήν*) · *τὸν δὲ θεὸν σέβε μου* (the god in me, my *ψυχή*). 261, 6, *τὴν ψυχὴν δ' ἀθανάτην ἔλαχον · ἐν γαίῃ μὲν σῶμα τὸ συγγενές, οὐράνιος δὲ ἤλυθεν ἡ ψυχὴ δῶμα κατ' οὐ φθίμενον κτλ.*; cf. 320, 6 ff.—594 (late epitaph of a doctor with philosophic leanings; found in Rome), 7 ff.: *οὐδ' ἄρα θνητὸς ἔην, ὑπ' ἀνάγκης ὑψιμέδοντος τύμβῳ εἰναλέῳ πεπεδημένος ἤνυσεν οἶμον. ἐκ ῥεθέων δ' ἅμα στείχων σεμνὸν ἔβη Διὸς οἶκον.* No sense can be made of the passage if *τύμβῳ* is understood as the real grave and this has led to altering or straining the sense of *εἰναλέῳ* (*εἰναλίῳ* Franz, *σιγαλέῳ* Jacobs). But the poet means: the dead man was (in his real nature, his soul) immortal, only the will of the gods had caused him (his soul) to be bound to the body and to complete his course of life in the body, after the end of which he will rise immediately (and return) to the realm of the gods. Read therefore *τύμβῳ εἰν ἀλαῷ πεπεδημένος*, fettered in the "dark grave" of the body: *σῶμα=σῆμα*. (Exactly as in Verg., *A.* vi, 734, the animae: clausae tenebris et carcere caeco.)—603: he who lies buried here *θνητοῖς ψυχὴν πείσας ἐπὶ σώμασιν ἐλθεῖν τὴν αὑτοῦ, μέλεος, οὐκ ἀνέπεισε μένειν.* That is: he has persuaded his (previously living and bodiless) soul to enter into the realm of mortal bodies (to occupy a body), but could not persuade it to remain there long—in this earthly life.

[142] Once at the most: *εἰ πάλιν ἔστι γενέσθαι . . . εἰ δ' οὐκ ἔστιν πάλιν ἐλθεῖν*—*Ep.* 304 (cf. above, chap. xii, n. 138).

[143] The epitaphs quoted in n. 141 have a theological meaning but do not allude to any specifically Platonic opinion or doctrines. There is no need to see Platonic influence (as Lehrs would: *Pop. Aufs.*², p. 339 f.) in the numerous epitaphs that speak of the ascent of the soul into the *aither*, the stars, etc. (notes 135, 136). It is true that Alexis 158 K. inquires whether the view that the body decays after death—*τὸ δ' ἀθάνατον ἐξῆρε πρὸς τὸν ἀέρα*—is not Platonic doctrine (*ταῦτ' οὐ σχολὴ Πλάτωνος*). But he has no real knowledge of Platonic teaching and calls Platonic that idea of the ascent of the souls of the dead into the upper regions which had long been popular in Athens—even before Plato's time. In fact Plato's doctrine has only the most distant resemblance to the popular one, and the latter originated and persisted without being influenced at all by Plato or his school.

[144] *Ep.* 650, 12. I belong to the company of the blessed which *τείρεσσι σὺν αἰθερίοισι χορεύει, λαχὼν θεὸν ἡγεμονῆα.* These last words must refer to a special relation of a pious kind to some god. We may note the conclusion of the *Caesares* of Julian (336 C): Hermes addresses the Emperor: follow the *ἐντολαί* of *πατὴρ Μίθρας* in life, *καὶ ἡνίκα ἂν ἐνθένδε ἀπιέναι δέῃ, μετὰ τῆς ἀγαθῆς ἐλπίδος ἡγεμόνα θεὸν εὐμενῆ καθιστὰς σεαυτῷ.* Cf. also the promise made in an Egyptian magic papyrus ed. Parthey, *Abh. Berl. Ak.* 1865, p. 125, l. 178 ff.: the ghost thus conjured up will after your death *σοῦ τὸ πνεῦμα βαστάξας εἰς ἀέρα ἄξει σὺν αὑτῷ, εἰς γὰρ ᾄδην οὐ χωρήσει ἀέριον πνεῦμα συσταθὲν* (i.e. commended) *κραταιῷ παρέδρῳ.* Cf. Pl., *Phd.* 107 D ff.: the souls of the dead are conducted each by the *δαίμων ὅσπερ ζῶντα εἰλήχει* to the judgment place: thence they go *εἰς ᾄδου μετὰ ἡγεμόνος ἐκείνου ᾧ δὴ προστέτακται τοὺς ἐνθένδε ἐκεῖσε πορεῦσαι.* Afterwards yet another, *ἄλλος ἡγεμών* as it appears, leads them back again. A blessed abode hereafter is found by *ἡ καθαρῶς τε καὶ μετρίως τὸν βίον διεξελθοῦσα καὶ ξυνεμπόρων καὶ ἡγεμόνων θεῶν τυχοῦσα*, 108 C. The same idea occurs on the monument of Vibia (in the Catacombs of Praetextatus in Rome): *Mercurius nuntius*

conducts her (and Alcestis) before Dispater and Aeracura to be tried: after that a special *bonus angelus* leads her to the banquet of the blessed (*CIL.* vi, 142). There is nothing Christian in this, any more than in the whole monument or its inscriptions. (The "angel" as an intermediate being between gods and men had long been taken from Jewish religion by heathen belief and philosophy: they were sometimes identified with the Platonic δαίμονες: see R. Heinze, *Xenokrat.* 112 f. These intermediate natures, the ἄγγελοι, have nothing to do with the old Greek conception of certain gods as "Messengers" or of the Hero Εὐάγγελος, etc. [cf. Usener, *Götternamen*, 268 ff.].) With the fanciful picture of Vibia we may compare (besides the Platonic passages mentioned above) what Luc., *Philops.* 25, has to say of the νεανίας πάγκαλος who leads the souls into the underworld (οἱ ἀγαγόντες αὐτόν less precisely in the parallel narrative of Plutarch, *de An. fr.* 1, ap. Eus., *PE.* 11, 36, p. 563 D).

145 Hermes the conductor of the souls as ἄγγελος Φερσεφόνης, *Ep.* 575, 1. Hermes brings the souls to Eubouleus and Persephone, *Ep.* 272, 9.—He leads the souls to the μακάρων ἠλύσιον πεδίον, 414, 9; 411; to the Islands of the Blest, 107, 2. He leads them by the hand to heaven, to the blessed gods, 312, 8 ff.

146 *Ep.* 218, 15, ἀλλὰ σύ, παμβασίλεια θεά, πολυώνυμε κουρά, τήνδ' ἄγ' ἐπ' εὐσεβέων χῶρον, ἔχουσα χερός. 452, 17 ff. Of the souls of the dead man, his wife and children it is said: δέχεο ἐς Ἀίδου (Hades does not admit everyone: cf. the dead man who prays οἱ στύγιον χῶρον ὑποναίετε δαίμονες ἐσθλοί, δέξασθ' εἰς Ἀίδην κἀμὲ τὸν οἰκτρότατον, 624), πότνια νύμφη, καὶ ψυχὰς προὔπεμπε, ἵνα ξανθὸς Ῥαδάμανθυς. To be thus received and conducted by a god or goddess is evidently regarded as a special favour. The abode of the εὐσεβεῖς is reached by those who have honoured Persephone before all other deities: *IG. Sic. et It.* 1561. Zeus too conducts the souls, *Ep.* 511, 1: ἀντί σε κυδαλίμας ἀρετᾶς, πολυήρατε κοῦρε, ἦξεν ἐς Ἠλύσιον αὐτὸς ἄναξ Κρονίδης (θεός, 516, 1–2). Speaking of a Ptolemy who has died young, Antipater Sid. says (*AP.* vii, 241, 11 ff.) οὐ δέ σε νὺξ ἐκ νυκτὸς ἐδέξατο· δὴ γὰρ ἄνακτας τοίους οὐκ Ἀΐδας, Ζεὺς δ' ἐς ὄλυμπον ἄγει. Apollo also: Parmenis buried by her parents says [νῦν μεγάλ]ου (to be restored in some such fashion) δέ μ' ἔχει τέμενος Διός, ὄρρά τ' Ἀπόλλων [λοιγ]οῦ (doubtful completion) ἄμειψεν, ἑλὼν ἐκ πυρὸς ἀθάνατον, *IGM. Aeg.* i, 142 (Rhodos).—Tibull. is clearly imitating Greek poetry when he says (1, 3, 57) sed me quod facilis tenero sum semper Amori ipsa Venus campos ducet ad Elysios (the poet himself explains why it should be Venus: he has specially honoured her. There is no need to imagine a Venus Libitina). Phleg., *Mirab.* 3, p. 130, 16 ff. West. [73, 1 Kell.]: Φοῖβος Ἀπόλλων Πύθιος . . . μοι ἐὸν κρατερὸν θεράποντ' (the daimonic wolf) ἐπιπέμψας ἤγαγεν εἰς μακάρων τε δόμους καὶ Περσεφονείης.

147 Isidote, hierophantis in Eleusis (grand-daughter of the famous sophist Isaios) is called by her epitaph (Ἐφ. Ἀρχ. 1885, p. 149, l. 8 ff.) ἔξοχον ἔν τ' ἀρεταῖς ἔν τε σαοφροσύναις· ἣν καὶ ἀμειβομένη Δηὼ μακάρων ἐπὶ νήσσους ἤγαγε, παντοίης ἐκτὸς ἐπωδυνίης. (l. 20 ἣν καὶ Δημήτηρ ὤπασεν ἀθανάτοις.)

148 By their noble death the gods show ὡς ἄμεινον εἴη ἀνθρώπῳ τεθνάναι μᾶλλον ἢ ζώειν, Hdt. i, 31; cf. [Pl.] *Axioch.* 367 C; Cic., *TD.* i, 113; Plu., *Cons. ad Apoll.* 13, 108 E; cf. Amm. Marc. 25, 3, 15.—The epitaph of Isidote alludes to the legend, l. 11: δῶκε (Demeter) δέ οἱ θάνατον γλυκερώτερον ἡδέος ὕπνου πάγχυ καὶ Ἀργείων φέρτερον ἠϊθέων.

[149] Γηραλέην ψυχὴν ἐπ' ἀκμαίῳ σώματι Γλαῦκος καὶ κάλλει κεράσας κρείττονα σωφροσύνην, ὄργια πᾶσιν ἔφαινε βροτοῖς φαεσίμβροτα Δηοῦς εἰναετές, δεκάτῳ δ' ἦλθε παρ' ἀθανάτους. ἦ καλὸν ἐκ μακάρων μυστήριον, οὐ μόνον εἶναι τὸν θάνατον θνητοῖς οὐ κακόν, ἀλλ' ἀγαθόν, Ἐφ. Ἀρχ. 1883, pp. 81–2 (third century A.D.). Below the statue of a daughter of this Glaukos, at Eleusis, there is an inscr., Γλαύκου δὲ γνωτὴ θεοειδέος, ὅς τε καὶ αὐτὸς ἱεροφαντήσας ᾤχετ' ἐς ἀθανάτους, Ἐφ. Ἀρχ. 1894, p. 205, n. 26, l. 11 ff.

[150] As a conventional formula: [D.H.] *Rhet.* 6, 5: ἐπὶ τέλει (of the funeral oration) περὶ ψυχῆς ἀναγκαῖον εἰπεῖν, ὅτι ἀθάνατος, καὶ ὅτι τοὺς τοιούτους, ἐν θεοῖς ὄντας, ἀμεῖνον ἴσως ἀπαλλάττειν.

[151] —τὸν ἀθάνατοι φιλέεσκον· τοὔνεκα καὶ πηγαῖς λοῦσαν ἐν ἀθανάτοις (we are reminded of the ἀθάνατος πηγή out of which Glaukos drew ἀθανασία: Sch. Pl., *Rp.* 611 C), καὶ μακάρων νήσους βάλλον ἐς ἀθανάτων, *Ep.* 366, 4 ff. There are two fountains in Hades, that (to the left) of Lethe, and (to the right) of Mnemosyne, from which cold water flows (l. 5): from the latter the guardians will give the suppliant soul water to drink καὶ τότ' ἔπειτ' ἄλλοισι μεθ' ἡρώεσσιν ἀνάξει: sepulchral tablet from Petelia (about third century B.C.), *IG. Sic. et It.* 638 (*Ep.* 1037; Harrison, *Proleg.* 661 ff.). Mutilated copies of the same original have been found at Eleuthernai in Crete, *BCH.* 1893–4, p. 126, 629; cf. above, chap. xii, n. 62.—This, in fact, is the "water of life" so often mentioned in the folk-lore of many countries; cf. Grimm, *D. Märchen*, n. 97, with *Notes* iii, p. 178, 328; Dieterich, *Abraxas*, 97 f.; *Nekyia*, 94, 99. This is the fountain from which Psyche also has to bring water to Venus (Apul., *M.* vi, 13–14); and it is certain that in the original Psyche-story it was not the water of the Styx that was intended (as Apul. supposes, but of what use would that be?), but the water of the fountain of life in Hades. It is a *speaking* fountain, *vocales aquae* (Apul. vi, 14), and, in fact, precisely the same as that mentioned in a unique legend of Herakles given in [Justin.] πρὸς Ἕλληνας 3 (p. 636, 7, ed. Harnack, *Ber. Berl. Ak.* 1896); Herakles is called ὁ ὄρη πηδήσας (? πιδύσας, "making it gush forth," would be more acceptable) ἵνα λάβῃ ὕδωρ ἔναρθρον φωνὴν ἀποδιδόν. Herakles makes the mountain gush forth by striking the speaking water out of the rock. This is exactly paralleled in the modern Greek stories given by Hahn, *Gr. u. alb. Märchen*, ii, p. 234; the Lamia who guards the water of life (τὸ ἀθάνατο νερό, the phrase often appears in these stories; cf. also Schmidt, *Griech. Märchen*, p. 233) "strikes with a hammer on the rock till it opens and she can draw the water of life". This is the same ancient fairy tale motif. The proper home of this water of life is probably the lower world, the world of either death or immortality, though this is not expressly stated in the Herakles legend nor in the fairy tale of Glaukos who discovered the ἀθάνατος πηγή (but probably also in the magic country of the West. Thus Alexander the Great finds the ἀθάνατος πηγή at the entrance to the μακάρων χώρα acc. to Ps.-Callisth. ii, 39 ff.; his story shows clear reminiscences of the Glaukos tale, its prototype, in c. 39 fin., 41, 2).—The Orphic (and Pythagorean) mythology of Hades (see above: chap. xi, n. 96; chap. xii, nn. 37–8; chap. vii, n. 21) then proceeded to make use of the folk-tale for their own purposes. In *Ep.* 658 the prayer also refers to the Orphic fable (*CIG.* 5772) ψυχρὸν ὕδωρ δοίη σοι ἄναξ ἐνέρων Ἀϊδωνεύς, and 719, 11, ψυχῇ διψώσῃ ψυχρὸν ὕδωρ μεταδός. They mean: may you live on in complete consciousness. (The same thing in the negative: the dead man dwells ἅμα παισὶ θεῶν καὶ λήθης οὐκ ἔπιεν λιβάδα, 414, 10:

οὐκ ἔπιον Λήθης Ἀϊδωνίδος ἔσχατον ὕδωρ, so that I can perceive the mourning of the living for my loss, 204, 11. καὶ θνήσκων γὰρ ἔχω νόον οὔτινα βαιόν, 334, 5.—Poetical allusion in *AP.* vii, 346: σὺ δ' εἰ θέμις, ἐν φθιμένοισι τοῦ Λήθης ἐπ' ἐμοὶ μή τι πίῃς ὕδατος.—Perhaps something of the sort already occurs in Pindar: see above, chap. xii, n. 37.)

[152] εὐψύχει κυρία καὶ δοίη σοι ὁ Ὄσιρις τὸ ψυχρὸν ὕδωρ, *IG. Sic. et It.* 1488; 1705; 1782; *Rev. Arch.* 1887, p. 201. (And once the line σοὶ δὲ Ὀσείριδος ἁγνὸν ὕδωρ Εἶσις χαρίσαιτο, inscr. from Alexandria: *Rev. Arch.* 1887, p. 199.) εὐψύχει μετὰ τοῦ Ὀσείριδος, *I. Sic. et It.* 2098. The dead man is with Osiris, *Ep.* 414, 5. Osiris as lord in the world of the blessed: *defixio* from Rome, *I. Sic. et It.* 1047: ὁ μέγας Ὄσειρις ὁ ἔχων τὴν κατεξουσίαν καὶ τὸ βασίλειον τῶν νερτέρων θεῶν.—It appears that the legend of the fountain of Mnemosyne and its cold water was independently developed by the Greeks and then associated subsequently with the analogous Egyptian idea or brought into harmony with it (certainly not as e.g. Böttiger, *Kl. Schr.*, thinks, originally belonging to the Egyptians alone and thence imported into Greece from Egypt). Egyptian Books of the Dead often speak of the cool water that the dead enjoy (cf. Maspero, *Ét. de mythol. et d'arch. égypt.* 1893, 1, 366 f.), as well as of the water drawn from the Nile and preserving the youth of the dead man: Maspero, *Notices et Extraits*, 24, 1883, pp. 99–100. The formula, "may Osiris give you the cold water" (everlasting life), does not seem to occur on original Egyptian monuments. It is prob. therefore modelled by Egyptian Greeks on their own ancient Greek formula.—On Christian inss. we often have the formula: *spiritum tuum dominus* (or *deus Christus*, or a holy martyr) *refrigeret*: see Kraus, *Realencykl. d. christl. Alterth.* s.v. *refrigerium.* This is probably, as has been frequently suggested, an imitation of the heathen formula, like so many features of early Christian burial usage.

[153] On sarcophagi in Isauria the lion is sometimes represented on the lid with the inscr. describing the contents: ὁ δεῖνα ζῶν καὶ φρονῶν ἀνέθηκεν ἑαυτὸν λέοντα καὶ τὴν γυναῖκα αὐτοῦ προτέραν, etc. On another sarcophagus: Λούκιος ἀνέστησε (three names) καὶ ἑαυτὸν ἀετὸν καὶ Ἄμμουκιν Βαβόου τὸν πατέρα ἀετὸν τειμῆς χάριν, *American School at Athens*, iii, p. 26, 91–2. These expressions must refer to something quite different from the otherwise not uncommon practice of representing lions or eagles on graves. I can only explain them on the supposition that the dead persons represent themselves and the relatives named in the forms which had belonged to them in the mysteries of Mithras, in which lions and lionesses formed the fourth grade, and eagles, ἀετοί (or ἱέρακες) the seventh (cf. Porph., *Abst.* iv, 16); these are elsewhere called πατέρες.

[154] The soul of a dead son (who as it appears from ll. 1, 2, 6 ff. had been killed by a flash of lightning and therefore removed to a higher state of being [see Append. i]) appears by night to his mother and confirms her own assertion, οὐκ ἤμην βροτός, *Ep.* 320. The soul of their daughter who has died ἄωρος and ἀθαλάμευτος appears to her parents on the ninth day (l. 35) after death, 372, 31 ff. (The ninth day marks the end of the first offerings to the dead: see above, chap. v, n. 84; cf. "Apparitions of the deceased occur most frequently on the ninth day after death": a German superstition mentioned by Grimm, 1812, n. 856.) It is significant that the daughter who thus appears in a vision has died unmarried. The ἄγαμοι, like the ἄωροι, do not find rest after death: see Append. vii and iii. The

soul of another unmarried maiden says distinctly that those like herself are especially able to appear in dreams: ἠϊθέοις γὰρ ἔδωκε θεὸς μετὰ μοῖραν ὀλέθρου ὡς ζώουσι λαλεῖν πᾶσιν ἐπιχθονίοις, *Ep.* 325, 7–8.—It becomes more general, however, in 522, 12–13: σώματα γὰρ κατέλυσε Δίκη, ψυχὴ δὲ προπᾶσα ἀθάνατος δι' ὅλου (thus the stone, *Ath. Mitt.* xiv, 193) πωτωμένη πάντ' ἐπακούει (cf. Eur., *Orest.* 667 ff.).

[155] ψυχὴ δὲ—says his son and pupil to the dead physician Philadelphos—ἐκ ῥεθέων πταμένη μετὰ δαίμονας ἄλλους ἤλυθε σή, ναίεις δ' ἐν μακάρων δαπέδῳ, ἵλαθι καί μοι ὄπαζε νόσων ἄκος, ὡς τὸ πάροιθεν, νῦν γὰρ θειοτέρην μοῖραν ἔχεις βιότου, *Ep.* 243, 5 ff. (*Inscr. Perg.* ii, 576).

[156] There is a striking conjunction of the most exalted hopes and the most utter unbelief on a single stone: *Ep.* 261.

[157] εἴ γέ τι ἔστι (ἐστέ) κάτω, *CIG.* 6442.—κατὰ γῆς εἴπερ χρηστοῖς γέρας ἐστίν, *Ep.* 48, 6; 63, 3. εἴ γ' ἐν φθιμένοισί τις αἴσθησις, τέκνον, ἐστίν—*Ep.* 700, 4. εἰ δέ τίς ἐστι νόος παρὰ Ταρτάρῳ ἢ παρὰ Λήθῃ, 722, 5. εἰ γένος εὐσεβέων ζώει μετὰ τέρμα βίοιο, *AP.* vii, 673.—Cf. above, chap. xii, n. 17.

[158] Call., *Epigr.* 15; *Ep.* 646; 646a (p. xv); 372, 1 ff.

[159] ἡμεῖς δὲ πάντες οἱ κάτω, τεθνηκότες, ὀστέα, τέφρα γεγόναμεν, ἄλλο δ' οὐδὲ ἕν, *Ep.* 646, 5 f.; cf. 298, 3–4. ἐκ γαίας βλαστὼν γαῖα πάλιν γέγονα, 75 (third century B.C.); cf. 438; 311, 5: τοῦθ' ὅ ποτ' ὤν (the I that was once living has now become these things, viz.), στήλη, τύμβος, λίθος, εἰκών. 513, 2, κεῖται ἀναίσθητος ὥσπερ λίθος (cf. Thgn. 567 f.) ἠὲ σίδηρος. 551, 3, κεῖται λίθος ὥς, ἡ πάνσοφος, ἡ περίβωτος.

[160] Ἕστηκεν μὲν Ἔρως (prob. on the monument) εὕδων ὕπνον, ἐν φθιμένοις δὲ οὐ πόθος, οὐ φιλότης ἔστι κατοιχομένοις. ἀλλ' ὁ θανὼν κεῖται πεδίῳ λίθος οἷα πεπηγώς, εἰχώρων ἁπαλῶν σάρκας ἀποσκεδάσας—ἐξ ὕδατος καὶ γῆς καὶ πνεύματος (here evidently not in the Stoic sense, but simply = ἀήρ) ἦα πάροιθεν· ἀλλὰ θανὼν κεῖμαι πᾶσι (all the elements) τὰ πάντ' ἀποδούς. πᾶσιν τοῦτο μένει· τί δὲ τὸ πλέον; ὁππόθεν ἦλθεν, εἰς τοῦτ' αὖτ' ἐλύθη σῶμα μαραινόμενον (inscr. in Bucharest; Gomperz, *Arch. epigr. Mitt. a. Oest.* vi, 30).

[161] πνεῦμα λαβὼν δάνος οὐρανόθεν τελέσας χρόνον ἀνταπέδωκα, *Ep.* 613, 6. (This is a commonplace of popular philosophy: "life is only lent to man": see Wyttenbach on Plu., *Cons. ad Apoll.* 106 F; Upton on Epict. 1, 1, 32 Schw.; cf. usura vitae *Anth. Lat. Ep.* ed. Bücheler, i, p. 90, n. 183.)

[162] Epitaph from Amorgos: *Ath. Mitt.* 1891, p. 176, which ends: τὸ τέλος ἀπέδωκα.

[163] δαίμων ὁ πικρὸς κτλ., *Ep.* 127, 3 (cf. 59). ἀστόργου μοῖρα κίχεν θανάτου, 146, 6. δίσσα δὲ τέκνα λιποῦσαν ὁ παντοβάρης λάβε μ' Ἅιδης, ἄκριτον ἄστοργον θηρὸς ἔχων κραδίην (Tyrrheion in Akarnania, *BCH.* 1886, p. 178).

[164] παύσασθαι δεινοῦ πένθους δεινοῦ τε κυδοιμοῦ· οὐδὲν γὰρ πλέον (ΠΑCΙΝ the stone as stated) ἐστί, θανόντα γὰρ οὐδένα (read οὐδὲν) ἐγείρει κτλ., ins. from Larisa, *Ath. Mitt.* xi, 451. εἰ δ' ἦν τοὺς ἀγαθοὺς ἀνάγειν πάλιν, ins. from Pherai, *BCH.* 1889, p. 404.

[165] οὐ κακός ἐστ' Ἀΐδης—comfort being derived from the fact that death is "common". *Ep.* 256, 9–10; 282; 292, 6; 298.

[166] εὐψύχει, τέκνον, οὐδεὶς ἀθάνατος, *IG. Sic. et It.* 1531; 1536 (cf. 1743 ad fin.); 1997 and frequent; *CIG.* 4463; 4467 (Syria). εὐψύχει Ἀταλάντη, ὅσα γεννᾶται τελευτᾷ, *IG. Sic. et It.* 1832. καὶ ὁ Ἡρακλῆς ἀπέθανεν, 1806.—Even on Christian graves the formula is frequent: εὐψύχει (ἡ δεῖνα), οὐδεὶς ἀθάνατος (see Schultze, *Die Katakomben*, 251).

[167] οὐκ ἤμην, γενόμην, οὐκ ἔσομ' οὐ μέλει μοι· ὁ βίος ταῦτα. *IG. Sic. et It.* 2190 (the original form of the ending is probably οὐκ ἔσομαι· τί πλέον; see Gomperz, *Arch. ep. Mitt. Oesterr.* vii, 149; *Ztschr. f. öst. Gymn.* 1879, p. 437); cf. *Ep.* 1117, οὐκ ἤμην, γενόμην, ἤμην, οὐκ εἰμί· τοσαῦτα· (this τοσαῦτα, or more commonly ταῦτα, is frequent in epitaphs as a formula of resignation—a summary of existence: "all life comes to nothing but this." See Loch, *Zu d. griech. Grabschr.* 289–95)—εἰ δέ τις ἄλλο ἐρέει, ψεύσεται· οὐκ ἔσομαι. *CIG.* 6265: εὐψυχῶ, ὅστις οὐκ ἤμην καὶ ἐγενόμην, οὔκ εἰμι καὶ οὐ λυποῦμαι (cf. also *Ep.* 502, 15; 646, 14; *AP.* vii, 339, 5–6; x, 118, 3–4). Frequent also in a Latin form: Non eris, nec fuisti, Sen., *Epist.* 77, 11 (see above, chap. xiv, pt. i, n. 68). Ausonius, p. 252, ed. Schenkl (ex sepulchro latinae viae): nec sum nec fueram; genitus tamen e nihilo sum. mitte nec explores singula, talis eris (probably this is how it should be read); cf. *CIL.* ii, 1434; v, 1813, 1939, 2893; viii, 2885, etc.; Bücheler, *Carm. lat. epigr.* i, p. 116.

[168] γνοὺς ὡς θνατοῖς οὐδὲν γλυκερώτερον αὐγᾶς ζῆθι, *Ep.* 560, 7. Coarser admonitions to enjoy the passing hour, *CIG.* 3846 (iii, p. 1070). *Ep.* 362, 5. παῖσον, τρύφησον, ζῆσον· ἀποθανεῖν σε δεῖ, 439, 480a, 7. An ins. from Saloniki, second century A.D., *Ath. Mitt.* 1896, p. 99, concludes—ὁ βίος οὗτος. τί στήκ(ε)ις ἄνθρωπε; ταῦτα βλέπων ΥΠΑΛΟΥΣΟΥ (ἀπόλαυσον? or ἀπολαύου?).

[169] εἰ καὶ . . . φροῦδον σῶμα . . . ἀλλ' ἀρετὰ βιοτᾶς αἰὲν ζωοῖσι μέτεστι, ψυχᾶς μαννύουσ' εὐκλέα σωφροσύνην, *Ep.* 560, 10 ff. σῶμα μὲν ἐνθάδ' ἔχει σόν, Δίφιλε, γαῖα θανόντος, μνῆμα δὲ σῆς ἔλιπες πᾶσι δικαιοσύνης (and elsewhere with variations): *Ep.* 56–8. Or only: . . τέλεσεν δὲ καὶ ἐσσομένοισι νοῆσαι στήλην, *Ath. Mitt.* 1891, p. 263, 3 (Thessaly). Homeric: see above, chap. i, n. 88, and cf. σᾶμα τόζ' Ἰδαμενεὺς ποίησα ἵνα κλέως εἴη . . . ancient inscr. from Rhodos: *Ath. Mitt.* 1891, p. 112, 243 (*IGM. Aeg.* i, n. 737).

[170] From an earlier period (*ca.* third century B.C.), *Ep.* 44: ἣν ὁ σύνευνος ἔστερξεν μὲν ζῶσαν ἐπένθησεν δὲ θανοῦσαν. φῶς δ' ἔλιπ' εὐδαίμων, παῖδας παίδων ἐπιδοῦσα. Fine also are 67 and 81b. But something like them appears even late: 647, 5–10. 556: a priestess of Zeus congratulates herself εὔτεκνον ἀστονάχητον ἔχει τάφος· οὐ γὰρ ἀμαυρῶς δαίμονες ἡμετέρην ἔβλεπον εὐσεβίην.—To recover for a moment the taste of the old robust spirit we may remind ourselves of Herodotos' story of Tellos the Athenian, the happiest of mankind. He was born in a prosperous city, had fine children and saw the children of all these children, none of whom died. And his happy life was crowned by a noble end. In a battle of the Athenians against their neighbours he was successful in putting the foe to rout and then he himself fell while fighting, so that his country buried him in the place where he fell and honoured him greatly. (Hdt. i, 30. Herodotos' Solon does indeed assign the second prize of happiness to Kleobis and Biton and their fortunate end: c. 31. A changed attitude to life makes itself felt in their story.)

[171] Mundus senescens, Cyprian, *ad Demetr.* 3 ff. The Christians lay the blame for the impoverishment and decay of life on the heathen. The latter in turn blame the recently arrived and now dominant Christianity for the unhappiness of the time: Tertull., *Apol.* 40 ff.; Arnob. 1; Aug., *CD.* It was already a vulgare proverbium—Pluvia defit, causa Christiani sunt, *CD.* ii, 3. The Emp. Julian found τὴν οἰκουμένην ὥσπερ λιποψυχοῦσαν and wished τὴν φθορὰν τῆς οἰκουμένης στῆσαι, Liban., *Or.* i, p. 617, 10; 529, 4.—The Christians returned the compliment: the reason why everything in nature and the life

of men was going awry is simply paganorum exacerbata perfidia (*Leg. Novell. Theodos. ii*, i, 3, p. 10 Ritt.).

[172] We know of a certain Nikagoras Minuc. f. (significantly enough an ardent admirer of Plato) temp. Const. δᾳδοῦχος τῶν ἁγιωτάτων Ἐλευσῖνι μυστηρίων, *CIG.* 4770. Julian, even as a boy, was initiated at Eleusis: Eunap., *V. Soph.*, p. 53 (Boiss.). At that time, however, in miserandam ruinam conciderat Eleusina, Mamert., *Act. Jul.* 9. Here again Julian seems to have restored the cult. Valentinian I, on the point of abolishing all nocturnal festivals (see *Cod. Theod. iii*, 9, 16, 7), allowed them to continue when Praetextatus Procons. of Achaea represented to him that for the Greeks ὁ βίος would be ἀβίωτος, εἰ μέλλοιεν κωλύεσθαι τὰ συνέχοντα τὸ ἀνθρώπειον γένος ἁγιώτατα μυστήρια κατὰ θεσμὸν ἐκτελεῖν, Zosim. iv, 3. (Praetext. was a friend of Symmachus and, like him, one of the last pillars of Roman orthodoxy: *princeps religiosorum*, Macr., *S.* i, 11, 1. He was himself *sacratus Eleusiniis*, and *hierophanta* there: *CIL.* vi, 1779; probably the Πραιτέξτατος ὁ ἱεροφάντης of Lyd., *Mens.* 4, 2, p. 148 R. [p. 65 W.], is the same person.) In 375 A.D. we hear of a Nestorius (probably the father of the Neoplatonic Plutarch) as ἱεροφαντεῖν τεταγμένος at the time (Zos. iv, 18). In 396 during the *hierophantia* of a πατὴρ τῆς Μιθριακῆς τελετῆς (whose oath should have excluded him from that office) the temple of Eleusis was destroyed by Alaric, incited thereto by the monks who accompanied him (Eunap., *VS.*, p. 52–3). The regular holding of the festival must then have come to an end.—Evidence of later celebration of the Eleusinia is not forthcoming. The expressions of Proclus, which Maass regards as "certainly" proving that the festival was still being held in the fifth century (*Orpheus*, 15), are quite insufficient to the purpose. Proclus speaks of various sacred ceremonies of initiation from which we μεμαθήκαμεν something; of a φήμη, i.e. written tradition, of certain unspecified Eleusinian θεολόγοι; of what the Eleus. mysteries ὑπισχνοῦνται to the *mystai* (just as we might speak in the present tense of the permanent content of Greek religion). These passages prove nothing: whereas the imperfects which he uses elsewhere clearly show that neither temple nor festival existed any longer in his time. (He speaks, *in Alc.*, p. 5 Crz., of what used to be in the temple of Eleusis and still more of what formerly occurred ἐν τοῖς Ἐλευσινίοις ἱεροῖς—ἐβόων κτλ., *in Ti.* 293 C.) The festival moreover cannot have gone on without the temple and its apparatus.

[173] The Orphic hymns in the form in which we have them all belong as it seems to one period, and that can hardly have been earlier than the third century A.D. They are all composed for practical use in the cult, and that presupposes the existence of Orphic communities (see Schöll, *Commun. et coll. quib. Graec.* [*Sat. Saupp.*], p. 14 ff.; Dieterich, *de H. Orph.*).—It must be admitted that they were not purely and exclusively Orphic communities for which the poems were written. These hymns, called "Orphic" a potiori, make use in parts of older Orphic poetry (cf. *H.* 62, 2 f., with [Dem.] 25, 11).

[174] Probably all these cults promised immortality to their *mystai*. This is certain in the worship of Isis (cf. Burckhardt, *Zeit Constantins d. G.*², p. 195 ff.). Apul., *M.* xi, 21–3, alludes to symbolic death and reawakening to everlasting life as the subject of the δρώμενα in the Isis mysteries. The initiated is thus *renatus* (21). In the same way the mystai of Mithras are said to be *in aeternum renati*: *CIL.* vi, 510; 736. Immortality must certainly have been promised. Acc. to Tert., *Pr. Haer.* 40, the mysteries of Mithras

included an *imago resurrectionis.* By this the Christian author can only understand a real ἀνάστασις τῆς σαρκός. Did these mysteries promise to their ὅσιοι a resurrection of the body and everlasting life? This belief in the ἀνάστασις νεκρῶν (always a difficulty for the Greeks: *Act. Ap.* xvii, 18; 32; Plotin. 3, 6, 6 fin.) is in fact ancient Persian (Theopomp. *fr.* 71–2; Hübschmann, *Jb. Prot. Theol.* v, p. 222 ff.), and probably came to the Jews from Persia. It is possible then that it may have been the essential idea of the Mithras mysteries.—Hopes of immortality as they appeared to the *mystai* of Sabazios are illustrated by the sculptures of the monument of Vibia (in the Catac. of Praetextatus), and of Vincentius: numinis antistes Sabazis Vincentius hic est. Qui sacra sancta deum mente pia coluit (Garrucci, *Tre Sepolcri,* etc., tab. i–iii, Nap. 1852).—It is difficult to see why Christian archeologists should regard this Vincentius as a Christian. He calls himself a worshipper of "the gods" and an *antistes Sabazii* (there cannot be the slightest objection to giving this meaning to numinis antistes Sabazis. The difficulties raised by Schultze, *Katakomben,* 44, are groundless: Sabazis = Sabazii is no more objectionable or doubtful than the genetives Clodis, Helis: see Ritschl, *Opusc.* iv, 454–6. The arrangement of words, *n. a. Sab.*, is due to the exigencies of metre).

[175] ἡ ὄρεξις τοῦ ἀγαθοῦ εἰς ἓν ὄντως ἄγει καὶ ἐπὶ τοῦτο σπεύδει πᾶσα φύσις, Plot. 6, 5, 1. πάντα ὀρέγεται ἐκείνου καὶ ἐφίεται αὐτοῦ φύσεως ἀνάγκῃ . . . ὡς ἄνευ αὐτοῦ οὐ δύναται εἶναι, 5, 5, 12; 1, 8, 2. ποθεῖ δὲ πᾶν τὸ γεννῆσαν (the νοῦς desires the πρῶτον, the ψυχή the νοῦς): 5, 1, 6.

[176] αἱ ἔξω τοῦ αἰσθητοῦ γενόμεναι (ψυχαί), Plot. 3, 4, 6. In death ἀνάγειν τὸ ἐν ἡμῖν θεῖον πρὸς τὸ ἐν τῷ πάντι θεῖον, Porph., *V. Plot.* 2. Return εἰς πατρίδα, Plot., 5, 9, 1.

[177] 2, 9, esp. § 16 ff.

[178] τὸ μὲν γὰρ αἰσχρὸν ἐναντίον καὶ τῇ φύσει καὶ τῷ θεῷ, 3, 5, 1.

[179] Flight from the ἐν σώματι κάλλος to the τῆς ψυχῆς κάλλη, etc., 5, 9, 2. And again in the fine treatise, π. τοῦ καλοῦ, 1, 6, 8. Though even here it is in a different sense from that in which Plato speaks in the *Symp.* of the ascent from καλὰ σώματα to καλὰ ἐπιτηδεύματα, etc. Plotinos protests energetically against the idea that his own sense of beauty makes him any the less φεύγειν τὸ σῶμα than the hatred of beauty cultivated by the Gnostics: 2, 9, 18. He too waits here below, only a little less impatiently, for the time when he will be able to say farewell to every earthly habitation: ib.

[180] . . . καὶ οὕτω θεῶν καὶ ἀνθρώπων θείων καὶ εὐδαιμόνων βίος ἀπαλλαγὴ τῶν τῇδε, βίος ἀνήδονος τῶν τῇδε, φυγὴ μόνου πρὸς μόνον, 6, 9, 11 fin.

APPENDIX I

In many legends death by *lightning* makes the victim holy and raises him to godlike (everlasting) life. We need only remember the story of Semele who now *ζώει ἐν Ὀλυμπίοις ἀποθανοῖσα βρόμῳ κεραυνοῦ* (Pi., *O.* ii, 27), or that of Herakles and his vanishing from the pyre of wood lighted by Zeus' flash of lightning (see partic. D.S. 4, 38, 4–5), or the parallel accounts of the translation or death by lightning of Erechtheus (above, chap. iii, n. 39). The primitive, popular belief finds unusually clear expression in the words of Charax ap. Anon. *de Incred.* xvi, p. 325, 5 ff. West., who says of Semele, *κεραυνοῦ κατασκήψαντος ἠφανίσθη· ἐκείνην μὲν οὖν, ὁποῖα ἐπὶ τοῖς διοβλήτοις λέγεται, θείας μοίρας λαχεῖν ᾠήθησαν.* (In this account Semele is *immediately* raised to heaven by the flash of lightning—a version of the story frequently given by later authors: *Ζεὺς τὴν Σεμέλην ἐκ τῆς γῆς εἰς τὸν Ὄλυμπον κομίζει διὰ πυρός*, Aristid. 1, p. 47 Dind. [*O.* 41, 3 K.]. Cf. Philostr., *Imag.* i, 14; Nonnus, *D.* viii, 409 ff. The passage of Pindar quoted above would also admit of a similar interpretation.) Generally speaking, *ὁ κεραυνωθεὶς ὡς θεὸς τιμᾶται* (Artem. 2, 9, p. 94, 26) as one *ὑπὸ Διὸς τετιμημένος* (ib. 93, 24). The belief in such elevation of a mortal through the disruption and purification of his body by the sacred fire of lightning (a *πῦρ καθάρσιον* of the highest kind—see chap. i, n. 41) need not be of late origin simply because it so happens that only late authorities speak of it in unmistakable terms (as Wilamowitz thinks, *Ind. Schol. Gotting. hib.* 1895, pp. 12–13). Such lofty conceptions were by this time no longer the product of popular imagination. Besides, it is quite clearly referred to in the above-mentioned story of Semele (see esp. D.S. 5, 52, 2) and in those of Herakles, Erechtheus, Asklepios. In the same way lightning struck the tomb of Lykourgos (as afterwards that of Euripides) as *θεοφιλέστατος καὶ ὁσιώτατος* (Plu., *Lyc.* 31). When the statues of the Olympic victor Euthymos at Locri and Olympia are struck by lightning it shows that he has become a Hero: Pliny, *NH.* vii, 152. The body of the person struck by lightning remains uncorruptible: dogs and birds of prey dare not touch it: Plu., *Smp.* 4, 2, 3, p. 665 B; it must be buried in the place where the lightning struck it (Artem., p. 95, 6; cf. Fest., p. 178b, 21 ff.; Plin., *NH.* ii, 145). Every detail shows plainly that the *διόβλητος* was regarded as holy. This, however, does not prevent death by lightning from being regarded on other occasions as the punishment of crime—as in the cases of Salmoneus, Kapaneus, etc.; though in some even of these cases the idea is occasionally present that the lightning's victim is raised to a higher existence. This is distinctly so when Euripides in *Suppl.* makes a character call Kapaneus, who has been killed by lightning, a *ἱερὸς νεκρός* (935) and his *τύμβος* (*rogus*) *ἱερός* too (981). *ἱερός* never means "accursed" like the Lat. *sacer*: it is invariably a title of honour. Kapaneus is here called "holy" just as Astakides, on his translation to everlasting life, is ἱερός in Kallimachos; and as Hesiod speaks of the ἱερὸν γένος ἀθανάτων (with τύμβος ἱερός cf. S., *OC.* 1545, 1763). We must not fail to observe that in this passage, where a *friend* of Kap. is supposed to be speaking, the latter is certainly not regarded by Eurip. as an impious person (as he is generally in Tragedy, and by Eurip. himself in *Phoen.*, and even in *Suppl.* the enemy so regards him (496 ff.), though acc. to this speaker Amphiaraos too is snatched away in atonement for his crime). Euripides in fact makes him highly praised by Adrastos (861 ff.) as the very opposite of a ὑβριστής; and it is obvious that Euadne's sacrifice of her life which immediately follows is not intended to be offered for the benefit of a criminal and enemy of the gods. For these reasons Euripides ennobles the character of Kapaneus and, consequently, the death of the Hero by lightning can no longer stand for his punishment, but is on the contrary a distinction. He becomes a ἱερὸς νεκρός. This, however, could not have been done by Eurip. unless the view that such a death might in certain circumstances bring honour on the victim and elevate him to a higher plane of being, had been at that time widespread and generally recognized. Eurip. therefore provides the most distinct evidence for the existence of such a belief in his time. (As one of the exalted dead Kapaneus is to be separated from the rest of the dead and burnt παρ' οἴκους τούσδε: 935, 938, 1009—i.e. before the ἀνάκτορον of the Goddesses at Eleusis: 88, 290.)—Finally Asklepios, in all the stories that are told of his death by lightning (and already in Hes. *fr.* 109 Rz.), is never regarded as entirely removed from this life: he lives on as Hero or god for all time, dispensing blessings. Zeus allows him to live on for ever immortal (Luc., *DD.* 13), and acc. to later versions of the story, in the constellation Ophiuchus (Eratosth. καταστ. 6; Hygin., *Astron*, ii, 14); the real and primitive conception evidently being that he was transported to everlasting life by Zeus' lightning-flash. So Min. Fel. 22, 7, says quite rightly: Aesculapius, ut in deum surgat, fulminatur.

APPENDIX II

μασχαλισμός

ἐμασχαλίσθη is the word used by Aesch., *Cho.* 439, of the murdered Agamemnon. Soph., *El.* 445, says ὑφ' ἧς (Κλυταιμνήστρας) θανὼν ἄτιμος ὥστε δυσμενὴς ἐμασχαλίσθη—also of Agamemnon. What particular abomination was meant by this brief statement must have been immediately understood by the Athenian public of the day. A more detailed account is given by Phot. and Suid. μασχαλίσματα (cf. Hesych. s.v.; Apostol., *Pr.* xi, 4), and they give Aristophanes of Byzantium as their authority. (Not from Aristophanes—for they differ in many particulars—but from a closely related source come the two versions of the Scholion to Soph., *El.* 446 and *EM.* 118, 22 f.) According to their authority μασχαλισμός is something done by the murderer (οἱ φονεύσαντες ἐξ ἐπιβουλῆς—Aristoph.) to the corpse of the murdered man. He cuts off the extremities of his victim, strings the severed parts on a chain and puts them on.—On whom ? on himself ? or the murdered man ? Aristophanes' words are undecisive : the Schol. Soph., *El.* 445, speaks in the first version of " himself " (ἑαυτοῖς, p. 123, 17 Papag.) and in the second of " him ", i.e. the murdered man : περὶ τὴν μασχάλην αὐτοῦ ἐκρέμαζον αὐτά [τὰ ἄκρα], p. 123, 23 ; cf. 124, 5. This too is probably the meaning of Schol. Ap. Rh. iv, 477 ; *EM.* 118, 28–9, speaks distinctly of hanging the chain round the neck of the dead man. This is, in fact, the most probable version. The murderer hung the limbs, strung together on a rope, round the neck of his victim and then drew the rope under the armpits (μασχάλαι) : a proceeding which is far from being " impossible " (as has been said), as anyone may discover by trying it for himself. The murderer then crossed the ends of the rope over the breast of his victim and after drawing them under the armpits fastened them behind his back. From this process of drawing under the armpits the whole procedure is called μασχαλισμός, and the μόρια of the dead man thus fastened to his body are his μασχαλίσματα (Aristoph.).

Anyone who wishes to reject this description of μασχαλισμός (as some have done recently) must first of all show from what source Aristophanes of Byzantium—whom no one who knows him would accuse of improvizing such details or of concealing his ignorance by invention—can have got his information if not from actual report and historical tradition. The possibility that he arrived at it by straining the meaning and giving a private interpretation of his own to the words μασχαλίζειν and μασχαλισμός is excluded by the nature of these words. They offer no hint whatever in the direction of the special meaning suggested by his account. We cannot indeed say (as Wilamowitz does on A., *Cho.* 439) that " grammar " forbids us to accept the explanation of what happened in μασχαλίζειν given by Aristoph. To say : ἐμασχαλίσθη, " he had to suffer μασχαλίζειν, μασχαλισμός," is equally correct whatever sense we give to the process of μασχαλισμός. But the word itself does not testify, by its mere form, to the absolute or exclusive correctness of Aristophanes' interpretation : it denotes without distinction absolutely any proceeding in which the μασχάλαι figure at all. Verbs in -ιζειν, derived from the names of parts of the body, can denote according to the circumstances the utmost variety of actions done to or with the part of the body concerned : cf. κεφαλίζειν, αὐχενίζειν, τραχηλίζειν, λαιμίζειν, ὠμίζειν, ῥαχίζειν, χειρίζειν, δακτυλίζειν, γαστρίζειν, σκελίζειν (and even πυγίζειν). What particular sort of activity applied to the μασχάλαι is indicated by the verb μασχαλίζειν cannot be decided from the mere form of the verb. This only makes it the more necessary to adhere to Aristophanes' interpretation, which must have been derived from some other source, i.e. from actual knowledge. It may be true that μασχαλίζειν, considered simply from the point of view of its form, might conceivably mean to tear the arm from the shoulder at the armpits (as Benndorf suggests, *Monument von Adamklissi*, p. 132 A)—though such an *ἐκμοχλεύειν τὸν βραχίονα ἐκ τῆς μασχάλης* should rather be *ἀπομασχαλίζειν* or *ἐκμασχαλίζειν*. But that out of its many possible meanings the verb should have just this particular one is not suggested by anything: least of all by the sculptured relief on which the gods appear to be tearing out the right arms of their defeated enemies. Such scenes according to Benndorf represent *μασχαλισμός*. But can the Greeks really have attributed to the gods this much execrated practice of cowardly murderers? We are not told by anyone that this scene represents *μασχαλισμός*—that is only a conclusion drawn from an apparent agreement between the representation and the view (itself as yet unproved) of what happened in *μασχαλίζειν*. Is the correctness of the meaning assigned to the word to be proved in its turn from its agreement with the representation? A most palpable argument in a circle!

There is no valid reason for rejecting the statement of Aristophanes; and there must be very good reason indeed for so doing before we may discredit such an authority. He gives his information with no uncertain voice and no suggestion of hesitation, and it must be regarded as the simple account of well-established facts. It would receive additional confirmation—if it needed any—from the very meaning and conception of the word *μασχάλισμα*. *μασχαλίσματα* must be the product of *μασχαλισμός*; they are, in fact, the severed *μόρια* of the murdered man, with which too Aristophanes identifies them. *Σοφοκλῆς ἐν Τρωΐλῳ πλήρη μασχαλισμάτων εἴρηκε τὸν μασχαλισμόν* (probably a mere oversight for *τὸν τράχηλον*): Suid. s.v. *ἐμασχαλίσθη* (Soph. *fr*. 566 = 623 P.). If *μασχαλίζειν* had consisted in the dislocation of the arm from its socket, it would be impossible to say what such *μασχαλίσματα* might be. They are without doubt identical with what are otherwise called, in descriptions of mutilations of the corpse of a murdered man, *ἀπάργματα* (Jason after the murder of Apsyrtos *ἀπάργματα τάμνε θανόντος*, A.R. iv, 477; cf. Schol. and *EM*. 118, 22 ff.), *ἀκρωτηριάσματα*, *τόμια* (*τὰ ἀποτμήματα καὶ ἀκρωτηριάσματα τοῦ νεκροῦ*, Hesych.). These expressions allow us to conclude that the whole procedure is intended to offer the murdered man as a sacrifice to some sort of *ἀποτρόπαιοι*. The *μασχαλίσματα* are the *ἀπαρχαί* of this sacrificial victim. Indeed, Aristoph. of Byzantium, ap. Phot. [Suid.] *μασχαλίσματα*, definitely states that *μασχαλίσματα* was the name given to *τὰ τοῖς μηροῖς ἐπιτιθέμενα ἀπὸ τῶν ὠμῶν* (not *ὤμων* as the edd. give; as also Nauck, *Arist. Byz.*, p. 221) *κρέα ἐν ταῖς τῶν θεῶν θυσίαις*. This refers—though it does not seem to have been remarked by those who have hitherto dealt with the passage—to the parts of the body which were cut off from the raw flesh of the *ἱερεῖον* before the sacrifice, laid on the severed *μηροί* of the victim, and burnt up completely with these: the *ὠμοθετεῖν* in fact so often mentioned in Homer (*A* 460 f.; *B* 423 f.; *γ* 456 ff.; *μ* 360 f.; *ξ* 427 f.). If these *ὠμοθετούμενα* could also be called (in a comparison) μασχαλίσματα, that again shows that at the μασχαλισμός there was no tearing out of an arm from its socket, but that in reality the extremities of the murdered man (—ἀκρωτηριάσαντες μόρια τούτου) were hewn off and a piece cut off ἐκ παντὸς μέρους τοῦ σώματος as the grammarians following Aristophanes say. Only in this case is the proceeding like that which took place at the ὠμοθετεῖν when the sacrificers ἔκοψαν μικρὸν ἀπὸ παντὸς μέρους (Aristonic. in Schol. *A* 461; Apollon., *Lex. Hom.* 171, 8; *Lex. Rhet.* ap. Eust. *A* 461, p. 134, 36: ὠμοθέτησαν· τὸ ἀφ' ἑκάστου μέλους τοῦ ἱερείου ἀπετέμοντο καὶ ἀπήρξαντο ἀπ' ὠμοῦ [so the last word should be written here too, though Eustath. found—and was surprised—ὤμου] καὶ ἐνέβαλον εἰς τὰ μηρία κατὰ τὴν θυσιάν). So too it is said of Eumaios: ὁ δ' ὠμοθετεῖτο συβώτης, πάντων ἀρξάμενος μελέων, *ξ* 427 f. (this is the passage in which ἡρμήνευσε [ὁ ποιητής], τί ἐστι τὸ ὠμοθετεῖν: Schol., B.L. *A* 461; it is this passage, and not *A* 461, which is meant by Hesych. too s.v. ὠμοθετεῖν, when he says ἐξηγεῖται δ' αὐτὸς Ὅμηρος; cf. also Dion. Hal. 7, 72, 15).

μασχαλισμός was then essentially an offering intended to avert evil or, what comes to the same thing, a kathartic offering (i.e. a symbol indicating such an offering). It was consummated by murderers ἐπὶ ταῖς καθάρσεσιν (Sch. S., *El.* 445); ὑπὲρ τοῦ τὴν μῆνιν ἐκκλίνειν as Aristoph. Byz. says (p. 221 N.); τὸ ἔργον ἀφοσιούμενοι as we are told by Apostolius, *Prov.* xi, 4. All these mean the same thing. But besides these there may still have been another intention present in the minds of the superstitious. The mutilation of the murdered man took place according to Sch. S., *El.* 445 (in the second version; there is something similar even in the first, p. 123, 18 f.) ἵνα, φασίν, ἀσθενὴς γένοιτο πρὸς τὸ ἀντιτίσασθαι τὸν φονέα. The mutilation of the corpse was transferred to the ψυχή that was leaving the body—such is the ancient conception to which Homer too is not a stranger (cf. e.g. *λ* 40 ff.). If the dead man is mutilated he will not, for example, be able to hold or throw the spear which in Athens was borne before the murdered man at his funeral (if he left no kinsman as avenger behind him) and was then set up beside his grave ([D.] 47, 69; Eur., *Tro.* 1147 f.; Poll. viii, 65; Ister ap., *EM.* 354, 33 ff.; *AB.* 237, 30 f.)—certainly for no other purpose than that of supplying the dead man himself with a weapon with which to take vengeance on his own account since no one else would βοηθεῖ him. (Thus among the Tasmanians a spear was planted on the grave of the dead that he might have a weapon ready for fighting: Quatrefages, *Hommes fossiles et hommes sauvages*, p. 346.) Probably the Greek murderer when he ἐμασχάλιζεν, calculated in exactly the same fashion as the Australian negro who cuts off the thumb from the right hand of his fallen foe in order that his soul may no longer be able to hold a spear (Spencer, *Princ. of Sociol.* i, p. 212).

In Soph., *El.* 446, the murderer after the μασχαλισμός also wipes the bloody instrument of death on the head of the murdered man. Murderers did this ὥσπερ ἀποτροπιαζόμενοι τὸ μύσος τὸ ἐν τῷ φόνῳ

(Schol.). There are passages in the Odyssey which allude to the custom (*μέγα ἔργον, ὃ σῇ κεφαλῇ ἀναμάξεις, τ* 92) as well as in Herodotos and Demosthenes (see Schneidewin on *Electra*). Their meaning is quite correctly given in Eust. on *Od.* τ 92: *ὡς εἰς κεφαλὴν δῆθεν ἐκείνοις (τοῖς πεφονευμένοις) τρεπομένου τοῦ κακοῦ.* Evidently a mimic version of *εἰς κεφαλὴν σοί.* Something similar is intended when the murderer sucks the blood of the murdered man three times and spits it out again three times. Ap. Rh. describes such a scene (iv, 477 f.); and something similar occurred in Aesch. (*fr.* 354; *EM.* refers to this in immediate connexion with *μασχαλισμός*). Here too the object is the *κάθαρσις* of the murderer, the expiation of the impious deed. (*ἡ θέμις αὐθέντῃσι δολοκτασίας ἱλέασθαι,* A.R.; *ἀποπτύσαι δεῖ καὶ καθήρασθαι στόμα,* A.) Spitting three times is a regular feature in magic charms and counter-charms: in this case the blood of the murdered man and with it the power of vengeance that rises up out of the blood, is averted. (despuimus comitiales morbos, hoc est, contagia regerimus, Plin., *NH.* 28, 35.)—What "savage" tribe ever had more primitive ideas or a more realistic symbolism than the Greek populace—and perhaps not populace only—of classical times in the sinister backwaters of their life into which we have here for a moment descended?

✗ APPENDIX III

ἀμύητοι, ἄγαμοι AND DANAÏDES IN THE UNDERWORLD

In Polygnotos' picture of the underworld were to be seen the figures *τῶν οὐ μεμυημένων, τῶν τὰ δρώμενα Ἐλευσῖνι ἐν οὐδενὸς θεμένων λόγῳ*—an old man, a *παῖς*, a young and an old woman, who bear water to a *πίθος* in broken pitchers: Paus. 10, 31, 9–11. The myth is evidently founded upon an etymological play on words—those who have neglected the "completion" of the holy *τέλη* and are *ἀτελεῖς ἱερῶν* (*h. Cer.* 482) must perform the vain labour in the realm of Persephone of carrying water in broken vessels: the *Δαναΐδων ὑδρείας ἀτελεῖς* (*Axioch.* 371 E). It can only have been an oversight that made Pausanias forget to say that the *πίθος* is *τετρημένος*, for this is essential to the story (see Pl., *Gor.* 493 BC; Philetair. ap. Ath. 633 F, 18 [2, p. 235 K.]; Zenob., *Prov.* ii, 6, etc.), and certainly cannot, as Dieterich, *Nekyia*, 70, imagined, be replaced by the *κατεαγότα ὄστρακα*. That the *οὐ μεμυημένοι*, the *ἀμύητοι*, as the inscription on the picture called them (Paus. § 9), were in fact those who had neglected the Eleusinian mysteries is only a conclusion of Pausanias' (or of his authority), as we see from the way he speaks in § 11; but it is probably the right conclusion. The Orphics took over the Eleusinian fable, but exaggerated it to the point of absurdity: they *τοὺς ἀνοσίους καὶ ἀδίκους κοσκίνῳ ὕδωρ ἀναγκάζουσι φέρειν* in Hades (Pl., *Rp.* 363 D; *Gor.* 493 BC). In this they followed a hint given by a popular proverb—representing one of the *ἀδύνατα*—*κοσκίνῳ ὕδωρ φέρειν* (which is also Roman: cf. Plaut.,

Pseud. 102; as an "ordeal": Plin., *NH.* 28, 12). It is not until later (nor in surviving literature before the *Axiochus*, 371 E: though perhaps a little earlier on vase paintings from South Italy) that the story occurs in which it is the *daughters of Danaos* who are punished in Hades by having to fill the leaking vessel. The reason given for this punishment is their murder of the sons of Aigyptos in the marriage bed: but why did the punishment take this particular form? Clearly in the case of the Danaides their non-fulfilment of an important τέλος is requited in the ever ἀτελεῖς ὑδρεῖαι. Their marriage union was uncompleted through their own choice (thus marriage itself was often called a τέλος and the wedding was preceded by προτέλεια and compared with the τέλη of the mysteries). In this it is certainly implied that their deed had not been expiated, and they themselves had not found other husbands, but had as it were immediately after their impious deed been sent down to Hades (cf. Sch. Eur., *Hec.* 886, p. 436, 14 Dind.). The daughters of Danaos came to the underworld as ἄγαμοι. To die before marriage was regarded as the height of ill-luck by the common people (cf. Welcker, *Syll. ep.*, p. 49): the essential reason being that those who die thus leave behind them nobody who is called upon to keep up the cult of their souls (E. *Tro.* 380). Other ideas may have been vaguely combined with this. Thus, on the graves of ἄγαμοι a λουτροφόρος was set up—a figure of a παῖς or a κόρη λουτροφόρος, or a vessel called the λουτροφόρος which has been identified with certain *bottomless* vases (see Furtwängler, *Samml. Sabouroff*, on Pl. lviii–lix; cf. Wolters, *Ath. Mitth.* xvi, 378 ff.). Can this have referred to a similar fate awaiting the ἄγαμοι after their death, a fate such as was imputed to the Danaides in particular as mythical types of those who are ἄγαμοι by their own fault?—an ever unsuccessful carrying of water for the λουτρόν of the bridal bath. (Dieterich, *Nekyia*, 76, with some probability takes this as the reason for the water-carrying.)

Of these two myths, was the one which appears later in order of time—the story of the Danaids—merely a subsequent development out of the earlier one (even said to occur on a black-figured vase), which told of the vain water-carrying of the ἀμύητοι? I cannot be so sure of this as I once was. I cannot indeed admit (with Dümmler, *Delphica*, 18 ff., who, however, fails to prove an earlier date for the story of the Danaids' jar) that it would be difficult to imagine how a special class of human beings came to be replaced later on by certain mythical representatives such as the Danaids were. But it is a very suspicious fact that the Danaids do *not* as a matter of fact represent the particular class of mankind—the ἀμύητοι—whose place they are supposed to have taken as their mythological representatives. They are not ἀμύητοι at all, but ἄγαμοι. The ἄγαμοι and their ἀτελεῖς ὑδρεῖαι in Hades must have been familiar in popular belief: in addition to this the mystical fable of the similar behaviour of those who had neglected the τέλος of initiation may have sprung up, but certainly not as the model of the ἄγαμοι story, more probably as a subsequent rehandling of it for the purposes of mystical edification. (The story of the ἄγαμοι has a much more primitive and popular flavour; and it alone gives a definite relation between the special labour of water-carrying in Hades and the nature of their default on earth.) The mythical fate of the ἄγαμοι was then forgotten owing to the competing interest of the story of the ἀμυητοι, which, in fact, absorbed it, when a poet—for a poet it must have been—took up what still-surviving custom and its accompanying legend applied to the ἄγ. in general and transferred it to the *Danaides*. This version of the myth was then victorious in the general consciousness both over the popular tradition about the ἄγαμοι and the mystery-fable of the ἀμύητοι.—It remains to be said that the Danaids (and the ἀμύητοι too in a lesser degree) were supposed to be *punished* by their ἀτελεῖς ὑδρεῖαι. This, so long as it was a matter of the ἄγαμοι simply, cannot have been the meaning of that fate of purposeless toil in their case any more than it was in the case of Oknos. Even Xenophon, *Oec.* vii, 40, lets us see that the vain toilers are not as a matter of fact intended to inspire horror, as sinners, but rather pity. His words are: οὐχ ὁρᾷς, οἱ εἰς τὸν τετρημένον πίθον ἀντλεῖν λεγόμενοι ὡς οἰκτίρονται, ὅτι μάτην πονεῖν δοκοῦσι; νὴ Δί', ἔφη ἡ γυνή, καὶ γὰρ τλήμονές εἰσιν, εἰ τοῦτό γε ποιοῦσιν. This gives us the attitude of mind from which the whole story originally grew up.

APPENDIX IV

THE TETRALOGIES OF ANTIPHON

I ought not to have admitted the doubt suggested in chap. v, n. 176, as to the genuineness of the Tetralogies traditionally ascribed to Antiphon. I have examined more carefully the well-known linguistic variations between the Tetralogies and speeches i, v, and vi of Antiphon, and also the recently noticed divergences (see Dittenberger, *Hermes*, 31; 32) of the Tetralogies from Athenian law (for which the author, like the declamation-writers of later times, substitutes occasionally a "*ius scholasticum*"—a purely fanciful creation but one more suited to pleading *in utramque partem*). All these objections seem to me, on maturer consideration, insufficient to make us reject the identity—otherwise so well established—of the author of the Tetralogies with the author of the Speeches.

APPENDIX V

RITUAL PURIFICATION EFFECTED BY RUNNING WATER, RUBBING WITH ANIMAL OR VEGETABLE SUBSTANCES (σκίλλα, FIGS), ABSORPTION OF THE *materia peccans* INTO EGGS.

For the purpose of ritual purification it is necessary to have water drawn from running springs or streams, or from the sea: θάλασσα κλύζει πάντα τἀνθρώπων κακά, Eur., *IT.* 1193. (Hence in the exalted semi-oracular language of bardic poetry ἡ ἀμίαντος = θάλαττα, Aesch., *P.* 578. At a sacrifice ὁ ἰαρεὺς ἀπορραίνεται θαλάσσᾳ, sacrificial calendar from Kos : *Inscr. Cos*, 38, 23.) Various details on this point in Lomeier, *De lustrat.* c. 17. In the water thus drawn from running sources the power of washing off and carrying away the evil still seemed to be inherent. When the pollution is unusually severe it has to be purged by the water from several running springs : κρηνάων ἀπὸ πέντε, Emped. 452 M. = 143 D. ; ἀπὸ κρηνῶν τριῶν, Menand., *Δεισ.* 530, 22 K. ; Orestes se apud tria flumina circum Hebrum ex responso purificavit (from the stain of matricide), Lamprid., *Heliog.* vii, 7—or else at Rhegion in the seven streams which combine to form one river : Varro ap. Prob., *ad Verg.*, p. 3, 4 Keil ; Sch. Theoc., prol., p. 1, 3 ff. Düb. (and cf. Hermann, *Opusc.* ii, 71 ff.). Even water from fourteen different springs might be used at a purification of murder : Suid. 476 BC Gaisf. (ἀπὸ δὶς ἑπτὰ κυμάτων, conclusion of an iambic or trochaic line). In all this the remarkable persistence of Greek ritual performances is shown once more. Even in a late period the same kathartic rules prevail. An order of the Klarian oracle of about the third century A.D. (ap. Buresch, *Klaros*, p. 9) commands those who seek its aid ἀπὸ Ναιάδων ἑπτὰ ματεύειν καθαρὸν πότον ἐντύνεσθαι, ὃν θειῶσαι πρόσσθεν (taken from *Il.* Ψ 533, but understood in a temporal sense) ἐχρῆν καὶ ἐπεσσυμένως ἀφύσασθαι ῥῆναί τε δόμους κτλ. And in a magical papyrus (about fourth century), ap. Parthey, *Abh. Berl. Ak.* 1865, p. 126, l. 234–5, instructions are given to collect ὕδωρ πηγαῖον ἀπὸ ζ' πηγῶν for magic purposes. (Then again in mediæval superstition : for the purposes of *hydromantia* " water must be taken from three running streams, a little from each ", etc.—Hartlieb ap. Grimm, p. 1770—probably a survival from classical antiquity : cf. Plin., *NH.* 28, 46, *e tribus puteis*, etc.) Cf. also and in general the completely analogous use of water in old Indian ceremonies of purification : Oldenberg, *Rel. Veda*, 423 ff. ; 489.—περιμάττειν, ἀπομάττειν : wiping-off of the uncleanness : see Wyttenb. ad Plu., *Mor.* vi, pp. 1006–7. In this use περιψῆν also occurs : in a transferred sense a φαρμακός is called a περίψημα = περικάθαρμα, *Ep. ad Cor.* 1, 4, 13. Washing-off with bran, earth, etc., is often mentioned. Otherwise the σκίλλα is used or the bodies of sacrificed dogs : ἐκάθηρέ τέ με καὶ ἀπέμαξε καὶ περιήγνισε δᾳδίοις (with περιήγν.) καὶ σκίλλῃ, Luc., *Necyom.* 7. The Superstitious Man is accustomed ἱερείας καλέσας σκίλλῃ ἢ σκύλακι κελεῦσαι αὐτὸν περικαθᾶραι, Thphr., *Ch.* 28 (16) fin. All sorts of medicinal properties were attributed to the σκίλλα. (The idea is elaborated farcically in the pamphlet of " Pythagoras " περὶ σκίλλης [D.L. viii, 47 ? κήλης Cobet], an extract of which is given by Galen π. εὐπορίστ. 3, vol. xiv, 576–9 K.) But above all it is regarded as καθάρσιος : Artem. iii, 50 ; καθαρτικὴ πάσης κακίας, Sch. Theoc. v, 121, and cf. Cratin., *Χείρ.* 232 K. Hence it is also ἀλεξιφάρμακον, ὅλη πρὸ τῶν θυρῶν κρεμαμένη, Diosc. ii, 202 fin. (see *Hermes*, 51, 628) ; such also was the teaching of " Pythagoras " : Plin., *NH.* 20, 101 ; of it may be buried at the threshold : Ar. *Δαναΐδ.* *fr.* 8 [255 H.-G.].

It is also λύκων φθαρτική: Artem. iii, 50 (cf. *Gp.* 15, 1, 6, with notes of Niclas). As being able to keep off daimones (in wolf-form) it was then used in religious "purification".—Figs are also used for the purpose of religious cleansing and scouring (*black* figs particularly inferum deorum et avertentium in tutela sunt, Macr. 3, 20, 2–3). Figs used ἐν καθαρμοῖς: Eustath., *Od.*, p. 1572, 57 (? is this the meaning of the περιμάττειν of the eyes with figs in Pherecr. ap. Ath. 3, 78 D [132 K.]). Hence Ζεὺς συκάσιος = καθάρσιος (Eustath.). Figs the best ἀλεξιφάρμακον: Arist. ap. Jul., *Ep.* 24, p. 505, 7 ff. From the specially magic properties of the fig comes the idea that fig-trees are never struck by lightning: Plu., *Smp.* 5, 9, p. 684 C; *Gp.* 11, 2, 7; Theoph. Nonn. 260, 288 (and cf. *Rh. Mus.* 50, 584); Lyd., *Mens. fr. fals.* 1, p. 181 W.; 4, 4, p. 69 W. The φαρμακοί at the Thargelia (above, chap. ix, n. 26) wear strings of figs round their necks (Hellad. ap. Phot., *Bibl.*, p. 534a, 5 ff.), and are beaten with branches of the fig-tree (κράδαι) and with σκίλλαι (Hippon. *frr.* 4, 5, 8; Hsch. κραδίης νόμος): here again the figs have a kathartic purpose (Müller mistakes this, *Dorians*, i, 346), as is shown also by the presence of σκίλλαι as well (cf. in general Theoc. vii, 107; v, 121). Before the φαρμακοί were driven out of the city as scapegoats they were thus "purified" with the above-mentioned κράδαι and σκίλλαι. The same thing is said in the story of the ravens which parodies this expiatory rite. The ravens are offered up to Λοιμός as a sort of φαρμακοί—περικαθαίροντας ἐπῳδαῖς ἀφιέναι ζῶντας, καὶ ἐπιλέγειν τῷ Λοιμῷ· φεῦγ' ἐς κόρακας (Arist. *fr.* 454 [496 Tbn.]; for a similar ἀποτροπιασμός (εἰς αἶγας ἀγρίας) see the commentators on Macar. iii, 59, Diogen. v, 49; cf. τὴν νόσον (regarded as a daimon), φασίν, ἐς αἶγας τρέψαι, Philostr., *Her.* 179, 8 Kays.).—Rubbing-off of the "impurity" was effected also with the dead bodies of puppies (σκίλλῃ ἢ σκύλακι, Thphr., *Ch.* 28 [16]). Those ἁγνισμοῦ δεόμενοι were rubbed down with the bodies of puppies (which had been sacrificed to Hekate): περιμάττονται, and this is περισκυλακισμός, Plu., *Q. Rom.* 68, p. 280 C.

It was believed that these materials (wool and the skins of animals were also employed) received into themselves the harmful and polluting substance. This is why *eggs* are also used as καθάρσια: e.g. in *P. Mag. Lond.*, n. 121, l. 522 ap. Kenyon, *Greek papyri in BM.* i, p. 101 (1893): γράφε τὸ ὄνομα εἰς ᾠὰ δύο ἀρρενικὰ καὶ τῷ ἑνὶ περικαθαίρεις (sic) σεαυτὸν κτλ. More in Lomeier, *Lustr.* (ed. 2 Zutph. 1700), p. 258 f. They were meant to absorb the impurity. ἀνελάμβανον τὰ τοῦ περικαθαρθέντος κακά, Auct. π. δεισιδ. ap. Clem., *Str.* vii, p. 844 P.

APPENDIX VI

HEKATE AND THE Ἑκατικὰ φάσματα, GORGYRA, GORGO, MORMOLYKE, MORMO, BAUBO, GELLO, EMPOUSA, ETC.

Hekate herself is addressed as Γοργὼ καὶ Μορμὼ καὶ Μήνη καὶ πολύμορφε: *Hymn.* ap. Hipp., *RH.* iv, 35, p. 102, 67 D.-S. Sch. A.R.

iii, 861, says of Hek. λέγεται καὶ φάσματα ἐπιπέμπειν (cf. Eur., *Hel.* 569; D. Chr. iv, p. 73 M. [i, p. 70 Arn.]; Hsch. ἀνταία), τὰ καλούμενα Ἑκάταια (φάσματα Ἑκατικά, Marin., *V. Procl.* 28) καὶ πολλάκις αὐτὴ μεταβάλλειν τὸ εἶδος διὸ καὶ Ἔμπουσαν καλεῖσθαι. Hekate-Empousa also in Ar. *Tagen. fr.* 500–1: Sch. Ar., *Ran*, 293; Hesych. Ἔμπουσα. Thus Hekate is the same as Gorgo, Mormo, and Empousa. Baubo also is one of her names: *H. Mag.*, p. 289 Abel. (Baubo probably identical with the Βαβώ mentioned among other χθόνιοι in an inscr. from Paros: Ἀθήναιον, v, 15; cf. the male personal names Βαβώ, Βαβεῖς. Βαυβώ can hardly be etymologically connected with βαυβών unpleasantly familiar in Herond. (though the mistake has been repeated in Roscher, *Myth. Lex.* ii, 3025); one does not see how a female daimon could be named after a male ὄλισβος. The nature of Hekate makes its more probable that she got her name from βαύ the noise of the baying hound: cf. βαυκύων, *P. Mag. Par.* 1911.) Baubo, too, is elsewhere the name of a gigantic nocturnal spectre: Orph. *fr.* 216 Ab.; Lob., *Agl.* 823.—Elsewhere these ἐπικλήσεις, or forms in which Hekate, Gorgo, Mormo, etc., appear, are found as the names of separate infernal spirits. Γοργύρα· Ἀχέροντος γυνή Apollod. π. θεῶν ap. Stob., *Ecl.* i, 49, p. 419, 15 W.; cf. [Apollod.] 1, 5, 3. Γοργώ is probably only the shortened form of this daimon (she is alluded to as an inhabitant of Hades as early as *Od.* λ 634; in the κατάβασις of Herakles [Apollod.] 2, 5, 12; χθονία Γοργώ, Eur., *Ion*, 1053). Acheron, whose consort she is, must have been regarded as the lord of the underworld. We also hear of a mother of the underworld god: in Aesch., *Ag.* 1235, Kassandra calls Klytaimnestra θύουσαν Ἅιδου μητέρα. In this very striking phrase it is impossible to take ᾅδου in its generalized sense (as Lob. does: *Aj.*³, p. 292), and the whole phrase as merely metaphorical = αἰνομήτορα. Why μητέρα in particular? And, above all, what would be the point of θύουσαν? Klytaimnestra, of course, it goes without saying, is only metaphorically called the "raging mother of Hades", i.e. a true she-devil; but the thing with which she is compared, from which the metaphor is taken, must have been a real figure of legend. In exactly the same way, in Byz. Greek, τῶν δαιμόνων μήτηρ is a figurative expression for a wicked woman: see Καλλίμ. καὶ Χρυσορρόη 2579 ed. Lambros; cf. ib., 1306, τῶν Νηρηίδων μάμμη. In German too "the devils mother", or grandmother, or the devil's wife or bride, are of frequent occurrence in a metaphorical sense: Grimm, p. 1007; 1607. But in all these cases the comparison invariably implies the existence of real legendary figures to which the comparison refers; and often enough in mediæval and modern Greek folk-lore these creatures actually occur. We may therefore conclude that the θύουσα Ἅιδου μήτηρ was a real figure of Greek legend. "Hades" in this connexion cannot be the god of the underworld, common in Homer and a regular poetic character elsewhere, the brother of Zeus and Poseidon. In that case his mother would be Rhea who certainly cannot be identified with the θύουσα Ἅιδου μήτηρ. In local mythology there were numerous other underworld gods any of whom might be loosely called Ἅιδης, the word being used as a general name for such deities. But the "raging" mother of the underworld god has the most unmistakable resemblance to Hekate who flies about by night on the wind (see above, chap. ix, p. 297 f.; below, App. vii) ψυχαῖς νεκύων μέτα βακχεύουσα (Reiss, *Rh. Mus.* 49, 181 n., compares her less well with the "huntsman of Hades"). It seems almost as if the two were identical: local legend could quite well have made Hekate the mother of the underworld god (just as she was the daughter of Admetos, or of Eubouleus, i.e. of Hades). If she is the same as Μορμώ (cf. the *Hymn.* ap. Hipp., *RH.* iv, 35) then she was also known to folk-lore as the foster-mother of Acheron. This title is applied to Μορμολύκα· τιθήνη of Acheron in Sophron *fr.* 9 Kaibel. But Μορμώ is simply the abbreviated form of Μορμολύκη as Γοργώ is of Γοργύρα, and cf. also Μομμώ Hsch., and with metathesis of ρ, Μομβρώ id. (Μορμολ. is mentioned together with Λαμία, Γοργώ, Ἐφιάλτης, as a legendary creature in Str., p. 19, and see Ruhnken, *Tim. Lex.*, p. 179 ff., Μορμολύκειον.) Μορμώ also in plural: ὥσπερ μορμόνας παιδάρια (φοβοῦνται), Xen., *HG.* 4, 4, 17; Hsch. μορμόνας· πλάνητας δαίμονας (i.e. "wandering", as in Hesiod, and like the Erinyes in the Pythagorean σύμβολον, and the ἀλάστωρ, the unquiet and wandering soul whose name is derived from ἀλᾶσθαι—so Lob., *Paralip.* 450). Besides this we have Ἑκάτας too in the plural: Luc., *Philops.* 39 fin. (perhaps only generalizing); τρισσῶν Ἑκατῶν, *P. Mag. Par.* 2825 f.; Ἔμπουσαι (with ἄλλα εἴδωλα), D.P. 725, etc., to say nothing of Γοργόνες. Μορμώ as a bogey to frighten children: Μορμὼ δάκνει, Theoc. xv, 40 (cf. [ἀνά]κλησις Μορμο[ῦς], a theatrical piece, probably a farce: *IGM. Aeg.* i, 125g). So too is the monster Λάμια that kidnaps children: Duris, *fr.* 35 (2 *FHG*); D.S. 20, 41; Heraclit., *Incred.* 34, etc. Some details in Friedländer, *Darstell. a. d. Sitteng.*[4], i, 511 f. (as a nickname Λαμώ: Sch. Ar., *Eq.* 62). Mormo herself is called Lamia, Μορμοῦς τῆς καὶ Λαμίας, Sch. Greg. Nz. ap. Ruhnken, *Tim. Lex.*, p. 182a. With Mormo and Lamia Γελλώ is also identified (Sch. Theoc. xv, 40), a ghost that kidnaps children mentioned already by Sappho, *fr.* 44; Zenob. iii, 3, etc. Καρκώ, too, is the same as Λάμια (Hesych.). Lamia is evidently the general name (see above, chap. iv, n. 115), while Mormo, Gello, Karko, and even Empousa, are particular Lamiai, who also merge into one another. Just as Mormo and Gello coincide, so also do Gello and Empousa: Γελλὼ εἴδωλον Ἐμπούσης, Hsch. (Empousai, Lamiai, and Mormolykai the same: Philostr., *V. Ap.* 4, 25, p. 145, 16 K.). Empousa, who appears in continually changing shapes (Ar., *Ran.* 289 ff.), is seen by human beings at night (νυκτερινὸν φάσμα ἡ Ἔμπουσα, *V. Aeschin.* init.; Philostr. *V. Ap.* 2, 4), but even more commonly at midday (like the Hekate of Lucian): μεσημβρίας ὅταν τοῖς κατοιχομένοις ἐναγίζωσιν, Sch. Ar., *Ran.* 293. She is, in fact, the *daemonium meridianum* known to Christian writers as Diana (Lob., *Agl.* 1092; Grimm, 1162). For devils appearing at midday see Rochholz, *Glaube u. Br.*, i, 67 ff.; Mannhardt, *Ant.*

Wald u. Feldc. ii, 135 f. ; Haberland, *Ztschr. Völkerpsych.* xiii, 310 ff. ; Drexler in *Myth. Lex.* ii, 2832 ff. ; Grimm, 1661. Hekate, in so far as she appears as an εἴδωλον in the upper world is identical with Emp. and with Borbo, Gorgo, Mormo, as well as Gello, Karko, Lamia. (Acc. to Sch. A.R. iv, 828 Stesichoros, ἐν τῇ Σκύλλῃ εἴδους [Εἴδους Bergk on Stes. *fr.* 13 quite unconvincingly] τινὸς Λαμίας τὴν Σκύλλαν φησὶ θυγατέρα εἶναι. Here Hek. herself seems to be described as " a kind of Lamia ", for she was generally regarded as the mother of Skylla, e.g. by Akousilaos [73 B, 27 *Vors.*], in the Hesiodic *Eoiai*, 172 Rz. [Sch. A.R.], and even in A.R. himself who in iv, 829, explains the Homeric Krataiis [μ 124] as merely a name of Hekate.)—The vagueness of feature and confusion of personality is characteristic of these ghostly and delusive apparitions. In reality the individual names (in some cases onomatopœic formations to suggest terror) were originally the titles of local ghosts. In the long run they all come to suggest the same general idea and are therefore confused with each other and are identified with the best known of them, Hekate. The underworld and the realm of ghosts is the proper home of these feminine daimones as a whole and of Hekate too ; most of them, with the possible exception of Empousa, give way entirely to Hekate in importance and are relegated to children's fairy-tales. In the case of Gorgyra (Gorgo) and Mormolyke (Mormo) this fact is clearly attested. Lamia and Gello carry off children and also ἀώρους from this life, like other daimones of the underworld, Keres, Harpies, Erinyes, and Thanatos himself. The Lamiai rise to the light from their underground lairs—λαμίας τινὰς ἱστοροῦντες (the oldest writers of histories) ἐν ὕλαις καὶ νάπαις ἐκ γῆς ἀνιεμένας, D.H., *Thuc.* 6. Empousa appears on earth at midday because that was the time when sacrifice was offered to the dead (Sch. Ar., *Ran.* 293 ; sacrifice to Heroes at midday : above, chap. iv, n. 9). She approaches the offerings to the creatures of the lower world because she herself is one of their number. (In the same way the chthonic character of the *Seirenes*—they are closely related to the Harpies—is shown by the fact that they too appear like Empousa at midday and oppress sleepers, etc., according to the popular demonology. See Crusius, *Philol.* 50, 97 ff.)

APPENDIX VII

The *Hosts of Hekate* cause fear and sickness at night : εἴτ' ἔνυπνον φάντασμα φοβῇ χθονίας θ' Ἑκάτης κῶμον ἐδέξω, Trag. Incert. *fr.* 375 (Porson suggested Aesch.). They form the νυκτίφαντοι πρόπολοι Ἐνοδίας, Eur., *Hel.* 570. (These πρόπολοι τᾶς θεοῦ are probably also referred to in the *defixio CIG.* 5773 ; Wünsch, *Tab. Defix.*, p. ixb.) They are nothing else than the restless souls of the dead wandering in the train of Hekate. Nocturnal terrors are produced by Ἑκάτης ἐπιβολαὶ καὶ ἡρώων ἔφοδοι, Hp., *Morb. Sacr.* (vi, 362 L.). Hence Orph., *H.* i, 1, calls Hekate ψυχαῖς νεκύων μέτα βακχεύουσαν. The souls which thus wander about with Hekate are in part those of the ἄωροι, i.e. of those who have died before the completion of their "destined" period of life, πρὶν μοῖραν ἐξήκειν βίου, Soph., *Ant.* 896; cf. Phrynich. in *AB.* 24, 22, and πρόμοιρος ἁρπαγή, *Inscr. Cos*, 322. Thanatos has acted unjustly towards them ἐν ταχυτῆτι βίου παύων νεοήλικας ἀκμάς, Orph., *H.* 87, 5–6. The period of conscious existence on earth which they had left incomplete they must now fulfil as disembodied "souls": aiunt immatura morte praeventas (animas) eo usque vagari istic, donec reliquatio compleatur aetatum quas tum pervixissent si non intempestive obiissent, Tert., *An.* 56. (They haunt the place of their burial: ἥρωες ἀτυχεῖς, οἱ ἐν τῷ δεῖνι τόπῳ συνέχεσθε, *P. Mag. Par.* 1408; cf. *CIG.* 5858b.) For this reason it is often mentioned on gravestones (and elsewhere: Eur., *Alc.* 168 f.) as something specially to be lamented that the person there buried had died ἄωρος: see *Epigr. Gr.* 12; 16; 193; 220, 1; 221, 2; 313, 2–3: ἄτεκνος ἄωρος, 336, 2; and cf. 372, 32; 184, 3; *CIG.* 5574 (see also App. iii and chap. xiv, pt. ii, n. 155, ἄγαμοι). Gello who herself παρθένος ἀώρως ἐτελεύτησε then becomes a φάντασμα, slays children and causes τοὺς τῶν ἀώρων θανάτους, Zenob. iii, 3; Hsch. Γελλώ. The souls of the ἄωροι cannot rest but must continually wander: see Plaut., *Most.* 499. They (ἀνέμων εἴδωλον ἔχοντες, *H. Hec.*, l. 15: *Orph.*, p. 290 Ab.) are the creatures which accompany Hekate in her nocturnal wanderings. The *Hymn.* to Hekate, p. 289 Ab. (cf. *P. Mag. Par.* 2727 ff.) addresses Hek. thus (10 ff.): δεῦρ' Ἑκάτη τριοδῖτι, πυρίπνοε, φάσματ' ἔχουσα (ἄγουσα Mein.), ᾗ τ' ἔλαχες δεινὰς μὲν ὁδοὺς (δεινάς τ' ἐφόδους ?) χαλεπάς τ' ἐπιπομπάς, τὴν Ἑκάτην σε καλῶ σὺν ἀποφθιμένοισιν ἀώροις κεἴ τινες ἡρώων θάνον ἀγναῖοί τε (καὶ Mein., but this position of τέ is a regular Hellenistic usage; occurs frequently in *Orac. Sibyll.*) ἄπαιδες κτλ. Thus the ἄωροι became the typical haunting spirits κατ' ἐξοχήν. Just as in this *Hymn.* they are summoned (with Hek.) for unholy purposes of magic, so an ἄωρος is sometimes expressly invoked in the *defixiones* which were placed in graves (esp. in those of ἄωροι: see the instructions given in *P. Mag. Par.* 332 ff., 2215, 2220 f.; *P. Anastasy*, l. 336 ff.; 353): λέγω τῷ ἀώρῳ τῷ κ[ατὰ τοῦτον τὸν τόπον, etc.]: Roman *defixio*, *I. Sic. et It.* 1047; ἐξορκίζω σε, νεκύδαιμον ἄωρε, leaden tablet from Carth., *BCH.* 1888, p. 299 (*Tab. Defix.*, p. xvi); cf. also *P. Mag. Par.* 342 f.; 1390 ff.; παράδοτε (the victim) ἀώροις, leaden tablet from Alexandria, *Rh. Mus.* 9, 37, l. 22; a lead tablet from Phrygia (*BCH.* 1893, p. 251) has: γράφω πάντας τοὺς ἐμοὶ ἀντία ποιοῦντας μετὰ τῶν ἀώρων· Ἐπάγαθον Σαβῖναν, etc. In the curses of *Epigr. Gr.*, p. 149, the Ἑκάτης μελαίνης δαίμονες alternate with ἄωροι συμφοραί; see also Sterrett, *Amer. Sch. Athens*, ii, 168.—Everything that has been said of the ἄωροι applies also to the βιαιοθάνατοι (or βίαιοι, a term found in the magical papyri; cf. also βιοθάνατον πνεῦμα, *P. Mag. Par.* 1950): they are a special kind of ἄωροι: they find no rest, see above, chap. v, n. 147; Tert., *An.* 56–7; Serv., *A.* iv, 386, quoting the *physici*; cf. also Heliod., 2, 5, p. 42, 20 ff. Bk. A βιαιοθάνατος, who has thus been deprived of his life, has to make special supplication for admission into Hades: *Epigr. Gr.* 625; cf. Verg., *A.* iv, 696 ff. Such souls become ἀλάστορες, wandering spirits: see above, Append. vi, p. 592; wandering of a βιαιοθάνατος, Plu., *Cim.* 1.—Finally the souls of unburied persons who have no share in the cult of the souls or home in the grave are also condemned to wander (cf. Eur., *Hec.* 31–50): see above, chap. v, p. 163. The ἄταφος is detained ἐνθάδε: Soph., *Ant.* 1070, and wanders about the earth: ἀλαίνει, Eur., *Tro.* 1083; cf. Tert., *An.* 56. Hence the souls of these ἄταφοι could be forced to appear and answer the sorcerer: Heliod., p. 177, 15 ff. Bk.; *rite conditis Manibus* the wanderings of the soul cease: Plin., *Ep.* 7, 27, 11; Luc., *Philops.* 31 fin.—The art of the μάντις and of the καθαρτής (and of the ἀπομάκτρια γραῦς, Plu., *Superst.* 3, p. 166 A) is supposed to keep off such nocturnal terrors; it is "purification" precisely because it drives away such unholy beings. It is also a kind of καθάρσιον that is employed when ἀπομαγδαλίαι (instead of to the dogs: Ath. 409 D) are thrown out ἐν τοῖς ἀμφόδοις γινομένοις νυκτερινοῖς φόβοις (Harmodios of Leprea ap. Ath. 149 C), i.e. to Hekate and her rout which also appears as a pack of hounds.

APPENDIX VIII

Disintegration of Consciousness and Reduplication of Personality

In that period of extreme excitement the Greeks must have had frequent experience of the abnormal but by no means unusual psychical state in which a division of consciousness takes place and becomes apparent. The single personality splits up into two (or more) distinct centres of consciousness; and these give rise to two personalities (succeeding each other, or contemporaneous), with a double will and a double intellect appearing in one man. Even unprejudiced psychological observers of our own time are unable to describe such phenomena, which appear (spontaneously or produced experimentally) in certain neuropathic conditions, except as a reduplication or multiplication of personality. A second self comes into being, a second centre of consciousness following or by the side of the first and normal personality, which is generally unaware of the existence of its rival. (Probably the most complete and cautious account of these matters is that given by Pierre Janet in *L'automatisme psychologique*, Paris, 1889.) When such phenomena appear in conjunction with marked religious or spiritualistic tendencies they are naturally explained in accordance with these intellectual preconceptions. The appearance in a man or woman of an intelligent will, unguided or unperceived by the normally dominant personality, is conceived as the entrance of a foreign personality into the individual; or as the expulsion of the real soul of the individual by such a demonic or spiritual visitor. Nothing, however, is commoner, in all ages, than the religious or spiritualist preconceptions that lead to such an explanation; and so what the Greeks called ἔκστασις or κατέχεσθαι ἐκ θεοῦ has been a very frequent explanation of such mysterious occurrences from the earliest times (and in the present day). It has appealed just as much to the person affected by such "reduplication of personality" as to those round about him (unless they have been scientifically educated). The actual experience of such phenomena is generally a fact; fancy begins only with the explanation offered. For the Greeks the Pythia was always the best known example of such "possession" of a human being by a foreign will or spirit which seemed to enter violently and from outside into the human individual, having little correspondence (as it usually happened) with the character or the intellect of the "medium" in his or her normal state of consciousness. The Sibyls, Bakides, *Βάκχοι*, the seers and priests of purification, Epimenides, Aristeas, and so many others, were further cases of the ascent of the soul to the divine or the entrance of a god into the soul. It was inevitable that the idea of an immediate relation between the soul and the divine, and of the divine nature of the soul itself, should grow up in connexion with such cases as these, and seem to be authenticated in them more than in any other way. Greece is not the only place where this has happened.

APPENDIX IX

The Great Orphic Theogony

The information about a coherent Orphic Theogony and Anthropogony which has come down to us from the statements of Neoplatonic philosophers and their contemporaries, is derived, as Lobeck very rightly concluded, from the *ἐν ταῖς ῥαψῳδίαις 'Ορφικαῖς θεολογία, ἣν καὶ οἱ φιλόσοφοι διερμηνεύουσιν* (Damasc., *Princ.*, p. 380 K.). This last statement means that they were explained in lectures given by the heads of the Platonic school since the time of Syrianos (*'Ορφικαὶ συνουσίαι* of Syrian.: Procl., *in Tim.* 96 B; Scholia of Proclus on Orpheus, *εἰ καὶ μὴ εἰς πάσας τὰς ῥαψῳδίας*: Marin., *V. Procl.* 27). Written commentaries were also published, more particularly in order to prove the *συμφωνίαν 'Ορφέως, Πυθαγόρου καὶ Πλάτωνος* (Syrianos wrote a book with this title, wrongly ascribed to Proclus by Suidas: see R. Schöll on Procl. *in Rp.*, p. 5. Probably the work of Syr. *εἰς τὴν 'Ορφέως θεολογίαν* is the source of Orph., *frr.* 123–4, which are traced back in the *Θεοσοφία*, § 50, to *Συριανὸς ἐν τοῖς ἑαυτοῦ πονήμασιν*. From Syr. also probably comes the citation from Orpheus *ἐν τῇ τετάρτῃ ῥαψῳδίᾳ*, ib., § 61). The older Neoplatonists before Syrianos took little notice of the Orphica. Plotinos gives no quotation at all (though perhaps an allusion in 4, 3, 12; see Lob., p. 555), Iamblichos quotes nothing from immediate acquaintance, Porphyrios, who read everything, gives a little (*frr.* 114; 123 Euseb. from Porph.; 211) and what he does give certainly comes from the Rhapsodiai. In fact, the Neoplatonics as a whole when they quote Orpheus from their own knowledge (and do not, for example, simply write "Orpheus" instead of "Pythagoras": see above, chap. x, n. 9) use the Rhapsodiai *only*, as Lobeck rightly maintains, p. 466 (Abel did not realize this, to the detriment of his collection of the *frr.*). The title of the poem they used can hardly have been Θεογονία. (This seems to occur as a title in *fr.* 188 [Clem. Al. from auct. π. κλοπῆς]. In *fr.* 108 it is only a description of contents; *fr.* 310 is spurious. In Suidas, Gaisford's MSS., we do indeed read of a θεογονία, ἔπη "ασ'": but the figure indicating the number of lines corresponds most suspiciously with that of the previous ὀνομαστικόν, and in any case would be insufficient for the great length of the ῥαψῳδίαι.) It seems extremely probable (as Lobeck already suspected, p. 716, 726) that the simple description: an Orphic poem divided into several Rhapsodiai, ἱεροὶ λόγοι ἐν ῥαψῳδίαις κδ' (Suid.), was the real title of the poem, which consisted of several ῥαψῳδίαι. This ἱερὸς λόγος (the plural only means that there were several books) is, however a different one (Lobeck missed this, p. 716) from the ἱερὸς λόγος which Epigenes (ap. Clem. Al., *Str.* i, 21, p. 144 P.) attributed to the Pythagorean Kerkops. (And again when Suid. attributes the 24 Rhaps. to the Thessalian Theognetos or to Kerkops he also means the *old* ἱερὸς λόγος not divided into Rhaps., and confuses this with the later and much extended ἱερὸς λόγος.) The older ἱερὸς λόγος is that alluded to by Cic., *ND.* i, 107, and prob. also by Plu., *Smp.* 2, 3, 2, p. 636 D (*fr.* 42); the quotation in *EM.* (*fr.* 44) from the 8th Bk. refers to the later ἱερὸς λόγος. But it is certain that the ἱερὸς λόγος in 24 Bks., the poem possessed by the Neoplatonists, from which by far the greater number of our fragments are taken, was not a work of the sixth century, written for instance (as Lobeck was inclined to think, 683 f.) by Onomakritos. It is even untrue—regrettably enough we might add—that as the Neoplatonists presumed (and Lobeck believed in consequence: p. 508, 529 f., 602, 613) Plato knew and made use of the "Rhapsodies". (This emerges with particular plainness from Gruppe's study of the question in *Jb. Philol. Supp.* xvii, 689 ff.). And when this is gone no other evidence for the earlier date of the Orphic Theogony in this form is left. And in the very few passages in which a real coincidence (and not a doubtfully assumed one) exists between the Rhapsodies and Pherekydes, Herakleitos, Parmenides (see Lob., p. 532; Kern, *Theogon.*, p. 52; Gruppe, p. 708) or Empedokles, the poet of the Rhapsodies is the borrower not the creditor. The age in which he lived cannot be precisely determined; the fact that Neoplatonic writers are the first to quote him does not settle the question; it is uncertain whether he lived after (as I think) or before the (otherwise unknown) Hieronymos whose statement about an Orphic Theogony is quoted by Damasc., *Princ.* 381 f. K. In any case Gruppe (p. 742) has correctly appreciated the character of the bulky poem (equalling or even surpassing the length of the Iliad), when he says that it consists in the main of a loosely connected patchwork of older Orphic tradition.

There are many points in which agreement between the Rhapsodies and older Orphic teaching and poetry is still demonstrable ; lines from older Orphic poems were taken over unaltered ; subjects from older Orphic Theogonies were combined, sometimes without regard for their divergent character ; different versions of the same motif occur together. Thus we have the *κατάποσις* (modelled eventually upon Hesiod) twice over : in the first version Zeus swallows Phanes, in the second the heart of Zagreus. Both mean the same thing ; the devouring of the heart of Zagreus may perhaps belong to the older Orphic legendary material, the devouring of Phanes to the later. The personality of *Φάνης*, however, cannot have been unknown even to the older stratum of Orphic poetry. D.S. 1, 11, 3, quotes a line of "Orpheus", which certainly was not taken from the Rhaps., in which *Φάνης* is mentioned (and identified with Dionysos). And in a gold tablet, folded up with the tablet bearing an inscription of Orphic character, *I. Sic. et It.* 642, and found in the same grave near Sybaris, there occurs in addition to other (illegible) matter a list of divine names which includes that of *Φάνης* (and also *Πρωτόγονος* here apparently distinguished from *Φάνης* with whom this figure of Orphic theology is generally identified) : see Comparetti, *Notizie degli scavi di antichità*, 1879, p. 157 ; 1880, p. 156. This establishes the existence of this figure of Orphic mythology as early as the third cent. B.C. (the prob. date of these tablets).—We may therefore employ the facts derived from the Rhapsodies with some confidence for the reconstruction of Orphic poetry and doctrine at those points at least in which coincidence with older Orphic teaching and the fantastic creatures of Orphic theology can still be proved. [I leave these remarks exactly as they stood in the first edition of this book, for they still fully correspond to my own opinion. Others in the meanwhile have expressed divergent views, esp. Gomperz, *Greek Thinkers*, i, p. 539. But that Gruppe's proof of the fact that Plato did not know the Rhapsodist Theogony is "wholly unsuccessful", is something which no one has yet sought to show upon intelligible *grounds*. Until such a disproof is forthcoming the belief in the early date of the Rhapsodies has no real ground on which to stand.]

APPENDIX X

Previous Lives of Pythagoras. His Descent to Hades

Pythagoras' miraculous power of remembering what had happened long ago in previous lives seems to be already alluded to in the lines of Empedokles, 430 ff. M. = *fr.* 129 D. The legend in which it was related how Pythag. showed that he had once been Emphorbos the son of Panthous who had been slain by Menelaos in the Trojan war, must, at any rate, have been put forward at an early period. The story is often told or alluded to : D.S. 10, 6, 1–3 ; Sch. V.

on *P* 28 ; Max. Tyr. 16 (i, 287 f. R.) ; Porph., *VP*. 26–7 ; Iambl., *VP*. 63 ; Philostr., *V. AP*. 1, 1, 1 ; 8, 7, 4 ; *Her*. 17, p. 192, 23 ff. Ks. ; Tatian, *Gr*. 25 ; Hor., *C*. 1, 28, 10 ; Ov., *M*. 15, 160 ff. ; Hygin. 112 ; Lact., *Inst*. 3, 18, 15 ; cf. also Call., *fr*. 83a (completely misunderstood by Schneider) who even calls Pythag. " Euphorbos ", as Hor. does and Luc., *DM*. 20, 3. The story is always told in such a way as to imply that no intermediate ἐνσωματώσεις of his soul had taken place between Pythag. himself and Euphorbos (they are definitely excluded in Luc., *Gall*. 17).—Why was Euphorbos in particular selected ? The fact that through his father Panthous he had a special connexion with Apollo, like Pythagoras (a true ψυχὴ Ἀπολλωνιακή : cf. also Luc., *Gall*. 16), can hardly have been sufficient reason (as Göttling, *Opusc*. 210 ; Krische, *Soc. Pythag*. 67 f. suggest).—Euphorbos was taken up and made one of a whole series of previous incarnations (Aithalides—Euphorbos—Hermotimos—Pyrrhos the Delian fisherman —Pythagoras) by Herakleides Pont. : D.L. viii, 4–5 (with which agree Hippol., *RH*. 1, 2, p. 12, 54 f. D.-S. ; Porph., *VP*. 45 ; Tert., *An*. 28, 31 ; Sch. Soph., *El*. 62). Starting with Aithalides (to whom Herakleides was perhaps the first to ascribe the gift of miraculous memory in addition to other miraculous powers) the power of ἀνάμνησις in life and death was transmitted through all the links in the chain down to Pythag. himself. (The story of the shield of Euphorbos was now transferred to Hermotimos for obvious reasons.) According to D.L. Herakleides φησὶν περὶ αὑτοῦ τάδε λέγειν (τὸν Πυθαγόραν). It is very possible that the language is here inexact and Herakleides did not (as the words of D.L. would strictly suggest) appeal to a statement of Pythagoras (in a book) but represented him as saying all this (in a dialogue). If this is correct, apart from the incarnation as Euphorbos which he took over from the tradition, Herakleides invented all the rest, according to his own fancy. The fable was then taken up with variations by others : in Sch. A.R. i, 645, two versions derived from the fiction of Herakl. but diverging in some points are mentioned (one being supported by οἱ Πυθαγορικοί, the other by Pythagoras himself—in a book ? Πυθαγόρας φησίν are the actual words). What Gellius 4, 11, 14, has to say on the authority of Klearchos and Dikaiarchos differs (except in the matter of Euphorbos) entirely from Herakleides (and the names given should not be altered). But it may, nevertheless, be essentially the same fable over again, this time in the form of a parody of Herakl. (which is not very likely in the case of Klearchos but suits Dikaiarch. very well). Encouraged by these predecessors Lucian in the *Cock* (19–20) carried still further the parody of the fabulous tale. The story of Herakleides seems to be seriously used in the γραφή in which Pythagoras αὐτός φησι δι' ἑπτὰ καὶ διηκοσίων ἐτῶν ἐξ ἀίδεω παραγεγενῆσθαι ἐς ἀνθρώπους, D.L. viii, 14. As Diels, *Archiv. f. Gesch. Philos*. iii, 468 f., shows to be very probable, this was in the ps.-Pythagorean book written in the Ionic dialect, not before the third century and divided into three parts, which D.L. quotes and makes use of (viii, 6 ; 9 ; 14 ; cf. also Sch. Pl., *Rp*. 600 B).

Pyth. here states that he appears on earth from the underworld "every 207 years", and the calculation may possibly be based on the series of lives invented by Herakleides and the Chronology of Apollodoros (in which case it could not be before the last century B.C.), thus: Pythag. born 572, Pyrrhos 779, Hermotimos 986, Euphorbos 1193 (in the first year of the *Τρωικά* acc. to Eratosthenes and Apollodor.), Aithalides 1490. It must indeed be admitted that this method of reckoning makes the gross error of calculating from birth to birth instead of from the death of A to the birth of B. (Other intervals are given in *Theologum. Arithm.*, p. 40 Ast [216 = 6^3: D.L. viii, 14, should not be altered to suit this as I once proposed]; Sch. Bern. Lucan. ix, 1, p. 289, 12 Us. [462, ? an error for 432 = 2 × 216; cf. *Theol. Arith.*, p. 40, 30])—The existence of a Pythagorean writing belonging to the period before Herakleides, in which these previous lives of Pythag. were mentioned cannot be certainly proved. It might be supposed (as I once supposed: *Rh. Mus.* 26, 558) that the conjunction of the legend of Pythagoras' previous lives with the descent of P. to Hades, which appears in Sch. Soph., *El.* 62, and Tert., *An.* 28, is ancient and original; in which case the previous lives would have been described in a Pythagorean *κατάβασις εἰς ᾅδου*. But the conjunction is quite arbitrary and is not such as would be likely in a Pythagorean book on the descent: the descent is, in fact, told as a parody, the form which had been given to it by Hermippos, and with the implication that it is untrue. Nor is it very likely that the previous lives would be described in connexion with a descent to Hades, considering that Pyth. remembered them while alive on earth and not in a condition of ecstasy, and did not learn of them in Hades. It would be more natural that, vice versa, an account of the previous lives should also include something about *τὰ ἐν ᾅδου*—the *ἀνάμνησις* included that also: cf. D.L. viii, 4 fin. (see the decisive objections to my previous view raised by G. Ettig, *Acheruntica*, Leipz. Stud. 13, 289 f.). This applies equally to the view of Diels[1] (*Archiv*, p. 469) that Herakleides (in his work *π. τῶν ἐν ᾅδου*) told of the previous lives of P. in connexion with the descent of P. to Hades and that Herakl. was the first to make P. go down to Hades. There is nothing to prove that Herakl. did this or to make it even probable. Without any

[1] What Diels, *Parmenides*, p. 15 (1897) says in support of his view might stand if we were willing to ignore the fact that Pythag., as has already been remarked, remembered his previous lives while he was still alive, and not in the ecstatic condition—not *ἔξω γενόμενος τοῦ σώματος*. But this is a fact, so that Diels' view remains untenable.—I cannot see what there is of a "rationalist" character (Diels) in the fact that Pyth. saw Hesiod and Homer in Hades undergoing punishment *ἀνθ' ὧν εἶπον περὶ θεῶν* (D.L. viii, 21). This is, in fact, an anti-rationalist, priestly invention (and so I see Dieterich also understands it, *Nekyia*, 130). This fact certainly does not tell against the view that the Hades poem had its origin in the sixth (or the first half of the fifth) century B.C.

grounds for doing so Diels supposes that what Pythagoras (acc. to Sch. Ambros. on α 371) "φησίν"· ἔξω γενόμενος τοῦ σώματος ἀκήκοα ἐμμέλους ἁρμονίας, was said by Pythag., not in a book going under his name, but in a dialogue by Herakleides (who is not even mentioned in that Schol.). There is no reason at all to doubt that these words (as Lobeck supposed, 944) came from a book ascribed to Pythagoras himself, in which he described his ekstasis and ecstatic visions (cf. Sch. Arist. 496b, 1 f., 13 ff. Br.). There is no further definite evidence for the existence of such a Pythagorean Κατάβασις εἰς ᾅδου (for the γραφή of D.L. viii, 21, has another and better interpretation, as already remarked). But a fairly early date for the origin of at least a legend about a descent of P. to Hades (and of quite definite statements about it with a propagandist aim) is attested by Hieronymos of Rhodos ap. D.L. viii, 21. (But we should not without more definite reason ascribe the invention of the fable itself to Hieron., as is done by Hiller, *Hier. Rh. frag.*, p. 25. What reason could Hieron. have had for inventing anything of the kind ?) Further, the lines of the comic poet Aristophon ap. D.L. viii, 38 [*fr.* 12 K.], already suggest that such legends were in existence in the third century B.C. Whether the work on the subject of Pythagoras' descent to Hades called forth the legend or whether the legend was already current and called forth the book, must remain undecided. But in any case the book included no account of the previous lives of Pythagoras: these (apart from the older legend of P. and Euphorbos) were first put forward by Herakleides Pont. (but not the Descent of P. to Hades).

APPENDIX XI

INITIATION CONSIDERED AS ADOPTION BY THE GOD

The Mystes whose soul is speaking in the first of the gold tablets found at Sybaris (Diels, No. 18) says, l. 7–8: ἱμερτοῦ δ' ἐπέβαν στεφανοῦ ποσὶ καρπαλίμοισι, δεσποίνας δ' ὑπὸ κόλπον ἔδυν χθονίας βασιλείας. This ὑπὸ κόλπον ἔδυν . . . can hardly mean anything else than: I seek (as ἱκέτης) the protection of her maternal bosom (or lap). It would certainly be attractive to take this (with Dieterich, *de hymn. Orph.*, p. 38) as referring to a symbolical act, corresponding to the ceremony in which in Greece and elsewhere, the adoption of a boy, his reception into a new γένος, was symbolically represented. (D.S. 4, 39, 2, in particular records the process; see Wesseling's learned note there; cf. also Preller, *Gr. Mythol.*[4] i, 702.) But such a *symbolical* proceeding if it was to bring about the association of the μύστης with the goddess must have taken place already in the ὄργια once held upon earth—here we are in Hades, and it is to say the least of it difficult to believe that this διέλκεσθαι τοῦ κόλπου can have been supposed to occur in Hades in the neighbourhood of the goddess herself (a fact which made a merely symbolical act of the kind supposed quite unnecessary).—Apart from this the views of Dieterich are quite sound: the ceremony was essentially regarded as an *adoption* of the μύστης by the goddess or the god, as a reception of the initiated into the divine γένος. The δράκων (who represents the god himself) διελκόμενος τοῦ κόλπου in the Sabazia seems actually to have had this meaning. Further the μύστης is sometimes called *renatus*, or *in aeternum renatus* (Apul., *M.* xi, 21; *CIL.* vi, 510; 736); the day of his initiation is his *natalis sacer* (Apul., *M.* xi, 24, where *natalem sacrum* should be read): in these circumstances we may venture to recall that the above-mentioned solemn rites of adoption also represented a *new birth* of the θετὸς υἱός from the womb of his new mother (see D.S. l.c. Hence Hera is called the δευτέρα τεκοῦσα of Herakles whom she adopted: Lycophr. 39; and hence also the adopted is called δευτερόποτμος, i.e. reborn: Hsch. s.v. ad fin.) This conception also provides the simplest explanation of the fact that the μυῶν, who has received the νέος μύστης into the divine γένος to which he himself already belongs, can be called the *pater* or *parens* of the μύστης (Apul., *M.* xi, 25; Tert., *Apol.* 8; *ad Nat.* i, 7)—he effects the entrance of the new member into his own family. (In Greek the name for such a mystic "father" seems to have been πατρομύστης, *CIG.* 3173, 3195.)—This conception of a *new birth* by initiation reminds us of the Christian idea of *rebirth* by baptism (which in its turn is developed from older Jewish ideas: see Anrich, *Ant. Mysterienwesen*, p. 111, n.). It is nevertheless one which the Greeks themselves had at an early date. The μύσται of the Eleusinia seem to have been not far from regarding initiation as an adoption into the divine γένος.

In the ps.-Platonic *Axiochus*, p. 371 D, we read in the description of the χῶρος εὐσεβῶν: ἐνταῦθα τοῖς μεμυημένοις ἐστί τις προεδρία καὶ τὰς ὁσίους ἁγιστείας κἀκεῖσε συντελοῦσι· πῶς οὖν οὐ σοὶ πρώτῳ μέτεστι τῆς τιμῆς, ὄντι γεννήτῃ τῶν θεῶν; καὶ τοὺς περὶ Ἡρακλέα τε (perhaps δέ would be better) καὶ Διόνυσον κατιόντας εἰς Ἅιδου πρότερον λόγος ἐνθάδε (i.e. at Athens) μυηθῆναι καὶ τὸ θάρσος τῆς ἐκεῖσε πορείας παρὰ τῆς Ἐλευσινίας ἐναύσασθαι.—Here Axiochos (for it is to him that Sokrates is speaking) is plainly described as γεννήτης τῶν θεῶν simply and solely because he belongs to the μεμυημένοι. According to Wilamowitz (*Gött. Gel. Anz.*, 1896, p. 984) he is called γεννήτης τῶν θεῶν only as a member of the γένος of the Εὐπατρίδαι to which he apparently belonged. But that anyone just on the strength of the by no means uncommon fact that he belonged to a γένος that happened to trace its earliest origin from a god (nor is it certain even that the Εὐπατρίδαι did this)—that anyone on this account should have dared to call himself a "member of the same family as the gods" is to say the least of it difficult to parallel. In this case at any rate nothing of the kind can be meant. From the general principle that the initiated have a προεδρία in Hades it is deduced, simply as conclusion from premiss, with a "surely then"—(πῶς οὖν οὐ—), that Axiochos too may hope to enjoy this same honour (τῆς τιμῆς—). It is then entirely impossible that, to account for this hope, a reason should be implied and expressed which, like the supposed descent of Axiochos from the gods, had nothing to do with the mysteries and the privileges of the *μύσται*. If it was the (alleged) descent of Axiochos from the gods which secured him *τιμή* in Hades it would be quite meaningless to accompany the mention of the *τιμή* thus secured to Axiochos with an allusion to the *τιμή* obtained on quite different grounds by the *μεμυημένοι* (which yet is mysteriously equivalent to that obtained by right of birth). This allusion, moreover, is put in such a way that it quite unambiguously includes the special case of Axiochos in the common denomination of the *μεμυημένοι* of whom he is said to be one. The fact, indeed, that the privileges of the *μεμυημένοι* is the only subject alluded to throughout is shown also by the third and last sentence : the famous cases of the initiation of Herakles and Dionysos are only mentioned as emphasizing still further the importance of *μυηθῆναι* for those *εἰς ᾅδου κατιόντας*.

Here then Axiochos can only be called *γεννήτης τῶν θεῶν* in so far as he is *μεμυημένος*. Why, indeed, he *πρῶτος*, before other *μεμυημένοι*, should have a claim to the honour of *προεδρία* is something that our text does not say and that can hardly be extracted from it. It certainly appears that Axiochos has a special privilege beyond that of other Mystai. Had he reached a specially high stage of the *τέλη* which was not open to everyone and at which kinship with the gods was first fully assured ? Did the family of the *Εὐπατρίδαι* undertake some active part in the *μύησις* which gave them a closer relation to the gods ? In any case his claim to be regarded as *γεννήτης τῶν θεῶν* must have depended on his having been initiated at Eleusis.

Now this kinship with the gods to which he thus attains can only be made intelligible, if, in accordance with the analogies adduced above, we regard the *μύησις* (or perhaps only its highest stages) as a symbolic adoption by the divinities, suggesting or representing entrance into the divine *γένος*. No one will maintain that *γεννήτης τῶν θεῶν* is a " very unnatural phrase " (Wil.) for one who has been " adopted " by the gods, who will recall the fact that at Athens the adopted person was inscribed *εἰς τοὺς γεννήτας* of the adopter (Is. 7, 13; 15; 17; 43), or, which is precisely the same thing, *εἰς τοὺς συγγενεῖς* of the adopter (Is. 7, 27; 1). Thereby he becomes himself *γεννήτης* of the members of the *γένος* into which he thus enters ; he is now their *γεννήτης*, or, as it is once expressed in an absolutely equivalent phrase, their *συγγενὴς κατὰ τὴν ποίησιν* ([Dem.] 44, 32).

Thus the fully initiated is *γεννήτης* of the divine family, *κατὰ τὴν ποίησιν*.

APPENDIX XII

Magical Exorcisms of the Dead on late κατάδεσμοι, φιμωτικά, etc.

Invocations and conjurings of *ἄωροι* and other *νεκυδαίμονες* of an earlier period are mentioned above (p. 594 f.). To a later period belong the *defixiones* found at Cyprus (Kurion) and edited in the *Proc. of the Soc. of Bibl. Archaeology*, p. 174 ff. The *defixiones* are there called παραθῆκαι, φιμωτικαὶ τοῦ ἀντιδίκου (i, 39, and frequently), or φιμωτικὰ καταθέματα (iv, 15, etc.). φιμοῦν and φιμωτικόν in this rude Egypto-Syrian Greek are equivalent to the terms, otherwise usual for such magic charms, καταδεῖν, κατάδεσμος (see above, chap. ix, n. 107). See also *P. Mag. Lond.* (Kenyon, *Greek Pap. in BM.*, p. 114), l. 967 ff. : in an appeal to a god (δεῦρό μοι καὶ) φίμωσον, ὑπόταξον, καταδούλωσον τὸν δεῖνα τῷ δεῖνι κτλ.—ib., p. 97, l. 396 ff. : φιμωτικὸν καὶ ὑποτακτικὸν γενναῖον καὶ κάτοχος· λαβὼν μόλυβον ἀπὸ ψυχροφόρου σωλῆνος ποίησον λάμναν καὶ ἐπίγραφε χαλκῷ γραφείῳ (bronze is a magic metal), ὡς ὑποκεῖται, καὶ θὲς παρὰ ἄωρον (see above, p. 594 f.): here follows the rest of the barbarous text.—On these Cypriote *defixiones* among the other invocations regularly appear those addressed to the souls of the unquiet dead, to the δαίμονες πολυάνδριοι (vi, 17, adds πεπελεκισμένοι καὶ ἐσ[ταυρωμένοι or ἐσκολοπισμένοι ? cf. Luc., *Philops.* 29]) καὶ βιοθάνατοι καὶ ἄωροι καὶ ἄποροι ταφῆς (τῆς ἱερᾶς ταφῆς, iv, 18) : thus i, 30 f., and frequently. The δαίμονες πυλυάνδριοι were probably the souls of executed criminals whose bodies were thrown out into the common burial grounds—as at Melite in Athens : Plu., *Themist.* 22—the πολυάνδρια (cf. Perizon. on Ael., *VH.* 12, 21). βιοθάνατοι εἴτε ξένοι εἴτε ἐντόπιοι are invoked, iv, 4. Invocation is made in common to : τύμβε πανδάκρυτε καὶ χθόνιοι θεοὶ καὶ Ἑκάτη χθονία καὶ Ἑρμῆ χθόνιε καὶ Πλούτων καὶ Ἐρινύες ὑποχθόνιοι καὶ ὑμεῖς οἱ ὧδε κατῳκημένοι ἄωροι καὶ ἀνώνυμοι (see *Rh. Mus.* 50, 20, 3) : i, 35, and frequently repeated with the same formula. What we have here is of frequent occurrence : a dead person is called upon to carry out a curse. An early example is *CIG.* 539 : καταδῶ αὐτοὺς (the persons to be cursed) σοί, Ὀνήσιμε (Attica, fourth century B.C.). The tablet in Böckh, i, p. 487, admits the reading Ὀνήσιμε as well as Ὀνήσιμη. The latter (as a nominative) is preferred by Wünsch, *Tab. Defix.*, p. ivb, p. 25 (n. 100), simply in order to expel every example of the invocation of a dead person to carry out a curse. But this is only a petitio principii ; and if we accepted Ὀνησίμη (as the name of the curser) at least the addition of some word like ἐγώ after αὐτοὺς σοί would be necessary—for which there is no room on the tablet. It will be necessary to retain the generally accepted vocative Ὀνήσιμε (to which the coming πάντας . . . τηρεῖν, l. 5–8, is much better suited than to the following Ἑρμῆ, l. 8, as in Wünsch's version). There is nothing remarkable in the invocation here of the individual νεκυδαίμων by name (thus doubling the force of compulsion exerted : cf. Kroll, *Rh. Mus.*, 52, 345 f.) to complete and carry out the curse : parallels are given above, p. 594 ff., and in the above-mentioned Cypriote φιμωτικά : cf. also *CIG.* 5858b, δαίμονες καὶ πνεύματα (i.e. " souls ") ἐν τῷ τόπῳ τούτῳ θηλυκῶν καὶ ἀρρενικῶν, ἐξορκίζω ὑμᾶς.

The custom of burying such magic defixions was astonishingly widespread. Defigi diris deprecationibus nemo non metuit, Plin., *NH.* 28, 19. In the places where Latin was spoken such abominations were indeed even more common than in Greek-speaking countries. (The Latin *defixiones* are collected now by Wünsch, *Tab. Defix.* xxv f.) The practice had a long life and is not quite dead even to-day. On the Roman side examples from the seventh and eighth centuries are by no means rare: see e.g. [Aug.] *Hom. de Sacrileg.*, § 20. For a Greek example see e.g. the story ap. Sophronius, *SS. Cyri et Ioannis Miracula* (saec. vi), chap. 55, p. 3625 Migne: magical objects were buried under the door-step of the victim's house; were discovered and dug up; whereupon the death immediately followed of—not the victim but—the magician.

12*th August*, 1897 (= 2nd German Ed.).

INDEX

The figures indicate pages, except where they follow a Roman numeral, in which case they refer to the numbered notes.

Selected titles: revised December, 1966

harper torchbooks

HUMANITIES AND SOCIAL SCIENCES

American Studies: General

CARL N. DEGLER, Ed.: Pivotal Interpretations of American History TB/1240, TB/1241

A. S. EISENSTADT, Ed.: The Craft of American History Vol. I TB/1255; Vol. II TB/1256

CHARLOTTE P. GILMAN: Women and Economics § TB/3073

JOHN HIGHAM, Ed.: The Reconstruction of American History Δ TB/1068

JOHN F. KENNEDY: A Nation of Immigrants Δ TB/1118

LEONARD W. LEVY, Ed.: American Constitutional Law TB/1285

ARNOLD ROSE: The Negro in America TB/3048

American Studies: Colonial

BERNARD BAILYN, Ed.: The Apologia of Robert Keayne: *Self-Portrait of a Puritan Merchant* TB/1201

LAWRENCE HENRY GIPSON: The Coming of the Revolution: 1763-1775. † *Illus.* TB/3007

PERRY MILLER & T. H. JOHNSON, Eds.: The Puritans: *A Sourcebook* Vol. I TB/1093; Vol. II TB/1094

EDMUND S. MORGAN, Ed.: The Diary of Michael Wigglesworth, 1653-1657 TB/1228

EDMUND S. MORGAN: The Puritan Family TB/1227

RICHARD B. MORRIS: Government and Labor in Early America TB/1244

WALLACE NOTESTEIN: The English People on the Eve of Colonization: 1603-1630. † *Illus.* TB/3006

American Studies: From the Revolution to 1860

RAY A. BILLINGTON: The Far Western Frontier: 1830-1860. † *Illus.* TB/3012

W. R. BROCK: An American Crisis: *Congress and Reconstruction, 1865-67* ° Δ TB/1283

GEORGE DANGERFIELD: The Awakening of American Nationalism: 1815-1828. † *Illus.* TB/3061

RICHARD B. MORRIS, Ed.: The Era of the American Revolution TB/1180

A. F. TYLER: Freedom's Ferment TB/1074

American Studies: Since the Civil War

MAX BELOFF, Ed.: The Debate on the American Revolution, 1761-1783: *A Sourcebook* Δ TB/1225

EDMUND BURKE: On the American Revolution. † *Edited by Elliot Robert Barkan* TB/3068

WHITNEY R. CROSS: The Burned-Over District: *The Social and Intellectual History of Enthusiastic Religion in Western New York, 1800-1850* TB/1242

W. A. DUNNING: Reconstruction, Political and Economic: 1865-1877 TB/1073

FRANCIS GRIERSON: The Valley of Shadows TB/1246

SIDNEY HOOK: Reason, Social Myths, and Democracy TB/1237

WILLIAM E. LEUCHTENBURG: Franklin D. Roosevelt and the New Deal: 1932-1940. † *Illus.* TB/3025

ARTHUR S. LINK: Woodrow Wilson and the Progressive Era: 1910-1917. † *Illus.* TB/3023

JAMES MADISON: The Forging of American Federalism. *Edited by Saul K. Padover* TB/1226

ROBERT GREEN MC CLOSKEY: American Conservatism in the Age of Enterprise: 1865-1910 TB/1137

ARTHUR MANN: Yankee Reformers in the Urban Age TB/1247

GEORGE E. MOWRY: The Era of Theodore Roosevelt and the Birth of Modern America: 1900-1912. † TB/3022

R. B. NYE: Midwestern Progressive Politics TB/1202

FRANCIS S. PHILBRICK: The Rise of the West, 1754-1830. † *Illus.* TB/3067

WILLIAM PRESTON, JR.: Aliens and Dissenters TB/1287

JACOB RIIS: The Making of an American ‡ TB/3070

PHILIP SELZNICK: TVA and the Grass Roots: *A Study in the Sociology of Formal Organization* TB/1230

TIMOTHY L. SMITH: Revivalism and Social Reform: *American Protestantism on the Eve of the Civil War* TB/1229

IDA M. TARBELL: The History of the Standard Oil Company. *Briefer Version.* ‡ *Edited by David M. Chalmers* TB/3071

GEORGE B. TINDALL, Ed.: A Populist Reader ‡ TB/3069

ALBION W. TOURGÉE: A Fool's Errand TB/3074

VERNON LANE WHARTON: The Negro in Mississippi: 1865-1890 TB/1178

Anthropology

JACQUES BARZUN: Race: *A Study in Superstition. Revised Edition* TB/1172

JOSEPH B. CASAGRANDE, Ed.: In the Company of Man: *Portraits of Anthropological Informants.* TB/3047

DAVID LANDY: Tropical Childhood: *Cultural Transmission and Learning in a Puerto Rican Village* ¶ TB/1235

EDWARD BURNETT TYLOR: The Origins of Culture. *Part I of "Primitive Culture."* § *Intro. by Paul Radin* TB/33

EDWARD BURNETT TYLOR: Religion in Primitive Culture. *Part II of "Primitive Culture"* § TB/34

W. LLOYD WARNER: A Black Civilization: *A Study of an Australian Tribe.* ¶ *Illus.* TB/3056

Art and Art History

EMILE MÂLE: The Gothic Image: *Religious Art in France of the Thirteenth Century.* § Δ *190 illus.* TB/44

ERICH NEUMANN: The Archetypal World of Henry Moore. Δ *107 illus.* TB/2020

DORA & ERWIN PANOFSKY: Pandora's Box: *The Changing Aspects of a Mythical Symbol* TB/2021

Business, Economics & Economic History

GILBERT BURCK & EDITORS OF FORTUNE: The Computer Age: *And Its Potential for Management* TB/1179

† The New American Nation Series, edited by Henry Steele Commager and Richard B. Morris.
‡ American Perspectives series, edited by Bernard Wishy and William E. Leuchtenburg.
* The Rise of Modern Europe series, edited by William L. Langer.
¶ Researches in the Social, Cultural, and Behavioral Sciences, edited by Benjamin Nelson.
§ The Library of Religion and Culture, edited by Benjamin Nelson.
Σ Harper Modern Science Series, edited by James R. Newman.
° Not for sale in Canada.
Δ Not for sale in the U. K.

THOMAS C. COCHRAN: The American Business System: *A Historical Perspective, 1900-1955* TB/1080
FRANK H. KNIGHT: Risk, Uncertainty and Profit TB/1215
ABBA P. LERNER: Everybody's Business TB/3051
HERBERT SIMON: The Shape of Automation TB/1245
PIERRE URI: Partnership for Progress: *A Program for Transatlantic Action* TB/3036

Historiography & Philosophy of History

JACOB BURCKHARDT: On History and Historians. △ *Intro. by H. R. Trevor-Roper* TB/1216
H. STUART HUGHES: History as Art and as Science: *Twin Vistas on the Past* TB/1207
ARNOLDO MOMIGLIANO: Studies in Historiography TB/1288
GEORGE H. NADEL, Ed.: Studies in the Philosophy of History: *Essays from* History and Theory TB/1208
KARL R. POPPER: The Open Society and Its Enemies △ Vol. I TB/1101; Vol. II TB/1102
KARL R. POPPER: The Poverty of Historicism ° △ TB/1126
G. J. RENIER: History: Its Purpose and Method △ TB/1209
W. H. WALSH: Philosophy of History △ TB/1020

History: General

L. CARRINGTON GOODRICH: A Short History of the Chinese People. △ *Illus.* TB/3015
DAN N. JACOBS & HANS H. BAERWALD: Chinese Communism: *Selected Documents* TB/3031
BERNARD LEWIS: The Arabs in History △ TB/1029
BERNARD LEWIS: Middle East and West ° △ TB/1274

History: Ancient and Medieval

HELEN CAM: England before Elizabeth △ TB/1026
NORMAN COHN: The Pursuit of the Millennium △ TB/1037
CHRISTOPHER DAWSON, Ed.: Mission to Asia △ TB/315
ADOLF ERMAN, Ed.: The Ancient Egyptians TB/1233
F. L. GANSHOF: Feudalism △ TB/1058
DENO GEANAKOPLOS: Byzantine East and Latin West △ TB/1265
DENYS HAY: Europe: Emergence of an Idea TB/1275
DENYS HAY: The Medieval Centuries ° △ TB/1192
SAMUEL NOAH KRAMER: Sumerian Mythology TB/1055
NAPHTALI LEWIS & MEYER REINHOLD, Eds.: Roman Civilization Vol. I TB/1231; Vol. II TB/1232
CHARLES PETIT-DUTAILLIS: The Feudal Monarchy in France and England ° △ TB/1165
HENRI PIRENNE: Early Democracies in the Low Countries TB/1110
STEVEN RUNCIMAN: A History of the Crusades. △ Vol. I TB/1143; Vol. II TB/1243

History: Renaissance & Reformation

JACOB BURCKHARDT: The Civilization of the Renaissance in Italy △ Vol. I TB/40; Vol. II TB/41
JOHN CALVIN & JACOPO SADOLETO: A Reformation Debate. *Edited by John C. Olin* TB/1239
G. CONSTANT: The Reformation in England △ TB/314
G. R. ELTON: Reformation Europe, 1517-1559 ° △ TB/1270
J. H. HEXTER: More's Utopia: *The Biography of an Idea. New Epilogue by the Author* TB/1195
HAJO HOLBORN: Ulrich von Hutten and the German Reformation TB/1238
JOEL HURSTFIELD, Ed.: The Reformation Crisis △ TB/1267
ULRICH VON HUTTEN et al.: On the Eve of the Reformation. *"Letters of Obscure Men." Introduction by Hajo Holborn* TB/1124
PAUL O. KRISTELLER: Renaissance Thought: *The Classic, Scholastic, and Humanist Strains* TB/1048
ROBERT LATOUCHE: The Birth of Western Economy TB/1290
GARRETT MATTINGLY et al.: Renaissance Profiles. △ *Edited by J. H. Plumb* TB/1162
J. E. NEALE: The Age of Catherine de Medici ° △ TB/1085
ERWIN PANOFSKY: Studies in Iconology △ TB/1077
J. H. PLUMB: The Italian Renaissance △ TB/1161
A. F. POLLARD: Henry VIII ° △ TB/1249
A. F. POLLARD: Wolsey ° △ TB/1248
A. L. ROWSE: The Expansion of Elizabethan England. ° △ *Illus.* TB/1220
G. M. TREVELYAN: England in the Age of Wycliffe, 1368-1520 ° △ TB/1112
VESPASIANO: Renaissance Princes, Popes, and Prelates: *The Vespasiano Memoirs* TB/1111

History: Modern European

MAX BELOFF: The Age of Absolutism, 1660-1815 △ TB/1062
ASA BRIGGS: The Making of Modern England, 1784-1867: *The Age of Improvement* ° △ TB/1203
CRANE BRINTON: A Decade of Revolution, 1789-1799. * *Illus.* TB/3018
D. W. BROGAN: The Development of Modern France. ° △ Vol. I TB/1184; Vol. II TB/1185
J. BRONOWSKI & BRUCE MAZLISH: The Western Intellectua[l] Tradition: *From Leonardo to Hegel* △ TB/300[1]
ALAN BULLOCK: Hitler, A Study in Tyranny ° △ TB/112[3]
E. H. CARR: German-Soviet Relations Between the Tw[o] World Wars, 1919-1939 TB/127[8]
E. H. CARR: International Relations Between the Tw[o] World Wars, 1919-1939 ° △ TB/127[9]
E. H. CARR: The Twenty Years' Crisis, 1919-1939 ° △ TB/112[2]
GORDON A. CRAIG: Bismarck to Adenauer TB/117[1]
FRANKLIN L. FORD: Robe and Sword: *The Regrouping o[f] the French Aristocracy after Louis XIV* TB/121[7]
RENÉ FUELOEP-MILLER: The Mind and Face of Bolshe[vism] vism TB/118[8]
HANS KOHN, Ed.: The Mind of Modern Russia TB/106[5]
WALTER LAQUEUR & GEORGE L. MOSSE, Eds.: Internationa[l] Fascism, 1920-1945 ° △ TB/127[6]
WALTER LAQUEUR & GEORGE L. MOSSE, Eds.: Left-Win[g] Intelligentsia Between the Two World Wars TB/128[6]
FRANK E. MANUEL: The Prophets of Paris: *Turgot, Con[dorcet,] dorcet, Saint-Simon, Fourier, and Comte* TB/121[8]
L. B. NAMIER: Facing East △ TB/128[0]
L. B. NAMIER: Personalities and Powers △ TB/118[6]
FRANZ NEUMANN: Behemoth TB/128[9]
DAVID OGG: Europe of the Ancien Régime, 1715-1783 ° △ TB/127[1]
PENFIELD ROBERTS: The Quest for Security, 1715-1740. * *Illus.* TB/301[6]
GEORGE RUDÉ: Revolutionary Europe, 1783-1815 ° △ TB/127[2]
LOUIS, DUC DE SAINT-SIMON: Versailles, The Court, an[d] Louis XIV △ TB/125[0]
A. J. P. TAYLOR: From Napoleon to Lenin: *Historical Es[says]* ° △ TB/126[8]
A. J. P. TAYLOR: The Habsburg Monarchy, 1809-1918 ° △ TB/118[7]
G. M. TREVELYAN: British History in the Nineteent[h] Century and After: 1782-1919 △ TB/125[1]
H. R. TREVOR-ROPER: Historical Essays ° △ TB/126[9]
ELIZABETH WISKEMANN: Europe of the Dictators, 1919-1945 ° △ TB/127[3]

Intellectual History & History of Ideas

ERNST CASSIRER: The Individual and the Cosmos i[n] Renaissance Philosophy. △ *Translated with an Intro[duction] duction by Mario Domandi* TB/109[7]
FRANK E. MANUEL: The Prophets of Paris: *Turgot, Con[dorcet,] dorcet, Saint-Simon, Fourier, and Comte* TB/121[8]
PHILIP P. WIENER: Evolution and the Founders of Prag[matism] matism. △ *Foreword by John Dewey* TB/121[2]

Literature, Poetry, The Novel & Criticism

JAMES BOSWELL: The Life of Dr. Johnson & The Journa[l] of a Tour to the Hebrides with Samuel Johnso[n] LL.D.: *Selections* ° △ TB/125[4]
RICHMOND LATTIMORE: The Poetry of Greek Tragedy △ TB/125[7]
J. B. LEISHMAN: The Monarch of Wit: *An Analytica[l] and Comparative Study of the Poetry of Joh[n] Donne* ° △ TB/125[8]

J. B. LEISHMAN: Themes and Variations in Shakespeare's Sonnets ° △ TB/1259
V. DE S. PINTO: Crisis in English Poetry, 1880-1940 ° △ TB/1260
C. K. STEAD: The New Poetic: *Yeats to Eliot* ° △ TB/1263
BASIL WILLEY: Nineteenth Century Studies: *Coleridge to Matthew Arnold* ° △ TB/1261
BASIL WILLEY: More Nineteenth Century Studies: *A Group of Honest Doubters* ° △ TB/1262
RAYMOND WILLIAMS: Culture and Society, 1780-1950 △ TB/1252
RAYMOND WILLIAMS: The Long Revolution △ TB/1253

Philosophy

G. E. M. ANSCOMBE: An Introduction to Wittgenstein's Tractatus. ° △ *Second edition, Revised* TB/1210
HENRI BERGSON: Time and Free Will ° △ TB/1021
FREDERICK COPLESTON: Medieval Philosophy ° △ TB/376
F. M. CORNFORD: Principium Sapientiae TB/1213
F. M. CORNFORD: From Religion to Philosophy § TB/20
WILFRID DESAN: The Tragic Finale: *An Essay on the Philosophy of Jean-Paul Sartre* TB/1030
MARVIN FARBER: The Aims of Phenomenology TB/1291
PAUL FRIEDLÄNDER: Plato: *An Introduction* △ TB/2017
W. K. C. GUTHRIE: The Greek Philosophers ° △ TB/1008
F. H. HEINEMANN: Existentialism and the Modern Predicament △ TB/28
EDMUND HUSSERL: Phenomenology and the Crisis of Philosophy TB/1170
IMMANUEL KANT: The Doctrine of Virtue TB/110
IMMANUEL KANT: Lectures on Ethics § △ TB/105
IMMANUEL KANT: Religion Within the Limits of Reason Alone. § *Intro. by T. M. Greene & J. Silber* TB/67
QUENTIN LAUER: Phenomenology TB/1169
GABRIEL MARCEL: Being and Having △ TB/310
GEORGE A. MORGAN: What Nietzsche Means TB/1198
MICHAEL POLANYI: Personal Knowledge △ TB/1158
WILLARD VAN ORMAN QUINE: Elementary Logic. *Revised Edition* TB/577
WILLARD VAN ORMAN QUINE: From a Logical Point of View: *Logico-Philosophical Essays* TB/566
BERTRAND RUSSELL et al.: The Philosophy of Bertrand Russell Vol. I TB/1095; Vol. II TB/1096
L. S. STEBBING: A Modern Introduction to Logic △ TB/538
ALFRED NORTH WHITEHEAD: Process and Reality: *An Essay in Cosmology* △ TB/1033
WILHELM WINDELBAND: A History of Philosophy Vol. I TB/38; Vol. II TB/39
LUDWIG WITTGENSTEIN: Blue and Brown Books ° TB/1211

Political Science & Government

KENNETH E. BOULDING: Conflict and Defense TB/3024
CRANE BRINTON: English Political Thought in the Nineteenth Century TB/1071
F. L. GANSHOF: Feudalism △ TB/1058
SIDNEY HOOK: Reason, Social Myths and Democracy △ TB/1237
DAN N. JACOBS, Ed.: The New Communist Manifesto & *Related Documents. Third edition, Revised* TB/1078
DAN N. JACOBS & HANS BAERWALD , Eds.: Chinese Communism: *Selected Documents* TB/3031
HANS KOHN: Political Ideologies of the 20th Century TB/1277
ROBERTO MICHELS: First Lectures in Political Sociology. *Edited by Alfred de Grazia* ¶ ° △ TB/1224
BARRINGTON MOORE, JR.: Political Power and Social Theory: *Seven Studies* ¶ TB/1221
BARRINGTON MOORE, JR.: Soviet Politics—The Dilemma of Power ¶ TB/1222
BARRINGTON MOORE, JR.: Terror and Progress—USSR ¶ TB/1266
KARL R. POPPER: The Open Society and Its Enemies △ Vol. I TB/1101; Vol. II TB/1102
PETER WOLL, Ed.: Public Administration and Policy TB/1284

Psychology

ALFRED ADLER: The Individual Psychology of Alfred Adler △ TB/1154
ARTHUR BURTON & ROBERT E. HARRIS, Editors: Clinical Studies of Personality Vol. I TB/3075; Vol. II TB/3076
HADLEY CANTRIL: Invasion from Mars TB/1282
SIGMUND FREUD: On Creativity and the Unconscious § △ TB/45
C. G. JUNG: Symbols of Transformation △ Vol. I: TB/2009; Vol. II TB/2010
JOHN T. MC NEILL: A History of the Cure of Souls TB/126
KARL MENNINGER: Theory of Psychoanalytic Technique TB/1144
MUZAFER SHERIF: The Psychology of Social Norms TB/3072

Sociology

JACQUES BARZUN: Race: *A Study in Superstition* TB/1172
BERNARD BERELSON, Ed.: The Behavioral Sciences Today TB/1127
ALVIN W. GOULDNER: Wildcat Strike ¶ TB/1176
CLARK KERR: The Uses of the University TB/1264
R. M. MAC IVER: Social Causation TB/1153
ROBERT K. MERTON, LEONARD BROOM, LEONARD S. COTTRELL, JR., Editors: Sociology Today: *Problems and Prospects* ¶ Vol. I TB/1173; Vol. II TB/1174
ARNOLD ROSE: The Negro in America TB/3048
PHILIP SELZNICK: TVA and the Grass Roots TB/1230
GEORG SIMMEL et al.: Essays on Sociology, Philosophy, and Aesthetics. ¶ *Edited by Kurt H. Wolff* TB/1234
HERBERT SIMON: The Shape of Automation △ TB/1245

RELIGION

Ancient & Classical

HENRI FRANKFORT: Ancient Egyptian Religion TB/77
G. RACHEL LEVY: Religious Conceptions of the Stone Age *and their Influence upon European Thought* △ TB/106
MARTIN P. NILSSON: Greek Folk Religion TB/78
ERWIN ROHDE: Psyche △ Vol. I TB/140; Vol. II TB/141
H. J. ROSE: Religion in Greece and Rome △ TB/55

Biblical Thought & Literature

W. F. ALBRIGHT: The Biblical Period from Abraham to Ezra TB/102
C. K. BARRETT, Ed.: The New Testament Background: *Selected Documents* △ TB/86
C. H. DODD: The Authority of the Bible △ TB/43
GEORGE ADAM SMITH: Historical Geography of the Holy Land TB/138

The Judaic Tradition

MARTIN BUBER: Eclipse of God △ TB/12
MARTIN BUBER: Hasidism and Modern Man TB/839
MARTIN BUBER: Moses △ TB/837
MARTIN BUBER: The Origin and Meaning of Hasidism △ TB/835
MARTIN BUBER: Pointing the Way △ TB/103
MARTIN BUBER: The Prophetic Faith TB/73
MARTIN BUBER: Two Types of Faith ° △ TB/75
SOLOMON GRAYZEL: A History of the Contemporary Jews TB/816
JOSHUA TRACHTENBERG: The Devil and the Jews: *The Medieval Conception of the Jew and its Relation to Modern Anti-Semitism* JP/22

Christianity: Origins & Early Development

AUGUSTINE: An Augustine Synthesis △ TB/335
ADOLF DEISSMANN: Paul TB/15
EDWARD GIBBON: The Triumph of Christendom in the Roman Empire § △ *Illus.* TB/46
MAURICE GOGUEL: Jesus and the Origins of Christianity. ° △ Vol. I: TB/65; Vol. II: TB/66

EDGAR J. GOODSPEED: A Life of Jesus TB/1
ROBERT M. GRANT: Gnosticism and Early Christianity △ TB/136
ORIGEN: On First Principles △ TB/311
SULPICIUS SEVERUS et al.: The Western Fathers △ TB/309

Christianity: The Middle Ages and The Reformation

JOHN CALVIN & JACOPO SADOLETO: A Reformation Debate. *Edited by John C. Olin* TB/1239
G. CONSTANT: The Reformation in England △ TB/314

Christianity: The Protestant Tradition

KARL BARTH: Dogmatics in Outline △ TB/56
RUDOLF BULTMANN et al.: Translating Theology into the Modern Age TB/252
SOREN KIERKEGAARD: On Authority and Revelation TB/139
SOREN KIERKEGAARD: The Journals ° △ TB/52
SOREN KIERKEGAARD: The Present Age § △ TB/94
SOREN KIERKEGAARD: Purity of Heart △ TB/4
SOREN KIERKEGAARD: Repetition △ TB/117
SOREN KIERKEGAARD: Works of Love △ TB/122
JOHN MACQUARRIE: The Scope of Demythologizing: *Bultmann and his Critics* △ TB/134
JAMES M. ROBINSON et al.: The Bultmann School of Biblical Interpretation: New Directions? TB/251
F. SCHLEIERMACHER: The Christian Faith △ Vol. I TB/108; Vol. II TB/109
PAUL TILLICH: Dynamics of Faith △ TB/42

Christianity: The Roman and Eastern Traditions

DOM CUTHBERT BUTLER: Western Mysticism § ° △ TB/312
A. ROBERT CAPONIGRI, Ed.: Modern Catholic Thinkers △ Vol. I TB/306; Vol. II TB/307
G. P. FEDOTOV: The Russian Religious Mind: *Kievan Christianity, the 10th to the 13th Centuries* TB/370
G. P. FEDOTOV, Ed.: A Treasury of Russian Spirituality TB/303
ÉTIENNE GILSON: The Spirit of Thomism TB/313
DAVID KNOWLES: The English Mystical Tradition TB/302
GABRIEL MARCEL: Being and Having TB/310
GABRIEL MARCEL: Homo Viator TB/397
FRANCIS DE SALES: Introduction to the Devout Life TB/316
GUSTAVE WEIGEL, S. J.: Catholic Theology in Dialogue TB/301

Oriental Religions: Far Eastern, Near Eastern

TOR ANDRAE: Mohammed § △ TB/62
EDWARD CONZE: Buddhism ° △ TB/58
ANANDA COOMARASWAMY: Buddha and the Gospel of Buddhism. △ *Illus.* TB/119
H. G. CREEL: Confucius and the Chinese Way TB/63
FRANKLIN EDGERTON, Trans. & Ed.: The Bhagavad Gita TB/115
SWAMI NIKHILANANDA, Trans. & Ed.: The Upanishads: *A One-Volume Abridgment* △ TB/114

Philosophy of Religion

NICOLAS BERDYAEV: The Beginning and the End § △ TB/14
NICOLAS BERDYAEV: Christian Existentialism △ TB/130
RUDOLF BULTMANN: History and Eschatology ° TB/91
RUDOLF BULTMANN & 5 CRITICS: Kerygma and Myth △ TB/80
RUDOLF BULTMANN and KARL KUNDSIN: Form Criticism: *Two Essays on New Testament Research* △ TB/96
MIRCEA ELIADE: The Sacred and the Profane TB/81
LUDWIG FEUERBACH: The Essence of Christianity § TB/11
IMMANUEL KANT: Religion Within the Limits of Reason Alone. § *Intro. by T. M. Greene & J. Silber* TB/67
K. E. KIRK: The Vision of God § △ TB/137
JOHN MACQUARRIE: An Existentialist Theology: *A Comparison of Heidegger and Bultmann* ° △ TB/125
PIERRE TEILHARD DE CHARDIN: Divine Milieu ° △ TB/384
PIERRE TEILHARD DE CHARDIN: Phenomenon of Man ° △ TB/383
PAUL TILLICH: Morality and Beyond TB/142

NATURAL SCIENCES AND MATHEMATICS

Biological Sciences

CHARLOTTE AUERBACH: Science of Genetics Σ △ TB/568
LUDWIG VON BERTALANFFY: Modern Theories of Development: *An Introduction to Theoretical Biology* TB/554
LUDWIG VON BERTALANFFY: Problems of Life △ TB/521
HAROLD F. BLUM: Time's Arrow and Evolution TB/555
JOHN TYLER BONNER: The Ideas of Biology Σ △ TB/570
R. W. GERARD: Unresting Cells. *Illus.* TB/541
ADOLF PORTMANN: Animals as Social Beings ° △ TB/572
O. W. RICHARDS: The Social Insects. △ *Illus.* TB/542
P. M. SHEPPARD: Natural Selection and Heredity △ TB/528
EDMUND W. SINNOTT: Cell and Psyche TB/546
C. H. WADDINGTON: How Animals Develop. △ *Illus.* TB/553
C. H. WADDINGTON: The Nature of Life △ TB/580

Geography

R. E. COKER: The Great and Wide Sea: *An Introduction to Oceanography and Marine Biology. Illus.* TB/551
F. K. HARE: The Restless Atmosphere △ TB/560

History of Science

MARIE BOAS: The Scientific Renaissance, 1450-1630 △ TB/583
A. HUNTER DUPREE: Science in the Federal Government: *A History of Policies and Activities to 1940* △ TB/573
O. NEUGEBAUER: The Exact Sciences in Antiquity TB/552
STEPHEN TOULMIN & JUNE GOODFIELD: Architecture of Matter ° △ TB/584
STEPHEN TOULMIN & JUNE GOODFIELD: Discovery of Time ° △ TB/585
LANCELOT LAW WHYTE: Essay on Atomism △ TB/565

Mathematics

E. W. BETH: The Foundations of Mathematics △ TB/581
H. DAVENPORT: The Higher Arithmetic △ TB/526
H. G. FORDER: Geometry: *An Introduction* △ TB/548
D. E. LITTLEWOOD: Skeleton Key of Mathematics: *A Simple Account of Complex Algebraic Problems* △ TB/525
GEORGE E. OWEN: Fundamentals of Scientific Mathematics TB/569
WILLARD VAN ORMAN QUINE: Mathematical Logic TB/558
FREDERICK WAISMANN: Introduction to Mathematical Thinking. *Foreword by Karl Menger* TB/511

Philosophy of Science

R. B. BRAITHWAITE: Scientific Explanation TB/515
J. BRONOWSKI: Science and Human Values △ TB/505
ALBERT EINSTEIN et al.: Albert Einstein: Philosopher-Scientist Vol. I TB/502; Vol. II TB/503
WERNER HEISENBERG: Physics and Philosophy △ TB/549
JOHN MAYNARD KEYNES: A Treatise on Probability. ° △ *Introduction by N. R. Hanson* TB/557
KARL R. POPPER: Logic of Scientific Discovery △ TB/576
STEPHEN TOULMIN: Foresight and Understanding △ TB/564
G. J. WHITROW: Natural Philosophy of Time ° △ TB/563

Physics and Cosmology

JOHN E. ALLEN: Aerodynamics △ TB/582
STEPHEN TOULMIN & JUNE GOODFIELD: The Fabric of the Heavens: *The Development of Astronomy and Dynamics.* △ *Illus.* TB/579
DAVID BOHM: Causality and Chance in Modern Physics. △ *Foreword by Louis de Broglie* TB/536
P. W. BRIDGMAN: Nature of Thermodynamics TB/537
C. V. DURELL: Readable Relativity △ TB/530
ARTHUR EDDINGTON: Space, Time and Gravitation TB/510
GEORGE GAMOW: Biography of Physics Σ △ TB/567
MAX JAMMER: Concepts of Force TB/550
MAX JAMMER: Concepts of Mass TB/571
MAX JAMMER: Concepts of Space TB/533
G. J. WHITROW: The Structure and Evolution of the Universe: *An Introduction to Cosmology* △ *Illus.* TB/504